the printma

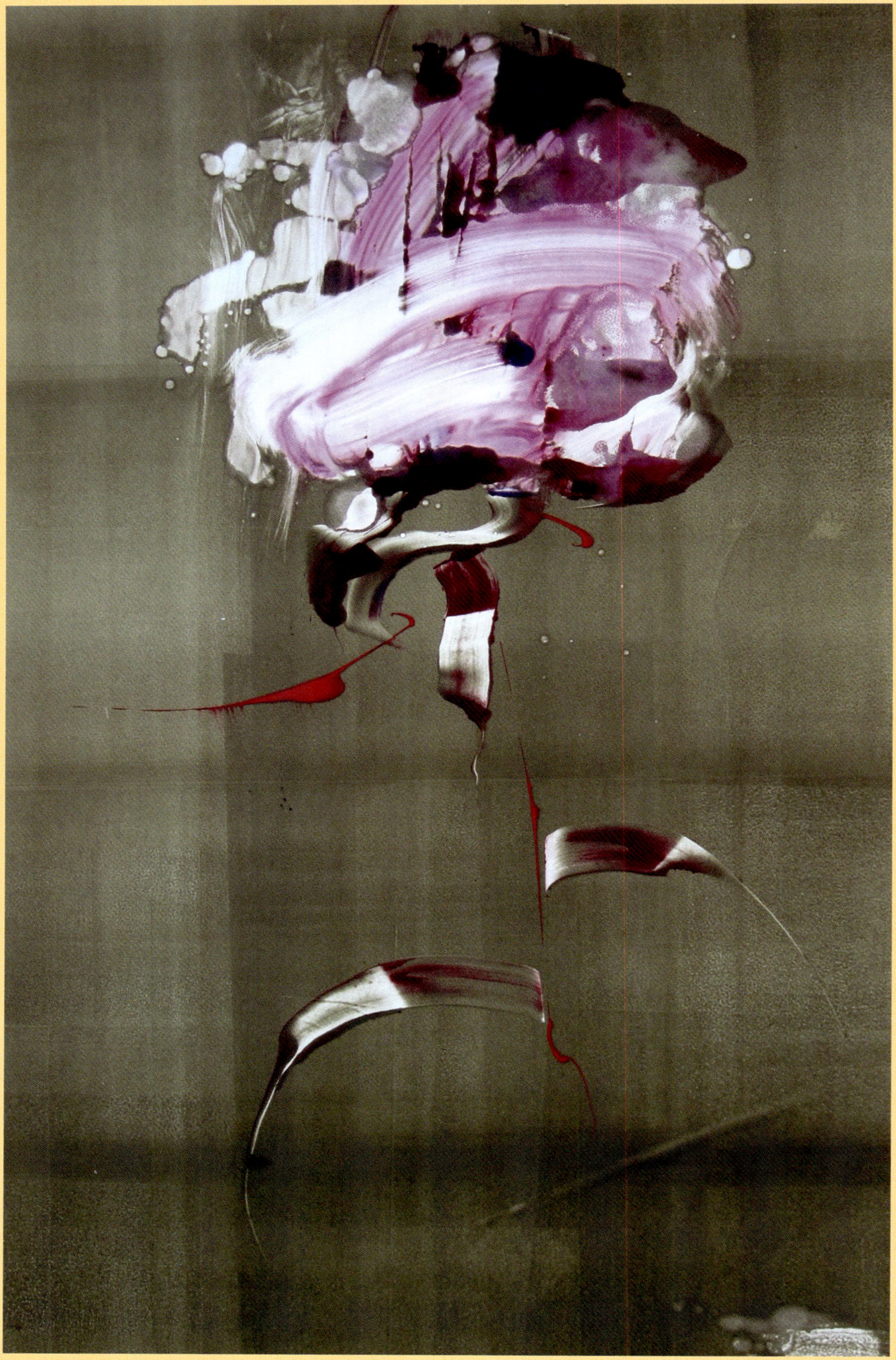

the printmakers' bible

COLIN GALE AND MEGAN FISHPOOL

B L O O M S B U R Y
LONDON • BERLIN • NEW YORK • SYDNEY

First published in Great Britain 2012
Bloomsbury Publishing Plc
50 Bedford Square
London WC1B 3DP
www.bloomsbury.com

ISBN: 978-1-4081-4067-3

A CIP catalogue record for this book is available from the British Library

Publisher: Susan James
Project manager: Davida Saunders
Copy editor: Lisa Carden
Cover design: James Watson and Sutchinda Thompson
Page design: James Watson
Layouts: Susan McIntyre

This book is produced using paper that is made from wood grown in managed, sustainable forests. It is natural, renewable and recyclable. The logging and manufacturing processes conform to the environmental regulations of the country of origin.

Printed and bound in China

FRONT COVER: (ABOVE LEFT) Carole Hensher, *Shiney Shoes*, 2007. Photo lithograph, 50 x 38 cm; (ABOVE RIGHT) Helen Clark, *Untitled*, 2007 (detail). Monoprint, 76 x 112 cm; (CENTRE RIGHT) Eileen Cooper, *Untitled*, 2008. Woodcut, 38 x 50 cm; (BELOW LEFT) Sarah Redman, *Untitled*, 2009. Monoprint, 76 x 76 cm; (BELOW RIGHT) Corinna Button, *On The Pull*, 2006. Collagraph, 76 x 112 cm

BACK COVER: (ABOVE RIGHT) Megan Fishpool, *Stravinsky*, 2008. Monoprint 56 x 60 cm; (CENTRE LEFT) Maria Carleton, *Diana Huntress*, 2011 (detail). Monoprint, 56 x 76 cm; (BELOW LEFT) Kate Boxer, *Blue Wolf*, 2007. Carborundum®, 76 x 112 cm; (BELOW RIGHT) Colin Gale, *Untitled Red and Yellow*, 2009. Photo etching, 56 x 76 cm.

FRONTISPIECE: Helen Clark, *Untitled Gold Flower*, 2011. Monoprint, 76 x 112 cm (30 x 44 in.).

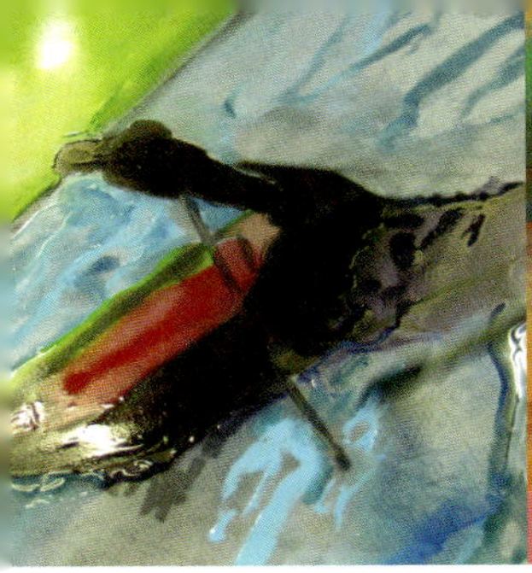
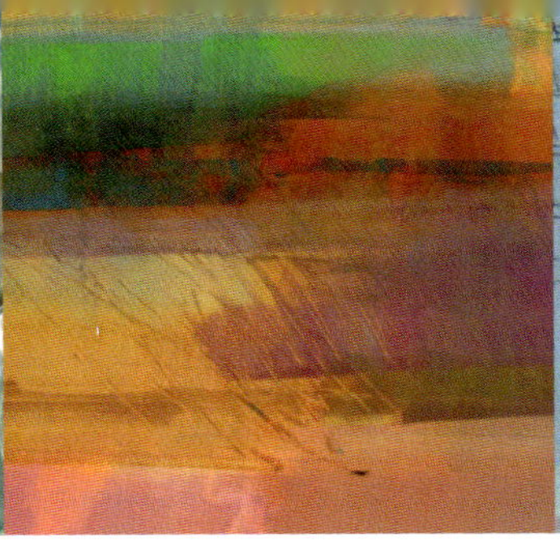
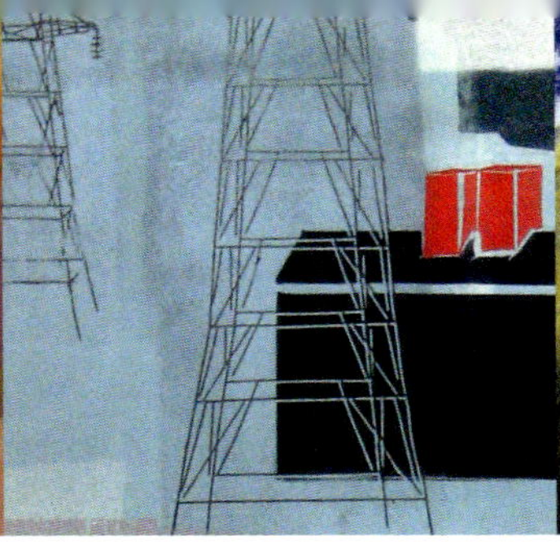
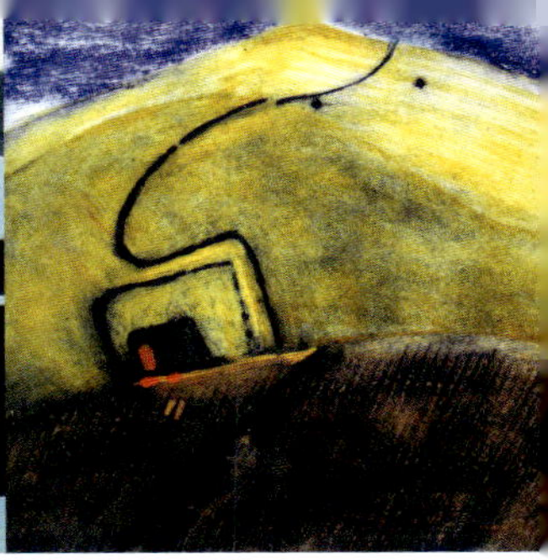

contents

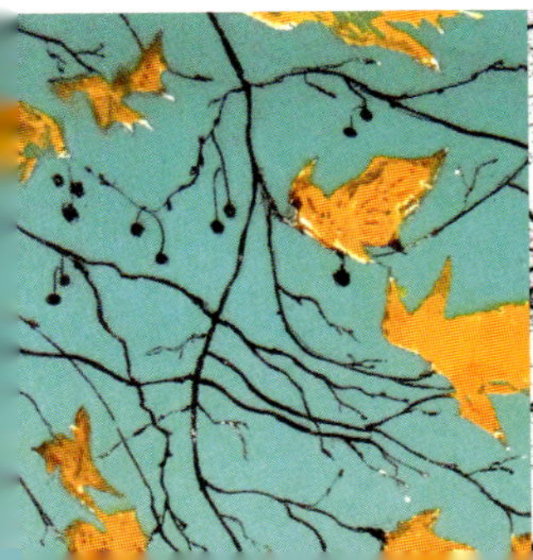
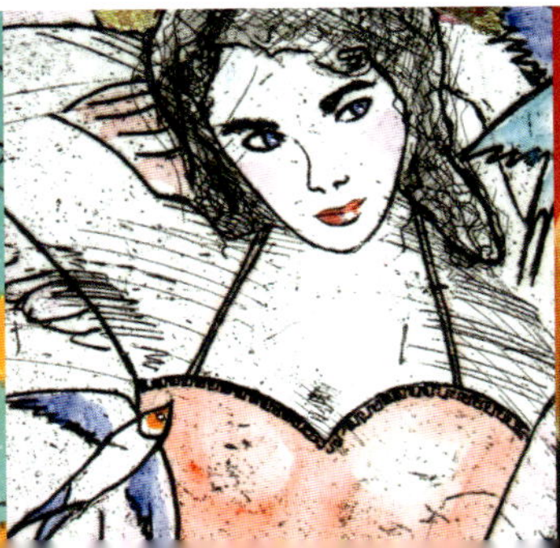
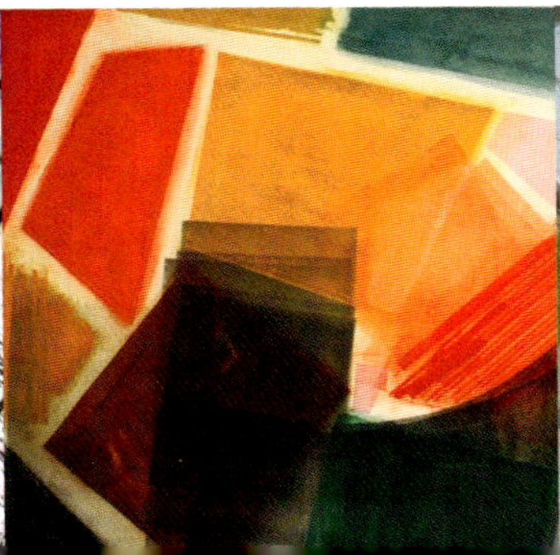
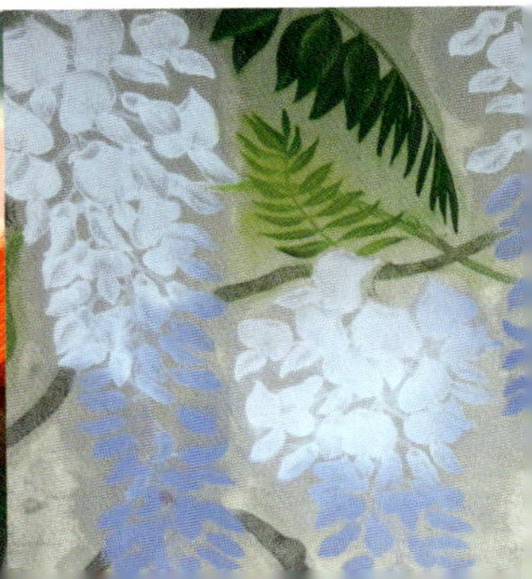

acknowledgements

With great thanks and appreciation to all of the artists who have agreed to have their work represented in this book.

Thank you to Scarlett Massel, Pellafort Press; Paul Croft, Aberystwyth University; Melvyn Petterson, Artichoke Print Workshop for advice given; and Bryan Poole, Marcelle Hanselaar, Paul Catherall and Sarah Redman for putting up with our cameras.

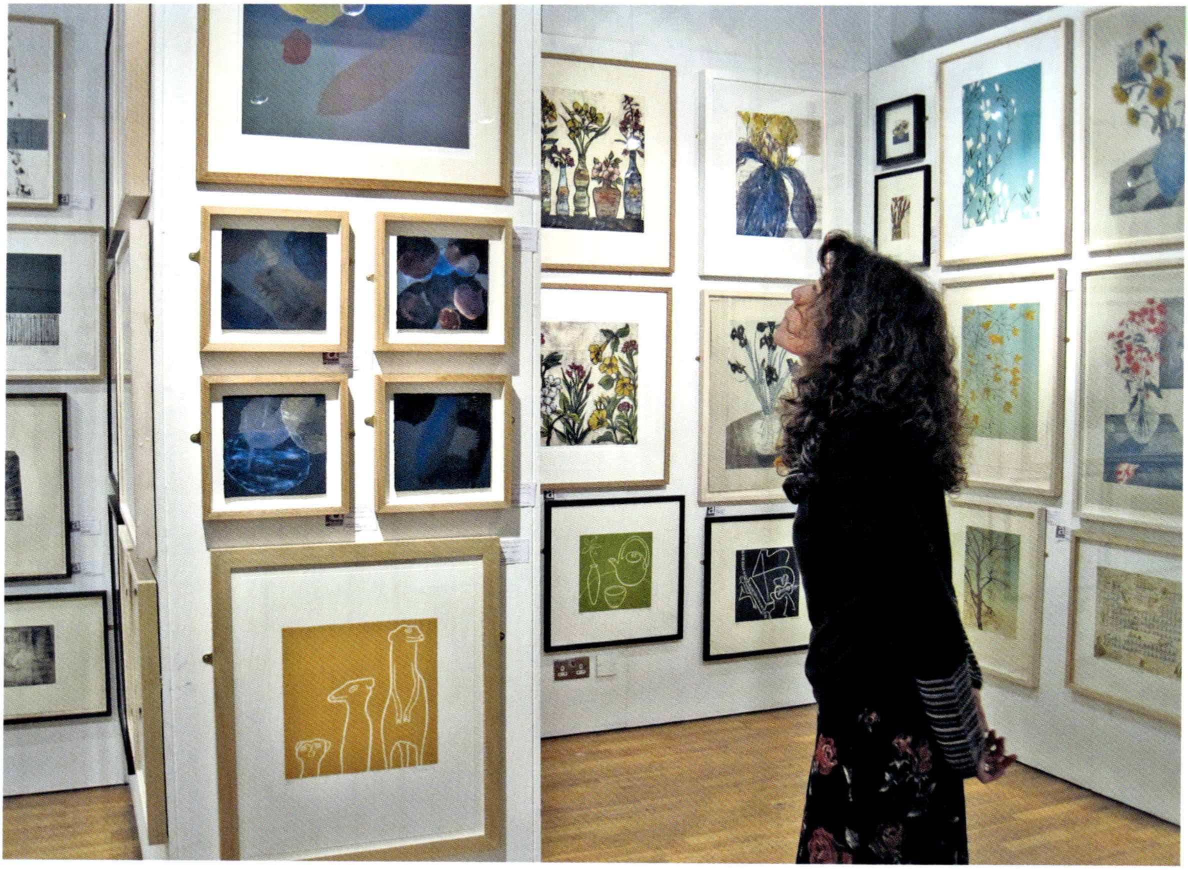

introduction

In its most simple definition, printmaking is a technical process that enables an artist to create a print. It is the story of how that process happens that makes printmaking fascinating and exciting, however!

As a concept, 'printmaking' encompasses many practical, 'how to...' technical processes. All processes of art (painting, sculpture, ceramics, even music and dance) need these to facilitate their execution and practice, and they involve materials, equipment and technical skills.

The aim of this book is to provide technical explanations, definitions, practical tips, 'how to...' steps, inspirational artist prints and reasons why printmaking will endure. Artists will continue to build on printmaking's impressive history and on its continual adaptations to, and absorption of, new materials, equipment and techniques.

Despite its title, this book is not a compendium of every possible element of printmaking: creating such a work would be impossible and we did not set out to write a book with that intention. In our view, a bible is a source of stories, information, histories and knowledge that inspire trust and confidence, and that is what inspires this book. It is a collection of information that can be referred to time and again and we hope that its practical and straightforward approach will appeal to everyone.

◀ **Artichoke Print Workshop.**

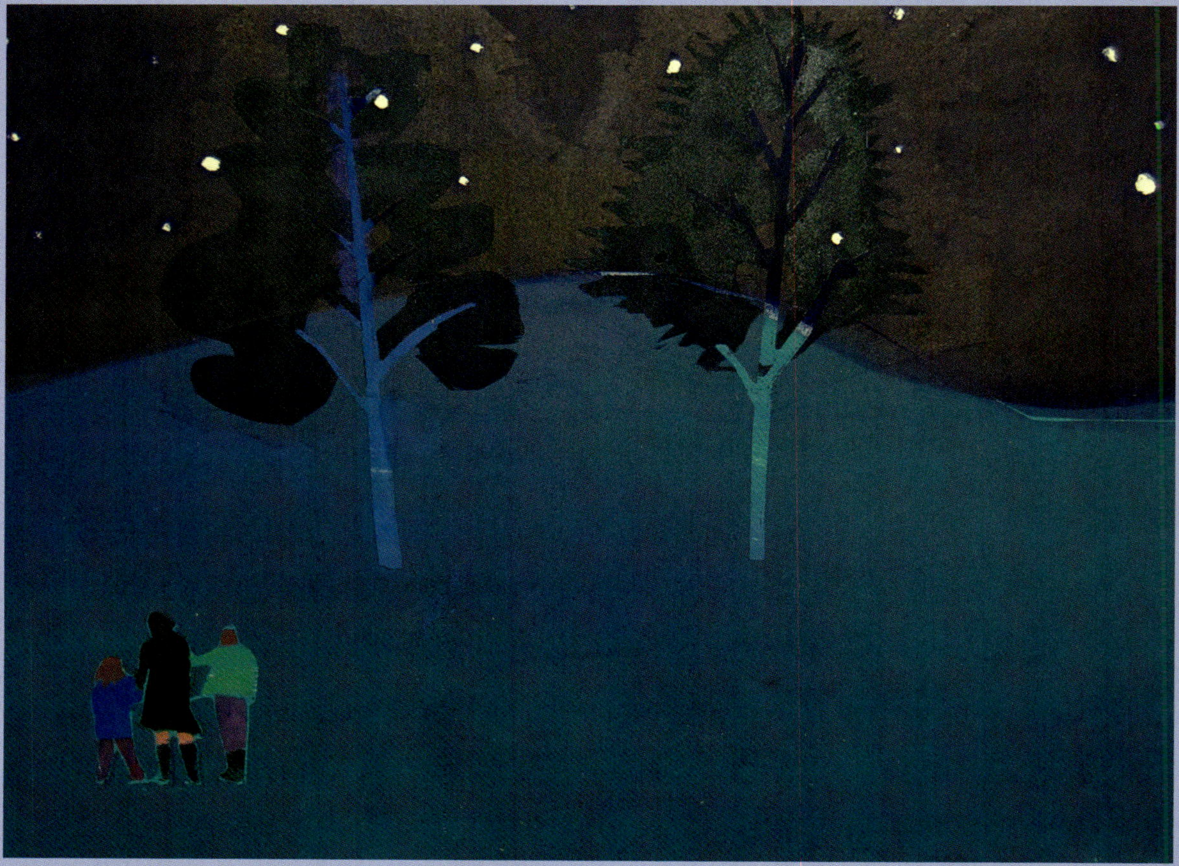

1

relief printing

A relief print is made by taking an impression from a matrix in which only the upper surface of the matrix has been inked. Relief printing is the oldest of all of the printmaking techniques. The urge to make an impression has been the source of printmaking's strength and longevity since the very first time someone pressed their hand into clay and made a record of it on another surface, thousands of years ago.

Relief printing is a technique in which the choices of both the surface of the block and how the image is cut into it, are essential.

◀ **Tom Hammick, *Nightwalk*, 2011. Reduction woodcut, 44 x 59 cm (19½ x 15¾ in.). Courtesy of Emma Hill, Eagle Gallery.**

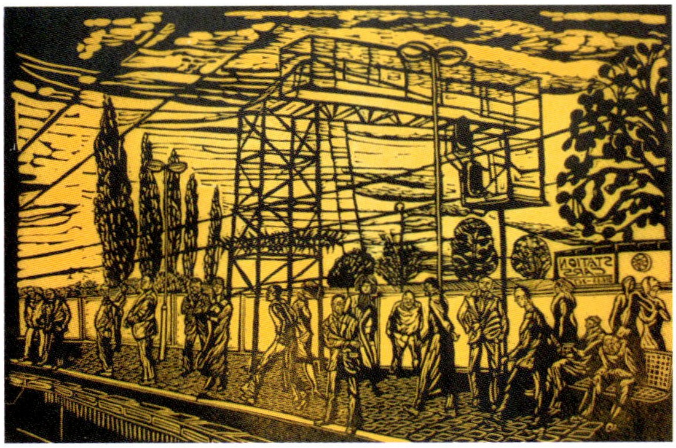

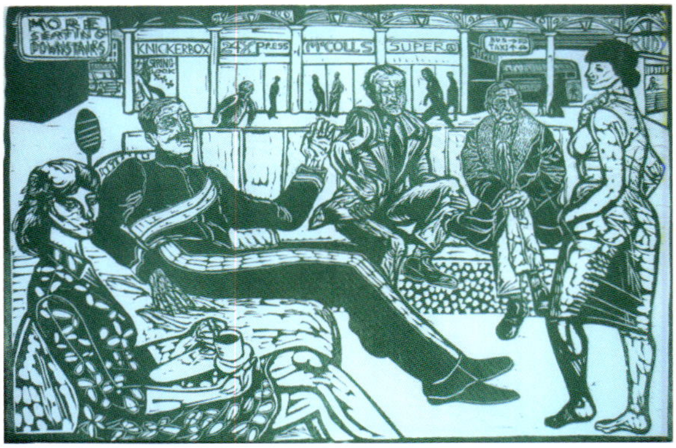

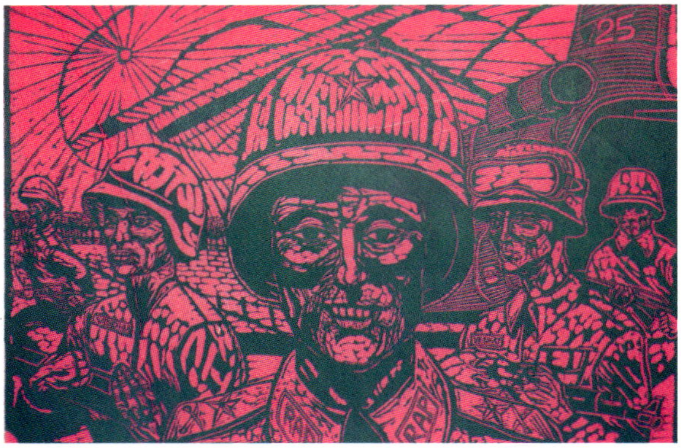

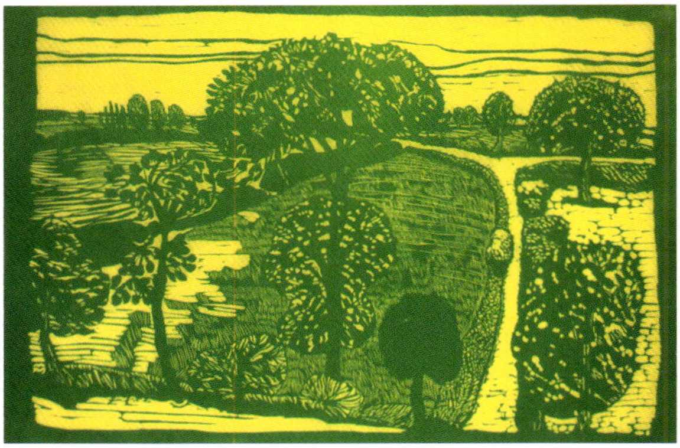

▲ TOP ROW

LEFT: **Rahil Sheik, *Ecclesiastes 3*, 2011. Linocut, 76 x 56 cm (30 x 22 in.).**

RIGHT: **Rahil Sheik, *Ecclesiastes 4*, 2011. Linocut, 76 x 56 cm (30 x 22 in.).**

▲ BOTTOM ROW

LEFT: **Rahil Sheik, *Ecclesiastes 5*, 2011. Linocut, 76 x 56 cm (30 x 22 in.).**

RIGHT: **Rahil Sheik, *Ecclesiastes 6*, 2011. Linocut, 76 x 56 cm (30 x 22 in.).**

The woodcut, the linocut and the wood engraving are types of relief printing, while copper engraving, like mezzotint, is a type of non-etch intaglio printing in which the substrate is inked in the manner of a relief print. (See Chapters 3 and 4 for full descriptions of copper engraving and mezzotint.)

Wood, and the material called linoleum, are the most popular and well-known substrates. Woodblocks were made in China, Japan and Egypt as early as AD 600; in England, the woodcut first appeared in the 15th century. Woodcuts find their origins in wood carving and stamping, which are as old as humankind.

Linoleum was invented in the late 1800s as a floor covering and by 1900 it had been incorporated into relief printing as a suitable material for cutting into. Lightweight and inexpensive, linoleum is available in pre-cut sizes and on rolls, which allows the artist to cut the printing block to the size required.

Rollers, dabbers, stippling brushes and spraying are ways of applying ink to the relief block surface. Inking the surface with a roller is the most common way of applying colour to a relief block.

▶ Relief printing is a popular printmaking technique. The artists at Artichoke Print Workshop in London have excellent facilities to use and we have watched them thrive as professional printmakers for many years.

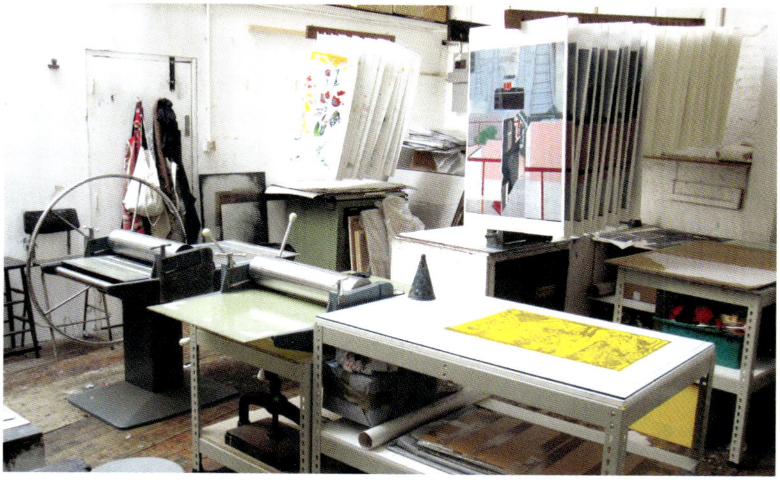

▶ Printmakers often commit themselves to one technique and specialise in it. Linocut is no exception. Some of the UK's best linocut artists work in professional studios and workshops to make their prints.

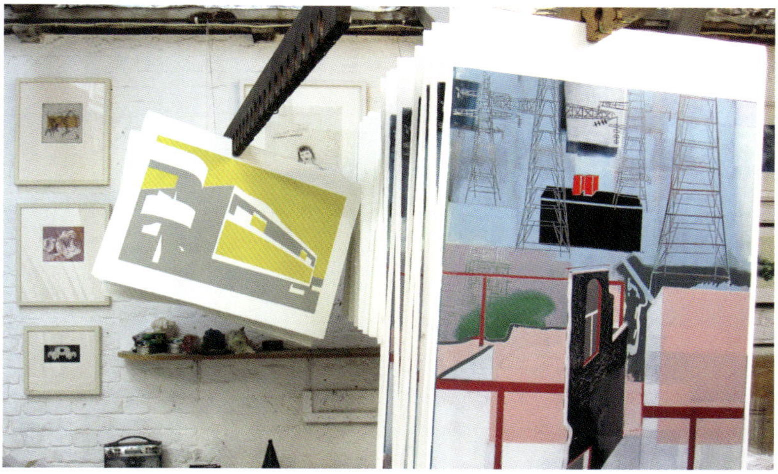

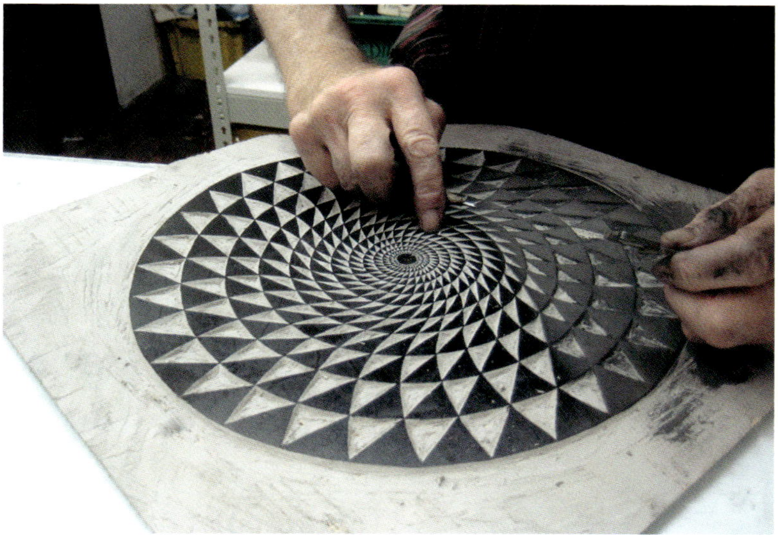

◀ Lino cuts very easily, enabling you to make complicated and intricate designs.

▼ Every little cut counts!

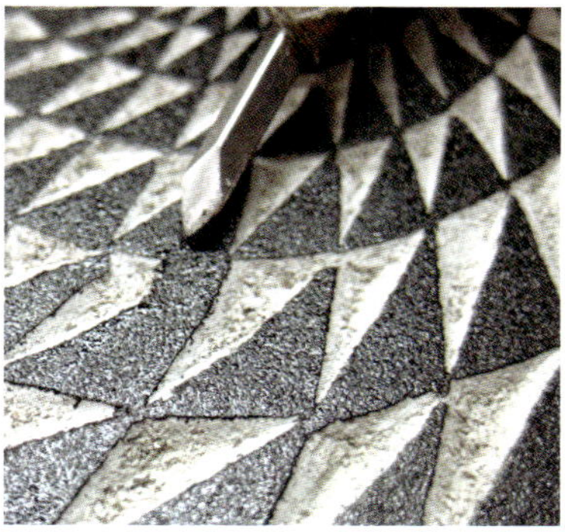

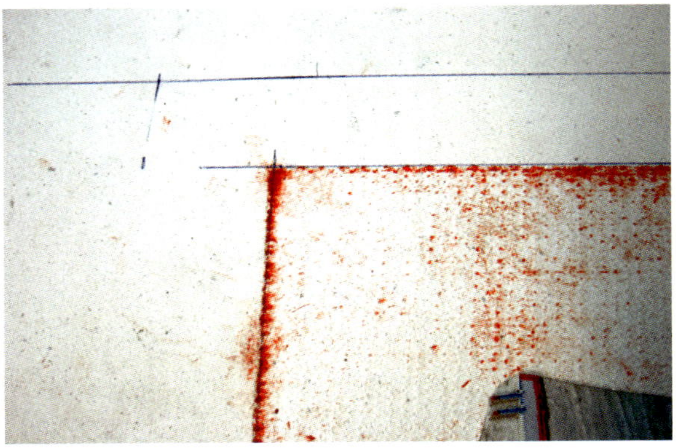
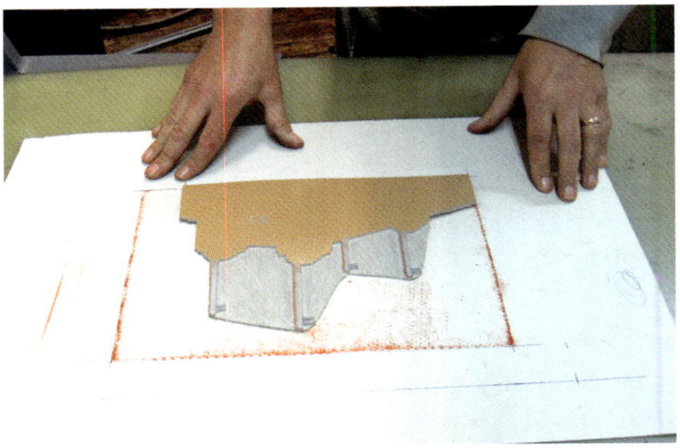
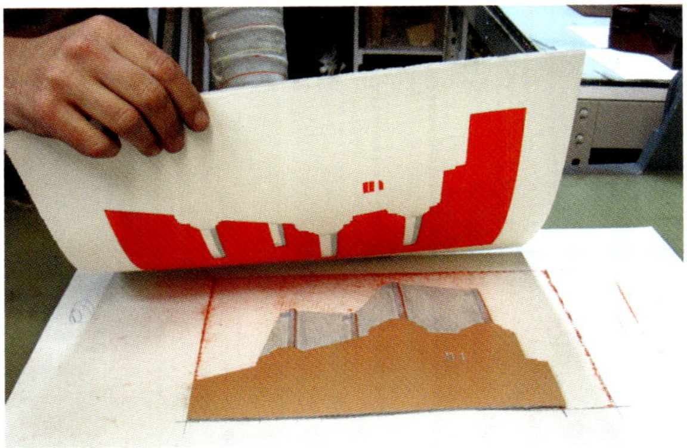
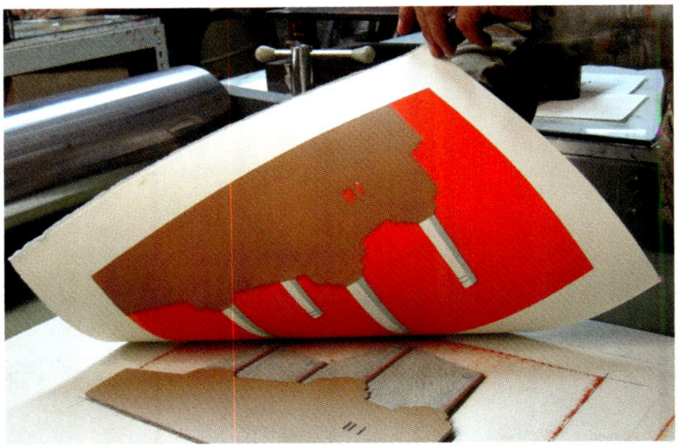

▲ TOP ROW

LEFT: Registration of an image in layers is a key element of relief printing.

RIGHT: It is very important to place the block inked with the next colour of the design to be printed in the correct position.

▲ BOTTOM ROW

LEFT: The second block is cut to fit with the first colour layer.

RIGHT: It takes years of practice to cut straight lines effortlessly in a lino block.

SUBSTRATES

A substrate is the base layer on which you place the technical media of your chosen process. In other words, it is the underlying layer on which the building of the image takes place. There is an enormous variety of material suitable for taking a relief print from: plywood, side grain, hardboard, MDF (medium-density fibreboard), linoleum, acrylic sheet, PVC (soft plastic) metals, flexo plates, polyboards and cardboard are often used by artists as relief blocks.

Linoleum

Linoleum is an inexpensive substrate. A man-made mixture of resin, linseed oil, powdered cork and pigment, it is heated and applied to hessian, jute or canvas backing with great pressure. The word derives from the Latin *linum*, meaning 'flax' and *oleum*, meaning 'oil'. It has a washable surface and has a smooth, semi-soft, compact surface that allows it to be cut. It is widely available. (For tips on drawing and cutting lino see p.21; for etching lino with caustic soda see pp.32–3.)

Plywood

Plywood is an inexpensive base. It is composed of several thin layers of wood which have been compressed together to form a lightweight sheet. This wood is easy to cut into, but has the trait of cutting easily in one direction (when you cut *with* the grain of the wood sheet) but then tearing and ripping into ragged shapes when you cut against the grain.

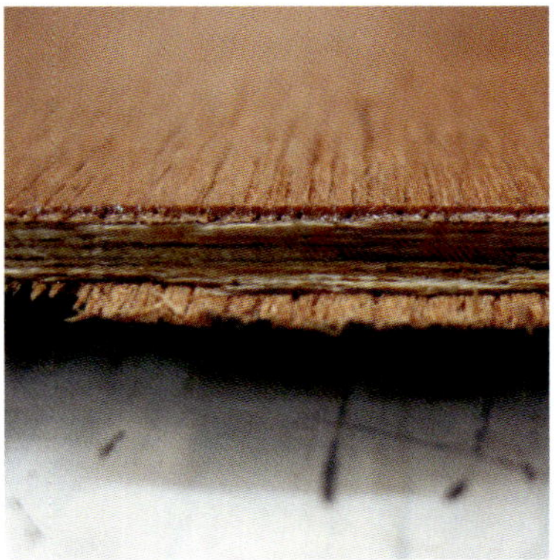

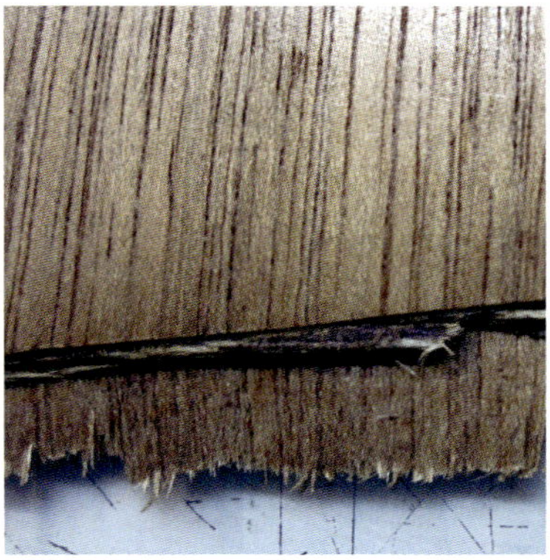

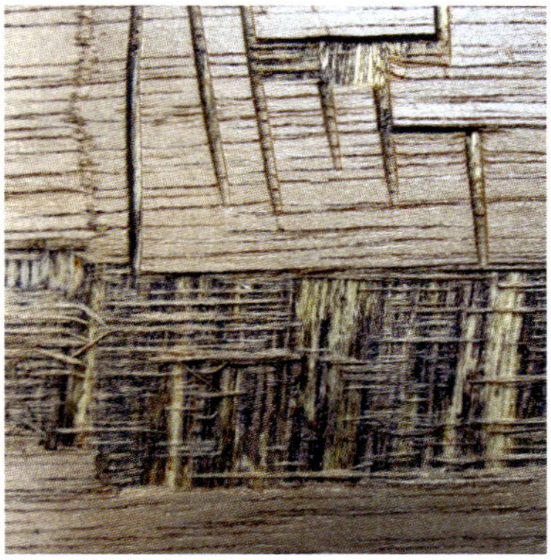

The unexpected cutting mishaps that result because of plywood's loose single grain direction can be used to the artist's creative advantage, unplanned accidental marks can add interesting shapes which can be incorporated into the composition.

▲ LEFT TO RIGHT

Plywood consists of several thin layers of wood laminated together.

It is easily shattered, which makes it ideal for abstract shapes or scruffy edges.

Because the grain in plywood runs one way only, it creates very unusual lines and broken areas when you cut across its grain. The plywood in this picture has been covered with a Ronseal water-based semi-gloss clear varnish.

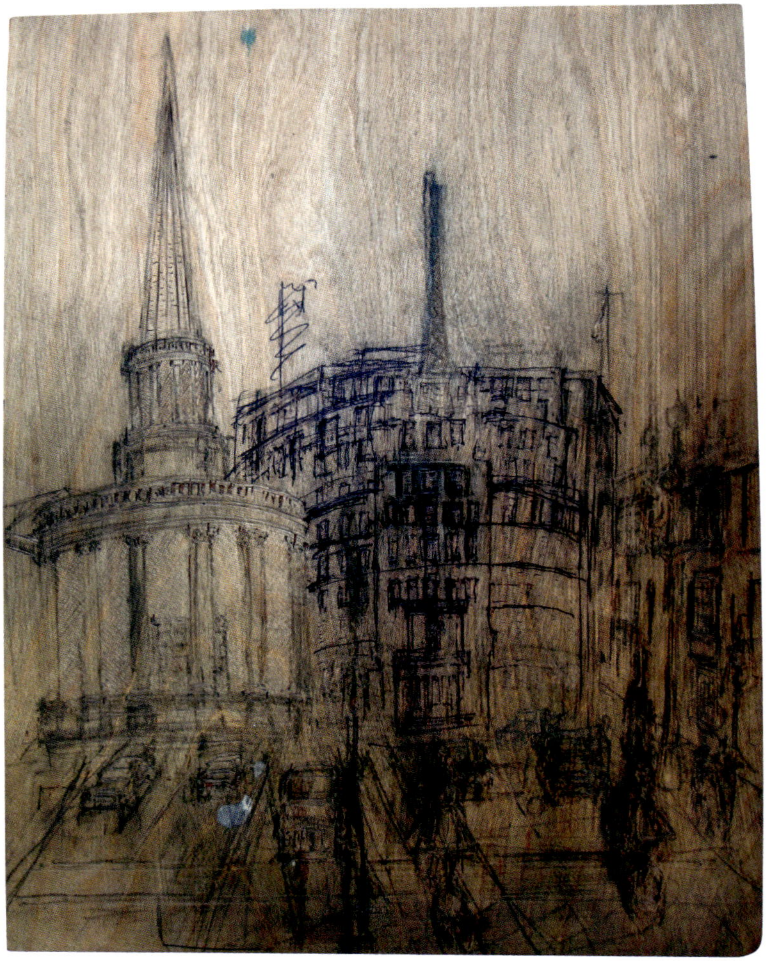

◀ The pencil drawing of the design on the surface.

▼ Coating the wood's surface with a very thin layer of varnish seals the surface of the wood and does not clog the surface texture of the grain.

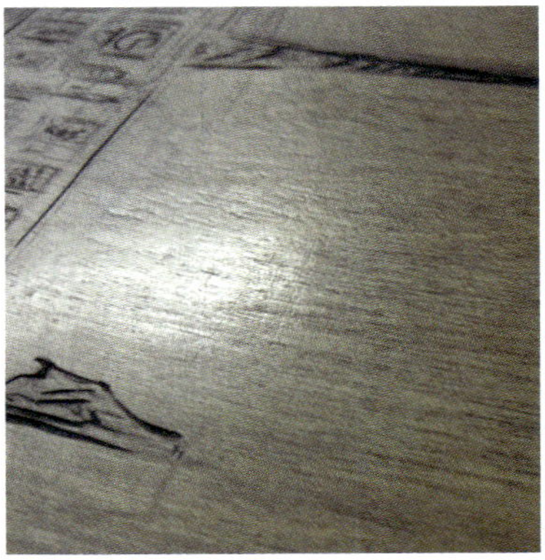

Veneer

Veneer is also a type of prepared wood. It is an extremely thin layer of wood that is used to cover another surface. It is relatively lightweight and pliable and may benefit from being mounted or laminated to a more rigid base.

Side grain

Side grain or long grain is wood that has been cut as a long length of wood. A plank of wood is the most familiar example of this. It is usually thicker than plywood. Side grain comes in both hard and soft varieties. Soft woods are easier to cut, as the name would indicate. Pine and birch are well known examples of this type of wood (pine is softer than birch), while maple and lemon wood are examples of hard woods.

End grain

End grain wood has been cut across the trunk of the tree. The cut surface reveals the tree's growth rings. End grain wood is used for wood engraving.

End grain blocks are used by wood engravers because cutting across the growth rings of the wood allows for a more precise and even cut than is possible when cutting across the side grain of wood.

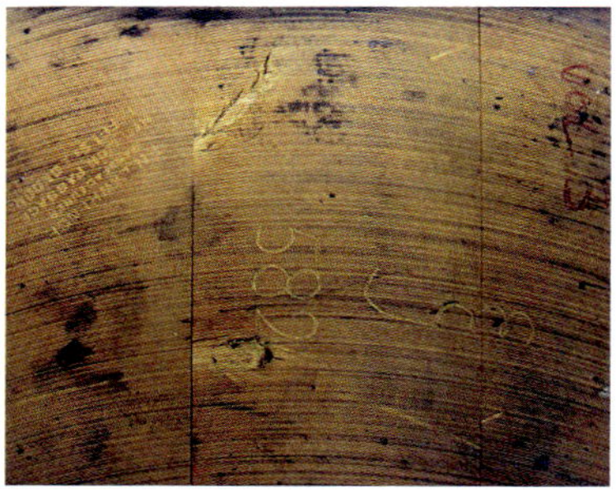

▲ This picture shows the concentric grain pattern of the wood block.

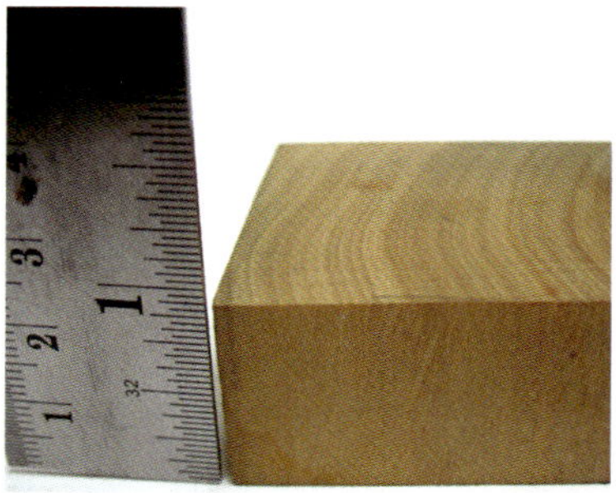

▲ The width of end grain blocks is approximately between three quarters of an inch to one inch and its height usually equals type height.

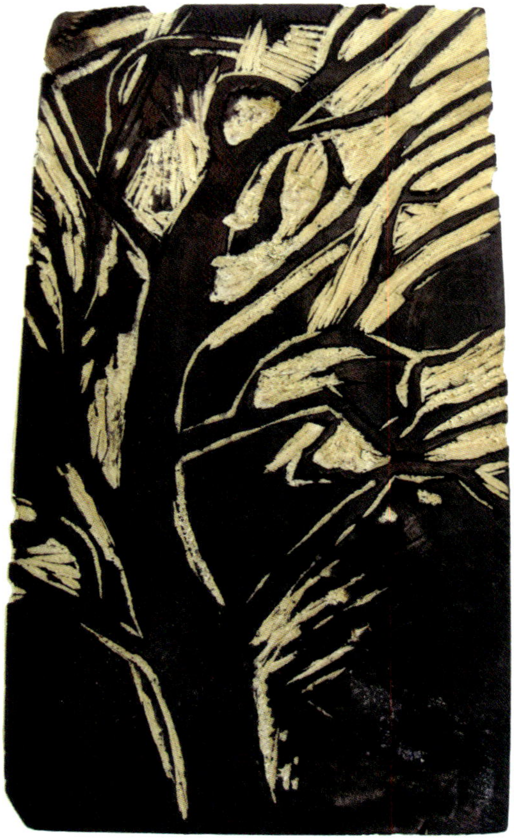

▼ Example of unpolished end grain texture in a wooden block. The crude image is accentuated by the coarse cutting method the artist has used on the block.

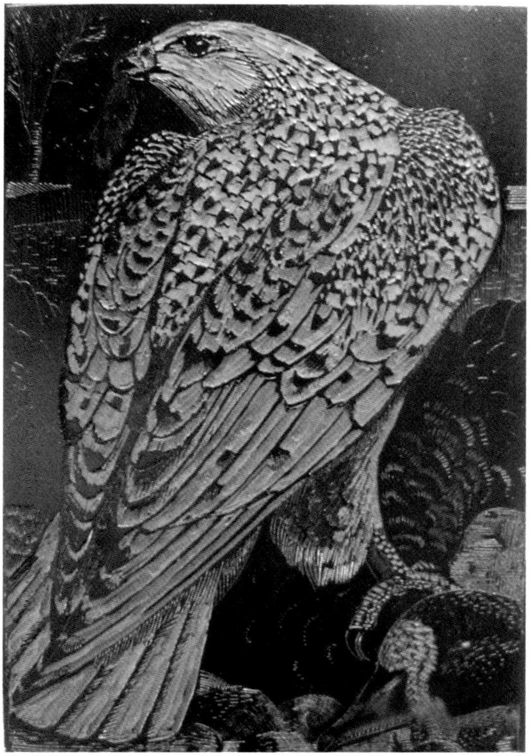

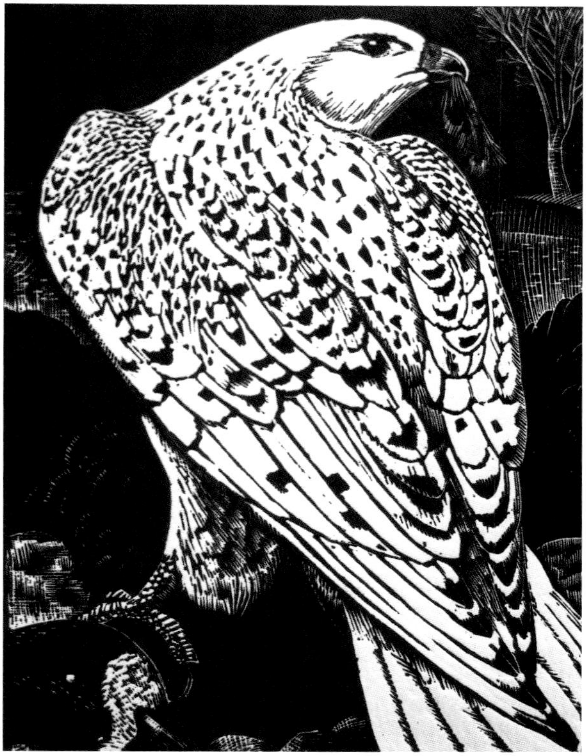

Apple, boxwood, cherry and American hardwood are all examples of end grains used for wood engraving. The outstanding feature of end grain wood is that it has a dense, compact surface ideal for fine and delicate marks to be made into it.

The width of end grain blocks is approximately 20 mm (between ¾–1 in.) and its height usually equals typeface height. Typeface height is measured in points; there are 72 points in an inch. In the early days of traditional letterpress typography (pre-19th century), the point constantly varied in size but printed texts show it was approximately 0.035 mm. This variation in size occurred because until the end of the 1800s, no one could agree on the length of a foot, the unit of measurement which contained the inch.

Most engravers recommend blocks of one inch type height because they are easier and lighter to handle, especially when several are being joined together for a larger block. If larger blocks are needed for larger images, small separate end grain blocks must be jointed together and glued. The end grain must then be sanded and polished until it is level. This is a great skill and it takes time to make by hand good quality large blocks for the engraver to use. As a result, these blocks are a very expensive item for a printmaker to purchase.

Prepared hardwood engraving blocks are available pre-polished on both ends from suppliers such as Intaglio Printmaker and T. N. Lawrence.

▲ LEFT The Tunnicliffe block pictured shows the skill of the artist cutting the image into the block.

▲ RIGHT The printed engraving from the block by the artist Charles Frederick Tunnicliffe (1901–79). Image courtesy of Abbot and Holder Ltd and Artichoke Trading Ltd.

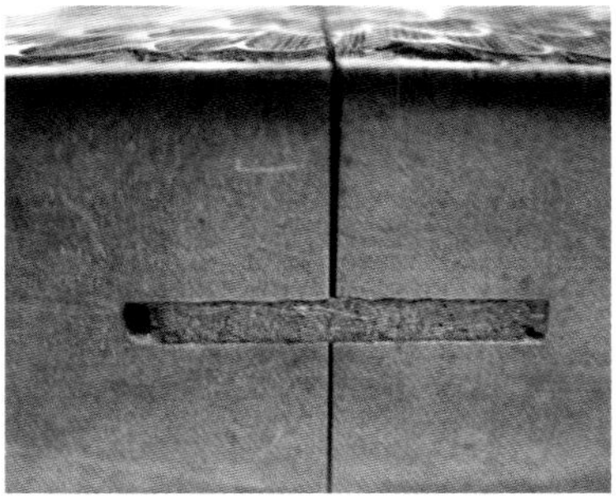

▲ If larger blocks are needed for larger images, small separate end grain blocks must be jointed together and glued.

Hardboard/MDF/OSB (oriented strand board)/ Particle board

These different types of hardboard have all been made from wood fibres that have been glued together with great heat.

MDF is an inexpensive wood composite that is readily available. It has a very smooth cutting surface with virtually no grain. The roughness revealed when it is cut into is uniform through the plate.

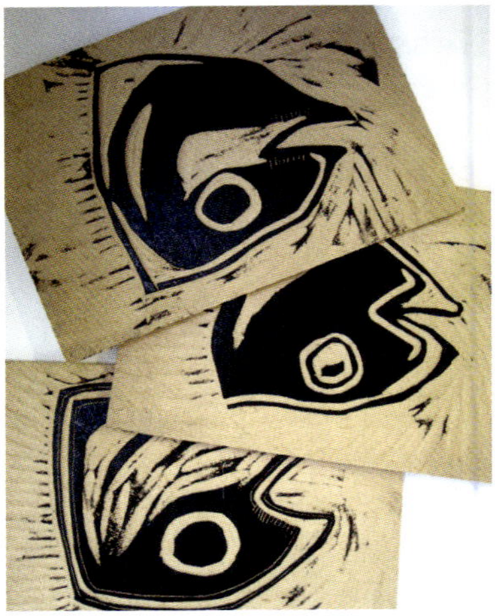

▲ Woodcuts on MDF.

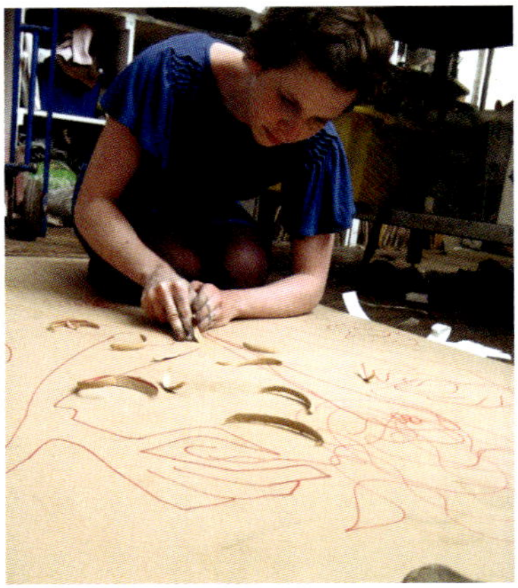

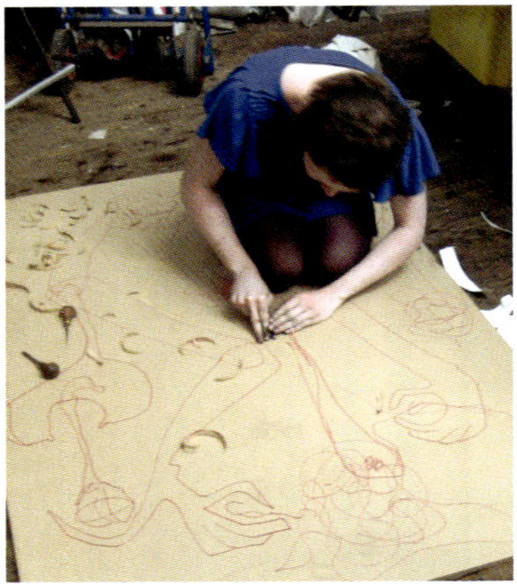

▲ LEFT TO RIGHT

Artist Mary Dalton demonstrates no matter what scale you work on, cutting the design into the substrate requires an energetic commitment.

A wood block this large is usually printed by hand. Most printmaking studios do not have presses with beds the size of this printing block 122 x 152.4 cm (48 x 60 in.).

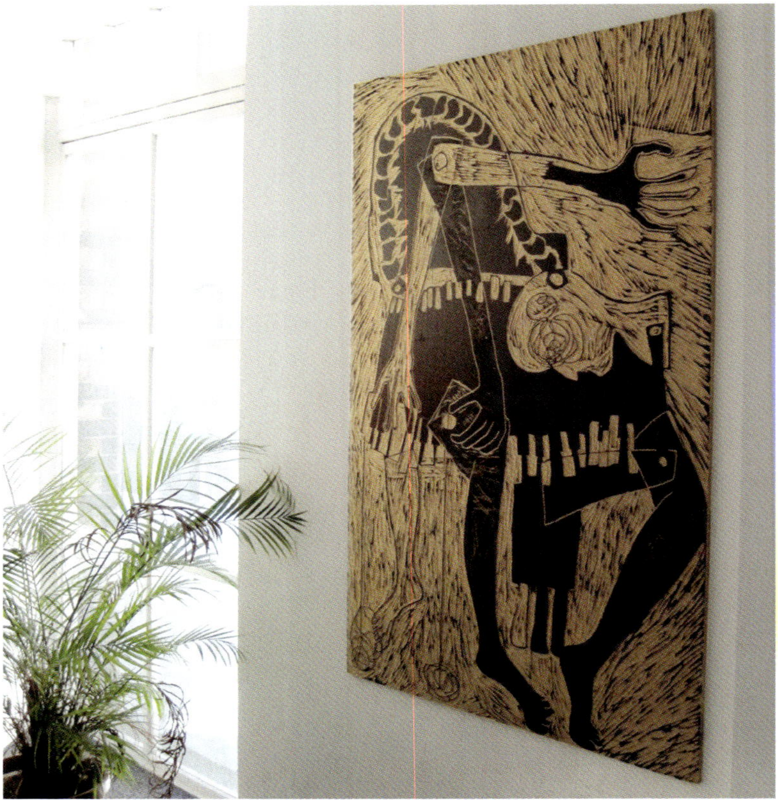

▶ MDF board allows images of great scale to be made. Working on a block this large is both dynamic and hard work!

Gesso/Whiting/Artex®

Gesso is a mixture of plaster dust and PVA (polyvinyl acetate) glue, which adheres to a substrate to create textures. Whiting is ground chalk, which can be combined with PVA glue to create a mixture which adheres to linoleum. Artex® ceiling paste (a plaster that is used to create texture on ceilings and walls; commonly available from DIY shops) and PVA can also be used.

PVC and acrylic relief blocks

PVC (soft plastic) blocks, acrylic sheets (engraving plastic) and polyblocks (polystyrene) now provide alternative surfaces for the printmaker to use as well as the traditional lino and wood surfaces.

Perspex (a thin acrylic sheet) can also be used. It can be mounted onto MDF board or laminated onto thick cardboard or mounting board to keep it rigid. The cut marks are not as smooth as those made on hardwood, but provide an acceptable alternative.

The resulting prints from Perspex blocks can be more inconsistent and variable than those printed from wood or linoleum. Flat areas of colour may smudge or blemish because the smooth plastic surface of the Perspex has no texture to grip the ink.

Tip

Using dampened printing paper on acrylic or PVC blocks often alleviates the problem of skids and ink movement marks.

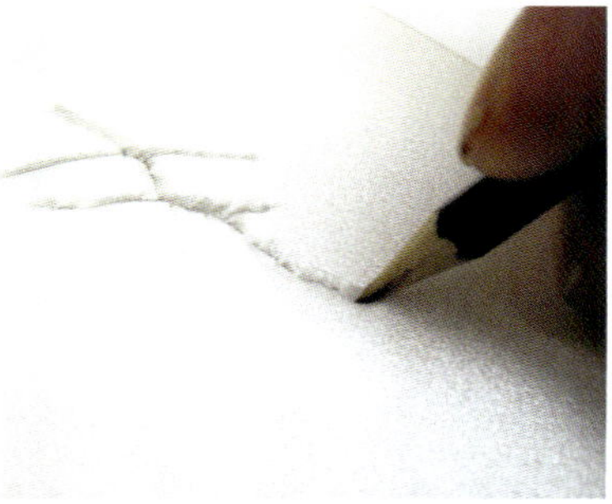

▲ The polyblock is a fun and unusual relief block. It marks easily. Even a pencil can make a mark on it.

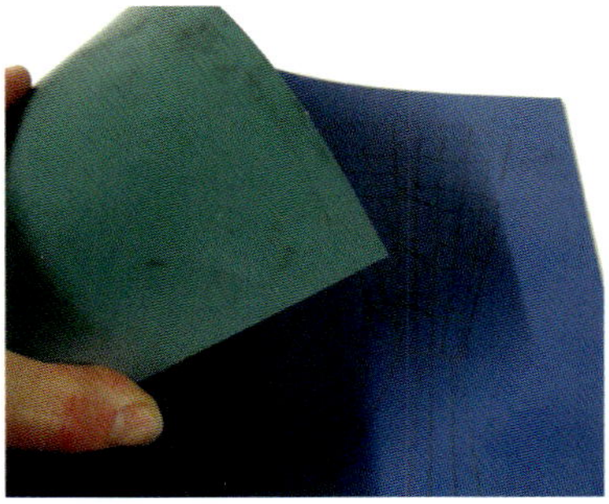

▲ PVC lino is very soft and flexible. It is extremely easy to cut and has no surface texture.

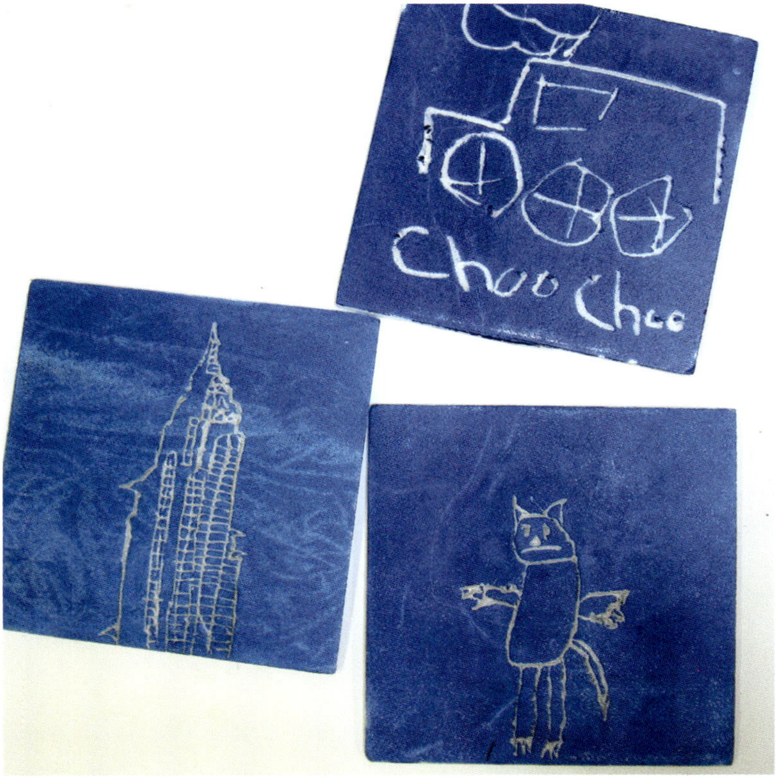

◀ The polyblock has a fair amount of surface texture. Images made with it are very immediate and striking.

Engraving plastic

Engraving plastic, or acrylic sheet, is a less expensive alternative to copper (traditionally used for engraving). It is perfectly flat and of a lightweight, thin and yet absolutely rigid construction. It has a black-coated side and a white-coated side. You cut into the black-coated side of the block, so that you can easily see the shape of the marks you are making to create the design. (You can also apply ink to the surface.) It does not have as much texture as an end grain block and this should be taken into account when printing the image. The pressure of the press being used should be adjusted accordingly as to alleviate any skidding or slipping marks that may appear in the final printed image.

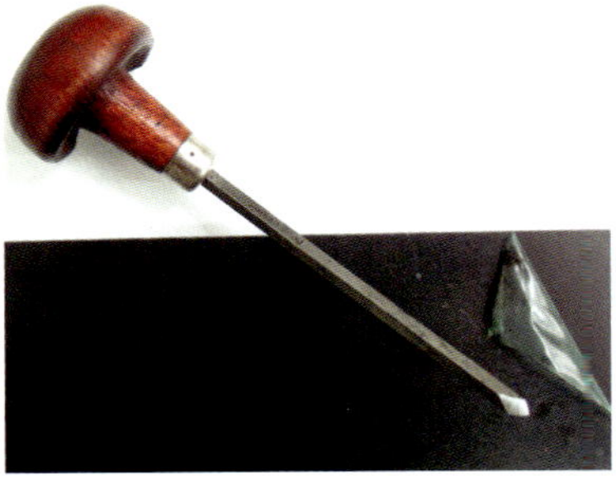

▲ Engraving plastic is lightweight and easy to cut.

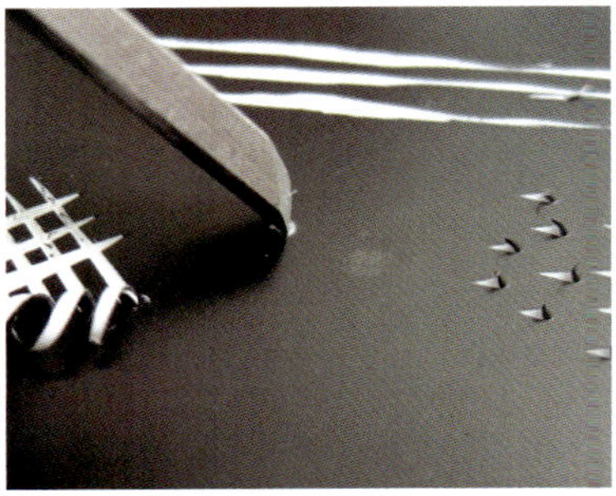

▲ An engraving tool cutting the surface of engraving plastic.

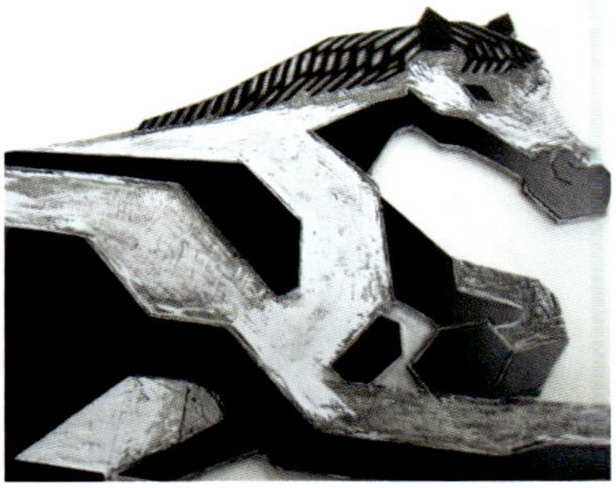

▲ Engraving plastic can be cut into shapes easily. The engraving plastic in this picture has been cut into a very complicated shape.

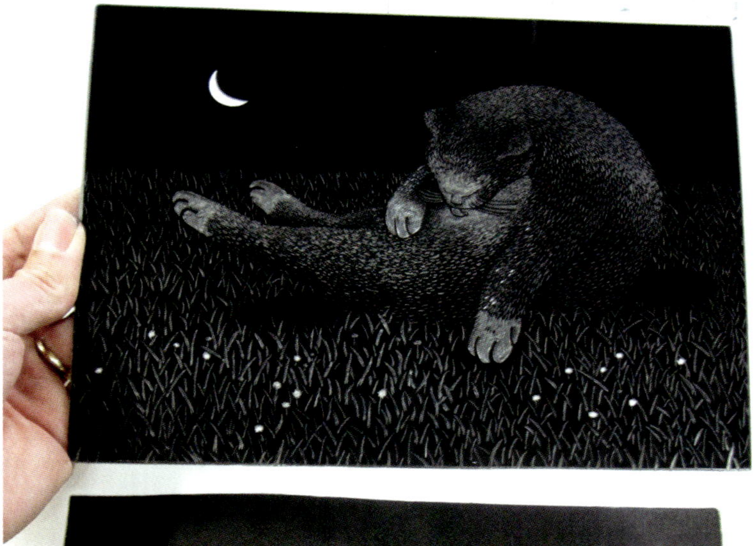

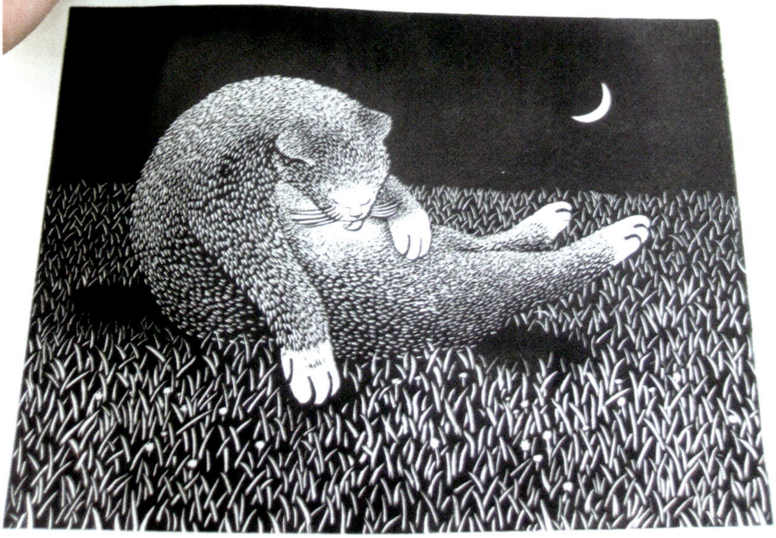

◀ A plastic engraving plate with image and printed image from plate by the artist Phil Solly.

TRANSFER METHODS FOR PLACING AN IMAGE ON A RELIEF BLOCK

Before cutting an image you will want to place it on the surface of the block as a guide. There are various methods of doing this.

Direct

Using a pencil, marker pen or biro, draw directly onto the block.

Gum arabic/Waterproof ink

Draw the image onto a piece of thin, smooth cartridge paper. Using a barely damp sponge, lightly coat the drawing with a very thin layer of gum arabic. Press this down firmly onto the block and leave it to dry. Finally, re-damp the paper. When the paper is removed, the drawing will remain on the surface of the block.

Lazertran®

Lazertran® is a man-made paper with a water-soluble coating. It can be used in inkjet printers and photocopiers. This makes it possible to put photographic images or digitally created images onto its surface. Once the image you wish to use has been printed or photocopied onto the Lazertran® it can be laminated (stuck onto) the relief block. Lazertran® can also be used on metals used for intaglio plates, lino blocks, acrylic plates and textile-based plates.

Carbon paper/Transfer paper

Place the carbon paper underneath your drawing and retrace the drawing, pressing down firmly and using a sharp pencil or biro. The thicker the paper the drawing is on, the more difficult it will be to make a successful transfer.

Tip

You can make your own transfer paper with tracing paper and red Conté® crayon.

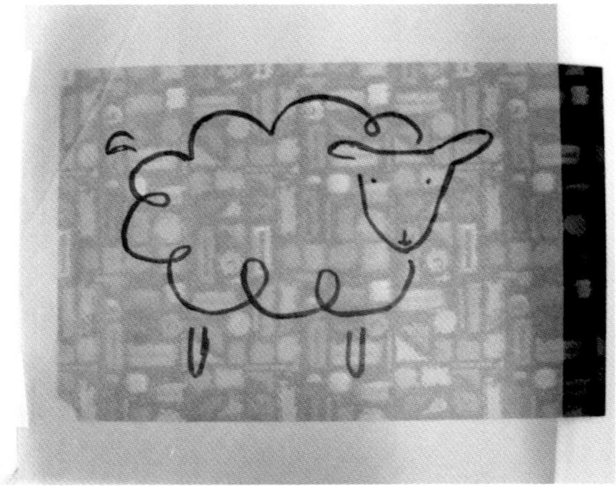

▲ Carbon paper is a very quick and direct way of transferring a drawn image onto a block. Simply retrace the original drawing with the carbon paper placed underneath it.

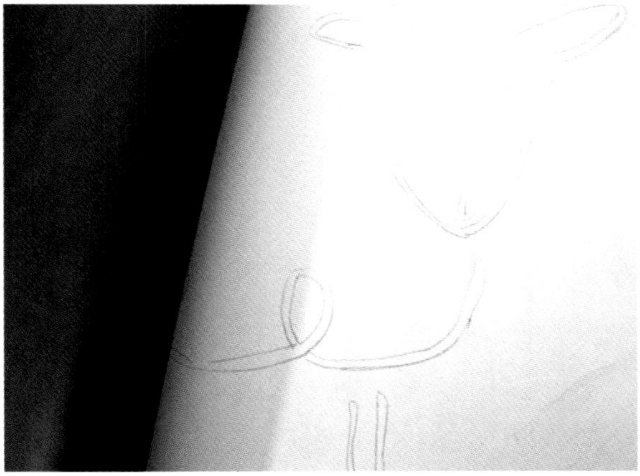

▲ The carbon offsets onto the surface of the block, creating a template of the image that can be followed easily with a cutting tool.

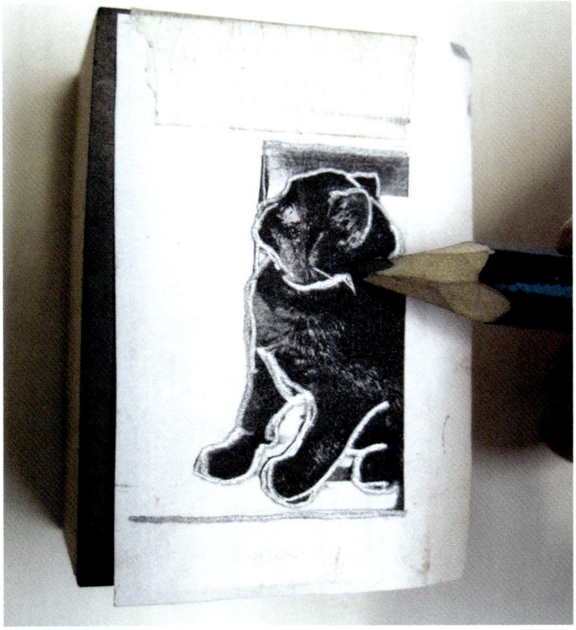
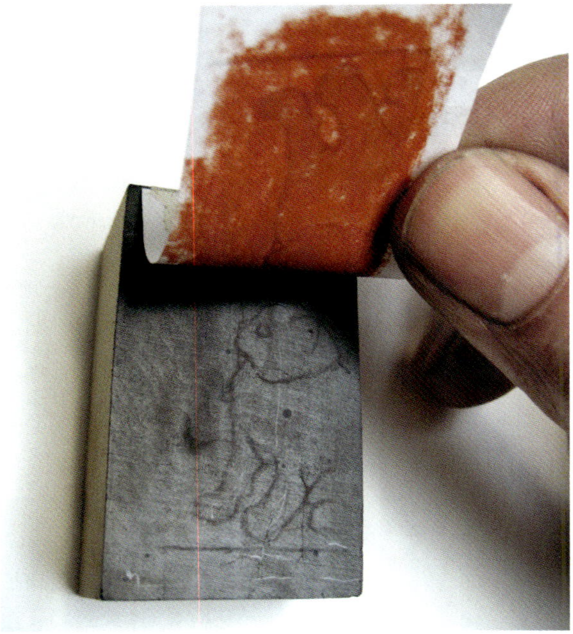

▲ LEFT TO RIGHT

This photocopy image has had red Conté® crayon rubbed on the back of it. A graphite pencil is used to trace around the image on the photocopy.

When the photocopy is lifted, you can see that the pressure of the pencil tip has offset the crayon onto the block in the shape of the image.

Photocopy transfer

Releasing a photocopy image from the surface of the paper it is on to a printing block is a process favoured by many artists. For many years, both acetone and screen wash were used to transfer a photocopied image to another surface. Changes in health and safety regulations mean that screen wash has been labelled a toxic substance, however, and it has been banned from schools and studios.

There are some alternatives, however. Oil of wintergreen/birch oil can be used and is sometimes successful. Saturate the paper image and run the image and block through the press. (You may have to do this several times.) Hand-burnishing may prove difficult as it will be a challenge to apply enough pressure for the drawing to be released. The oil will not sit on the paper and magically make the image appear on the block, unfortunately.

Methylated spirits can also be relatively successful in releasing imagery and text from some types of printed newspapers. But again, the use of recycled paper and modern printing inks rather than the old-style ink toner which was the key to releasing the image makes the process unsuccessful and frustratingly hit and miss.

Graphite transfer

Using newsprint or a lightweight cartridge paper (80 gsm) works most successfully. Choose a pencil with as much grease content as possible: B pencils with Numbers 3, 4, 5 and 6 work best. They contain the softest graphite, hence the most grease. H pencils contain very little or no grease so will only disappoint, especially if you spend a long time making

▶ LEFT TO RIGHT: Draw an image on semi-opaque paper. Drafting film, tracing paper or even tissue paper is suitable.

Turn over the drawing. Take a coloured piece of chalk and rub it over the drawn marks. (They are easy to see because the paper is semi-opaque.)

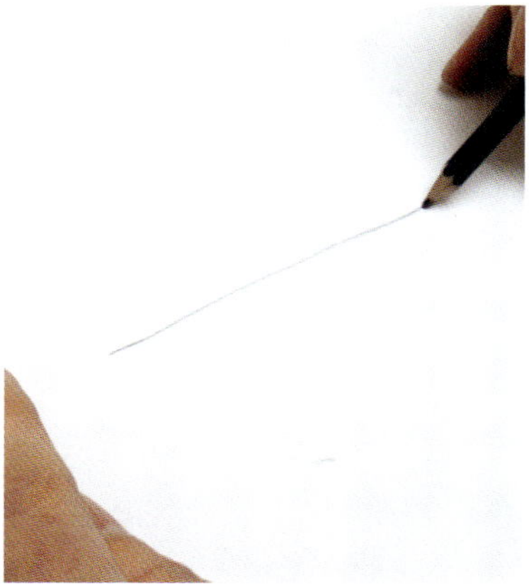

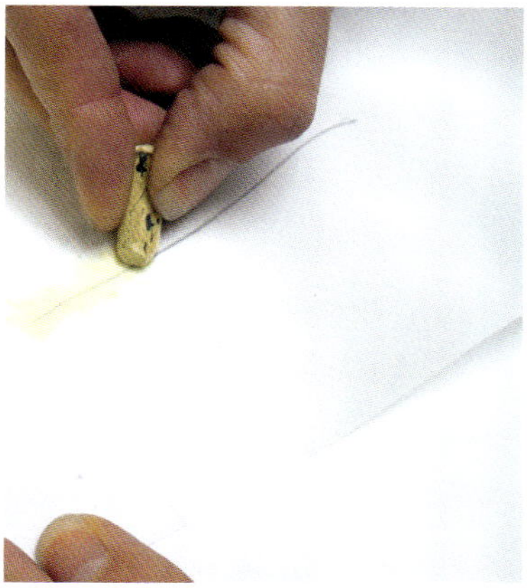

▶ LEFT TO RIGHT: Turn over the marked semi-opaque paper. Place it in position on the block. Re-draw following the lines you have previously made.

The pressure of the pencil offsets the yellow chalk onto the surface of the block. You now have a template to follow with your cutting tools. You can spray the block with aerosol fixative to fix the chalk temporarily. It is easily removed with a good quality hard-surface cleaner.

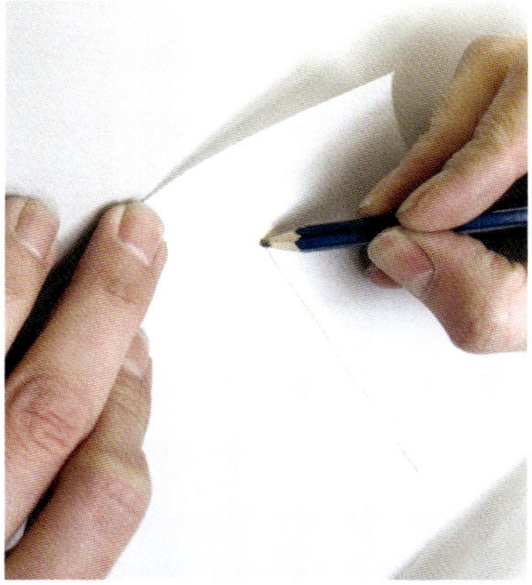

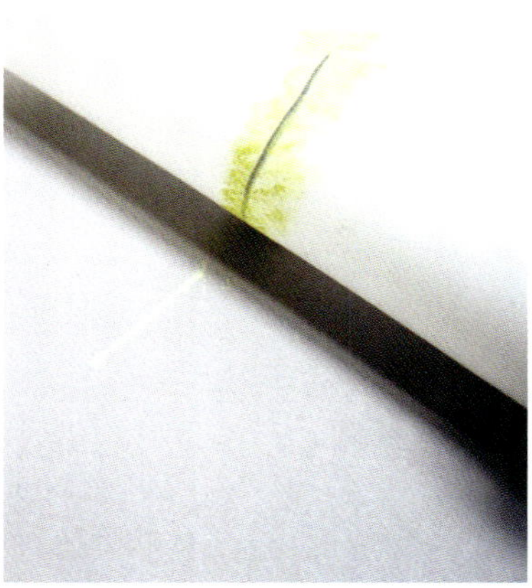

a terrific drawing and it does not transfer – or even worse, is damaged in the image transfer process. (This process can be used on wood blocks, metal plates [degrease metal plates with methylated spirits], cardboard and plastic substrates.)

Tip

If a greasy enough pencil is used – the B pencil number range, nos. 6, 7, 8 etc. – you can transfer the drawn image by hand burnishing it onto the block. This is particularly useful if you are using a wood block. You may also transfer graphite drawings successfully onto hard ground etching plates using this simple process.

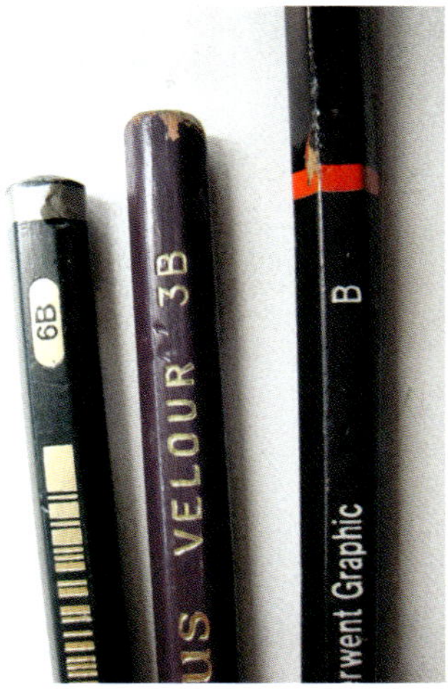

◀ B drawing pencils contain more graphite and make very greasy drawn lines. Graphite pencil numbers 3B–9B are the most suitable to use when making a drawing for a transfer. (See pp.99–101 for a full step-by-step illustration sequence.)

Offset transfer

Offsetting a proofed image from one printing substrate to another is a practical registration technique. It can be used for offsetting intaglio, lithographic and relief images onto a second printing block which will be used to advance the image.

This way of transferring an image is used to transfer an image from one block to another (in this case from an etched plate to lino) to aid in the progression of registering the design for the cutting of multiple blocks.

Tip

Dust the image on the surface of the lino block with French chalk after printing. This will stop the image from smudging while you cut it.

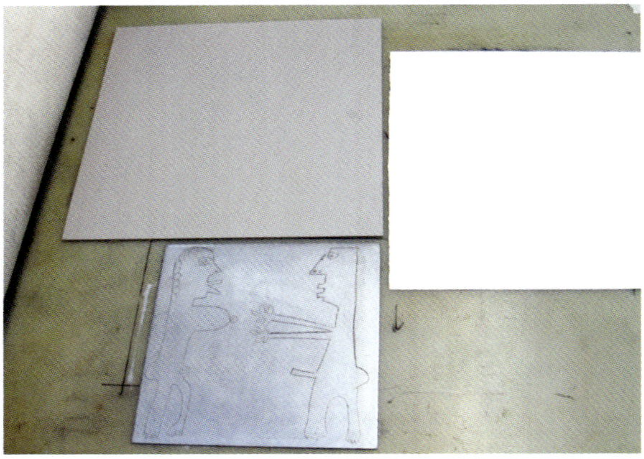

1 Ink and wipe the plate you wish to transfer so it is ready to print onto dampened printing paper.

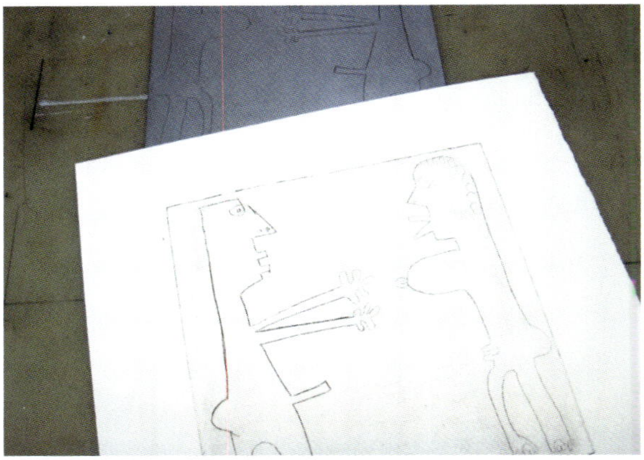

2 Place the paper over the plate/block and roll the paper and block through the press if it is a spring-roller press, or draw the swing arm towards you if you are using a Columbian or Albion press. Use firm, even pressure and a suitable lightweight paper if you are burnishing by hand.

3 Remove the paper that now has the printed image on it. Place it on the clean lino block, making sure the edge of the paper matches up with the lino block edges.

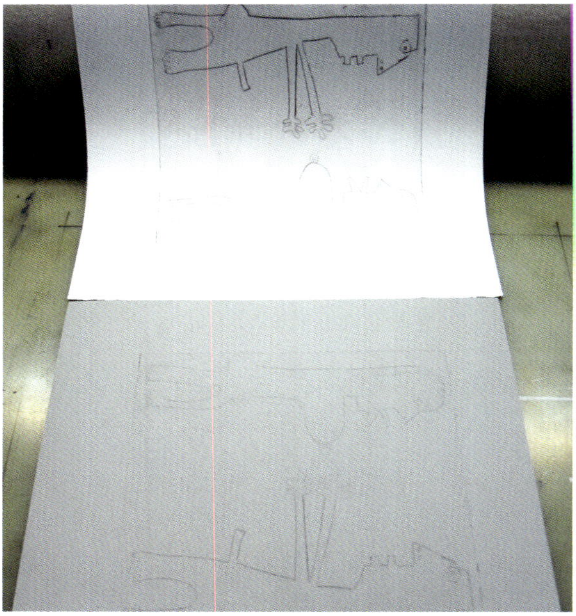

Tip

The paper used for relief printing is extremely varied and comprises hand-made papers, commercially produced papers and specialist papers as well as fabrics, textiles and alternative surfaces such as hard board, cardboard, plastic and wood. If you can somehow offset your printing block onto a surface, then pretty much anything can have a relief print printed onto it.

CUTTING AND INKING TOOLS

An extensive array of cutting tools are now available to the artist for mark making and cutting into a relief block, as well as home-made tools.

Tools used for woodcuts and linocuts are called cutters, blades and gouges. Jigsaws, chisels, handsaws, scalpels and Stanley® knives can also be used.

Tools used for wood (and metal) engraving come in a variety of styles and shapes, all of which have specific uses. They include burins, flat scorpers, spit sticks, round edge gravers, multi-line tools, flat gravers, round gravers, angle tint tools and elliptic tint tools.

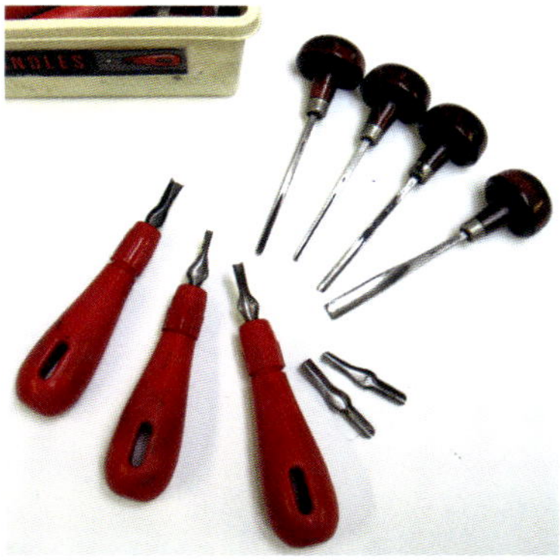

▲ **A variety of inexpensive lino cut tools with different cutting blades.**

▼ **Specific tools come readily available in sets. A set of Japanese cutting tools, which includes a baren, is pictured here.**

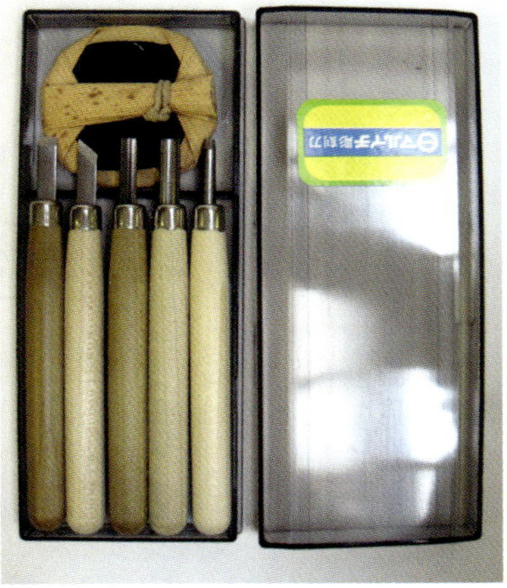

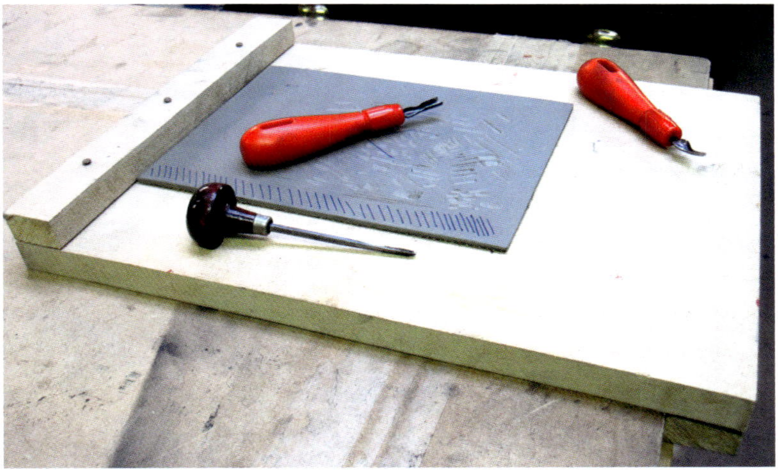

▲ **The bench hook is a device that supports the block during the cutting time. Hooks can be made easily out of off-cuts of MDF or other flat-surfaced smooth-grain wood. The hook is made so that it has a strip of wood on one of its underside edges and another on the topside at the end opposite. The block pushes against the topside strip and bottom strip pushes against the edge of the table it is on, thus keeping everything stable.**

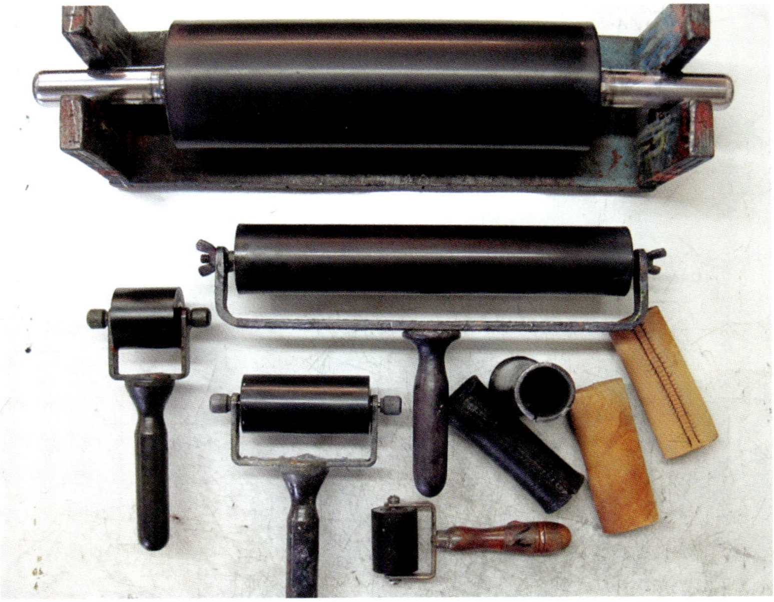

◀ **Rollers come in all sizes. They are an invaluable tool for inking up any relief print surface.**

CUTTING A WOODBLOCK

▶ LEFT TO RIGHT: A sharp cutting tool makes the cutting process easier.

A close-up of the cutting tool and block.

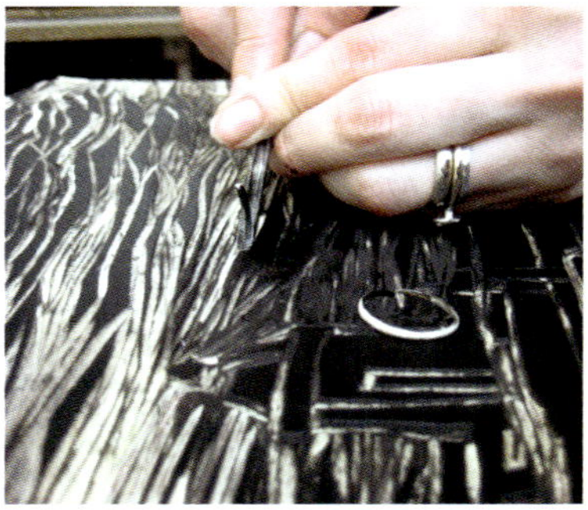

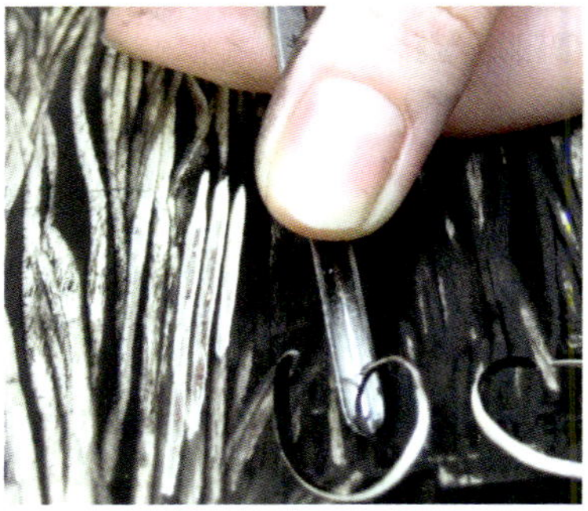

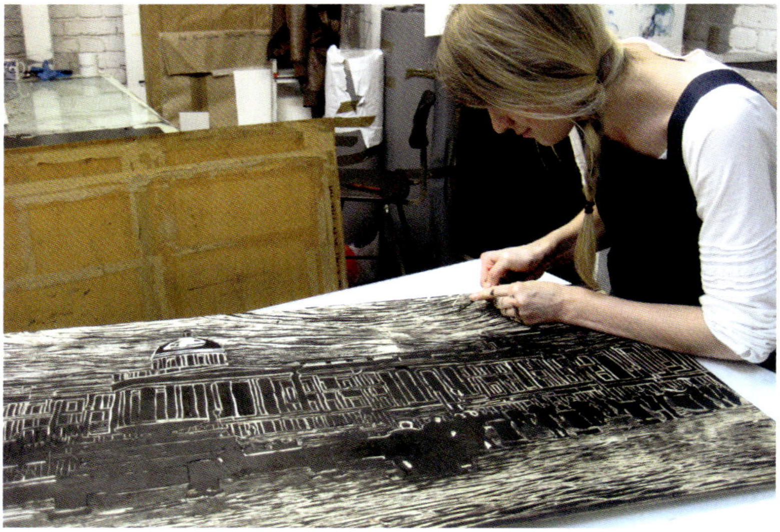

◀ The artist Natalia Avdeeva working on a large-scale woodblock. A woodblock of this scale takes time to complete.

▶ Natalia Avdeeva with a proof from the woodblock, which has been inked in oil-based black relief ink.

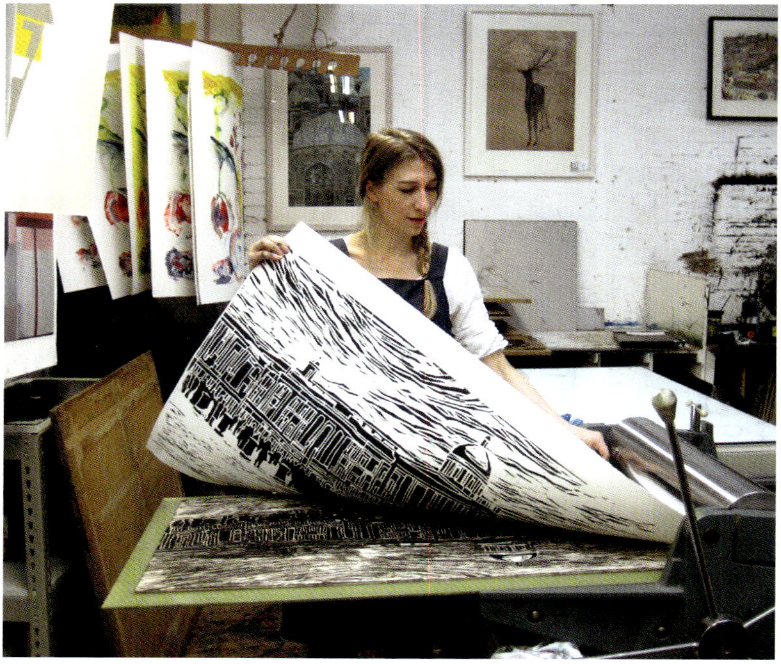

DRAWING AN IMAGE ON LINO

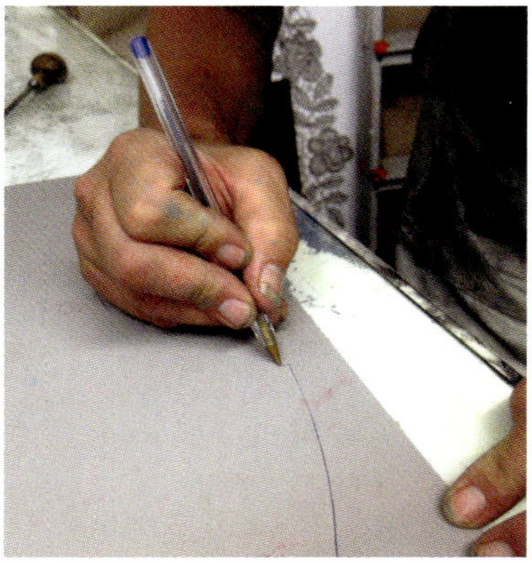

▲ A pencil drawing on the block makes a helpful guide.

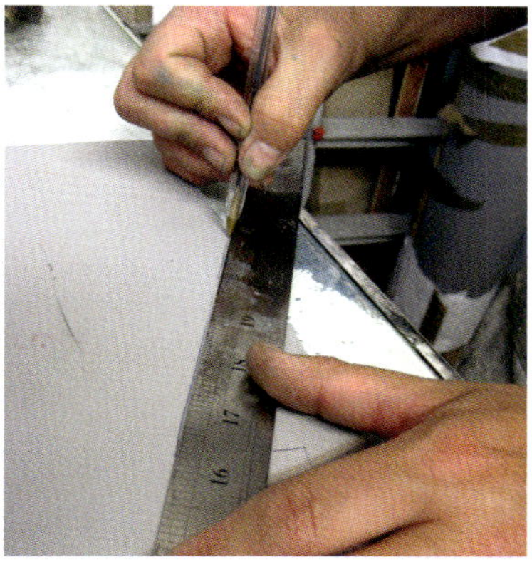

▲ A ruler can be used to draw straight lines.

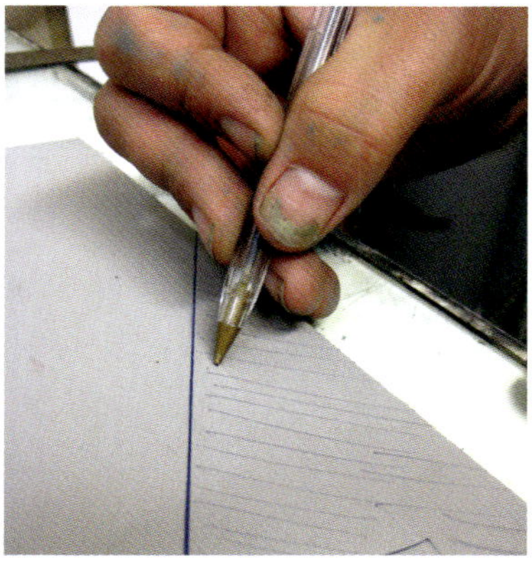

▲ Highlighting areas on the block by shading indicates the large areas to be cut away.

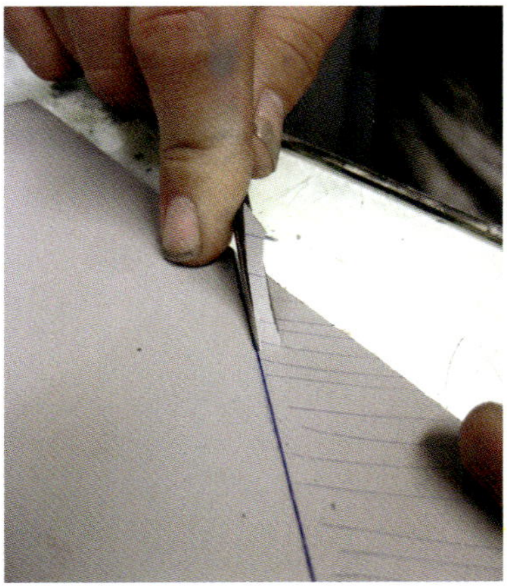

▲ Cutting straight lines in lino is a skill.

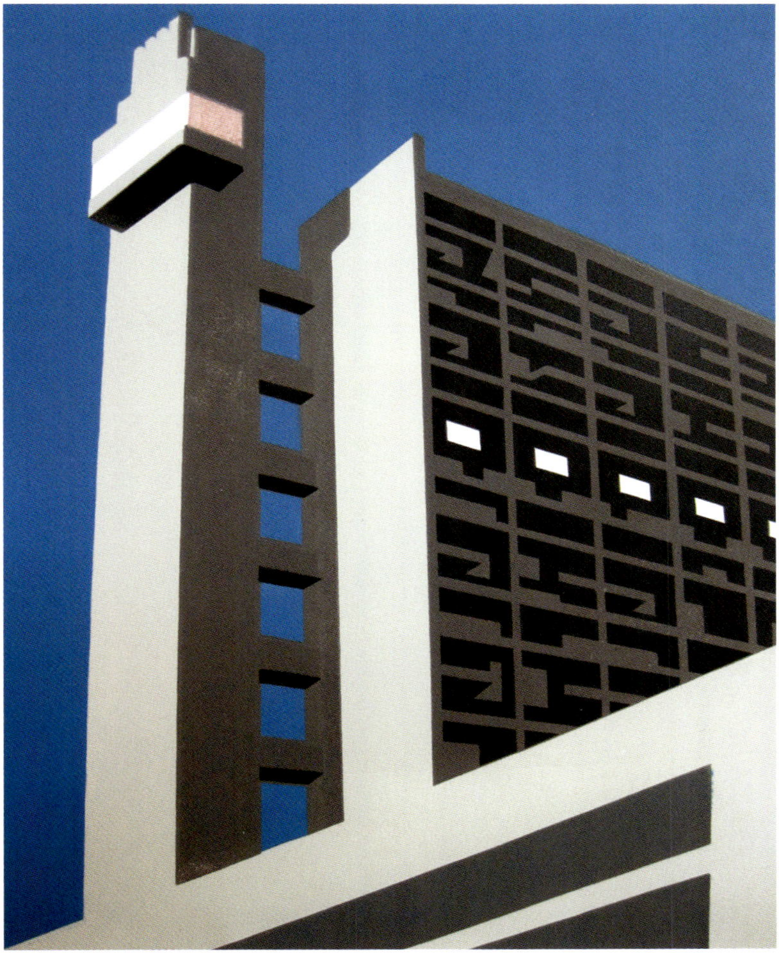

▶ Paul Catherall, *Trellick Blue II*, 2011. Linocut, 57 x 45 cm.

PRESSES

Relief prints are printed using conventional relief presses such as the Albion and the Columbian. Nipping presses and letterpress presses such as the Adana are also suitable, as are sprung-roller presses such as the Karsten Berglin machines used at Artichoke. Relief prints are also printed by hand (see p.29). A hard block or pad called a baren is used to apply pressure through the paper against the inked surface.

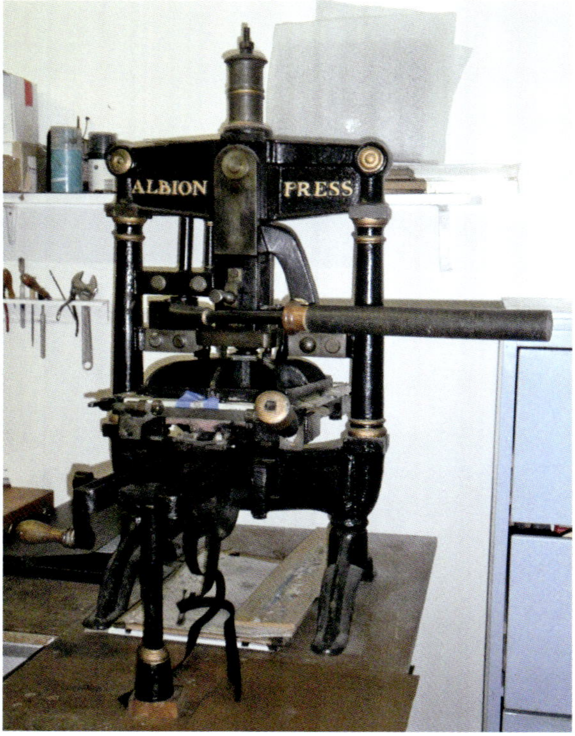

◀ The Albion is a traditional relief printing press. It comes in many sizes: this picture shows a tabletop Albion with a 38 x 25 cm (15 x 10 in.) bed.

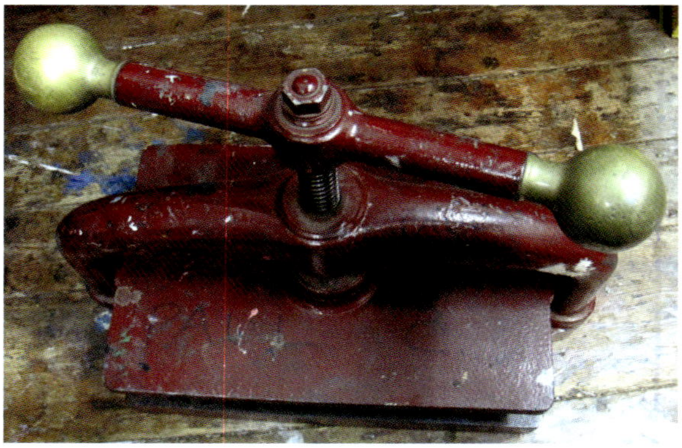

▲ Nipping presses have long been used by bookbinders and are very suitable for relief printing. They have a relatively small printing area but can be used inventively for stamping and embossing.

▼ Pressure is exerted by turning the handle of the nipping press, which lowers the top platen onto the block to be printed. You must use firm pressure to create an adequate printing pressure.

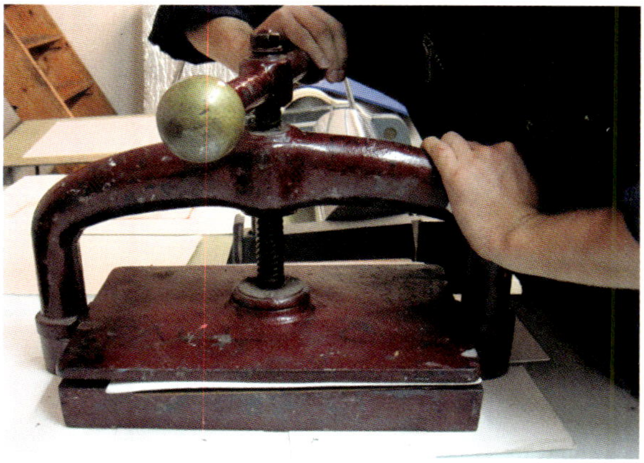

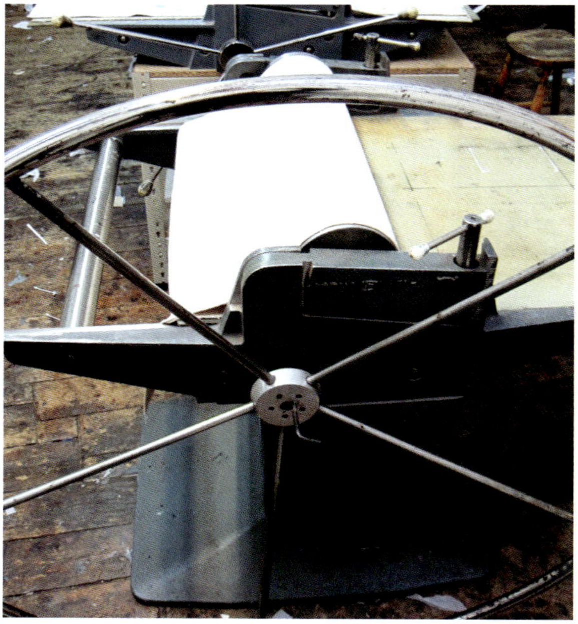

▲ The Kasten Berglin sprung-roller printing press is ideal for relief printing. It can print block heights of up to 5 cm (2 in.) and blocks of great length. The largest block we have printed using this press is 360 x 76 cm (12 ft x 30 in.).

Printing with cut plywood shapes

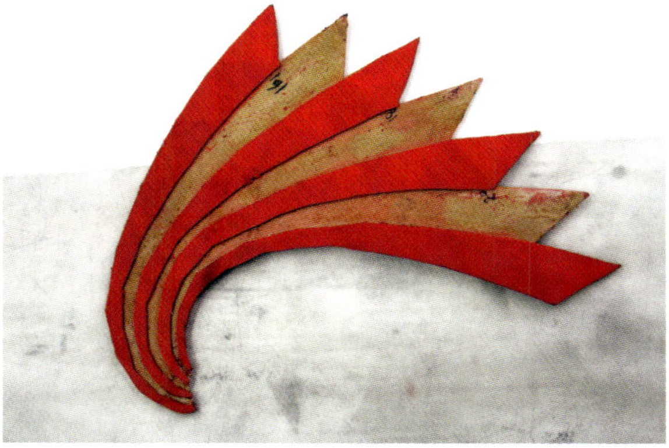

▶ The plywood has been cut into an intricate shape. The surface has been sealed with varnish, and red ink has been rolled onto the raised image area.

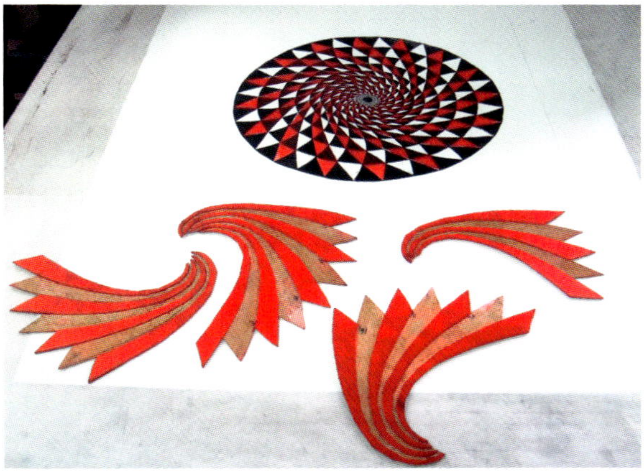

▲ Several complicated plywood pieces required for this image have been cut.

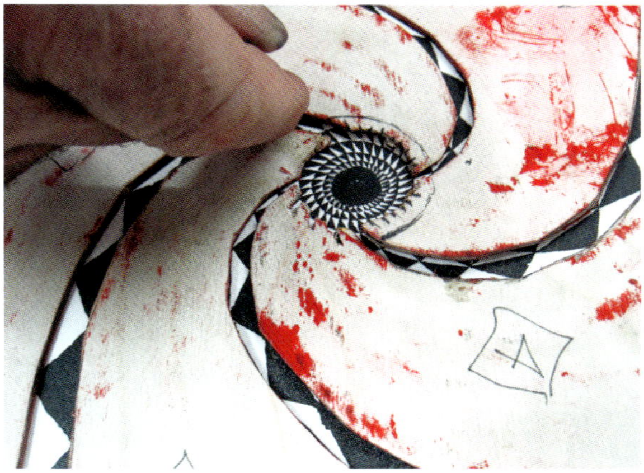

▲ The cut plywood shapes have been placed into position on the linocut image (previously printed).

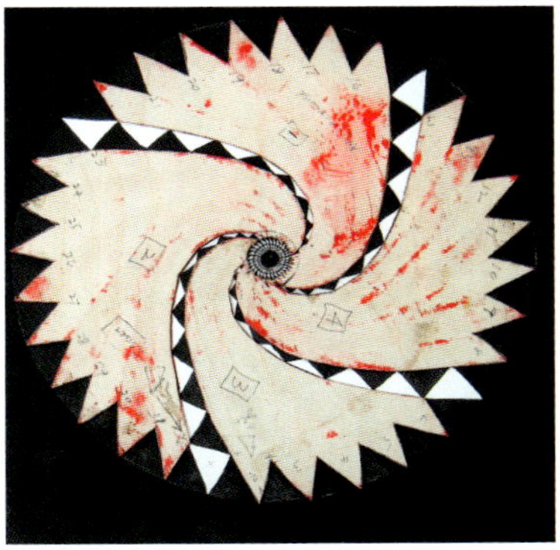

▲ The inked woodcut pieces have been placed face down on the linocut image.

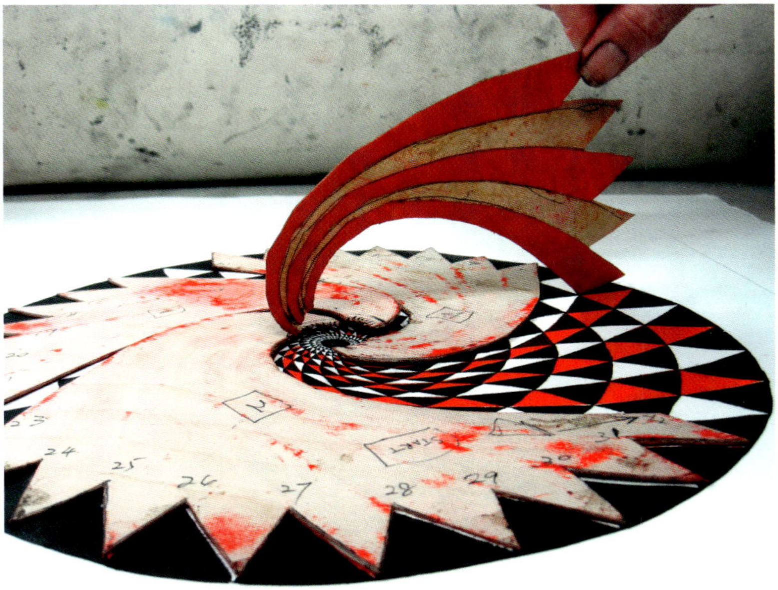

▶ The image was printed using a fixed-roller etching press with no pressure and a single blanket.

REDUCTION AND REGISTERED BLOCKS CUTTING METHOD

In the reduction method, the same block is used and cut away for each colour necessary to print the design. As a result, you must plan your design carefully beforehand and also print as many as you will need for the entire edition, as you cannot reprint previous colours because they will have been cut away.

Using the method of registered lino blocks is very popular. A series of blocks are cut, one for each colour necessary to make up the completed design. Each block is exactly the same size meaning that successive blocks to be printed can easily be placed in the correct printing position.

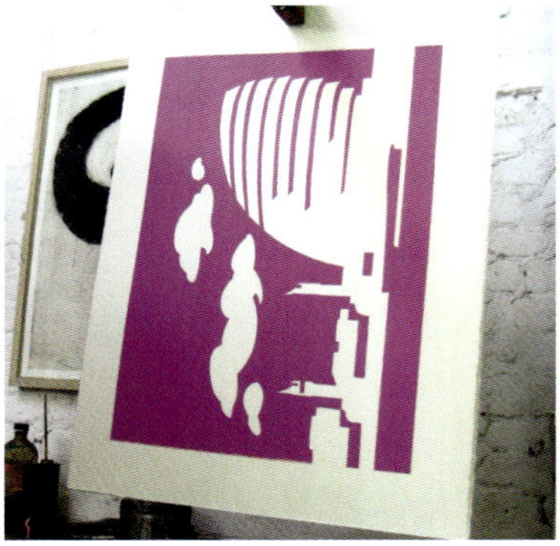

▲ A relief print can be made from many registered blocks. The pink is the first colour printed for this linocut image.

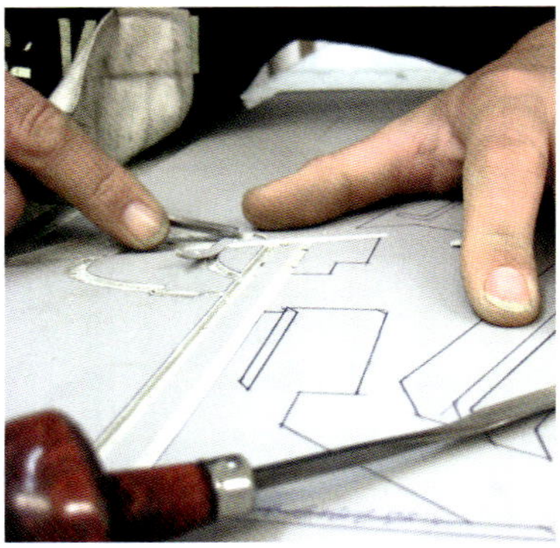

▲ The second block image areas to be cut away have been drawn with biro.

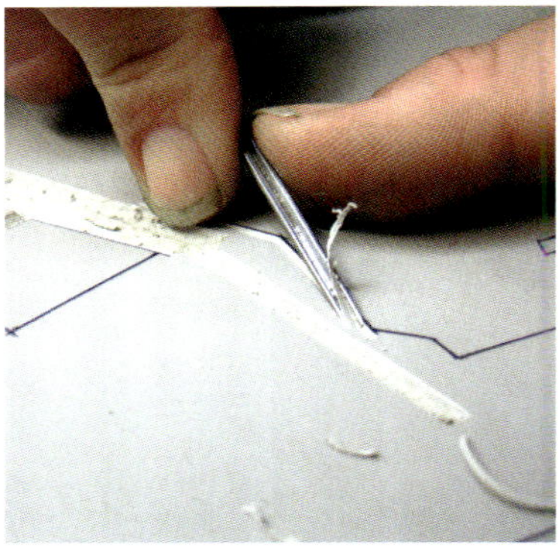

▲ The choice of cutting tools is solely up to the artist. Fine lines will dictate the cutting tool of choice, as will large, open areas that need to be removed.

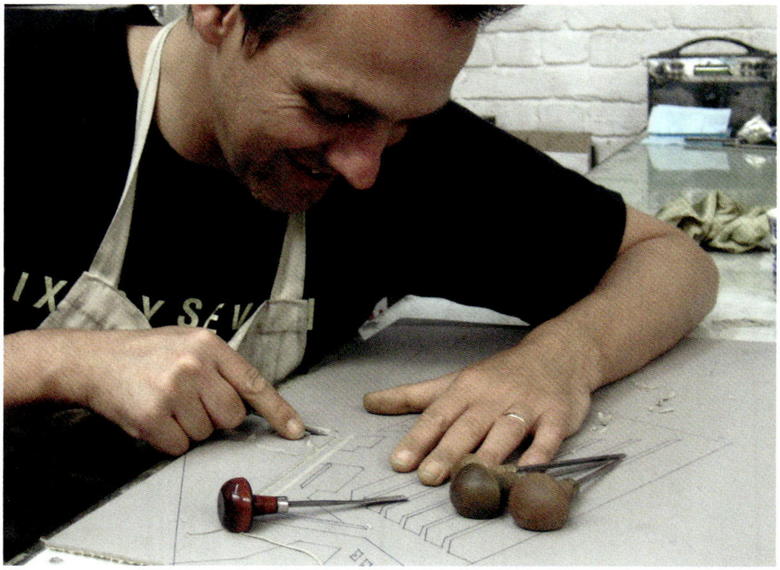

◀ The artist Paul Catherall shows the patience and care essential for the accurate cutting of lines, especially when there are several blocks to be made and registered to complete the image.

HAND BURNISHING

Relief prints can be printed by using hand pressure and a baren in a process known as hand burnishing. A baren is a smooth, flat, hand-held wooden disc or rounded oblong shape which is slightly cupped or has a handle across its back so that you can grip it. It is used to apply even pressure to the printing surface.

To make a relief print, ink the printing block and position the printing paper on the inked surface. Next place a piece of newsprint on top of the printing paper to prevent any friction, scarring or tearing of the paper by the baren. To make the print, grip the baren in your hand and place it flat side down on the newsprint covering the paper, using very firm pressure move the baren across all areas of the surface of the block. It is important to remember to pass the baren over the outer edges of the block to pick up its outline.

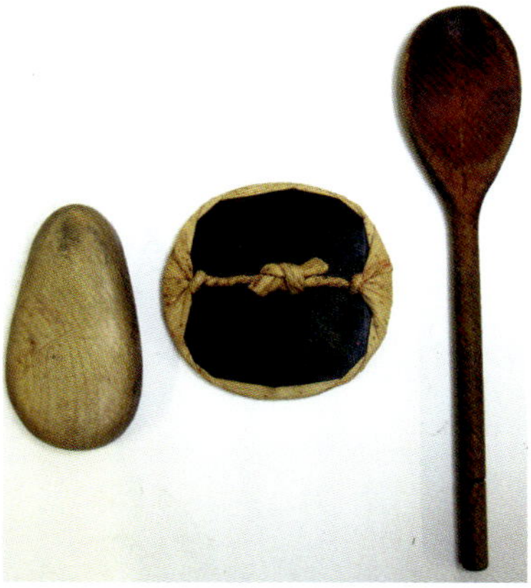

▲ This picture shows tools used for hand burnishing relief prints: a wooden burnisher, a baren and the indispensable wooden or metal spoon.

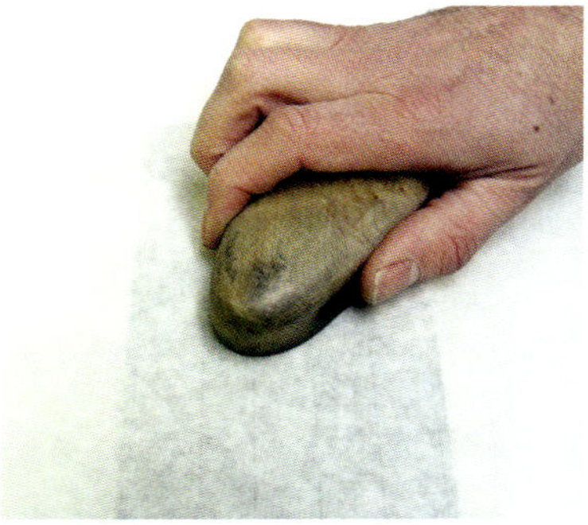

▲ A correct and comfortable way to hold a wooden burnisher.

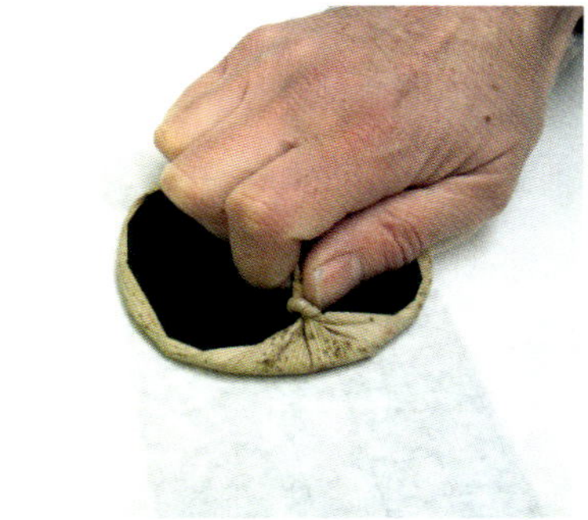

▲ A correct and comfortable way to hold a Japanese baren.

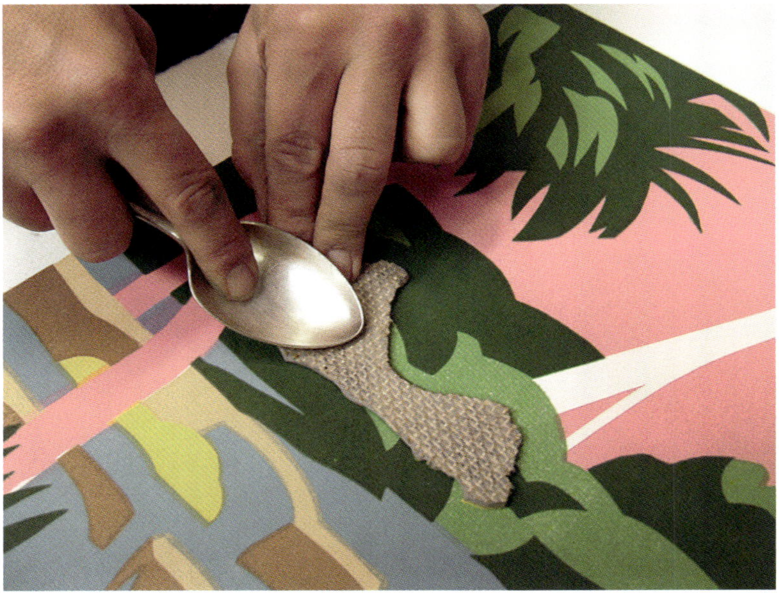

▶ A wooden or metal spoon is suitable to use to burnish a lino shape into a complicated multi-block lino colour scheme.

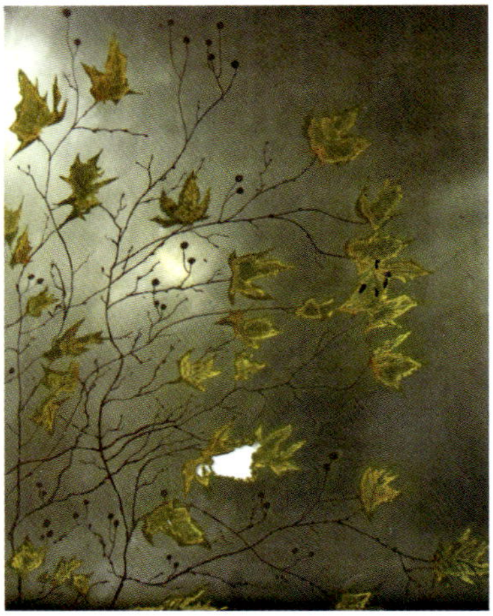

▲ **An open bite steel plate. Note the extremely ragged torn metal shapes. How well the plate is stopped out on both the front and the back helps to dictate how the lines and shapes will be bitten.**

ALTERNATIVE METHODS OF RELIEF PRINTING

Intaglio plates may be deliberately designed to be printed in relief. The simplest way to print an intaglio plate in relief is to surface roll the plate with an inked roller.

The design on the plate does not have to be deeply etched, although many artists desire a deeply etched line on the surface of the plate because it gives a more distinct and more embossed line.

A line or texture on the surface that has been deeply etched on a *steel* plate is called 'open bite'. (See Chapter 5.) On zinc and copper plates, however, 'open bite' creates a different affect. Normally the depth of texture achieved on zinc and copper is quite shallow, because both metals must be aquatinted (see Chapter 5) for the plate surfaces to hold tone.

Of course this process can be missed out and the surfaces directly etched with nitric acid or copper sulphate (in the case of zinc) or ferric chloride (copper). The destruction of the metal areas will take some time – many hours – after which deeply incised misshapen lines and open areas will occur where the unprotected areas of the plate have been destroyed.

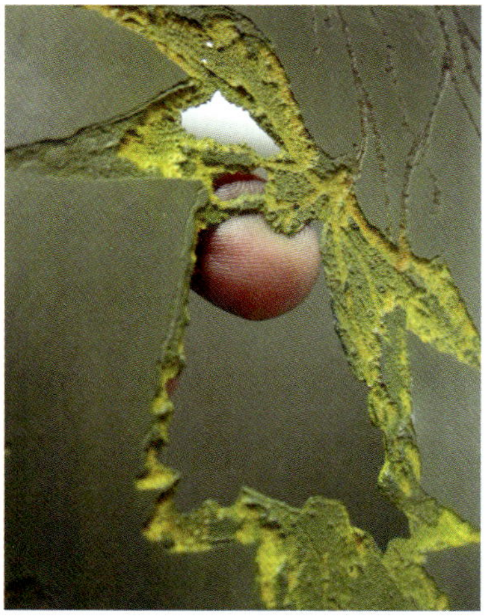

▲ **The open bite on this plate is extreme. It creates a very organic and pleasing affect to the image.**

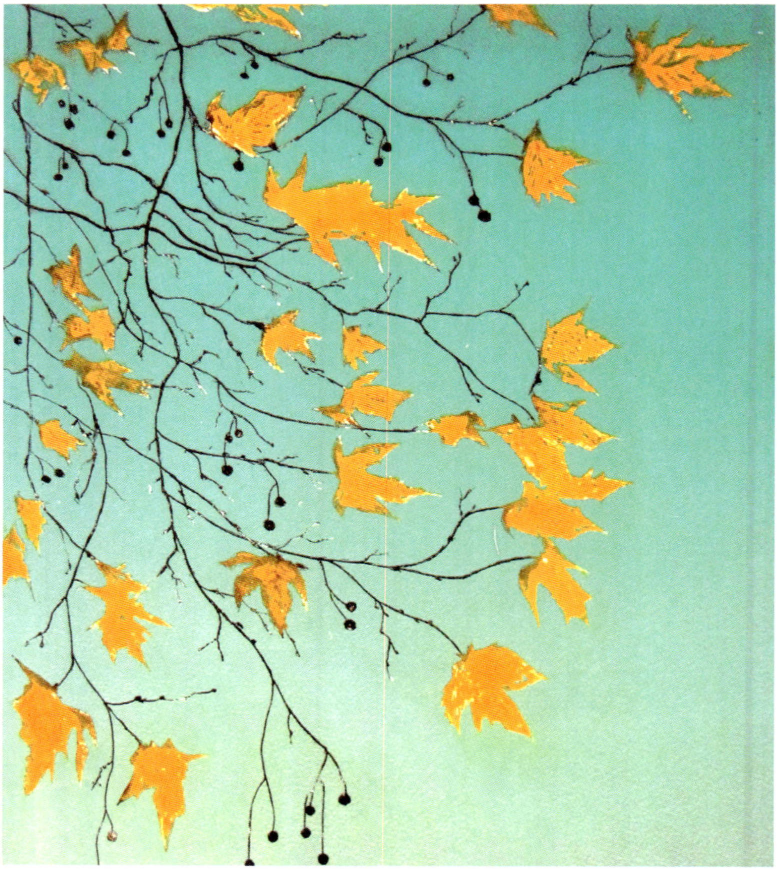

▶ **Peter Wareham, *Autumn Plane*, 2009. Open bite and emboss on steel, 41 x 48 cm (16 x 19 in.).**

Photopolymer film/photopolymer roll-on emulsion

It is as easy to deep etch plates which have straw hat varnish and stop-out varnish painted onto them as it is to deep etch plates which have photopolymer film laminated onto them or photopolymer emulsion rolled onto them. All of these grounds stop the mordant biting into the surface of the metal.

Photopolymer films and photopolymer roll-on emulsion work on the principle that the photopolymer element is laminated securely onto the plate.

The image is created on the plate using the normal exposure sequence appropriate for the positive of the image to be used. The areas of emulsion on the plate that are not hardened by the UV light stay soft and are washed away exposing the substrate area to be etched. The hardened areas are very durable and provide an excellent resist to the action of the mordant.

To make the image look like a relief-printed image, use a negative image rather than a positive one. This can be done with a photocopier or with many of the image-facilitating software programs available for all computers now with which you can invert the image.

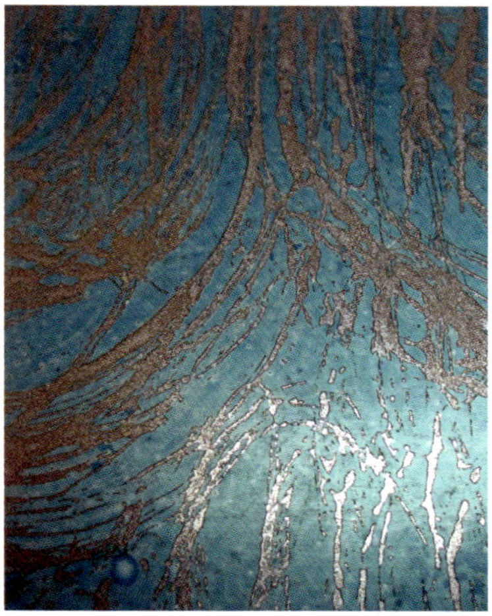

▲ To make the image look like a relief-printed image, use a negative image rather than a positive image.

Flexograph plate as relief print

Flexograph plates (also known as solar plates) are actually photo-sensitive relief plates. In recent times, other processes in printmaking have commandeered them: they are used in intaglio printing where they are equally successful as etching plates, for example. Originally, however, they were designed for commercial letterpress relief printing.

A flexography plate comprises a rubber-like (solid gel-like) photosensitive polymer emulsion, which is adhered to a non-reflective backing of thin steel. Different manufacturers' makes will use different substrates to which the emulsion is attached. They all can be processed the same way – in theory.

Sluicing the plate in a tray of room temperature water develops the image. The longer the image remains in the water, the more deeply dissolved the image becomes. The plate is then dried thoroughly, removing all traces of water with high heat.

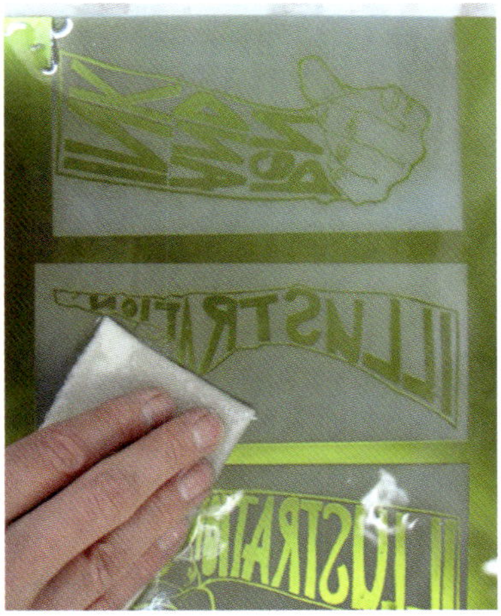

▲ Flexograph plates are actually photosensitive relief plates.

ETCHING LINO WITH CAUSTIC SODA (sodium hydroxide)

Etching linoleum with a caustic soda solution creates a variety of textures on the surface.

The areas protected by the stop-out varnish or beeswax applied to the lino block will print solid when ink is rolled onto the block.

The areas etched by the caustic solution will print as uneven textured tonal areas on the block. (Lazertran® transfer images are often used when etching lino with caustic soda.)

- To etch the lino, first degrease the lino block with methylated spirits or denatured alcohol (surgical spirit).
- Draw your image onto the lino.
- Paint stop-out varnish on the lino block. (Melting beeswax onto the lino block is also a way of protecting areas of the lino that you do not want the caustic to mark.)

It is essential to wear eye protection, nitrile gloves, a respirator (to filter air), face mask (to filter dust) and an apron at all times during this process.

Mixing the caustic soda solution

Two crucial notes here.

1. The solution will heat up considerably. Do not be alarmed.
2. Always add the caustic soda crystals to the water. *Never* add water to the caustic soda crystals.

We recommend the following mixture for making a caustic soda solution. Most caustic soda solutions are unsuccessful because the solution has not been made to the correct strength, the lino block has not been degreased or the solution has not been left on the block long enough.

Caustic solution

- Ceramic mixing bowl (a Mason pudding bowl is ideal)
- Long-handled wooden spoon
- 60ml cold water (4 tablespoons of water)
- 120–180ml caustic soda crystals (approximately 8–12 tablespoons)
- Decorators' wallpaper paste (this is a very fine powder available at DIY stores) or acrylic medium
- Glass jar with wide-mouth opening and screw-tight lid

Add the caustic soda crystals to the cold water *very* slowly – one tablespoon at a time.

Do not add another tablespoon of caustic soda until the previous tablespoon has dissolved. If the mixture is still too watery you may need to add more than the minimum eight recommended tablespoons of caustic soda to the solution. Continue to add more single tablespoons of caustic soda to the mixture until no more of the crystals will dissolve

– the mixture has now reached its saturation point and should be left to cool down (this will approximately 15 minutes).

Adding acrylic medium to the caustic mixture will make the mixture flow more easily (it will become loose and painterly). Adding wallpaper paste to the caustic mixture will make the mixture stiffer, which means shaped marks can be made more effectively.

Apply the caustic solution to the lino block. (Do not paint out the areas of the design in which the caustic soda is going to be applied.) Leave the solution on the surface of the lino block for at least two hours. To many, etching as a concept and the action of a plate being etched conjures up an immediate image of fierce action, but it actually takes a good while for the caustic to mark the surface of the lino.

Wash the lino thoroughly, first in a tray of water and then under running water to remove all traces of the caustic soda solution. Again, it is essential that you wear eye protection, nitrile gloves, a face mask and apron while doing this.

Tip

You may want to use two different glass jars to divide the caustic solution so you can add either acrylic medium or wallpaper paste.

OTHER RELIEF TECHNIQUES: FROTTAGE, EMBOSS, CASTING, STENCILLING

Frottage is the act of taking a rubbing from a raised, uneven surface using a transfer material (such as graphite, chalk, charcoal or crayon) onto a fabric, textile or paper substrate.

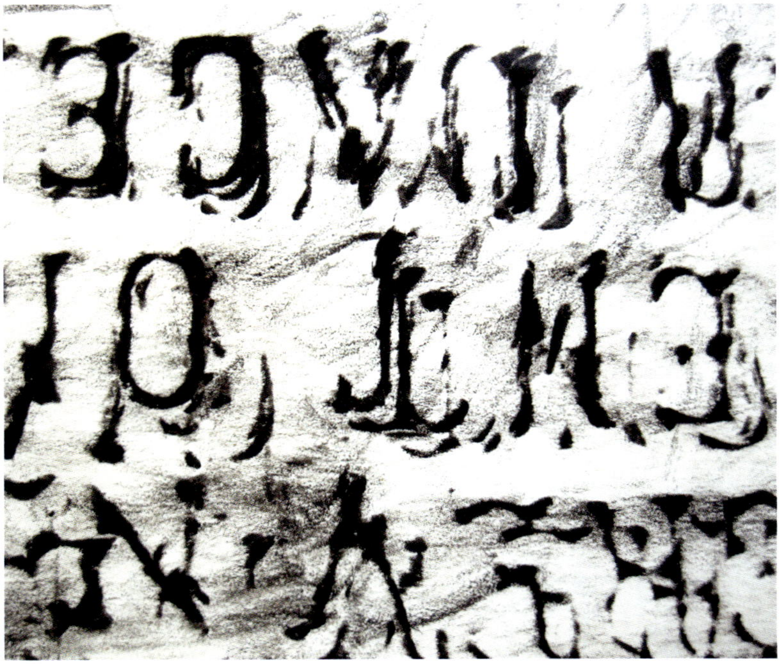

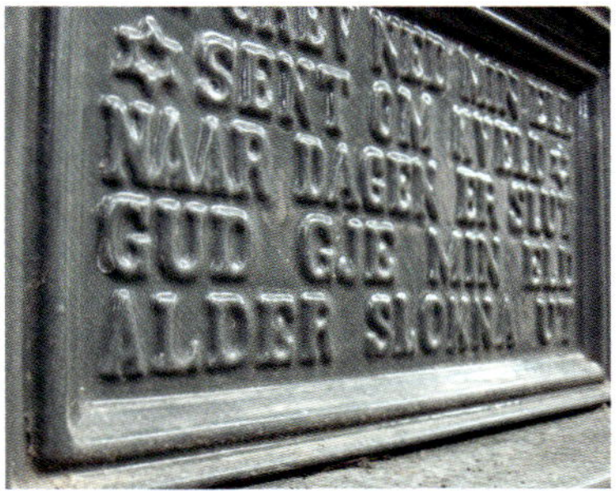

▲ Frottage surface to be rubbed.

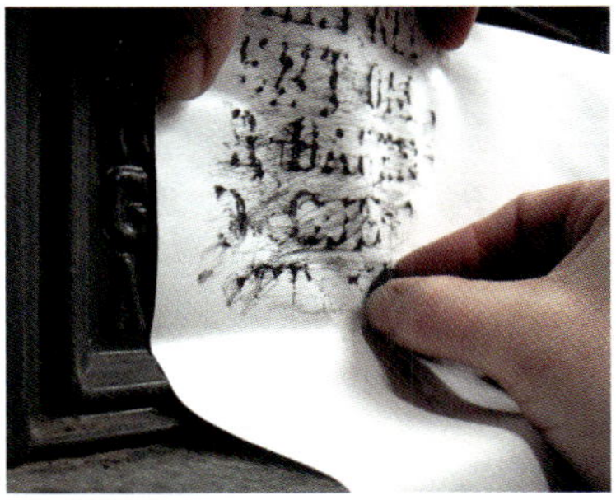

▲ A soft oil crayon is used to gently rub the raised letters on the surface of this old stove.

◀ Frottage image on newsprint.

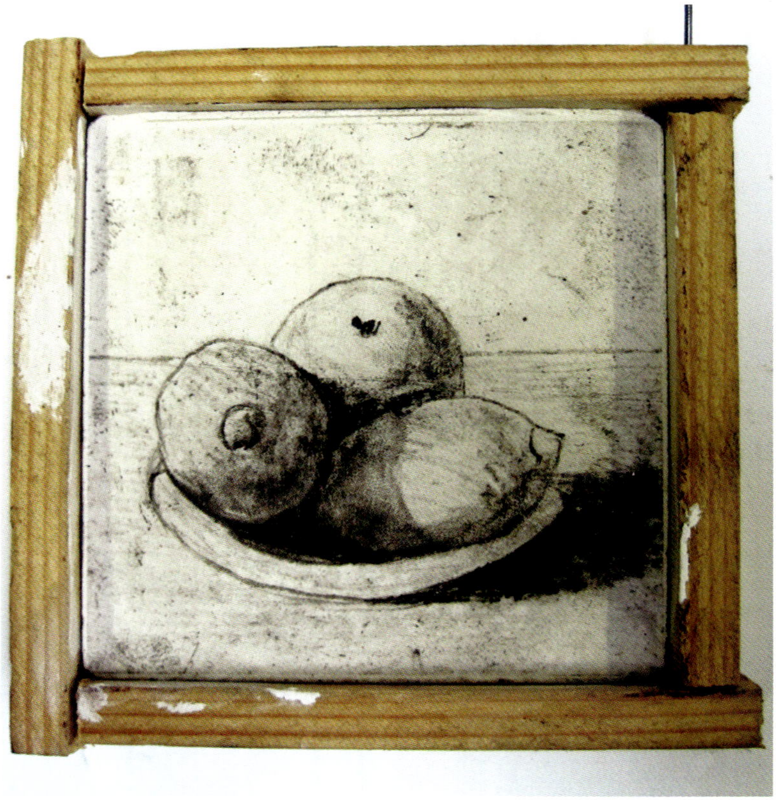

▲ **This plaster cast was taken of an inked etching plate. Black ink was used. Wooden strips were nailed together to create a shallow box into which the plaster was poured. This kept the wet plaster in a block shape until the plaster had set.**

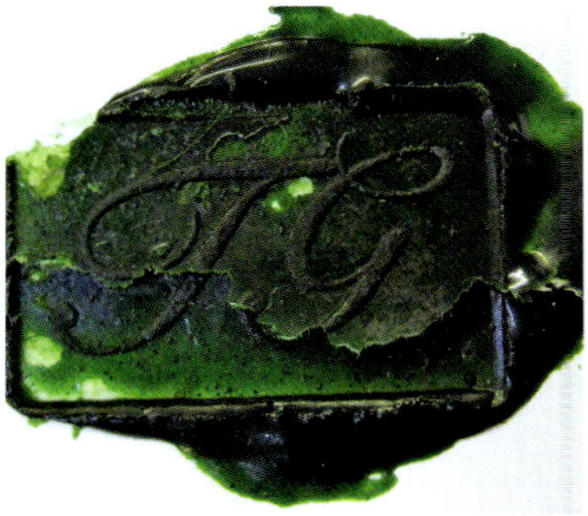

▲ **Seals with logos, names, initials and crests were once popular. Beeswax or tallow was melted and dripped onto paper, envelopes or folded sheets of paper. The seal with the sender's or maker's mark was then quickly pressed into the warm wax, leaving an impression in it.**

Casting involves creating a surface that can be printed on by filling in a contained area with a suitably liquid substance capable of hardening, such as plaster, wax or resins. An image from an inked plate can then be embedded into it.

In stencilling, a cut-out shape leaves an open area which can be filled by ink, powdered colour or liquid emulsions in order to create an image.

In processes featuring embossing or stamps, a raised or incised design is covered with a dampened paper or suitable shape-holding textile (hand-made papers). When the design and paper is run though a printing press, the intense pressure pushes the shape of the design into the surface of the paper. The 'punch' of the emboss is dependent on the degree of texture used in the design of the chosen substrate to be printed. Stamps are raised designs which can be used to make a marked indentation into a surface or inked in relief to leave a mark on a surface. (See the Chapter 10 for more information.)

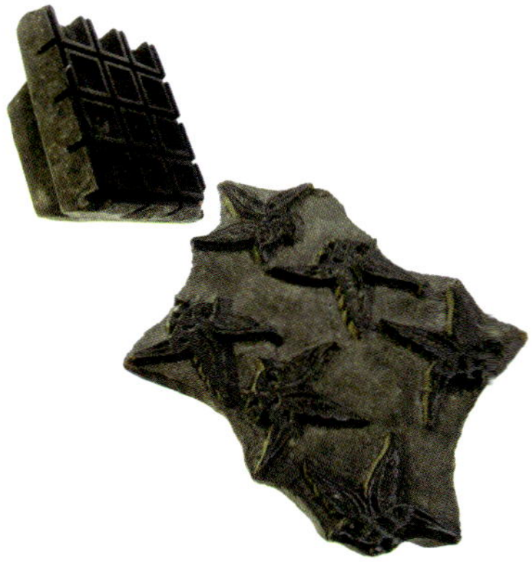

▲ **Textile blocks are used for printing on fabric and papers.**

LETTERPRESS

Letterpress is a printmaking process in which an impression is taken from raised, inked text. The letterpress format we are most familiar with (text arranged as books, newpapers etc.) was established when Gutenberg perfected the printing press (made of wood) and moveable metal type in 1452. Letter shapes made from wood have been dated to as early as the 1200s but were used primarily for stamping and embossing identity marks.

Artists' books are a direct evolvement of letterpress. They often contain many printed images which could be viewed separately as solo images, but they are deliberately designed to be books and so a work of art in themselves. They are often sadly undervalued as art objects.

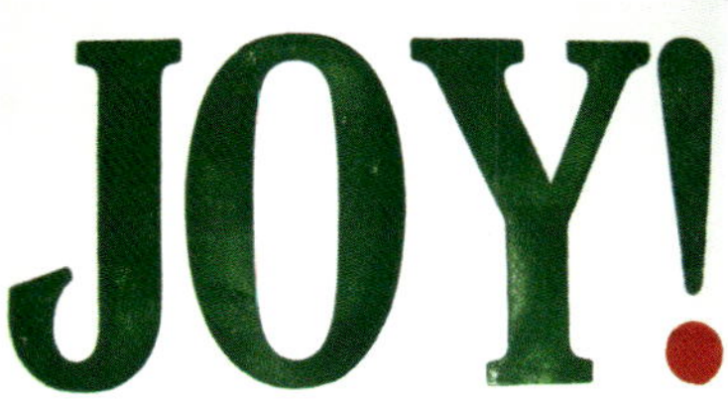

▲ Letterpress images are striking and immediate.

▼ Letterpress is used because of both its visual appeal and its graphic punch! Ralph Steadman's studio, England, UK.

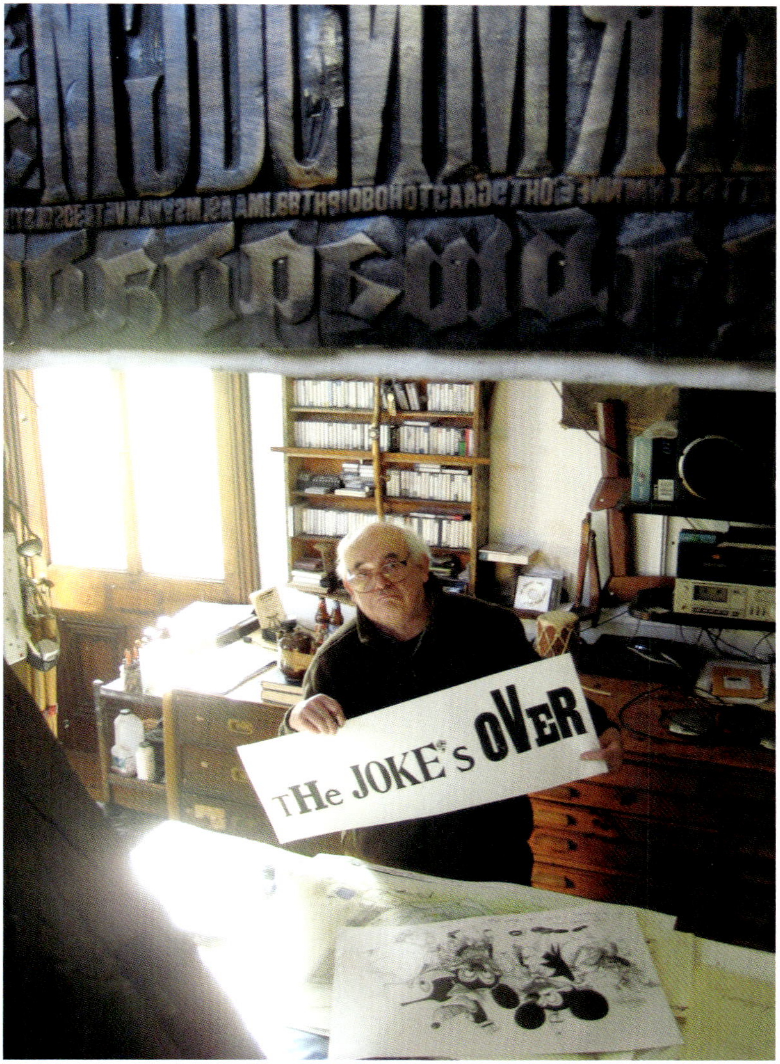

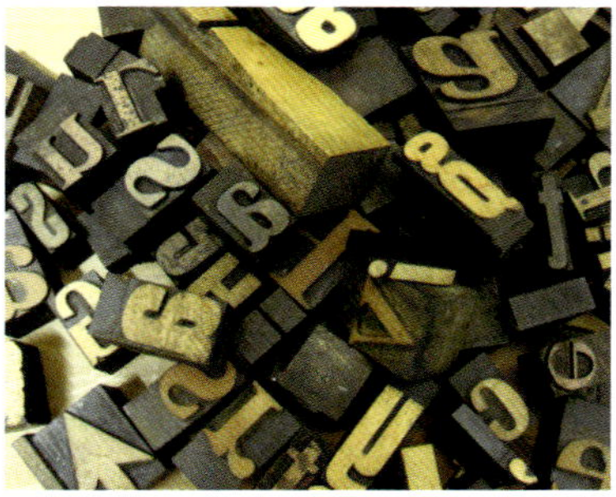

▲ Both wooden letterpress type and metal letterpress type were made for commercial printing.

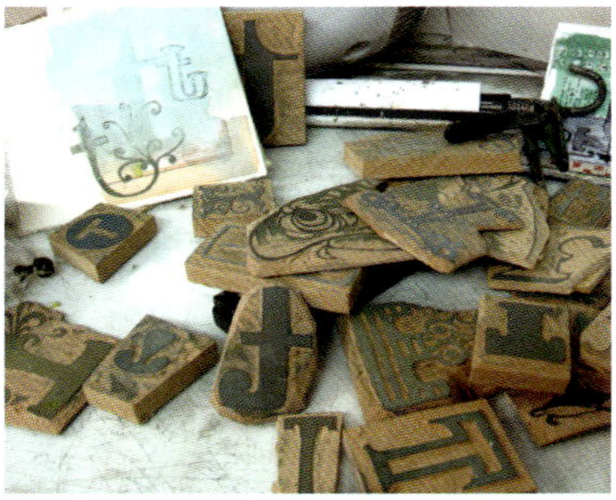

▲ These hand-made wooden letters by the artist Staffan Gnosspelius were made specifically for the text needed in the images he is making for a book's illustrations.

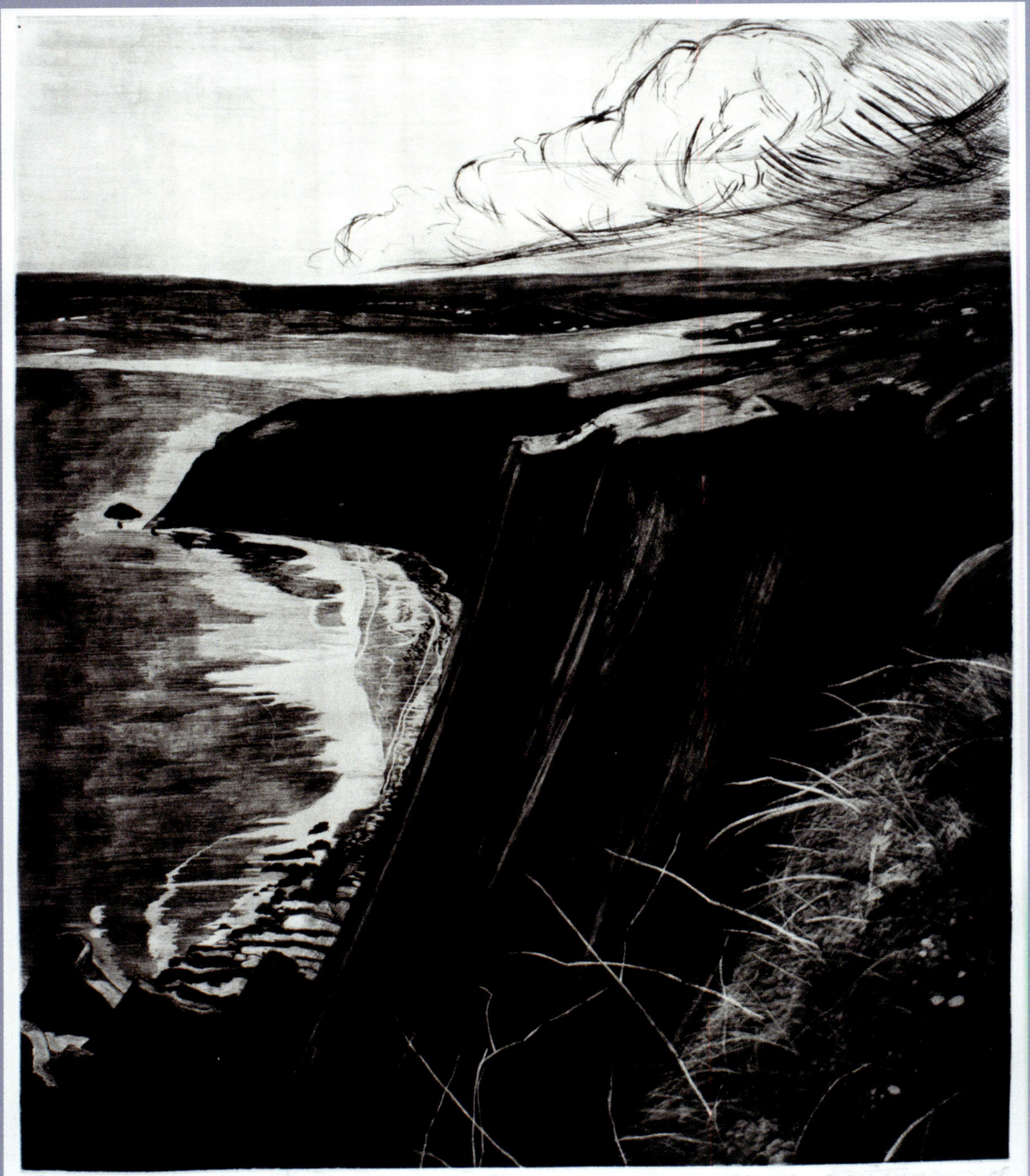

2

drypoint

Drypoint is an intaglio technique. Intaglio is a term used to describe printmaking techniques in which an image is incised into the surface of a plate, usually a metal plate is used.
When the technique of drypoint is used no acid or mordant is needed to create the image on the plate's surface, hence it is referred to as a non-acid intaglio technique.

◀ **Melvyn Petterson, *St David's Bay*, 2009. Drypoint, 76 x 112 cm (30 x 40 in.).**

Drypoint is a non-mordant technique. Marks are incised directly into the plate surface, which not only makes a rut, but kicks up burr. When the plate is inked, this rough burr also holds ink. The result is a line with a velvety, rich characteristic quite distinct from the sharp, clean line of an etching or engraving. Drypoint is beautiful as a technique used on its own, but is often combined with etching or engraving.

The first recorded drypoints were made by during the 15th century by a man referred to as 'The Master of Housebook'.

Fig. A

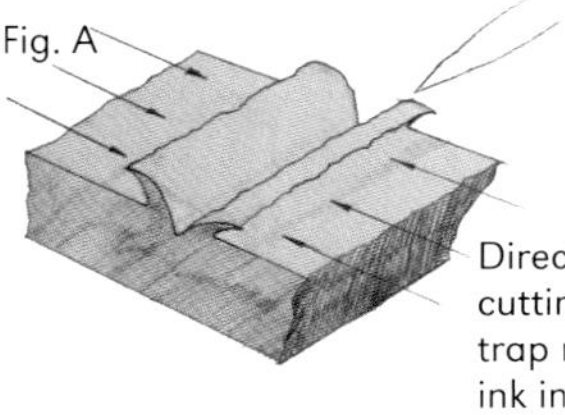

Fig. B

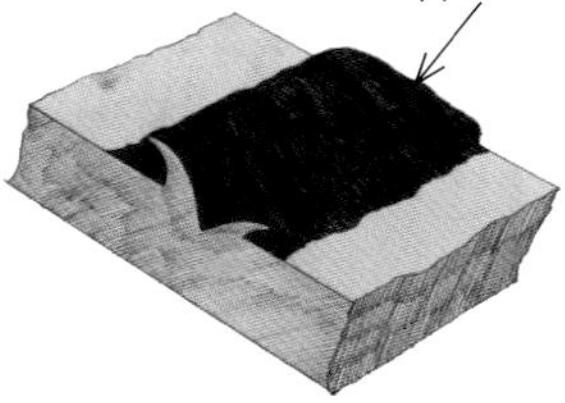

Fig. C

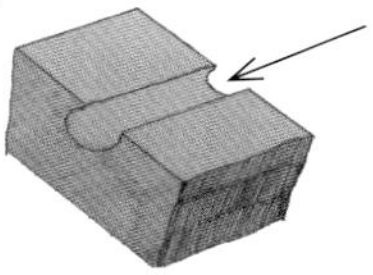

▲ **This teaching aid (Fig. A) shows the burr that is kicked up or displaced from the rut and the direction of wiping used to trap the maximum amount of ink. Fig. B shows ink trapped in the rut and underneath the burr. Fig. C shows the profile of a line made by acid biting, which removes metal. In drypoint, the deeper the line is cut (by pressing harder with the drypoint tool), the darker the line will print. When making a drypoint, the angle at which the tool is held makes a difference. Using a steep angle will kick up more burr, while a perpendicular angle will leave less. A very light line may have no burr at all.**

PLATES AND SURFACES

Drypoints are made on many surfaces, including copper, zinc, aluminium, laminated card and plastic. Which surface is used depends largely on how many prints (the size of the edition) the artist wishes to make, and the cost of purchasing the plates. When carving a drypoint line into a plate, you are dispersing metal rather than removing it: the rut made is displaced into the burr. As you draw the line into the plate surface, you are pushing metal away to the sides of the drawn mark – similar to the wake that follows a boat as it moves through the water.

A plate will, therefore, wear through wiping and press pressure. The burr is worn down and forced back into the rut, meaning that each impression becomes increasingly light. (This is why collectors prize early edition numbers from a drypoint edition.) It is impossible to give an exact number of prints that can be pulled from a specific surface before the burr wears down: that figure will relate to the hardness of the plate (for example, copper is hard while aluminium is soft), the nature of the marks made and how hard you press with the tools.

Drypoint card

The most inexpensive surface to drypoint on is laminated card. The card can be made using an office laminating machine with thin card similar to that used in a typical breakfast cereal box. Printmaking suppliers such as Intaglio in London sell drypoint card in various sheet sizes. It is an excellent way to introduce students or children to printmaking.

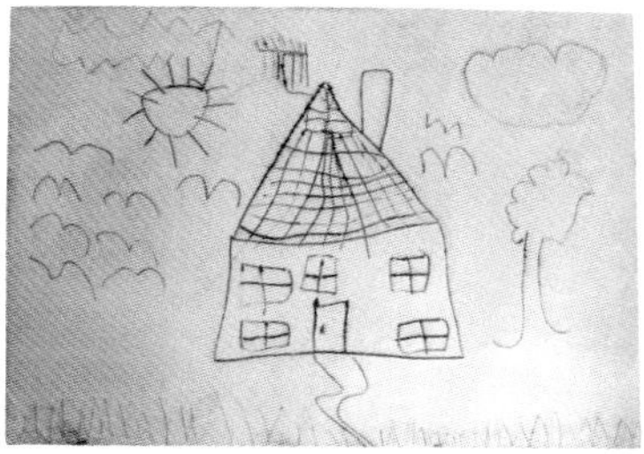

▲ **A drypoint card.**

Drypoint plastic

Drypoint plastic takes the form of plastic, Mylar® or Perspex in sheets ranging from 175 micron to 2mm thick. The number one advantage of these materials is that they are transparent, so a sketch or key design can be placed underneath as a guide for scratching the marks.

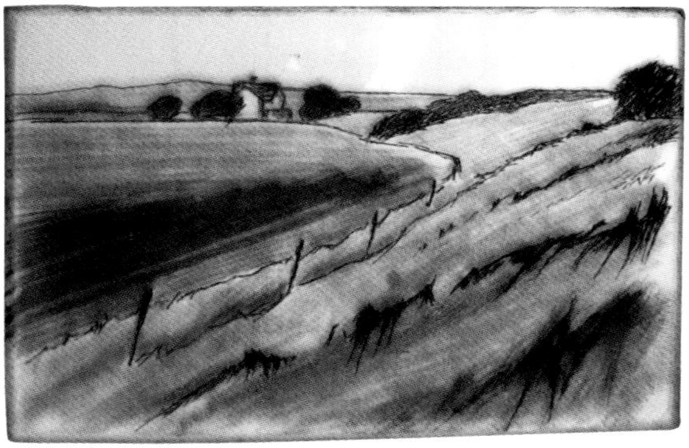

▶ **A 2 mm Perspex plate courtesy of Melvyn Petterson.**

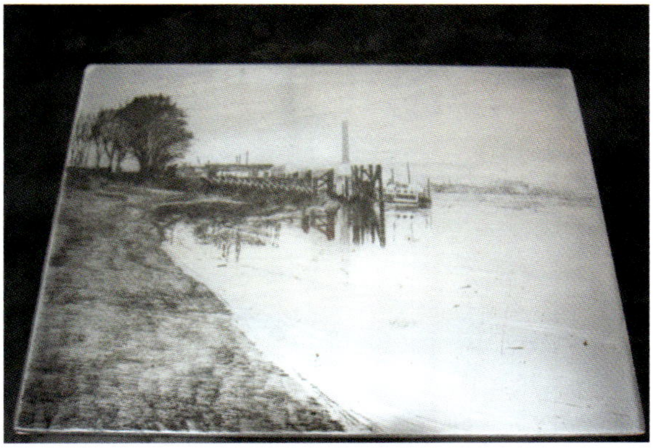

▲ A steel-faced copper plate by Melvyn Petterson.

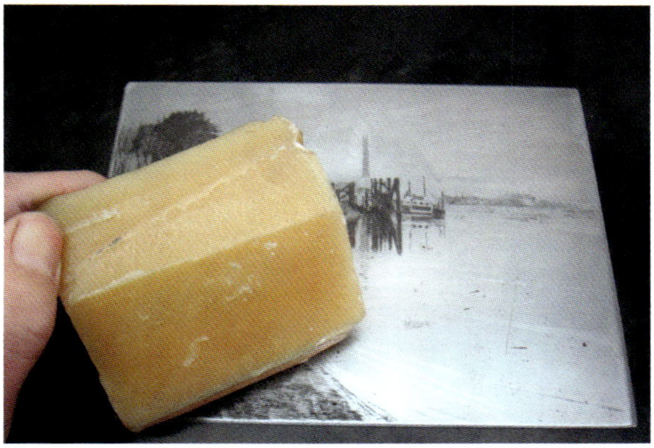

▲ It is important to protect a steel-faced plate after printing to prevent rust, as this can pit and mark the steel coating. Do this by removing all ink from a plate, placing it on a hotplate and covering the surface with melted beeswax.

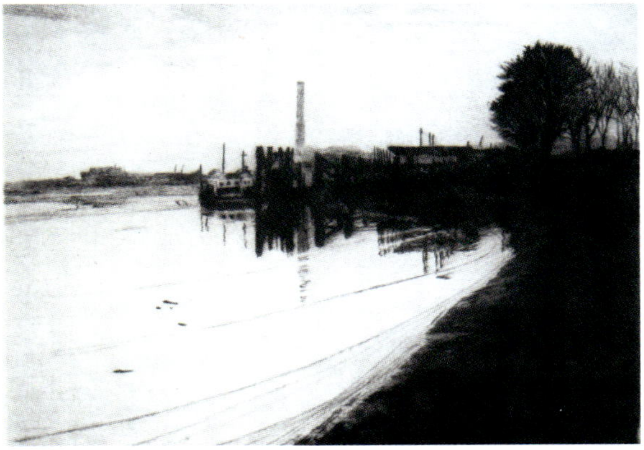

▲ Melvyn Petterson, *Greenwich Evening*, 1986. Drypoint on steel-faced copper, 20 x 15 cm (7¾ x 6 in.).

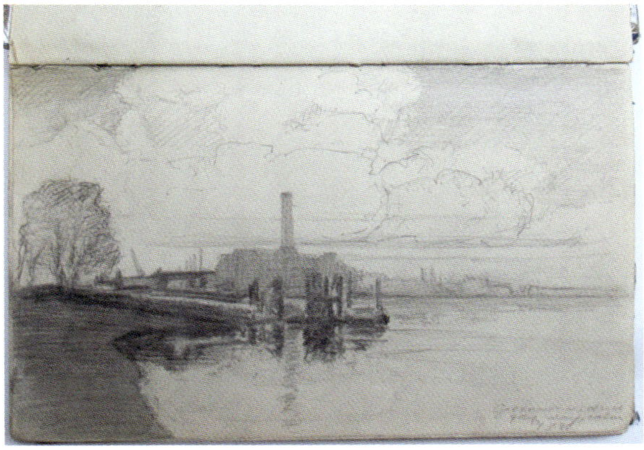

▲ Petterson's sketchbook shows the drawing made *in situ*. Note the artist was not concerned to reverse the image as he said 'the work was about the abstract shapes and atmosphere created by the failing evening light'.

Copper

Copper is the favoured drypoint metal for the artist wishing to make an edition of 30 or more. This is because copper can be steel-faced and zinc cannot (although you can copper-face zinc). Steel-facing is an electroplating process whereby the copper surface is covered with a thin film of iron that hardens the burr, making a larger edition possible. We have successfully editioned drypoints on steel-faced copper to 75 with no discernable loss of image detail.

Zinc and aluminium

Both zinc and aluminium are soft metals and are easy to work with using tools. It is possible to print editions with a good image quality of up to 30 in number. Aluminium will print with a slight surface tone as the surface is not highly polished.

TOOLS

Drypoint needles are the key tools used in drypoint. They are more substantial implements than etching needles. Etching needles simply cut through a layer of ground, while drypoint needles physically carve into the plate surface and cut a deep line that will hold a good amount of ink. The pressure exerted on a drypoint needle would break the tip of an etching needle.

A solid steel tool is the most commonly used. Carbide-tipped and diamond points are designed for frictionless drawing on metal plates. Although very hard, diamond points can be easily shattered when drawing hard at right angles or into and across other lines. They are best used carefully for finer detail work. A very good improvised drypoint tool can be made by filing a 15 cm (6 in.) nail to a sharp point.

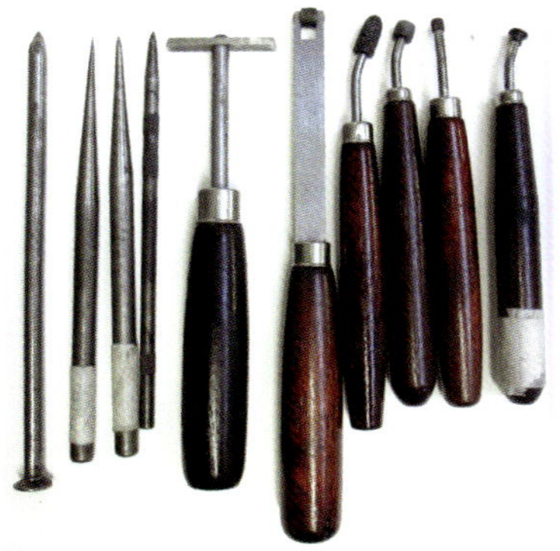

▲ **Assorted tools used for drypoint.**

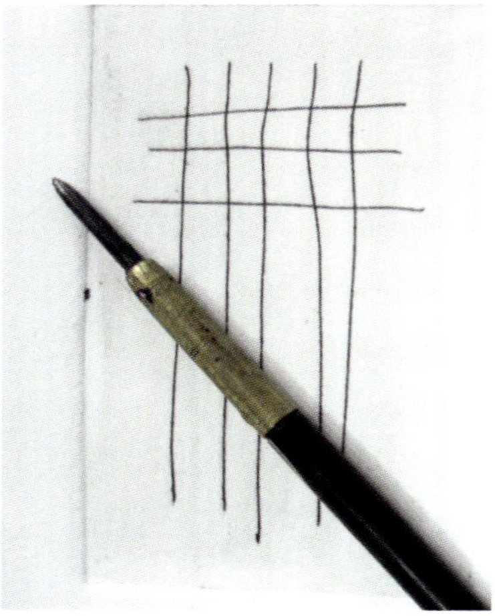

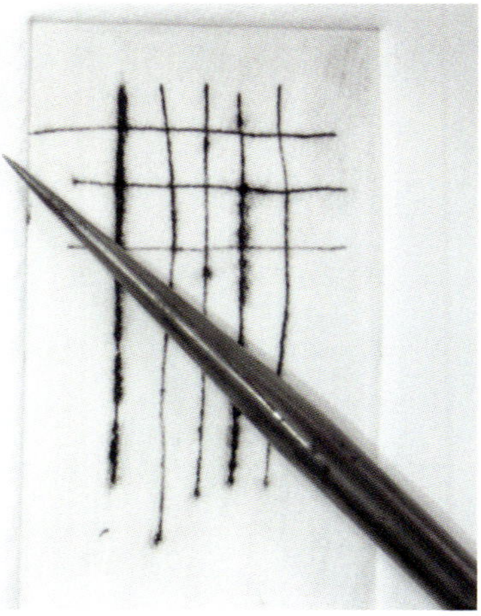

◀ LEFT TO RIGHT: **Etching needle and printed line.**

Drypoint needle and printed line.

Roulette wheels

Roulettes are used for making tones. The tools have spinning heads which rough up the plate surface, leaving behind textures and dots that hold the ink.

Rakes

Often called 'halftone rakes' or 'lining rakes', these implements have teeth which cut parallel lines when they are dragged across the plate surface.

Sandpaper

DIY sandpaper or sanding sheets for wood or metal come in varying grades (for example, 400 = rough, 1800 = fine) and are useful for laying down large areas of tone. They can be used by rubbing them directly onto the plate surface in selected areas or can be run face-down on a plate through the etching press to add a tone to the plate. The latter technique was used successfully by the American printmaker Martin Lewis. Lewis disliked beginning work on a 'clean' plate and preferred working on one that had already had a slight tone pressed into it.

▲ The sandpaper technique creates an all-over tone on the plate surface. This picture shows a zinc plate with the 'sandpaper aquatint' tones that can be built up. The sandpaper was run through the press over four times.

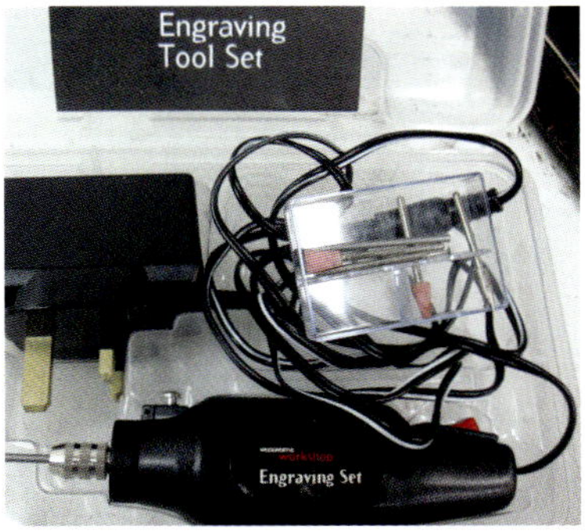

▲ Electric engraving tool sets come with multiple heads that can be used to make lively and vibrant marks. (Dremmel is a popular brand and widely available.)

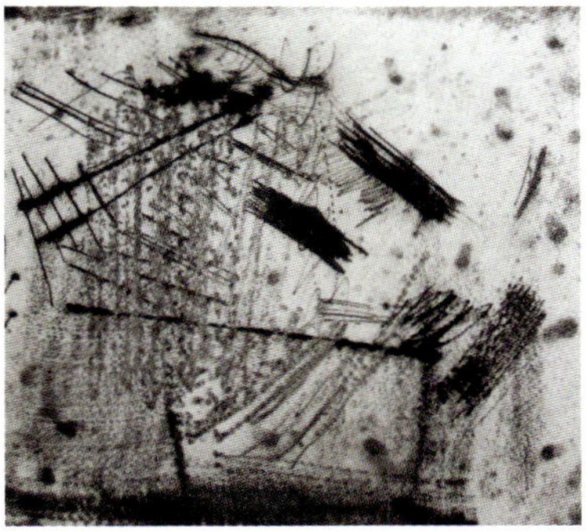

▲ A range of lively marks has been produced by the engraving tool.

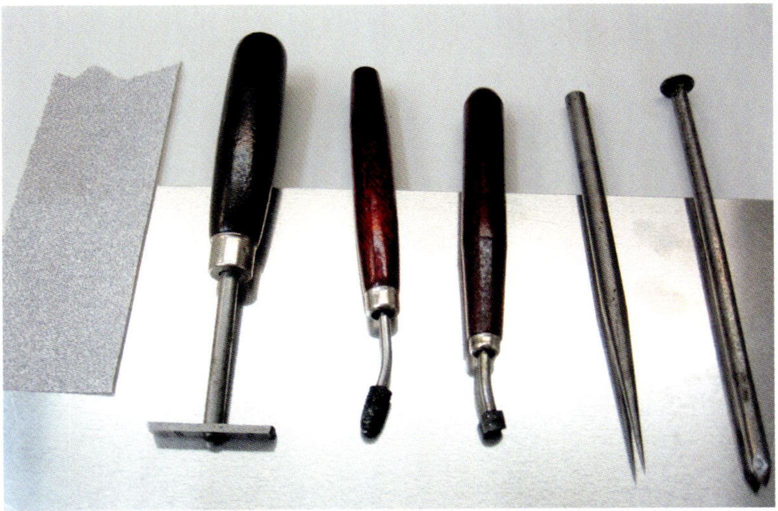

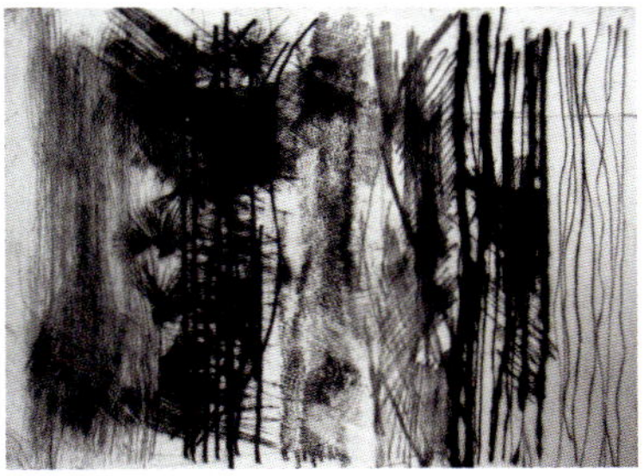

These pictures show an aluminium plate with tools (left) and the printed marks each tool makes (above). From left to right, they are: sandpaper; halftone rake; irregular roulette; fine, regular roulette; steel drypoint tool; sharpened 6 in. nail.

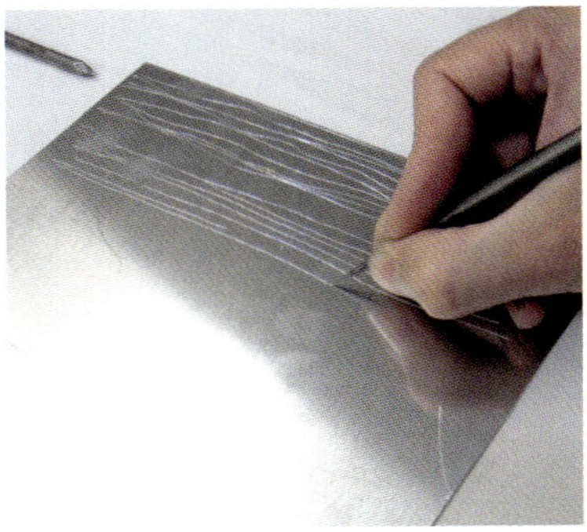

▲ Scoring lines with the drypoint needle.

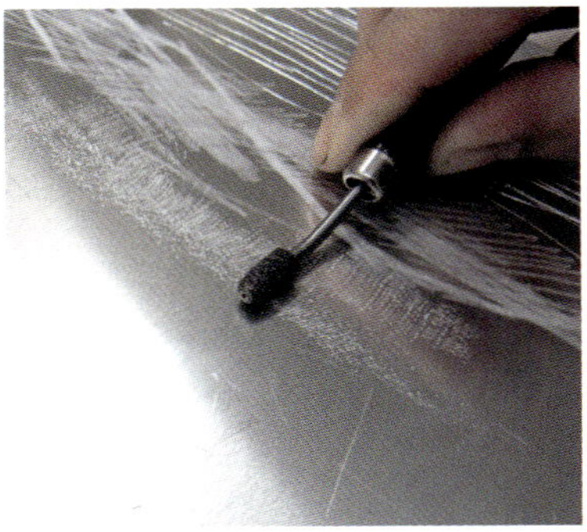

▲ An irregular roulette.

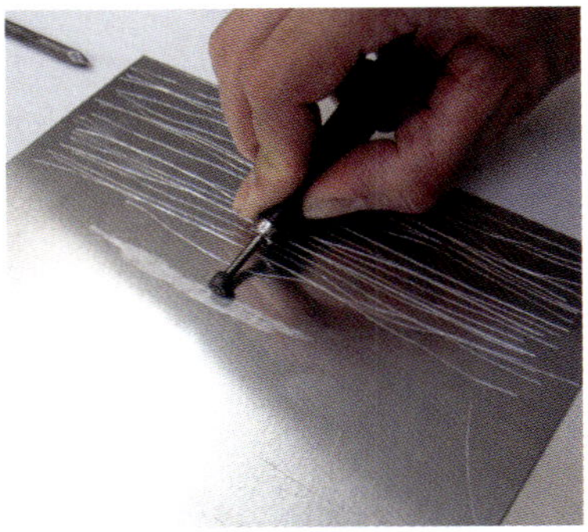

▲ Using the fine, regular roulette.

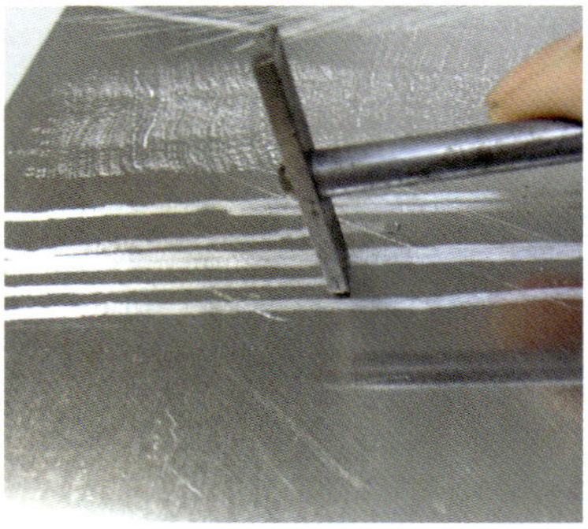

▲ Dragging a halftone rake grade 85 LPI (lines per inch).

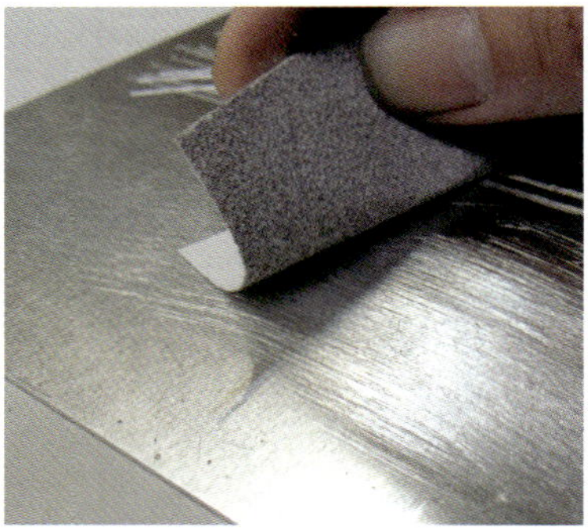

▲ Scuffing the surface of the aluminium with sandpaper.

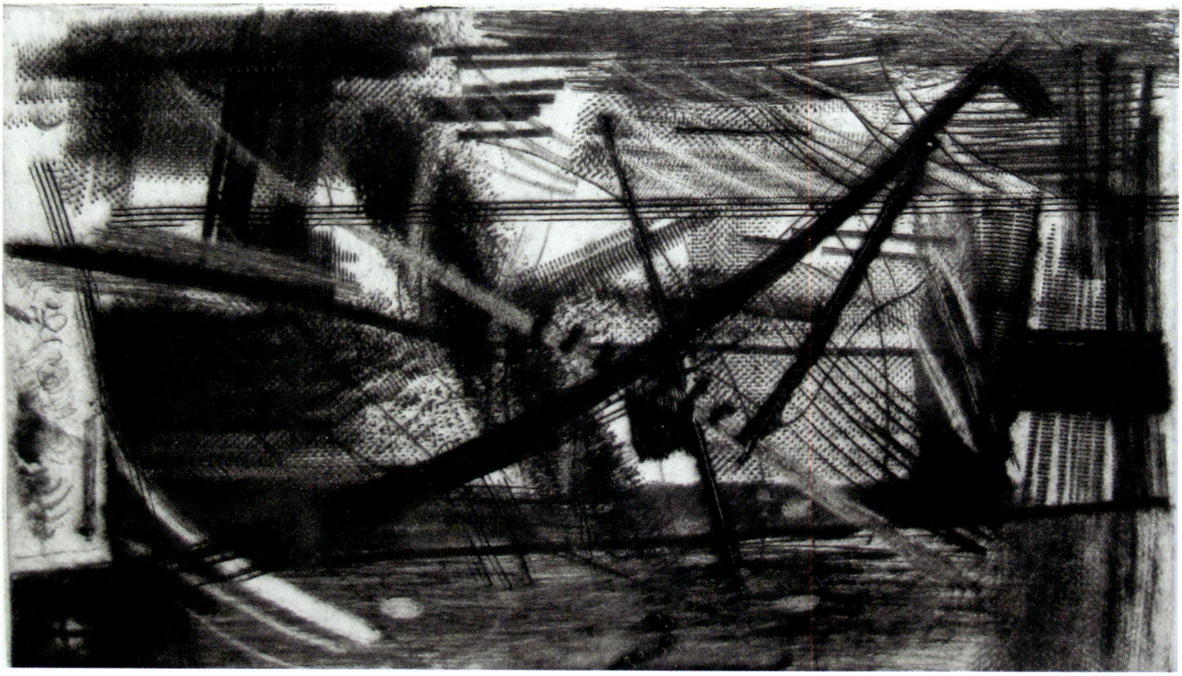

▲ The resulting print has been made with all of the tools mentioned above. It shows the richness of mark-making that can be achieved using drypoint.

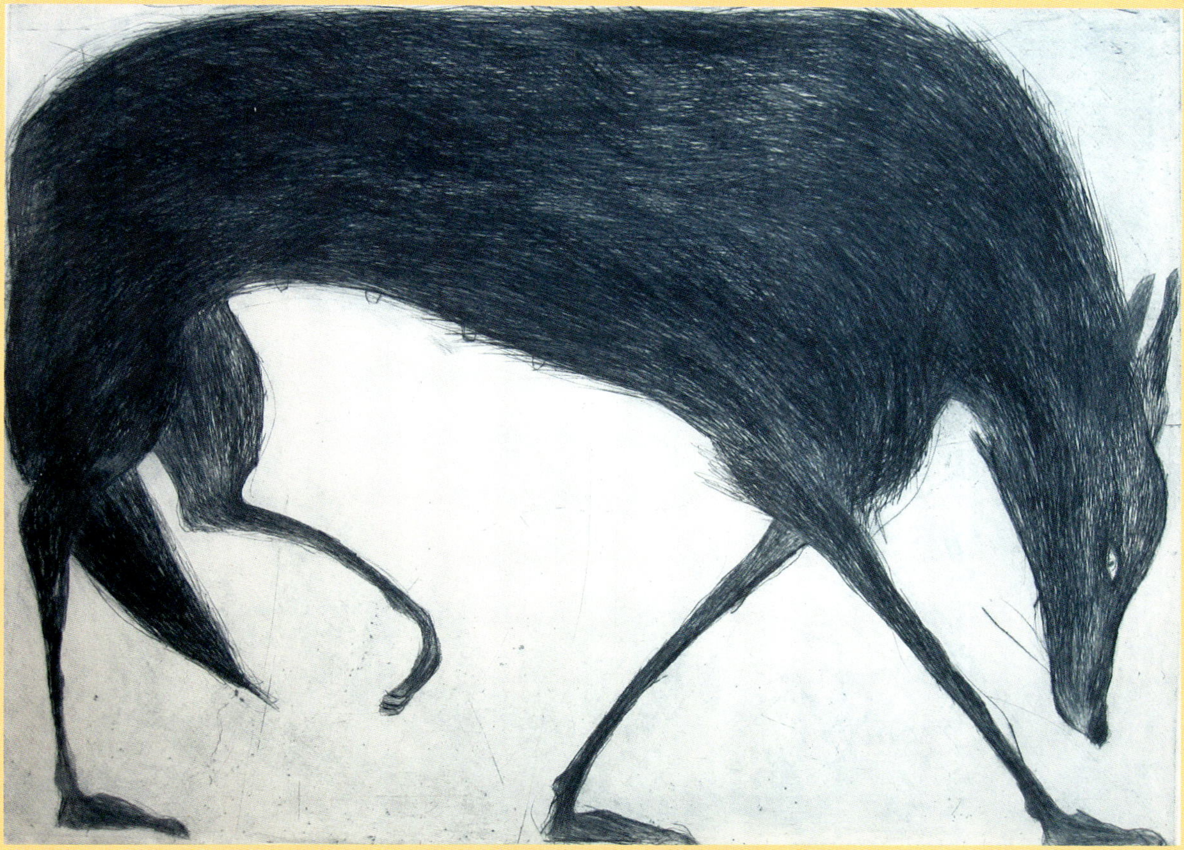

▲ Kate Boxer, *Blue Wolf*, 2009.
Drypoint, 112 x 76 cm (44 x 30 in.).

▶ Printing *Wolf*, an edition of 30, drypoint on aluminium.

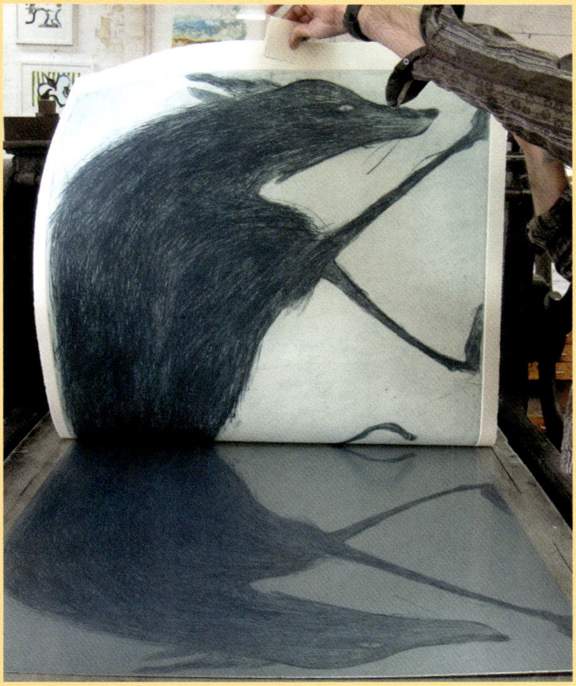

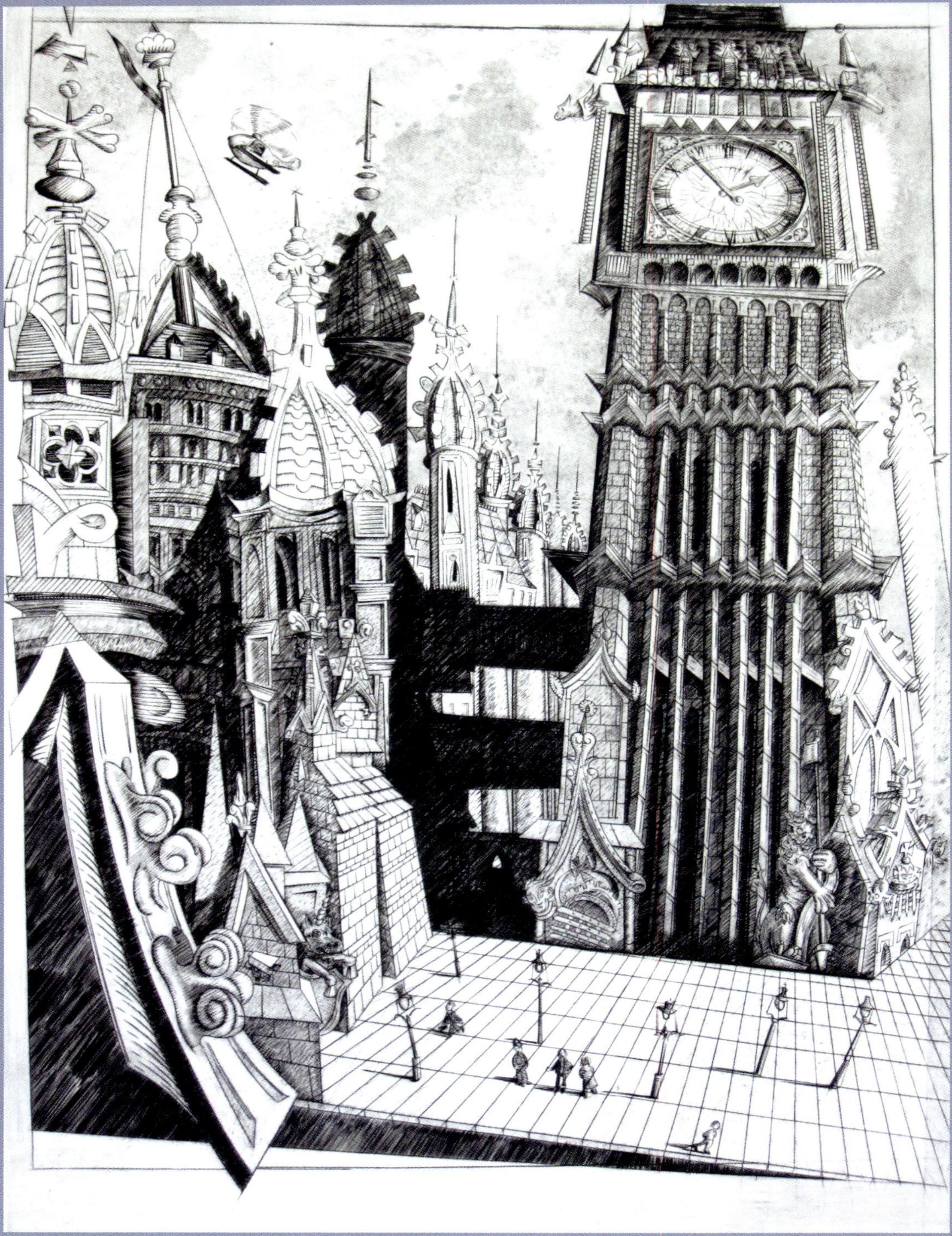

3

engraving

Often overlooked by printmakers, engraving is a technique capable of producing exquisite lines that are crisp, even and as fine as a hair if needed. Engraving is a non-mordant intaglio technique. It differs from drypoint in that only the line below the surface holds ink. Any burr produced during cutting is removed using a scraper tool (in drypoint, the burr is relied upon to hold ink). It is possible to combine engraving with other techniques such as etching.

◀ **Brendan Hansbro, *Houses of Parliament*, 1996. Engraving on copper with flower of sulphur tints, 44 x 60 cm (17¼ x 23½ in.). Flower of sulphur is a way of gaining very subtle tints on copper. The powder is sprinkled into olive oil that has been painted onto the copper and then left for several hours.**

Engraving can be done on wood and copper using tools called gravers and burins. In copper engraving, lines are cut into the surface of the plate and when inked, print as black (or coloured) lines onto (white) paper. In wood engraving, the lines are cut into the wood surface and when inked, print as white lines in/on a black background. Woodcut (also called wood block) is, as discussed on pp.14–15, a relief process where the image is cut into the long grain of the wood.

History of engraving

In the 19th century when copper became too expensive to use for engraving (after all, electricity had arrived and the world needed electrical wiring), steel was used instead. Steel engravings were being made from the late 18th century mainly for the production of banknotes. In the 19th century, steel engraving became a much-used technique. Steel engraving had several advantages over copper engraving: not only was steel harder than copper, so the wear and tear on the image was reduced, but its added longevity meant many more prints could be pulled from the plate.

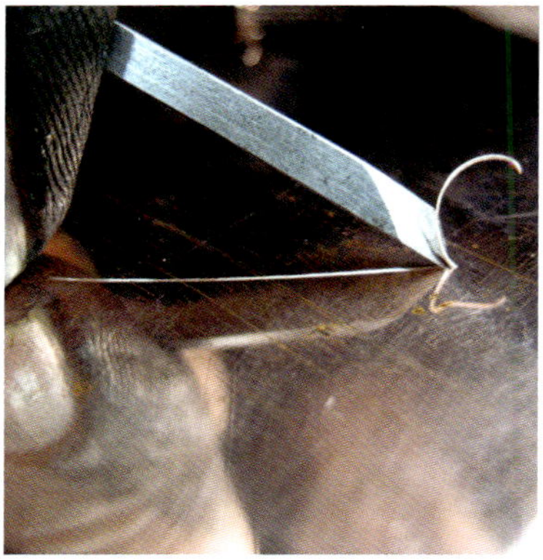

▲ **The engraving of copper plates and the engraving tools used to do so have changed little in the history of this excellent technique.**

Not all steel engraved plates were made by hand, however. Machines called 'ruling machines' were used to make a tight-knit sequence of parallel lines across the surface of a plate. This meant that even greater tonal detail could be given to an image.

The advent of photoengraving in 1814 and chromolithography in 1837 ushered in new ways of making an image quickly. Photoengraving superseded steel engraving. This process introduced a sensitised metal plate on which an image could be placed and then etched. It meant that images no longer needed to be hand-drawn, as the subject matter could be photographed and transferred to the sensitised plate. (Steel plates were also used in this process.)

Chromolithography ('chromo' means 'colour') replaced the need to colour images by hand as each component colour in an image was now placed onto separate lithographic plates. Each colour was then printed in a registered sequence to rebuild the image as a whole.

Mezzotint is a type of copper and/or steel engraving which allows tone to be added into an image. It is thought to have been invented in the 17th century by Ludwig von Siegen (c. 1609–80). In the technique of mezzotint, rather than lines being cut into the surface of the metal, an all-over texture is laid down across the entire surface using a curved tool with serrated teeth called a 'rocker'.

Every tone imaginable can be created in an image using this technique, and as a result it became extremely popular in the 18th century and was used in the commercial reproductions of well-known artists' work. (See Chapter 4 for more information.)

Engraving tools

Engraving differs from drypoint in that only the line below the surface holds ink. Any burr that may be produced during cutting is removed using a scraper tool. In drypoint, the burr is relied upon to hold ink.

Handling engraving tools correctly is extremely important as each tool is created to do a specific task and create a specific mark. Once you understand the identity and individuality of each tool, your portfolio of mark-making becomes endless.

There are many fascinating engraving tools with equally fascinating names, spit sticker to name just one. The spitsticker (literally 'the spike on the belt') is a tool with an ellipsis-shaped end point. It is available in many sizes. It is very effective and creates close parallel lines, complicated sets of curved lines and the types of generally drawn lines that are necessary to make an image. It is the 'pencil' of the engraving toolbox.

The multiple lining tool has a series of grooves on its cutting end. It can make between three and six lines at the same time, depending on the number of grooves the tool has. It is used for making tones and tints on the plate (see the 'crosshatching' definition in Chapter 5, p.70) and also makes fascinating stippling marks.

▼ A close-up of a lozenge-shape graver and a flat graver.

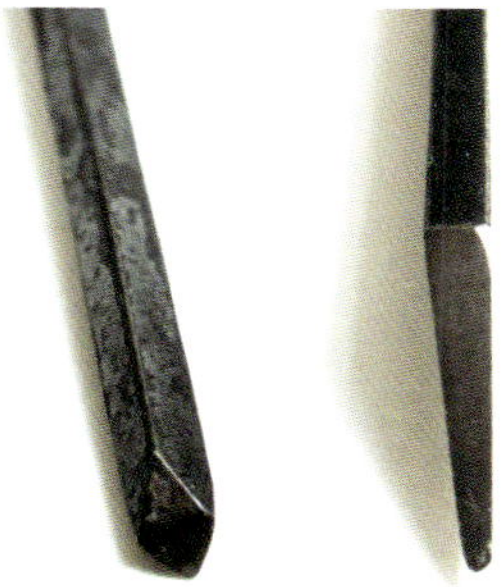

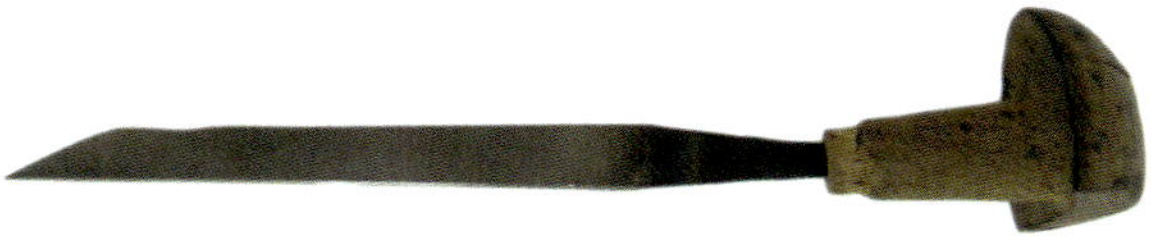

▲ A side-on view of a flat graver.

▶ For good engraving, it is essential that tools are kept sharp. Use a smooth sharpening stone with a little light oil.

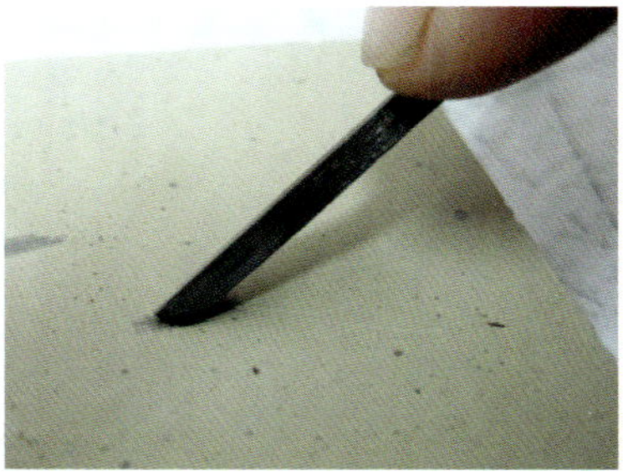

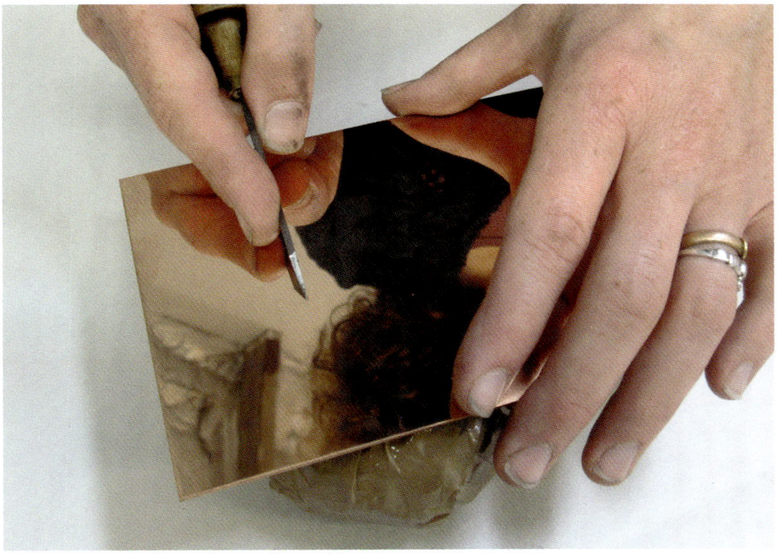

▲ The burin is held between the index finger, middle finger and thumb, with the handle lodged in the palm of the hand. When cutting, the pressure comes entirely from the arm pushing through the palm. Always cut slowly. To end a stroke, depress the hand to lift the point of the tool. Curves are cut by turning the plate with the non-cutting hand – the tool hand hardly moves. This skill takes considerable practice!

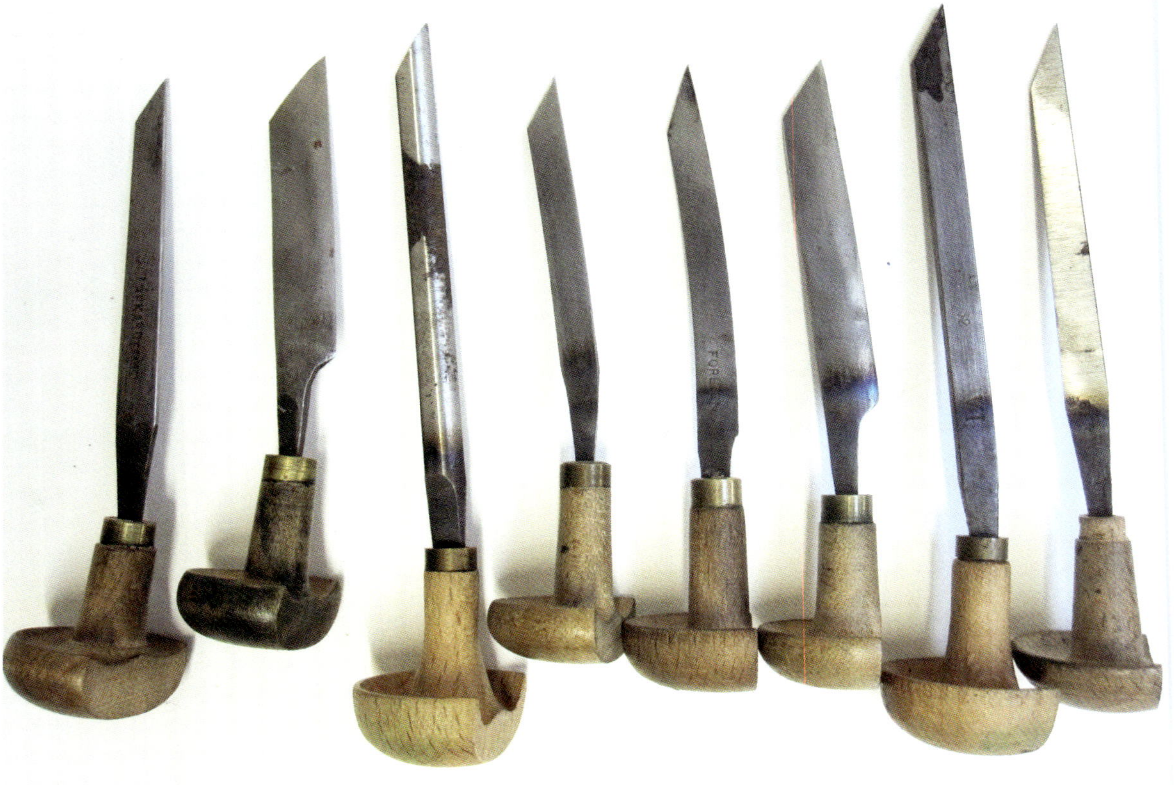

▲ A variety of engraving tools. Each particular cutting edge makes a specific mark on the plate. They are either lozenge-shaped (diamond) or square-shaped, which make a V-shaped line. Engraving tools include flat gravers, round gravers (also called 'scorpers'), angle tint tools, elliptical tools, multiple line tools and spitstickers.

▶ This is a correct way to place the engraving tool in your hand, with the handle of the tool lodged in your palm. Grip the shaft firmly. The pressure when cutting comes entirely from the arm pushing through the palm. *Always cut slowly.* To end a stroke, depress the hand to lift the point of the tool. Curves are cut by turning the plate with the non-cutting hand: the tool hand hardly moves. This skill takes considerable practice!

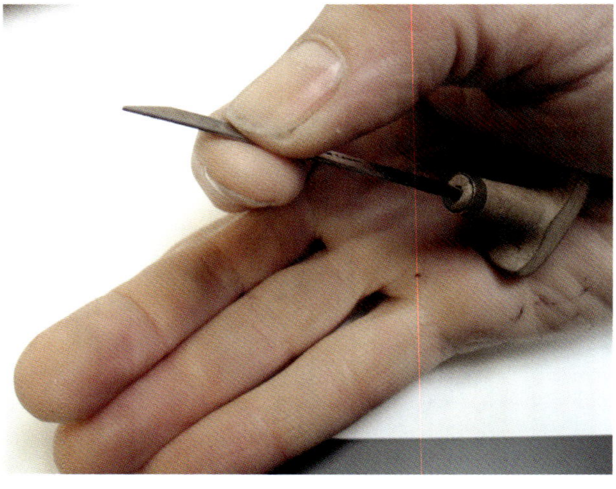

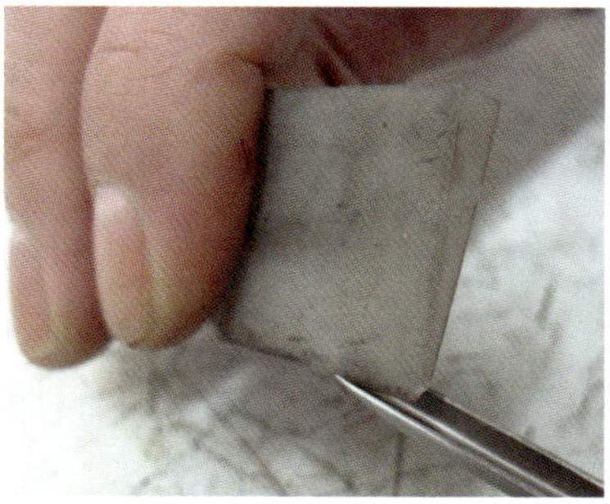

▲ An Arkansas stone is the perfect sharpening stone for engraving tools (and lino cutting tools). It has angled ends so that it can fit the smallest tips and not damage the cutting angle of the tool.

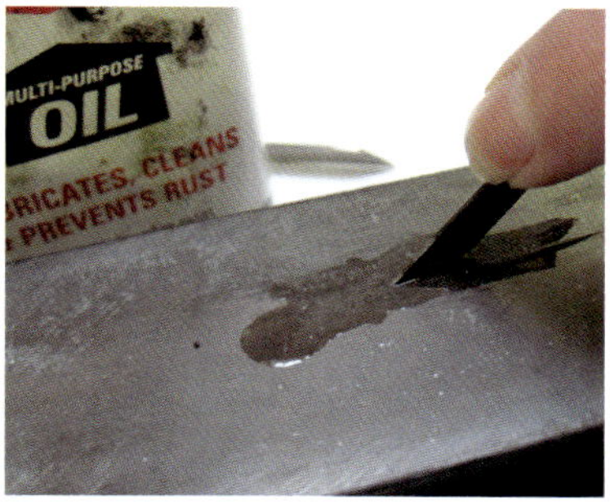

▲ Sharpening a burin.

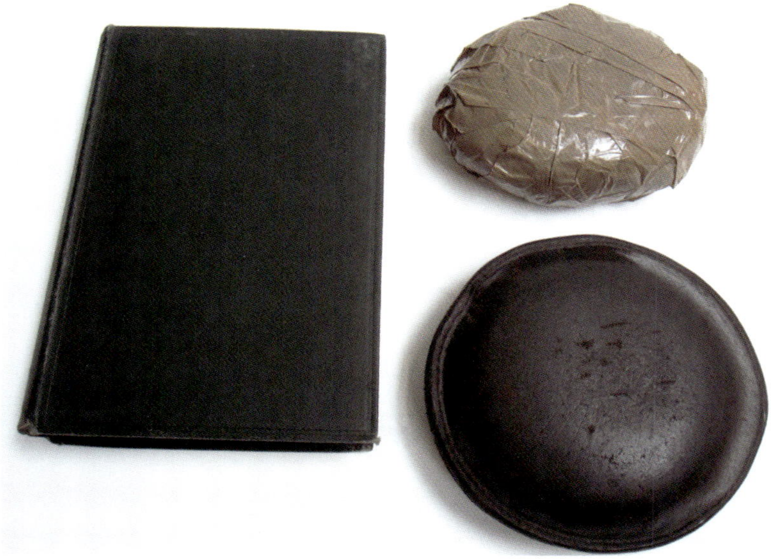

▶ The sandbag (leather is traditional but they can be easily home made by filling a small plastic bag with sand and then wrapping it tightly with packing tape) – and the ever dependable book if no sandbag is to hand – is used to support the block and to move it easily while cutting the surface, especially when making spirals or complicated curving lines. Being able to spin the plate to follow the curved motion of the chosen engraving tool is a great skill.

A sharpening stone is used to sharpen engraving tools. It is necessary to do this to keep the cutting edges or shape of the tools' cutting ends honed to perfection.

Traditionally, the copper plate was placed on a leather bag filled with sand so that the plate could be turned and manipulated as it was cut with the engraving tool. If you cannot obtain a leather sandbag, improvise one by filling a piece of cloth with sand and binding it tightly with brown packing tape. Alternatively, use a hardback book that is smaller than the plate.

Engravers are also making use of new plate technology such as engraving plastic. See Chapter 1 for more information.

Note that you can also use engraving tools to cut lino blocks. This is down to the personal preference of the artist and how they use the required tools.

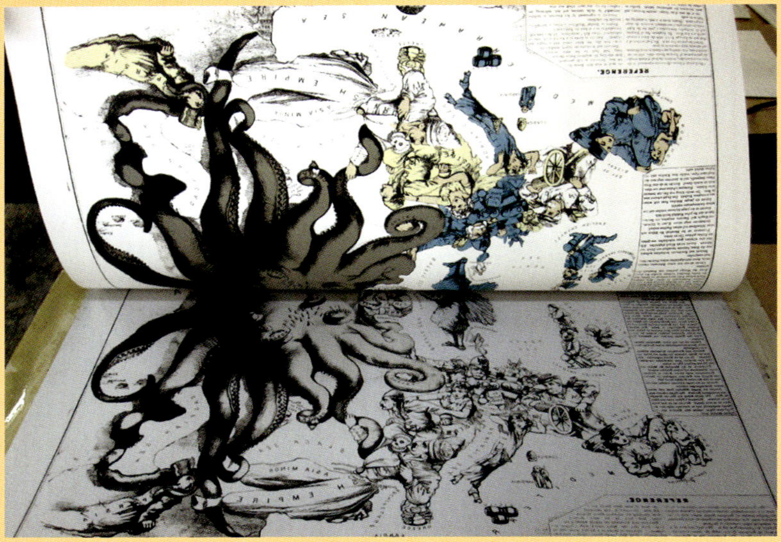

◀ The Octopus Map was made at Artichoke Print Workshop in 2011 for the BBC Four programme *The Beauty of Maps* ('Serio-comic maps', Series 4). The map is made using chromolithography. The only concession to the passing of time was the positives of the image that were made for the image. It was a true testament to the skill of draftsmen of that time, as the layers of the image would have been drawn by hand onto several separate plates.

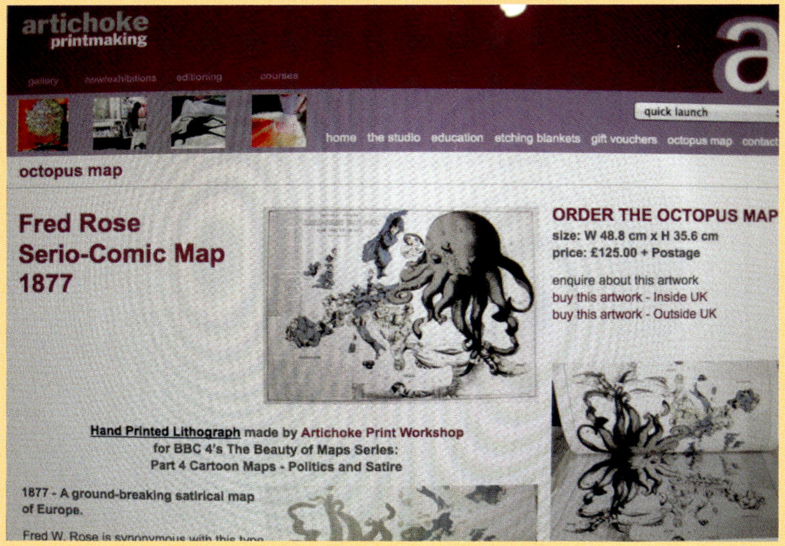

◀ The map can be viewed online at www.artichokeprintmaking.com/?octopus-map-88, where you can follow the production of the map as a live animation. Yes, it really was made by hand!

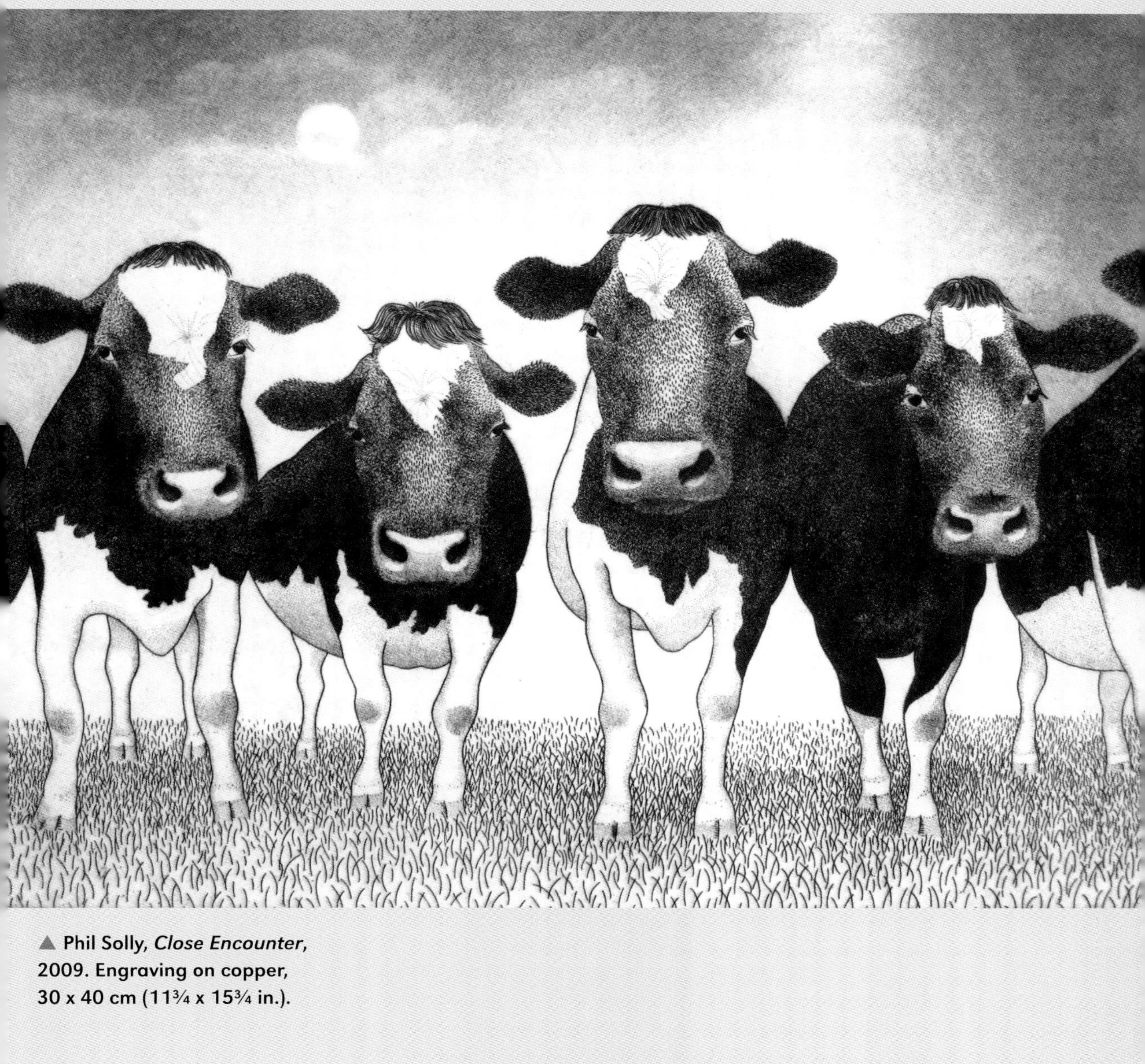

▲ Phil Solly, *Close Encounter*, 2009. Engraving on copper, 30 x 40 cm (11¾ x 15¾ in.).

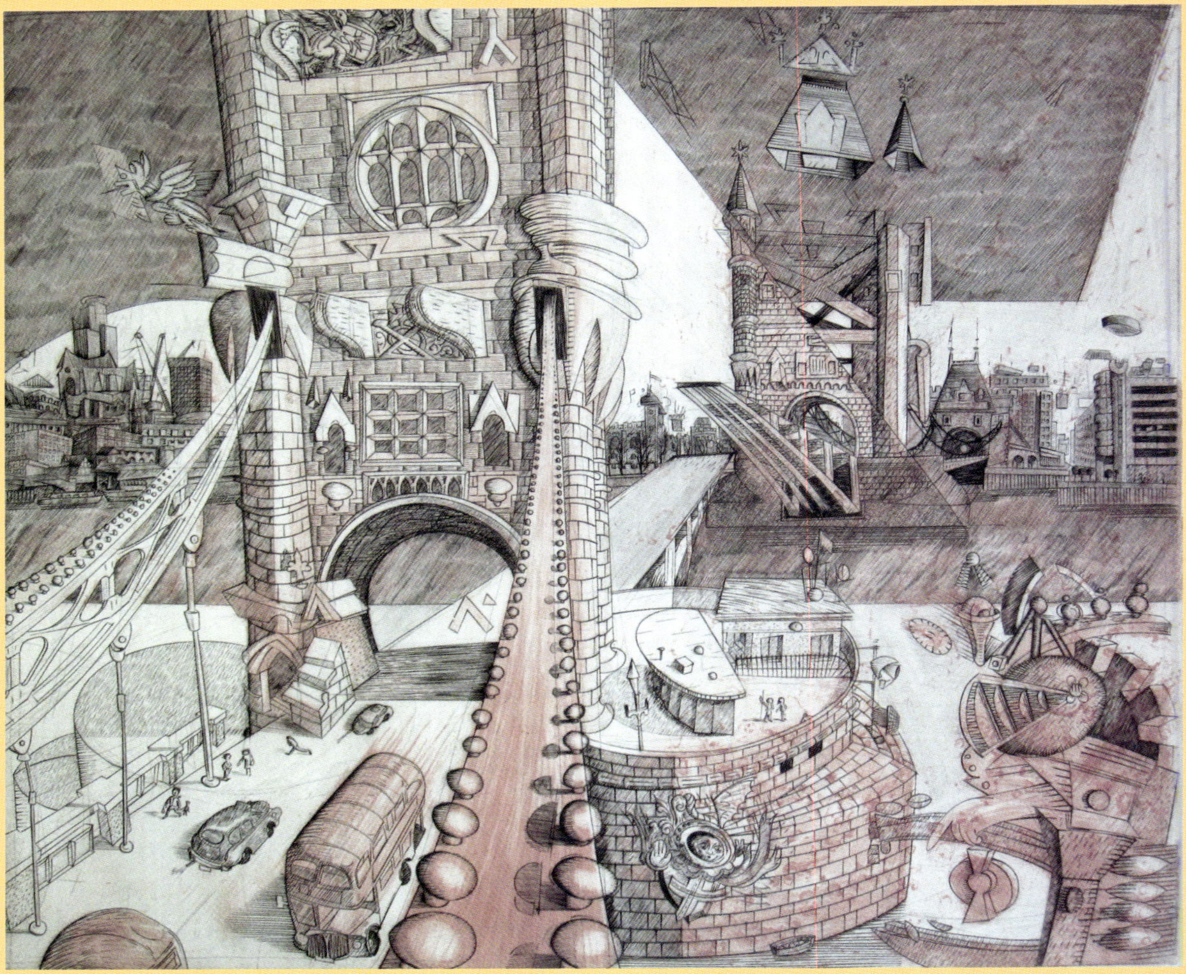

▲ Brendan Hansbro, *The Tower Bridge*, 1999. Engraving on copper with roulette and flower of sulphur tints, 52 x 44 cm (20½ x 17¼ in.).

▶ A William Washington engraving on copper, showing detail of the Houses of Parliament with bomb damage, 1943. Image courtesy of Abbot and Holder Ltd and Artichoke Trading Ltd.

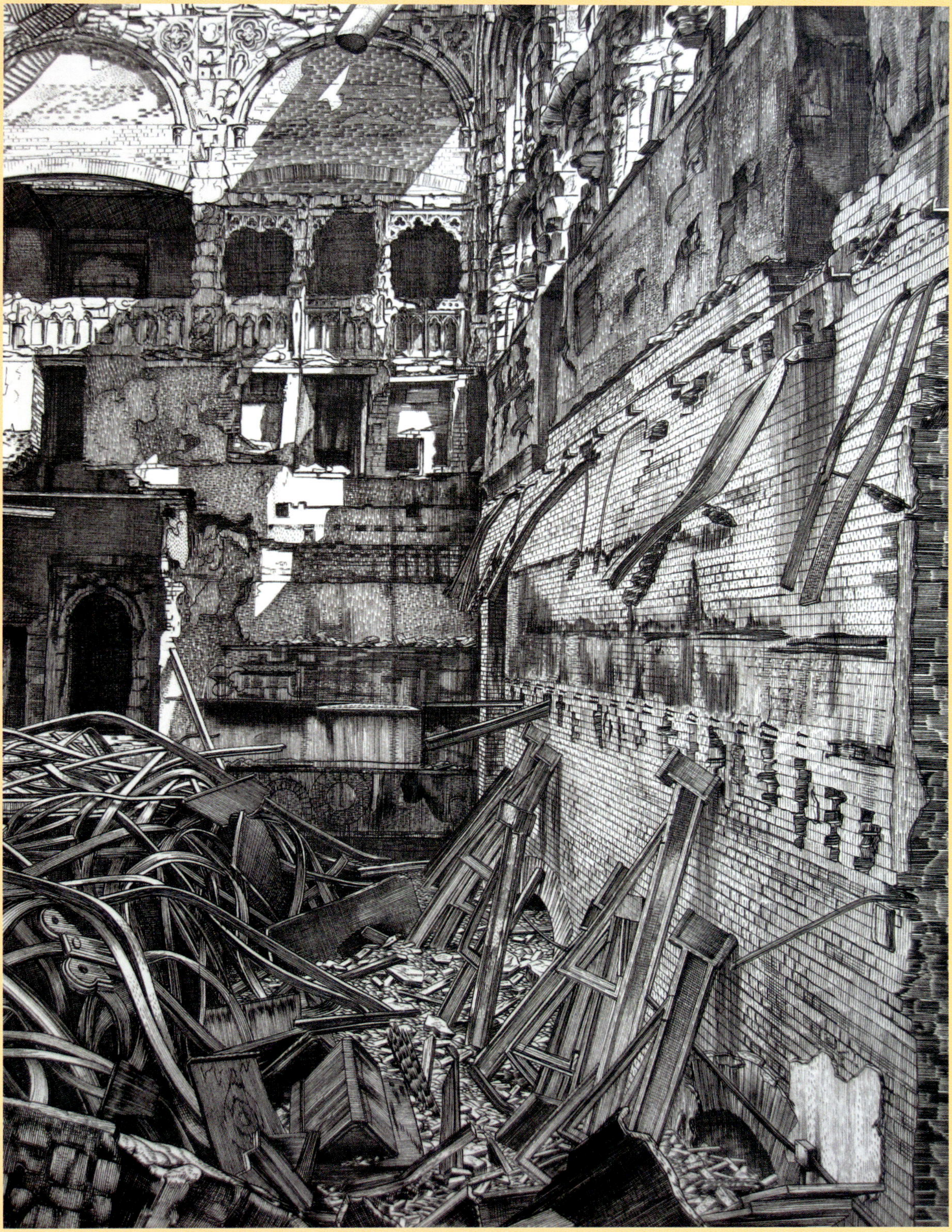

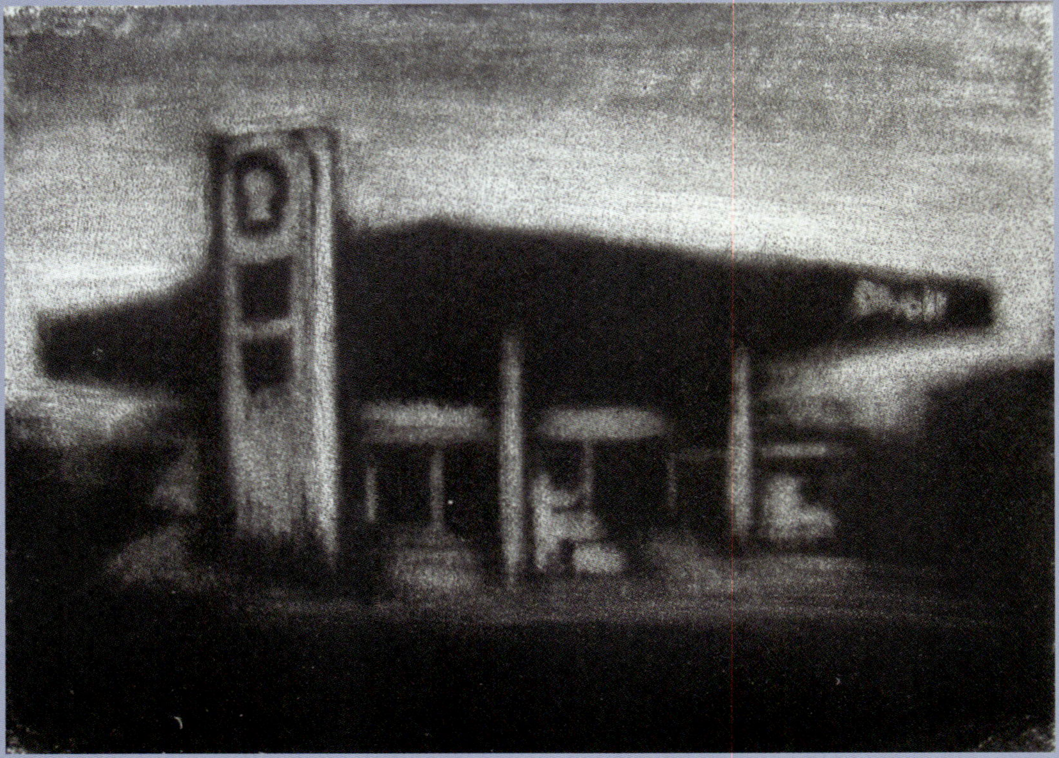

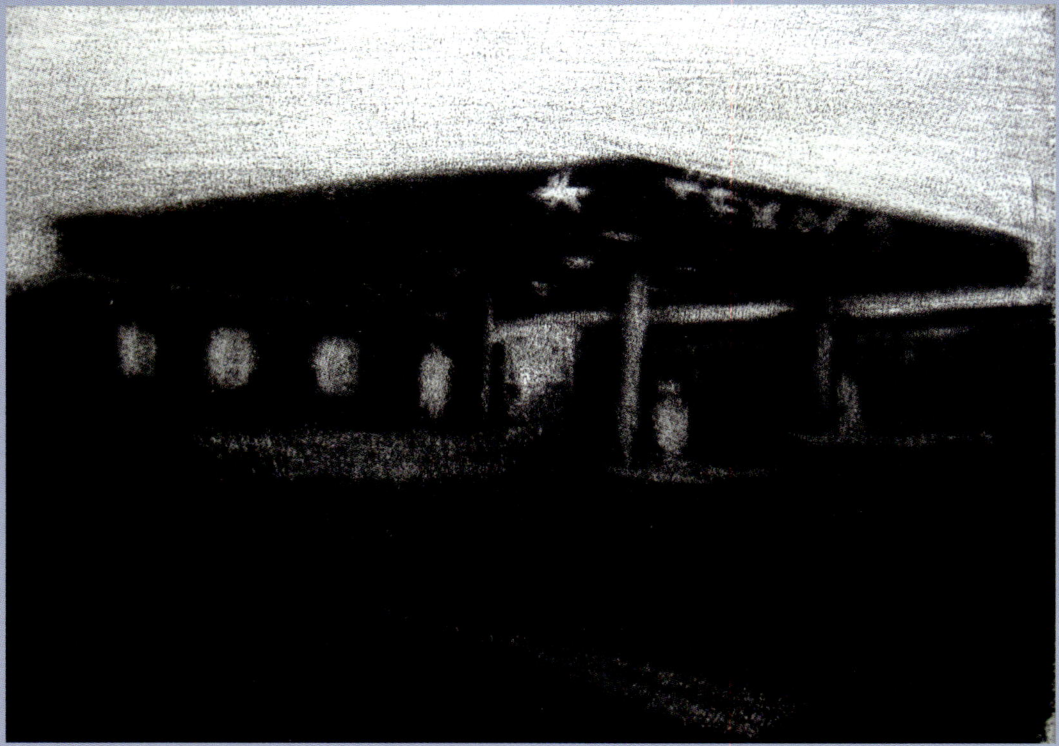

4

mezzotint

Mezzotint images are recognised by their dramatic tones and the intrinsic element of diffused light. This soft, smoky chiaroscuro style is the mezzotint's most compelling visual appeal.
It is a technique in which the artist creates the image by drawing the light elements of the image first. The artist works from dark to light, unlike all other intaglio techniques, which progressively make the image darker in tone.

◀ TOP: **Rosie Prince, *Shop*, 2011. Mezzotint on copper, 12 x 8 cm (4¾ x 3¼ in.).**

◀ **Rosie Prince, *Texaco*, 2011. Mezzotint, 10 x 7 cm (4 x 2¾ in.).**

The 18th century was the heyday of mezzotint. England virtually monopolised the use of the mezzotint, primarily in the reproductive print industry.

Stung by the declaration that engravers were not capable of original genius or original works, the engraver John Landseer stated, 'Engraving is no more an art of copying painting than the English language is an art of copying Greek to Latin. Engraving is a distinct language of art.'
(*The Mezzotint History and Technique*, Carol Wax, Harry N Abrams Inc., 1990).

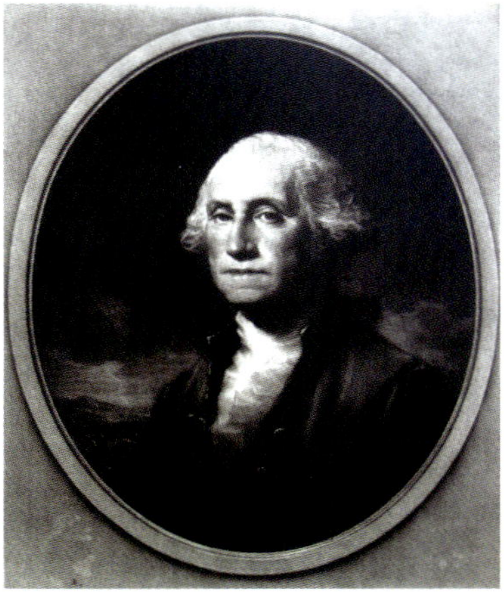

▲ Gilbert Stuart (1755–1828), *George Washington*. Mezzotint, 30 x 39 cm (11¾ x 15¼ in.).

The rise of the original mezzotint had begun. But even in the 1800s, its survival was sorely tested by the arrival of new printmaking processes – photoengraving and photolithography. It took until the end of the 19th century for the technique to experience a revival. Sir Frank Short is credited with this, as it occurred during his time as an etching instructor at the Royal College of Art (1891–1924).

Contemporary artists who have used the medium include Joseph Pennell, Martin Lewis, M. C. Escher, Susan Rothenburg, Robert Motherwell, Bill Jacklin and Chuck Close.

ROCKING THE MEZZOTINT PLATE

Mezzotint is a non-acid intaglio technique. The ground on a mezzotint is made by creating a rough burr texture over the entire surface of the metal plate (usually copper) using a tool called a 'rocker'. If you imagine placing your hand on a sheet of sandpaper, this is what the surface of a prepared mezzotint plate feels like.

The number of directional passes with which the rocker marks the plate determines how rough and dense the burr on the plate becomes. A hand-rocked plate ensures concentrated pressure, creating a healthier burr on the plate surface. Pre-rocked (pre-prepared) plates are available but they are expensive. Due to the time involved in preparing a plate, it is recommended that only copper be used. Copper is harder than zinc and can be steel-faced easily, thus protecting the integrity of the plate from wear throughout an edition.

▼ From left to right: 40 gauge rocker; 85 gauge rocker; tip ball burnisher; medium flat burnisher; medium-size scraper.

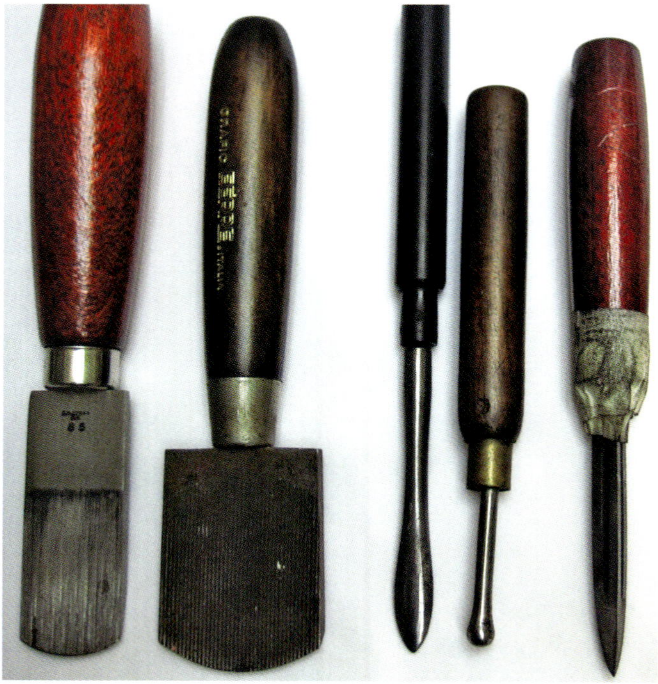

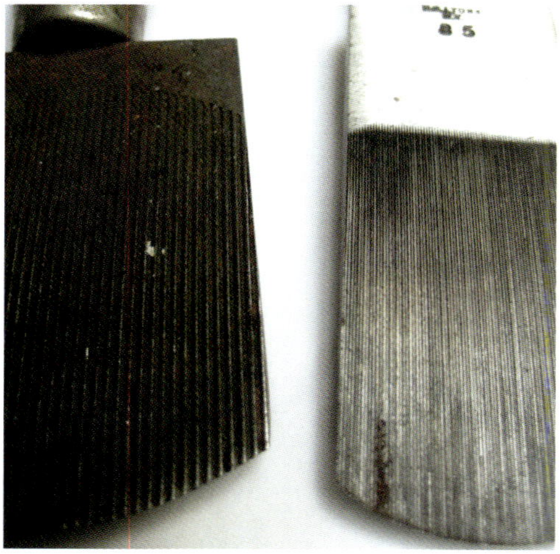

▲ A 40 gauge rocker and a 85 gauge rocker. The chiselled, serrated teeth of the rocker are created by fluted grooves. The gauge of the rocker is the size of the pattern the cutting end makes. An 85 gauge rocker will make an extremely fine rocking line.

▶ The correct way to hold a rocker is so that the fluted side faces the wrist and the direction of the angle of the rocker leans away from the bevelled side. (The fluted side of the rocker is the side with the ridges.) The weight of pressure applied to the rocker during the rocker motion produces the indentations which create the burr that covers the entire plate.

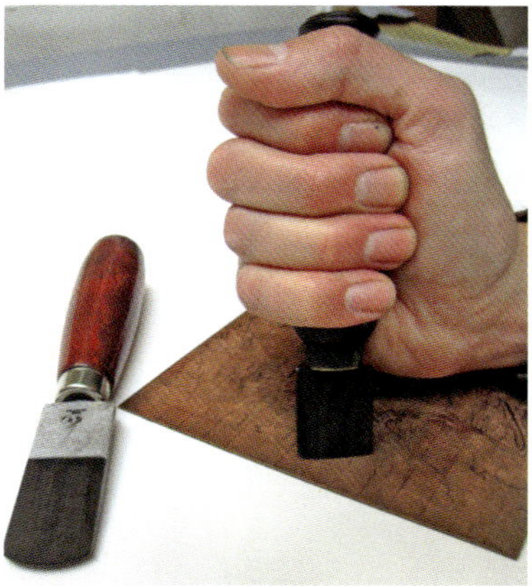

▶ Anchoring a rocker in a rocker pole ensures that the rocker is at a constant angle. (Commissioned rocker pole, K&S Engineering Ltd.) This is important as rocking a mezzo plate is time-consuming. Rocker arms are no longer commercially available, but it is possible to source a second-hand one or to have one made by a metal worker, as shown in our example.

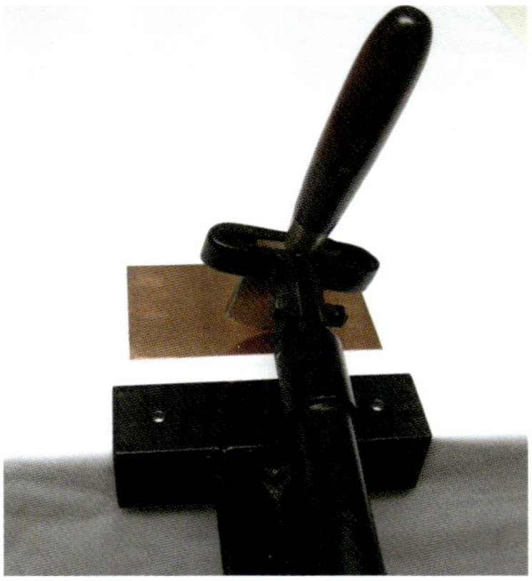

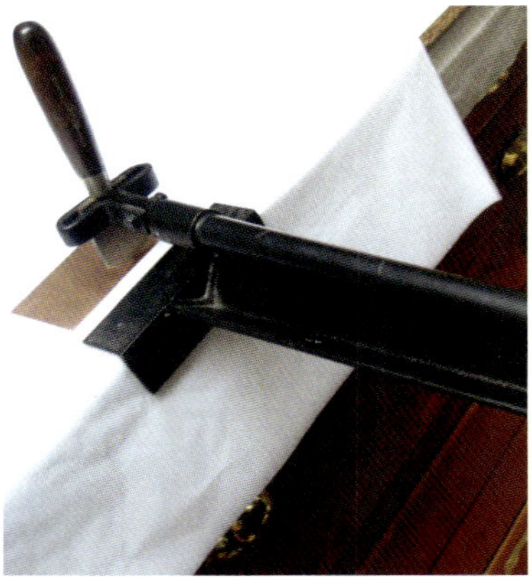

▶ The grid pattern drawn on the plate is a guideline used for the rocker when creating the burr. The grid can be drawn quickly using a ruler and a permanent marker pen. Each individual square of the grid is rocked in sequence. The plate is turned and the rocker begins the second 'pass' in another direction. Each 'pass' is a different direction in which the rocker moves. (It is a bit like cutting a pie into sections.) For example, the first four passes would be: 1 = horizontal; 2 = vertical; 3 = left diagonal; 4 = right diagonal. The more passes that are made on the plate, the denser the ground (the roughened surface of the plate) becomes.

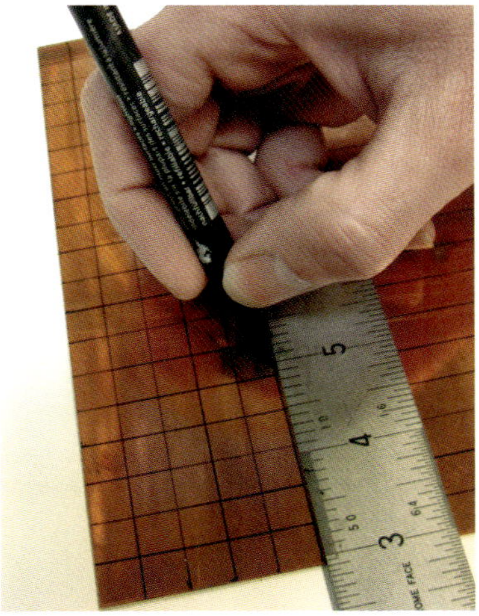

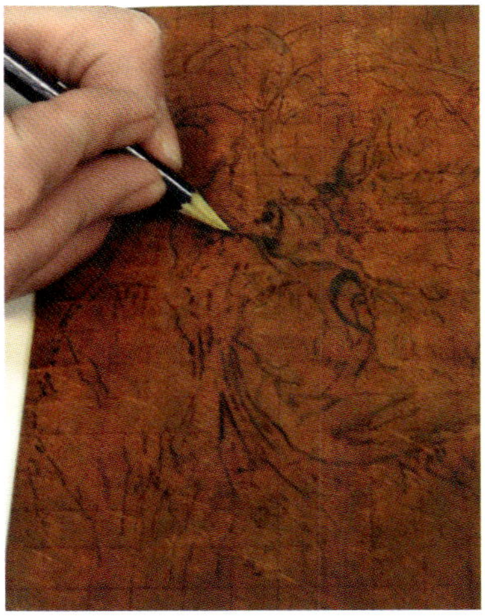

A rocker arm is used on medium- to large-sized plates to maintain a consistent cutting angle and to alleviate strain on the arm. Pre-rocked plates are available but they are expensive. However, it is considered that hand-rocking a plate creates a superior ground (the rough surface or burr on the plate) than a machine-rocked plate.

TRANSFERRING THE IMAGE ONTO THE MEZZOTINT PLATE

Use carbon paper to transfer the image onto the rocked plate. Lay carbon paper underneath the plate and then place both on the rocked plate. Trace over the image with a pencil: the carbon drawing will appear on the plate as a guide to follow when burnishing the image.

▼ The outline of the image is transferred to the plate after tracing over it with carbon paper.

Tip

An easy way to reverse the image prior to drawing it is to scan the image into Photoshop®. Go to the 'Image' menu, choose 'rotate canvas' and then choose: 'flip horizontally'. You can then print this out.

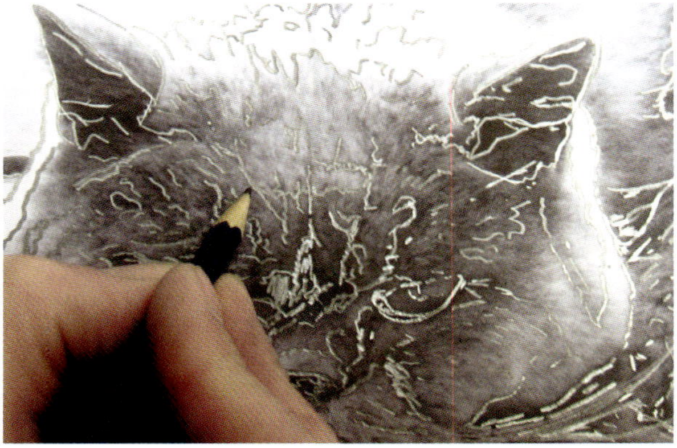

BURNISHING THE MEZZOTINT PLATE

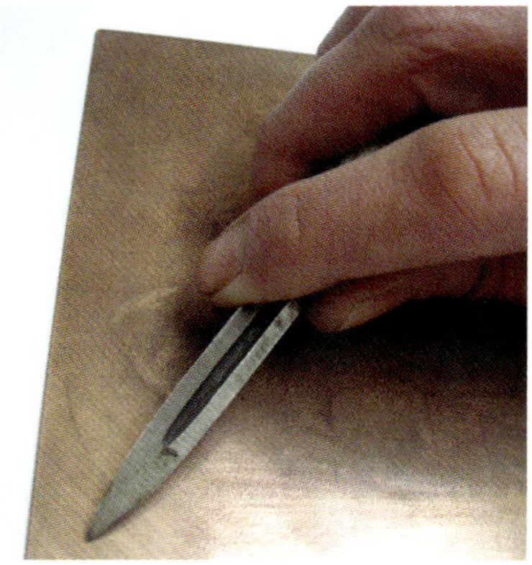

▲ Scrapers create soft, dull tonal areas of texture which look very good when combined with the shimmering highlights the burnisher makes. The scraper can also be used to restore tone to the image when the burnisher has flattened (made too shiny) an area.

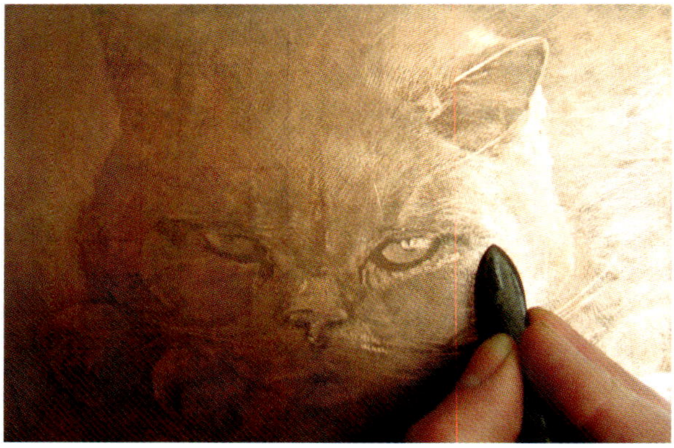

▲ Flat burnishers are ideal for creating broad tonal areas. Ball burnishers create a thin white line. Note that exerting too much pressure may create a groove on the plate. The groove will hold ink and print as a black shape.

Tip

Steel wool and sand paper (carborundum® paper), jewellers rouge, pumice stone, Arkansas stones, Dremel® drills and even kitchen scouring pads can be used to add tonal effects to the mezzotint plate. Always remember to remove the copper dust created on the plate when scraping areas, so that the metal filings do not scratch the image.

▶ The finished mezzotint plate image before inking and printing. The shiny highlighted areas will print as the white areas in the image.

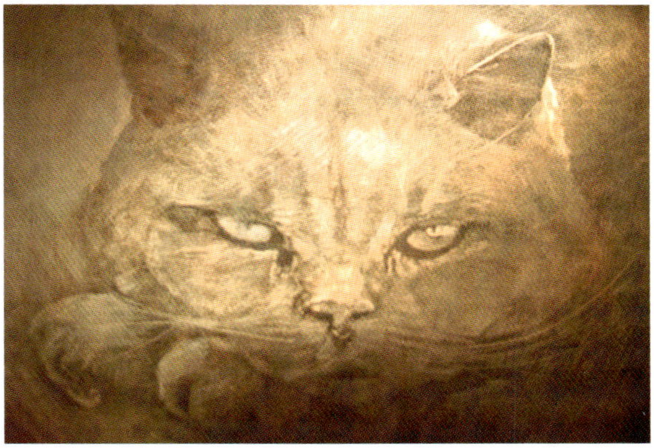

PRINTING THE MEZZOTINT PLATE

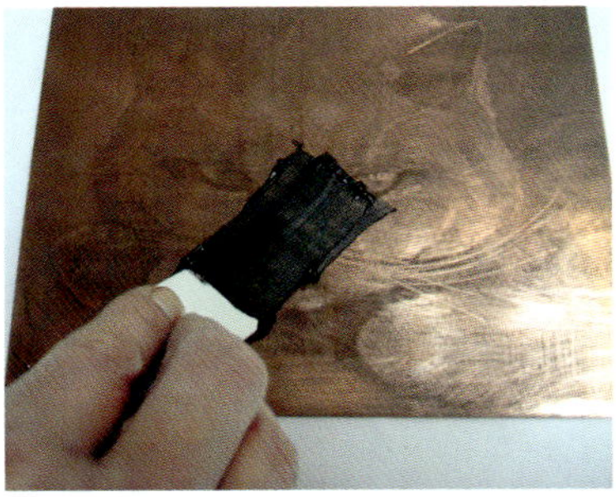

▲ Ink is carded onto the mezzotint plate. The card allows the ink to be dragged uniformly across the plate surface and forces ink evenly into the highly textured areas.

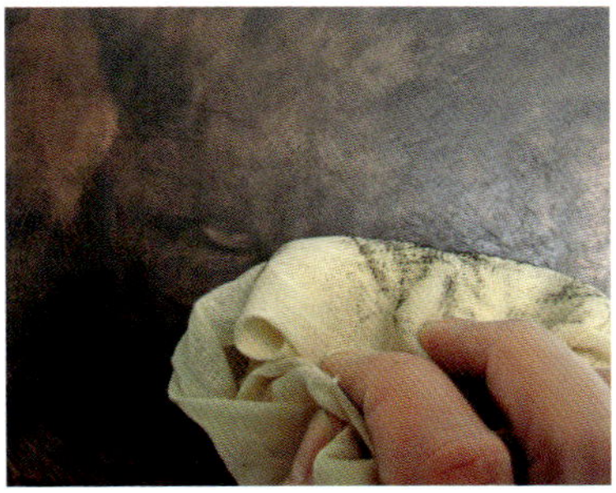

▲ Scrim or tarlatan (starched woven cotton). The rounded ball of scrim should fit comfortably in your hand. Scrim removes the excess ink on the plate and allows you to give special attention to all of the textured details in the image. A general wipe reveals the actual state of the image on the plate. A second clean with scrim is then used for the final stages of wiping, which accentuate the highlights in the image.

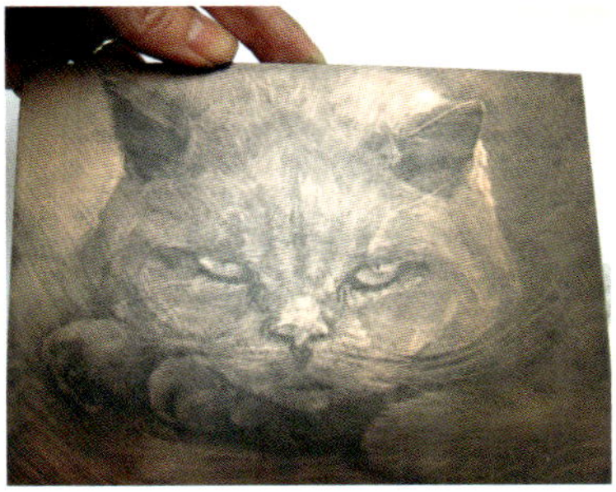

▲ The inked mezzotint plate ready to be printed. A mezzotint plate will yield 20–25 prints.

Tip

The most effective way to eliminate 'plate tone' (the film of ink that still adheres to the plate after wiping) and create sharp white areas in the image is to use the 'palm' method or hand-wiping. Lightly coat the base of your palm area with whiting and whisk it lightly across the plate using gentle, even strokes. Tissue paper and nylon stockings can also be used to remove plate tone.

▶ The inked plate is placed on the bed of the press and a printing paper of good weight and rag is used to take an impression. After printing, the desired quantity of prints of the image, the mezzotint plate should be cleaned very well. Ink left in the texture of the mezzotint will harden and impair the texture on the plate. A soft toothbrush should be used; never use a harsh scrubbing brush.

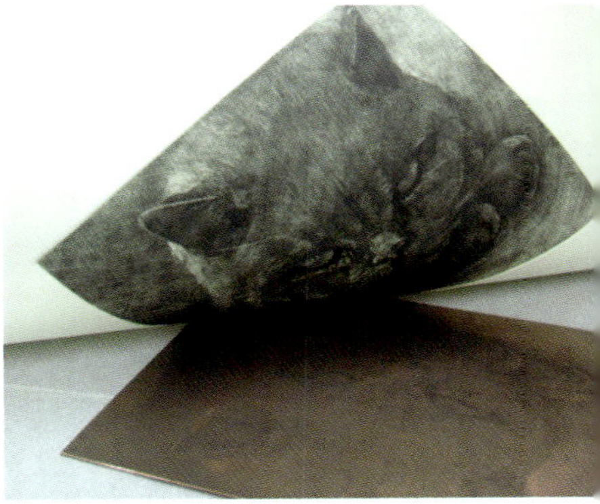

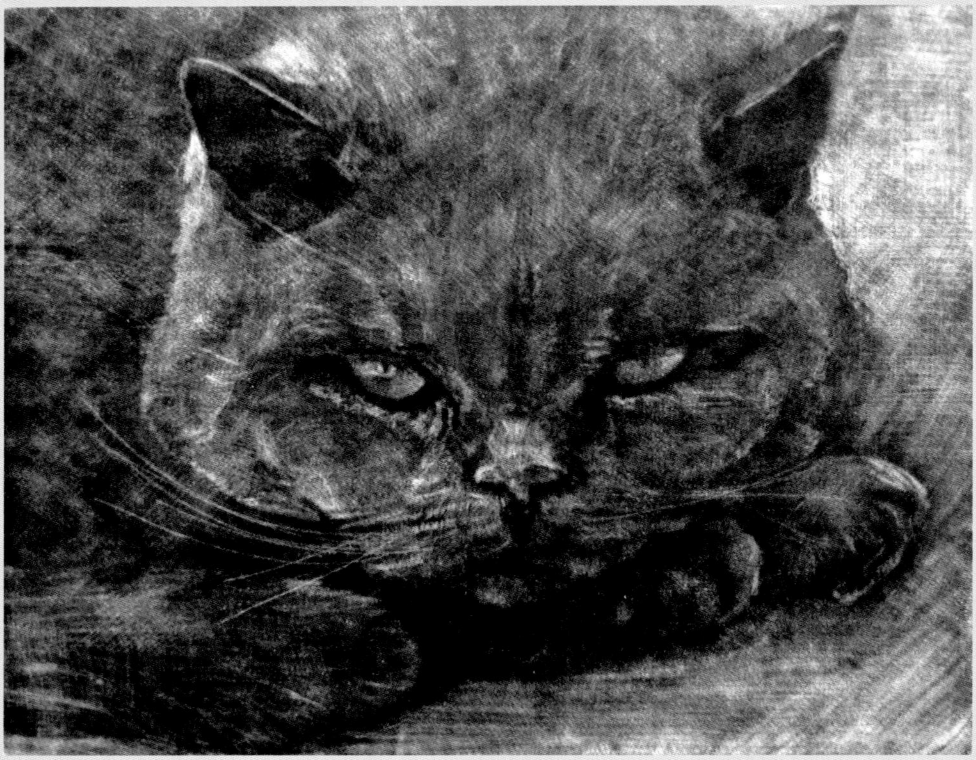

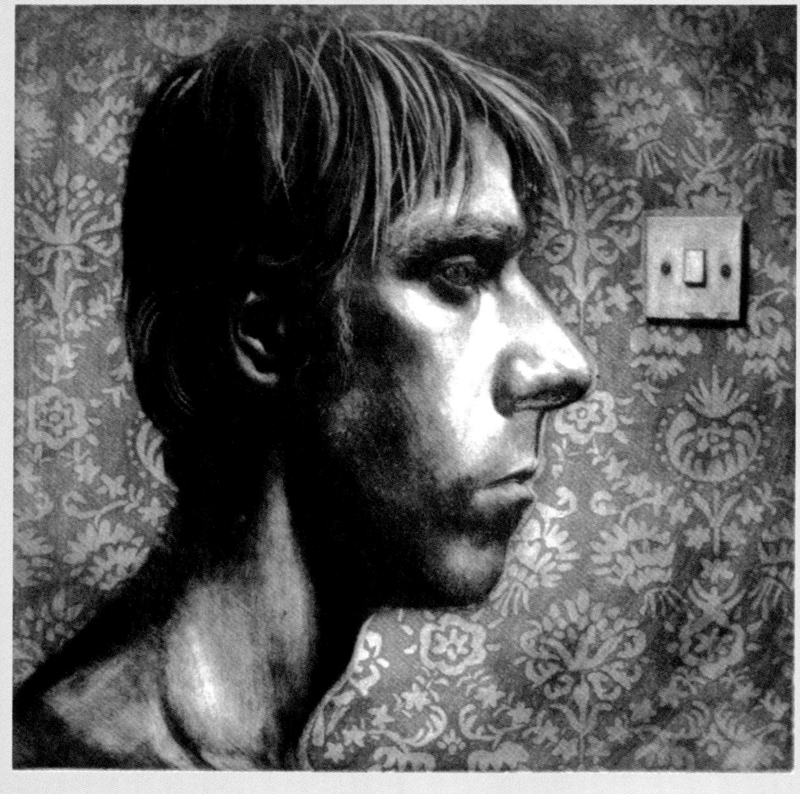

▲ Colin Gale, *Blue Boy*, 2010. Mezzotint, 18 x 14 cm (7 x 5½ in.).

◀ Stuart Pearson-Wright, *Self-Portrait*, 2006. Mezzotint and relief, 20 x 20 cm (7¾ x 7¾ in.).

▶ TOP: Paul Emsley, *Rhino*, 2008. Mezzotint, 71 x 114 cm (28 in. x 45 in.).

▶ BOTTOM: Philip Solly, *Highland Encounter*, 2008. Mezzotint and engraving, 56 x 60 cm (20 x 23½ in.).

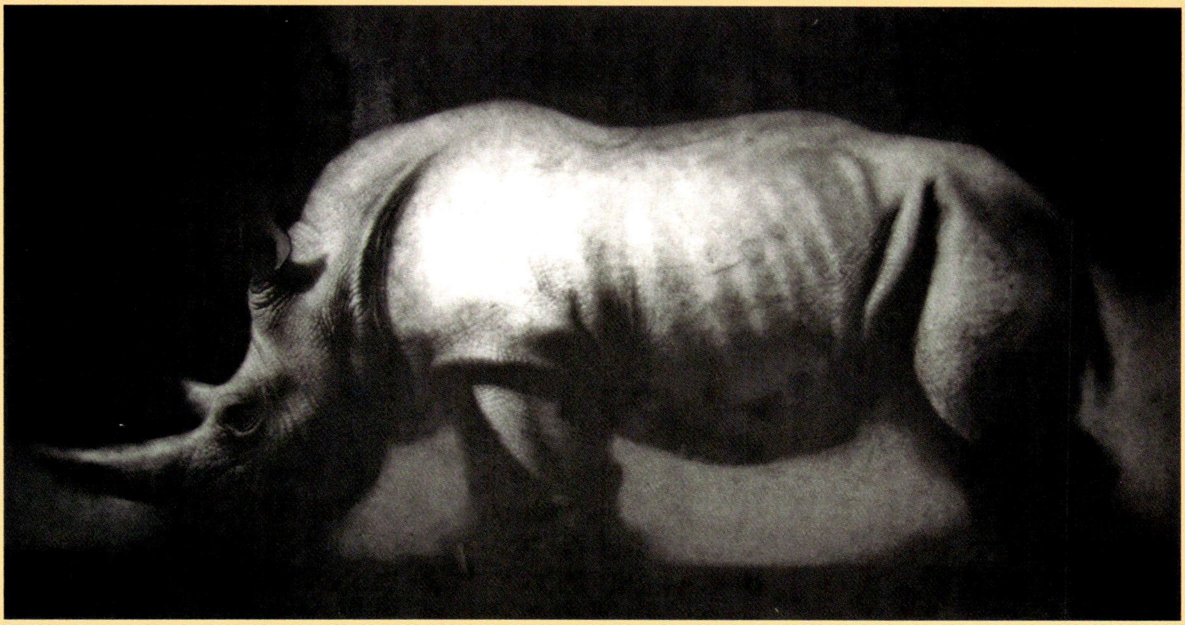

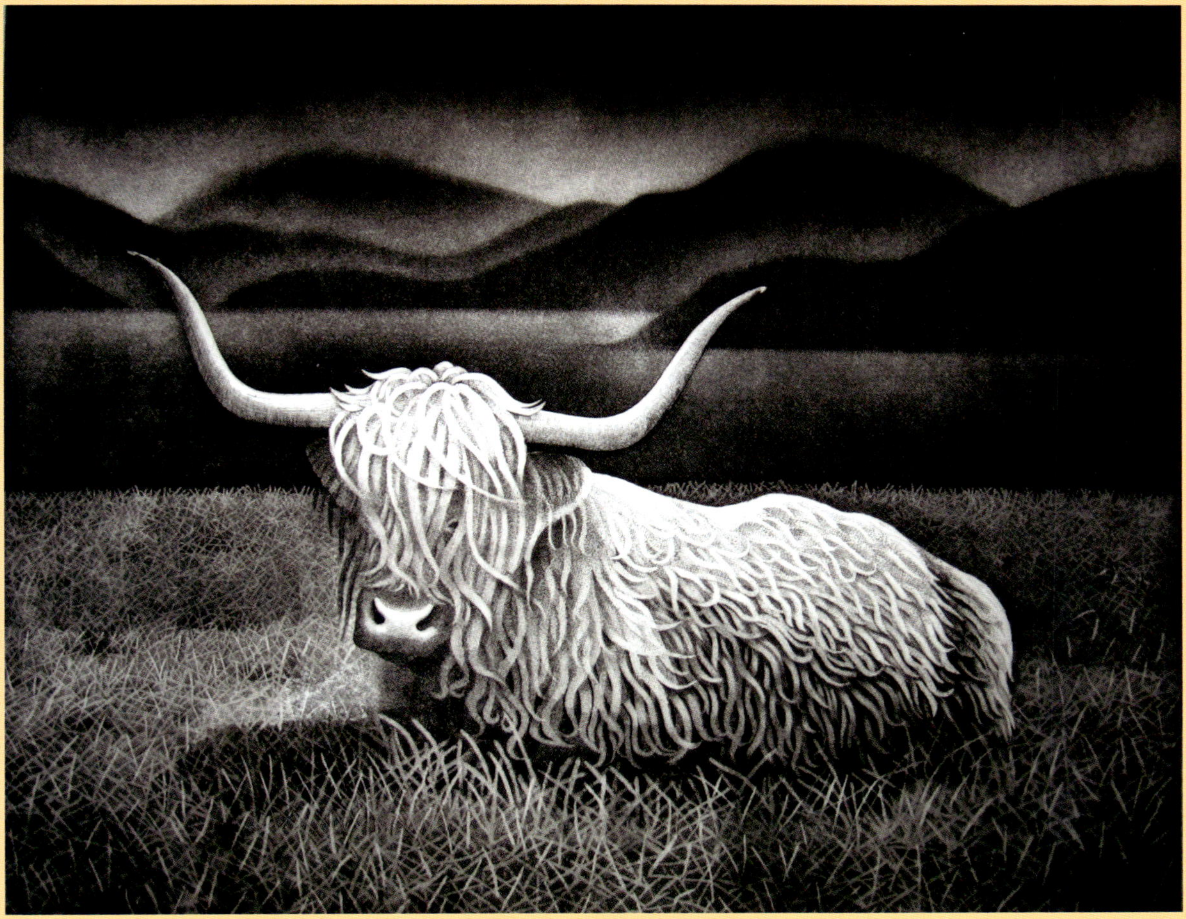

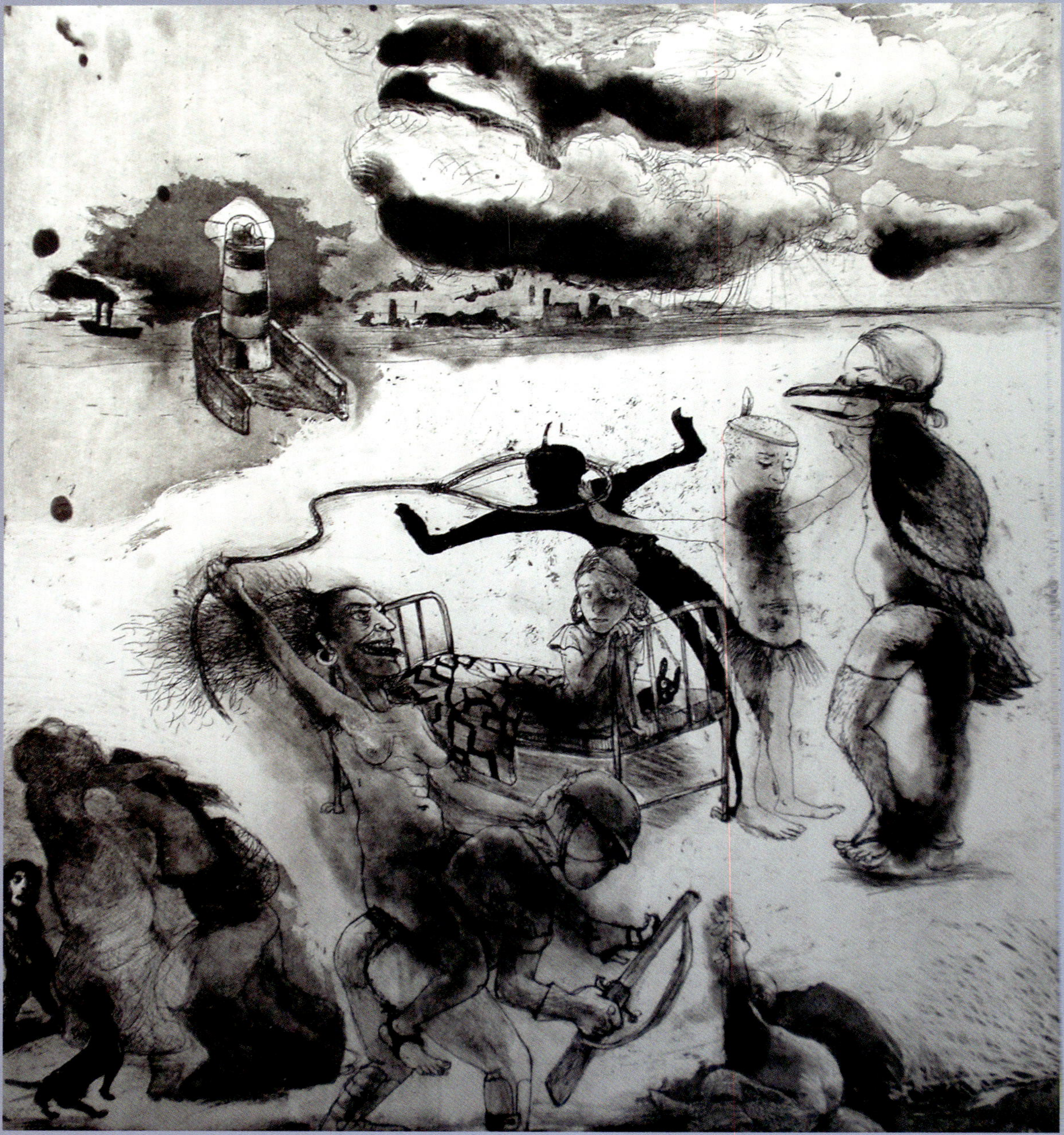

5

etching

Intaglio is an umbrella term for a number of printmaking techniques which include drypoint, etching, aquatint, engraving, mezzotint, photoetching and flexograph. Drypoint, engraving, mezzotint and flexograph are all no-mordant intaglio techniques. Aquatint, etching and photoetching are all intaglio techniques in which a mordant is used to create marks on the surface of a metal plate that has been covered in a waxy or liquid ground.

Intaglio decoration on metal for armour and weapons was commonplace for centuries and these skills transferred naturally to printmaking once paper went into commercial production. The first European paper mill opened in 1264 in Fabriano, Italy.

◀ **Marcelle Hanselaar, *Loss of Innocence 4*, 2011. Etching/aquatint on zinc, 50 x 45 cm (19½ x 17¾ in.).**

hard ground etching

Hard ground etching is the most common technique used to make lines on a metal plate. The ground provides a resist to the mordant that bites the metal. To make a mark, a sharp metal tool is used to scratch through the ground revealing the metal beneath. When the plate is placed into the mordant (an acid or salt) it bites the metal where the lines have been drawn through the ground. During printing it is these bitten lines or ruts that hold the printing ink that is then tranferred to paper using a press.

Plates are first cut to size using a treadle metal guillotine. The guillotine is an essential piece of workshop equipment as it is not possible to cut plates by hand. Remember that the plate dimension is the first drawing decision, so get this right! Once you cut the metal, you cannot glue it back together again.

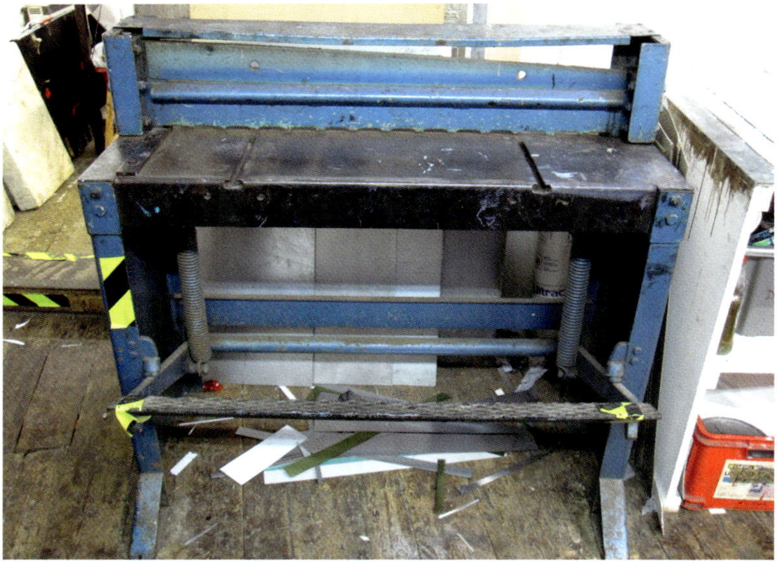

◀ **A treadle guillotine for cutting metal plates.**

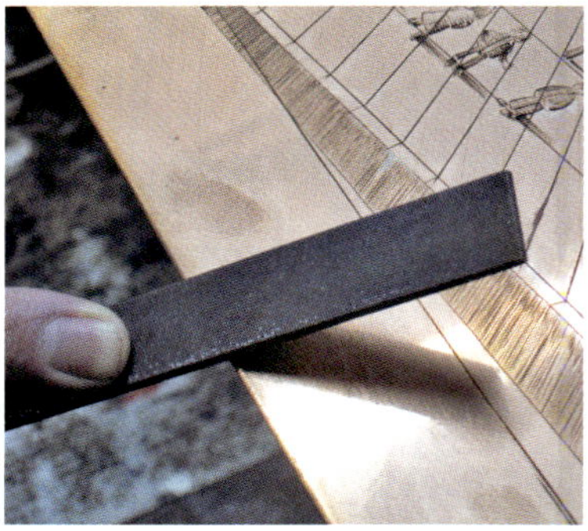

▲ **Filing the edges of the plate.**

FILING

The next stage is to bevel the edges of the plate. This removes the sharp edges which can cut fingers, damage rollers and potentially cut through the printing paper and press blankets. Hold the plate firmly on a desk top with one hand and file the edges at a 45 degree angle. (It is easier to do this standing up, so that your body weight is pressing down on the plate.) Bevel all edges (top side of the plate only) and round the corners slightly. It is not essential to have perfect edges at this point, as the edges will become slightly corroded during etching. Most workshops have a designated filing area to prevent filings contaminating areas where inking takes place. Filings scratch plates and can ruin work.

Before applying hard ground to an etching plate (be it a traditional hard ground wax or an acrylic-based ground), it is essential to degrease the plate surface thoroughly. Any traces of grease left there will repel the ground applied, resulting in 'foul biting' (the term used for areas or spots of the plate that the acid attacks and bites where it is not intended to do so). Metals such as copper and zinc are inherently greasy on the surface. Steel is covered with a thin, oily film to prevent rust or oxidisation. Even grease from fingertips after handling the plate will result in grounds not adhering to the plate surface.

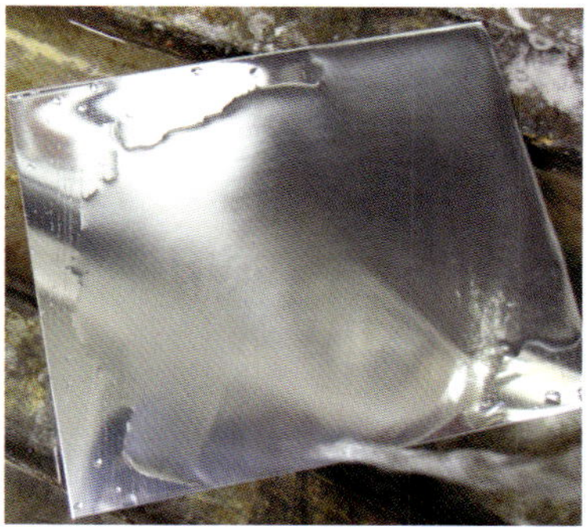

▲ A zinc plate with water on the surface. The water is repelled particularly at the greasy edges of the plate.

To see how greasy a metal plate is, simply place it under a running tap. The water will repel around any greasy areas on the plate, particularly at the edges.

The methods and recipes below are suitable for the four types of metal used in etching: copper, zinc, steel and aluminium. Degreasing methods vary from workshop to workshop and there are many ways it can be done. No method is entirely right or wrong and the removal of grease is the most important end result.

The most common, tried-and-tested method of degreasing (and also the cheapest) is to use whiting powder (calcium carbonate or chalk). Degreasing should take place in a sink used for processing plates. It is useful to have wooden battens in the base of the sink on which plates can be placed. These wooden battens keep plates raised off the bottom of the sink, which helps prevent the grit or dirt in the sink from coming into contact with the plate surface. (Both of these could hinder degreasing and will cause unintended scratches on the plate.)

THE TRADITIONAL METHOD OF DEGREASING

Whiting powder is mixed with water to which household ammonia is added. The water and ammonia is pre-mixed at a ratio of approximately 100 parts water to 10 parts ammonia for use in the studio and can be stored indefinitely in a large container ready for use. Mix the whiting

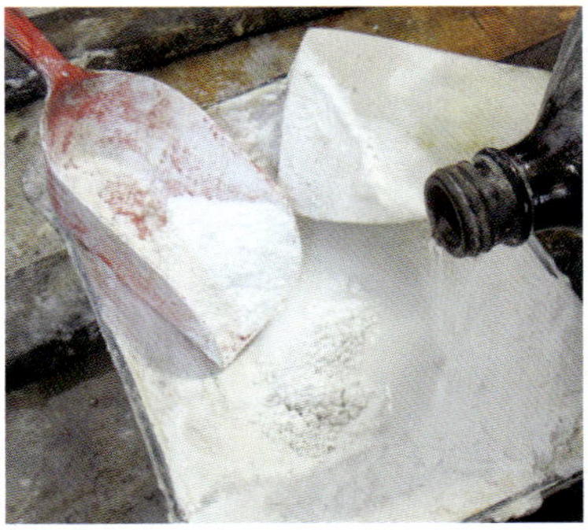

▲ Mixing whiting powder with a water/ammonia mix.

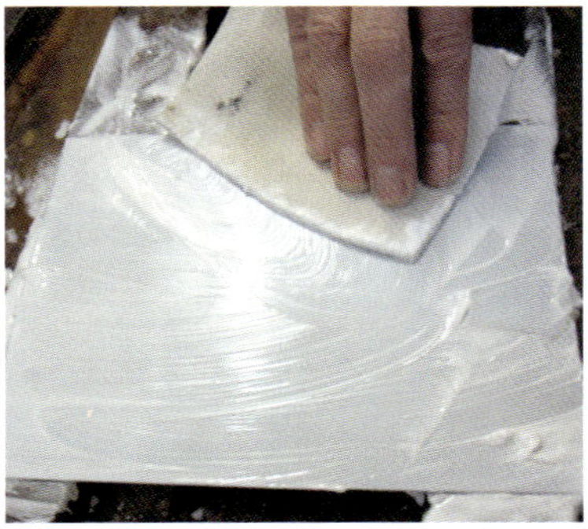

▲ Degreasing a plate using whiting.

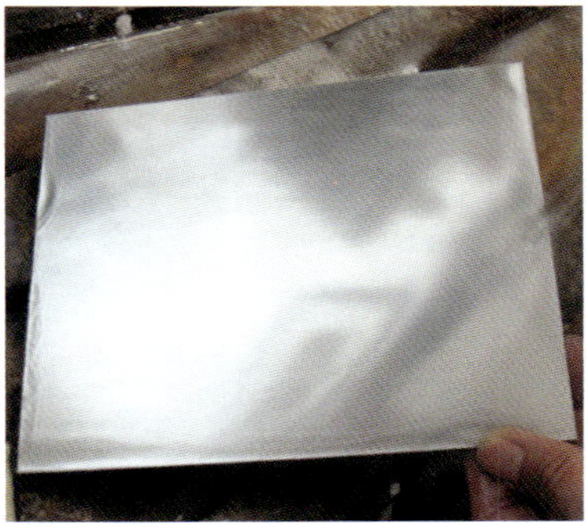

▲ Water will run off in an unbroken film when a plate is degreased properly.

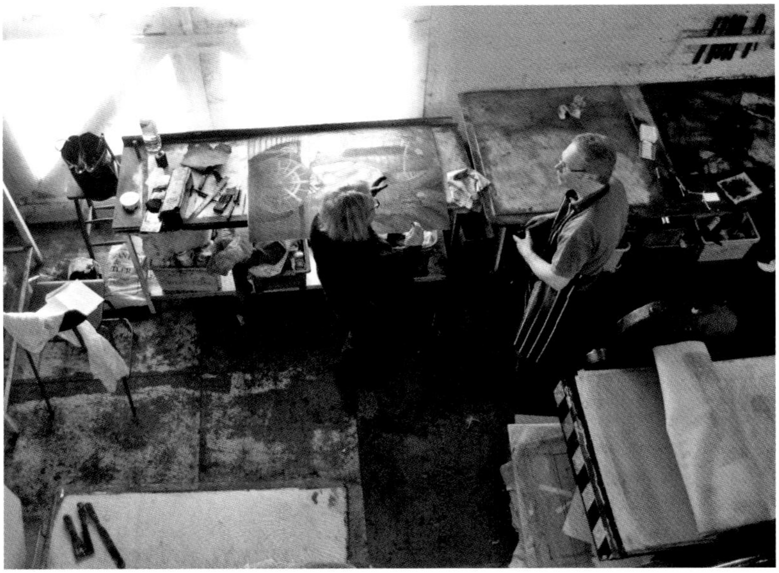

◀ Ana Maria Pacheco working on a large copper plate at Artichoke in 2011.

and water into a thick paste and apply to the plate surface with a clean cotton cloth or cotton wool (paper towels are suitable too). Rub firmly, concentrating on the edges. Rinse the plate well with water. Dry the plate using a hairdryer or fan.

Salt and vinegar on copper

If copper plates become tarnished, use white vinegar and salt mixed together to remove the tarnish before proceeding to degreasing with whiting powder. Dry the plate quickly using a hairdryer or fan. If this does not work, use liquid metal polish with a soft rag.

WAX HARD GROUND

Wax hard ground is still the most practised of hard ground techniques. Its tradition of quality mark-making dates back to Rembrandt and Goya. We have yet to see any method that betters the quality and sensitivity of a needle drawing a mark through hard ground wax.

Hard ground wax is a mixture of beeswax, bitumen and resin. It is supplied in small 'cakes' or balls.

To apply the ground, a degreased plate is placed face-up onto an electric hotplate. The hotplate should be warm enough to begin melting the ground when it is pressed onto the surface of the plate.

Using a hard rubber or nitrile PVC roller that is kept specifically for this job, begin rolling the ground to an even layer. Cover the entire plate as evenly as possible. Remove the plate by pushing it off the hotplate onto a 'jigger' – in printmaking, this is normally a home-made wooden box the height of the hotplate – and allow to cool.

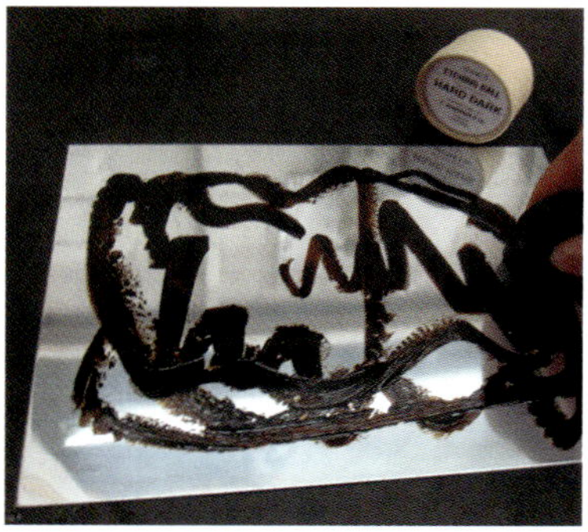

▲ Melting a wax ground onto a zinc plate.

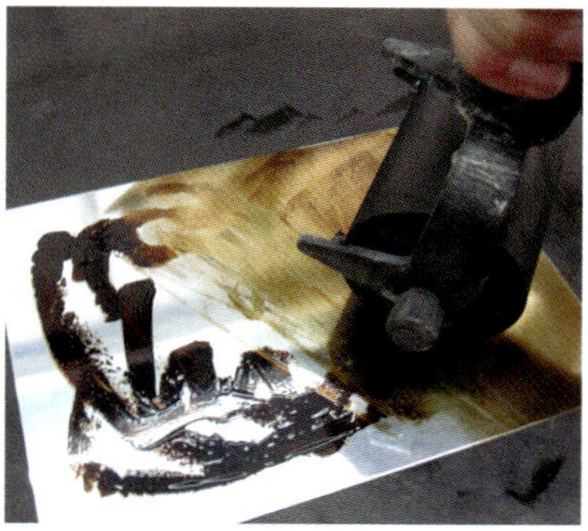

▲ Rolling the ground to cover the plate surface.

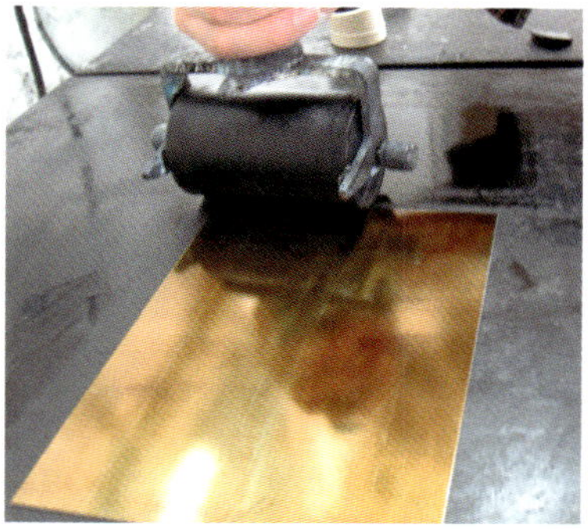

▲ Roll as evenly as possible.

Tip

If the roller has hard ground coated on it from previous use (this is common in a studio with many artists), roll the roller repeatedly across the surface of the hotplate to warm up the ground already on the roller. The hard ground roller should be cleaned every time it is used: dust, grit, ink, hair and chalk become embedded into the ground that covers it, preventing the even rolling of a clean ground on the plate surface. Regular cleaning will also prevent an excess of ground building up on the roller (an unnessary waste). To clean the roller, warm it on the hotplate and remove the excess ground with a cotton rag. Use a small amount of solvent (white spirit) on a clean rag to give the roller a final wipe.

Smoking the plate

Smoking a wax hard ground is carried out for two reasons. The first is visual: the blackening of the ground makes the needled marks made on the surface highly visible, particularly with copper, which is similar in colour to the brown wax. Second, smoking makes the ground more resistant to the mordant used to bite the plate.

▼ Smoking a plate held using a hand vice.

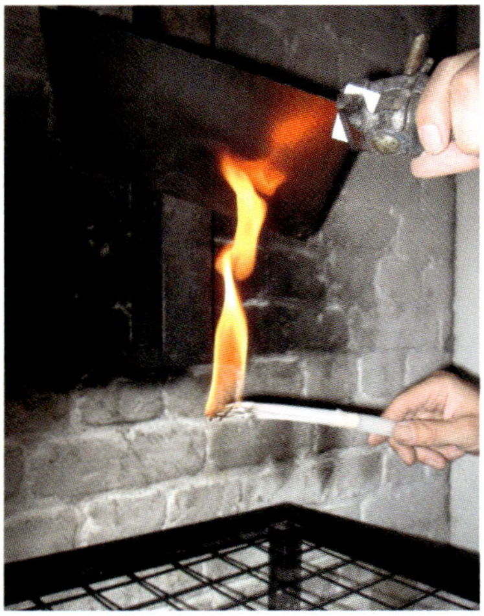

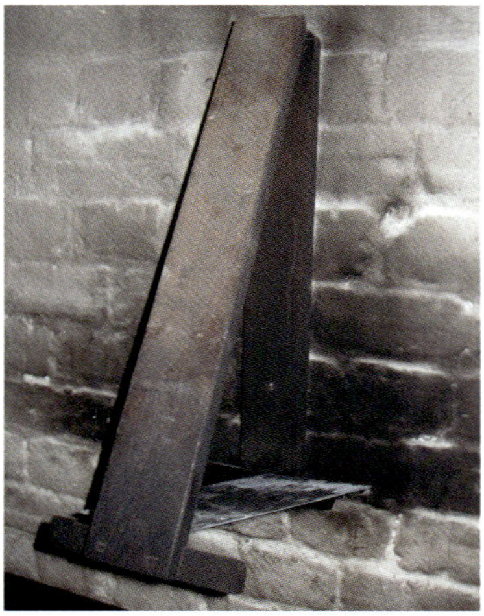

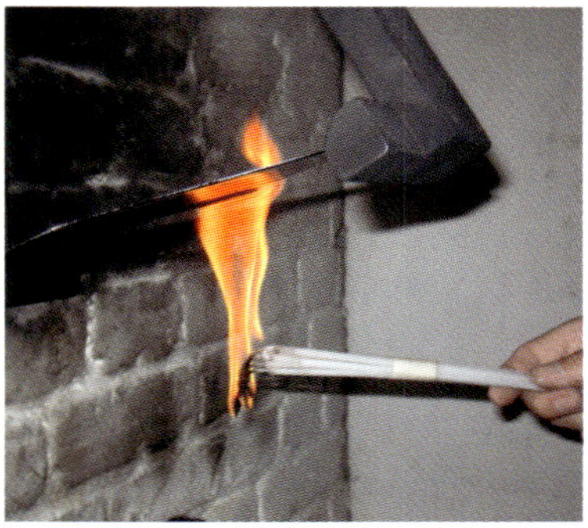

▲ Smoking a plate held with a hinged wall bracket.

◀ A hinged wall bracket.

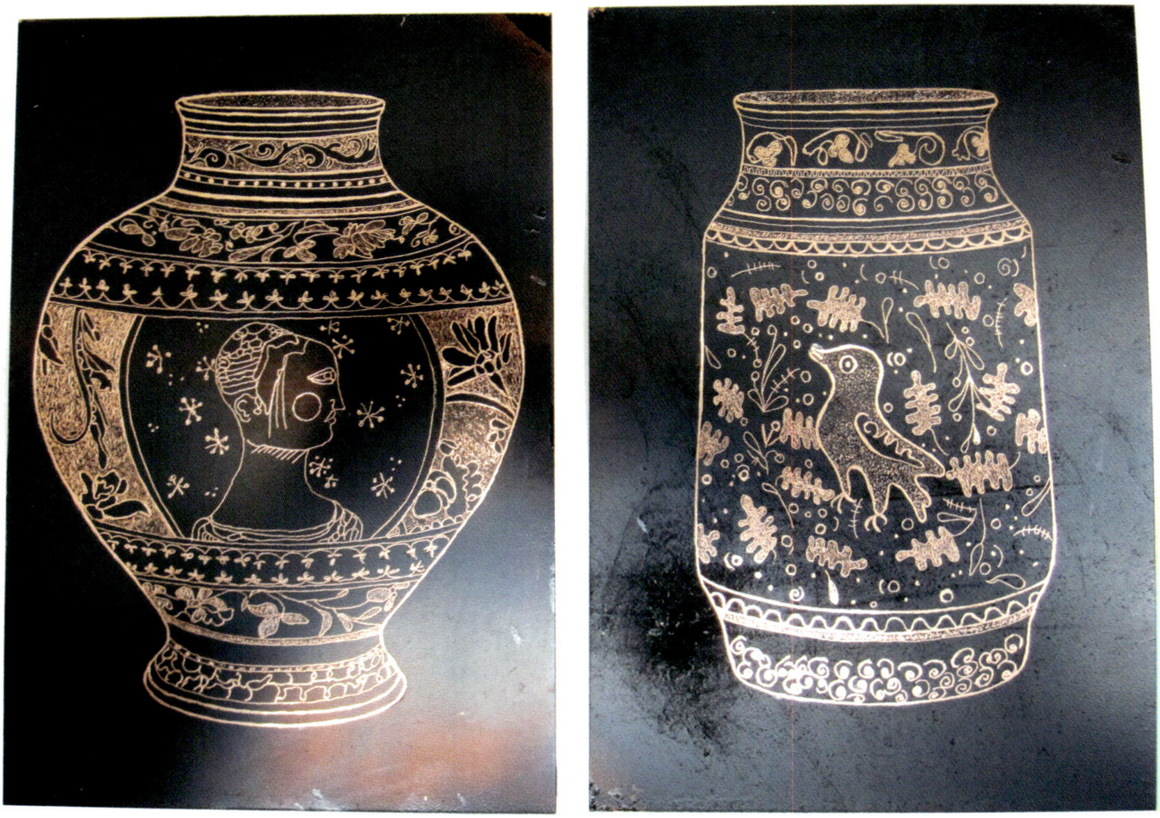

▲ **Alessia Bertacco, two 8 x 12 cm (3¼ x 4¾ in.) plates drawn on smoked hard ground ready for biting, 2011.**

To smoke the plate, it must be suspended ground-side facing down. Use a hand vice (for small plates only) or a hinged wall bracket. A bunch of wax lighting tapers (usually six to eight of them) are tied with tape and the bunch of tapers held so that the tip of the flame touches the ground. The flame is moved systematically across the wax surface. You will observe the wax changing from a dull to a shiny black. Allow the plate to cool for several minutes before handling.

ACRYLIC HARD GROUND

This method of etching has the advantage of not needing a hotplate.

Ready-mixed acrylic hard grounds are available and brands include Lascaux® Hard Resist and Z-Acryl Hard Ground Emulsion. These are flow-coated onto plates that have been lightly sanded and degreased. Sand the plate by hand with very fine sandpaper or use an orbital sander – this will help the ground to key onto the plate and prevent it from chipping. Then degrease the plate.

Stand the plate upright in a plastic tray. Starting at the top, pour the liquid ground directly from the bottle and allow the emulsion to run down the plate until the surface is evenly coated. Remove the plate from the tray and allow to dry naturally in a vertical position.

Pour any excess emulsion back into the bottle, clean the tray with paper towels and rinse with water.

Acrylic hard ground can be removed by soaking the plate in a tray of sodium carbonate in water.

HOUSEHOLD HARD GROUND

When coloured with black Indian ink or food colouring, floor varnishes such as Pledge® Future and Klear® can be flow-coated onto a lightly sanded and degreased plate. It is common to add artists' acrylic binder medium (one part medium to five parts floor varnish) to add flexibility and strength. Without the medium, we have found that these coatings are quite brittle and cause flaking of the line when needled through. It is probably wiser to use the purpose-made, branded acrylic grounds as they are well formulated and reliable.

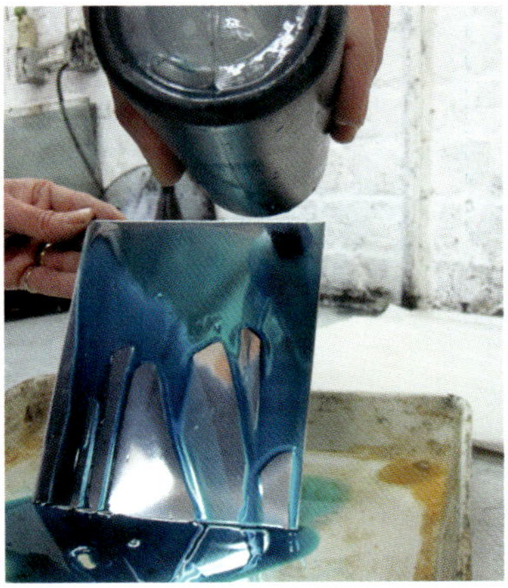

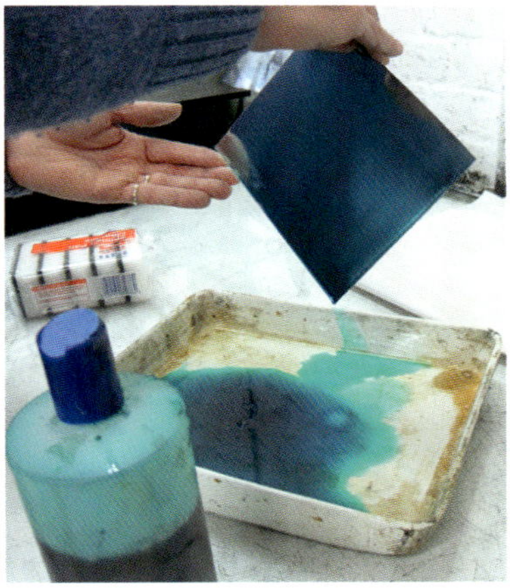

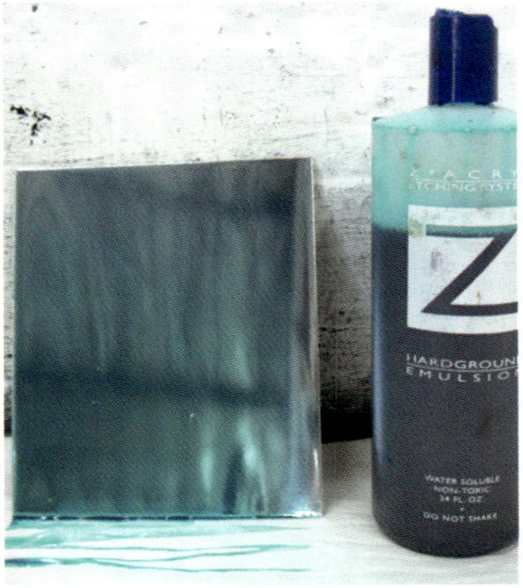

▲ LEFT TO RIGHT

Flow-coating a plate using acrylic liquid ground.

DRAWING THE PLATE

Before commencing a drawing, bear in mind that the image will print in reverse (a mirror image). Approaches to drawing are an individual choice, of course: some artists simply choose to be direct and 'wade in'. Picasso for instance, didn't even worry that his etched signature would print in reverse! For some, subject matter or gestural approaches to mark-making image-reversal may not be a factor, but for an image that needs to read topographically left to right, correct image reversal is essential. There are two methods which will help the artist easily 'reverse' the image onto a prepared plate.

The first method is to use a mirror to reverse a sketch or a photograph. The image is placed facing the mirror and the artist draws the image seen in the mirror rather than the actual photograph or sketchbook page image.

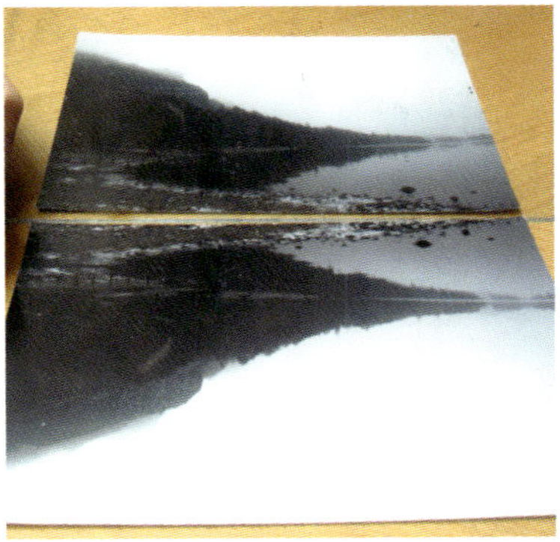

▲ A photograph of Lake Derwent reversed in a mirror.

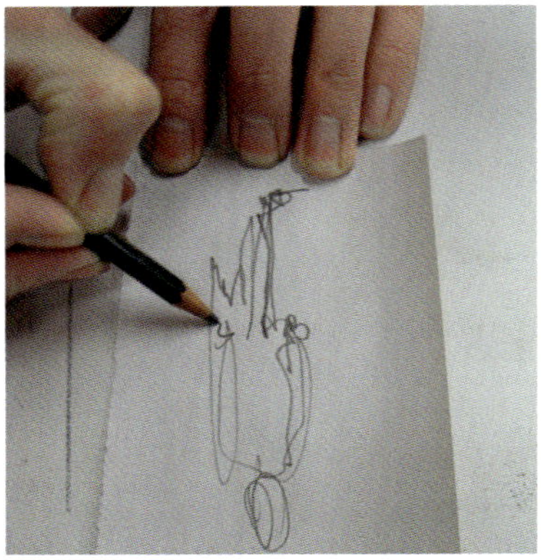

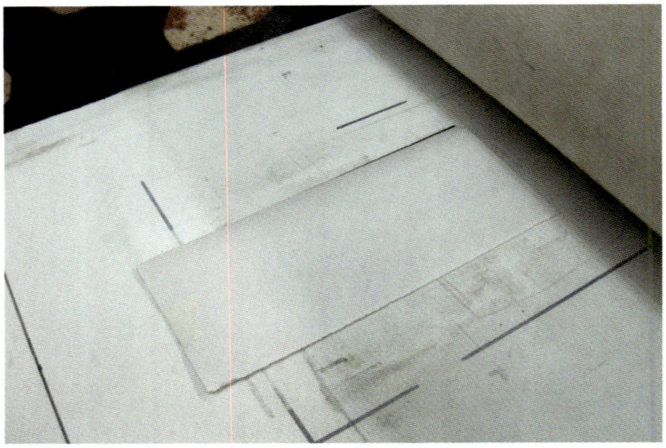

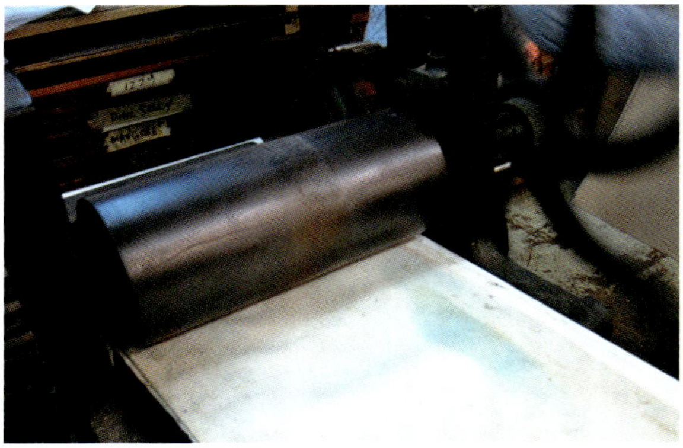

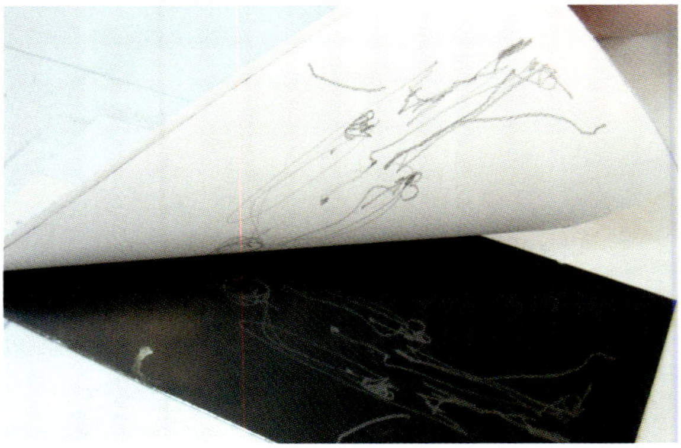

A second method is to transfer a pencil drawing onto a smoked hard ground wax. To do this, make a drawing in soft pencil on thin, smooth paper. Place the drawing on top of the prepared hard ground plate and run this through an etching press (with slightly reduced pressure than that required for normal printing). The greasy carbon from the pencil will be transferred onto the smoked ground, providing an excellent guide to follow with the etching needle.

▲ TOP ROW, LEFT TO RIGHT

A soft pencil onto thin paper.

The drawing placed face-down on the smoked plate.

▲ BOTTOM ROW, LEFT TO RIGHT

Roll through the press with slightly reduced pressure than for regular printing.

The graphite is transferred to the plate surface; the drawing appears in reverse.

MARK-MAKING

The ideal needle for etching should be fine and slightly rounded or blunt. It is not intended to dig into the metal surface as in drypoint (see pp.41–7). The needle simply cuts through the hard ground wax/emulsion (acrylic) to reveal the bare metal surface. The ruts or grooves in an etched plate are created by the biting action of the mordant. (See pp.75–80.)

A variety of tools can be used to remove ground. In fact, anything that makes a mark can be employed. When needling the plate, dark areas are created by lines that are close together – this is called 'cross-hatching'. This drawing technique is used because if the lines are joined together, the acid will etch a wide rut (open area) in the plate which means the ink will not be held correctly in the groove of the line. The shape of this open area is referred to as 'open bite'.

▶ Colin Gale's tools for drawing through hard ground. On the left are improvised tools including a dart, a gramaphone needle glued in a wooden stick, two dissecting needles for very fine lines and a heavy round file with a sharp point. The group on the right contains shop-bought needles (note the variety in points). On the far right is a scraper burnisher, essentially a correcting tool but great to draw with, too.

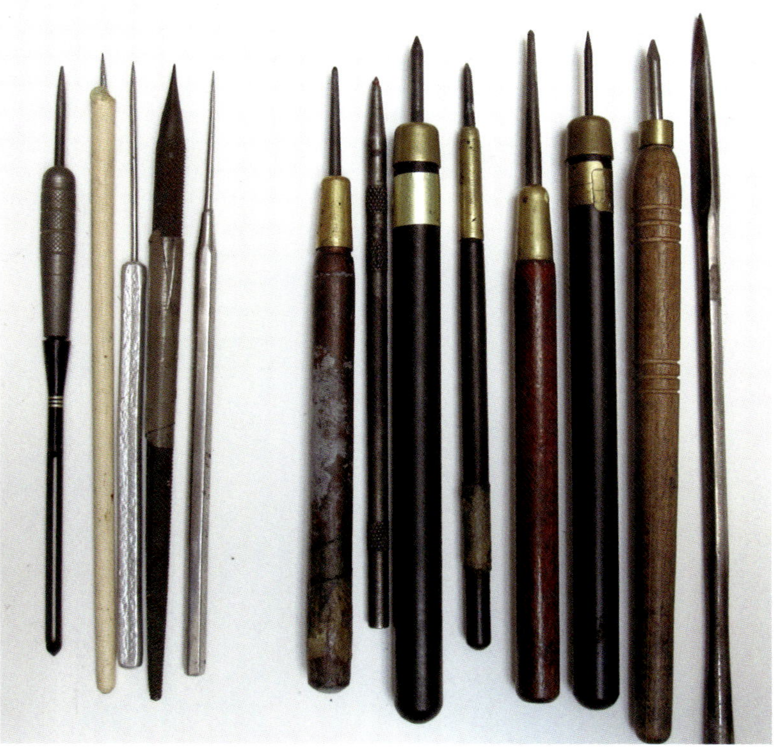

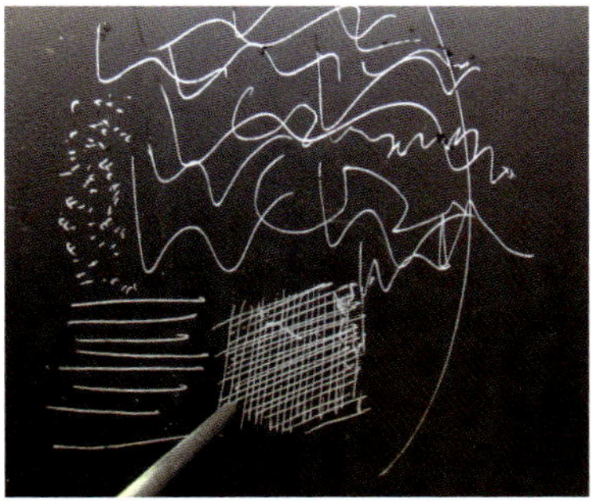

▲ Needling through a smoked wax hard ground on zinc.

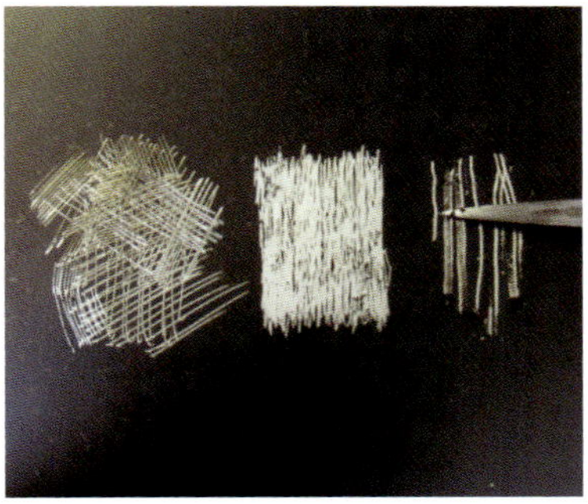

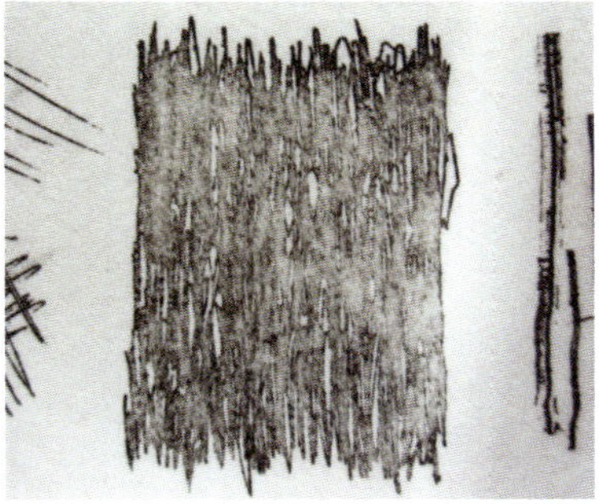

▶ LEFT TO RIGHT: A hard ground plate with (left) cross-hatching; (middle) cross-hatching that is too close and which will lead to open bite; (right) marks made using a triangular scraping tool.

The printed result from the plate on right, showing open bite in the central section.

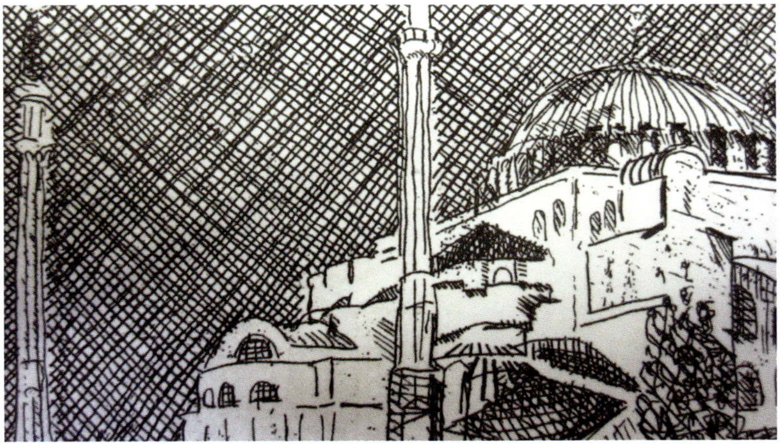

▶ An example of cross-hatching in an etching on zinc by Steve White (detail). The plate was drawn outside on location in Marrakech.

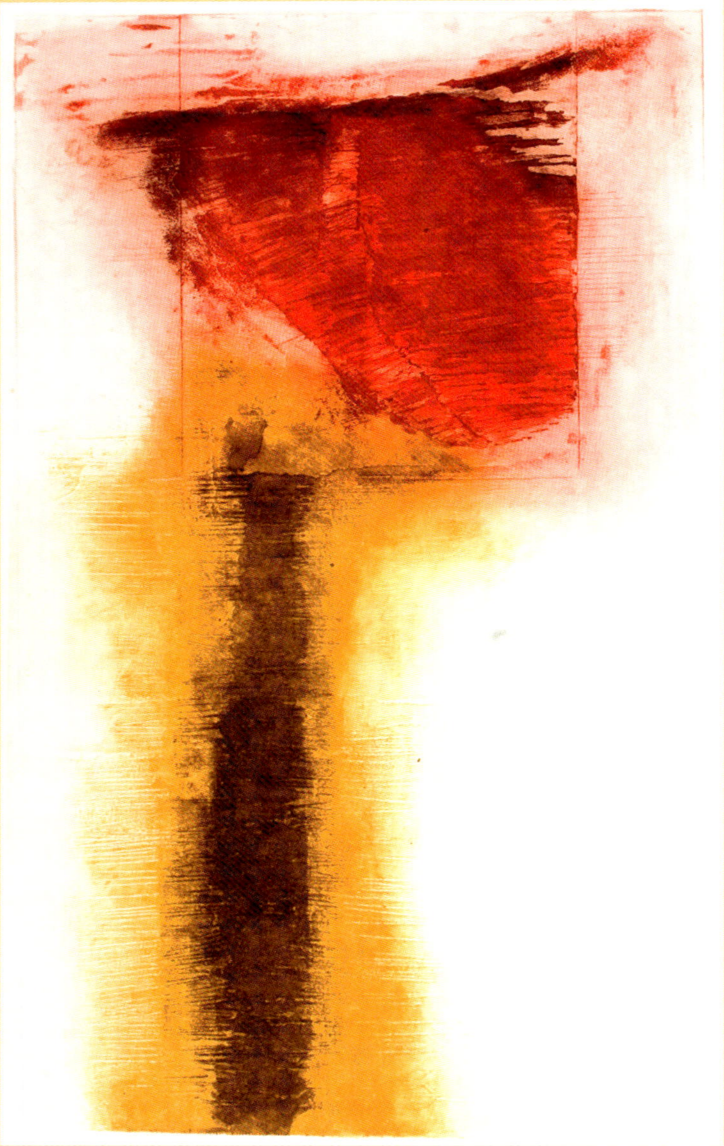

▲ **Megan Fishpool, *Ovid*, 2001. Open bite on steel, 70 x 50 cm (27½ x 19¾ in.).**

Open bite may be used creatively as in this example where the image is drawn through wax hard ground on steel.

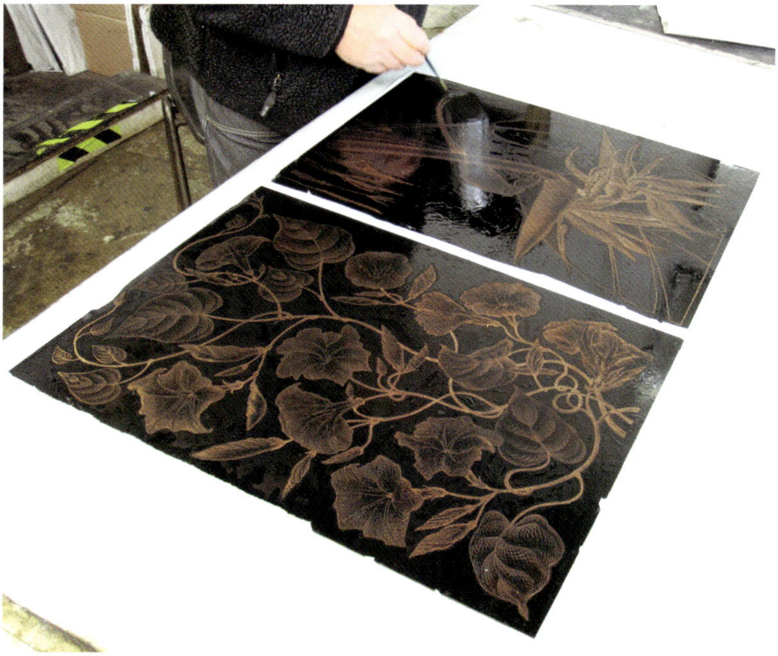

◀ Bryan Poole stopping out blemishes in the wax ground prior to biting the copper plates in ferric chloride. Better safe than sorry!

CORRECTING MISTAKES

At the drawing stage, mistakes on the hard ground plate can be corrected easily by painting over the lines with liquid stop-out varnish or acrylic emulsion. It is important to make any corrections – including the spotting out of blemishes and scratches – before the drawn plate is placed in the acid. Once bitten, any mistakes will need painstaking removal using a scraping and burnishing tool (see p.74).

ETCHING THE PLATES

Once the plate is drawn, it must be placed into a mordant (an acid or salt) so that the lines can be bitten. Before this happens, the back of the plate *must* be protected from the action of the biting otherwise the metal will be attacked from behind as well. This will weaken the plate structure and spoil the acid itself.

Traditionally, the back of plates have always been painted out with a stop-out varnish or plate-backing resist (straw hat varnish, packing tape or sticky back plastic, for example). Lean the plate with the drawn side facing the wall. Use a soft brush to coat the back of the plate. Take care not to let the liquid creep or dribble onto the image side of the plate.

A recommended way of stopping out the back of a plate prior to etching is by using plastic packing tape. Overlap the strips of tape across the entire back surface of the plate. This method is considerably quicker than applying a liquid resist and cuts out the solvents or chemical strippers needed to remove varnish or resists. It is easily removed.

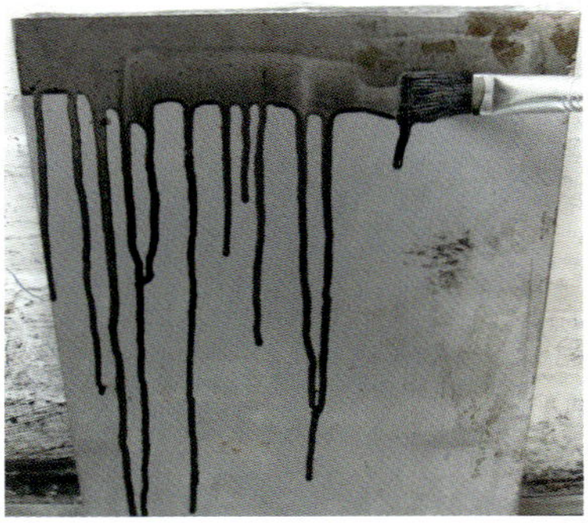

▲ Stopping out the back of a plate with straw hat varnish. Straw hat is a methylated spirit-based varnish and can be made by mixing one part shellac (often sold as Button Polish) with one part methylated spirit, plus a little black spirit dye to add colour.

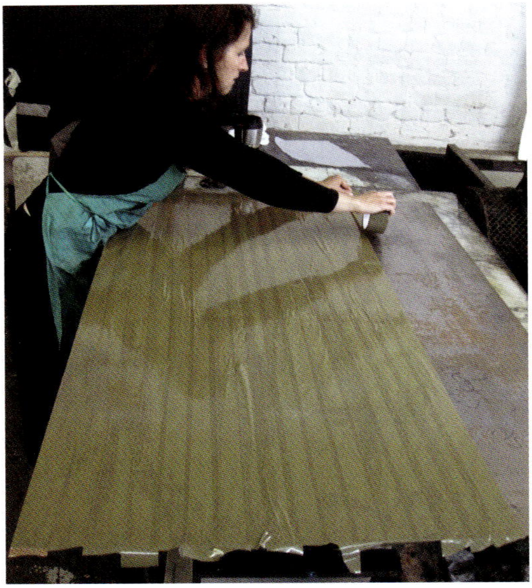

◀ Stephanie Newell-Nebbia using packing tape to seal the back of a large steel plate prior to etching the plate in nitric acid. The plate is now immersed in a bath of mordant. The mordant is unable to assail the ground but attacks the plate where the drawing has revealed the bare metal surface. The choice of mordants is discussed below.

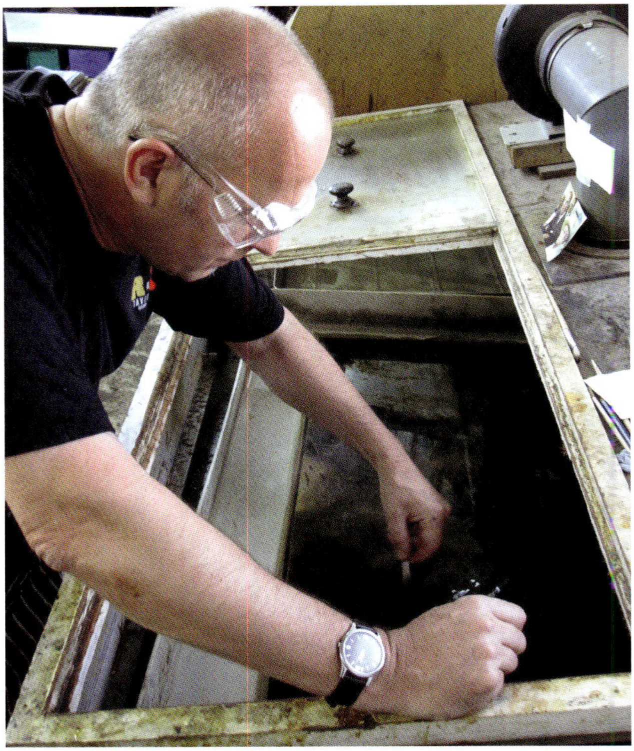

▶ Simon Reddington etching a zinc plate in dilute nitric acid. The plate is being etched in an acid extraction booth, which takes away any fumes. Note the use of eye protection which must be worn at all times when handling any etching mordant. Simon is feathering the plate to remove bubbles formed by the etching process (please note that he has *chosen* not to wear gloves). The acid used here is at a diluted concentration that cannot burn the skin. Perversely, acid splashes are more common when wearing heavy duty gloves as these make for clumsy handling of a plate.

ETCHING THE PLATE, CORRECTING BITTEN MISTAKES

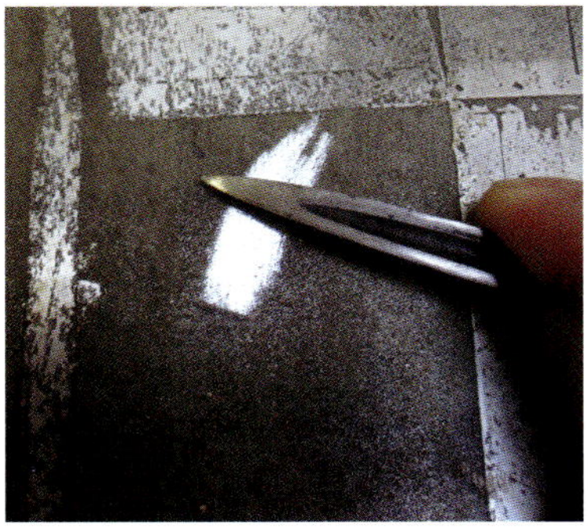

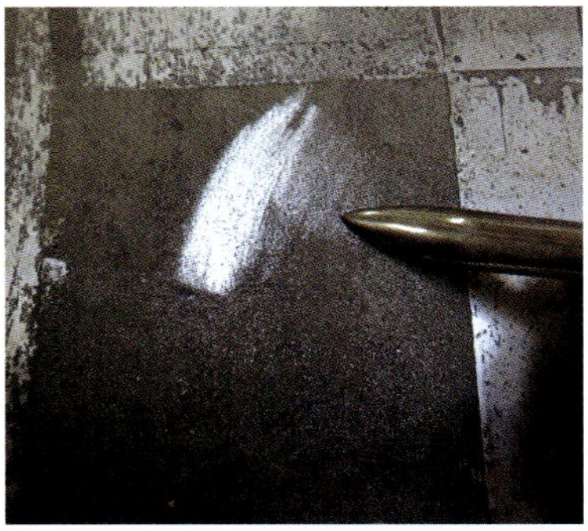

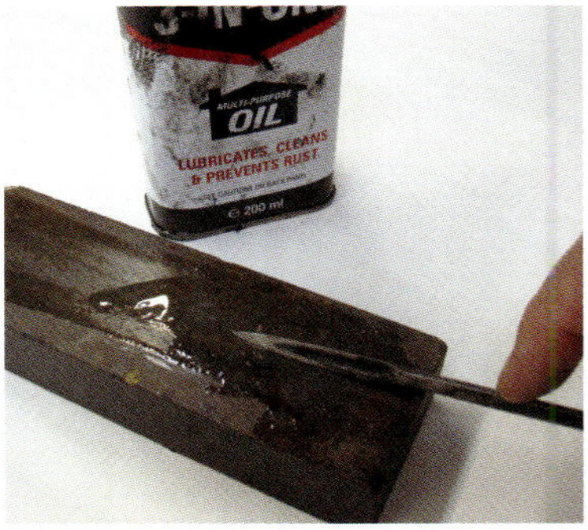

▲ Bitten lines and tones may be removed from a plate by physically scraping them back. The metal becomes flat again and is unable to hold ink. To do this, use a triangular scraping tool followed by a burnishing tool to rub down any remaining rough areas.

▲ Keep the scraper tool keen-edged by using a sharpening stone with a little oil.

mordants

Mordants are corrosives. A mordant is capable of biting, burning or corroding. The most popular mordants used in the printmaking studio are nitric acid, copper sulphate and ferric chloride (also known as iron perchlorate).

These mordants are mixed with water. In the correctly mixed ratios, they are extremely suitable for etching copper, zinc, steel and aluminium. A printmaking studio will usually recommend the corrosives to use with a specific metal and have fume cupboards with specific mordants ready-mixed to a ratio they find is best for plate-making.

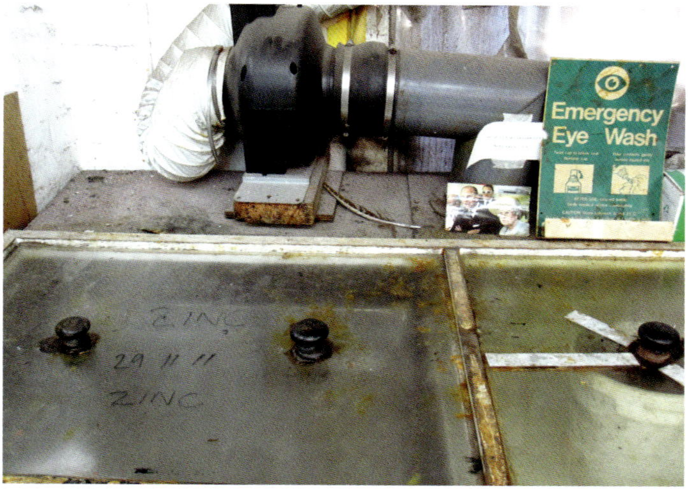

▲ A fume cupboard with acid-proof extraction fan. A fume cupboard is a priority for all printmaking workshops that use nitric acid. Nitric acid mixtures must always be kept in fume cupboards whether they are being used or stored for future use.

Ferric chloride is distinguished by its copper colour in liquid form. It has a light metallic smell. (Copper sulphate crystals resemble blue instant coffee!) Nitric acid is a clear, colourless liquid immediately distinguishable by its stinging, acrid vapour.

Ferric chloride reacts favourably, safely and benignly with copper. It is a favoured choice of many printmakers to use for making their intaglio images. We use nitric acid and ferric chloride because we feel they are the most practical and cost effective mordants available, and they work the best for the projects we undertake. Health and safety issues are part of most skilful crafts; care and common sense are crucial and should always be a part of what you are doing and how you use your tools and interact with your environment.

The mordants, resins, solvents, inks, grounds, printing presses etc. used in printmaking have changed little in their make up composition or application over many centuries. Most often, they still provide the most efficient way of making a technique work successfully. The roads of Babylon were paved with bitumen (really!) and we still use bitumen on our roads today. In powder form, it was used for aquatinting plates from 1730 onwards. We still use it for grounds (hard and soft), stop-out resists and in lithography (asphaltum).

Copper sulphate is used in all aspects of industry and everyday life. You dash through it at the swimming baths before you leap into the pool. It keeps your book bindings from rotting. It's what gives all the glassware in our homes pretty colours. It's the colour green in a firework. In printmaking, it is used to etch metal plates.

METALS AND MORDANTS

Aluminium

Aluminium is not a metal traditionally associated with etching. Its molecular structure is soft and cannot etch as fine as other metals can. Aluminium produces a rough bite that will suit certain artistic aims, however. It is inexpensive, too – approximately one fifth the cost of copper. Aluminium can be bitten using copper sulphate or ferric chloride.

Aluminium mordant recipe

100g copper sulphate
100g salt (sodium chloride)
1 litre water

Copper

Traditionally, copper is the favoured metal choice for etching. The texture of copper is fine and hard, meaning it bites very cleanly. It has the bonus of being able to be steel-faced which is always the best option if large editions (over 30 in number) are to be printed from the plate. The drawback with copper is the high purchase price. Copper is available polished but this adds even more to its cost.

Copper is usually bitten in ferric chloride. This has been tried and tested both commercially and by artists for decades.

When ferric comes in contact with copper, it creates a sediment which, during long biting times (30 minutes or more), may begin to block the lines created by the action of the acid. To address this, some artists bite plates upside-down, supported by Blu-Tack® stuck onto the plate corners to lift the plate from the bottom of the tray.

Other studios use vertical tanks so that the sediment drops out. However, they are difficult to use in a busy studio as it is impossible to see what is happening inside – not useful when several people need to use the tank at once. Clumsy studio users drop plates into the tank and they fall to the bottom of the tank, which means paddling about in the ferric unnecessarily. Or they forget about the plate entirely, creating an excess use of the ferric which entails cleaning the tanks when not absolutely necessary. The tanks are large, cumbersome and not space-efficient in a busy studio.

At Artichoke, we bite copper face-up in flat trays and have never found the sediment issue a problem as we inspect a plate's bite every 20 minutes and then rinse it with water. This avoids any problems entirely. Flat trays can be stored away after use and the acid can be bottled when not in use so that the water content does not evaporate. We find it a completely flexible system that caters for small and large plates as needs demand.

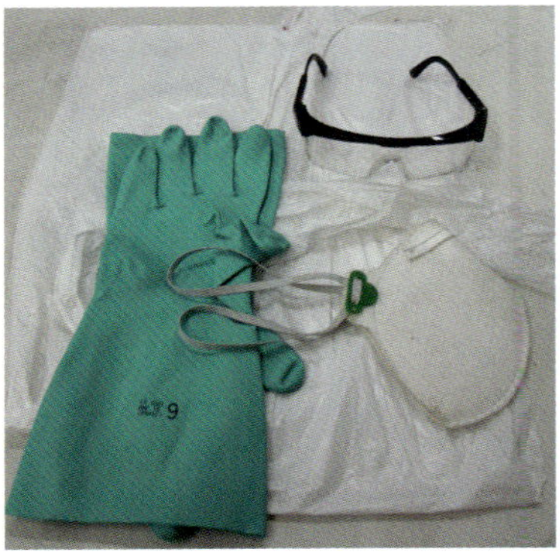

▲ **The appropriate safety attire must always be used and worn when handing any mordant. Safety equipment includes nitrile gloves (nitrile is resistant to both acids and solvents), eye protection, a paper face-mask for when handling powders and crystals, and a plastic apron.**

▶ **TOP: Margaret Sellars, *Untitled*, 2011. Etching on aluminium bitten in copper sulphate, 112 x 76 cm (44 x 33 in.).**

▶ **BOTTOM: Detail of the rough etch produced with the copper sulphate/salt mix.**

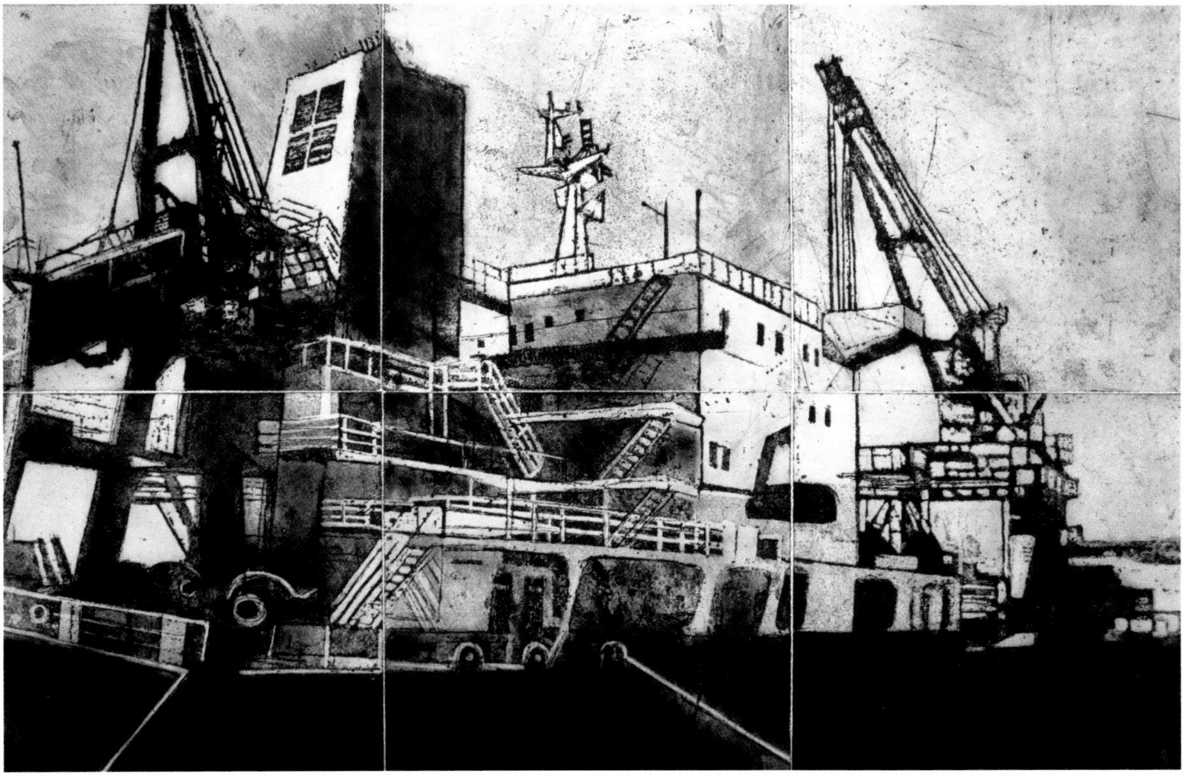

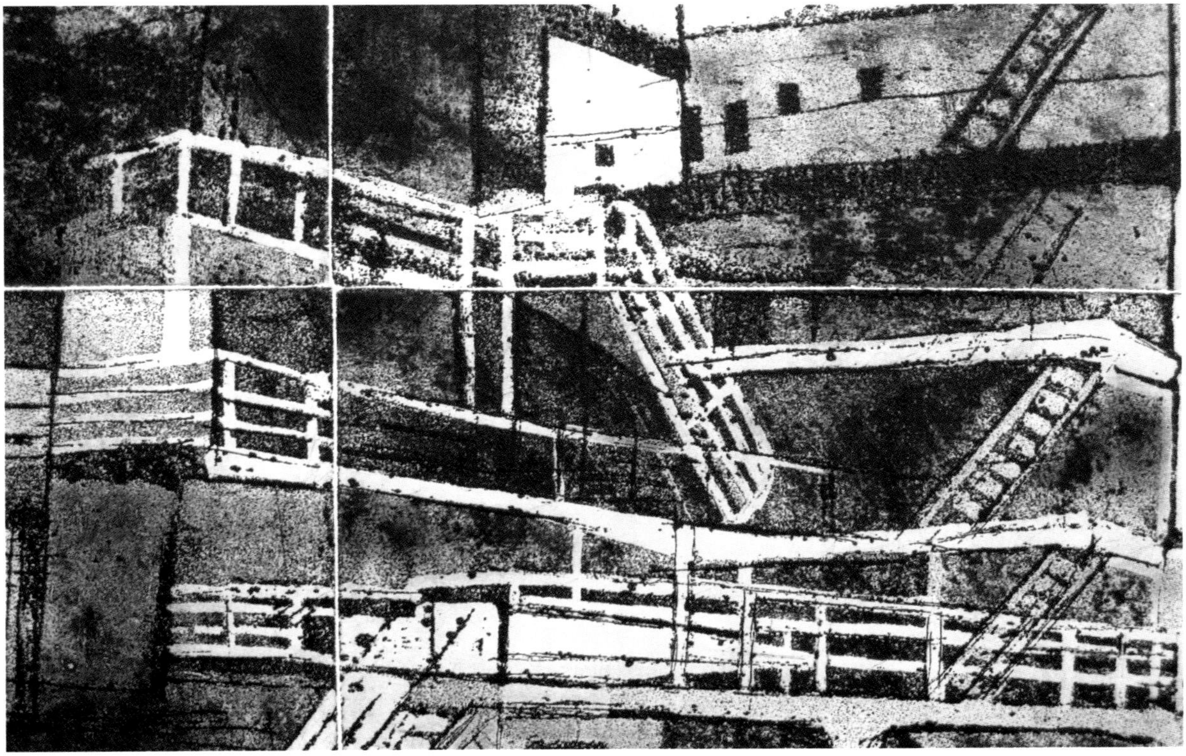

Nitric acid can be used on copper but the concentration (ratio) needs to be very strong: approximately one part acid to two parts water. This strength makes it an extremely hazardous mordant to use and for this reason, we would not recommend it.

Historically, an acid called Dutch Mordant was much used. (It is the mordant Rembrandt would have used, in fact.) Dutch Mordant bites extremely finely, with no widening of the lines. It has not been popular recently as the gas given off during mixing is extremely toxic, but we have included a recipe below as it is still a useful option for fine work. Hunter Penrose in London still supply Dutch Mordant ready-mixed in five-litre containers.

Ferric chloride for copper $FeCL_3$
2 parts water
1 part ferric
45 degree baume

This is suitable for both line and aquatint.

Ferric is best purchased as a liquid from chemical suppliers but it can also be purchased in crystal form. Mix 60g ferric crystals with 100ml water to give approximately 45 degree baume. Do this outside in open air as chlorine gas is given off when they are first mixed together. Wear safety clothing at all times.

Ferric can be measured using a baume hydrometer, which measures the specific gravity of liquid. The quickest mixture for copper is approximately 37 degree baume.

Dutch Mordant for copper
20 parts hydrochloric acid HCl
4 parts potassium chlorate $KClO_3$
80 parts water

John Buckland-Wright recommends the above recipe in his book, *Etching and Engraving* (London: Studio, 1953). Dutch Mordant is very rarely used nowadays, as it has been largely substituted by ferric chloride.

Zinc

Zinc is a popular choice for both beginners and experienced printmakers. It is not as expensive as copper and available in sheets that are polished and coated, giving a pristine surface to work on. Zinc is a relatively soft metal and it is fast-biting in mordants.

Zinc mordant recipes

Nitric acid
10 parts water
1 part nitric acid *or*
18 parts water
1 part nitric acid (to give a slow bath more controllable for aquatint)

When mixing acid always add the acid to the water. Fume extraction should be used when mixing nitric solutions.

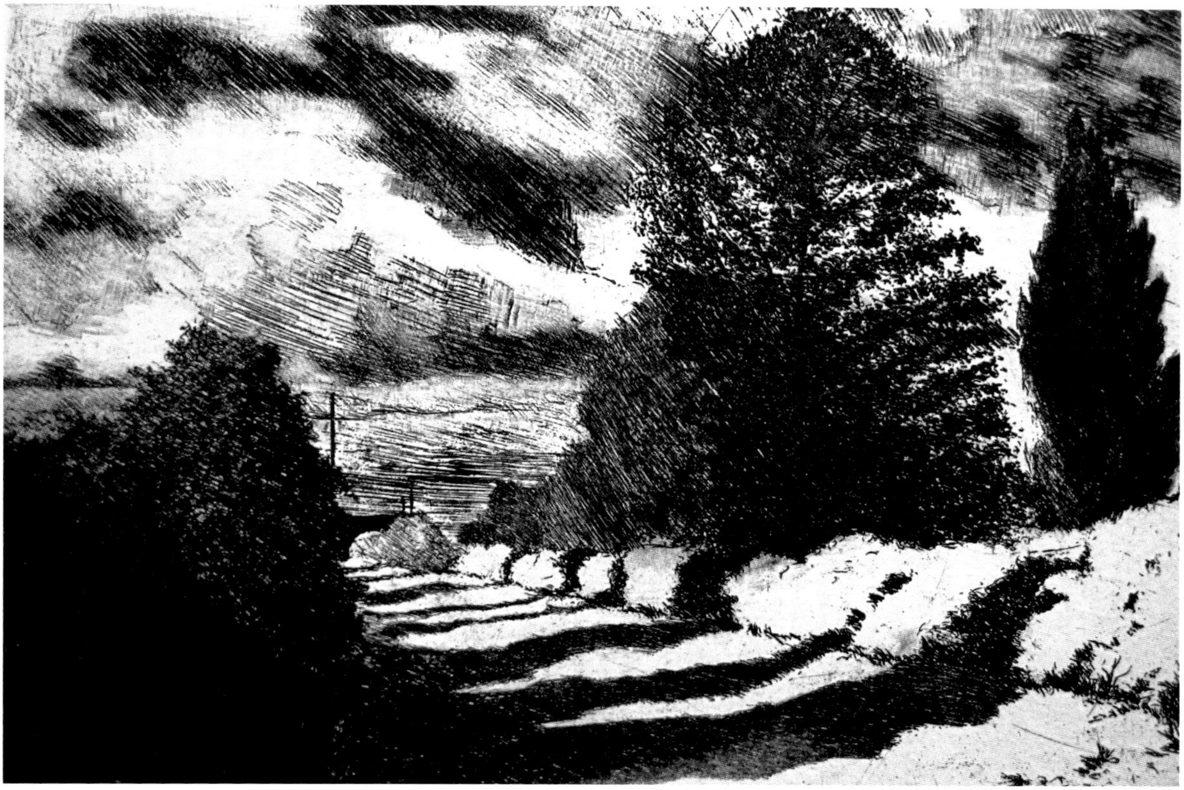

▲ Melvyn Petterson, *Sunburst*, 2006. Etching on zinc bitten in nitric acid, 20 x 15 cm.

Ferric chloride mordant recipes
'Edinburgh Etch' for zinc
1 litre ferric
7 litres water
400 gram citric acid
= approximately 20/30 degree baume

Use anhydrous (water-free) citric acid. Slowly dissolve the citric in water and make up to 7 litres. Add the ferric to the water.

Citric acid
Citric acid ($C_6H_8O_7$) is a clear, colourless, crystalline acid obtained mainly through the fermentation of carbohydrates or from the juices of lemons, limes and pineapples. It is used to prepare citrates (the salts used in beverages, flavourings in foods and in metal polishes). It speeds up the action of the etch and inhibits the forming of sediment.

Copper sulphate recipe for zinc
'Bordeaux Etch'
50–100g copper sulphate powder ($CuSO_2$) to one litre of water.

Steel

Nitric acid is the only reliable and quick way to bite mild steel. We have found that a mixture of eight parts water to one part nitric works well. The acid needs to be fresh and can become quickly exhausted if large areas of open plate are being bitten. As with aluminium, steel is inexpensive to purchase, making it an ideal choice for large works.

Due to the metal's innate structure, steel will open bite with natural pits that will hold ink. This is very useful for large plates that would not fit into an aquatint box. The disadvantage of using mild steel is that it does not have a polished surface, which means the highlight areas of image on the plate will always hold a tone and print grey.

To achieve white highlights on steel, it must be polished. To polish steel, use wet and dry sandpaper and rub by hand. Start with medium grade and finish with fine grade: it takes time but is worth it! Steel works very well with colour ink as it is so hard that light colours such as yellow do not become tainted while rubbing or wiping them into the plate textures, as colours such as these are prone to do with softer metals such as zinc.

Steel mordant recipe

8 parts water 1 part nitric acid

Add the acid to the water. Always use a fume extraction unit.

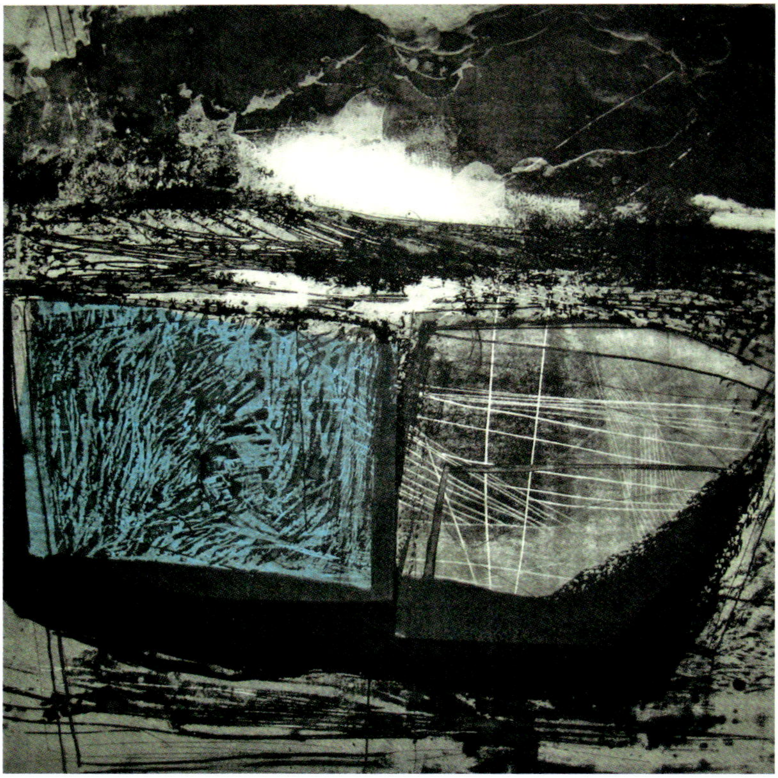

◀ **Morgan Doyle, *Untitled*, 2010. Etching on steel, 90 x 90 cm (35 x 35 in.).**

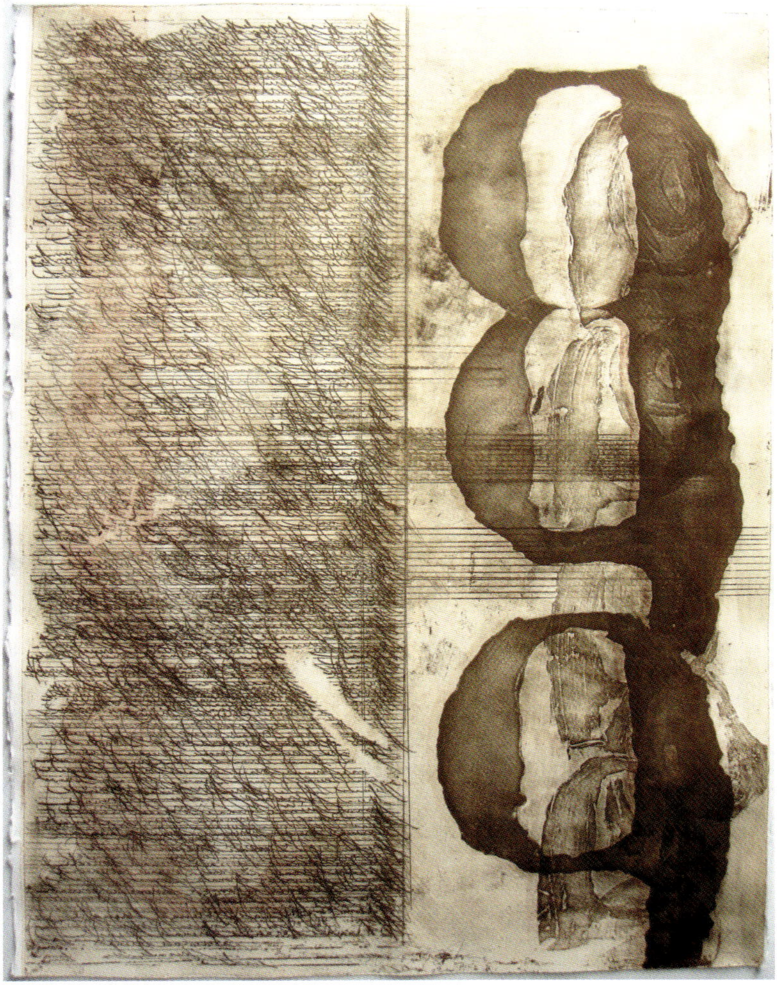

◀ Megan Fishpool, *Suite 49*, 2009. Etching on steel, 60 x 90 cm (23½ x 35 in.).

GALVANISED ('GALV') ETCH

Galvanised etch (or electro etch) is a surface finish which can be used on steel, copper or zinc. You need very expensive, special equipment for this process.

For steel plates that have been galv etched, you can use the Bordeaux etching mordant (see p.79).

The process involves attaching the metal plates to be etched to the terminals of batteries or a battery charger. The current flows from one plate to the other as they lie in a conducting fluid which facillitates the process. The positive and negative elements of the ions in the metal's make-up re-arrange themselves on the opposite surface of polarity. It is a reasonably complicated process and there are very few printmaking workshops with the equipment and ability to host it.

DISPOSAL OF ACIDS

Spent acids – in other words, those which no longer have any energy left to mark the plate surface – need to be disposed of safely.

Printmakers need to be practical and realistic about this. As individuals, we are all responsible for minimising our impact on the environment. Professionally, for many of us, printmaking is our livelihood. We do our best, then, to be responsible about the waste disposal methods we use and the products and materials we choose to use in our workshop environment.

Perspective is needed at all times. All of the printmaking activity in the UK combined would not have the same impact as a small factory. Individuals use detergents, bleaches, cleaners, fuel, paints and so on in the home every day on a much greater scale than they do in a printmaking workshop, and without the attendant hysteria. We all accept that a safe and healthy working environment is a priority. We hope that all printmaking workshops are maintained with reasonable diligence and safety awareness.

There are companies that deal with the removal of chemical waste and you can pay them to take away unrecyclable waste. (Companies will collect from a business but not from an individual.) After a company collects that waste, what happens to it?

We were told a story by a printmaking technician from one of the major London art schools. The school in question spent many years diligently saving and storing the ferric sludge they used at the college. It was then turned over to a chemical 'disposal' company.

A day later, the college's underground carpark flooded as all of the drains were blocked and backed up with dirty brown-yellow liquid: they'd tipped it down the drain. We are not for a moment suggesting that all disposal companies are negligent but suggest that we all have a different idea of what 'safe disposal' really means.

Ferric chloride is, in itself, not classified as a hazardous waste material. Once it is used to etch copper, however, it then contains dissolved copper and the classification changes.

In practice, most printmakers dispose of their acids by neutralising them into a benign substance. For nitric, use calcium carbonate (chalk) and water it down thoroughly before disposing of it down a designated processing sink. Copper sulphate is poured into a glass container and left until the sludge of copper and zinc hydroxide have settled to the bottom of the container. The liquid is then poured off and neutralised using sodium carbonate (washing crystals). The solid can be disposed of as solid waste.

As ever, common sense is the best way forward and we recommend that you talk to your local authority for guidelines on the safe disposal of spent acids and any hazardous waste material.

developing an image

An image created with any printmaking technique is in a constant state of flux. It is impossible to have a completely preconceived idea of exactly what the final image will look like. The artist cannot have complete control over the medium being used, but can only build on unexpected results or accept that alternative technical steps may have to be taken. Even the most innovative artist has to work within the technical and physical constraints of the chosen medium.

Typically a plate will be proofed, added to and re-worked over a period of time, with each resulting proof a defining 'state' of that image.

Marcelle Hanselaar, artist, painter and printmaker, says: '[I] start with a drawing/composition but have no idea how it is going to look at the end. I work from what I see on the proof. I add tone, more figures, redraw/scrape away etc. on each proof, until slowly, like in a painting, the image comes into its own.

'The medium does give me ideas on how to proceed, and that's why I use so many grounds and aquatints on each plate. So sometimes, like in *The Drowning Pool*, the image will change drastically over a few months.'

The following series of illustrations documents the development of two etchings made by Marcelle Hanselaar. They are an excellent example of how an image is built up from an initial line etching and given form through the various layers of aquatint that were placed on the plate.

The Drowning Pool

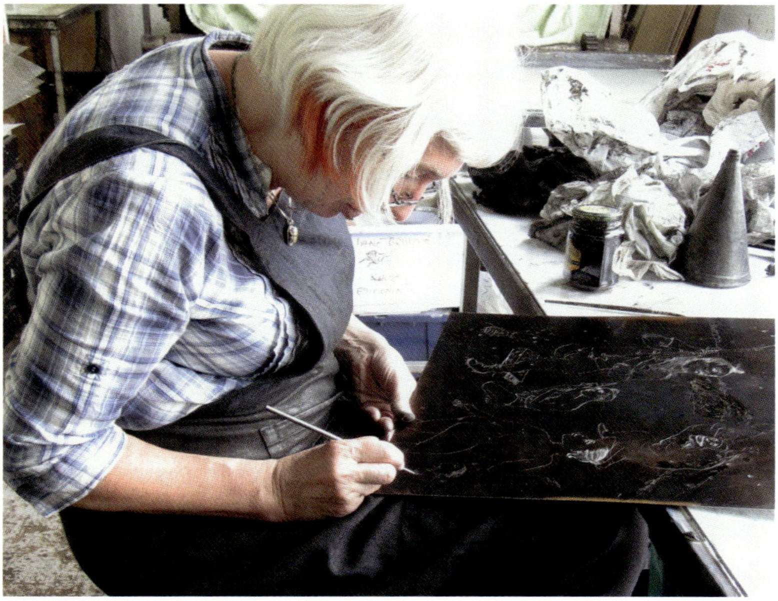

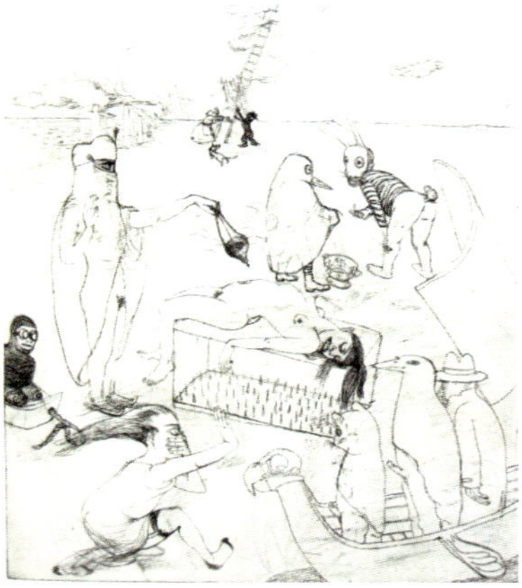

◀ The artist drawing through a hard ground.

▲ The first state: wax hard ground etching.

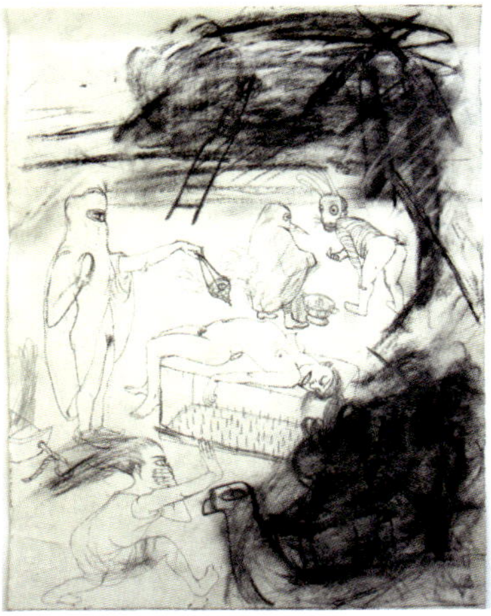

▲ The first state proof is drawn over with charcoal to realise new forms.

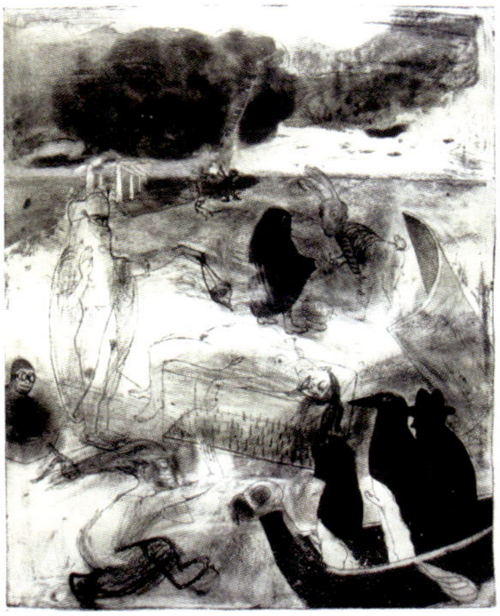

▲ More drawing, some roulette, aquatint and spit bite are added.

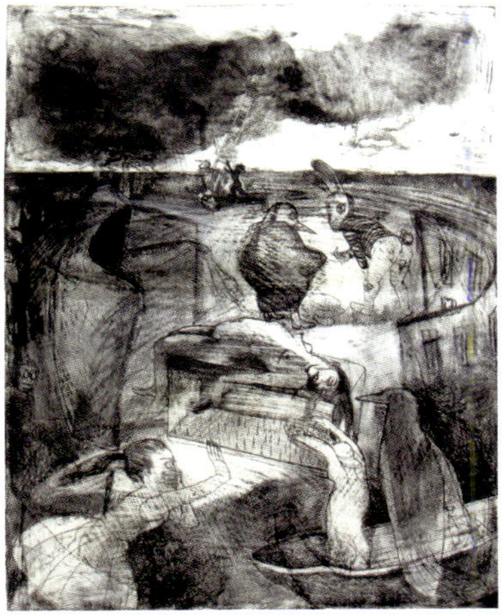

▲ Aquatint is added but then heavily scraped back. The left-hand figure is almost obliterated and transformed into a ghostly apparition.

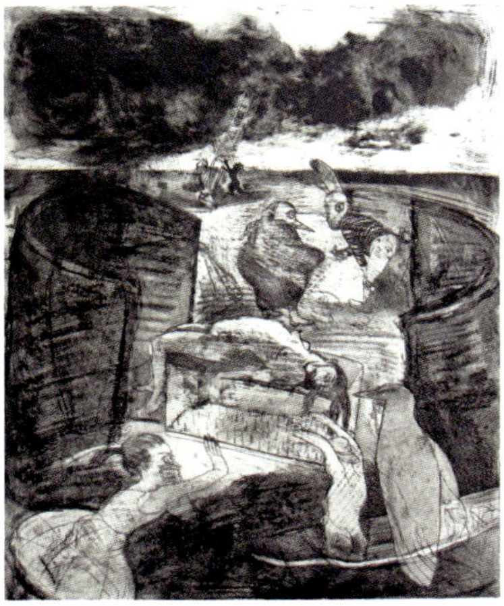

▲ The semi-circular 'screen' takes shape.

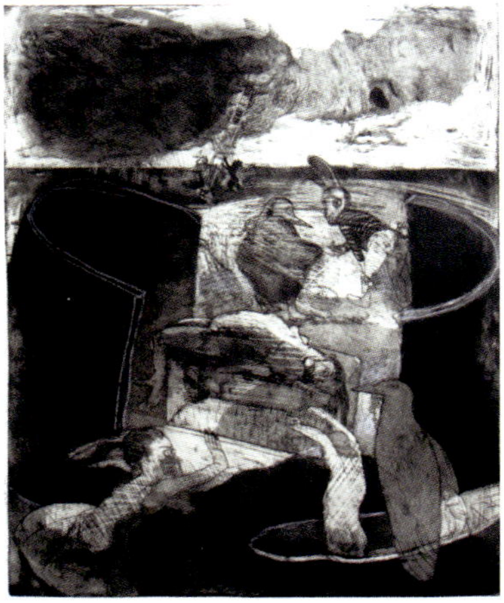

▲ Dark aquatints simplify the composition. White chalk is used to indicate where scraping is needed.

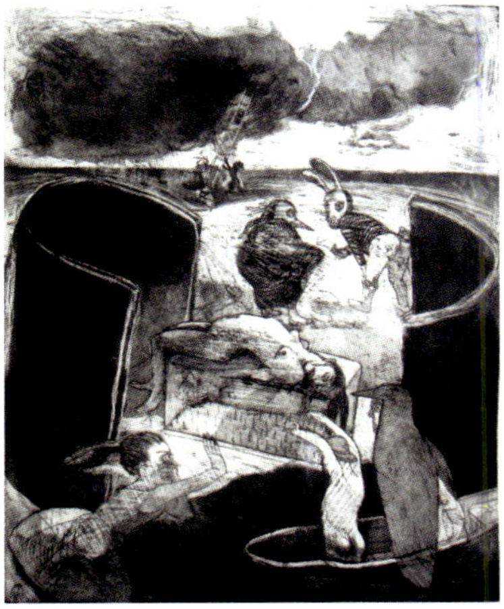

▲ The final proof with minor white chalk additions.

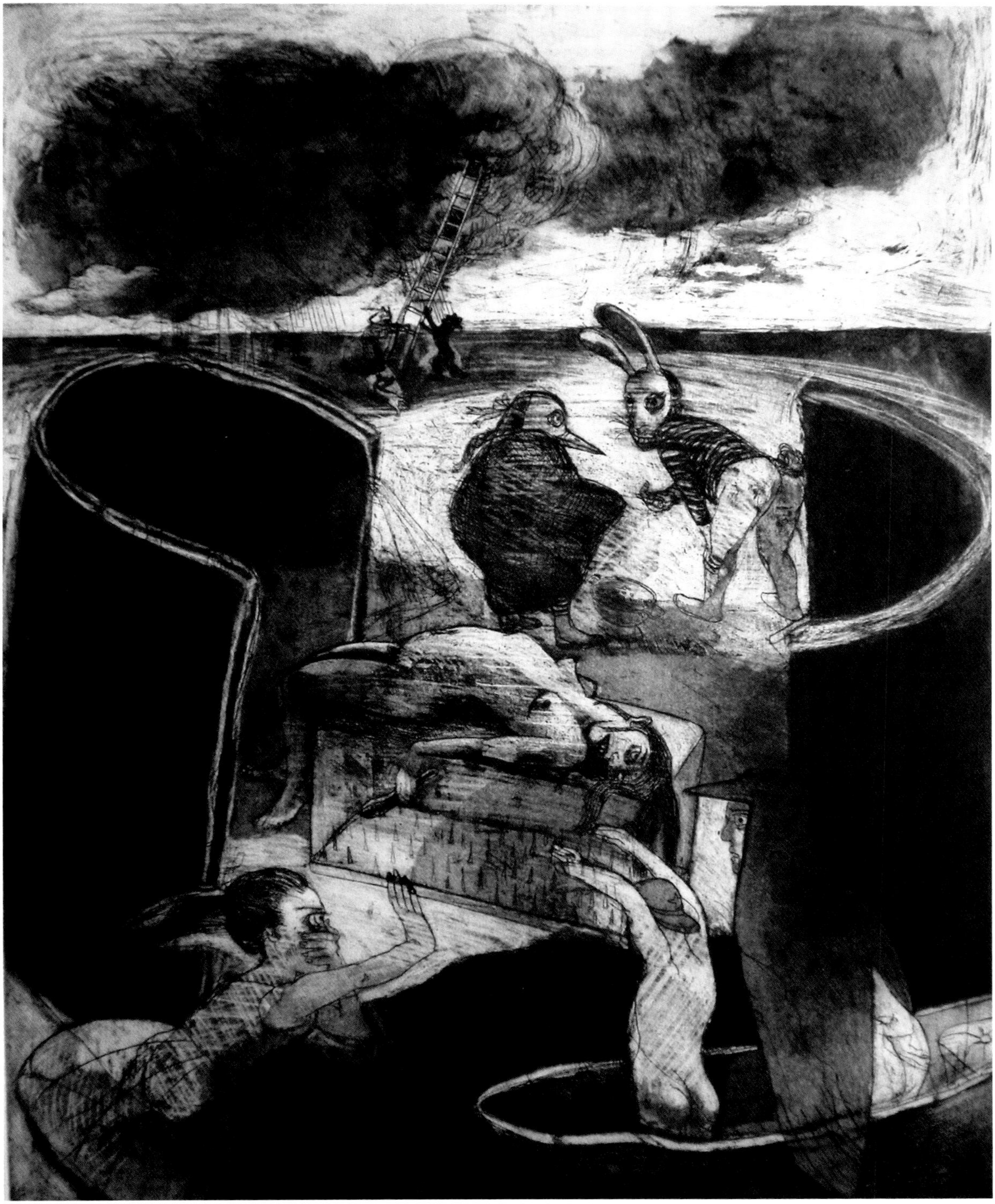

▲ Marcelle Hanselaar, *The Drowning Pool*, 2011. Etching/aquatint on zinc, 50 x 40 cm (19½ x 15¾ in.).

Loss of Innocence 4 by Marcelle Hanselaar

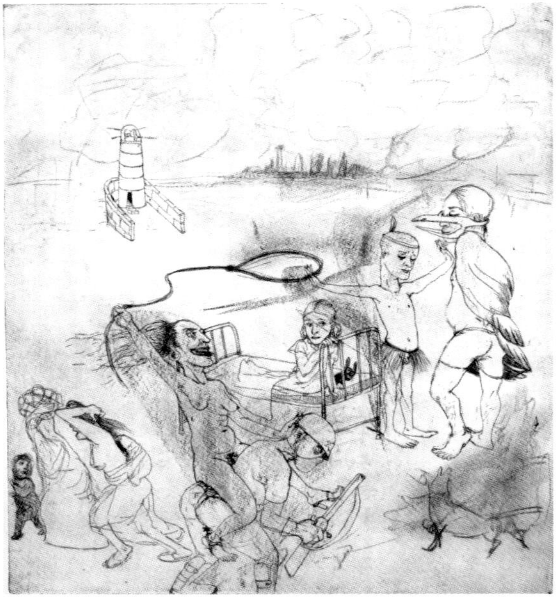

▲ The first state with charcoal additions.

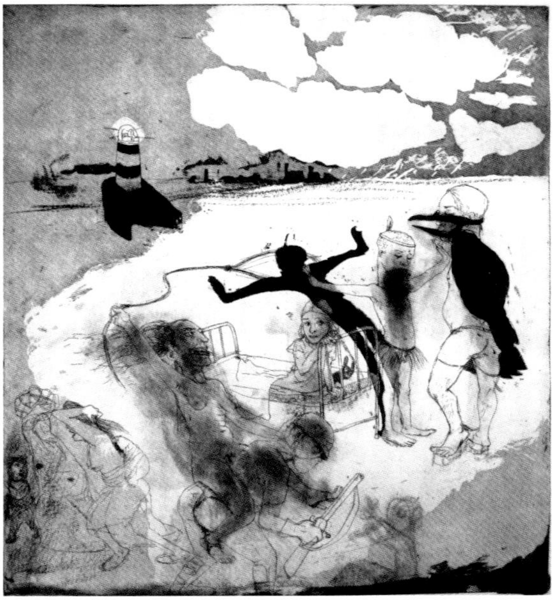

▲ Second state. Aquatint and spit bite have been added. Again, the proof is worked with charcoal.

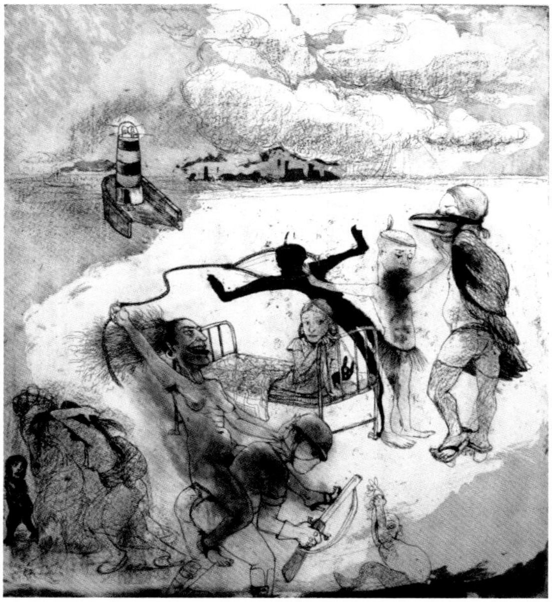

▲ Third state. The plate has been reworked with hard ground and more figures added.
There has been a second application of spit bite and the aquatint has been lightened by scraping. Charcoal is used on the proof to work out where to add and darken tones.

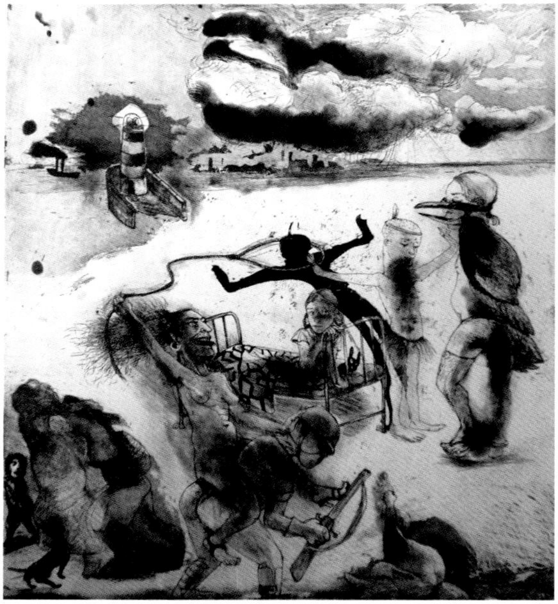

▲ The final state. Aquatint and spit bite with scraping are used to resolve the image, and a roulette used for tonal gradations. (Also see p.62.)

intaglio printing

In intaglio printing, the image is made by wiping ink into the grooves on the plate, and then forcing the ink from the plate onto dampened paper with use of a printing press.

TAKING THE FIRST PROOF

The moment the print is pulled from the plate, many thoughts race through your head. It can be a moment of exhilaration or exasperation, but usually the emotion is somewhere between these two. Remember it is *extremely* rare for an image to be considered completed the very first time it is pulled from the plate. Most plates made with any printmaking technique will go through many re-workings, either by adding lines or new tones, or by removing areas deemed unsatisfactory. These progressive stages are referred to as 'states' and many never see the light of day, as they are thrown away or kept for the artist's personal archive.

State proofs are a valuable insight into an artist's thinking as well as a fascinating record of the 'technical battle' between a medium and an artist's intention as the medium is pushed to the artist's intention. Rembrandt, for example, left a remarkable collection of drypoints which record changes in a single image each time he took a print from the plate.

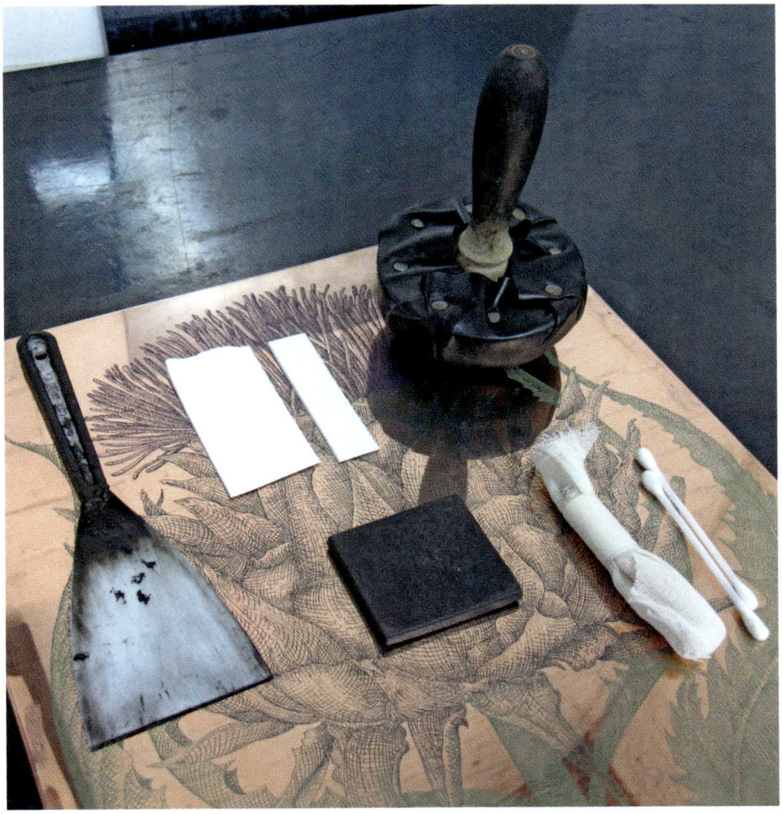

◀ An array of inking implements, including plastic scraper, card strips, rubber squeegee blade, leather dabber, scrim 'dolly' and cotton buds.

Printmaking is always a balance between artistic intention and the technical constraints within a particular medium. However, creating and solving this balance can lead the artist down new avenues where prints become hybrid as they move across different mediums.

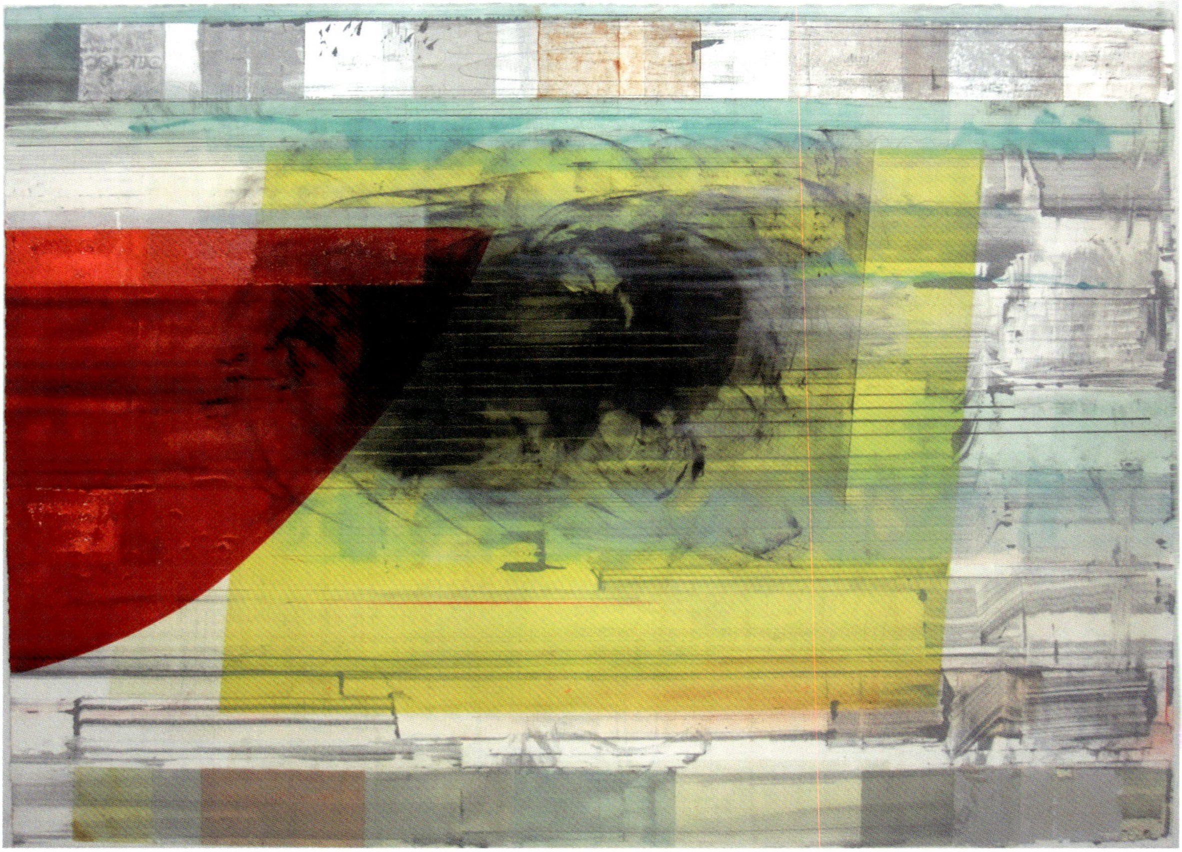

▲ **Colin Gale, *Untitled hybrid print*, 2011. Drypoint, monoprint, Chine-collé and pencil, 76 x 56 cm (30 x 22 in.).**

INKING A PLATE

Once a plate is removed from the mordant, it is rinsed with water to remove all traces of the mordant. All grounds and varnishes on the front and back of the plate (including any plastic backing tape on the back) must be removed.

The mordant will invariably have attacked the edges of the plate, making them rough and pitted (no matter how well you think you have stopped out the plate!). At this stage, the edges are still filed as proofs will be printed to confirm the various stages as the image progresses. The plate will be re-worked and re-bitten so it is not necessary to have perfect edges at this stage.

What tool you use to ink a plate is a matter of personal preference. Many different tools and implements can be used to push ink into the bitten areas, but remember that they must be semi-pliable so that they do not scratch the plate surface.

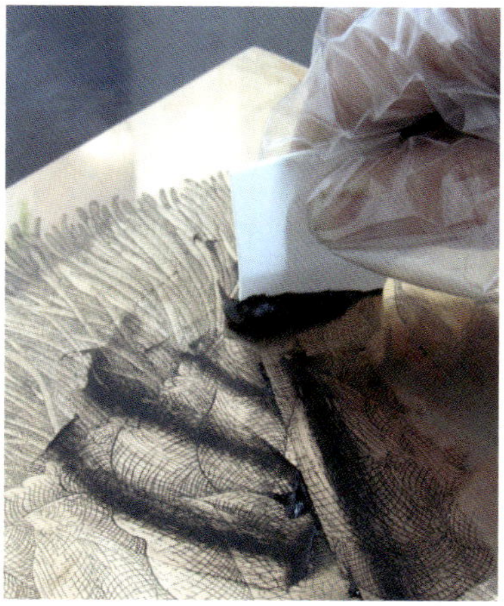

◀ Inking a copper plate with card off-cut.

▶ Taking a pad of scrim (tarlatan), the ink is rubbed onto the plate in a circular motion. This action simultaneously pushes ink into the lines and removes excess ink from the non-image areas of the plate surface. The scrim is a semi-starched cotton material with an open weave and is designed to catch or hold excess ink during wiping.

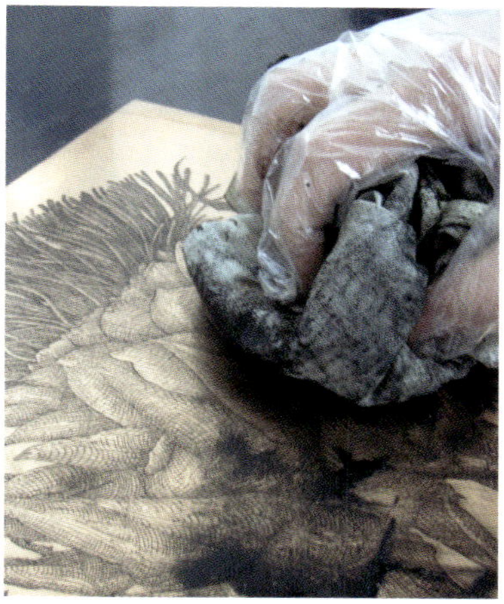

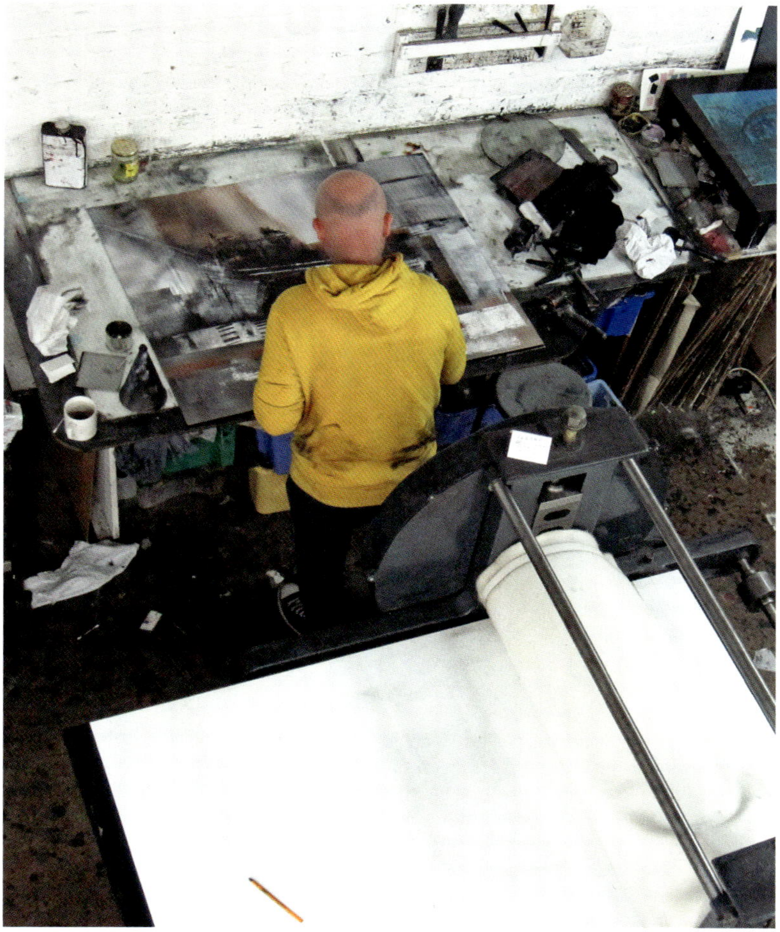

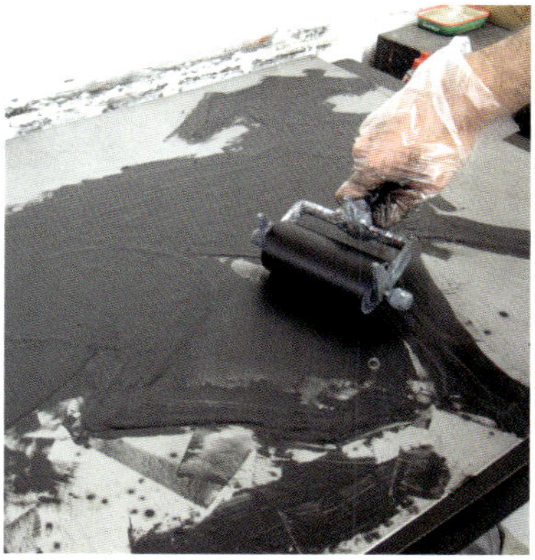

▲ For very large plates, it is quicker to ink the plate using a roller.

◀ Morgan Doyle working on a large steel plate at Artichoke.

As we work in a communal studio, we find that offcuts of mount or matt card are entirely suitable for inking a plate. They are plentiful, quick and easy to cut and can simply be thrown away after use.

PLATE TONE

How a plate is wiped is down to personal choice in the main, but can also be dictated by the type of image produced and how the finished result is intended to look. A plate may be wiped leaving a thin film of ink (known as 'plate tone') over the entire surface to give more 'atmosphere' to the image by softening the contrast between ink and paper. This is achieved by wiping with scrim only. The amount of ink left on the plate surface is judged visually before it is printed.

To achieve the desired plate tone often takes several printed proofs and experimentation with varying amounts of ink. To increase plate tone, adding a little medium copperplate oil may be beneficial, as it will help to hold a thin film of ink over the plate surface. Also consider using a highly pigmented ink (such as Charbonnel® Black 55985) to increase intensity of plate tone.

Images that require a very graphic 'clean' look usually benefit from tissue wiping and hand wiping. A plate's non-image areas need to be free of any traces of ink film if the print is to be clean and show only the paper tone in contrast to the printed bitten lines and tones. We find that using a sequence of scrim wiping, followed by tissue wiping and then finishing with hand wiping works well. These latter two techniques remove all traces of ink film from the plate surface.

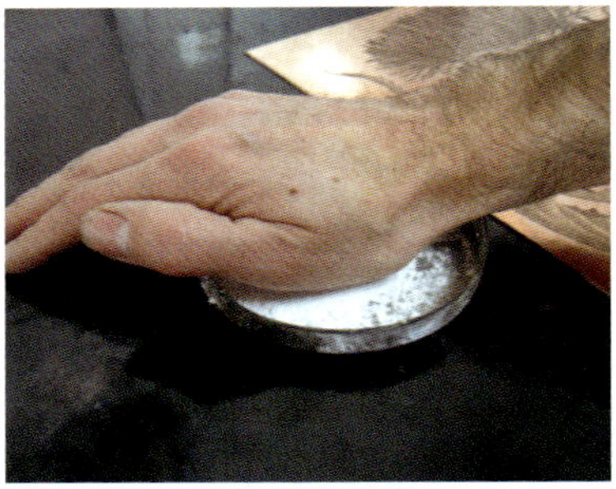

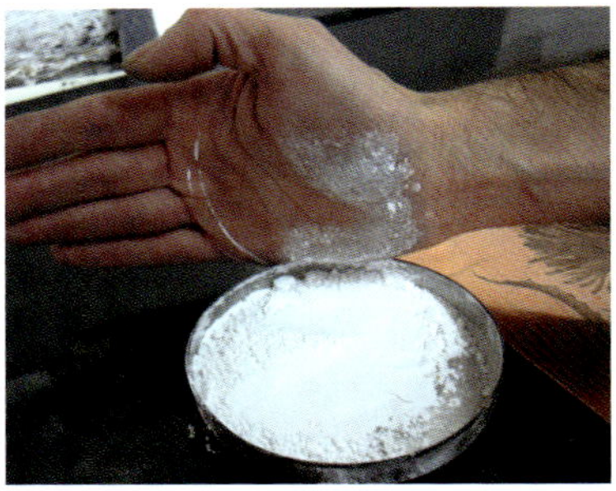

▲ Hand wiping. Use a container such as a metal ink-tin lid or a ceramic saucer to hold whiting chalk. Dab the palm of your hand into the whiting, then dust off the excess chalk with a clean rag. (The aim is just to have a very fine dusting of chalk on your palm.)

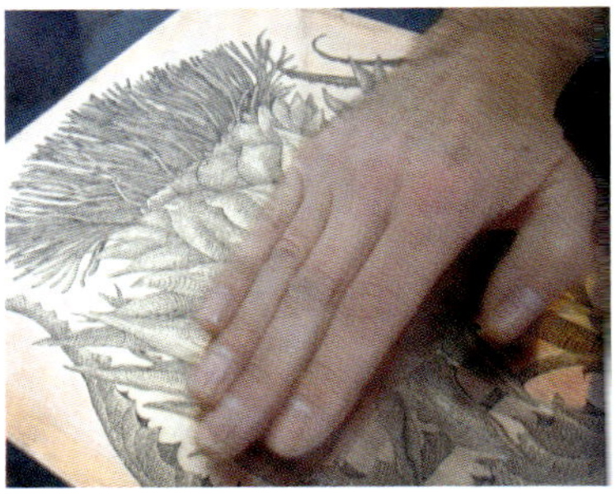

▲ Using fast and light strokes, drag your palm over the plate surface. This action will lift any remaining ink film from the plate. The plate in this illustration is *Cardoon*, by Bryan Poole.

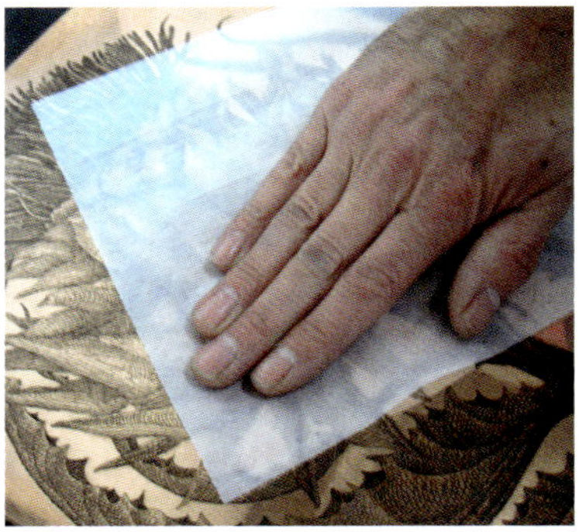

◀ Wiping the plate using tissue. Use a clean square of tissue and keep the hand flat. When editioning a plate, prepare a stack of tissue by tearing down several tissue sheets with a metal straightedge.

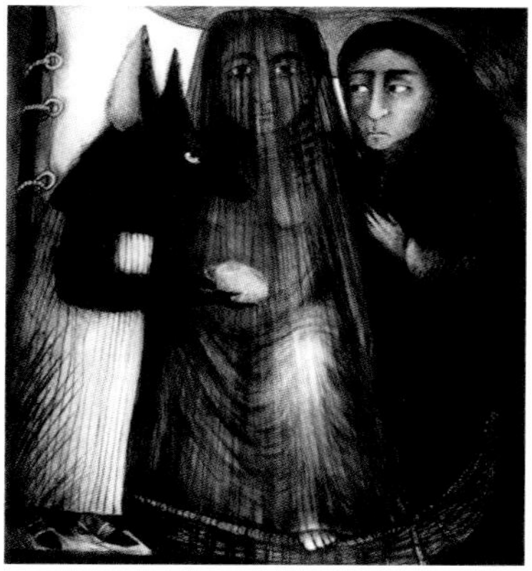

◀ Ana Maria Pacheco, *Dark Event VII*, 2007. Drypoint, 68 x 60.7 cm (26¾ x 24 in.). Courtesy of Pratt Contemporary Art Limited.
Plate tone on drypoint plates is particularly desirable. It takes a good eye to read the surface of a plate and decide how the light and dark tones will look and when to stop wiping ink from the surface. The artist Ana Maria Pacheco is a skilled printmaker and her dark, brooding drypoints take full advantage of plate tone.

▼ Stuart Pearson-Wright, *Domestic Scene*, 2006. Detail, drypoint on copper, 58 x 100 cm (22¾ x 39½ in.).
This plate was inked using Charbonnel® Black 55985 and then scrim-wiped only to leave plate tone. Note the contrast with the paper tone on the left. The highlights on the bath rim are wiped out using a cotton bud so that they show the paper tone when printed.

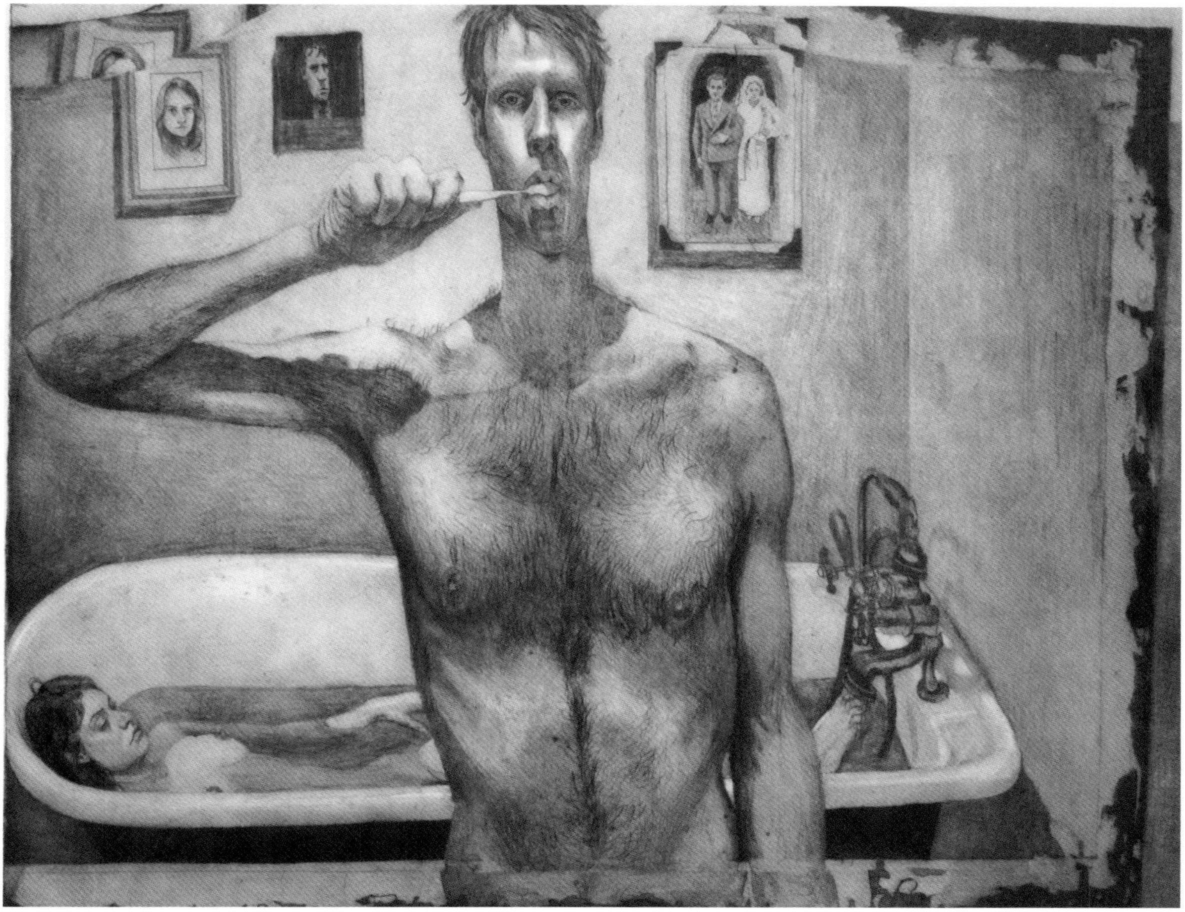

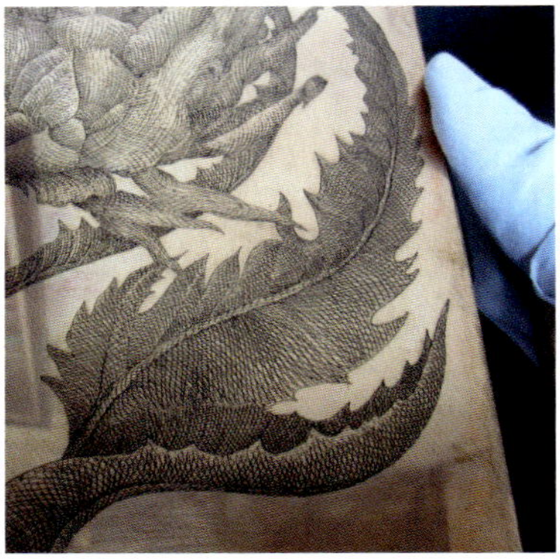

▲ **Before printing, wipe the edges of the plate using a cotton rag. Poke a finger into a clean piece of rag and wipe each edge until no ink is transferred to the cotton rag.**

PLATE REGISTRATION

To register a plate so that it prints onto a sheet of paper squarely, it is necessary to mark out the bed of the press or to prepare a registration acetate. A black permanent marker is used to mark the corners and sides of the printing sheet. The plate is then placed squarely between these marks. Draw round the corners of the plate with the permanent marker. The bed or acetate now shows where to lay the inked plate and where the paper should be placed ready for printing.

Note that the permanent marker must be dry *before* the print is taken or the marks may transfer to the paper during printing. If this becomes a problem, dust the lines with whiting or French chalk.

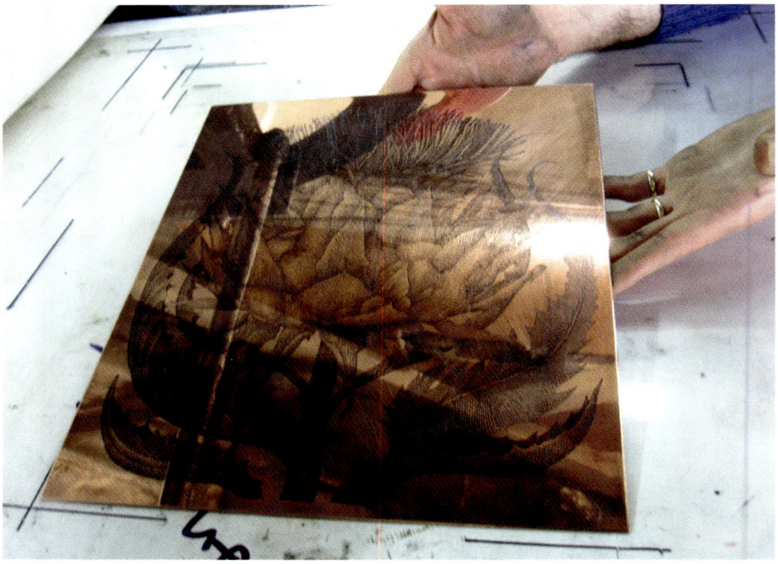

▶ **The inked plate by Bryan Poole being positioned on the registration acetate on the press bed.**

PAPER

Mould-made paper is the most useful paper to employ for etching. It is made from cotton fibre rather than wood pulp, and this is important: cotton fibres are able to stretch under great pressure, but wood pulp paper compresses. Paper is available in many shades from bright white to black. Popular paper brands for etching include Somerset, BFK Rives, Hahnemühle and Zerkall.

Printmakers have their favourites and tend to stick with them. At Artichoke, we use a lot of Somerset 300gsm for etching. We like the choice of shades and surfaces if offers us: it has a particularly soft, white, texture. Also, soaking time is not crucial: whether it is in the water for a few minutes or a few hours, it still performs consistently. Finally, the paper is tough: it cleans up easily (ink scuffs, handling marks etc.) with a sponge when wet, and with an eraser when dry. This fact alone cuts down on wastage both in paper and labour time.

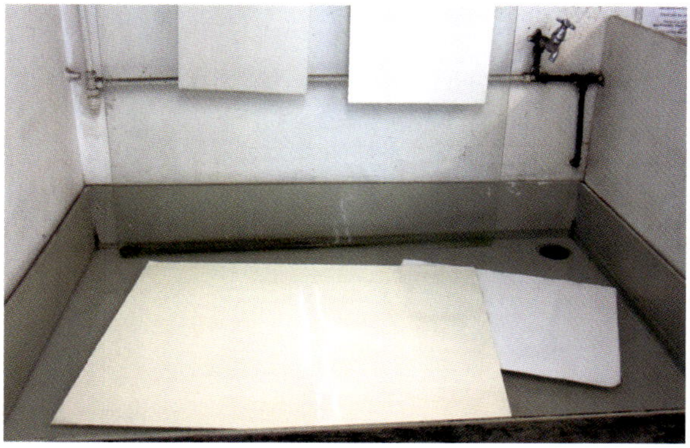

▲ Any paper used for etching needs to be soaked in clean water in a tray or sink used only for this express purpose. Paper soaking time varies with each brand depending on the amount of size a paper contains, but around ten minutes would be a good average soaking time for most papers. Size is a type of glue applied to the surface of the paper or internally to give it strength. Soaking the paper fluffs up the fibres so that they are able to press down into the etched lines and pick up the inked information.

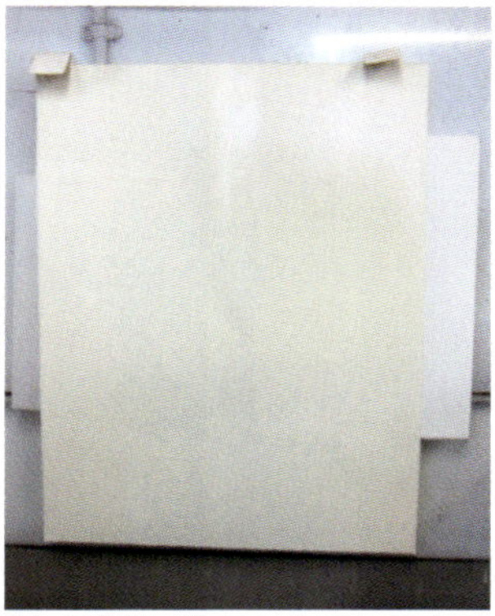

▶ After soaking, the paper is drained on a sheet of thick acetate such as Perspex.

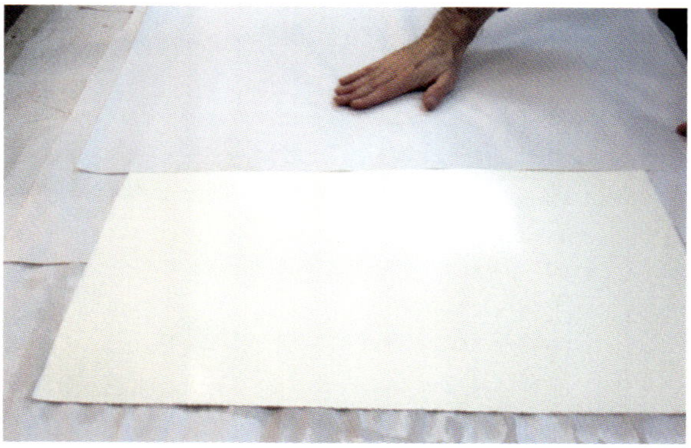

▲ The excess water is now blotted from the paper's surface. Excess water could repel the ink, resulting in a poor impression. Traditionally, cotton blotting paper has been used. Today, blotting paper is made from wood pulp and in our opinion does not perform as well as the old cotton type (it has a great tendency to crease). A more cost-effective blotting option for a busy studio is newsprint. It is very absorbent, dries quickly and is inexpensive – which means it is not a disaster when it gets dirty and has to be thrown away.

PRINTING

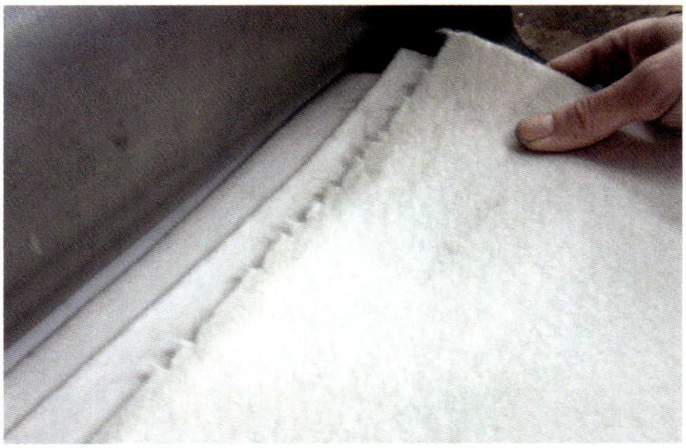

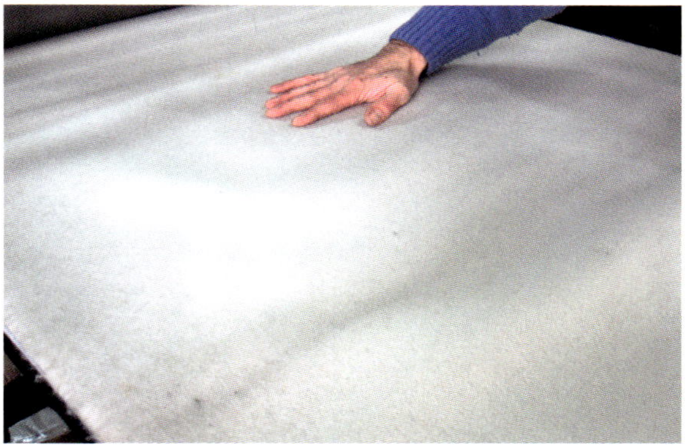

▲ Make sure the blankets are positioned squarely on the press. If the press pressure is uneven, the blankets will creep to the tighter side causing blankets to become bunched up between the press frame and roller. For a heavy roller press, step the blankets before winding them through. Ensure the blankets are lying flat on the bed.

▶ The damp paper is lowered into position as marked by the registration sheet. It is easiest to handle and place the paper correctly by holding it at two diagonal corners. The use of paper grips (torn down from paper offcuts) keeps the paper free of fingermarks.

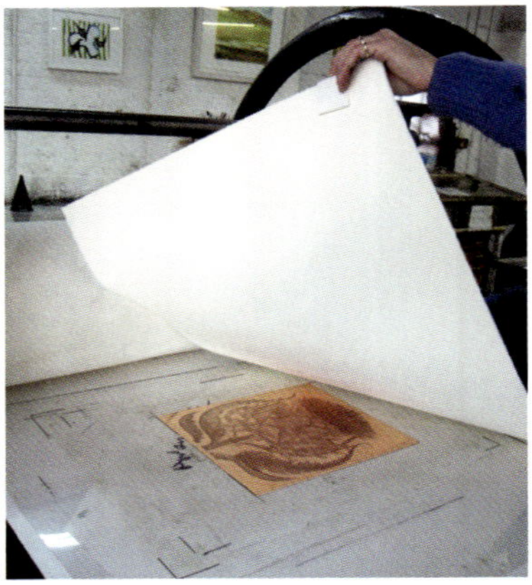

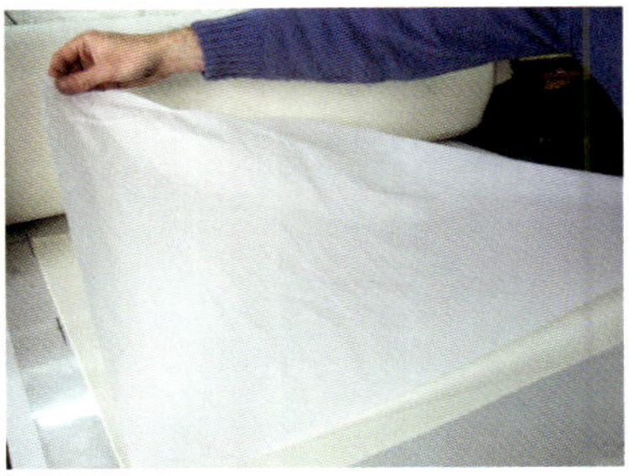

▲ Place a clean sheet of tissue paper over the printing paper to keep it clean.

▶ Stand square on to the press and grip the handle with both hands. Push the handle forward using your hands and arms, not your wrist! Step forward as you do this and step back as you pull the wheel towards you. Moving in this way means that the lower back, shoulders and wrists are not put under excess strain.

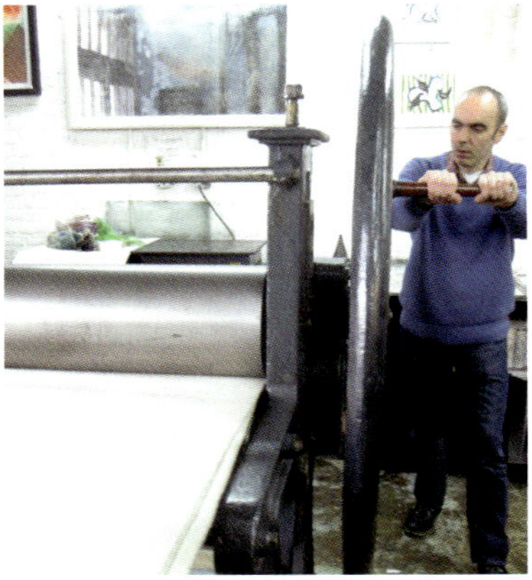

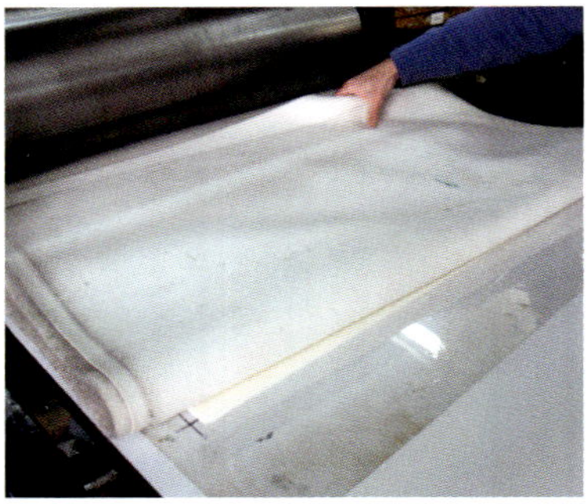

▲ Fold the blankets back and place them over the roller.

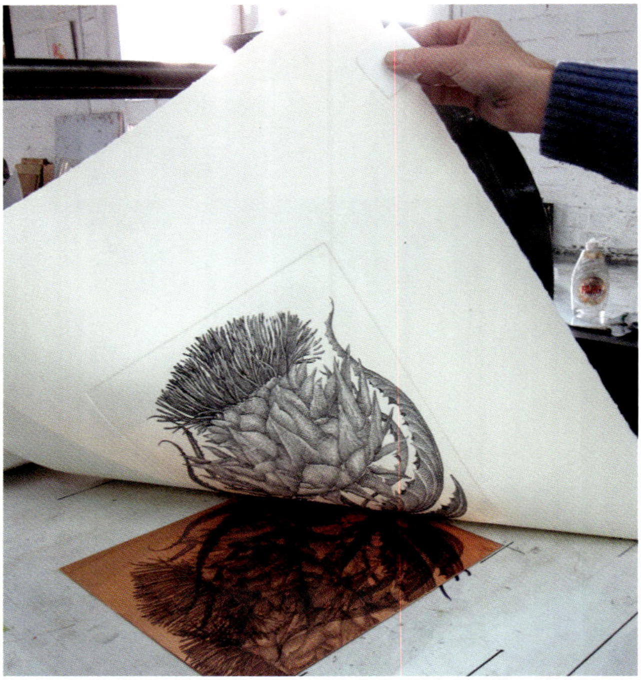

▶ The paper is lifted from one corner.

DRYING PRINTS

Prints must be placed between boards and under weight so that they dry flat. Cotton blotting paper has been used traditionally on either side of a print. If the blotting paper has creases in it, your prints will too. An alternative to blotting paper is archival mill board that is 4–5 mm thick.

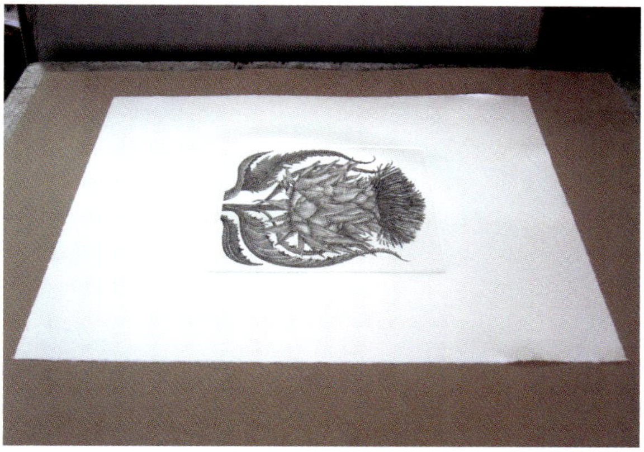

▲ The freshly pulled print is placed on archival mill board.

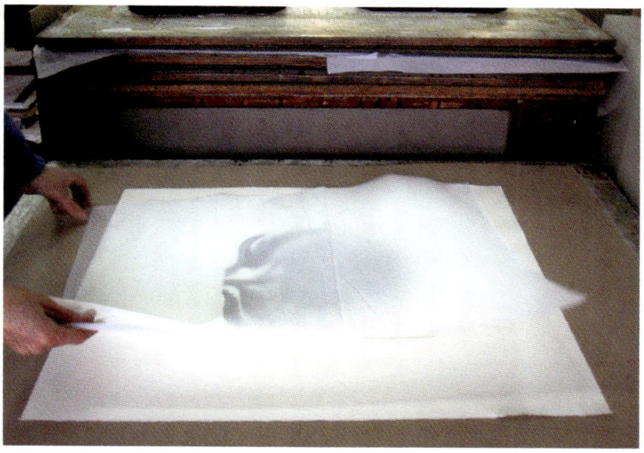

▲ Place a clean sheet of tissue over the print to prevent the wet ink offsetting onto the top board.

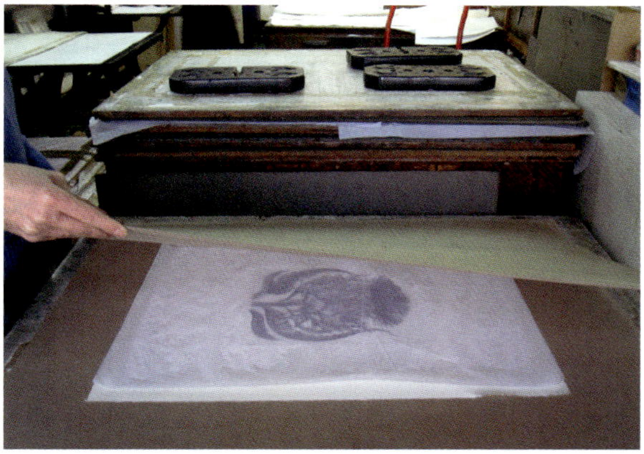

▲ Place a sheet of mill board over the print.

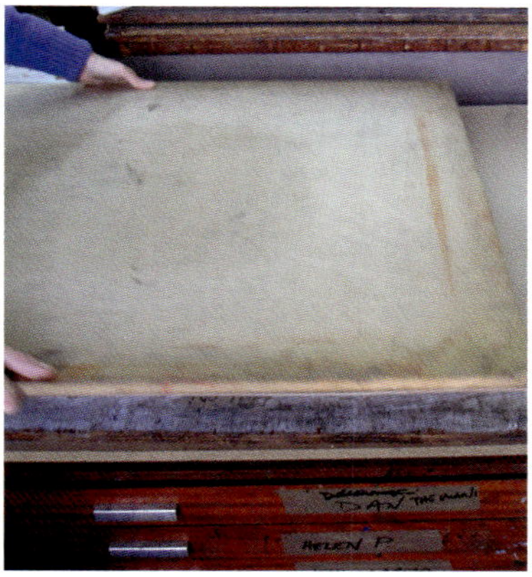

▶ A heavy board of MDF. is placed on top.

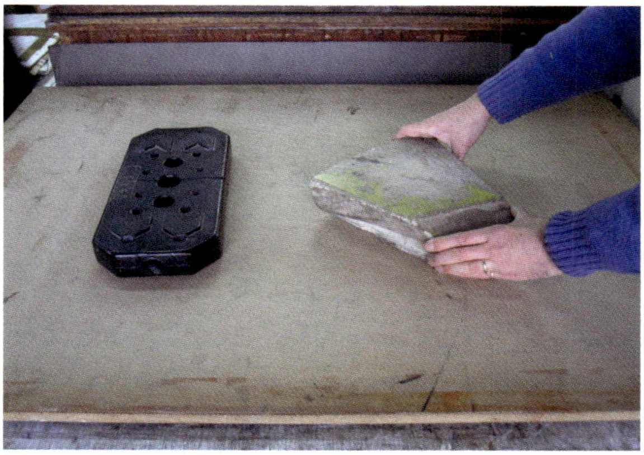

▶ Weights are placed on top to keep the stack flat. Prints need between three and seven days to dry well, depending on atmospheric conditions in the room or studio and the number of prints in the stack. The more prints in the stack, the longer the prints will take to dry.

printing in colour from one plate

The technique for printing many colours from one plate is called à la poupée. Small inking tools called 'dollies' are used to apply many individual colours to a single plate surface, hence the name of the technique (which means 'with a doll' in the original French). There are historical examples of Victorian intaglio prints that have 54 colours on one plate!

The image in this sequence (by the artist Bryan Poole) charts some of the many stages in making *Wisteria* (2011), a nine-colour etching and aquatint from one copper plate.

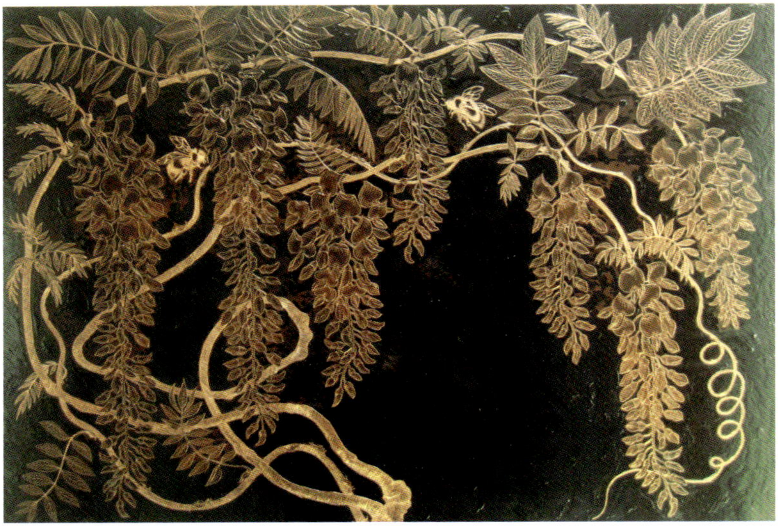

◀ The completed line drawing through wax ground on copper. The non-image area has been meticulously painted over with stop-out varnish to prevent any risk of foul biting. This is a necessary and wise precaution for this type of image, as it is important to have a clean, crisp image in the final print. Although time-consuming (it took two whole days to stop out the plate!), it is still quicker than having to make repairs with a scraper burnisher tool.

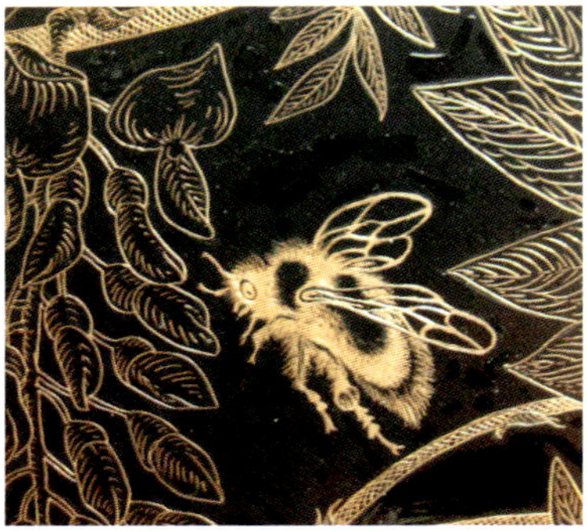

▲ A close-up of the bee prior to etching in ferric chloride.

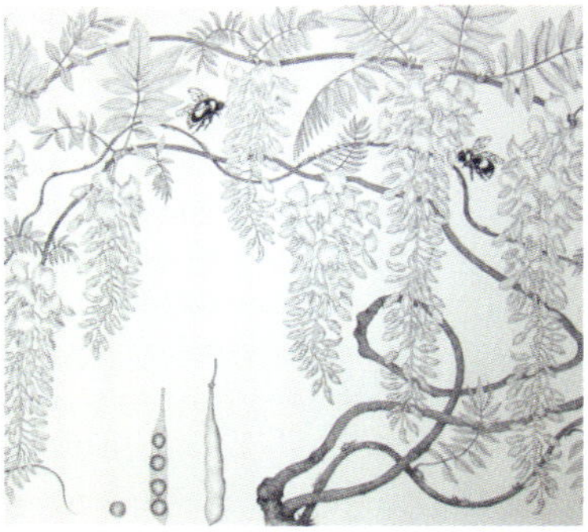

▲ The first state: line work.

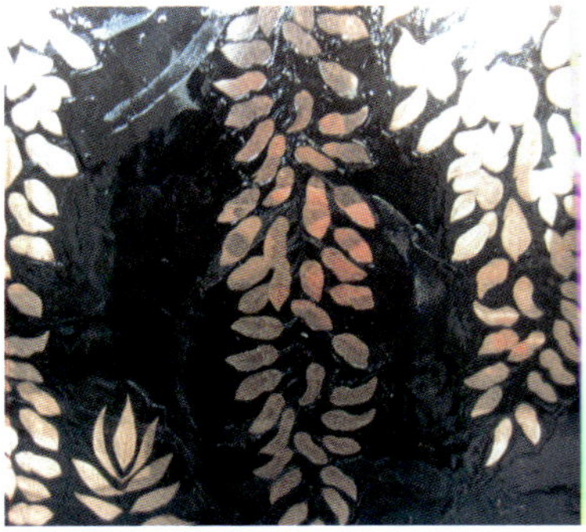

▲ The plate is now stopped out so that tone can be added to the flowers and leaves using aquatint.

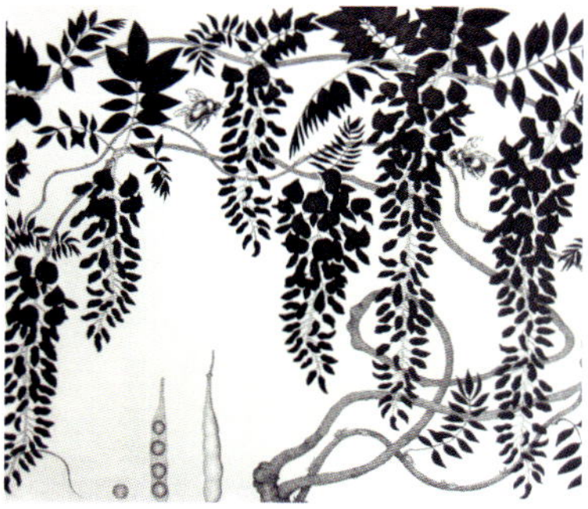

▲ The second state: a strong black bite was aimed for. Highlights are now burnished into the aquatint to provide the modelling on the leaves and flower petals. The finished plate is steel-faced to ensure an edition of 100 can be consistently pulled.

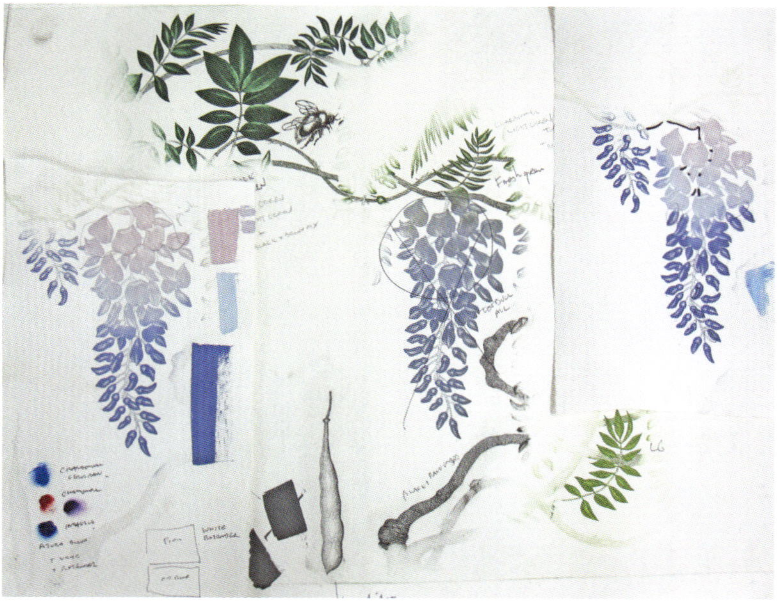

▲ Colour notes are prepared by taking several proofs from the plate. Three colours are used for the flowers, a pink and two blues. Both transparent white and opaque white ink is used to gain the subtlety needed. It took one day to proof the colours.
The leaves are inked using three different greens. A dark grey and brown are used for the seed details and branches, and black for the two bees.

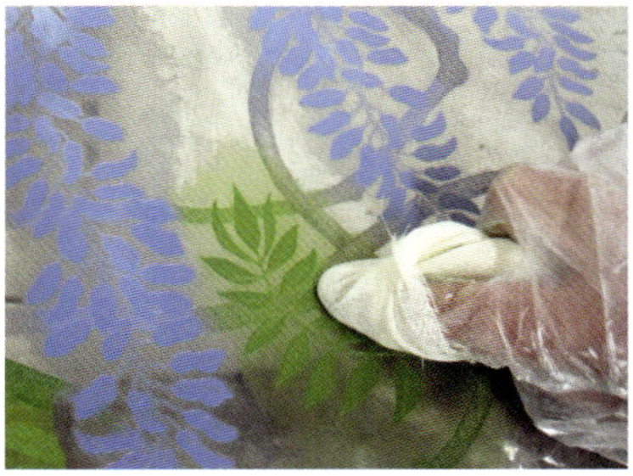

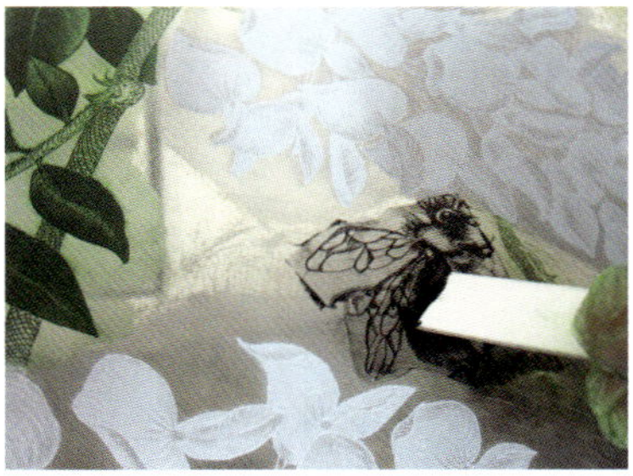

▲ Small pieces of scrim and card are used to ink the plate. Great care is needed to keep each specific colour area clean.

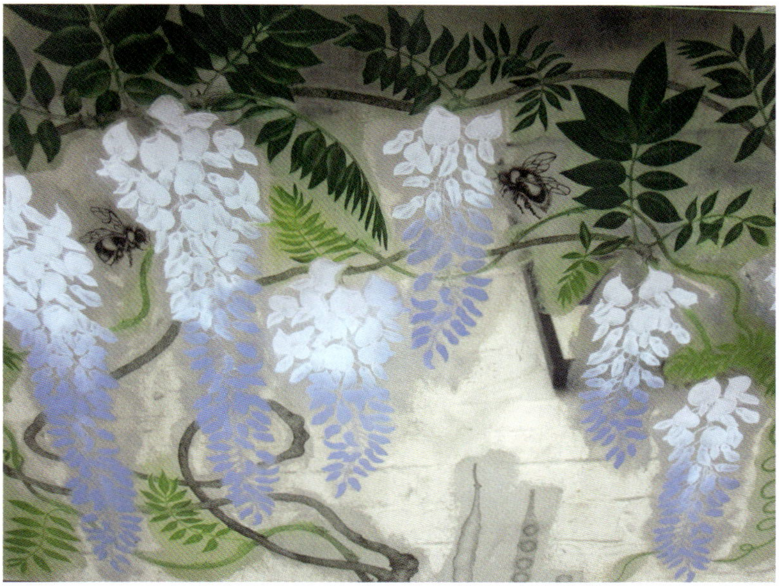

▲ The inked plate is ready for hand-wiping.

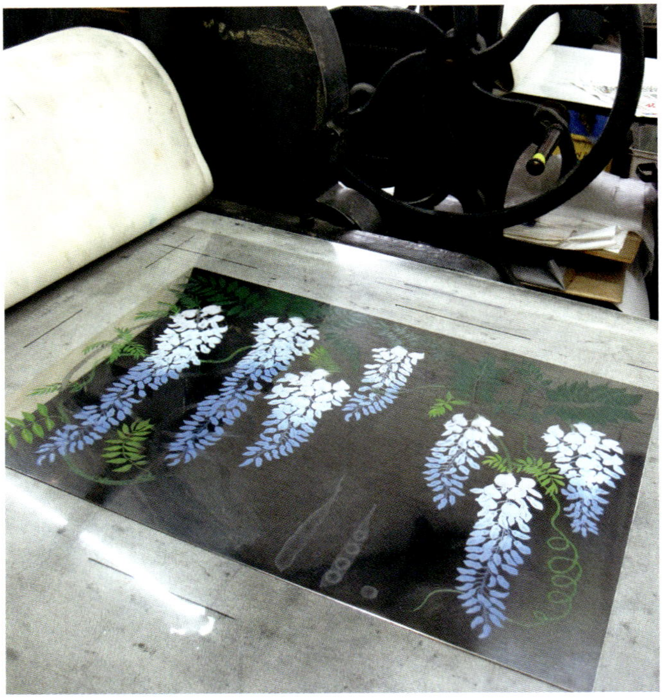

◀ The inked plate on the press bed ready for printing. Each impression taken from the plate takes an hour and a half to complete. This is the total combined inking time and printing time.

▼ Bryan Poole, *Wisteria*, 2011. Etching and aquatint, 56 x 76 cm (22 x 30 in.).
The finished print prior to hand touching with watercolour by the artist. Proofed and printed by Colin Gale at Artichoke.

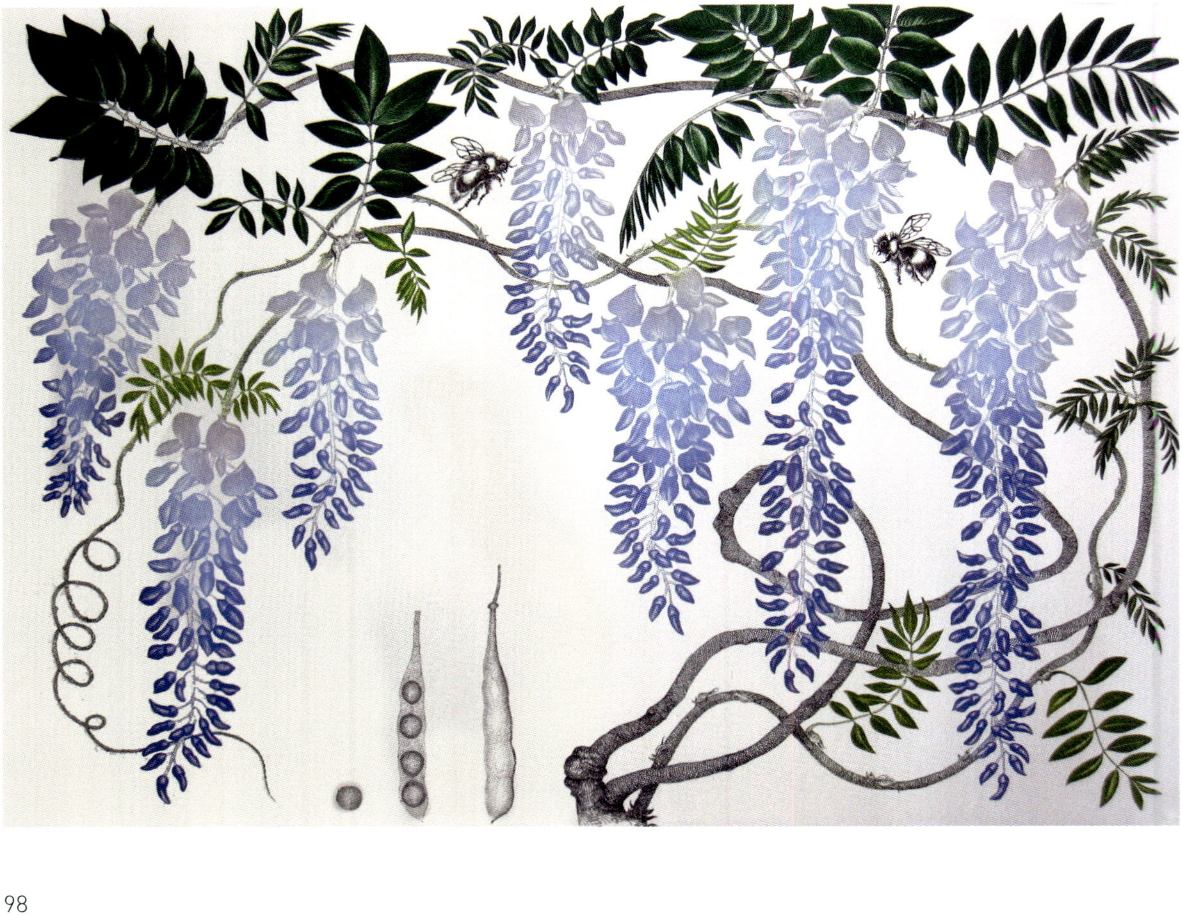

intaglio multiplate printing

When printed colours need to be clean and separate in an image with no possibility of blending where they meet, or when two different techniques are mixed, it is necessary to make more than one plate. Each plate holds different colour or mark information and is printed in a separate pass through the press (but on the same sheet of paper).

The illustration below shows how plates of the same size can be registered together, accurately and simply. Registration blocks can be obtained from engineers/metal fabricators or cut from lengths of standard stock 6 cm steel.

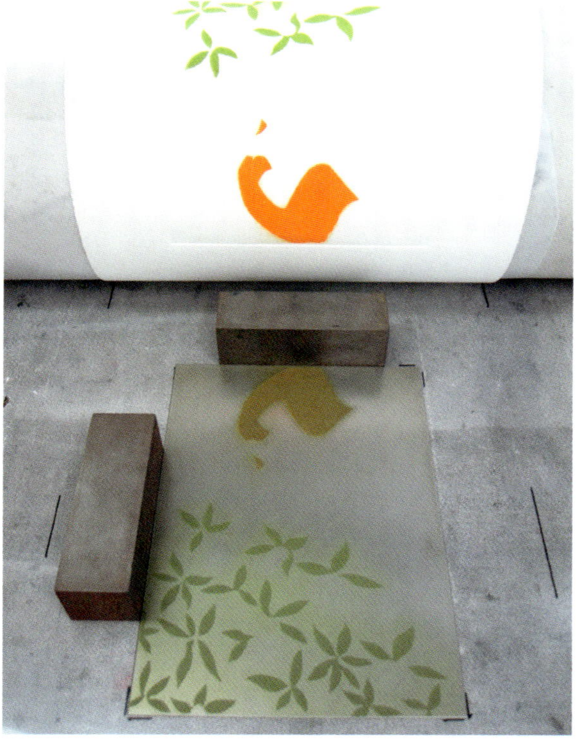

▲ The green and orange are inked on the first plate. The two colours are several centimetres apart and so can be inked and wiped without fear of contaminating each other. The first plate is run through the press, making sure that the paper is still trapped under the press roller. A steel block is placed at the bottom of the plate and another at the side of it.

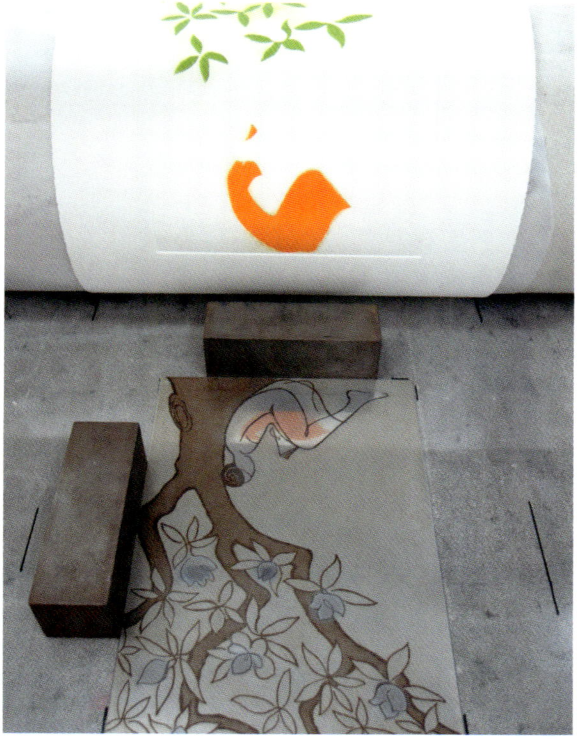

▲ The first plate is removed and replaced with the second inked plate, which butts up against the heavy steel blocks.
The blocks are removed, the trapped paper lowered over the plate and the press is wound.

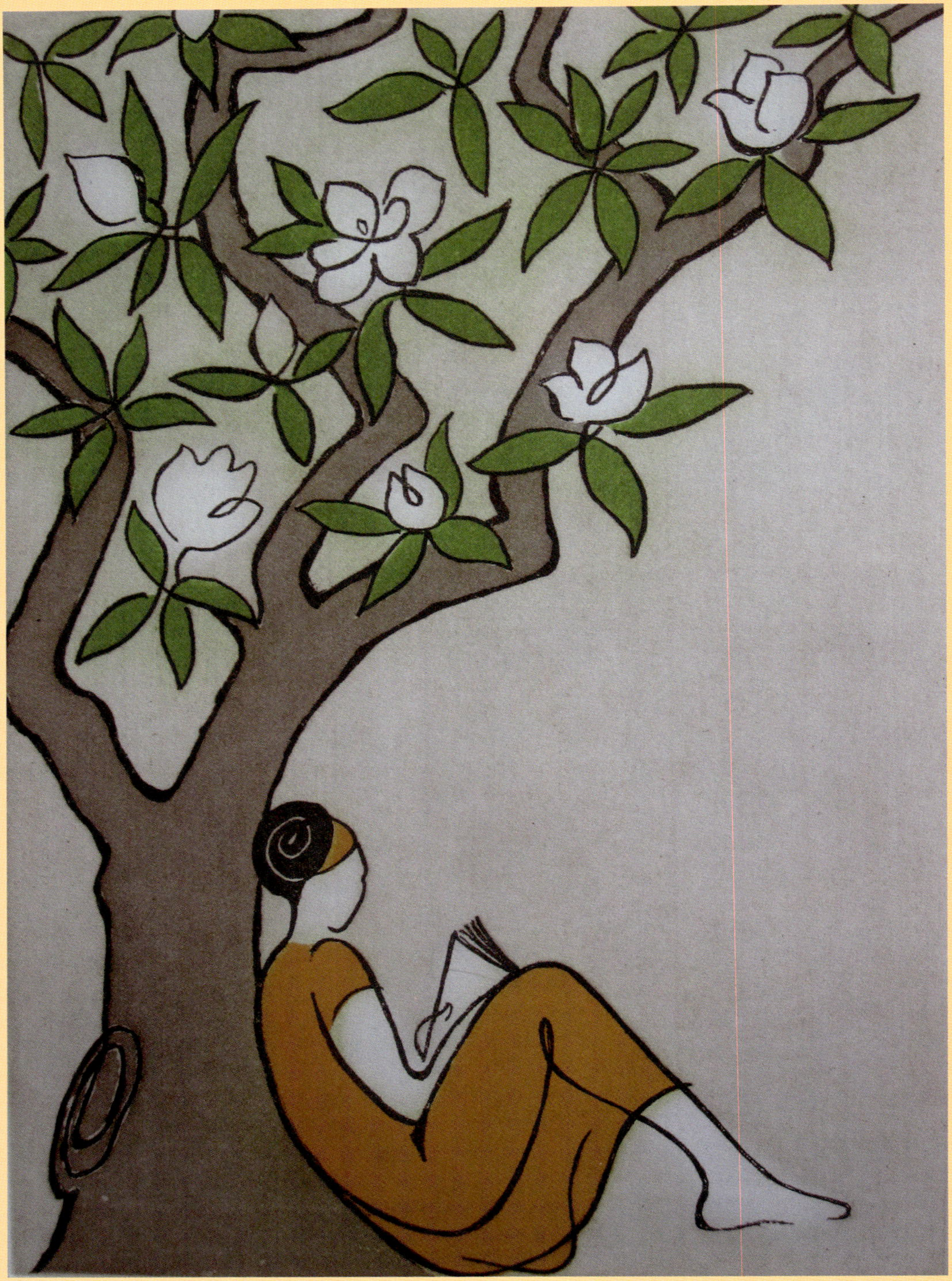

▲ Paula Cox, *Magnolia Tree*, 2009. Etching and aquatint on zinc, 20 x 28 cm (7½ x 11 in.).

The brown plate was printed with plate tone. The magnolia flowers and flesh parts were wiped using a cotton bud.

INTAGLIO MULTIPLATE PRINTING

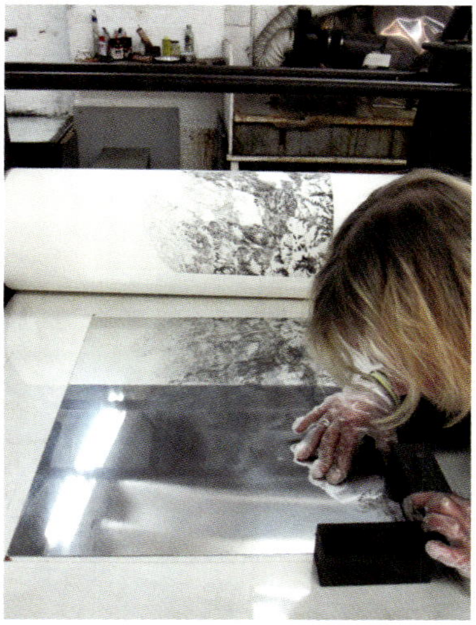

▲ Marianne Ferm placing registration blocks against the first plate.

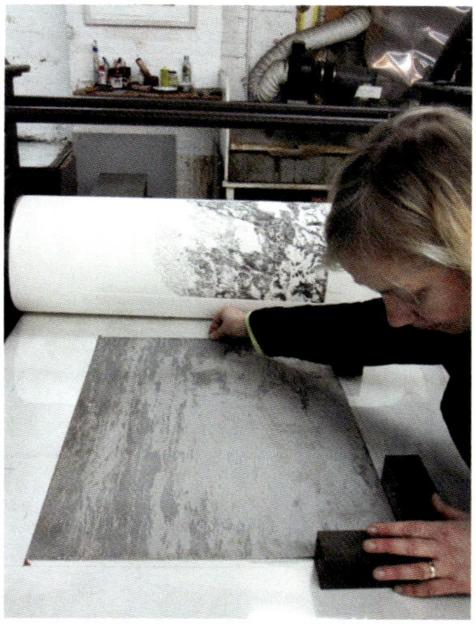

▲ The second plate with the emboss (there is no ink) is placed against the blocks.

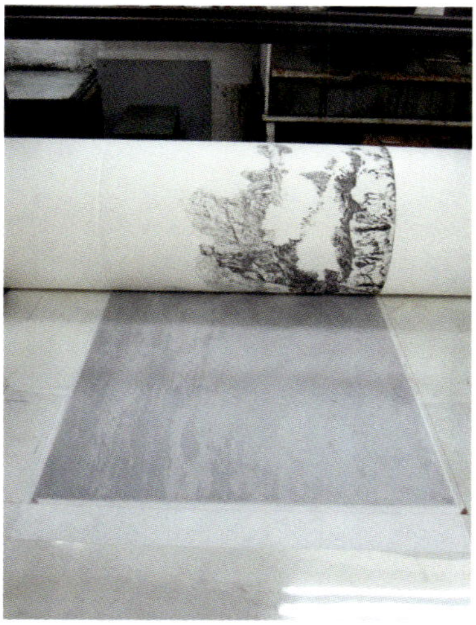

▲ The second plate being rolled through the press.

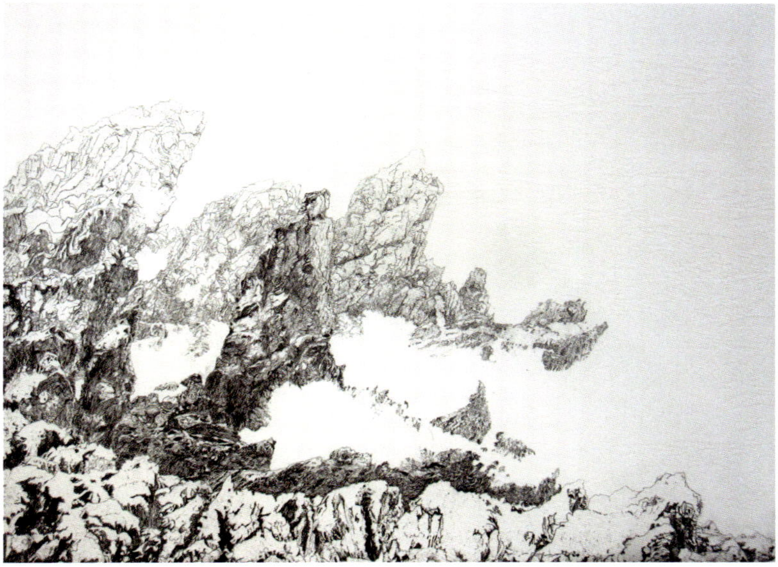

▲ Marianne Ferm, *Next – The – Oceans II*, 2010. Etching and embossing, 86 x 70 cm (33¾ 27½ in.).

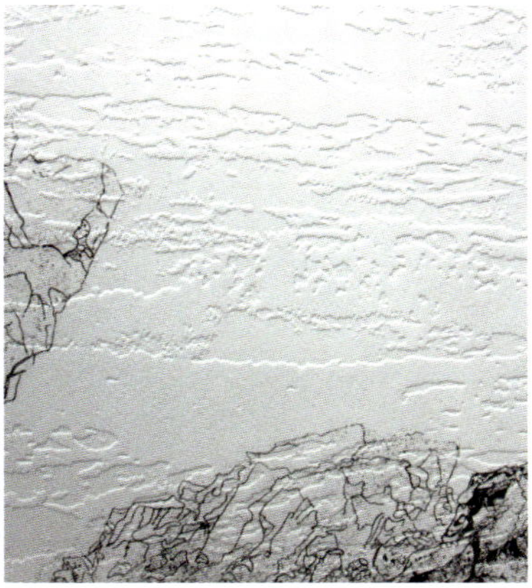

▲ A close-up showing the paper embossing.

aquatint

THE HISTORY OF AQUATINT

Aquatint was developed commercially as a faster method – compared with mezzotint or engraving – of biting tones into a plate surface. The name of the process derives from the Latin words for water and colour (*aqua* and *tint* respectively).

Goya was the first artist to employ aquatint as a means of artistic expression when he combined aquatint with hard ground line work at the end of the 18th century.

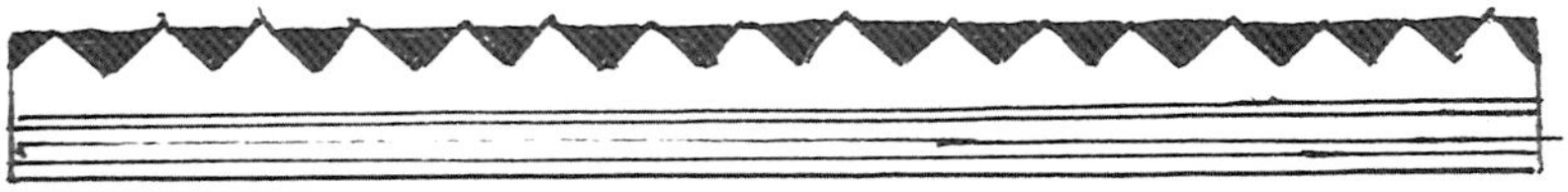

A cross section of a bitten aquatint plate showing the 'tooth' that holds the printing ink.

WHY IS AQUATINT NEEDED?

Aquatint is needed to facilitate the biting of small pits in a plate surface, which in turn enables ink to be held in an even and consistent manner. As in all mordant biting techniques, the deeper the pits or ruts, the more ink is held and the darker the tone or line appears. Using aquatint allows the artist to create tones which can range from the barest hint of grey to a deep black.

MAKING AN AQUATINT TEST STRIP

Making an aquatint test strip is a good idea for the following reasons:

- It gives artists an overview of a mordant's biting times and how the mordant reacts with a particular plate surface.
- It acts as a useful guide for future biting times.
- It helps us calculate accurate biting times on the day (mordant strength varies from day to day), particularly for light tones.

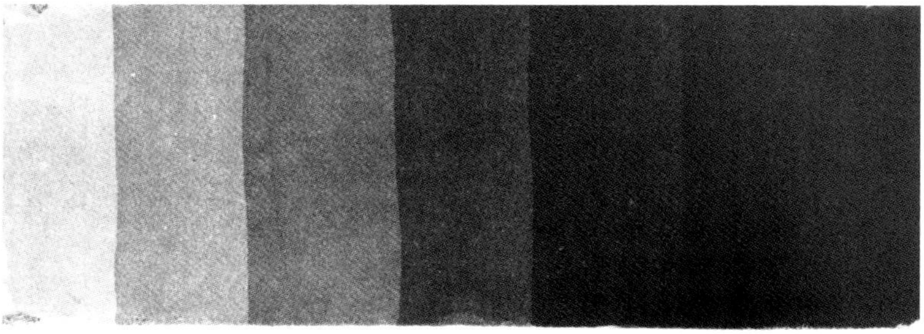

A printed test strip for zinc in a nitric acid solution of 12:1 (12 parts water to one part acid) in steps from 15 seconds to 10 minutes.

Making a test strip is not just a tedious exercise done by beginners. A plate that needs subtle light tones can be over bitten easily, and fixing it will mean many hours' work on the plate surface with a scraper and burnisher. On a soft metal such as zinc, even 15 seconds too long in the mordant (or 15 seconds less than needed) can make an enormous visual difference.

Always remember that how the mordant bites is unpredictable for a variety of reasons. Factors such as room temperature (mordant reacts faster when warmer), how many times the mordant has been used previously (the more use, the weaker it will be) and the density of the aquatint grain laid on the plate can all have a significant impact. Because of the very nature of aquatint resin, it will vary each time you make one, so even the most experienced printmaker cannot predict accurately the tone of a light aquatint.

When you are applying an aquatint, it is wise to include an offcut of metal that receives the same resin dust or aquatint spray as the main plate and at the same time. The offcut can then be bitten and printed first. This test strip is then used as an accurate guide to biting times for the main plate.

To make the test strip

Step 1 is to degrease the plate. The aquatint is then applied to the degreased plate and the plate bitten, in this case for 15 seconds. The plate is then removed from the mordant and dried. A strip approximately 3 cm (1¼ in.) wide is then painted over with stop-out varnish.

The plate is then returned to the mordant. It is usual to double the timing for each following strip (30 seconds for this first one, one minute for the next, two minutes for the third and so on). Work methodically across the plate, biting and stopping out at given intervals. Don't forget to make a record of the times on a separate piece of paper: these times are then transferred onto the printed test strip.

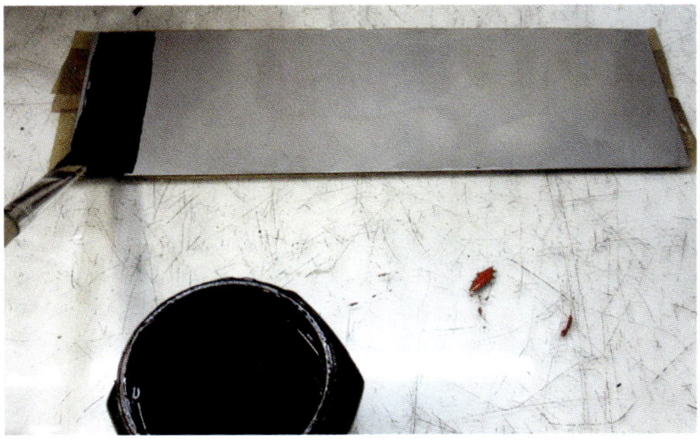

▲ **The first bitten strip being sealed with stop-out varnish.**

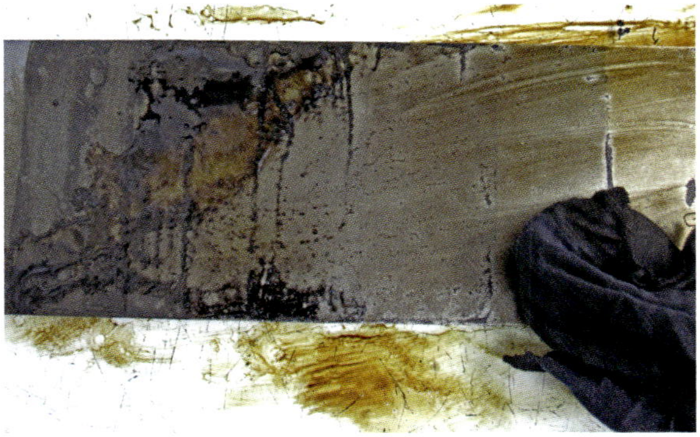

▲ **The bitten test strip is cleaned first with white spirit to remove the varnish and then with methylated spirit to remove the resin ground.**

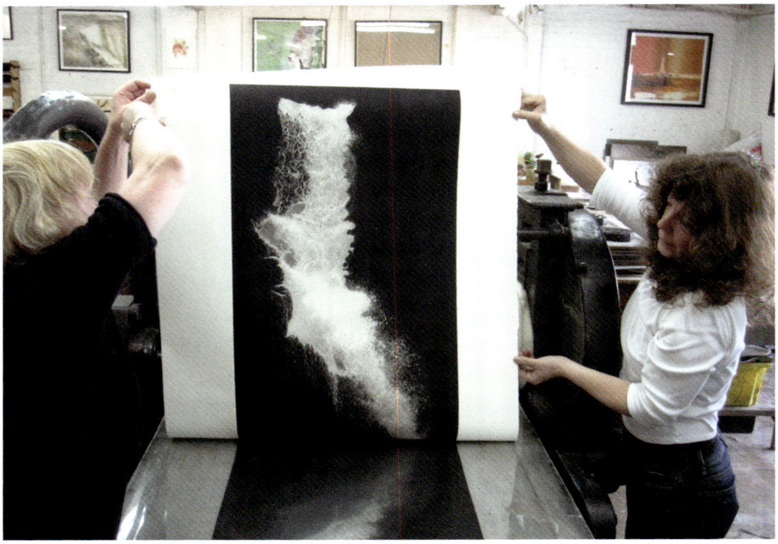

▶ Marianne Ferm and Megan Fishpool pulling an aquatint on zinc. Large-scale works often require two pairs of hands!

TRADITIONAL RESIN AQUATINT

Powdered resin dust is applied using an aquatint box, then fused to the plate with heat. This method is still widely practised and extremely reliable. A dust mask should always be worn when handling powdered resin.

Resin can be applied to a blank plate, to a plate that has bitten work on it already, or to a plate where the image to be bitten has already been stopped out.

When handling resin, be sure to use a face mask. The resin has a tendency to stick to the inside walls and griddle of the box. Take a long metal strip – a plate offcut salvaged from under the workshop guillotine will do! – then loosen the resin by scraping the walls and metal griddle inside the aquatint box.

▼ This picture shows a copper plate by Bryan Poole with bitten line work and painted-on stop-out. The stopped-out areas resist the mordant. The areas showing bare metal will be bitten by the mordant.

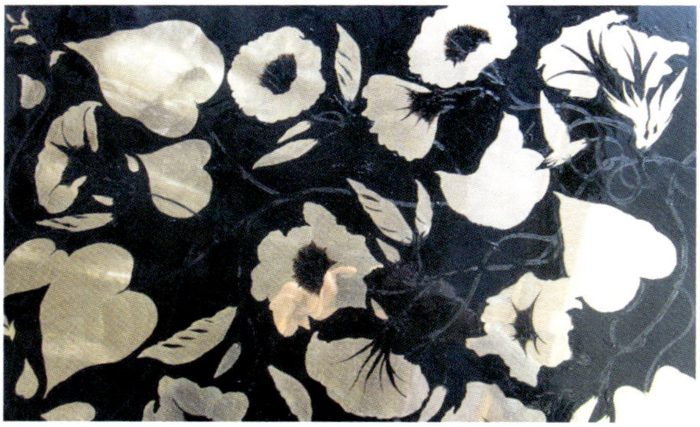

▶ An aquatint box at Artichoke. It is preferable to have an aquatint box in a separate room to contain the spread of resin dust.

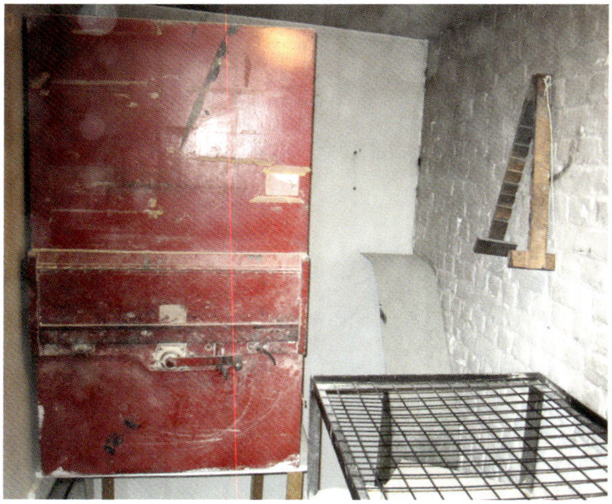

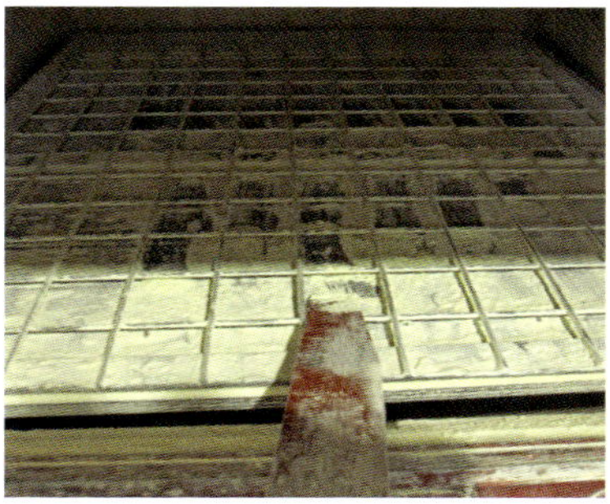

▲ Loosening the resin using a metal strip.

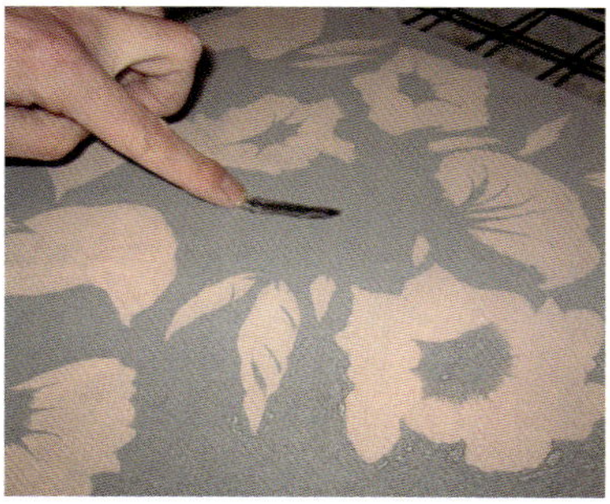

▲ This photograph illustrates the typical amount of resin covering the plate on removal from the aquatint box before fusing.

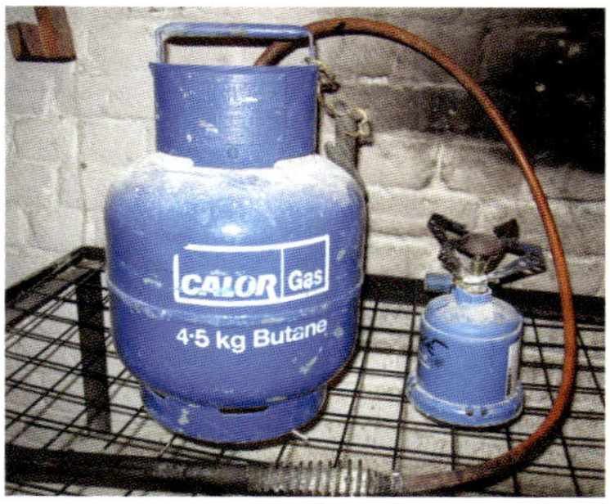

▲ Calor® gas and gas poker; camping gas heater.

The door to the box is now closed and the handle turned vigorously a dozen times or so. This sends up a cloud of dust inside the box. The degreased plate is now placed inside the box, the door closed and the dust allowed to settle on the plate surface. The plate should remain in the box for approximately four minutes.

The plate is removed from the box and placed face up on a wire rack. The plate is now heated from underneath using a gas poker or camping gas burner (useful for very small plates).

Heat the whole plate gently from underneath. Then, beginning at one edge of the furthest corner, melt the resin systematically. Move the heat in one direction across the plate. The resin will become transparent as it melts. It is important to remove the heat on the plate once the resin has melted or it will become too fluid and fuse together. If this happens, the plate surface will become sealed from the action of the mordant. The aim is to have tiny dots of resin around which the mordant bites. Once all the resin has turned transparent, turn off the heat. Leave the plate to cool for several minutes. It will be extremely hot!

The plate is removed from the mordant, rinsed with water and dried. The bite can then be inspected with a magnifying glass known as a 'linen tester'. Examining a plate in this way is the only reliable way of judging whether the aquatint texture achieved will produce a strong black.

▼ LEFT TO RIGHT: Unfused resin on plate with flame from gas poker.

The heat of the gas poker gently fuses the resin onto the surface.

The fused resin is clear and the unfused resin appears dusty.

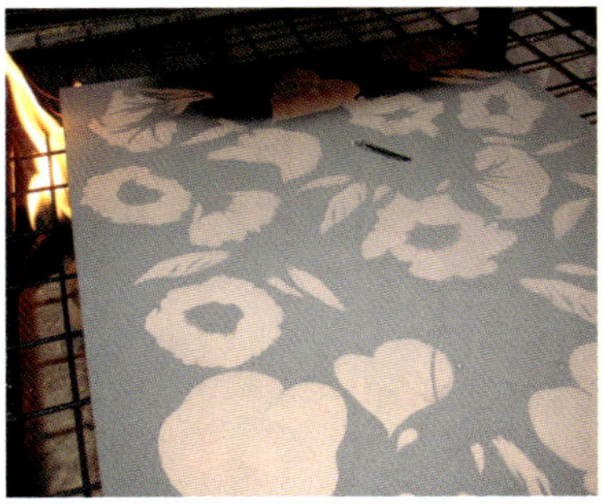

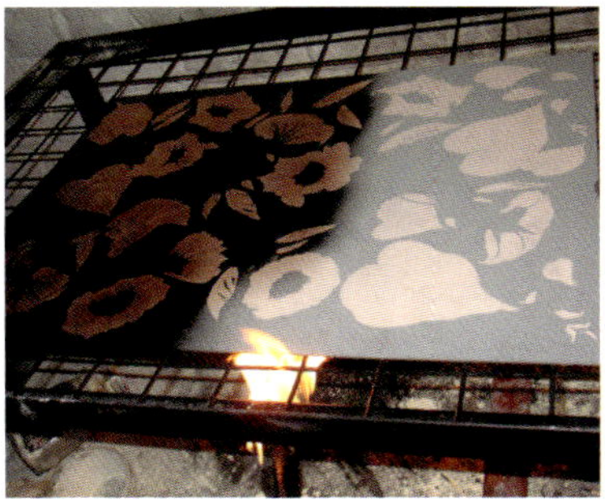

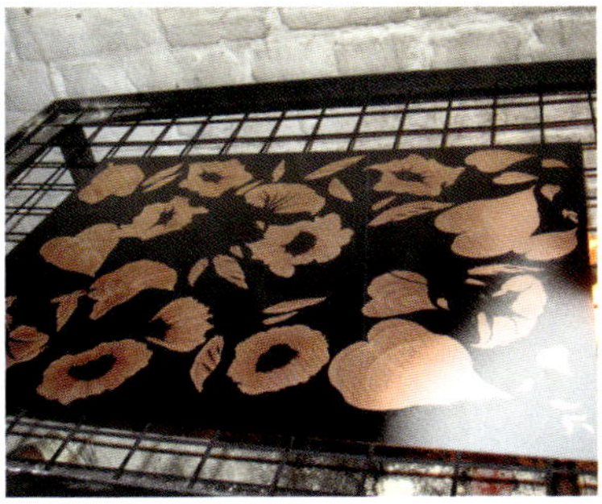

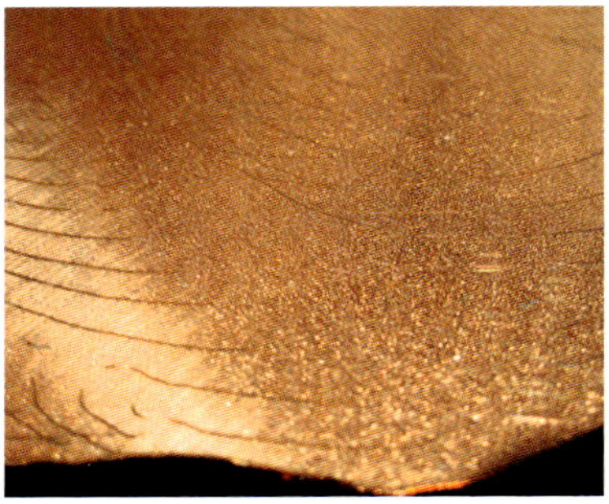

▲ A close-up of the fused resin on the copper plate.

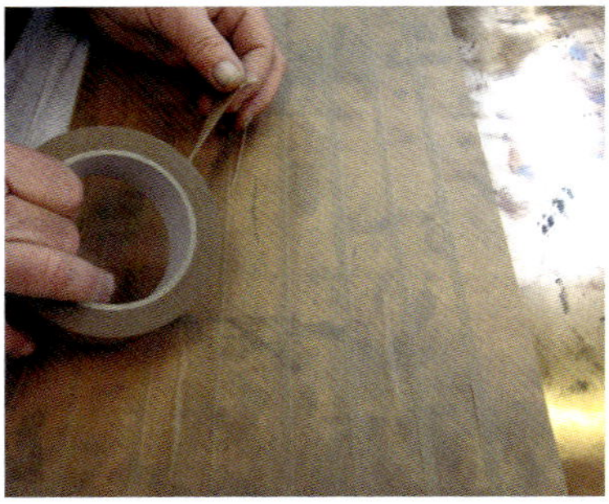

▲ The back of the plate is sealed with packing tape.

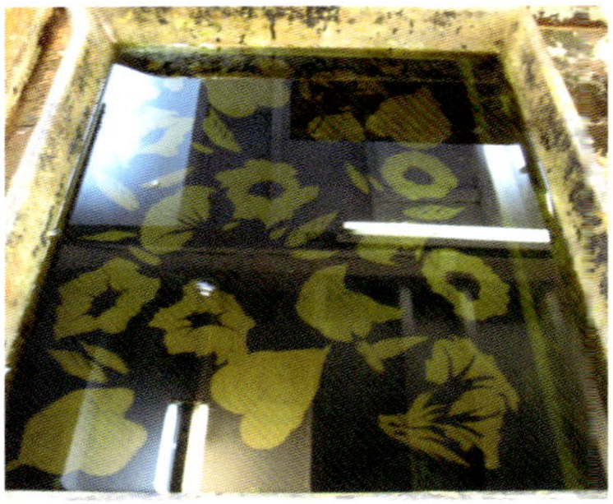

▲ The copper plate is bitten in ferric chloride. Biting times are judged by referring to an aquatint test strip. Several tones may be bitten by stopping out areas of the plate to fix them before returning the plate to the mordant.

A strong black is achieved before the resin globules become undercut by the action of the mordant. The resin globules gradually become smaller as the metal surrounding each resin globule is bitten. If the plate is bitten for too long, these globules are undercut and disappear, leading to open biting of the plate surface. An open bite means the loss of the tooth structure which holds the ink, which leads to a dull grey printing result.

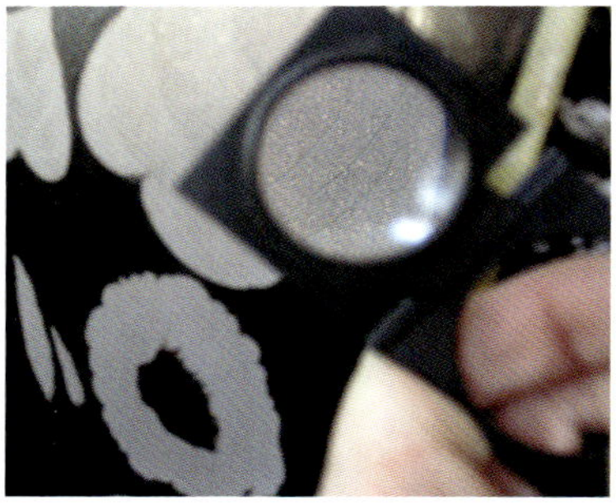

▲ Examining the resin globules using a linen tester.

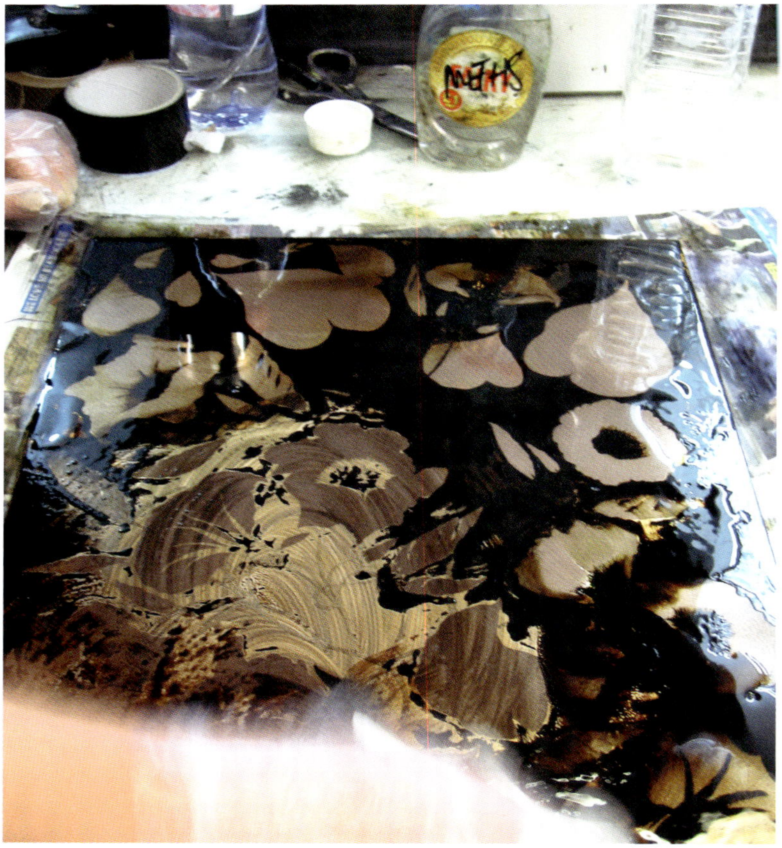

▶ After biting, both the stop-out and the resin must be removed from the plate before proofing. In this example, the stop-out is removed with white spirit and the aquatint resin with methylated spirits.

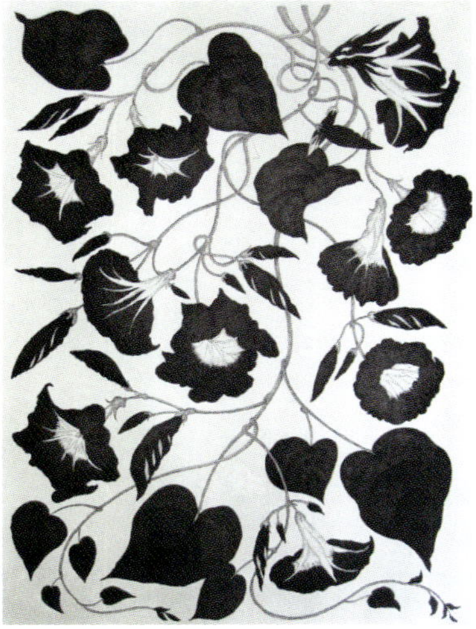

◀ The black and white proof. A proof is pulled to check that biting has been successful. As the image is to be printed in colour, we chose a bite that would print strongly in black. The aquatint now needs to be hand-burnished to create the highlights on the leaves and petals before colour proofing can begin.

▶ Bryan Poole at work hand-burnishing the highlights. Note the use of a hand-held magnifying glass and 3-IN-ONE® oil to lubricate the burnishing tool.

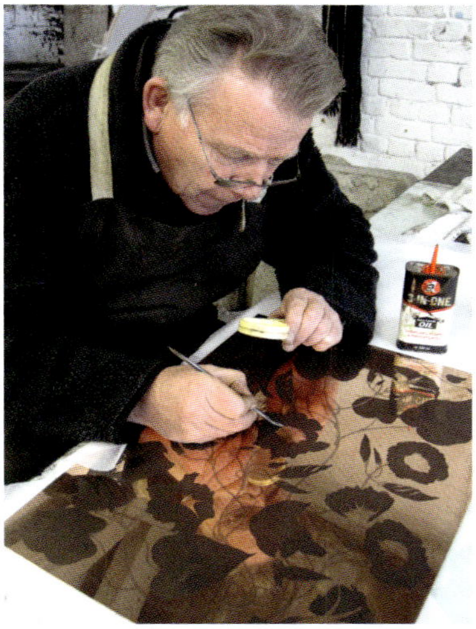

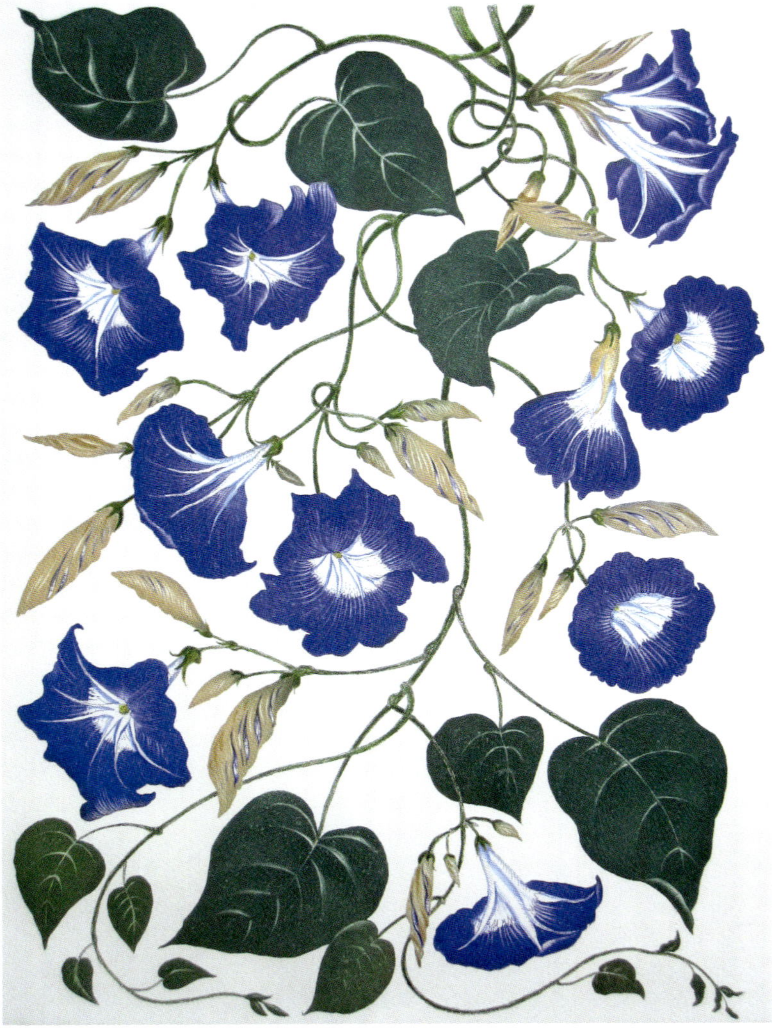

Tip

Always place small plates on a larger plate before placing them in the aquatint box. This will ensure an even distribution of resin dust over the edges of the plates. It also facilitates easier handling as fingers will not disturb the dust when they are removed from the box.

◀ Bryan Poole, *Ipomoea purpurea, Morning Glory*, 2012. 76 x 56 cm.

HAND-SHAKEN AQUATINT

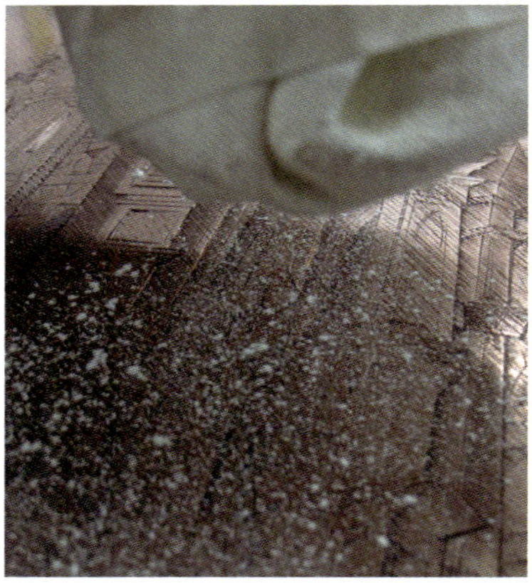

◀ LEFT: A close-up of a printed section of coarse aquatint.
RIGHT To lay a hand-shaken aquatint, take a container (such as an empty jam jar) and part fill it with powdered resin. Cover the top with two or three layers of scrim/tarlatan. The more layers you make, the finer the hand-shaken resin will be. Tape the scrim to the sides of the jar. With the jar inverted, tap the side. The scrim sieve allows the resin to fall randomly onto the degreased plate. The resin is now fused to the plate with heat prior to biting.

▼ A coarse aquatint on a zinc plate by Margaret Sellars being feathered in a mordant bath. The highlights have been stopped out using bitumous stopping-out varnish.

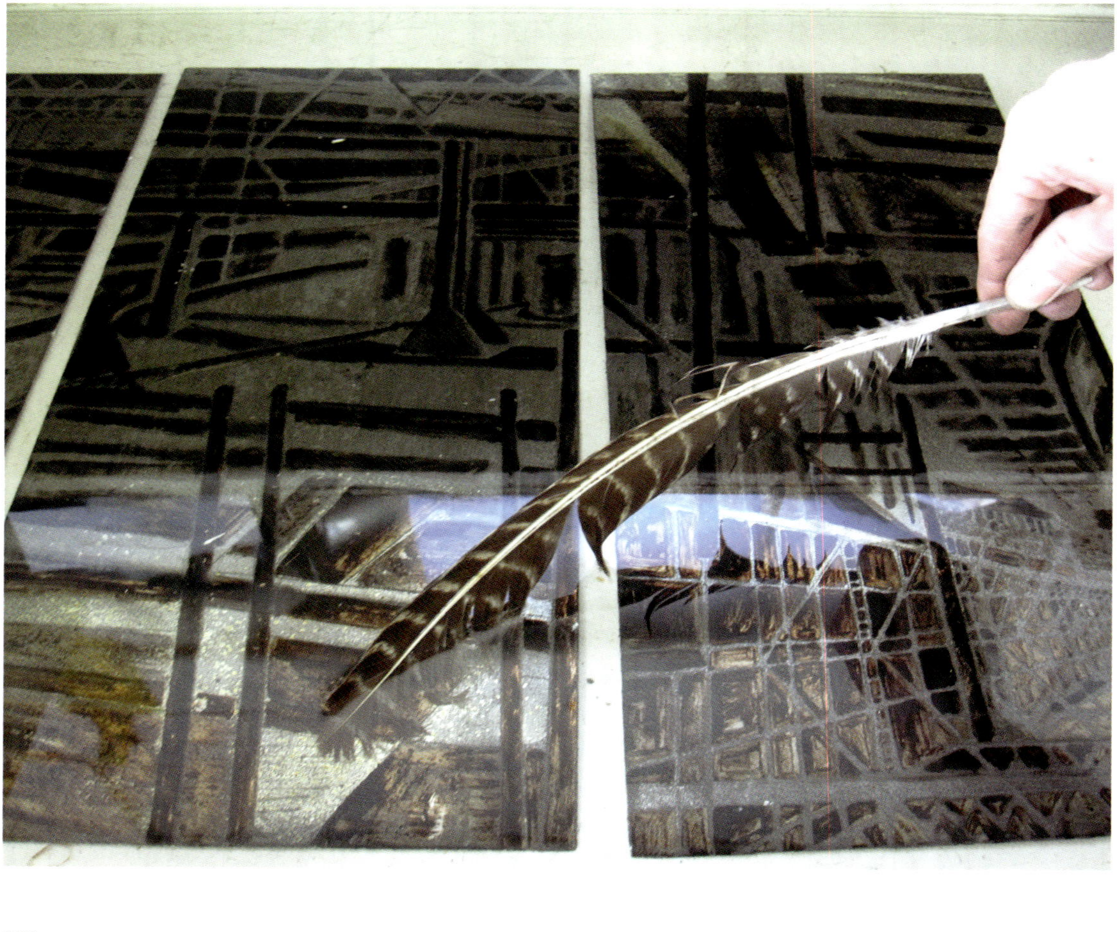

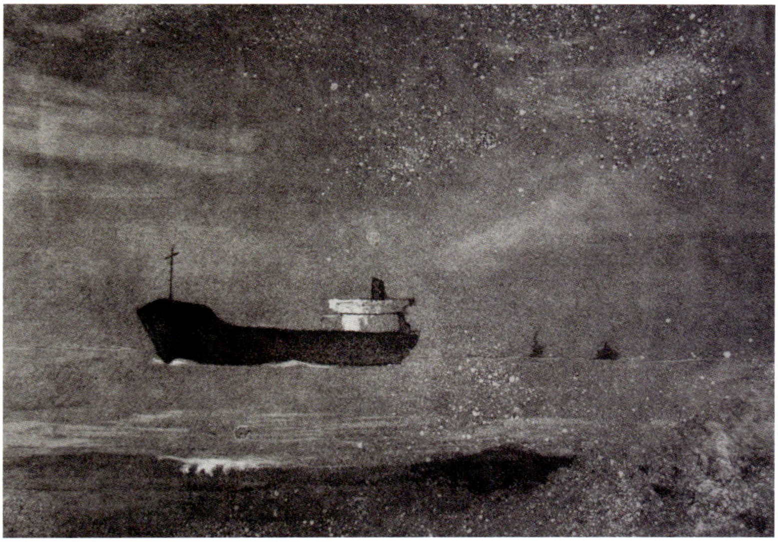

◀ Etching detail by David Parry. A hand-shaken aquatint has been used effectively in the sky and sea of this night scene.

ACRYLIC-RESIST AQUATINT

This method is commonly used when no aquatint box is available or when health and safety concerns prevent the use of one. A resist (such as Lascaux® Aquatint Spray Resist or Hunt Speedball Screen Filler) is sprayed onto a degreased plate using an airbrush. This method throws up some interesting creative possibilities beyond that of laying a flat tone. For example, the airbrush can be used to make graduated tones, patterns and designs with the use of simple paper or card stencils.

When spraying, aim for a 50% coverage of filler on the plate. This means that approximately half the plate area is sealed with filler which resists the acid and half the surface is bare metal which will be bitten.

Follow manufacturer's recommendations for use. Screen fillers usually need to be diluted with water. Don't be afraid to experiment with varying dilutions: in theory, a finer result is achieved with a greater dilution.

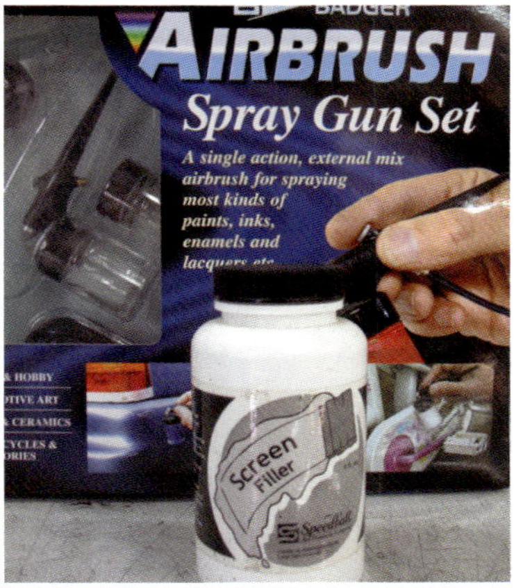

▲ A Badger™ airbrush and Speedball Screen Filler.

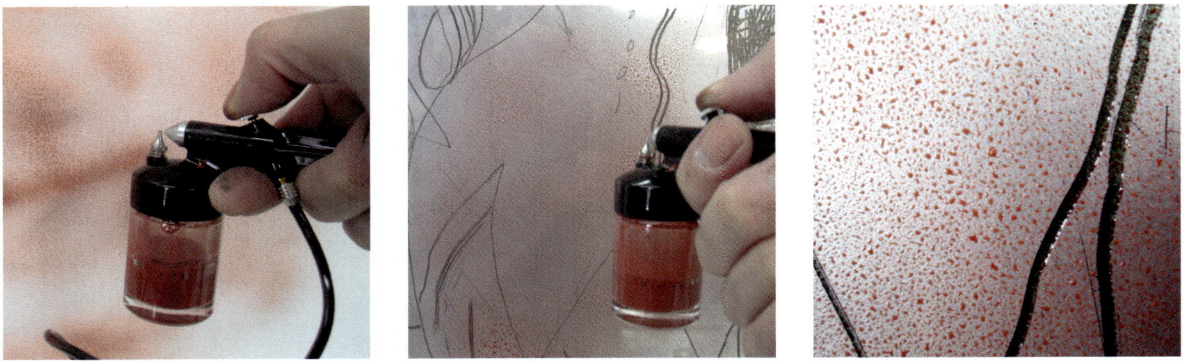

▲ Experimenting on sheets of paper allows us to both practise with the airbrush and test the dilution of screen filler. The screen filler is diluted with water (approximately 70% screen filler to 30% water).

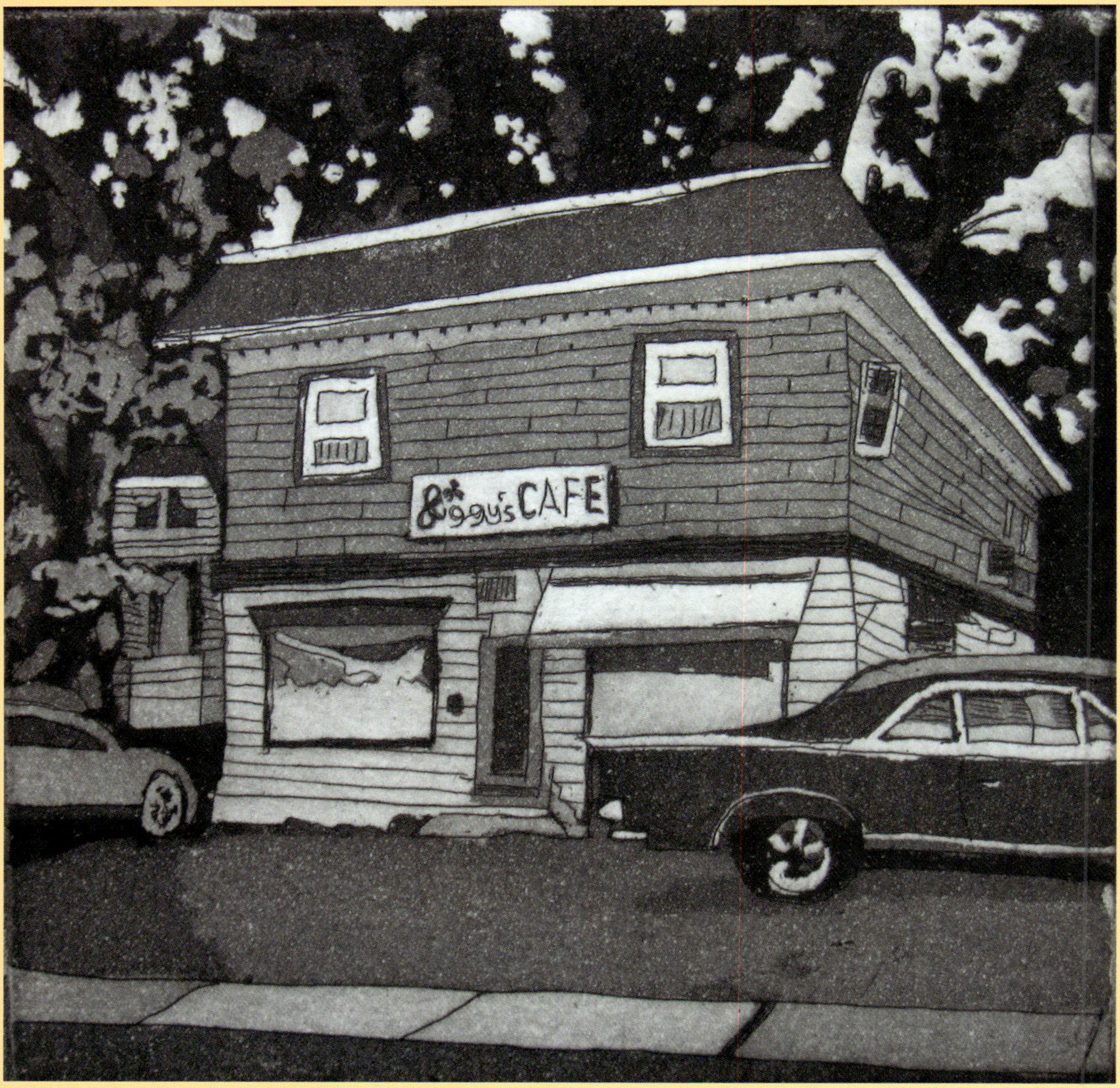

These two Suzy Flood etchings and aquatints are on copper bitten in ferric chloride.

▲ Suzy Flood, *Jiggy's*, 2011. Etching and aquatint, 9 x 9 cm (3½ x 3½ in.).

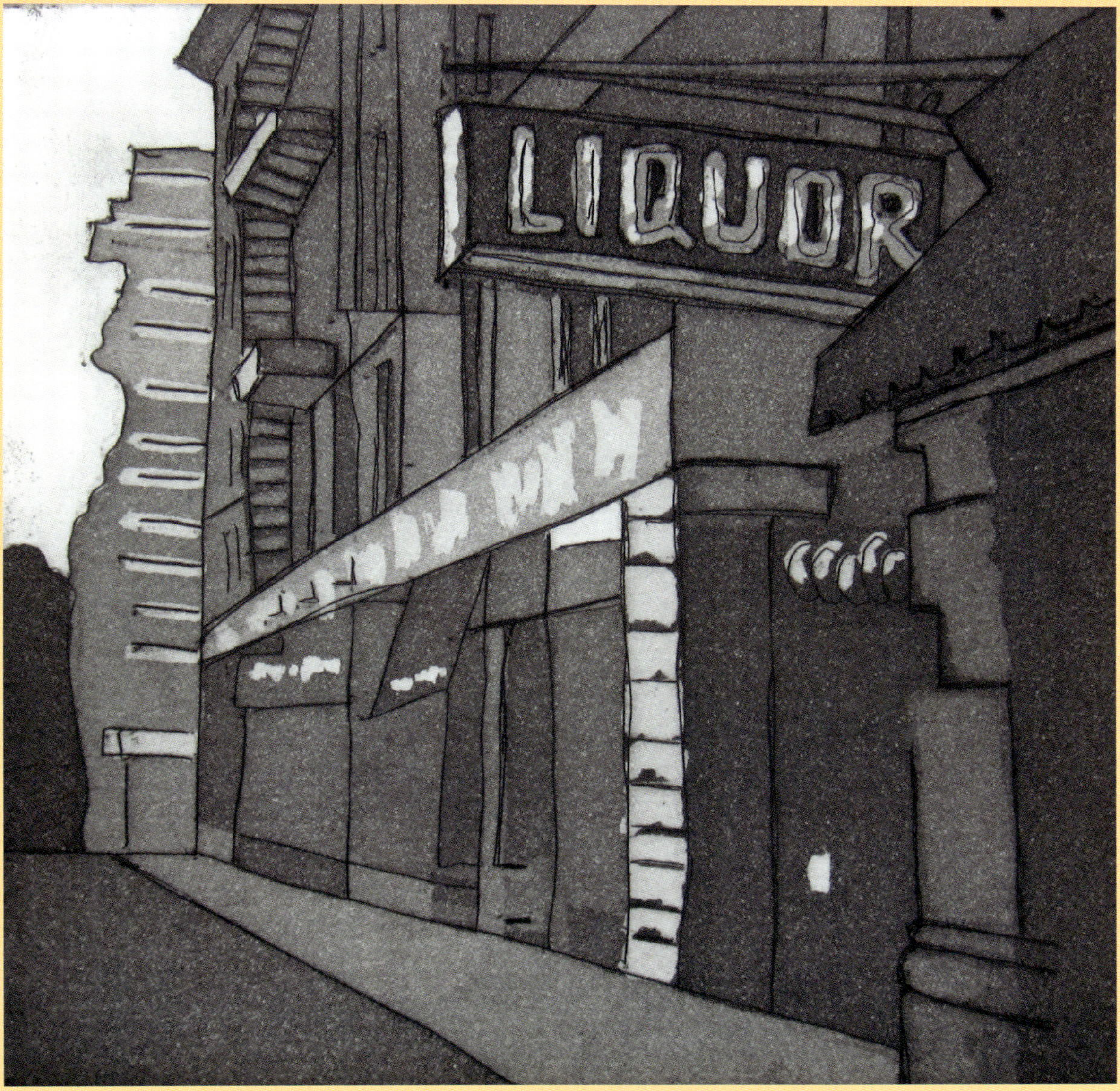

▲ Suzy Flood, *Liquor*, 2011.
Etching and aquatint, 9 x 9 cm
(3½ x 3½ in.).

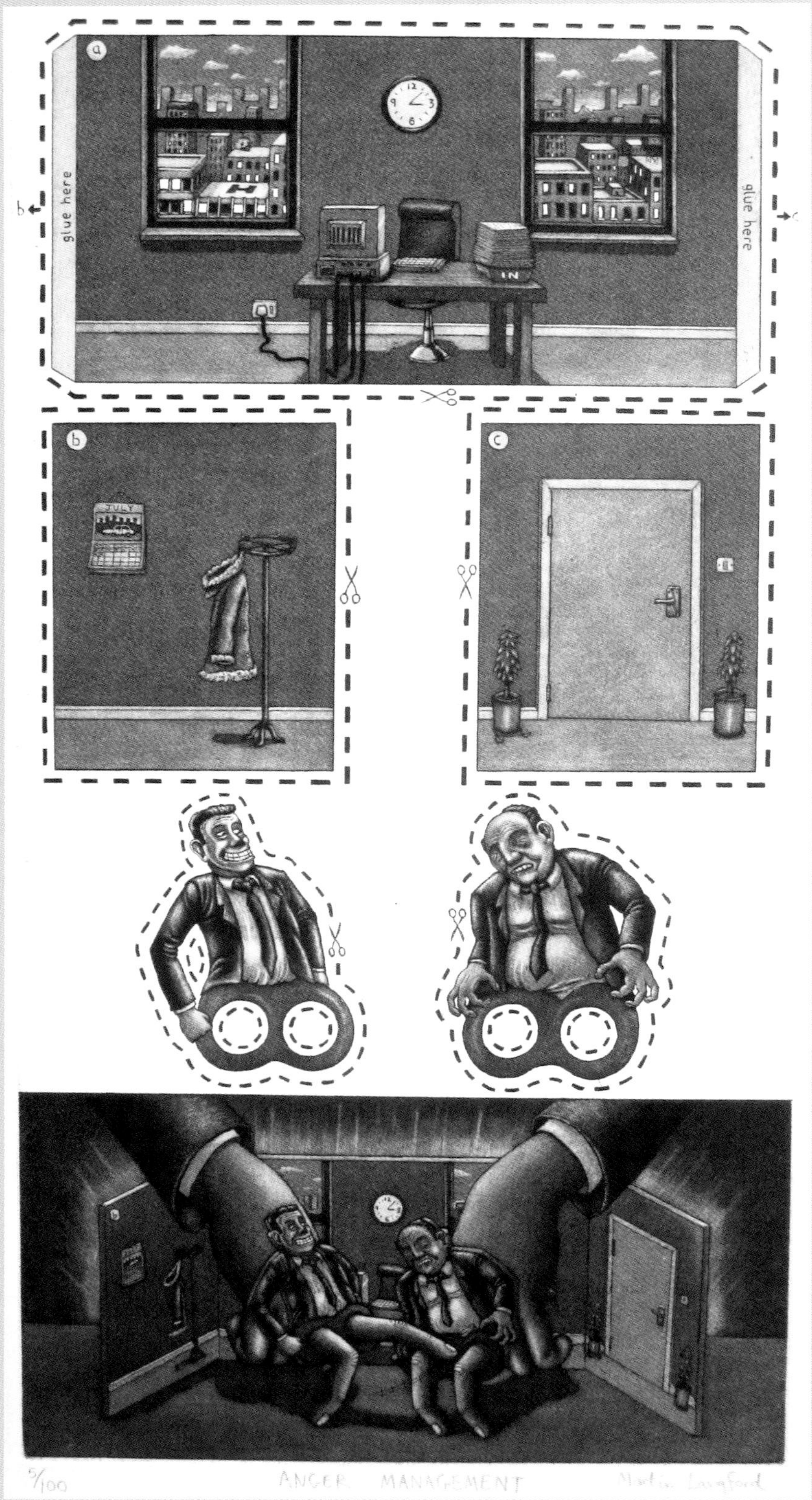
a
glue here
glue here
IN
b
c
JULY
ANGER MANAGEMENT

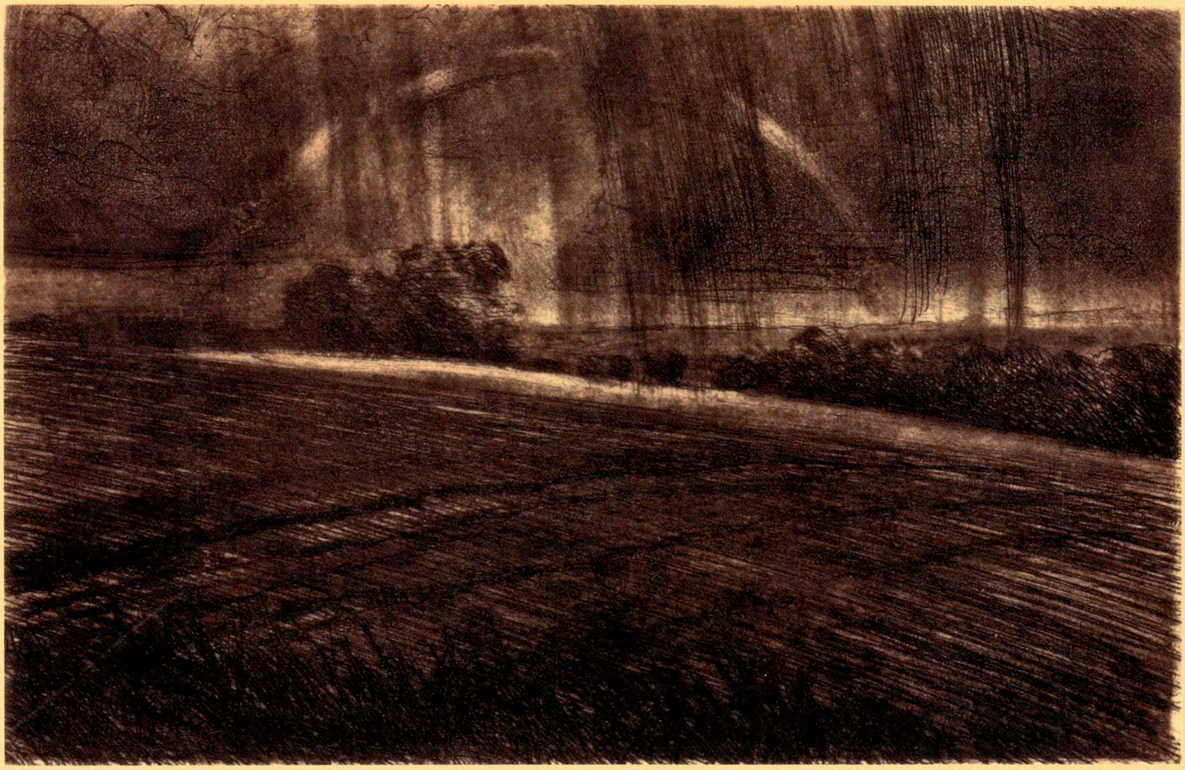

▲ Melvyn Petterson, *Rainbow IV*, 2009. Etching and aquatint on zinc, 14 x 21 cm (5½ x 8¼ in.).

◀ Martin Langford, *Anger Management*, 2008. Aquatint on copper, 24 x 46 cm (9½ x 10¼ in.).

soft ground

Soft ground was developed in Europe in the mid 18th century as a way of producing pencil-type lines in a bitten plate. (It was superseded in the early 19th century by lithography, a technique which richly exploits drawn marks. See Chapter 6). The technique can be used on its own but is regularly combined with other intaglio techniques. Traditionally, a ground of soft wax is used and this is still the most common way of producing a soft ground etching. More recently, water-soluble resists (acrylics) have been developed which work on a similar principle to wax soft ground.

WAX SOFT GROUND

Wax soft ground is composed of similar ingredients to wax hard ground (see p.66) but with the addition of tallow. Hard and soft grounds look very similar but to tell the difference, simply dig your nail into the ground. It will be obvious which is hard and which is soft as your nail will press easily into the soft ground.

Soft ground doesn't dry, which means it can be lifted from the plate surface by placing textures onto the surface of the soft ground on the plate. Alternatively, the ground on the plate can be covered with thin paper to remove areas of ground or embed a texture into it.

▼ Claire Burbridge, *Dress* (detail), 2000. Lace material and patterned wallpaper pressed into wax soft ground, 50 x 99 cm (19½ x 39 in.). Copper bitten in ferric chloride. The plate was inked using two colours.

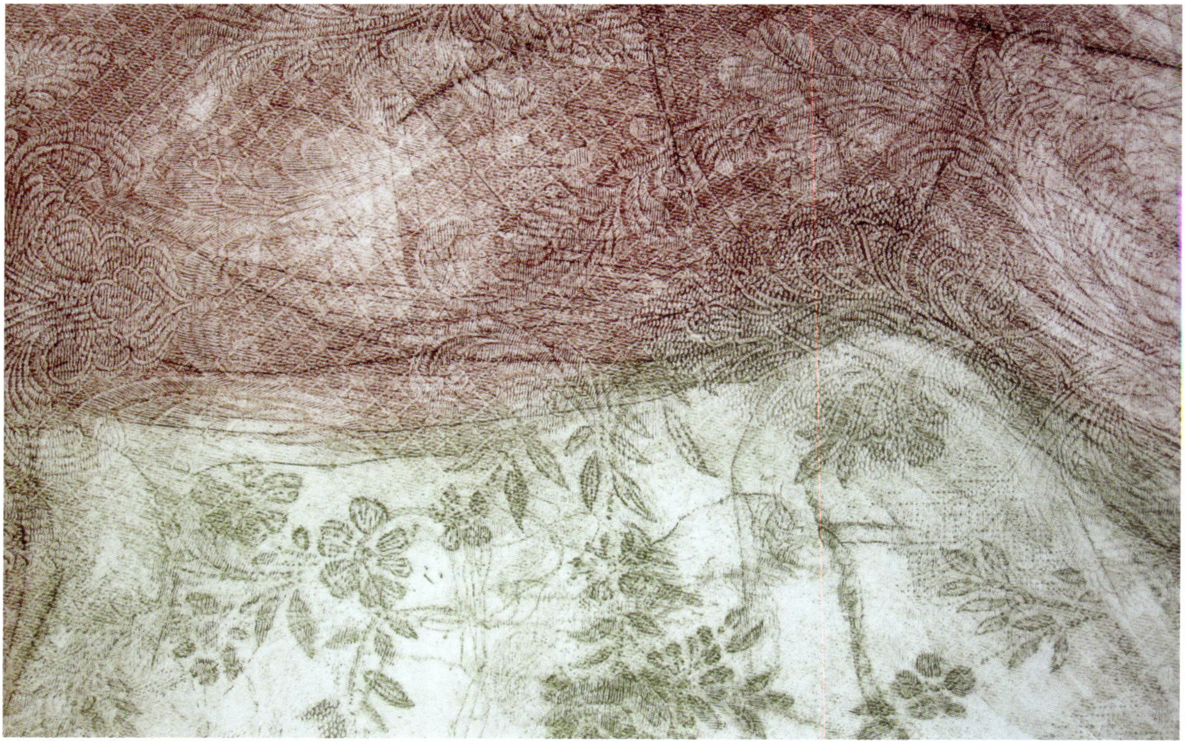

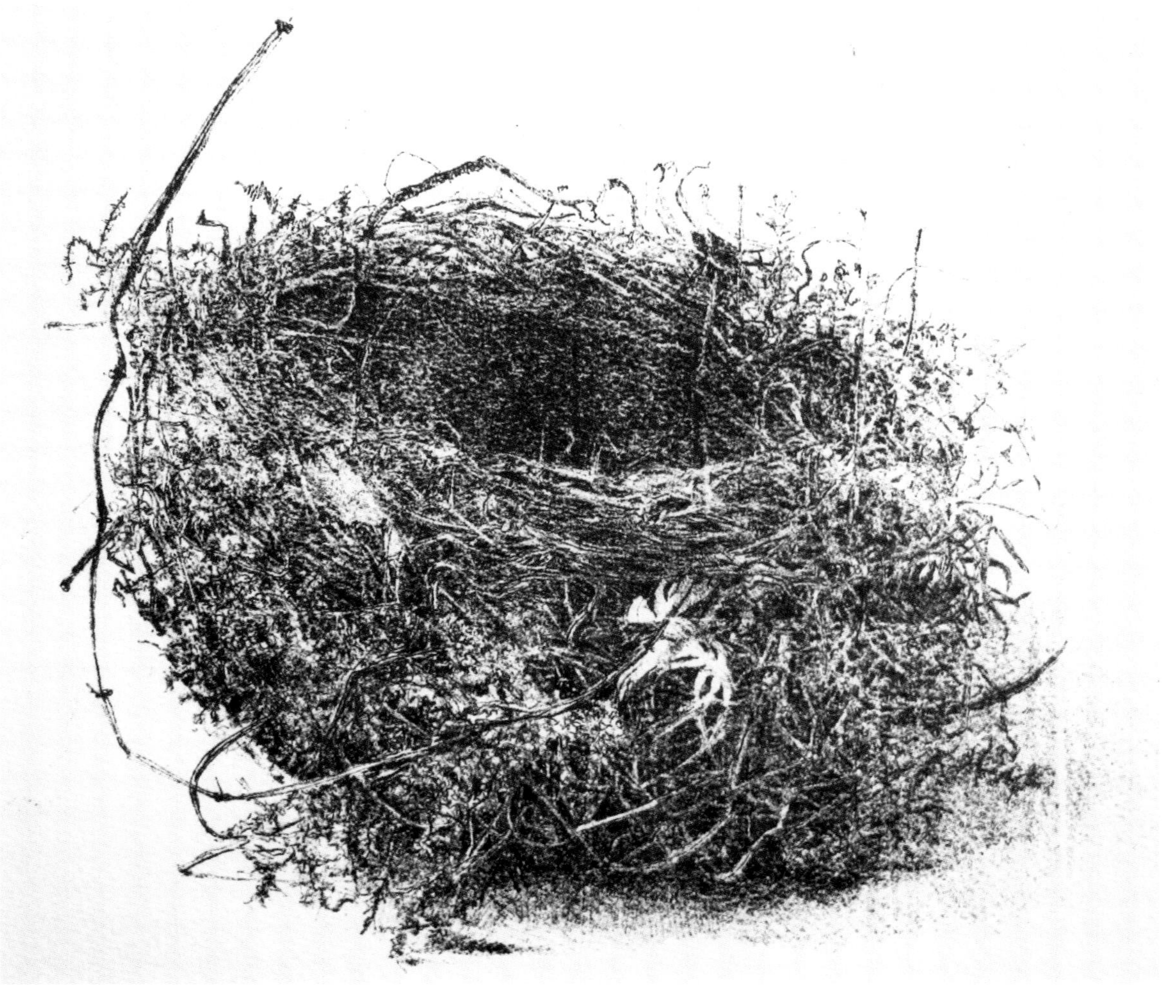

Soft ground can be used on copper, zinc, steel and aluminium. We always recommend degreasing the plate before applying any type of ground or resist including soft ground.

Textured materials can be pressed into the soft wax to leave their impression. If the textures are thin – for example, fabric, crumpled paper or leaves – they can be run through the press over the soft ground plate. The textures will remove the wax, leaving exposed metal which will allow acid to bite in those areas.

To press a texture into soft ground using an etching press, it is important to adjust the pressure on the press to slightly less than that used for printing, as too much pressure will strip all the soft wax ground from the plate. Place the grounded plate face-up on the press bed. Carefully lay the material to be transferred onto the plate surface, then lay a sheet of greaseproof baking paper over the material and plate to prevent any ground from transferring onto the press blankets.

▲ Camilla Clutterbuck *Bird's Nest*, 2009. Soft ground etching on zinc, 20 x 15 cm (7¾ x 6 in.). This fine drawing was made using an HB propelling pencil through newsprint. It was bitten in 10:1 nitric acid for 20 minutes.

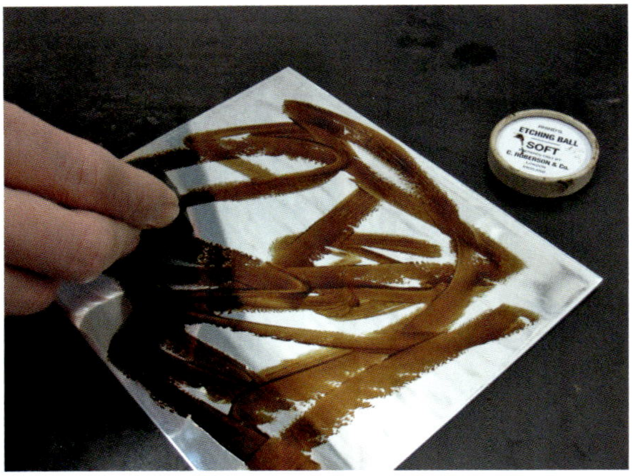

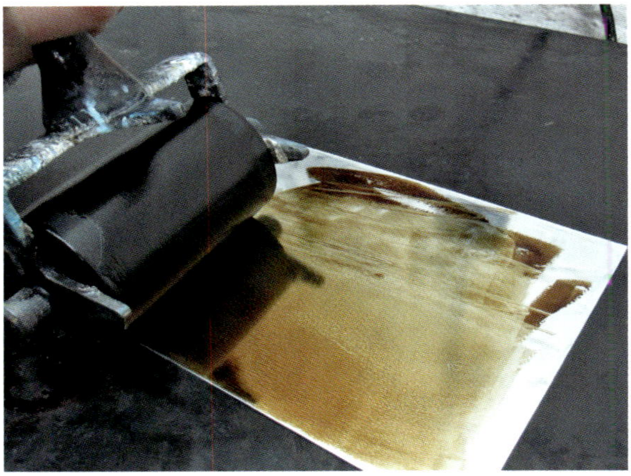

▲ The degreased plate is placed onto a warm hotplate. (The hotplate does not need to be anywhere near as hot as it must be when melting a hard ground.) The soft ground ball is pressed onto the warm plate surface.

▲ The soft ground is rolled out thinly using a clean roller. When the plate has ground on the entire surface, it is removed carefully and allowed to cool.

The usual way of working is to place a thin sheet of paper over the grounded plate and to draw with a pencil. Where the marks are drawn, the soft wax lifts from the plate surface and is offset onto the paper. (The marks produced will still have the characteristics of a pencil mark.) Marks will, of course, vary according to hand pressure and the hardness of the pencil used. Thicker paper will produce a wider softer mark while thin paper will produce a sharper, finer mark. (You will have to apply firmer pressure when using thicker paper.)

▶ A thin sheet of paper or newsprint is placed over the grounded plate. It is a good idea to tape the paper to the table at one end so that it can be lifted and the plate inspected to make sure that bare metal is being revealed by the offsetting of the ground. When the drawing is completed, the plate is bitten in the selected mordant or acid. The wax ground is removed with white spirit or lithotine (a petroleum-based solvent) before printing.

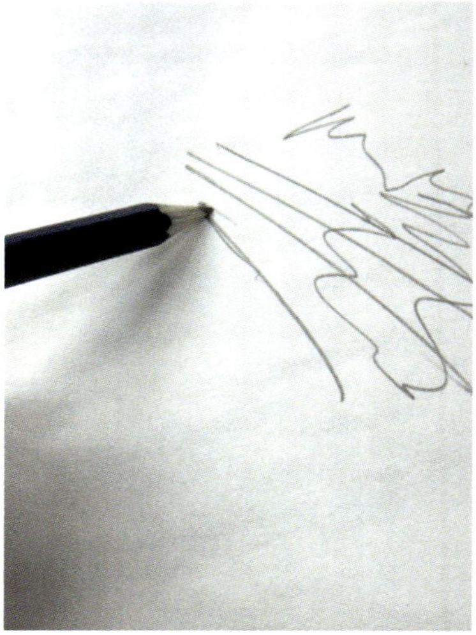

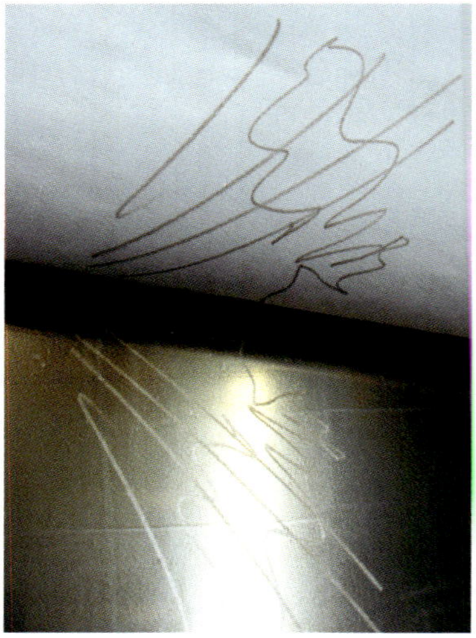

Note that lithotine is a solvent used mainly for washout in lithography. It is similar to kerosene and mineral spirits.

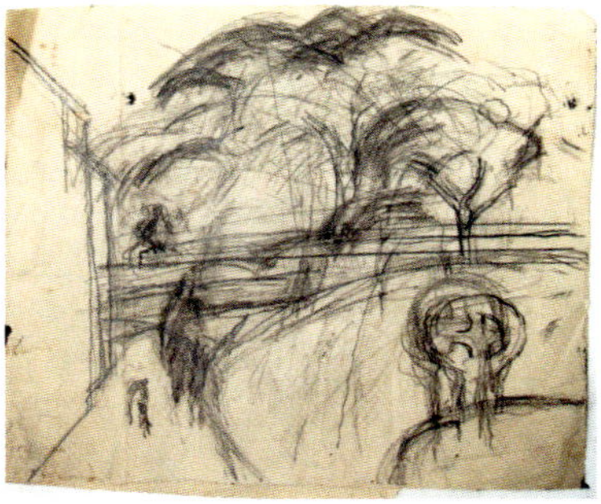

▲ A newsprint drawing by Susan Einzig used to offset the soft ground wax together with the first printed proof (right).

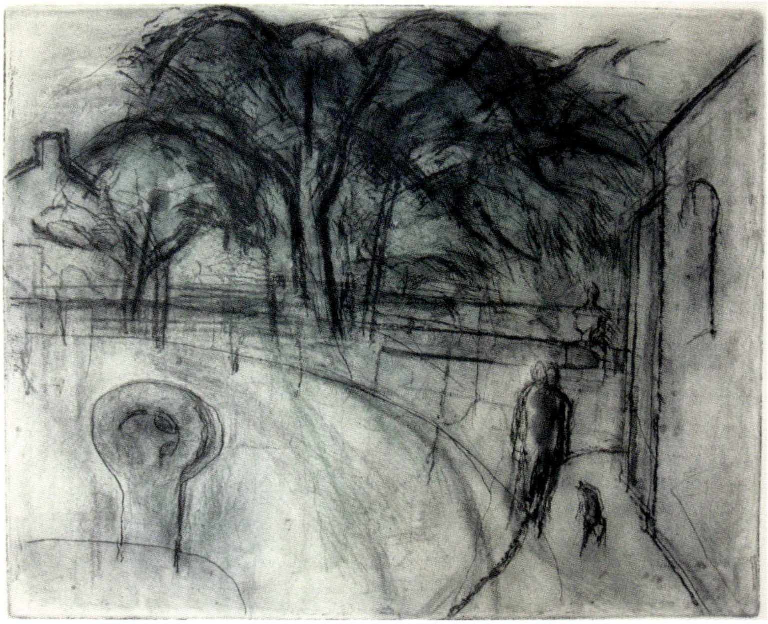

ACRYLIC SOFT GROUND RESISTS

Other options for soft ground techniques include water-soluble resists and pastes such as Lascaux® Soft Resist or Baldwin's Ink Ground. Graphic Chemical Water-Based Block Printing Ink can be used with the addition of artists' acrylic medium – approximately one third medium to two thirds ink.

None of these products require the use of a hotplate to apply them to a plate and solvents are not necessary for cleaning. The resists are rolled on or, in the case of Lascaux® Soft Resist, painted onto a degreased plate and marks are made by working through sheets of thin paper to lift the resist from the plate surface. Being water-soluble, a variety of experimental textures can be made by working directly into the ground's surface using utensils such as brushes, a sponge or textured cloth moistened with water.

Baldwin's Ink Ground and Graphic Chemical Water Based Block Printing Ink can also be used as hard ground when dry. To dry the ground, heat in an oven at approximately 140°C/275°F. If an oven is not available, use an electric hotplate or an electric paint stripper (also called a heat gun and available at DIY stores). If the ground begins to smoke the heat is too high and should be reduced. Alternatively a 'homemade oven' can easily be created using a cardboard box with a hole cut in the side, into which is inserted a hair dryer. Using this method it will take 10–15 minutes to dry the ground.

SOFT GROUND ETCHING USING WATER-BASED RELIEF PRINTING INK

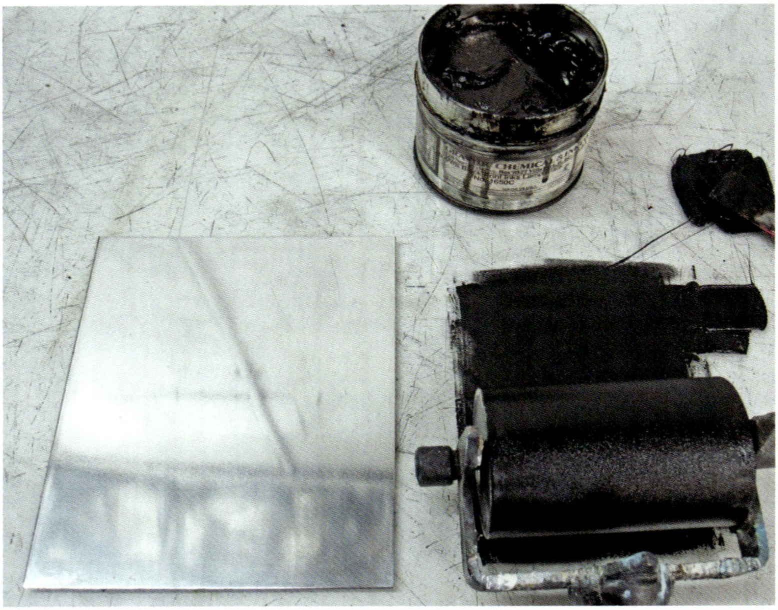

◀ A roller is used to roll water-based block printing ink onto a zinc plate. (Black Graphic Chemical water-based block-printing ink is being used in this picture.)

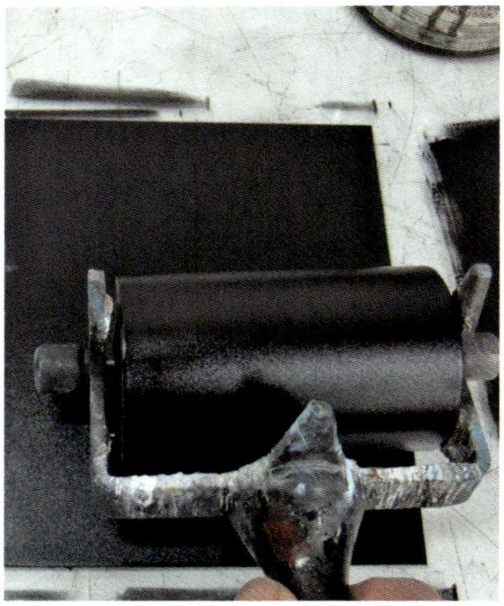

▲ The water-based ink is rolled thinly onto the degreased zinc. The roller and inking glass are cleaned with a sponge and water.

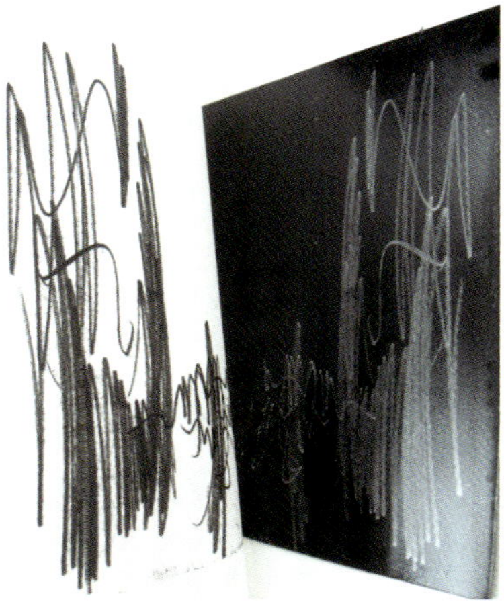

▲ Newsprint is used to offset marks made with a hard pencil.

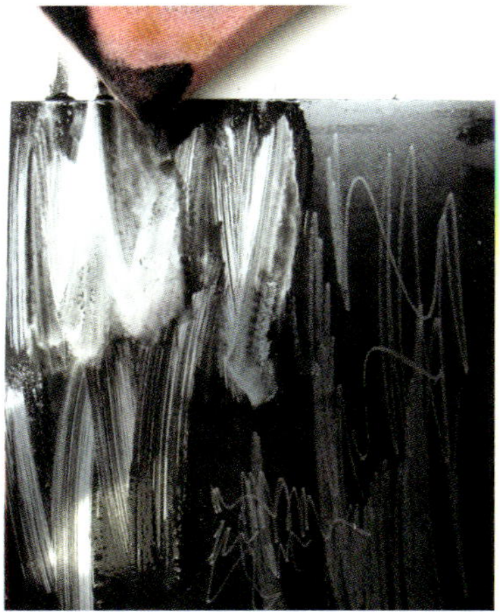

▲ A sponge (any ordinary kitchen sponge can be used) moistened with water is used to create marks and textures into the resist. As the ink is black, it is very easy to see the marks being made.

Once you have completed making the image, the plate needs to dry. The ink on the plate will take a long time to dry naturally so it is best to 'cure' the ink using an electric paint stripper or heat gun. Alternatively, place the plate in a warm oven or on a warm hotplate. The ink will turn a matt black when it is dry on the plate. Curing time will vary but from experience, we recommend the image can be removed from the heat when it is touch-dry.

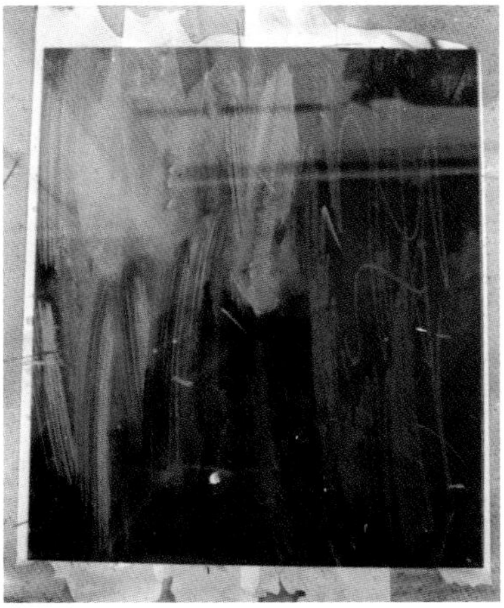

◀ The plate being etched in a solution of copper sulphate. The water-based coating is removed from the bitten plate by soaking in a bath of sodium carbonate (washing crystals). The mixture ratio is 4–5 heaped teaspoons of sodium carbonate to half a litre of room-temperature tap water.

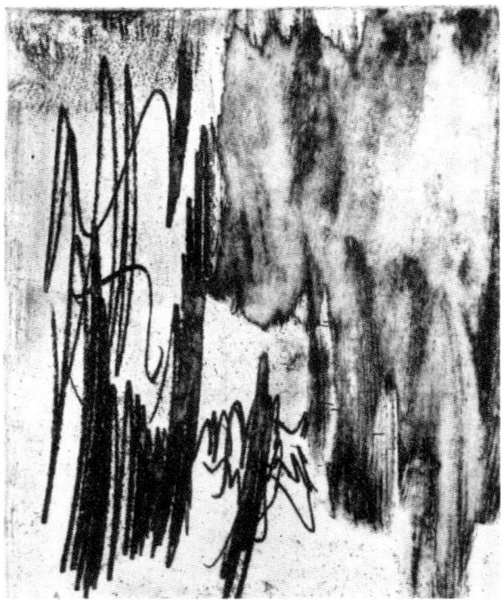

▶ An inked impression of the bitten plate.

▼ Rachel Lindsey Clark, *Tower Bridge*, 2002. Soft ground etching, 30 x 25 cm (11¾ x 9¾ in.).

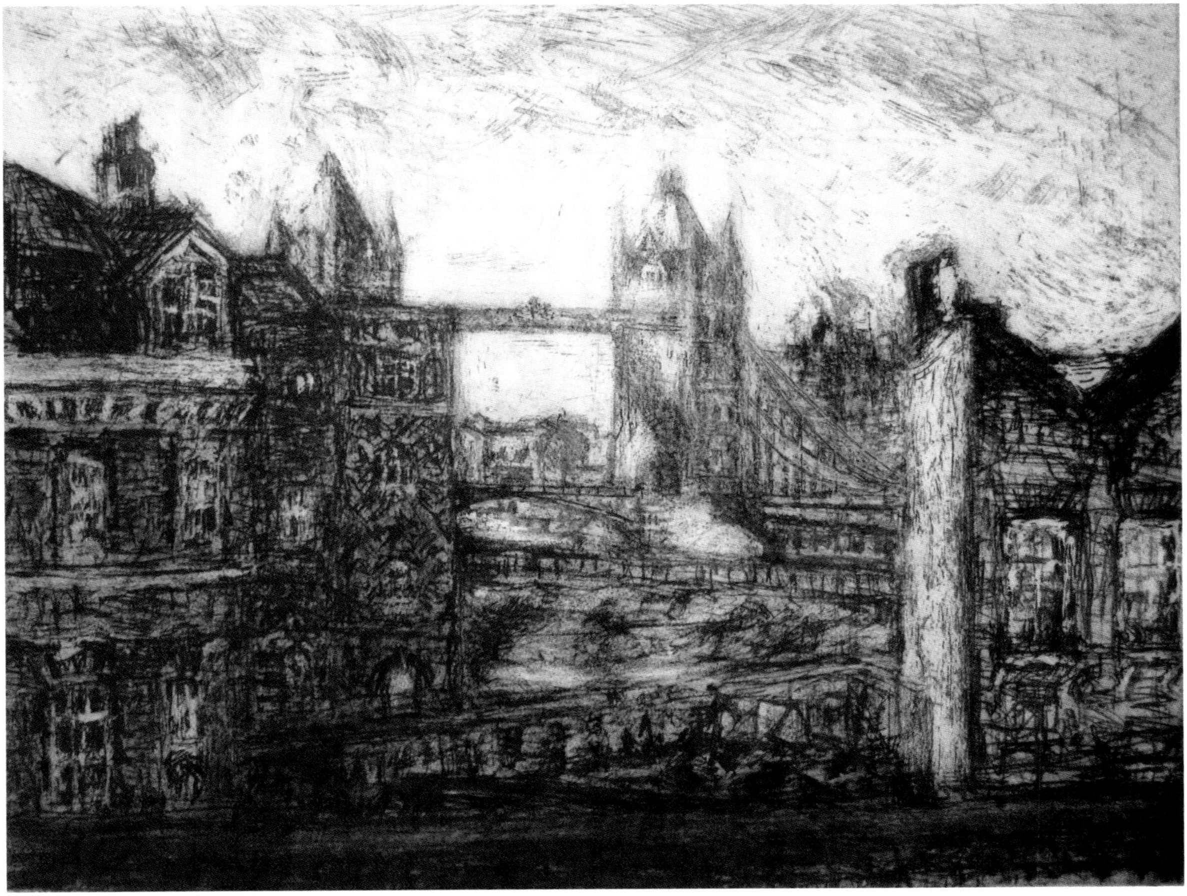

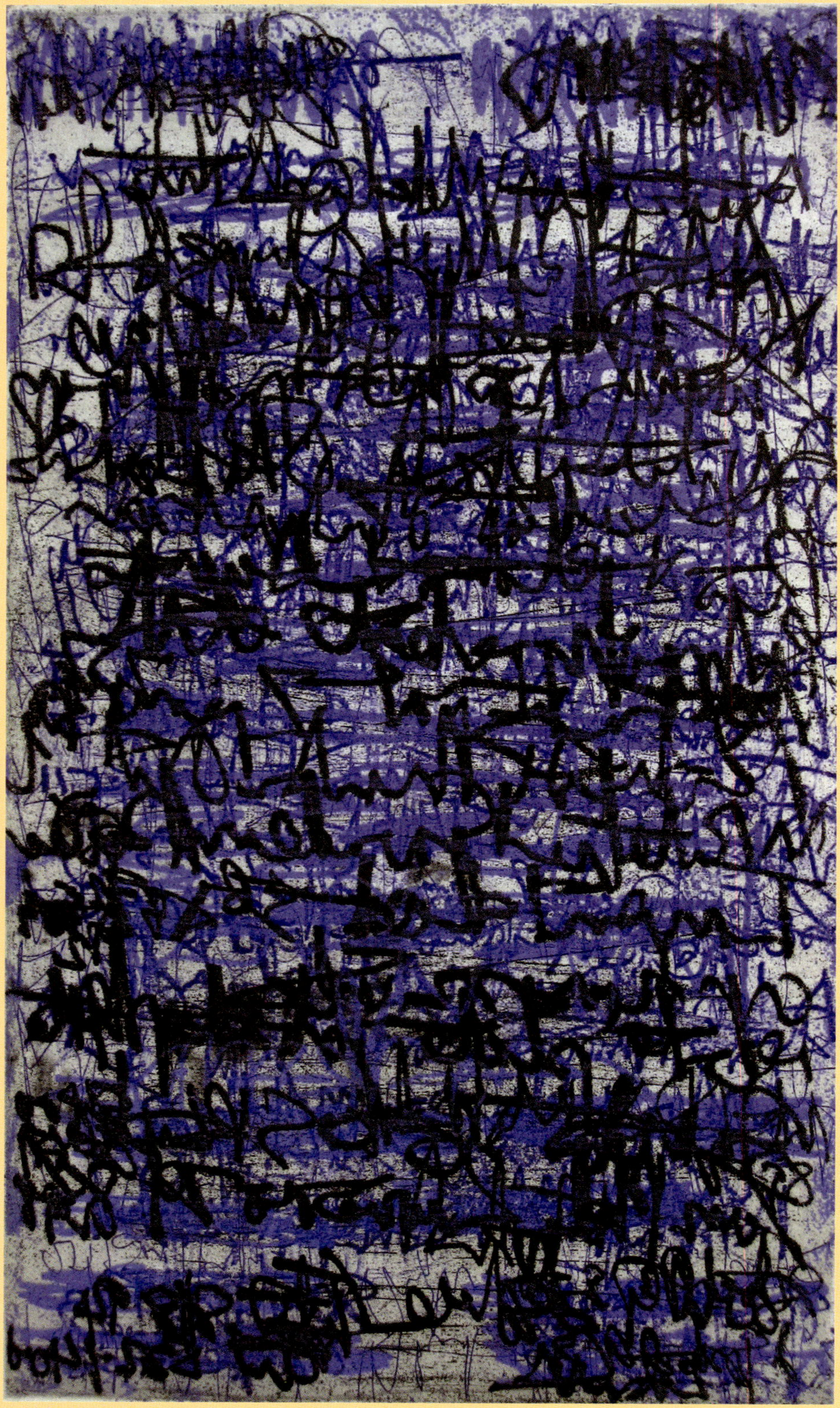

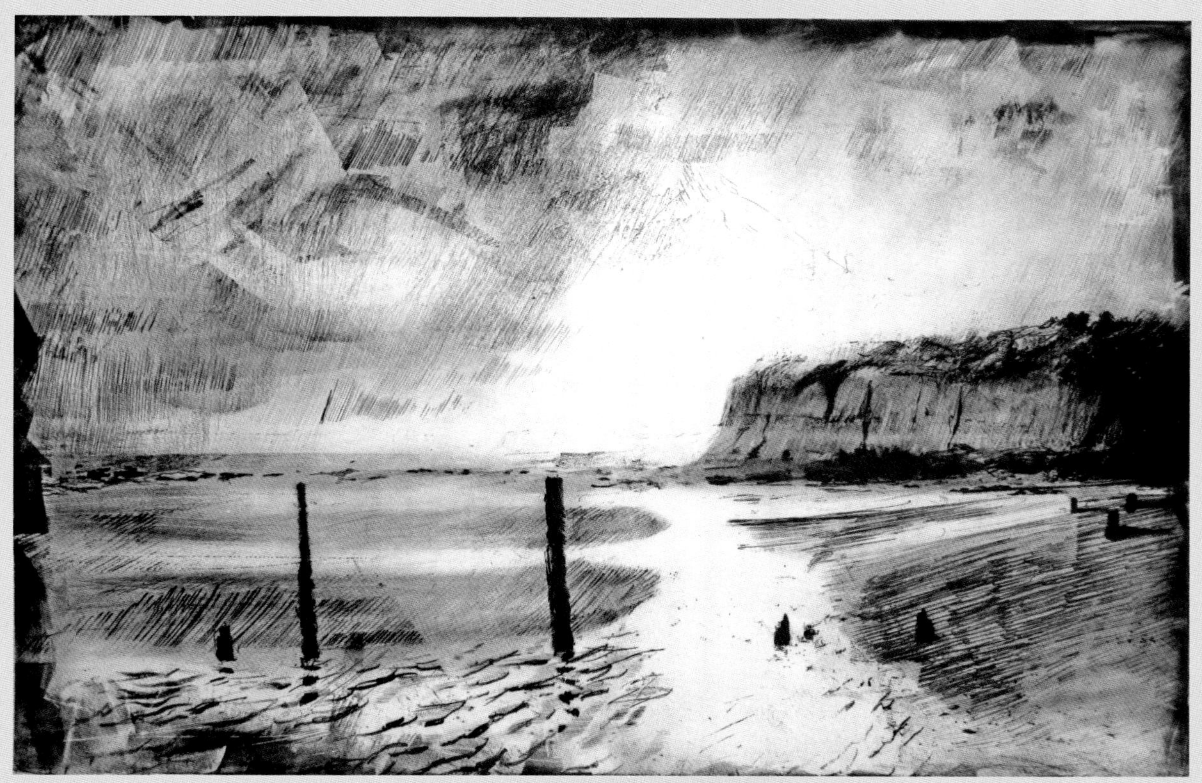

▲ Stephen Robson, *Pett Level II*, 2011. Soft ground etching, 90 x 60 cm (35½ x 23½ in.).

▶ Stephen Robson pulling *Pett Level II*, 2011.

◀ Colin Gale, *Untitled*, 1999. Soft ground etching printed from 3 plates, 15 x 25 cm (6 x 9¾ in.).

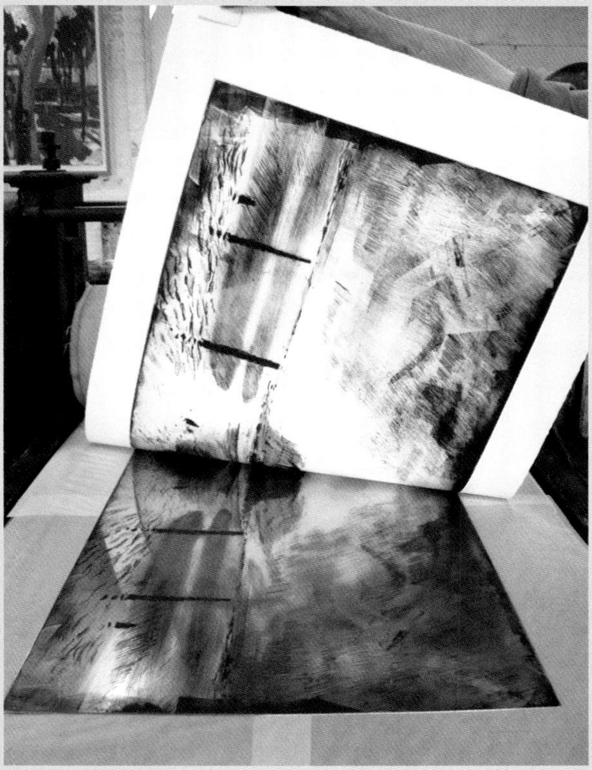

sugar lift aquatint

Sugar lift is an aquatint technique which enables the artist to create positive marks of a gestural and calligraphic nature. It is useful because the marks that you paint are the marks that will actually print as a black (or tone). Artists who favour this methoc often develop their own sugar lift recipes, often choosing to jealously guard their secret!

The technique is a relatively simple one. The sugar mixture must be viscous enough to be painted accurately onto a plate. It should be able to dissolve easily in water and ideally should be tinted with a colour (so that it can be seen on the plate surface). There are three methods of sugar lift: the first is the traditional sugar lift recipe; the second and the third involve using one of two ready-mixed products – photo opaque and Camp Coffee.

For all sugar lift techniques, *you must* degrease the plate. This process works equally well on copper, steel, zinc and aluminium. First, and before any of these sugar lifts can be used, an aquatint is laid on the plate. This gives a good grainy key for the sugar lift mixture as well and also provides the texture necessary for the acid biting that follows.

◀ **Fusing aquatint resin onto a zinc plate.**

▼ **Granulated white sugar being added to warm water.**

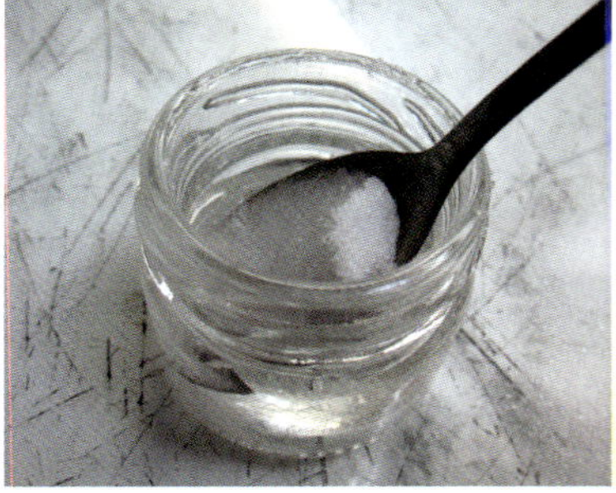

TRADITIONAL SUGAR LIFT RECIPE

This traditional sugar lift recipe makes a sugar-saturated solution that is coloured with water-soluble black ink. To make the mixture, quarter-fill a small jar with warm water. Start to spoon in measures of white granulated sugar. Stir the mixture thoroughly, dissolving each spoonful of the sugar. Add more sugar until no more sugar can be dissolved. The mixture is now saturated.

Next, add a few drops of water-soluble black drawing ink and stir. The ink is added purely as a visual aid for painting the mixture onto the plate surface.

PHOTO OPAQUE METHOD

Photo opaque is a water-based, plum-coloured liquid, used commercially for spotting out pin holes or scratches in the solid black areas of photographic positive films. It is available in small quantities from graphic and printmaking suppliers. Photo opaque is ready to use straight from its container, although the mixture may need to be thinned slightly. To do this, simply stir in a small amount of tap water.

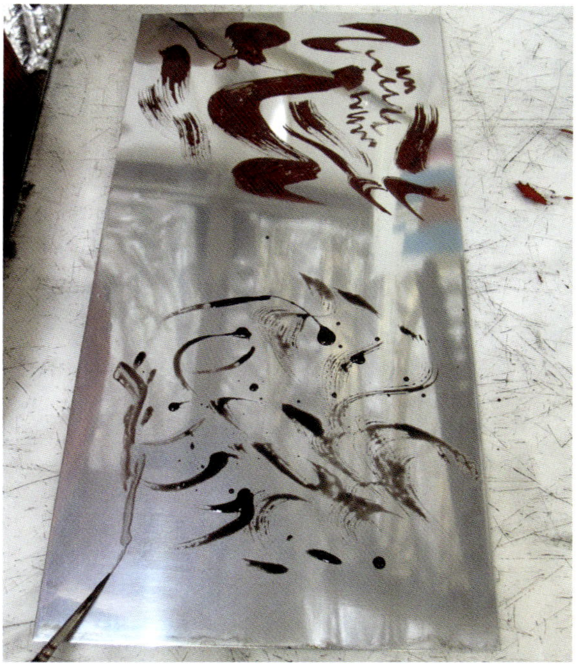

▲ A zinc plate with sugar lift brush marks. The top half of the plate is treated with photo opaque and the bottom half of the plate treated with the traditional sugar and ink recipe. Allow the sugar lift marks on the plate to dry. (The sugar mixture will take considerably longer to dry than the photo opaque.)

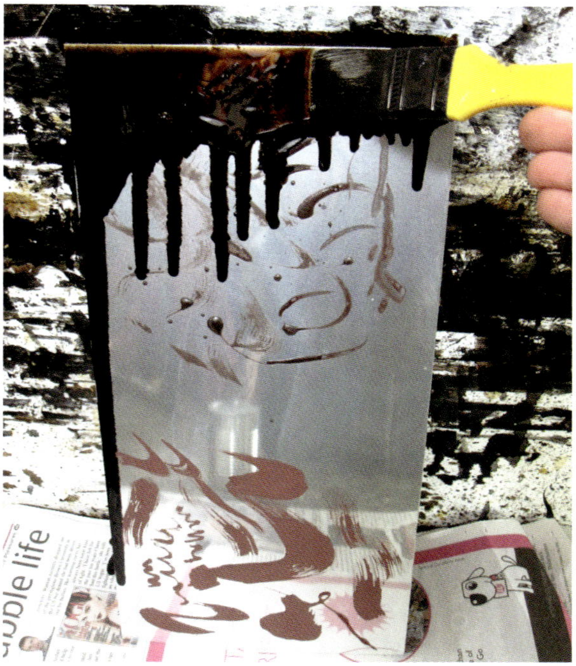

▲ Stand the plate against a wall. Flood a thinned mixture of stop-out varnish and white spirit (thinned 50:50 with white spirit) over the whole plate, starting at the top and using a soft brush to move it across the plate. Allow the stop-out mixture to dry.

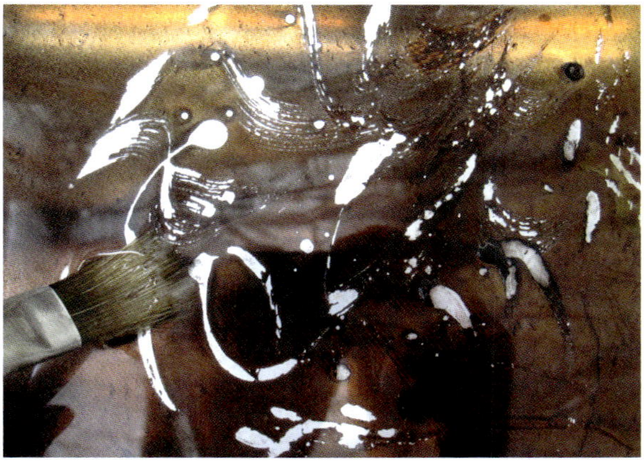

▶ To lift the painted-on stop-out mixture, place the plate onto a tray containing hot (but not boiling) water. Leave the plate to soak for several minutes before lightly teasing the painted areas using a clean brush or cotton cloth. The water will gradually dissolve the sugar or opaque solution, lifting the stop-out. Note that if you have not degreased the plate, this is the point where you will find out why it is necessary. All of the time spent applying the sugar lift will be sadly wasted as all will lift away completely from the plate surface.

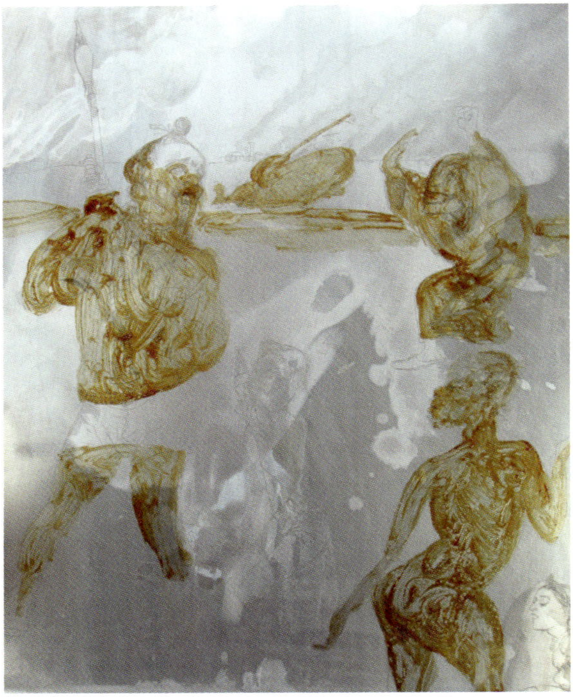

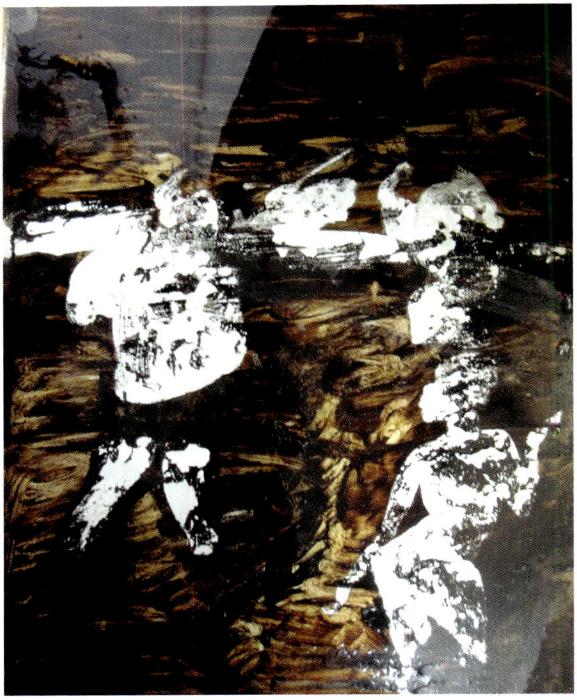

▲ LEFT TO RIGHT: **Zinc plate with painted-on Camp Coffee by Marcelle Hanselaar.**

The sugar lift marks on the plate being 'lifted' in warm water.

Camp Coffee

Camp Coffee (bottled coffee syrup) is a coffee and chicory essence which has had sugar added to it in its manufacturing stage. It can be used straight from the bottle and creates a smooth, slightly gritty texture when it is painted on the plate. It takes longer to dry than photo opaque but less time to dry than a traditional sugar lift mixture. It is a legitimate food product and makes a unique cup of coffee which can be made while you wait for the mixture to dry on the plate!

LITHO CRAYON LIFT TECHNIQUE

Using the litho crayon lift technique adds useful textural marks to the plate's surface as the marks are drawn rather than painted. Standard lithographic crayons are used. (See Chapter 6.)

This technique works along similar principles to sugar lift techniques *except* that solvent is used to lift the oil-based drawn work.

The plate is degreased and an aquatint ground is laid on the plate. Draw directly onto the aquatint ground with the crayon. Straw hat varnish diluted with methylated spirit (a 50:50 ratio is good) is used to coat the plate.

When the straw hat varnish is dry, the crayon work is lifted by pouring on white spirit (lithoine or paraffin). Leave the solvent to sit on the plate for a few minutes before gently rubbing with a soft cotton cloth moistened with more solvent. The solvent dissolves the lithographic crayon marks. The plate is now ready for etching.

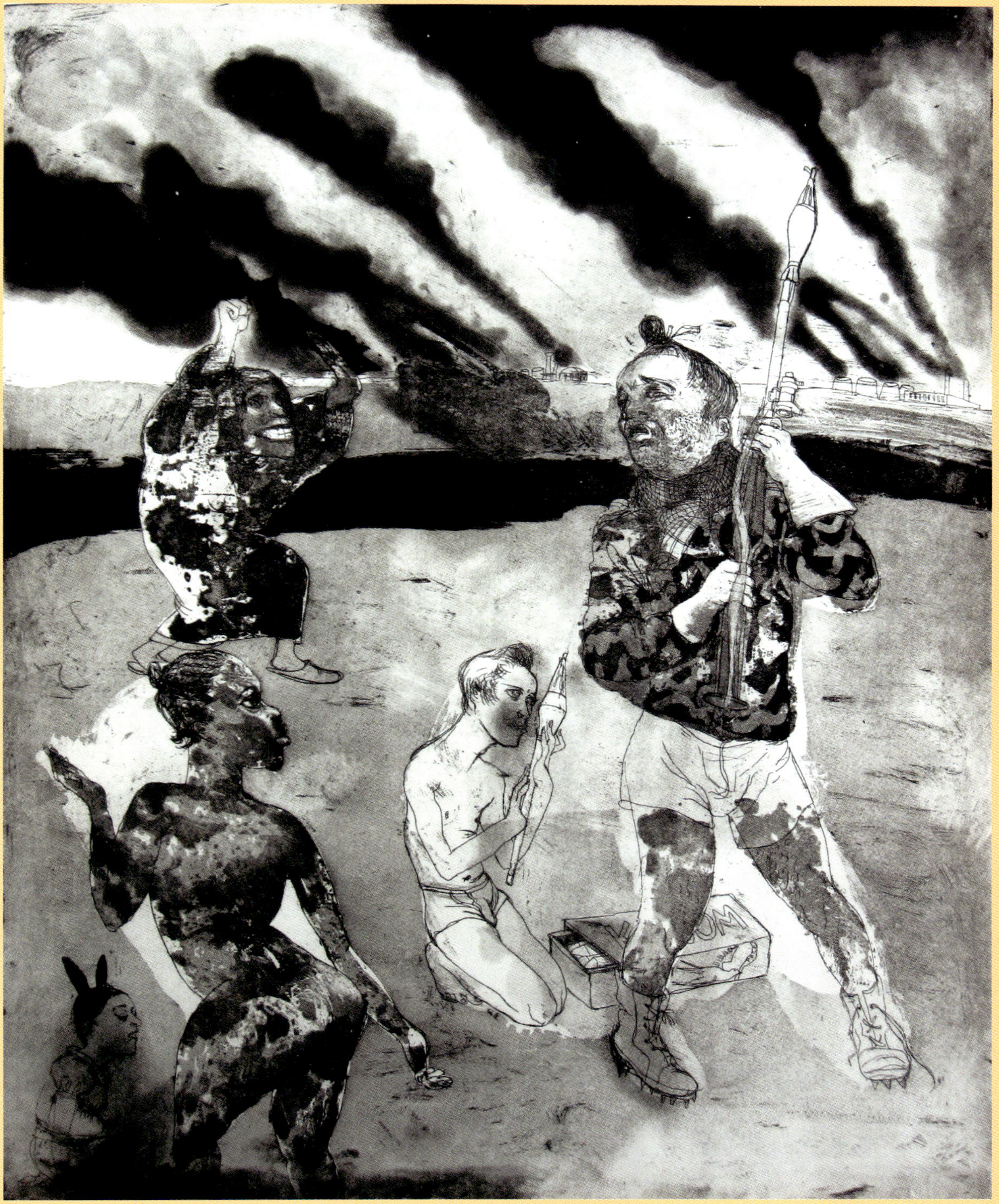

▲ Marcelle Hanselaar etching and aquatint (state 2) using Camp Coffee.

spit bite

Spit bite is an aquatint technique whereby the mordant is painted directly onto the plate surface. It produces wonderful smokey tones that have wash-like characteristics. The technique is called 'spit bite' as artists used to spit on the plate and add the mordant to it to control its spread. Acid may be painted on directly or applied through a surface tension breaker for more control, such as liquid gum arabic or washing-up liquid (which do the job of the spit).

First, a fine aquatint resin or spray must be applied to the plate. The appropriate mordant for the metal used is mixed in small glass containers. Artists like to mix two or three different strengths of mordant and use brushes of varying sizes to apply it.

If you are attempting spit bite for the first time, we recommend you make a test plate to get a feel for the technique. Painted-on acid is quickly exhausted, so multiple applications are needed to build up the tones. Very subtle areas can be created by wetting the plate first: this disperses and weakens the acid as it is applied.

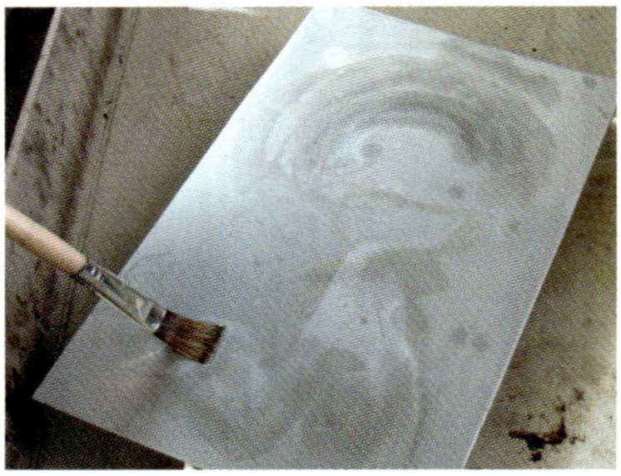

▲ Nitric acid painted on to zinc. Two mixtures were used: a 10:1 for the lighter areas and a 4:1 for the darker ones. If nitric is used, this technique must be practised in a fume cupboard. As with all mordants, always wear personal safety protection: goggles, gloves and an apron.

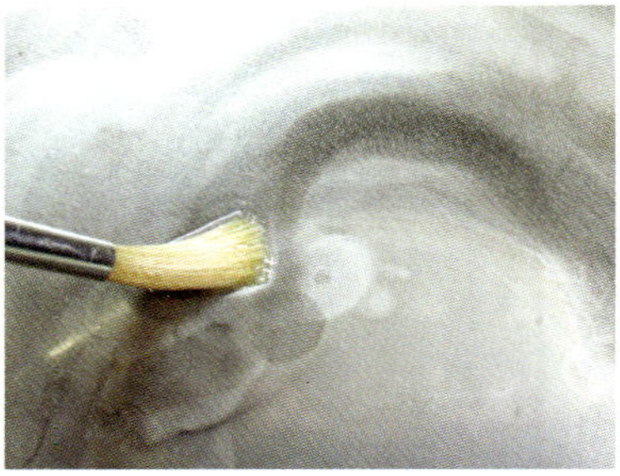

▲ A strong acid mixture is applied with a smaller brush for the darker tones.

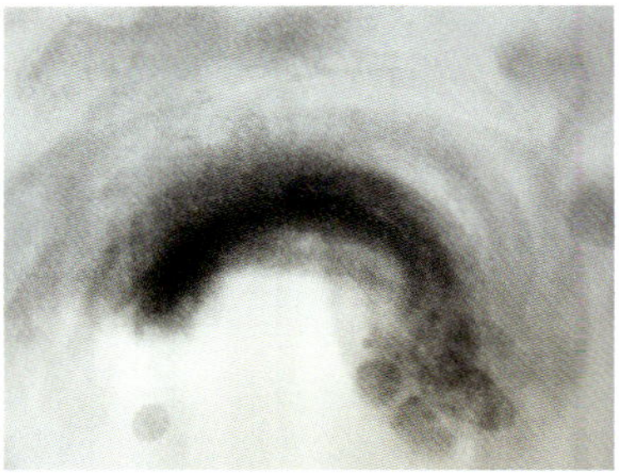

▲ A detail of the print taken from the zinc test plate.

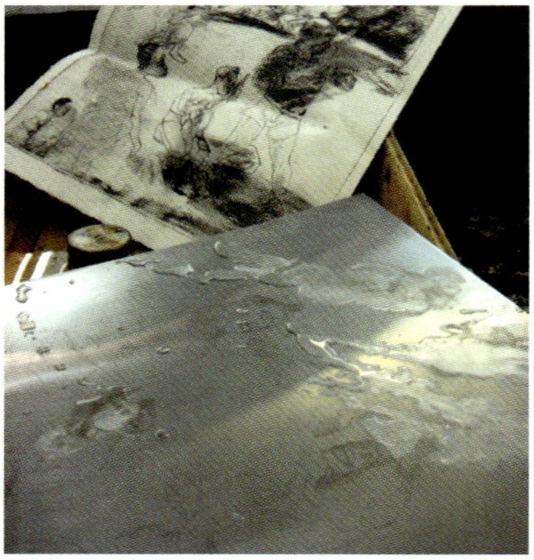

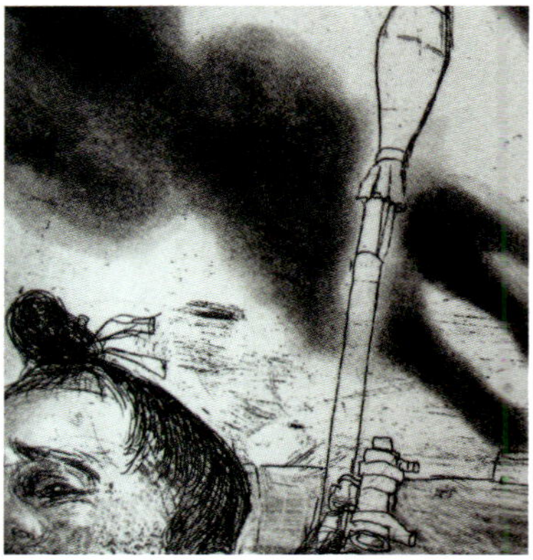

▲ A detail (left) showing spit bite on a plate with a proof in the background and a detail (right) of the resulting print. Marcelle Hanselaar, 2011.

▶ Marcelle Hanselaar, *Loss of Innocence, War*, 2011. Etching and aquatint on zinc edition of 30, 40 x 50 cm (15¾ x 19½ in.). The brooding sky and background were applied using spit bite.

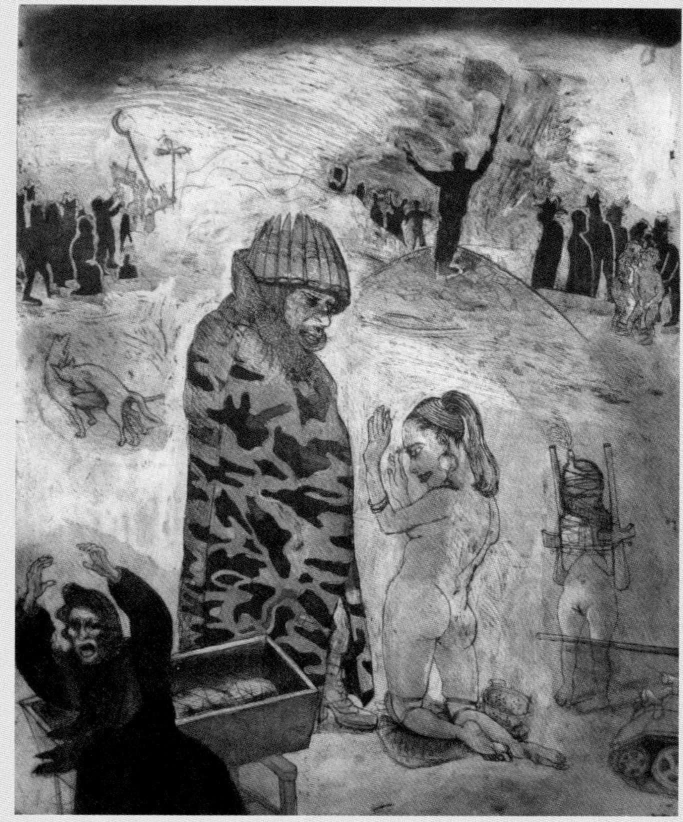

▼ Melvyn Petterson, *Rain near Castleneau*, 2007. Etching and aquatint on zinc using spit bite, 21 x 13 cm (8¼ x 5 in.).

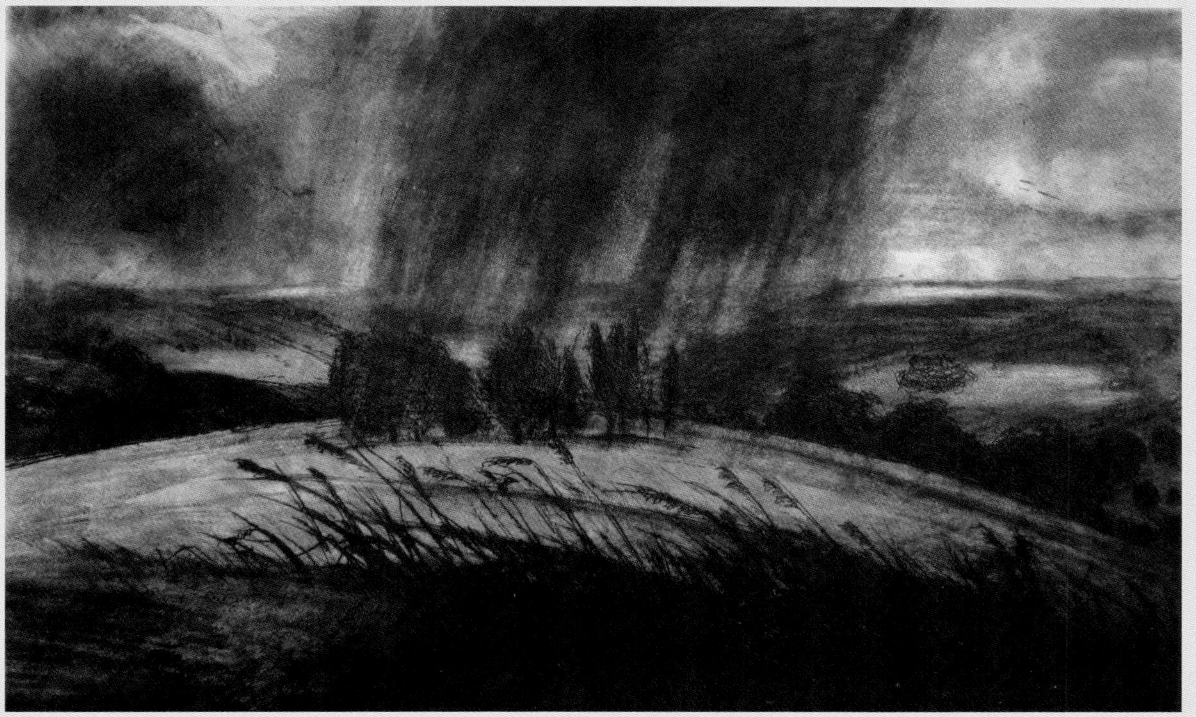

photo etching and photo polymer intaglio

These two processes allow marks and images from an art work positive to be transferred onto a plate by exposure to ultraviolet light. An exposure unit (also called a 'print down frame') is used. Most colleges and workshops will have one of these and they are designed primarily for exposing photo screens, but can be used for photo etching and photo lithography too. The exposure unit is a straightforward piece of machinery: a box with a glass top containing a mercury vapour or metal halide lamp that emits ultra violet light. The UV light is used to harden light-sensitive emulsion on a plate or screen when exposed with artwork called a positive.

The positive may be a computer-generated print-out, made by a photocopier or hand-drawn on to transparent Mylar® or acetate.

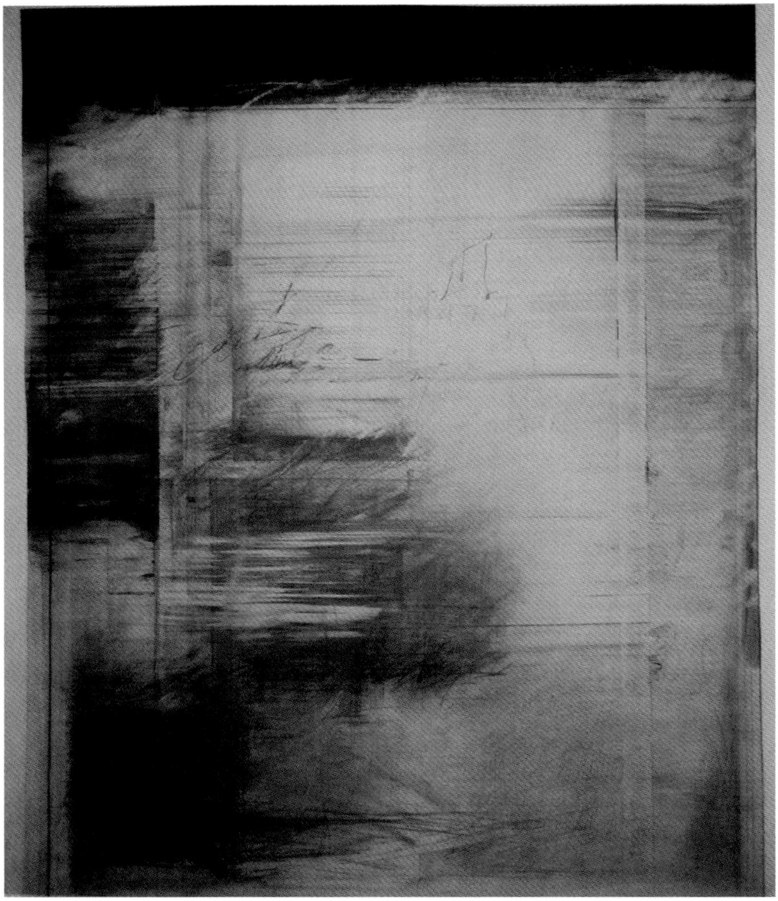

◀ **Megan Fishpool, *Muse*, 2009. Photopolymer intaglio, 74 x 90 cm (29¼ x 35½ in.).**

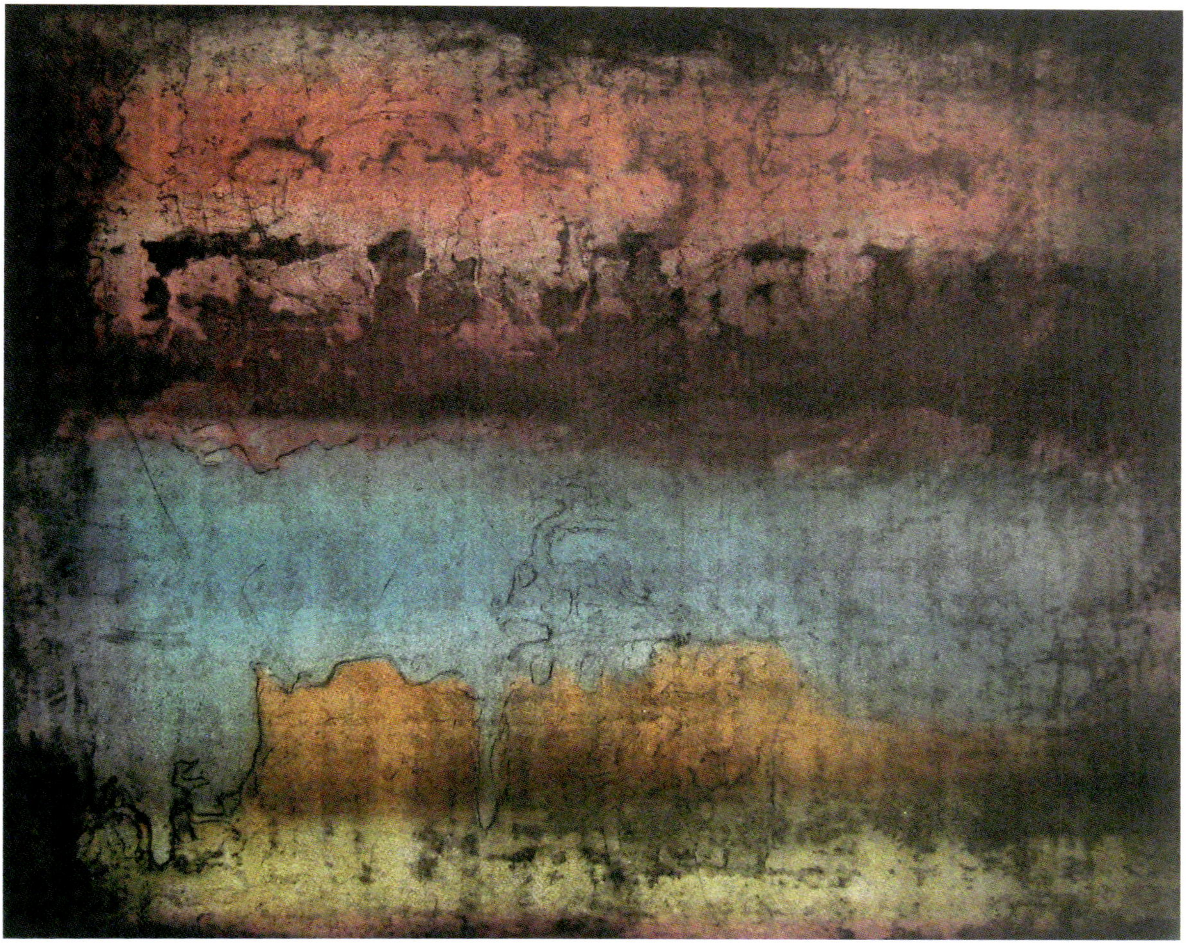

▲ Colin Gale, *Untitled Red and Green*, 2009. Photoetching, 72 x 60 cm (28¼ x 23½ in.).

When an image is transferred onto the plate using an emulsion that has been applied/rolled on by hand and then etched in a mordant, this process is called photo etching. If a photopolymer plate (also referred to as a solar plate or flexography/flexo plate) is used, the resulting image is not called an etching as no mordant is involved. They are instead referred to as intaglio prints (intaglio type, intaglio gravure or polymer gravure). As artists, we use both of these processes depending on the nature of the marks we wish to produce.

In general, photopolymer plates suit images such as photographs and drawings with fine marks that require a high definition result. This process mirrors photo gravure, a technique invented in the 19th century and no longer practised widely: it is extremely time-consuming, requires a dark room and uses harmful chemicals such as ammonium dichromate. By contrast, photopolymer intaglio plates come ready-coated, are quick to process and use only water to process them.

The roll-on emulsion used for photo etching is basically a stencil process and produces a cruder result in terms of mark definition than solar plates. This is due to the simplicity of the emulsion stencil (black and white areas, i.e. minimal tones) and the action of the acid. This method of photo etching is used when the artist prefers the results and marks from a plate that has been physically etched.

ARTWORK POSITIVES

The following types of positive can be used across all photo-based printmaking media including photo etching, screen printing and photo lithography. The key factor in all positive making is that the marks are opaque to light (they are dark enough to stop light penetrating through). When drawing, use black opaque materials. When using a computer or photocopier, increase the contrast and when printing out, select the 'quality' setting. Both will increase the opacity or 'darkness' of the positive.

Hand-drawn marks

▶ **These marks have been made on transparent, grained Mylar® plastic sheet such as True Grain. Materials include: (from left to right) dark pencil, drawing ink, pastel, litho crayon, black ink and acrylic paint.**

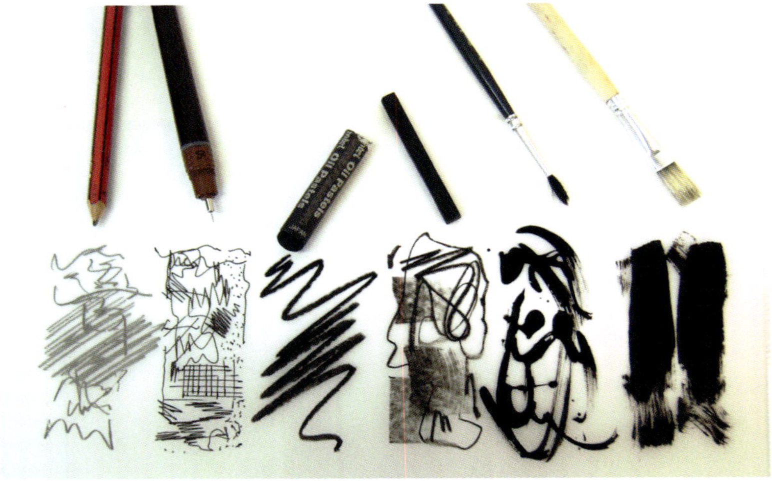

Photocopies

▶ **Photocopies on acetates. Specialist bureaux can output these to A0 size from images on a CD or memory stick. They are a very cost-effective option.**

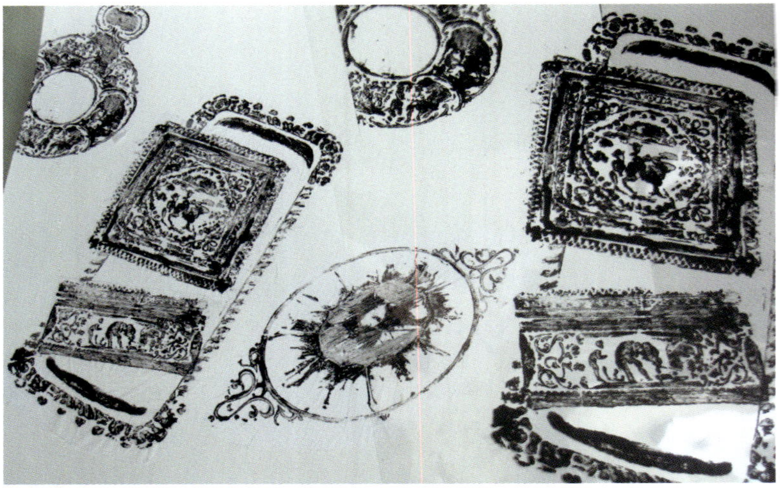

The quality of printed black is usually good on paper. However, exposure times must be increased so that the exposure light penetrates the copier paper. This technique is used extensively for photo screen printing. Copier paper is not recommended for flexo plates as they may pick up the copier paper grain – the plates are extremely sensitive to the most subtle of marks.

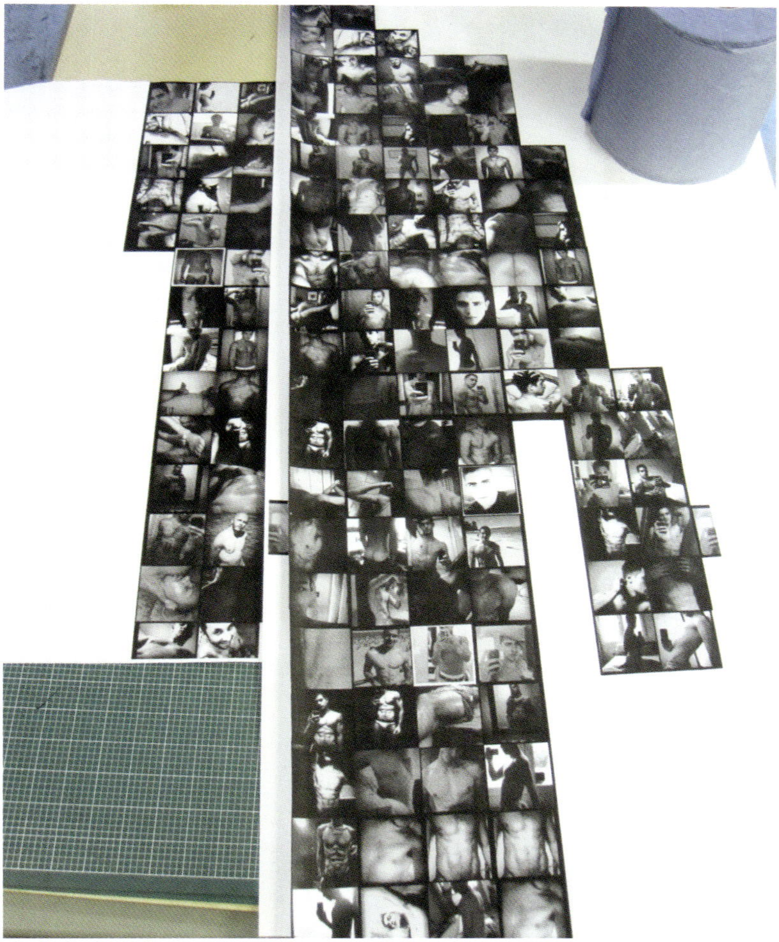

◀ Photocopies on paper. Large paper positive by Tony Broad on 80gsm paper for screen printing.

▼ One trick is to oil the photocopy all over using vegetable oil to make it semi-transparent.

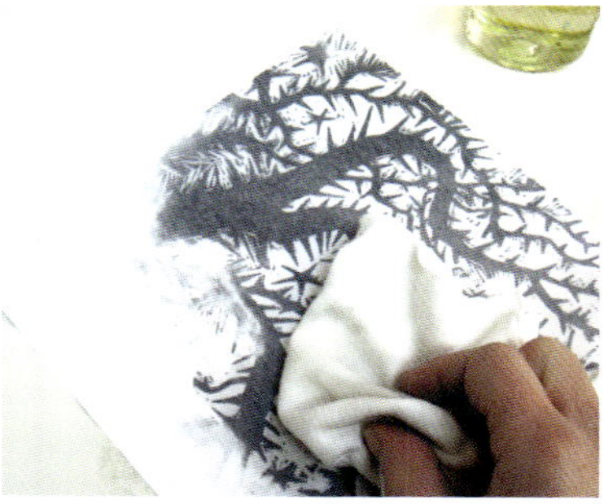

Photocopy on tracing paper

▶ A semi-transparent media. As with paper copies, more exposure time must be given. Tracing paper is easily available from stationers in A4 pads and can be put through an inkjet printer or a photocopier.

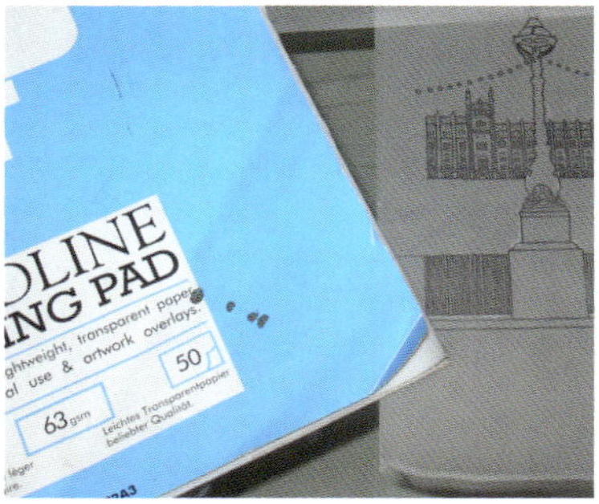

Computer-generated

▶ Transparent film can be purchased for inkjet printers. The type that has a grain on one side works well. Use a graphics bureau for larger outputs. Image by Giulia Zaniol.

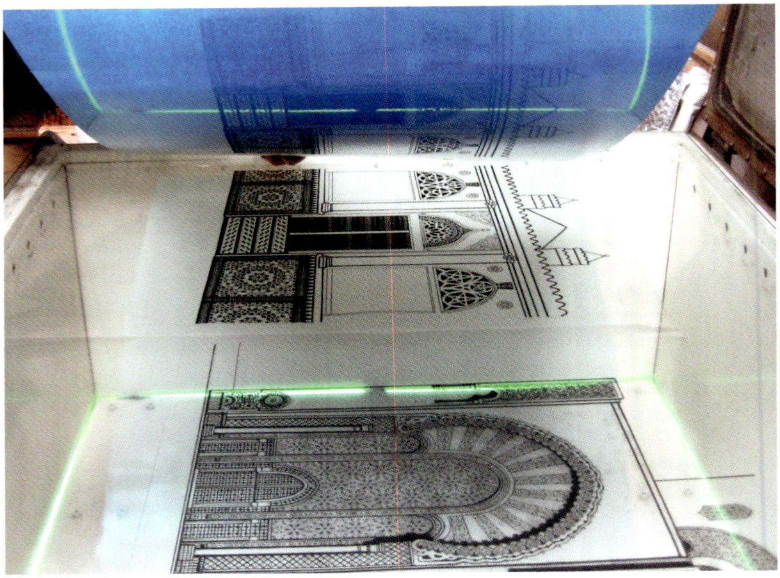

Image setters

Graphics bureaux have image-setting machines. These use high-quality laser-printed 'wet processed' films. This is the most expensive of all the options for positives, but will give results of the best quality. The machines are capable of printing very fine halftones for use with flexo plates.

▼ Colin Gale, *Tommy* (left) and *Fritz*, (right) 2009. Intaglio gravure detail, made using 200dpi halftones output from an image setter, 20 x 32 cm (7¾ x 12½ in.).

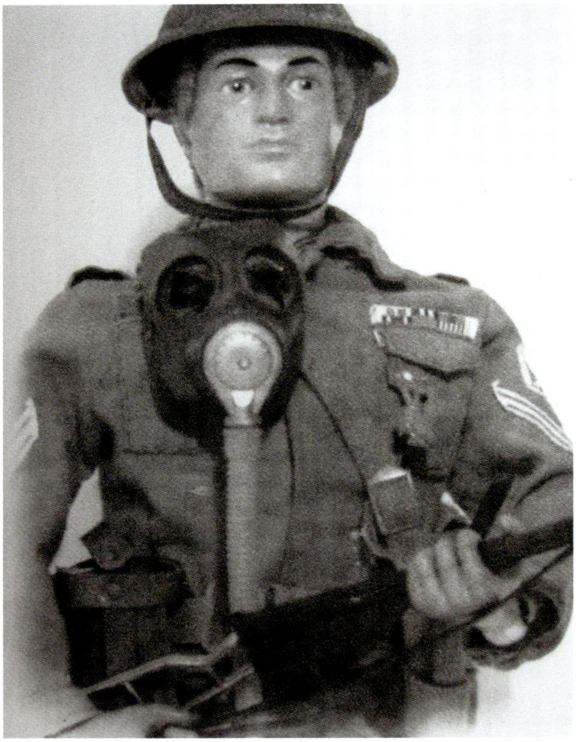

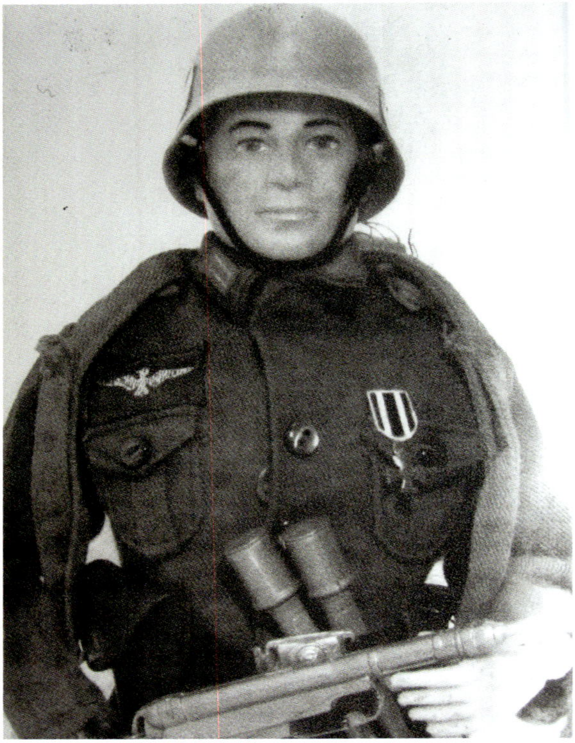

Photo etching using roll-on emulsion

These acrylate resin emulsions are designed for the copper circuit board industry. They can be applied to any of the usual metal surfaces used by printmakers. Although they are light-sensitive, a dark room is not needed but it is wise to avoid direct sunlight and to replace the lid on the container immediately after use. The product used is called Photoimageable Blue Etch Resist.

Method

As you would when applying any ground to a plate, you must first degrease the plate well.

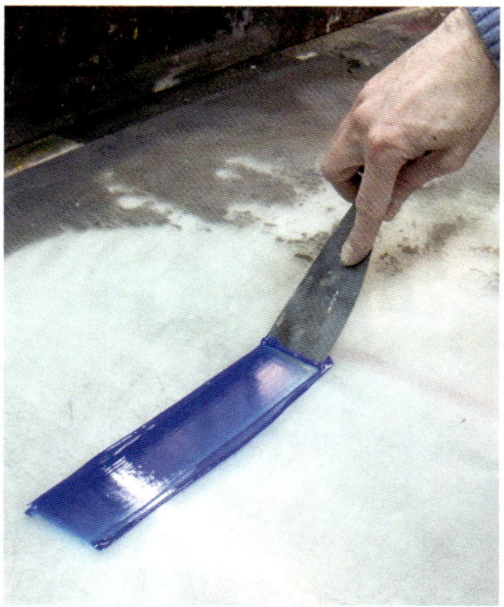

▲ Take the emulsion from the container using a metal palette knife and spread it thinly onto glass.

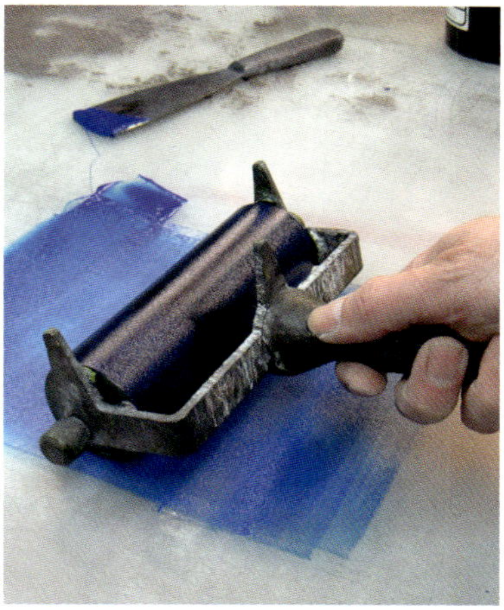

▲ Roll the emulsion into a thin, even slab using a good-quality hard roller. The consistency of emulsion should be similar to that of printing ink when inking a lino or relief print.

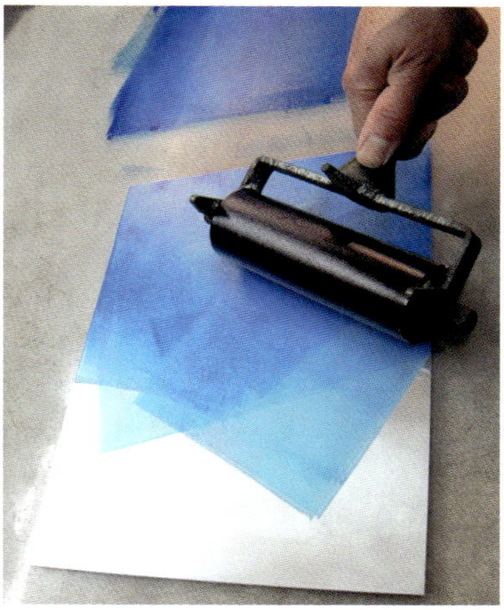

▲ Using good hand pressure, coat the degreased plate evenly.

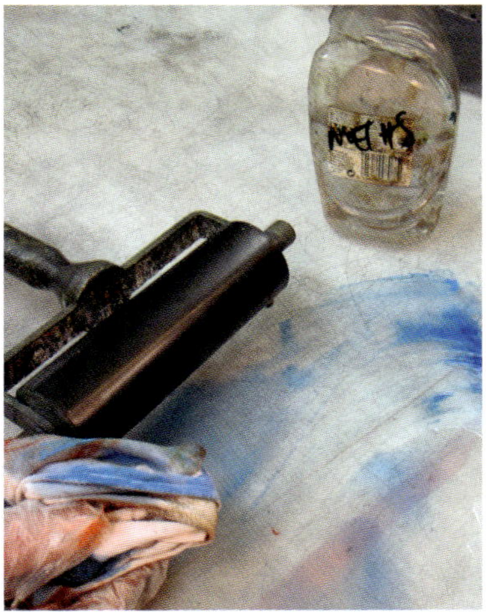

◀ Clean the roller and glass with methylated spirits.

▶ Place the plate on a tabletop with the emulsion side facing away from you and heat the back with a hairdryer. (This reduces the drying time considerably.) Cover the plate with a board to prevent any light coming into contact with it and then leave to dry thoroughly overnight.

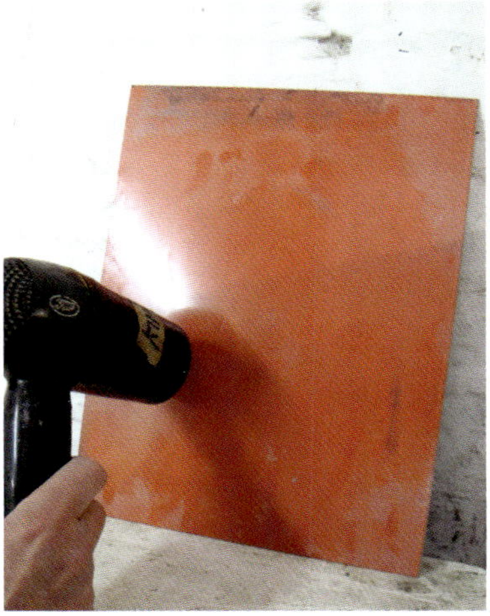

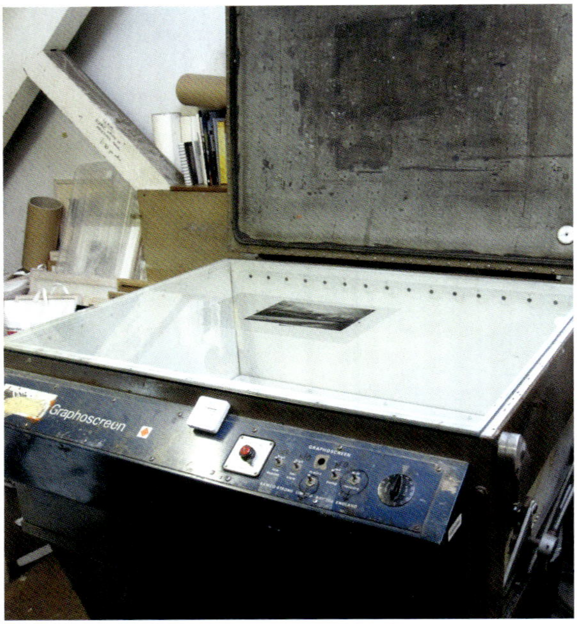

▲ When the plate is dry, expose it and the artwork positive in an exposure unit. Place the positive on the glass. The image should be as you want it to print in the final result (remember the image will be reversed on the plate). Place the plate emulsion side down on the positive. Expose the plate (exposure times will vary with different units so no guide can be given here). The emulsion has a very wide exposure latitude so times do not have to be as accurate as they are with photopolymer or flexo plates. It is always wise to make a test strip using an offcut of metal coated at the same time as the main plate is coated.

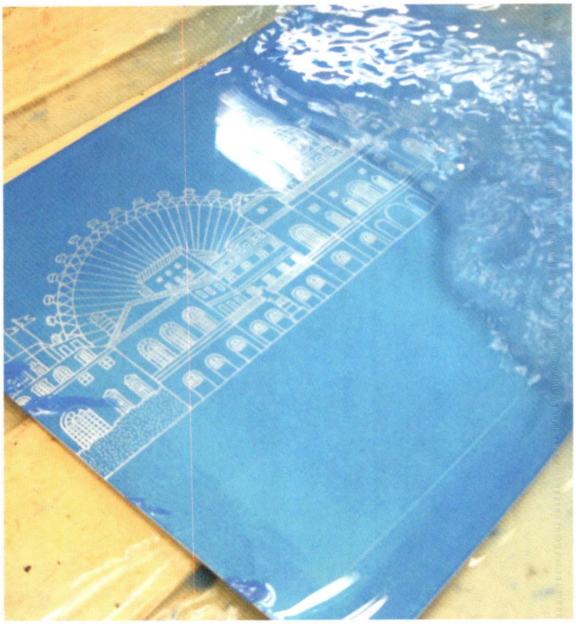

▲ The exposed plate is developed in a tray of water mixed with sodium carbonate (use two heaped teaspoons per litre of water). The image will develop quite quickly. Rub lightly with a soft sponge for a few seconds then agitate the tray until bare metal can be seen in the image areas. Remove the plate from the developing solution, rinse the plate under running water and dry quickly using a hairdyer. Plate image courtesy of Giulia Zaniol.

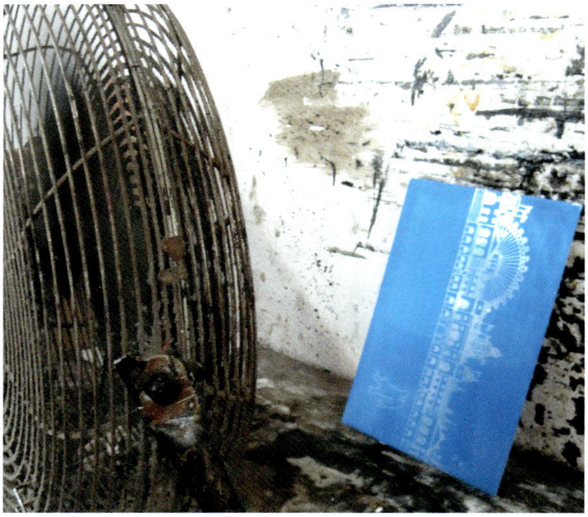

◀ After drying, allow the plate to stand for 20 minutes under a cool fan so that the emulsion hardens fully. The plate is then ready for biting in mordant. Don't forget to stop out the back of the plate! If the plate has lines or areas wider than 2 mm, it will need to be covered in aquatint resin or aquatint resist spray (see pp.102–9) before biting.

▶ Printing a photo etching on zinc by Jo DePear. The positive used was a photocopy acetate. A clean background was needed for this image, so the blue emulsion was stripped from the plate before printing. The emulsion on the plate was then removed by using liquid household paint stripper.

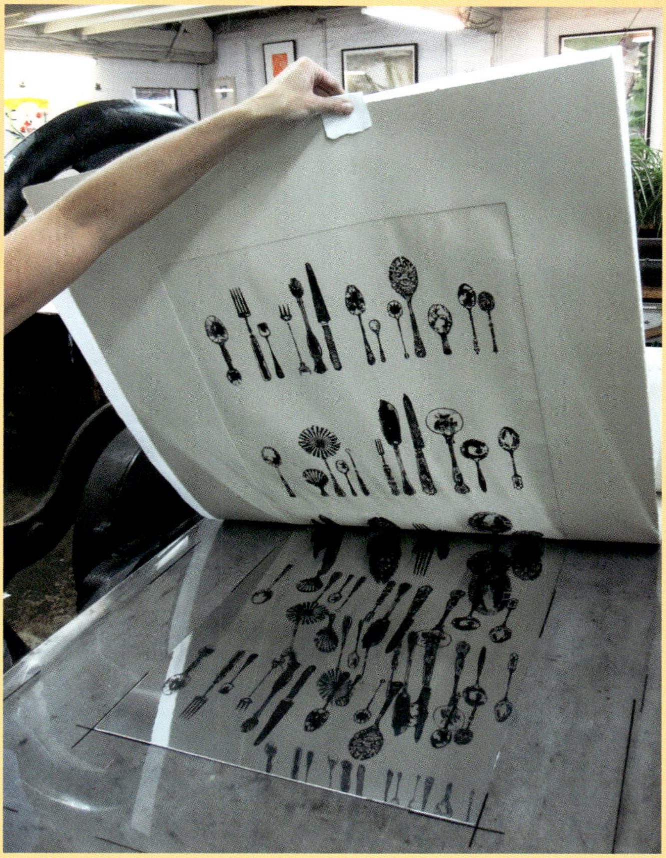

▼ Colin Gale, *Untitled*, 2003. Red and black photoetching printed from two plates, 120 x 60 cm (47¼ x 23½ in.).

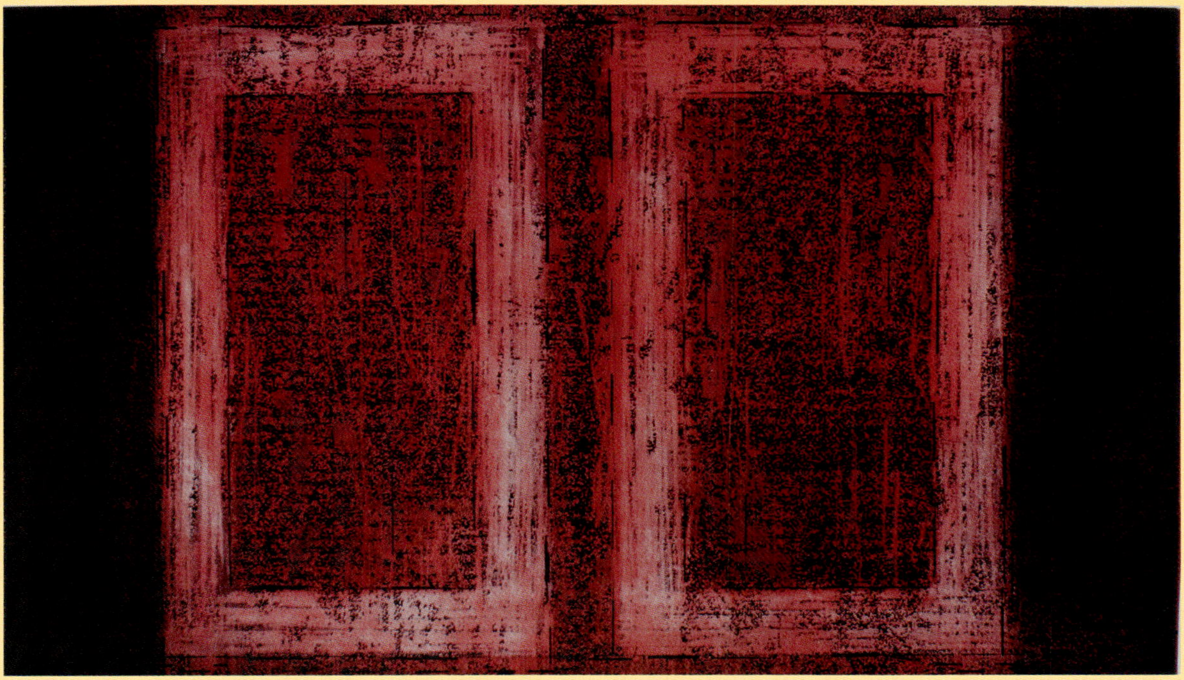

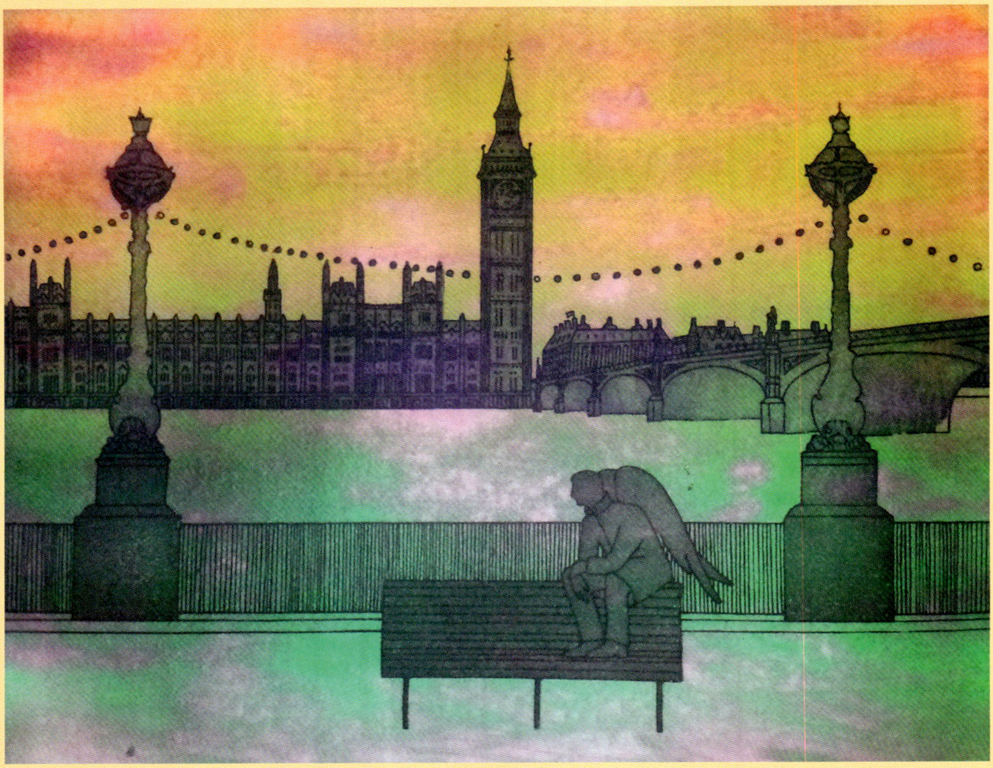

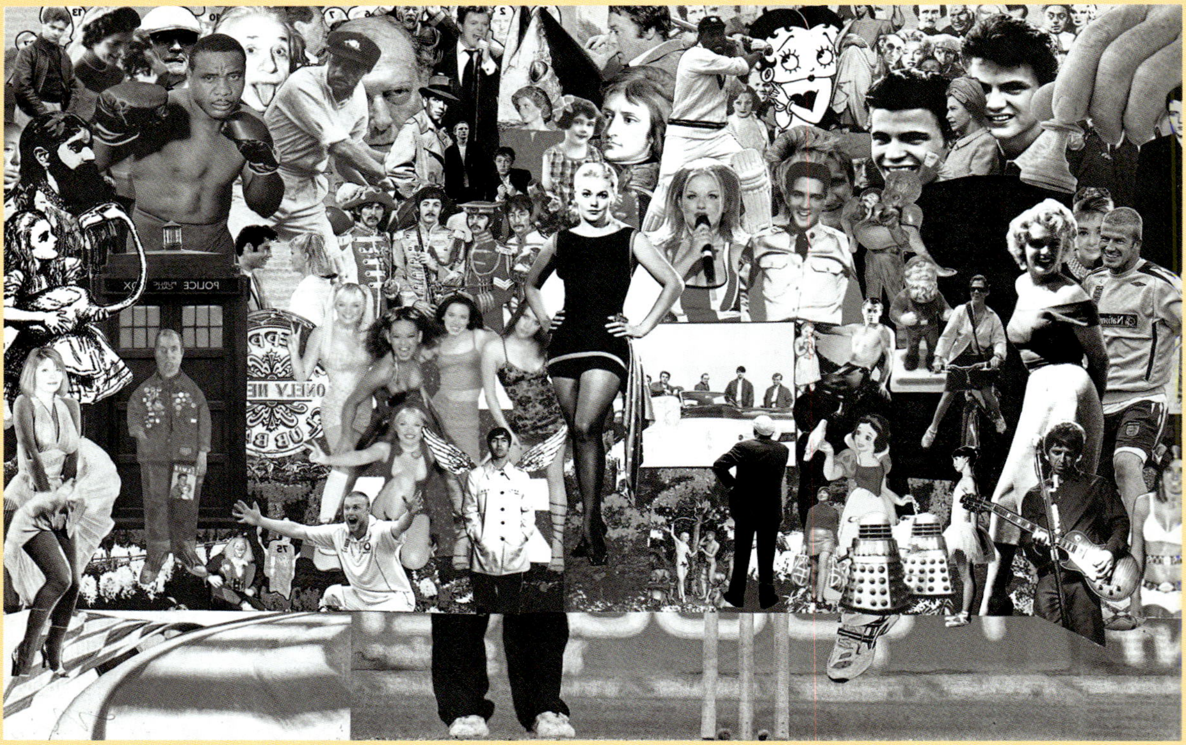

◀ TOP: Giulia Zaniol, *Royal Palace of Whitehall*, 2012. Photoetching and aquatint printed using two plates, 30 x 21 cm (11¾ x 8¼ in.).

◀ BOTTOM: Megan Fishpool, *Happy Birthday Peter Blake*, 2008. Photo intaglio, 56 x 76 cm (11¾ x 7¾ in.).

▶ Printing *Emirates* photoetching on zinc printed in black. Note it is not always necessary to strip the emulsion from the plate for printing.

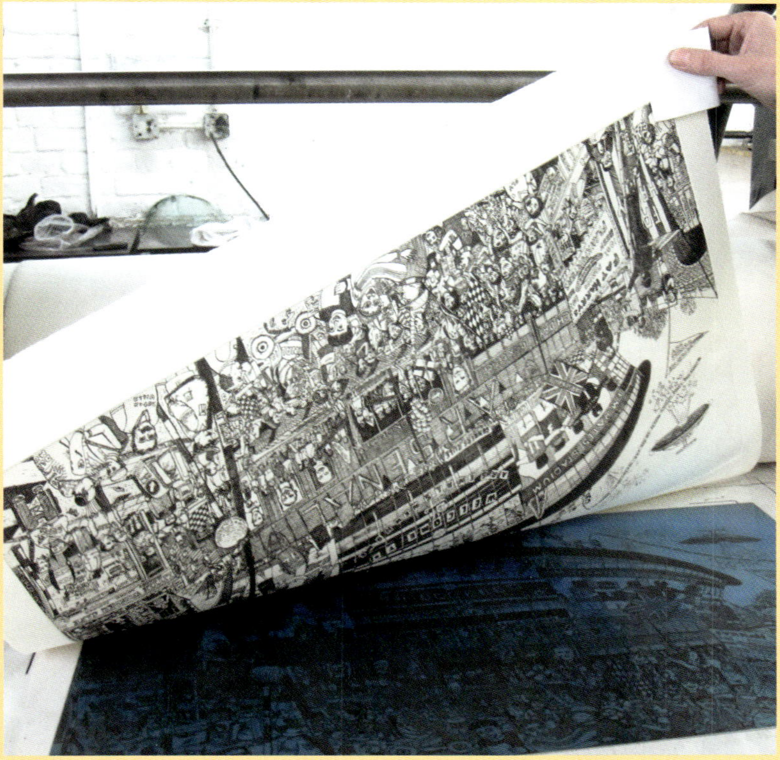

▼ Mick Davies, *The First Game at The Emirates*, 2009. Hand-coloured photoetching, 56 x 76 cm (22 x 30 in.).

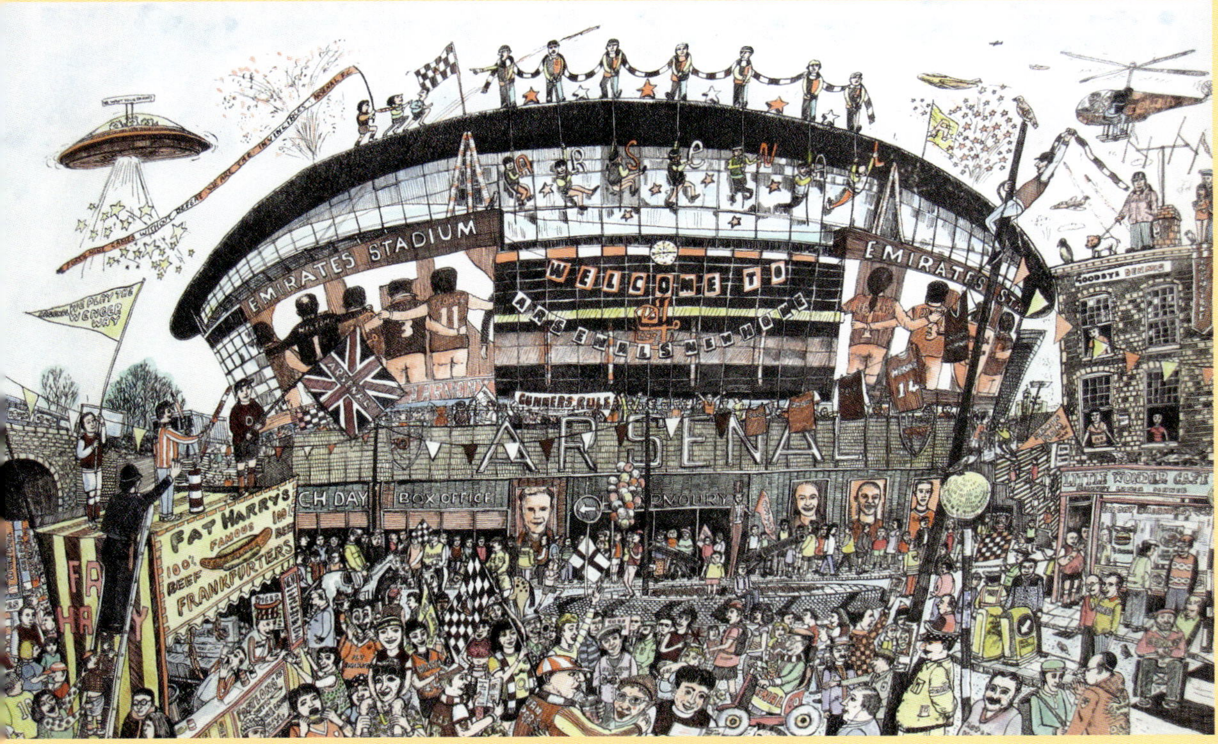

flexograph/solar plate

Flexograph plates are commercial products used in the printing of packages and packaging. These plates are of particular use to printmakers due to the wide range of marks – both hand-drawn and photographic – that may be utilised. One advantage of using them is that the surface of the plates requires no chemicals to process it: tap water only is needed! The plates may be used for relief printing or, more commonly, for intaglio printing. They are capable of holding very subtle detail which is usually rarely obtainable from traditional etching techniques.

Printmakers commonly refer to the plates as 'solar plates'. Weather permitting they can be exposed using sunlight. However, this can be unreliable and so the use of a UV exposure unit is required and recommended. Note that once they have been exposed incorrectly, the plates cannot be used again.

The plates consist of a steel backing with a light-sensitive photopolymer emulsion coating. Printmaking suppliers sell the plates in standard sizes from A4 up to 103 x 128 cm. The plates can be cut easily using a metal guillotine. If a guillotine is not available, they may be cut by hand: score the plate repeatedly using a heavy-duty cutting knife (Stanley® knife) guided by a heavy metal straightedge. Although the plates are light-sensitive, they will not be damaged during the time it takes to cut them. It is absolutely essential to avoid direct sunlight, however, so wrap the plates carefully in thick paper until needed.

The plates are commonly supplied in two thicknesses, KM 73 and KM 95 – the figures refer to the plates' gauge, 0.73 mm and 0.95 mm respectively. We recommend you use the heavier gauge for larger works as it will provides more stability in handling (the plates dent and bend very easily). The plates come supplied with a protective plastic coating which is removed prior to exposing.

HALFTONE SCREEN

Making a flexography plate involves a two-stage exposure process. First, the plate is exposed to a halftone screen. This screen consists of an irregular pattern of opaque dots, which simulates the random dot composition of a fine aquatint. Second, the plate is exposed to the transparent media containing the drawn information, which is referred to as the positive, see p.128.

As with traditional etching, the intaglio line (groove) must contain a tooth-like texture in order to hold the printing ink. The halftone screen exposes a dot 'tooth' structure over the entire plate surface. The structure of this texture holds the dark tone information which is to be etched onto the plate's surface. It provides a rich, velvety black coverage. The second exposure, using a positive acetate (the image), creates the highlight areas.

The exposure time for the halftone screen (once ascertained) will be the same for all positives used. (The exposure time is the same whether the image is photographic or hand-drawn.) If you are using a communal studio, it is likely that this time has already been worked out by the studio and the exposure time is confirmed to the user by the technician.

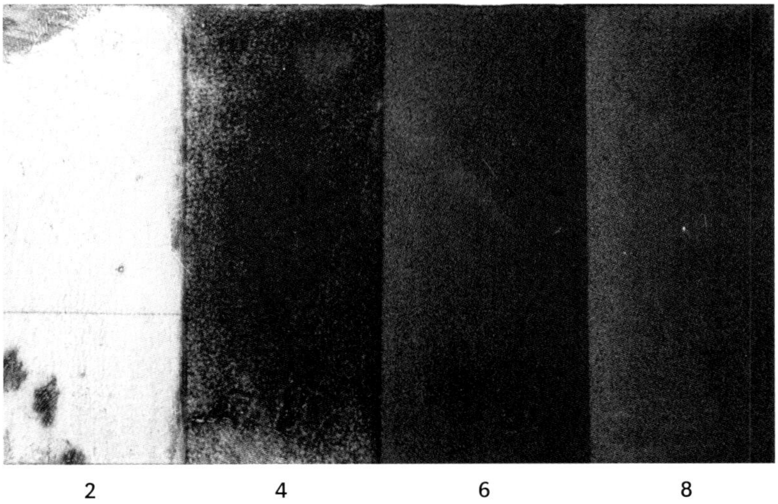

◀ A printed half tone screen test strip. The plate was exposed in two minute bursts. A good even black was achieved at six minutes.

Making an exposure test strip

To make an exposure time test strip, cut a small strip of flexo plate. Remove the plastic coating and place it face-down on the halftone screen. The edge of the strip must be placed off the screen so that it can be taped to the exposure unit glass (this prevents it from moving). Expose the plate in minute intervals or light units. Slide a sheet of thin copier paper under the plate to block out each exposed timed interval along the strip.

As noted above, making a test strip is essential if you are to ensure the correct exposure time for your image. If the image is over-exposed – given too much light time – then detail will be missing in the plate. If it is under exposed – too little light time – the image will print too dark with tone in the non-image (background) areas.

Exposure times vary according to the media holding the drawn or printed information. For example, an image on clear acetate will need a different exposure time to an image on grained drawing acetate. This is because the grain in the acetate will register as a grey texture or light grey tone. Typically, an image on grained acetate will require a longer exposure time than clear acetate.

This drawing of a tortoise by Elizabeth Cope has been made using lithographic crayons onto grained acetate. A craft knife blade has been used to scrape marks and highlights into the crayon work.

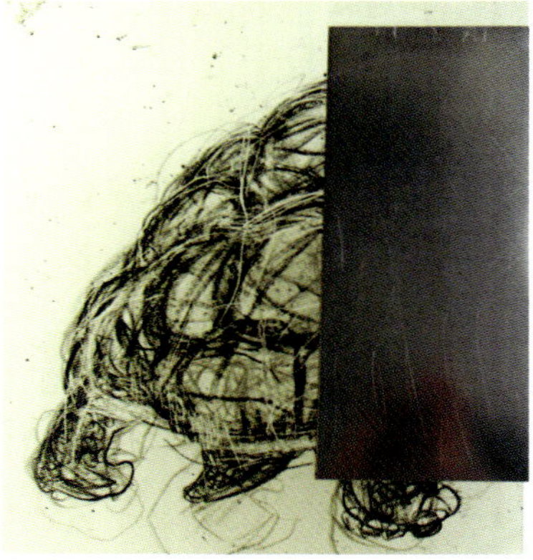

▲ The off-cut of flexo plate strip is exposed to a halftone screen. To make the test strip, first lay the drawing onto the glass top of the exposure unit. The off-cut is placed over the drawing. The plate is taped to the drawing at the top to prevent it from moving. A sheet of thin A4 copier paper is placed next to the plate ready to be slid underneath the plate to mark each minute of exposure on the test strip.

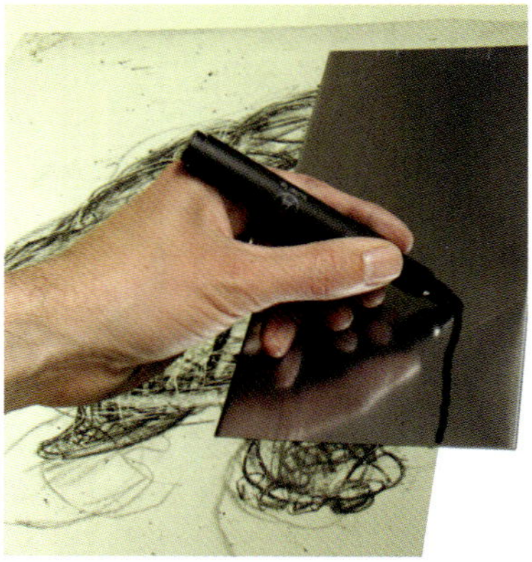

▲ The off-cut is exposed for one minute. The copier paper is then slid under the plate one-fifth from the edge (mentally divide the plate into equal portions depending on how many exposures you will make). A line is drawn with a permanent marker indicating where the paper edge is located. This is the first exposure time. The plate is then exposed for another minute (the second exposure time). The copier paper acts as a block, protecting the one minute segments already completed on the strip from the UV light. The paper strip is moved again for each minute of exposure.

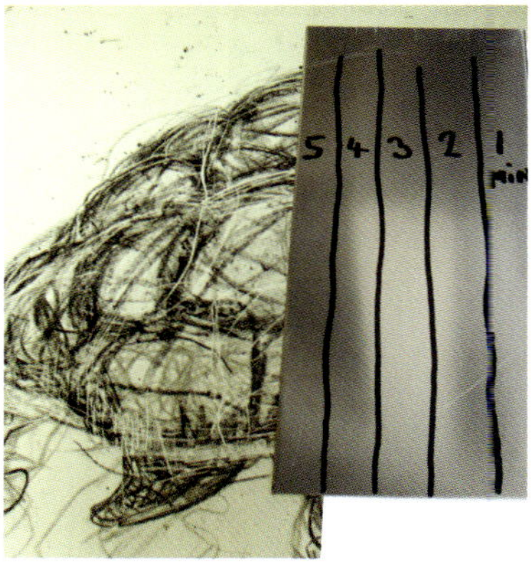

▲ This completed test strip has been exposed in 'steps' of one minute. The cumulative total test time is five minutes. It is important to record the time steps on the back of the plate using the permanent marker.
Note that the exposure times in this example are in minutes and not light units: the exposure unit we use is manually operated and the timer unit marks the time in minutes and seconds.

▶ The exposed plate is developed in a bath of tap water. Manufacturers' recommendations are to use water at a temperature of 20–25°C. In practice, we have found it necessary to warm the cold tap water only in winter. Developing time is approximately three minutes. During this time, it is necessary to rub the plate gently using a clean sponge or heavy cloth. The image will appear quite quickly on the plate and a cloudy sediment will be seen floating in the water.

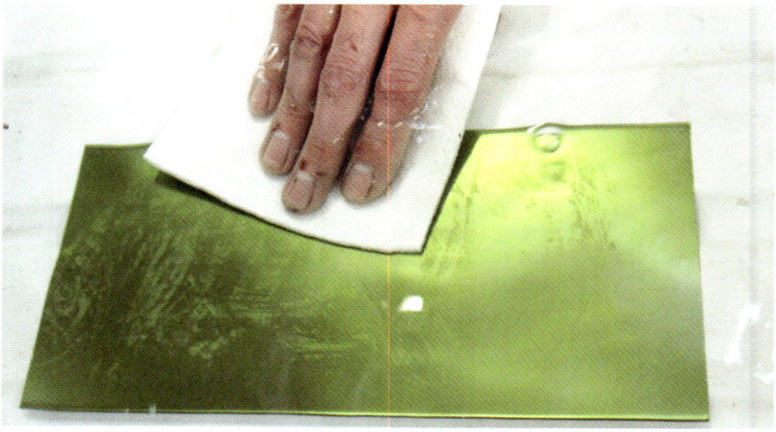

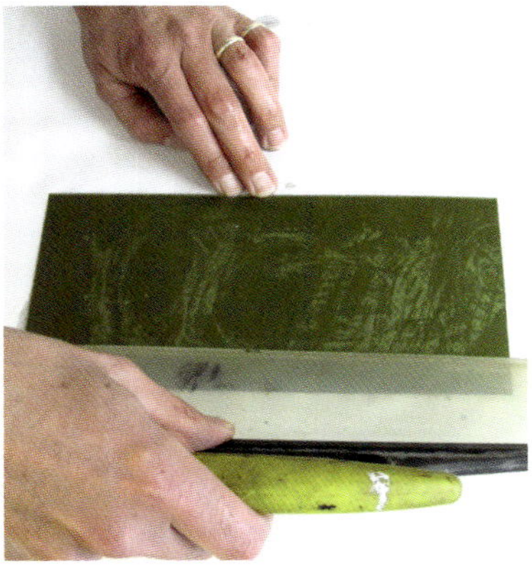

▲ The plate is removed from the water. Use a plastic squeegee to remove the excess water quickly.

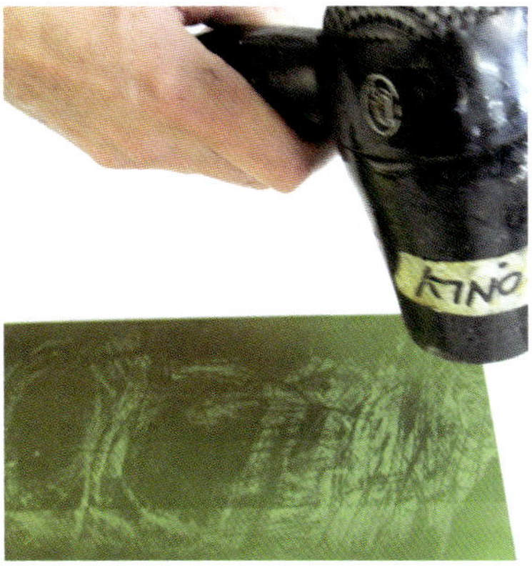

▲ The plate is dried immediately using an electric hairdryer . It is important that the plate is dried as quickly as possible. Water marks can become etched into the plate's surface if drying does not occur evenly and rapidly.

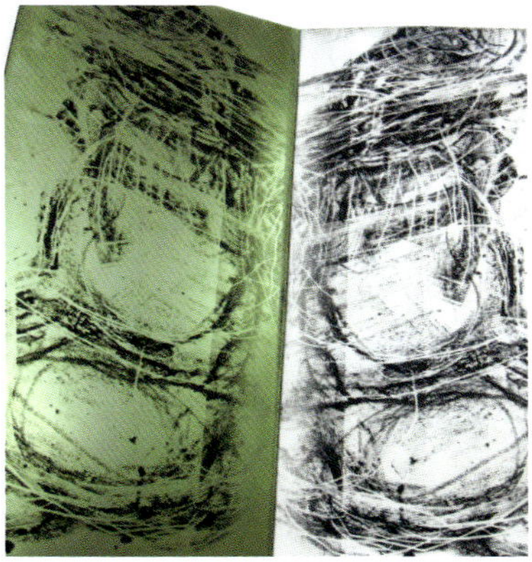

▲ The dried plate is inked and wiped in the traditional manner used for intaglio images. We recommend you wipe the surface with tissue in order to remove all plate tone so that the image tones can be assessed accurately.

▶ The exposure times that were written on the back of the test strip are transferred to the printed test strip. The strip is then compared with the original drawing. To select the required exposure time, you will need to assess the image's detail and the tone of the non-image (background) areas required. Look at the the original positive image for comparison. In this example, the one minute strip contains good detail but the background tone is too dark. The three minute strip has good clean background tone, but drawing detail has been lost. It is therefore decided that two minutes will be the correct exposure time for this drawing.

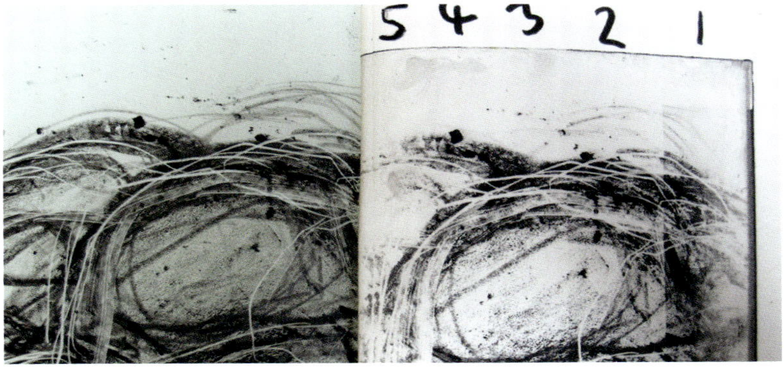

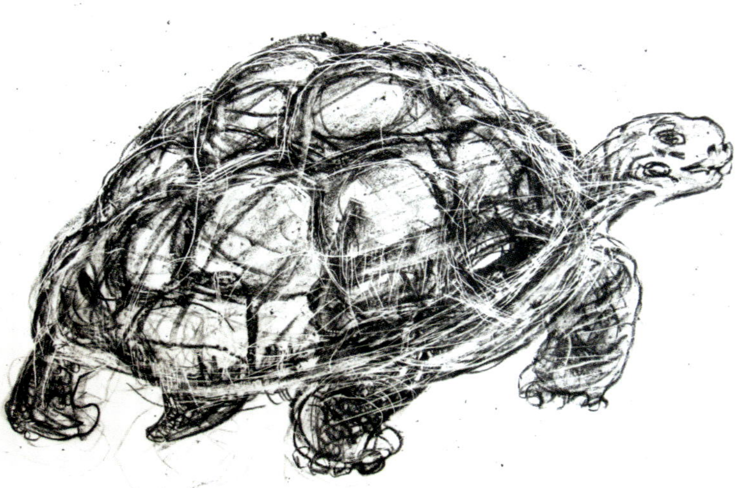

▶ The final print on Somerset paper. The plate was exposed to the halftone screen for six and a half minutes and two minutes to the original drawing.

PRINTING

Flexo plates do have one drawback in comparison to metal plates, and that is that they are a 'sandwich' of polymer and steel. As a result, it is not possible to bevel the edges as you can with a metal plate. Extra care and time must be spent wiping the edges prior to printing.

▶ **Once made, the flexo plate is inked and printed in the same manner as any other intaglio plate. We recommend finishing by wiping the plate with tissue paper and the flat of the hand. As the plates are dark green in colour and thus close in tone to the black ink, wiping with tissue ensures that detail is not obscured by any plate tone left on the surface after scrim wiping.**

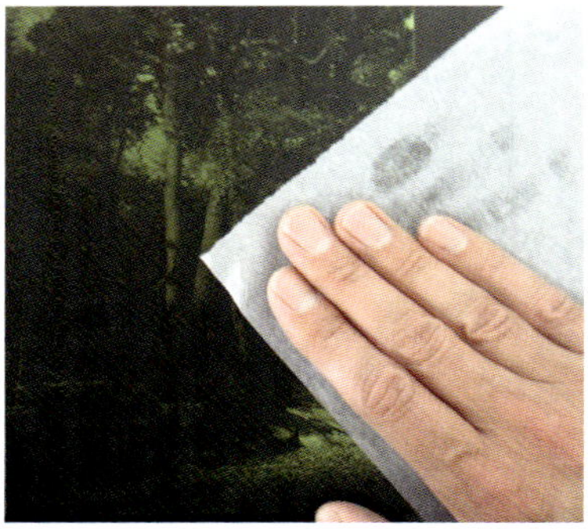

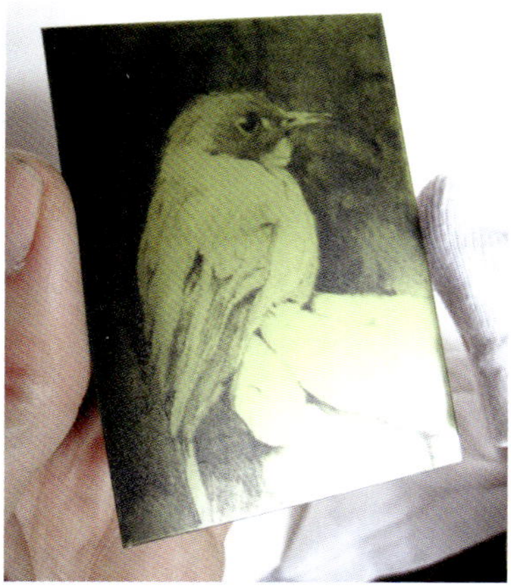

▲ **Wiping the edges of a small flexo plate using a cotton rag.**

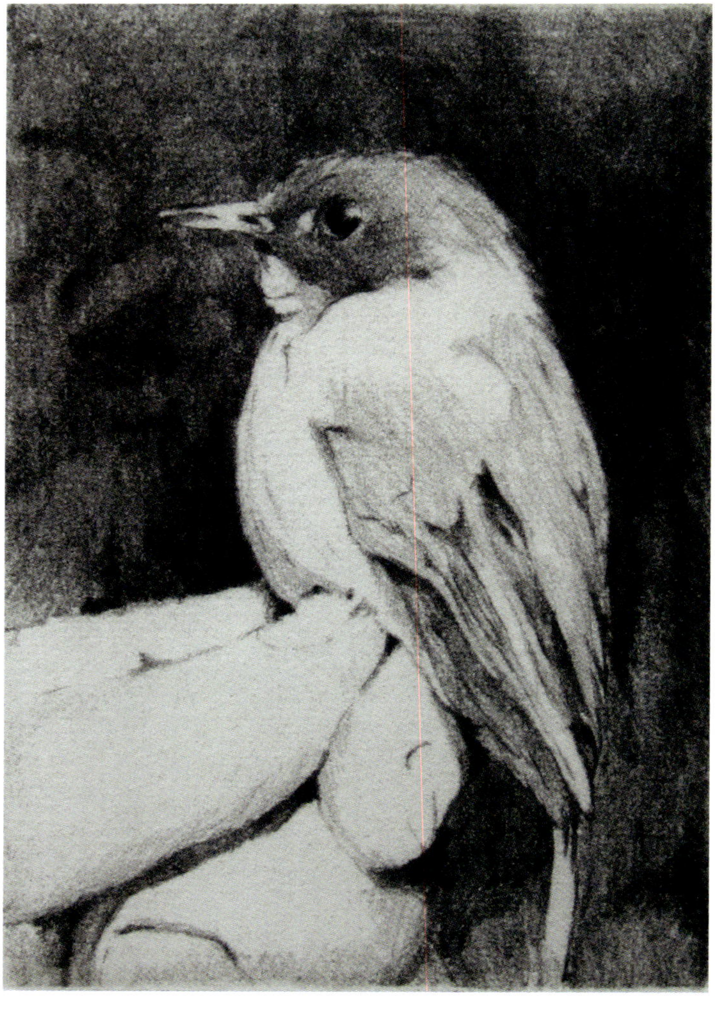

▶ **Axel Antas, *New to Nature*, 2011. Intaglio gravure, 5 x 7 cm (2 x 2¾ in.).**

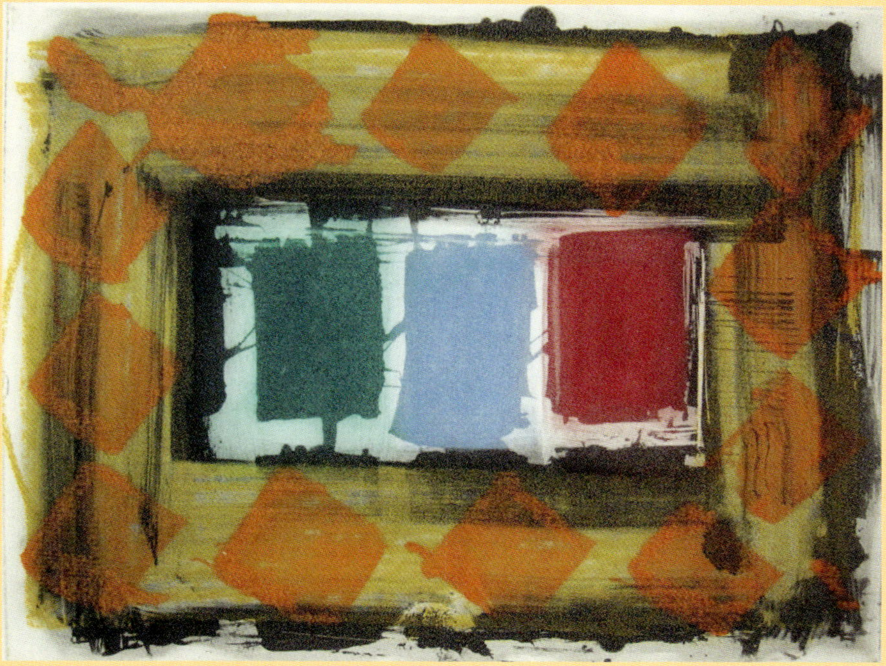

▶ Colin Gale, *Untitled*, 2011. Intaglio gravure and monoprint, 15 x 12 cm (6 x 4¾ in.).

▼ Colin Gale, *City Scape*, 2011. Intaglio gravure and monoprint, 76 x 56 cm (30 x 22 in.).

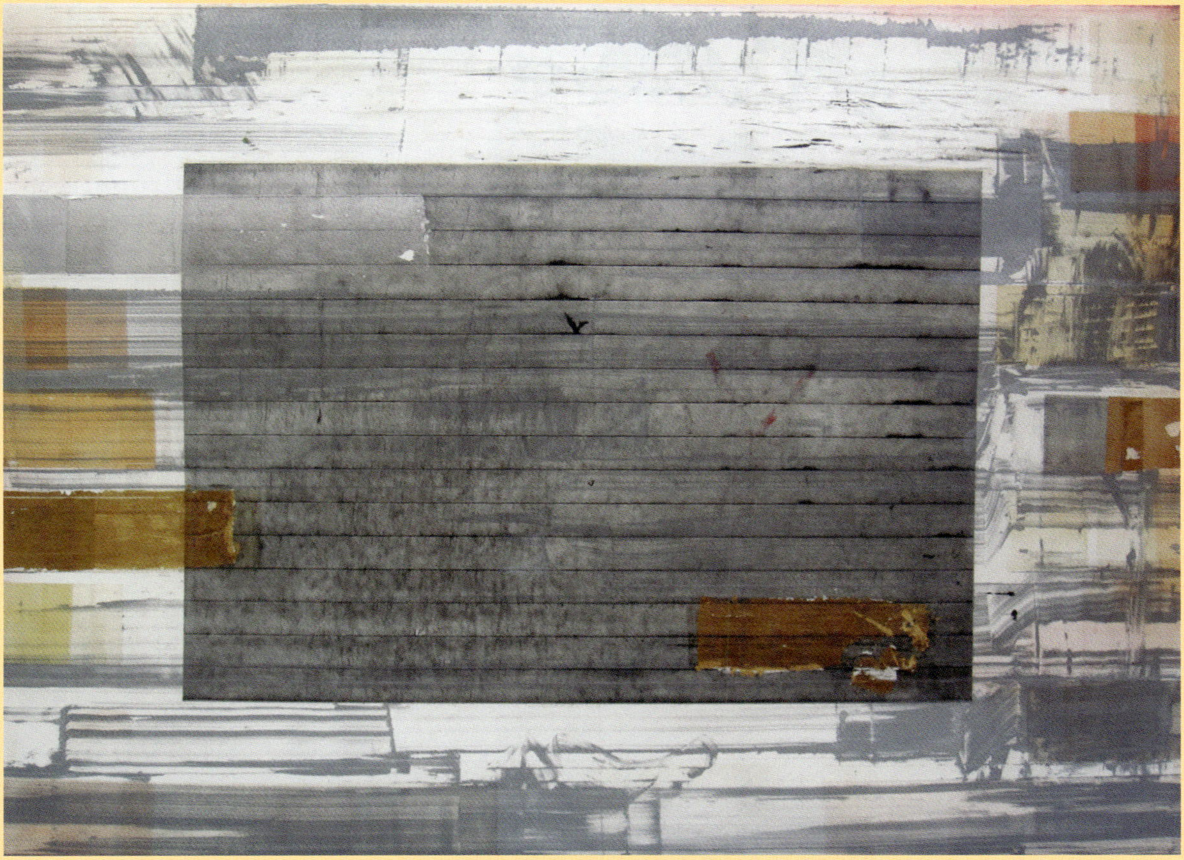

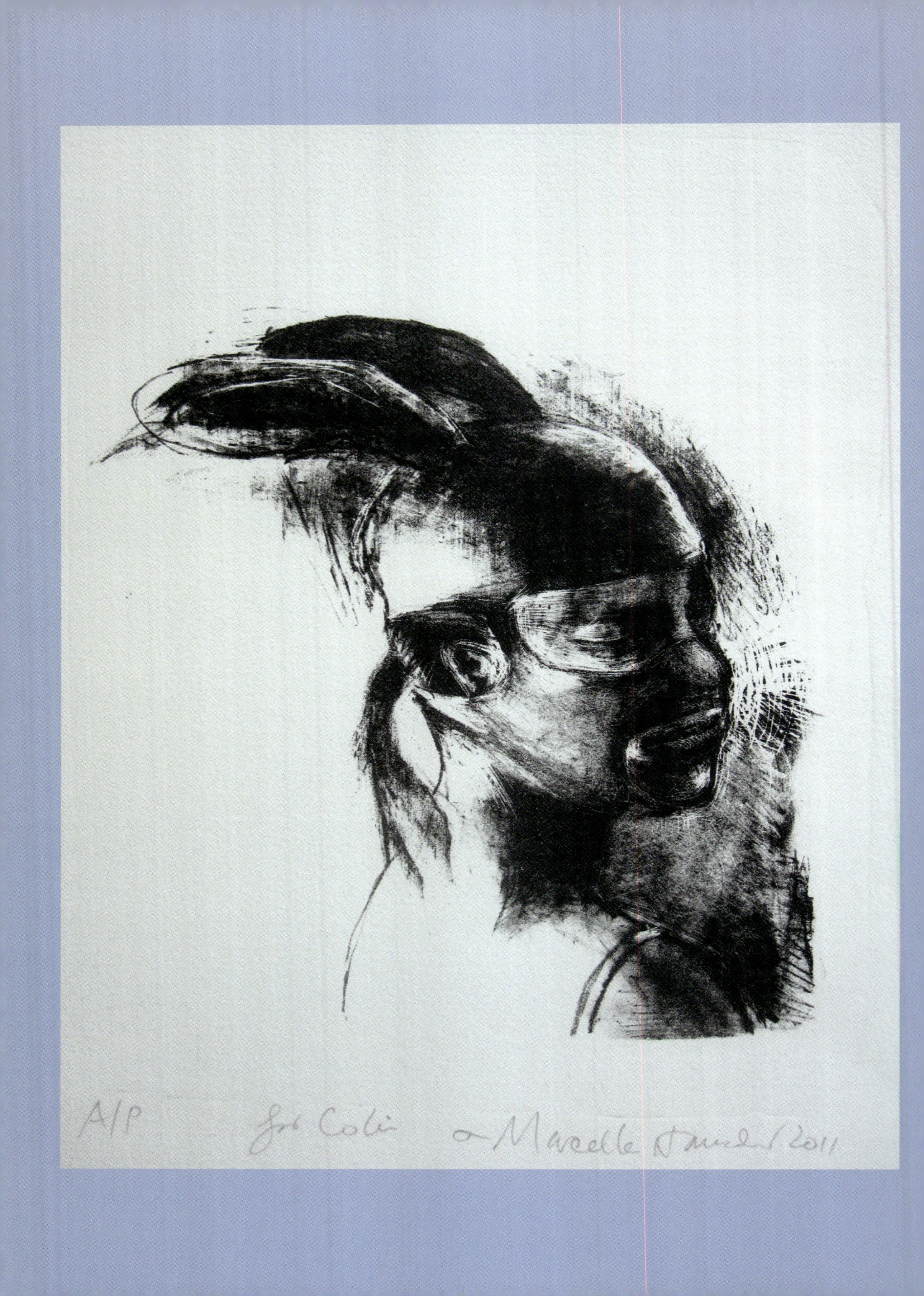
A/P
for Colin

6

lithography

Lithography is well known as a commercial printing process. It was invented by Alois Senefelder (1771–1834), who was looking for a method to print his theatrical works. As well as the commercial process, Senefelder created what can also rightly be called 'the art' of lithography for his personal use and left a rich legacy of processes and methods that we, as fine artists, have embraced. Nowadays we combine lithographic materials and techniques used in the past with technical advances, such as waterless lithography/algraphy, that print-makers can use in processes in the studio.Even with the advent of photography, lithography remains a supremely beautiful autographic printmaking form because of the direct contact with the stone and grained plate that the process demands.

◀ **Marcelle Hanselaar, *For Colin*, 2011. Stone lithograph, 28 x 38 cm (11 x 15 in.).**

stone lithography

Invented in 1798 by Alois Senefelder, stone lithography employs limestone quarried from the Solnhofen Valley in Bavaria, Germany. Although limestone is geographically common, the limestone in Bavaria is particularly pure in structure and is without faults or impurities which would spoil a painted or drawn mark. The stones were formed in the Jurassic Period, so are approximately 200 million years old. Stones vary in colour from grey/blue – which are the hardest and densest – to creamy white colours. Stones were used commercially before the advent of metal plates. They were used typically to print packaging labels and for posters and maps. When they were eventually superseded by metal lithographic plates, their creative potential was spotted by artists and they were saved from being used for garden paths or patios.

CHOOSING A STONE

When choosing a stone, your first decision relates to size and dimension. A stone should be at least 5 cm thick, as thin stones are liable to crack under the pressure exerted by the press. It is wise to check how level or flat large stones are: a badly grained stone may be dipped or concave in the centre, which will lead to printing problems. To check whether a stone is level, use a straightedge and a strip of tissue paper. Place the tissue strip in the centre of the stone and lay the straightedge on top. Pull the tissue gently. If the stone is flat, the tissue will not slide. If the tissue moves easily, the stone is dipped in the centre. A dipped stone will require a considerably longer graining cycle as the edges of the stone will have to be lowered first – in fact, it may be worth selecting an alternative stone.

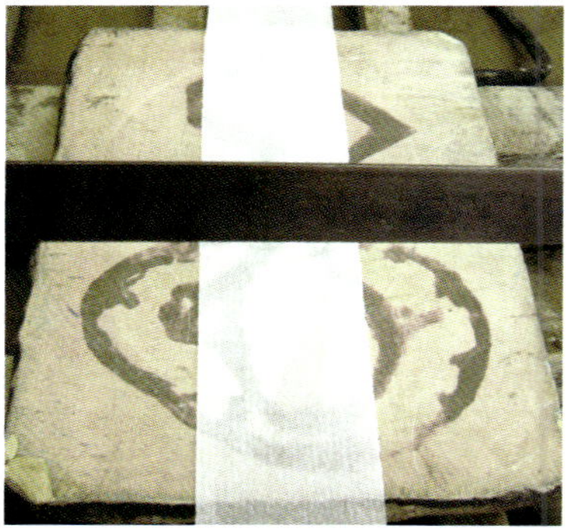

▲ **Checking the surface of the stone is level with a straightedge and tissue strip.**

REGRAINING A STONE

In stone lithography, the greasy drawing becomes chemically and physically embedded into the stone's surface.

For each new image, it is necessary to remove the previous drawing by physically removing a minute layer of the stone's surface. This is achieved by 'graining', using an abrasive grit called carborundum® (aluminium oxide). There are two methods to achieve this. One uses a tool called a levigator, the other uses two stones together.

The aim of graining a stone is to remove the previous image as quickly as possible and to apply a grained texture on which to work. Some manuals recommend graining with three grades of carborundum®: coarse (80 grain), followed by medium (180 grain) and then fine (220 grain). The difficulty with this triple sequence is that if only one single grain of coarse grit remains on the stone or levigator before you proceed with the next grade of grit, scratches will occur. If the scratches are not polished away during the three regraining steps, they will appear as

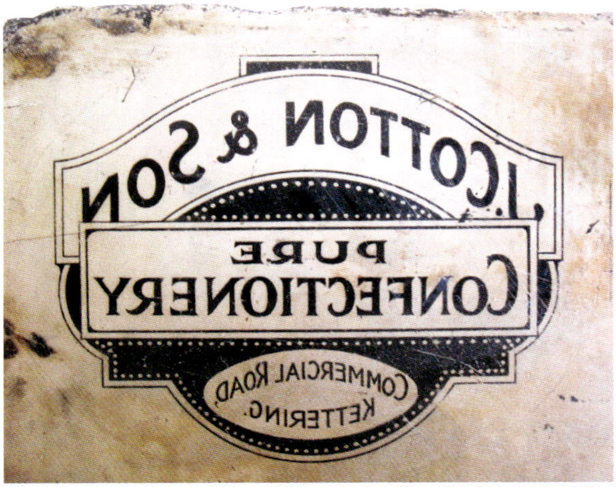

▲ **Stone with original Cotton & Son confectionery label. Note the reversal of the imagery.**

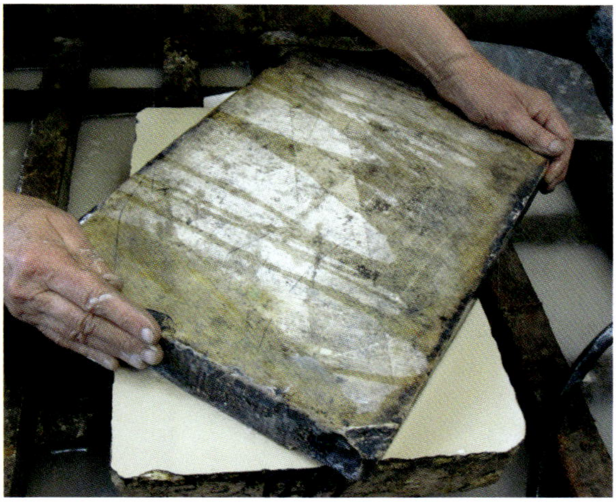

▲ **Graining stone on stone.**

white marks in the drawing during proofing and remain there until the final print of the image from the stone is taken. The scratches made by the mixed sizes of grit are below the surface on the stone and will not hold the drawing materials used to create the image. You cannot force excess crayon or tusche into them to make them disappear, unfortunately.

We find that triple graining is very time-consuming: it is vital to clean away each different grit by rinsing with water, and meticulous attention to detail is needed. There is much anecdotal evidence that students are put off stone lithography because they perceive that graining is an arduous and lengthy task, which it can be if you use this method. Regraining and polishing a stone ready for use should take you no longer than 15–20 minutes. We use the following method: it is much faster than triple graining and greatly reduces the risk of scratches occurring.

Using coarse grit (number 80 grain), grain the stone until the previous image has gone. Check the stone to make sure that everything has been removed completely.

The levigator

The levigator consists of a heavy, circular cast-iron disc with wooden handle. The levigator is spun over the wet stone together with an abrasive grit (coarse carborundum®) which slowly grinds down the stone surface, removing any trace of the previous image.

To use the levigator, begin by wetting the stone thoroughly with water. Sprinkle a little coarse carborundum® onto the stone and lift the levigator, placing it over the grit. (Take care to *lift* the levigator rather than slide it. Sliding the levigator across the surface of the stone merely pushes the grit wastefully over the edge of the stone into the graining sink.)

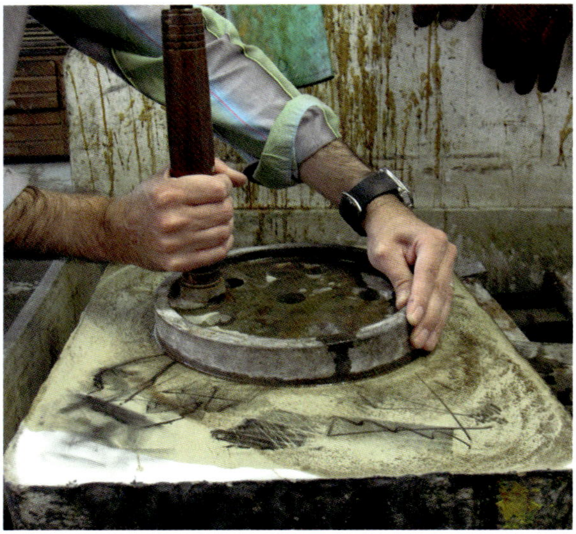
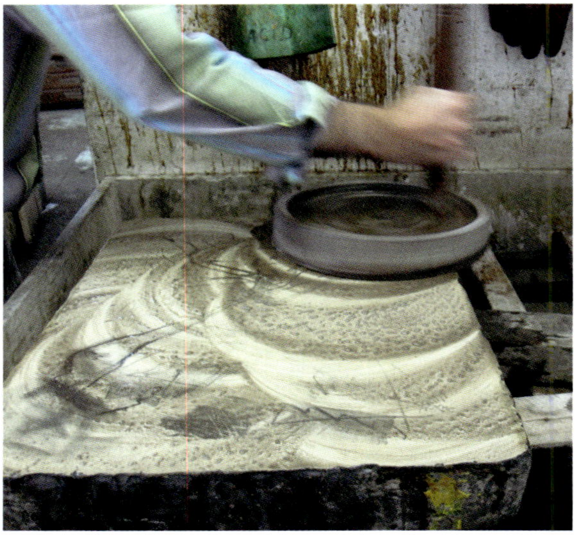

▲ Graining using a levigator.

You will need a strong firm grip to move the levigator. Grip the wooden handle towards the bottom with one hand and with the other, grip the iron disc of the levigator and pull it around anti-clockwise towards your body. This motion initiates the levigator spin, but at the same time turn the levigator faster with the hand holding the handle.

The key to success in this procedure lies in building up enough momentum so that while the disc is spinning, it may be guided slowly around the stone in a systematic pattern.

Pay attention to the sound made during graining. When the grit is biting into the stone, a sharp, rough sound is heard. When the sound becomes dull and the action feels smooth, the abrasive is worn and fresh grain must be added.

Tip

Concentrate on the corners of the stone. You may otherwise end up with a dipped (or concave) centre to the stone, which will produce an uneven surface for printing.

Stone-on-stone graining

This method is suitable for smaller stones. Two stones of similar size are grained, one on top of the other. Although generally slower than graining with a levigator, this method has the advantage that two stones are grained for the price of one (as it were).

Coarse carborundum® (number 80 grain) is placed between two wet stones. The top stone is rubbed manually over the bottom stone in a 'figure of eight' pattern until all traces of the previous image are removed.

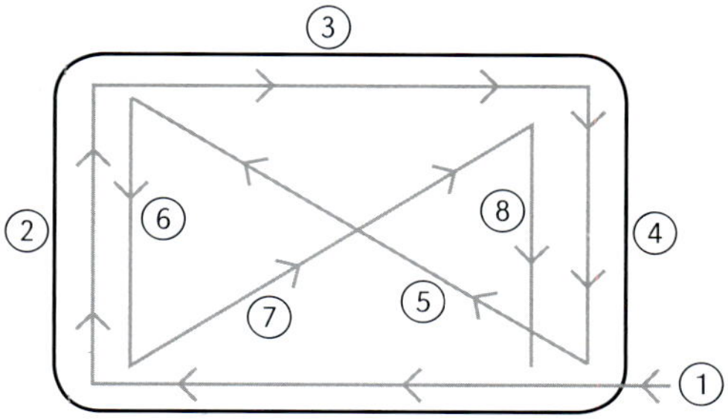

▶ A 'figure of eight' graining pattern for stone.

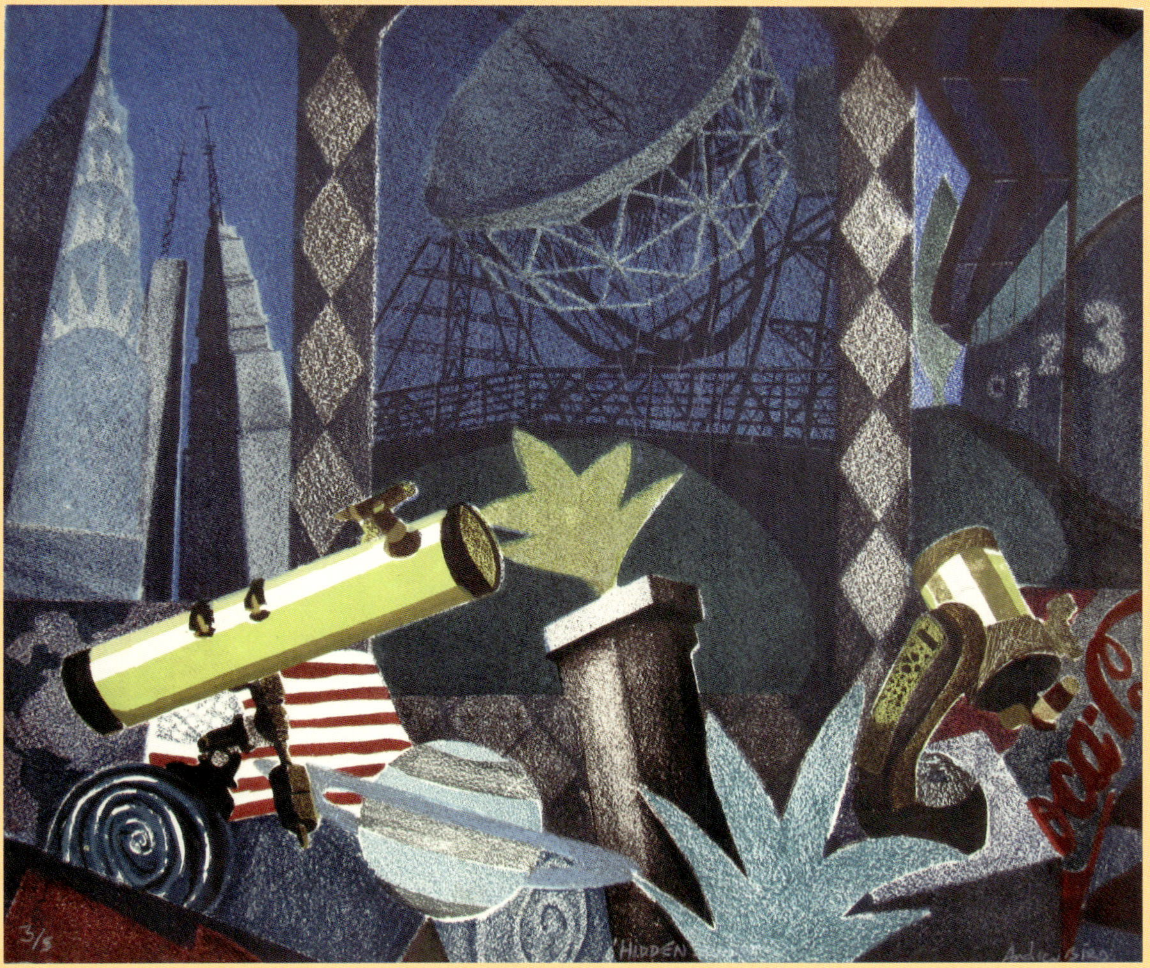

▲ Andrew Bird, *Hidden Place*, 2000. Stone lithograph, 50 x 40 cm (19½ x 15¾ in.). Drawn on a coarse grain surface.

▶ Detail showing texture on a coarse grain stone.

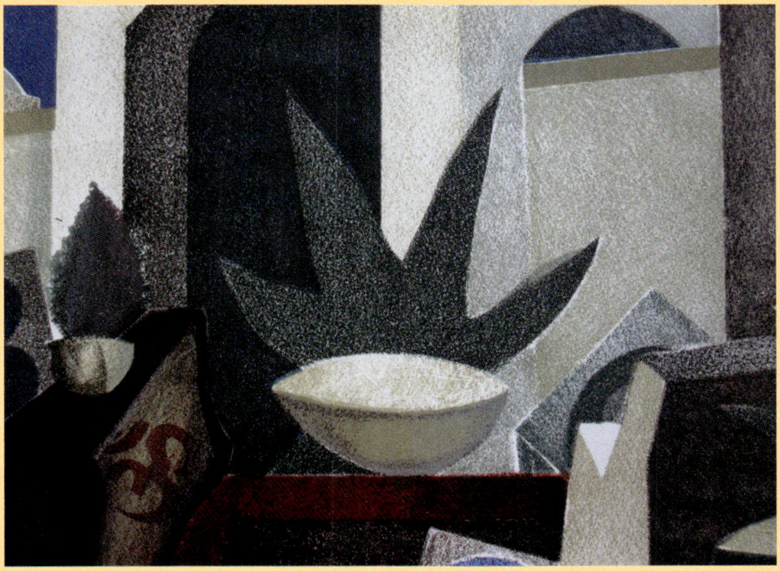

Checking the stone for image removal

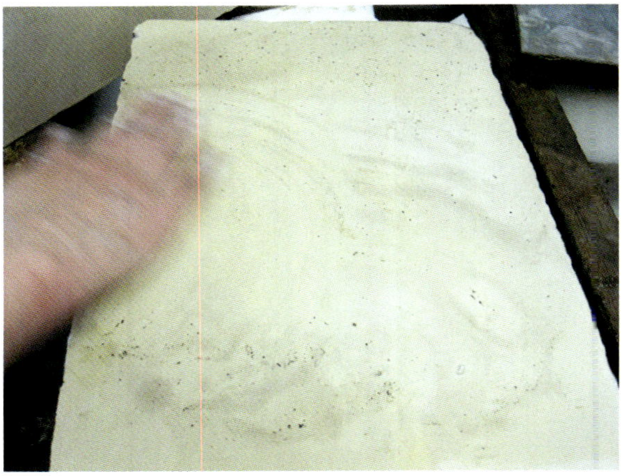

▶ It is important that all traces of the former image are ground away, otherwise the previous image may reappear through your drawing. Even though graining removes the image, it is possible for greasy residue from the previous drawing to remain present. To check this, rub some asphaltum liquid over the wet stone surface. If grease (drawing) is still present, the asphaltum will highlight it, in which case further coarse graining will be required.

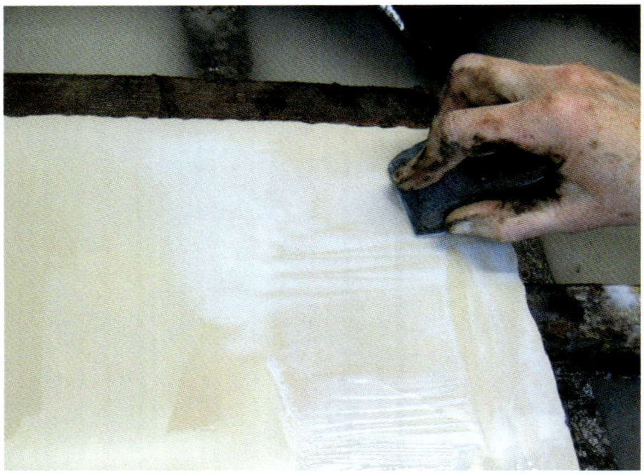

Polishing the stone

◀ When all traces of the previous image have been removed, the stone is now polished using a lump of smooth honing stone such as 'snake stone' or 'Arkansas stone' – these are dark grey, hard smooth volcanic rocks geographically common globally and used for polishing and honing. Rinse the stone thoroughly with water before firmly massaging the polishing stone systematically over the whole surface. This process takes just a few minutes and polishes away the coarse surface. It also removes any scratches created by the carborundum®.

ADDING GRAIN

One of the advantages of using a stone rather than a metal plate is that you can choose the texture of the surface you wish to draw on. You can give a stone a coarse, medium or fine surface by choosing one of the grits to rub over the newly polished stone surface. You will need a small stone (a broken piece of stone is often kept for this procedure), coarse, medium or fine grain carborundum® and water. For example, an expressive, gestural image would suit a coarse or medium grain, while a delicate line drawing would benefit from a fine grain surface. Take the required grain, sprinkle it onto the stone and add water. Place the smaller stone on top of the polished stone and using both hands rub the two stones together for several minutes.

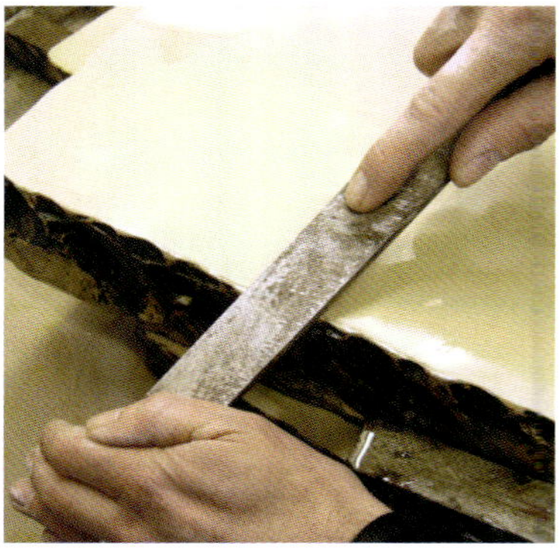

File the edges

▶ The next stage is to bevel or file the edges of the stone so that they stay clean during printing. At an angle of 45 degrees, use a rough file to round off the stone's edges.

PREPARING THE STONE FOR DRAWING

Counter etching

For a stone to accept a drawing mark, it must be prepped or 'counter-etched'. Flood the stone with acetic acid mixed with water at a ratio of nine parts water to one part acetic acid. Leave the counter-etch solution on the stone for approximately two minutes (a slight fizzing action will be observed), then rinse thoroughly with water.

Dry the stone using a hairdryer or a hand-held drying 'flag'.

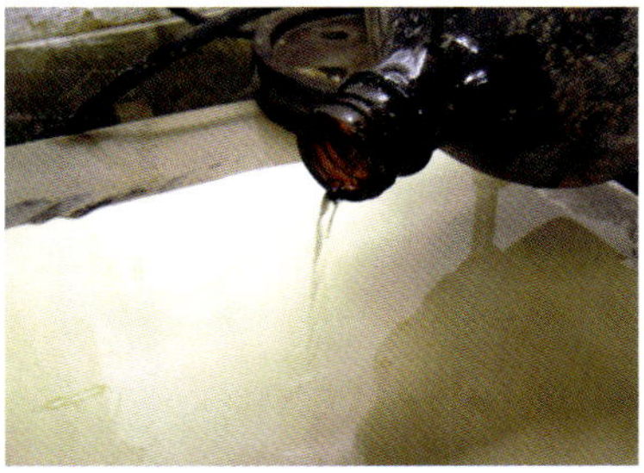

▲ Counter-etch solution (1:9) is poured onto the stone.

DRAWING THE IMAGE ON THE STONE

The wonderful thing about lithography is that such a wide range of marks and textures can be built up together without the separate processing that other techniques (such as etching) require. Painterly marks can exist alongside reticulated washes and crayon tones that are uniquely all processed together.

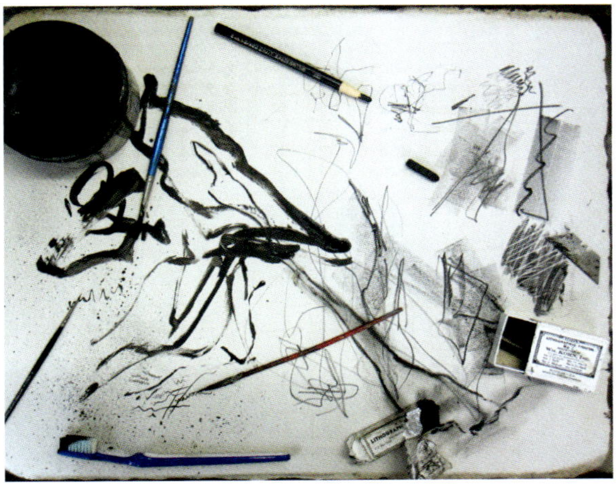

▲ A selection of marks made on a stone together with drawing materials and implements.

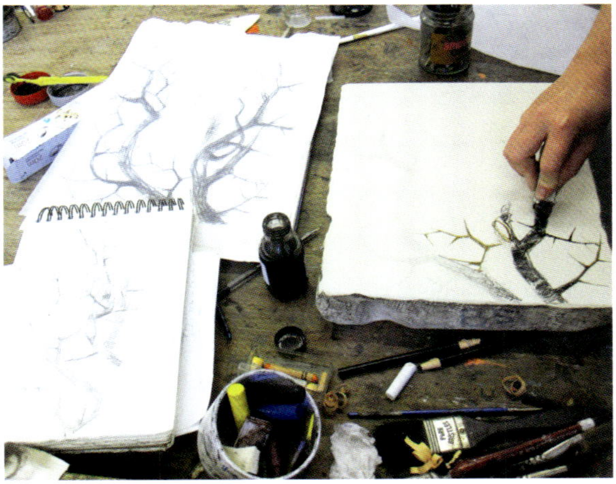

▲ Drawing on the stone using a litho crayon.

Use coloured chalk, red Conté® crayon or wax free transfer paper to map out your composition. As they have no grease content, these materials will have no effect on the stone: they act purely as a guide, enabling you to compose the image on the stone's surface.

Lithographic drawing materials are composed of grease (tallow), soap, wax, shellac and black pigment. They are easily available from printmaking suppliers and the main brands are Charbonnel® and Korns.

Lithographic drawing materials can be generally separated into two categories: dry and liquid.

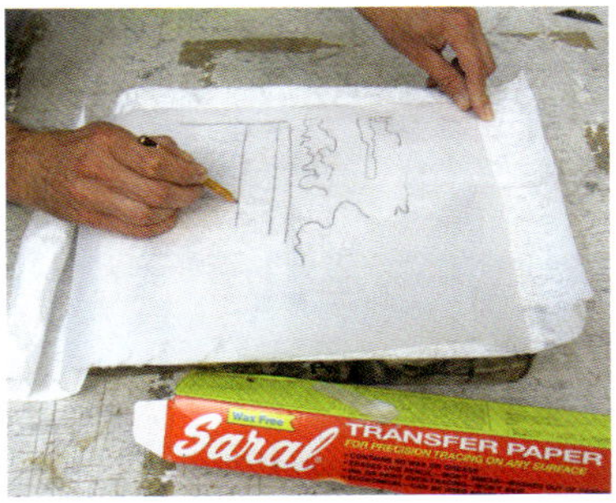

▲ A roll of Saral® Wax Free Transfer Paper is used to trace down a drawing.

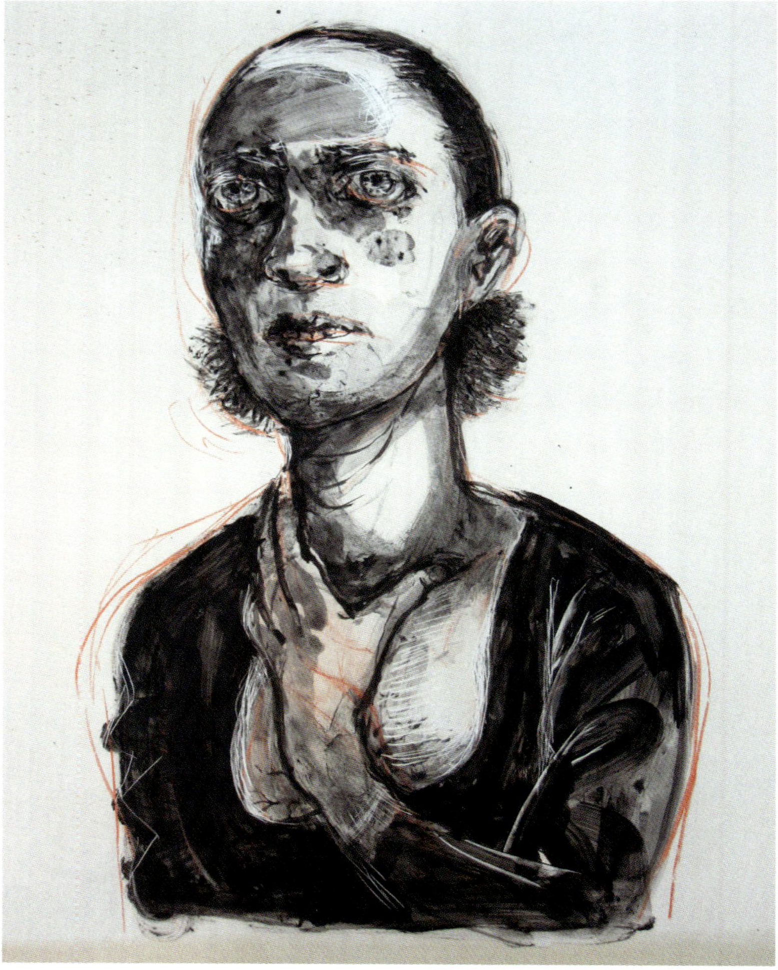

◀ Marcelle Hanselaar image drawn onto a lithographic stone. Note the red Conté® crayon, which was used to sketch out the initial composition.

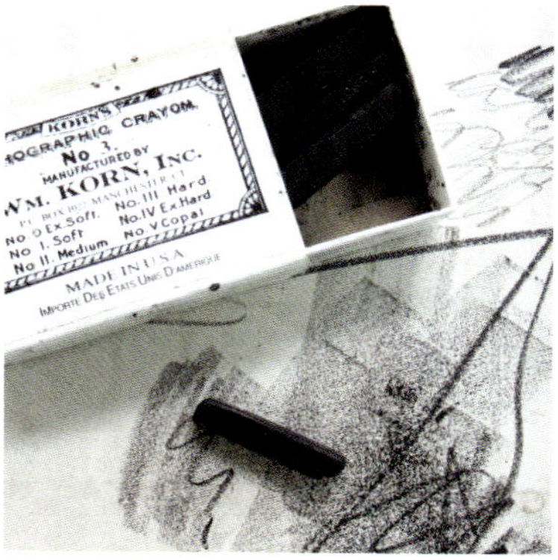

▶ Lithographic crayons are supplied in stick and pencil form. They are graded from soft to hard, by numbers 1–5. (Refer to the box as manufacturers' grading systems vary.) An extra-hard option is available called 'copal'. The crayons can be used flat on their sides to lay down tones, or by their end points for sharper lines.

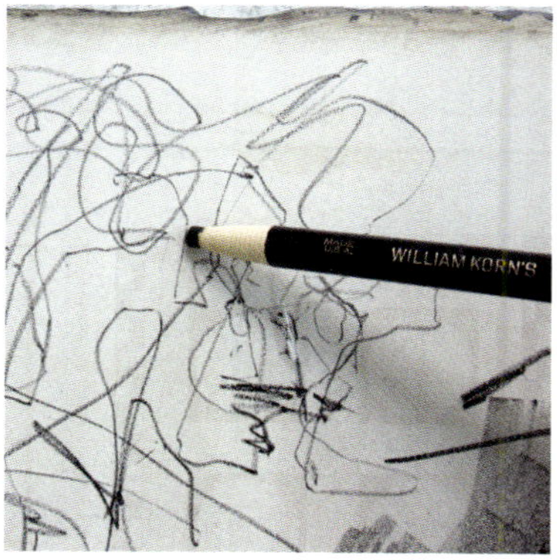

▲ Pencil crayons can be sharpened to a point and offer a different type of mark to the stick crayon, particularly if held at the end with the fingers.

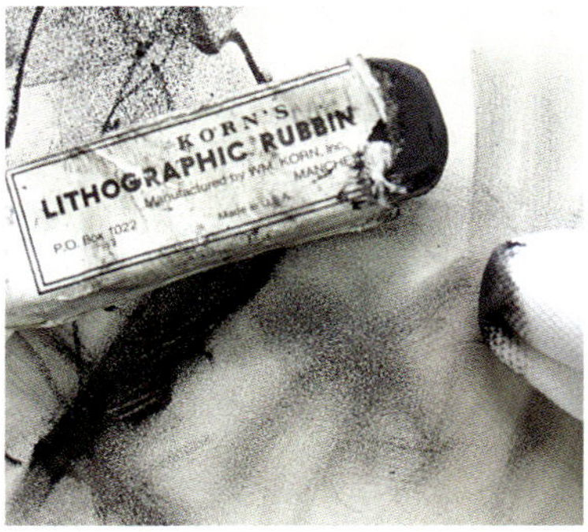

▲ Rubbing sticks are available in hard, medium and soft varieties. They can be applied and smudged using a rag wrapped around a finger.

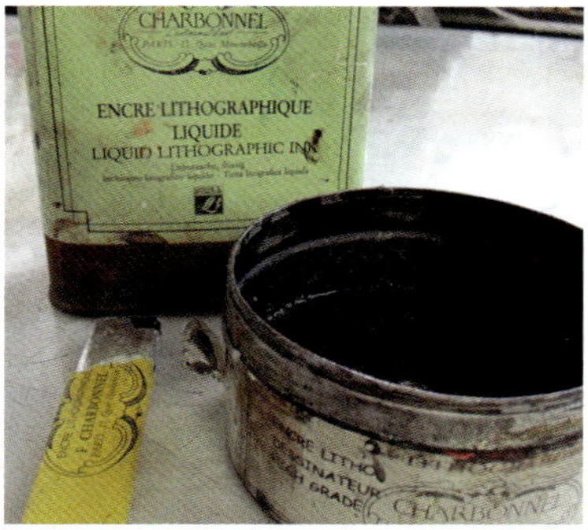

▲ Lithographic tusche and ink is supplied in stick form, as a paste in a tin or ready-mixed. Stick tusche and paste tusche is mixed with distilled water or solvent (pure turpentine) to the consistency of single cream. It can then be painted on using a brush, splattered with a toothbrush or drawn with a dip pen. The liquid can be dropped into a pool of distilled water and allowed to dry, producing amazing reticulated effects or washes.

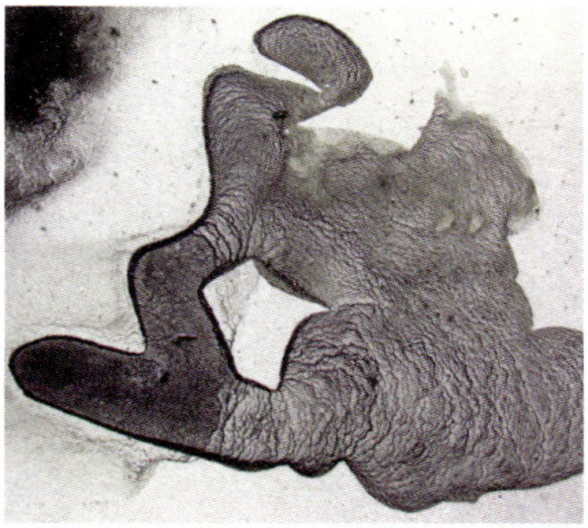

▲ Mixed tusche dropped into a pool of distilled water.

▼ A dip pen provides the finest line available to the lithographer – use with liquid ink.

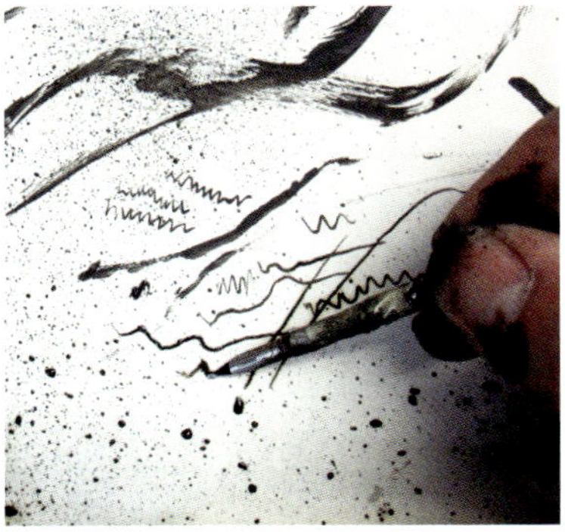

The mixed tusche may be thinned further to produce lighter, delicate washes. Whistler's lithographs of the Thames are good examples, but these works exist in many states due to the technical difficulties in fixing delicate washes to the stone. Delicate washes should be regarded as experimental as in practice they are very unpredictable in application and unstable during printing runs: they have a tendency to either not print at all or fill in and turn black as printing proceeds. For this reason, washes are not seen in early commercial stone lithographs, where crayon work was hand-tinted using delicate watercolour painting.

PROCESSING THE DRAWN STONE

Once the drawing is complete, it must undergo processing using gum arabic and nitric acid (the 'gum etch'). This processing is referred to as 'etching' but should not be confused with the biting of metal plates, however. In a lithography context, etching refers to the separation of the surface into opposites, the non-image areas that hold water and the drawn image areas that attract ink.

The first step is to dust the image with resin and then French chalk. The resin is an acid resist against the nitric content of the gum etch, while the French chalk protects the greasy drawing from smudging during the gum etch application.

Mixing a gum etch

Most stone lithography manuals have gum etch recipe tables. These indicate how types of drawing – broadly classified as light, medium and heavy – should be treated with an ounce of pure gum arabic to which is added drops of pure nitric acid.

A convenient way to measure an ounce of gum is to use a plastic top from a 5 litre container. The nitric is added using a dropper bottle. Remember that this is pure nitric acid, so eye and hand protection must be used.

Assess the drawing and mix batches of gum etch into light, medium and strong accordingly. If the drawing is broadly the same in character, one gum etch should suffice for the entire stone.

As every stone is geologically unique, gum etches must be tested on the margins of the stone or where there is no drawing so that the reaction can be assessed.

All etches used on stones react mildly to the stone's surface. The perfect strength etch produces a distinct reaction immediately on contact with the surface of the stone. A very strong etch will react fiercely, producing a full, bubbling, white froth. This is probably too strong an etch; to dilute it, add gum arabic. An etch that is weak will take many seconds to react with the stone and only a mild effervescence (froth) will be seen.

Standard etch table

light crayon and washes	6–12 drops	7–10 seconds effervescence (or none)
medium work	12–18 drops	5–7 seconds effervescence
heavy crayon and solvert washes	18–25 drops	2–5 seconds effervescence

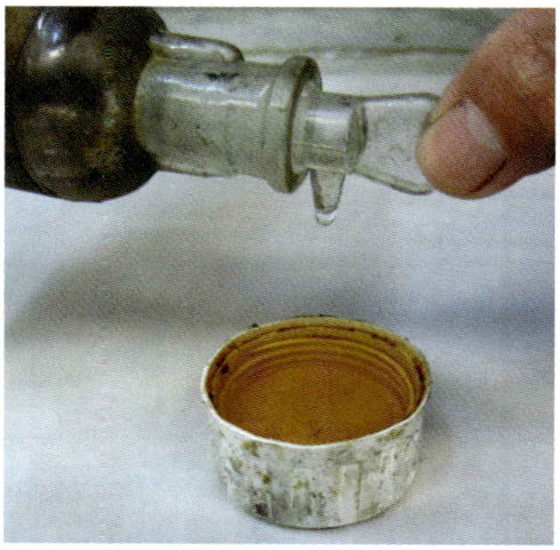

▲ An acid dropper bottle.

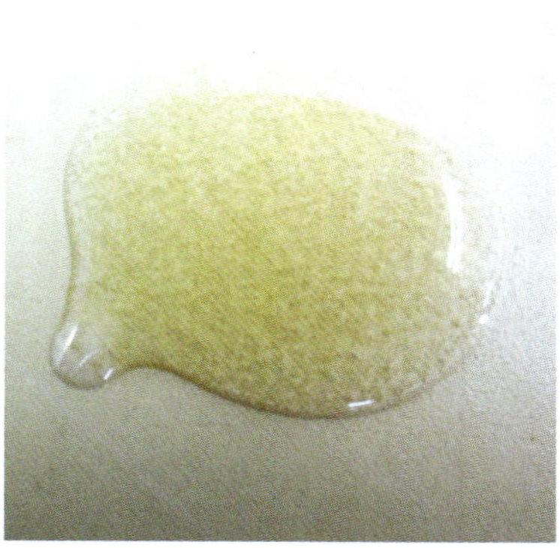

▲ A gentle effervescence after a few seconds of contact with the stone.

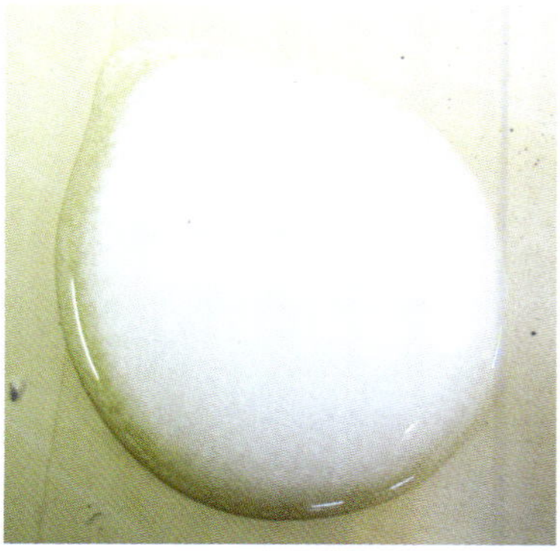

▲ A strong effervescence after a few seconds of contact with the stone.

Apply etches to the stone, beginning with the weakest etch. Ensure all the stone is covered and allow the etch to sit for one to two minutes before buffing down to a thin layer. This process is known as 'giving the first etch'.

Leave the buffed gum-etched layer to sit for at least one hour (preferably overnight).

PROOFING THE STONE

The drawing materials (the image) must now be washed out through the gum arabic. Often the gum etch is too thick, so it is recommended that this is sponged off and a thin layer of gum is applied. This fresh gum should be buffed down using a clean cloth. It is important that very little gum is sitting on top of the drawn areas as it will be difficult to wash out with solvent.

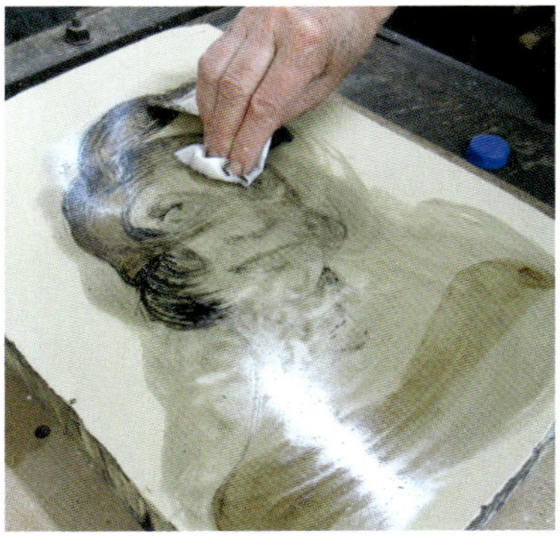

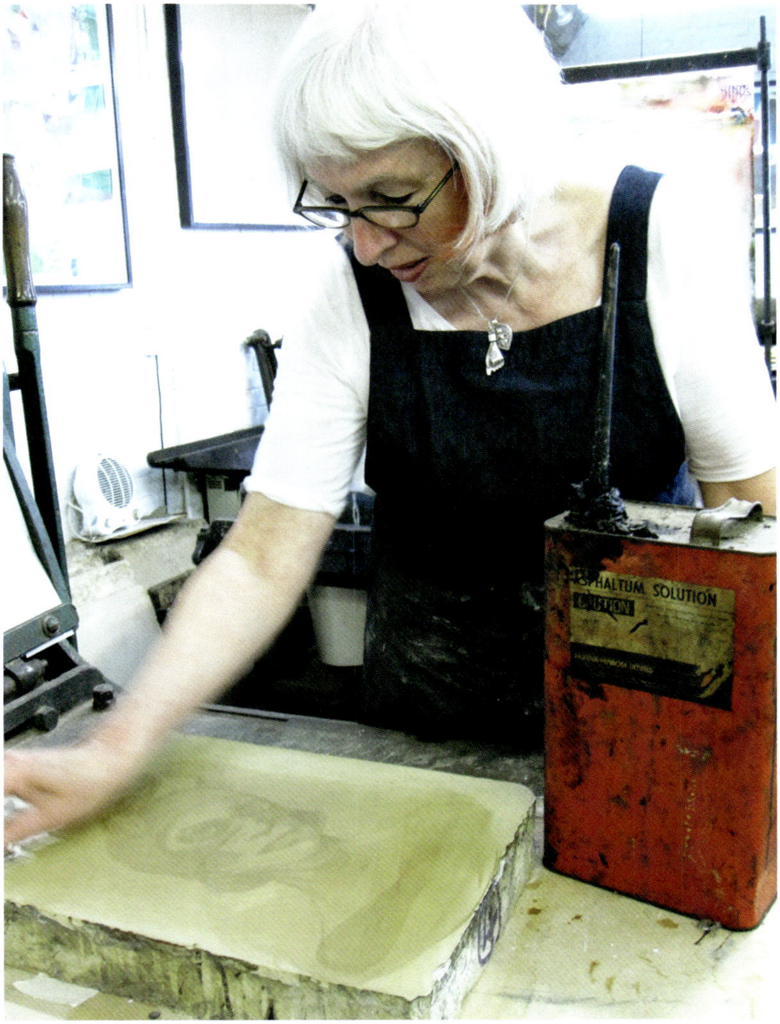

▲ Sprinkle the solvent (white spirit) onto the stone and rub gently with a clean rag, washing out the drawing material.

▶ The artist Marcelle Hanselaar applies a thin layer of liquid asphaltum to the image. This acts as a key for the ink that is to be rolled on to the stone.

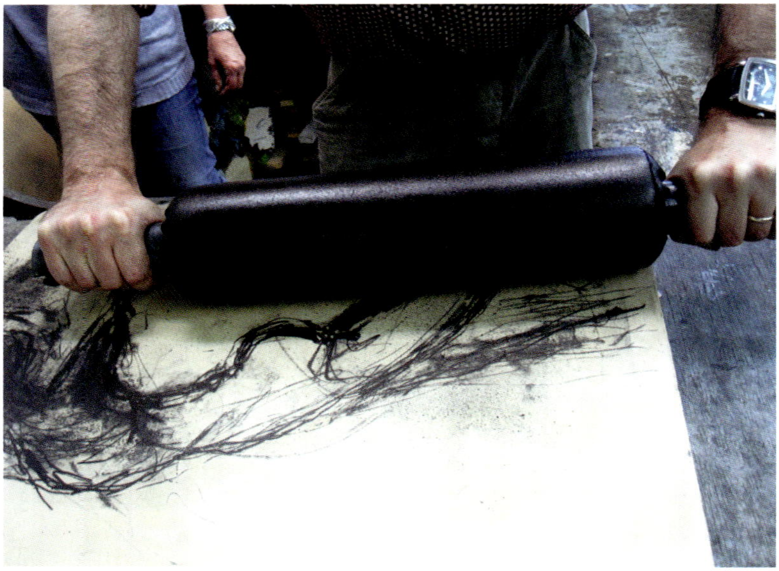

◀ Rolling a stone with a nap roller and proofing black (Senefelder's Crayon Black)

The stone is now rolled up in 'proofing black', a stiff black ink that contains no driers. An image can be rolled up for processing or storage without the ink drying on the stone, meaning the ink can be washed out easily and replaced with a printing colour when needed. The proofing black is applied using a leather nap roller. This type of roller has the rough or suede side facing out, imbuing it with good inking capabilities. The nap roller is kept specifically for this job and as non-drying black is used, the roller does not need to be cleaned.

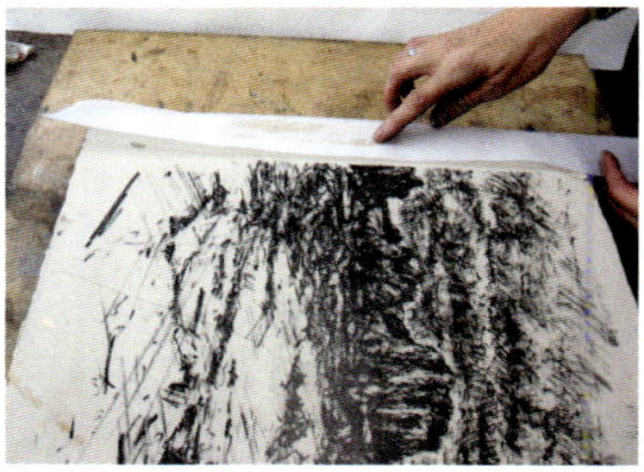

▲ Laying strips of tissue paper on the stone's edges.

Tip

To ensure clean margins when printing lay strips of tissue on the stone's edges.

A stone must be damped with a sponge and clean water before it is rolled up. The non-image areas that have been etched with gum retain the water and it is this water layer that repels the ink. It is crucial here to make a distinction between damp and wet. The stone must be evenly damp and not have pools or drops of water (wet areas) as these can emulsify (become small, separate globules) with the ink during rolling up, causing printing problems.

The ink is built up slowly over several proofs made on to newsprint. If the ink is applied too thickly, it will spread and fill in the fine detail. When the stone has received the first inking, the pressure on the press must be set because every stone is a different thickness. Slide the bed in until the scraper bar is positioned across the middle of the stone. The pressure screw should be turned sufficiently so that when the lever is engaged, a firm resistance is felt. The bed is then re-positioned so that the scraper bar is on the leading edge of the stone. Pressure is applied and the bed is cranked through. The first newsprint proof should be light grey in tone. The stone is re-damped, inked again and further proofs on newsprint are taken until the image reaches a full-strength black in the strongest tonal area. This typically takes between three and five pulls.

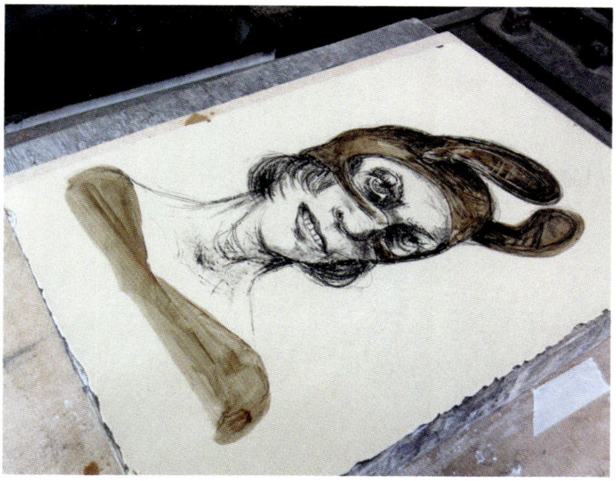

▲ The drawn stone prior to inking.

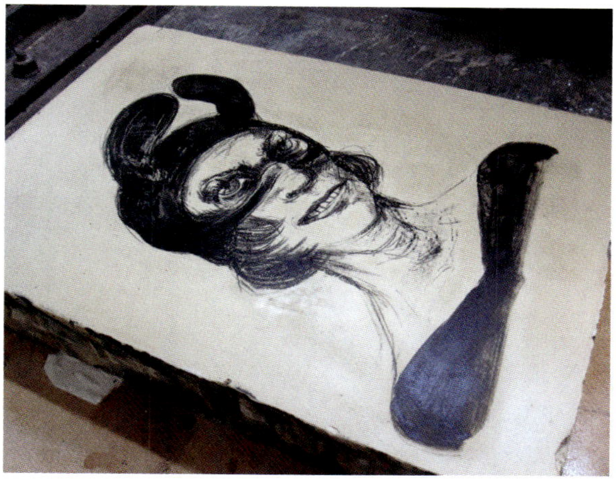

▲ The stone after it has been inked.

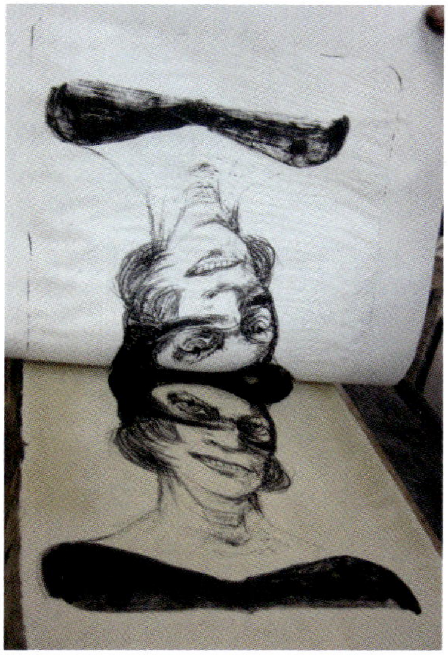

▲ Pulling a newsprint proof from the stone.

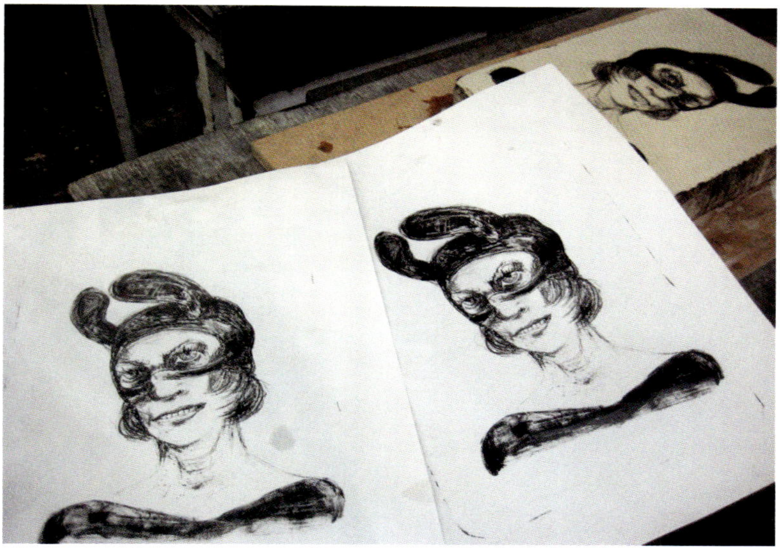

▲ The first two proofs on newsprint showing progression in tone from left to right. Also see p.162.

Once the image is proofed, the drawing is assessed (prior to giving the stone a second etch to stabilise it for printing/editioning). This is the time the artist makes decisions to change the image.

To add drawing

Dust the image with resin and French chalk to protect the image. Flood the stone with acetic acid nine parts water and one part acetic acid, and allow this to sit for two minutes before sponging off with clean water. This process is called 'counter etching' and removes the gum adsorb layer, which means the stone can once again accept grease (ie, the litho drawing materials).

To erase drawing

Drawing is most easily removed by scraping with a sharp blade. Be sure to scratch slightly into the stone surface to remove the mark completely. As well as removing unwanted marks, the blade may be used creatively to make highlights and to 'draw' with. Perhaps the most remarkable example of this is in some of Picasso's work, such as his *Bull* lithograph, where the stone is re-worked with a blade and printed in a series of eleven states.

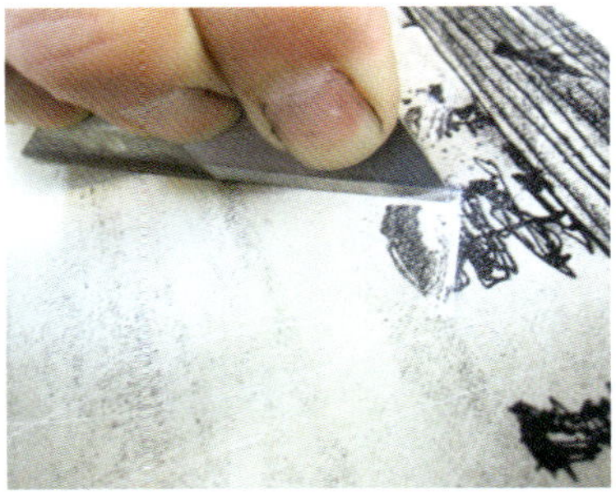

▲ Removing drawing with a sharp Stanley-type blade.

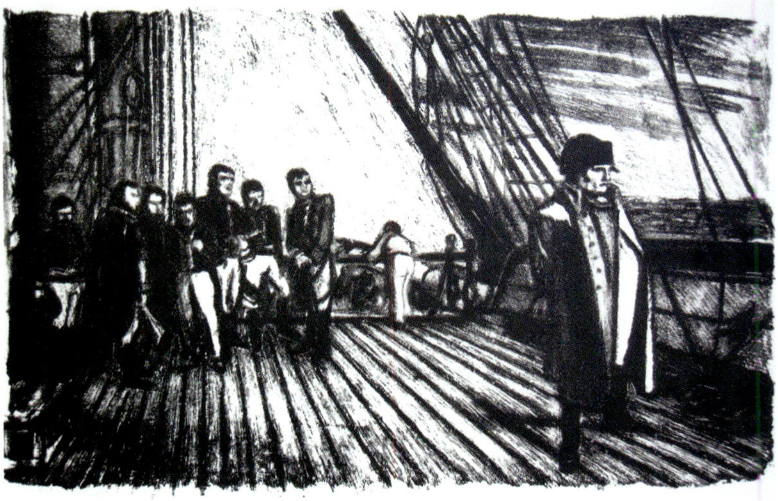

▶ Michael Jackson, *Napoleon onboard the Bellerophon*, 1999. Stone lithograph printed at Artichoke, 34 x 30 cm (13½ x 11¾ in.). Note the use of heavy scraping on the sail and deck.

Detail below.

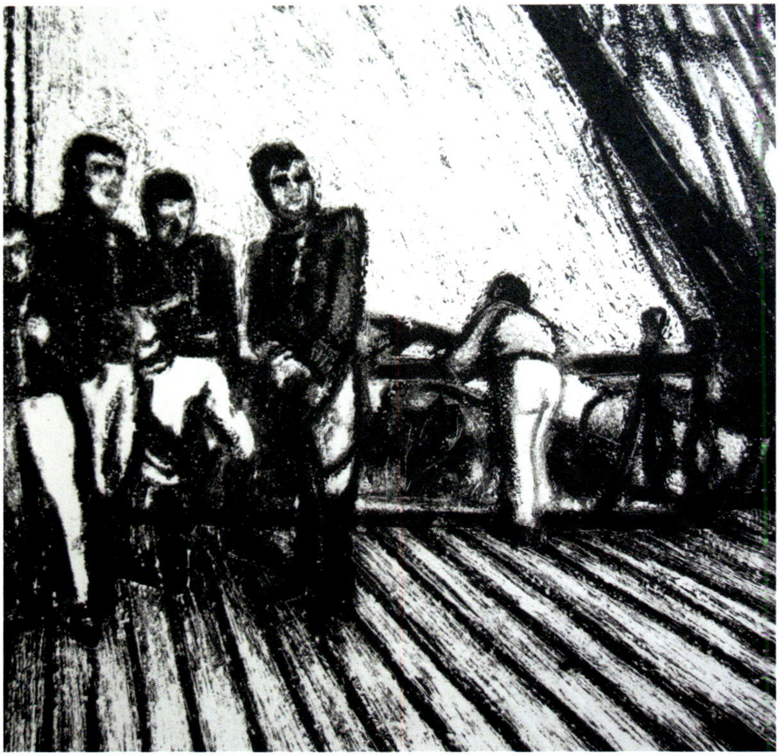

Chemical erasing

Marks may also be removed chemically by dipping a stone or rubber hone in dilute nitric acid (ten parts water to one part nitric). (If you are working in a studio that commonly uses etching, simply use a little from one of the etching baths, if available.) Chemical erasing is particularly useful for removing ink that may collect on the margins of stones during printing. Simply 'burn off' the unwanted marks with the nitric solution before applying a little gum etch. Allow to dry for several minutes before sponging off and proceeding with the printing.

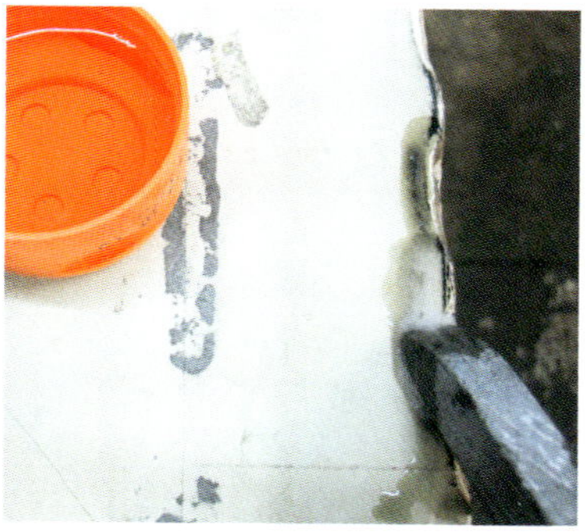

▲ Cleaning a stone edge with an Arkansas slip dipped into 10:1 nitric acid solution.

▼ Stone lithograph by Zeng, *Untitled*, 2005, 50 x 60 cm (19½ x 23½ in.). Strong chemical erasing was used to 'burn' the highlights.

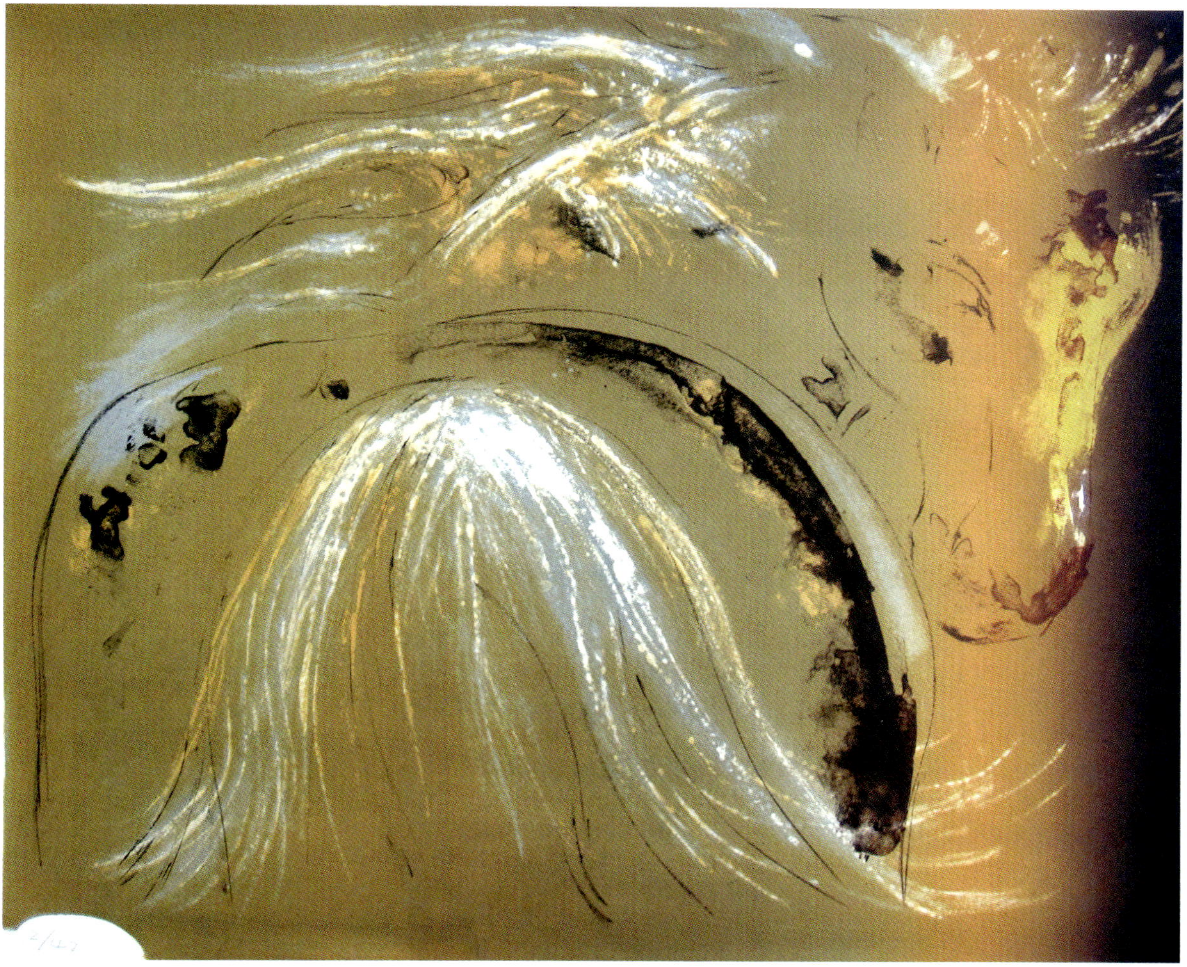

SECOND ETCH

If the drawing on the stone looks good after proofing with newsprint (or after adding to or erasing parts of the image), the stone is given a second etch.

A stone should be given a second etch to stabilise and fix the image more strongly before a print run is started. Any new drawing added should be dusted with resin and French chalk. The strength of the second etch (i.e., the number of nitric drops added) can be adjusted at this stage if needed. This is based on how the stone proofed up on the newsprint. If the first one or two proofs came up very dark quickly, this would indicate that the first etch was too weak. If the stone proofed very slowly, this may indicate that the first etch was too strong. If the stone proofed up evenly in three to five pulls on newsprint, it is a good indication that the first etch was the correct strength.

REGISTRATION

Each printing sheet should be registered with the stone to ensure even margins and the correct lining-up of colours. In an ideal world, a nine colour lithograph would be made by drawing down each of the nine colours on nine separate stones. In practice, however, due to the lack of availability of stones – all of which would have to be of a similar size – most colour stone lithographs are printed from a single stone. The first colour would be printed on the required number of sheets of paper before the stone is regrained and the next colour layer drawn on the cleaned stone. This process requires a key drawing to be made onto tracing paper, so that the design can be traced down in chalk onto the regrained stone for each colour necessary to complete the design.

One solution often employed in colleges is to use aluminium or zinc plates to print colour layers, with the final key layer printed on top from a stone. As stones are not available in large numbers, plate lithography is faster for groups or classes as many users can share the use of a direct plate press. Plates are the same gauge of metal and portable, which means they do not have to be inked on the press bed.

If the printing paper is smaller than the stone, use the T-bar registration method. A 'T' is scratched into the stone surface at one edge and a single line at the opposite edge. These marks are made with a sharp metal point and then transferred in pencil to the back of each printing sheet.

Pin registration

If the printing paper is larger than the stone, 'pin registration' is used. In this process, two holes are made very close to the edge of each end of the stone. A heavy drypoint needle is used to bore the hole. It should be deep enough so it is not grained off when making the subsequent colour layers. The position of these holes is then traced down onto the back of

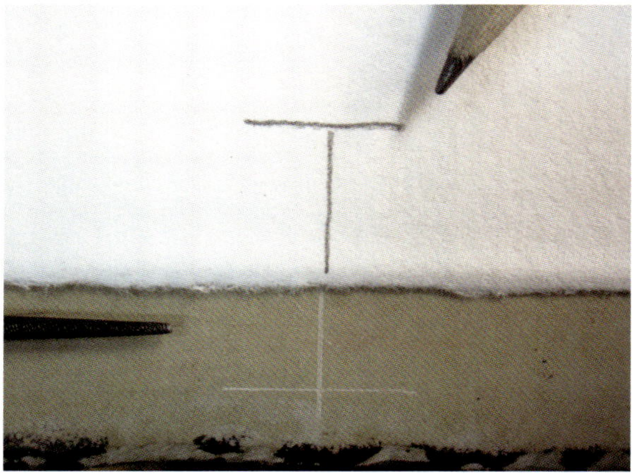

▲ Close up of T-bar registration.

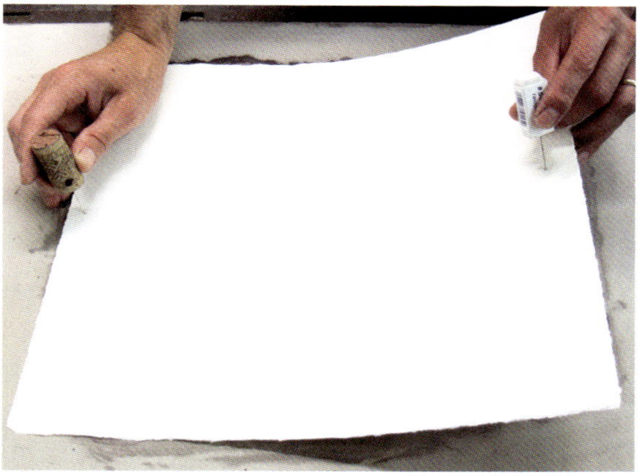

▲ Improvised registration needles using a cork and an eraser.

each printing sheet and a hole is pricked through the paper with a small needle. As each piece of paper is printed, two needles are poked through the paper and locate the holes in the stone.

Needles can be improvised using sewing needles glued into a length of wood or pushed into wine bottle corks or hard erasers.

PRINTING USING A COLOUR

After the stone has received its second etch and allowed to sit for at least an hour – and preferably overnight – it may be printed in colour. Mix the colour and prepare the paper before washing out the black proofing ink as described above. The colour ink may need thickening by adding magnesium carbonate and litho varnish as described on p.165. The colour must be built up to full strength by proofing onto newsprint (as done when proofing in black), before printing onto quality paper. Choose paper that is smooth with a hard surface: don't be afraid to experiment with different papers to find one that prints the image well. It seems to be a frustrating fact with lithography that the cheap newsprint often prints a more beautiful quality image than expensive printing paper!

STORING THE STONE

If the stone is to be used at a later date, it must be placed under non-drying black. Dust the image with French chalk and gum with pure gum arabic or a very light gum etch which will help stabilise the non-image areas.

To store the stone for later printing, strip the printing colour from the stone using sheets of newsprint before rolling the stone up in non-drying black. You do not have to wash out the colour before rolling on the proofing black. Make proofs onto newsprint until the black prints strongly.

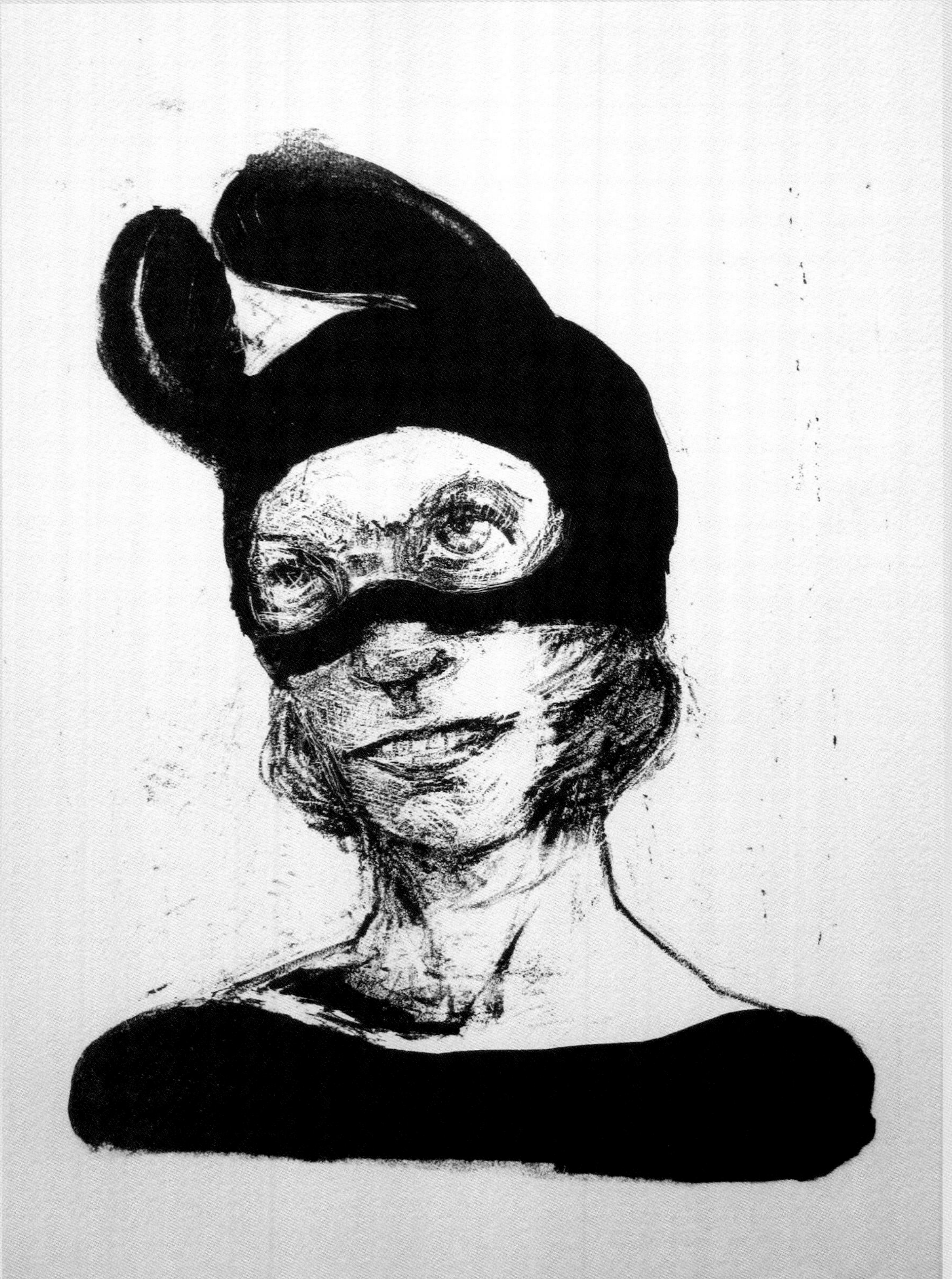

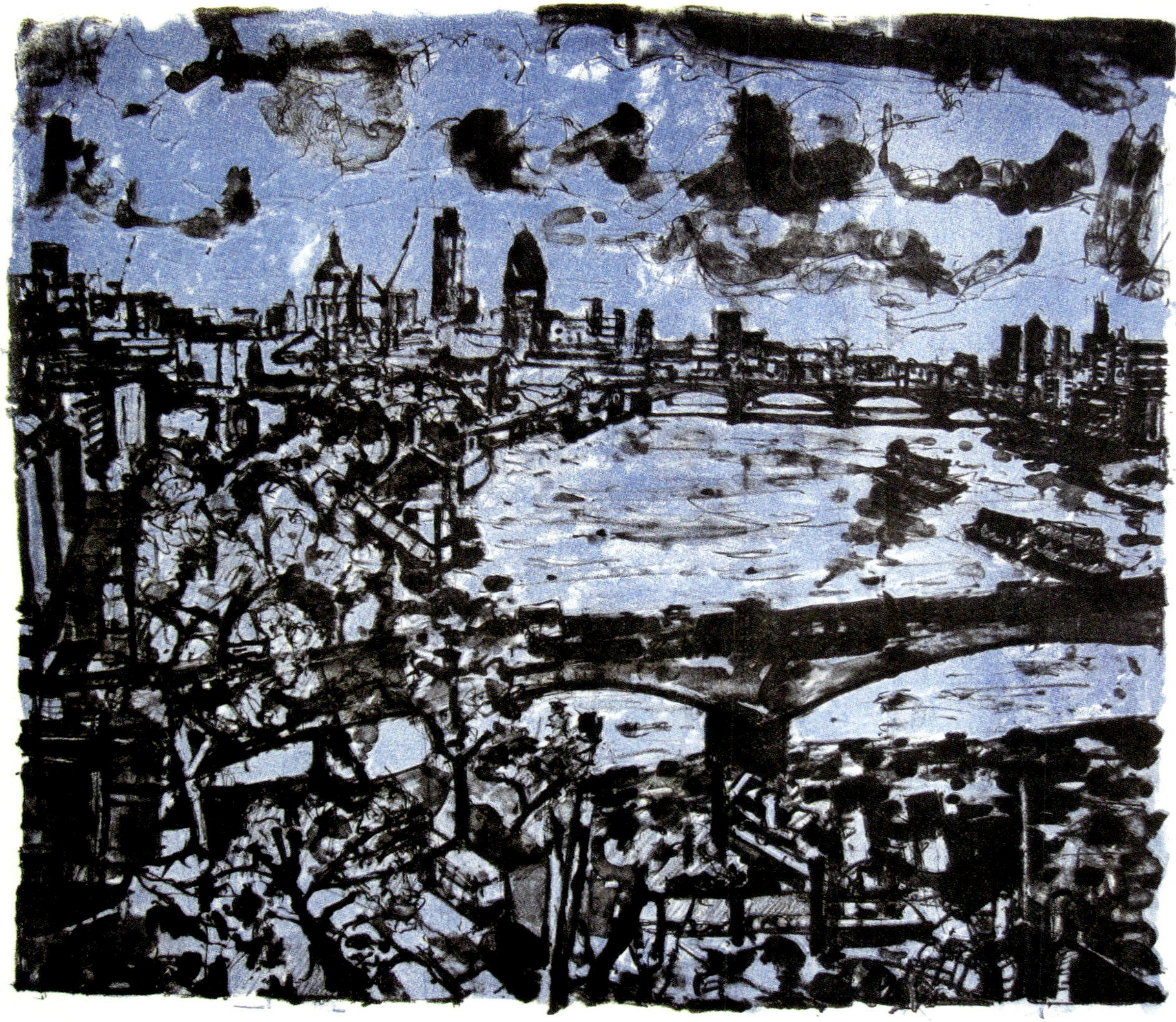

▲ Peter Spens, *View of the Thames from The Savoy*, 2006. Stone lithograph, proofed and printed by Colin Gale, 52 x 46 cm (20½ x 18 in.).

◀ Marcelle Hanselaar, *Untitled*, 2011. Stone lithograph, 24 x 30 cm (9½ x 11¾ in.).

plate lithography

The use of plates in lithography was driven by the commercial need for faster and more efficient methods of printing. The introduction of the steam-powered rotary press in the 1840s changed forever the task of printing commercial images by hand. Lithographic plates were lighter and easier to handle than stones and were extremely compatible with the technological innovation of steam-powered mass production. By the beginning of the 20th century, stone had been replaced completely by plates for commercial printing. Developments in photography married the two commercial processes and allowed photographic images to be produced on an industrial scale.

Modern-day hand lithography (plates printed by hand) has derived directly from these early commercial processes. Artists have kept the process of using plates alive even as the commercial industry moves towards making the production of plates increasingly unviable commercially.

There are three main options for hand printed plate lithography: ball-grained aluminium plates, zinc plates and photosensitised aluminium plates (which are still used by some in commercial lithography).

▼ A George Mann motorised direct press (*c.* 1930) at Artichoke.

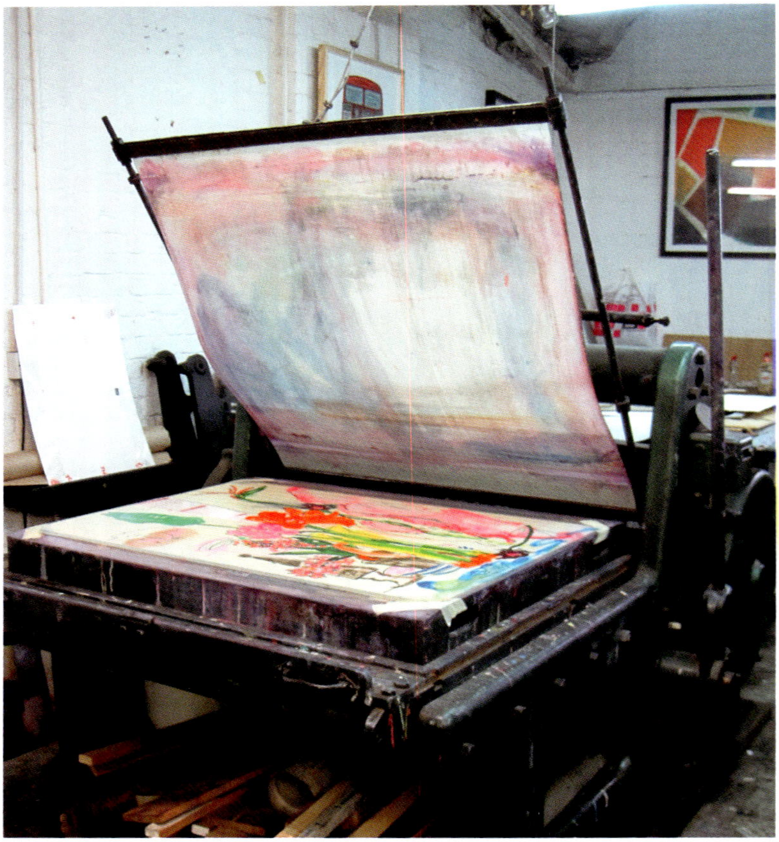

An artist in the studio will most often use grained plates of aluminium or zinc for hand-drawn lithography. Grain is applied to the metal plates in a hopper-type machine which contains ball bearings and an abrasive (aluminium oxide). The hopper shakes violently and the ball bearings, which are moving constantly across the surface of the metal, embed new texture onto the surface of the metal. It is an *incredibly* loud process!

Historically, aluminium has been used in the US and zinc in the UK, but this situation is starting to change. Increasing numbers of British colleges and workshops are choosing to adopt aluminium plates now that the plates can be easily imported from the US and Holland. The regraining of zinc plates is expensive and commercially only one supplier does it in the UK.

Grained litho plates have a similar surface to that of a typically grained stone. Drawing and processing methods for ball-grained plates will feel very familiar to printmakers used to stone lithography.

BALL-GRAINED ALUMINIUM AND ZINC PLATES

Both of these metals are used in similar ways but they each require different processing chemicals and have their own working characteristics.

An advantage of the zinc plate is that each plate can be used several times for different drawings before the grain becomes too worn down to use. The plate is not thrown away but is instead regrained and used again. For this reason, zinc plates usually remain the property of the workshop and are used time and again by many artists. We have had our zinc plates in the studio for over 20 years now and they are still regrained and used on a regular basis.

Zinc is inherently a greasy metal and is less easy to desensitise than aluminum. 'Desensitising' is the term that refers to the ability of the non-image areas to repel ink. Due to zinc's greasiness, printing can be a problem and scumming (a situation in which the non-image areas take on ink where they should not) occurs easily.

Aluminium plates are used only once and then must be discarded or recycled. (Unfortunately, the plate manufacturers will not take them back, so you will have to take them to your local recycling centre yourself.) Aluminium is easier to desensitise than zinc, making it a more stable surface to print on. Problems such as scumming are less likely to occur.

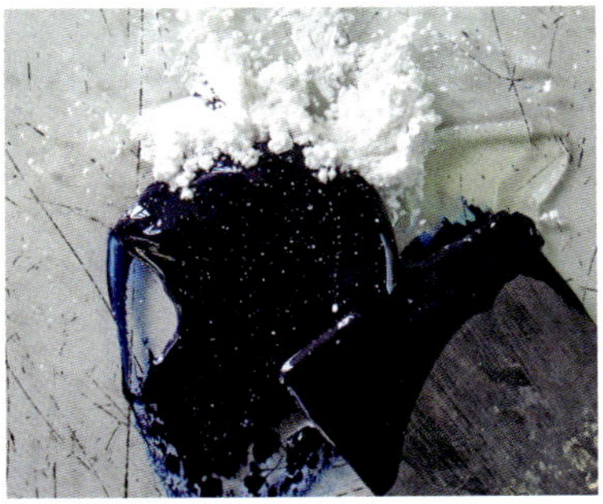

▲ **Mixing magnesium carbonate and heavy varnish into ink.**

INK

Roll-up black

For those producing hand-printed plate lithography, a specially formulated ink is available. Commercial lithographic ink is often used but for hand-printed lithography this should be modified or 'shortened' by the addition of magnesium carbonate and a tiny amount of heavy varnish (linseed oil varnish, no. 7 or 8) because it is too 'runny'. Note that commercial lithographic inks are designed to be used on fast-running machines, so their consistency is 'long' or runny. Graphic Chemical make two different types of lithographic black ink: Roll-up Black for plates and Senefelder's Crayon Black for stones. Charbonnel® Conservation Litho Ink is non-drying for preparation of stones and plates.

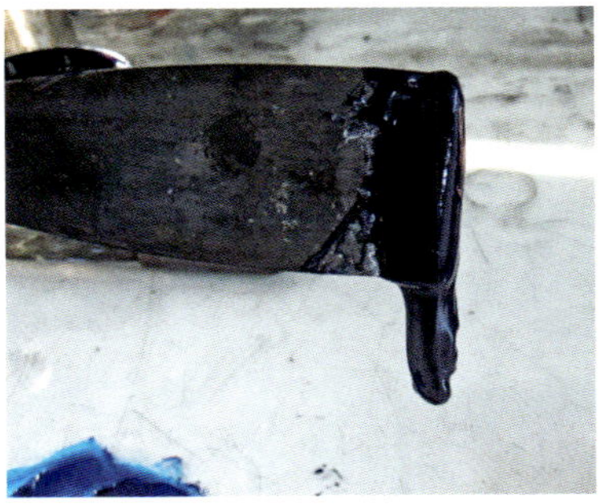

▶ **If mixed correctly the ink should drop off the palette knife and break at 5 cm (2 in.) into its fall from the knife's edge. If it does not, the ink is either too short (stiff/thick) or too long (runny).**

PHOTO ALUMINIUM PLATES

These plates are used by the commercial lithographic sector for printing graphics. The most useful for the printmaker are the positive working plates, which are pre-coated with a light-sensitive emulsion and exposed to an acetate positive (either hand-drawn or photographic). Positive plates are made by many suppliers and are typically 0.3 mm thick. Bespoke chemical systems are used to process them.

Aluminium plate lithography

To process an aluminum plate, follow the steps below.

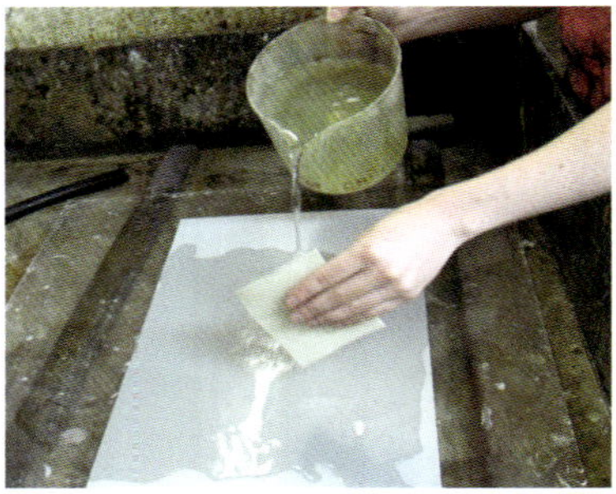

1 Place the plate face-up in a sink, raised off the bottom to ensure it stays free of any chemical residue or grit.

2 Flood the plate with hot water and wipe the surface with a clean, soft pad of cotton or muslin.

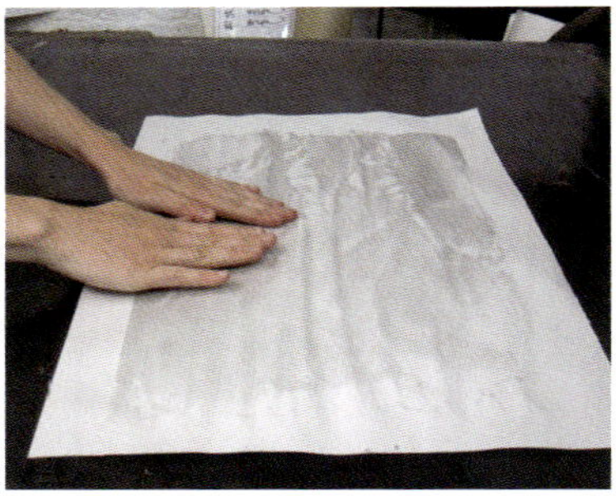

3 Remove the plate from sink and blot immediately with clean newsprint.

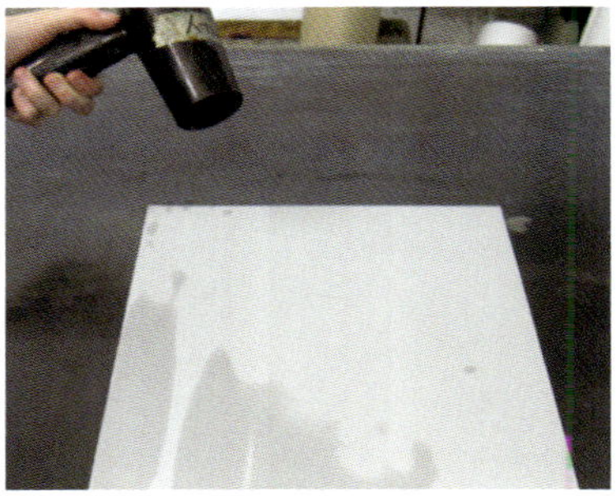

4 Dry the plate quickly with a hairdryer. This is important and will prevent oxidisation of the plate surface.

DRAWING ON THE PLATE

All conventional lithographic drawing materials may be used, including crayons and tusche. See p.151 for further information on drawing materials. Photocopier toner can also be used to create subtle wash marks. (It is hard to obtain old-style photocopier toner as so many photocopiers using toner are being replaced by inkjet printers and digital scanners.) Toner can be mixed with surgical spirit in varying diluted solutions and applied with a brush.

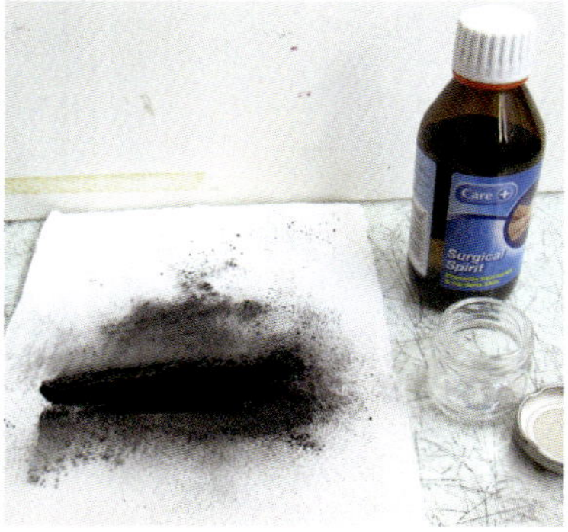

▲ **Toner, surgical spirit and an empty jam jar.**

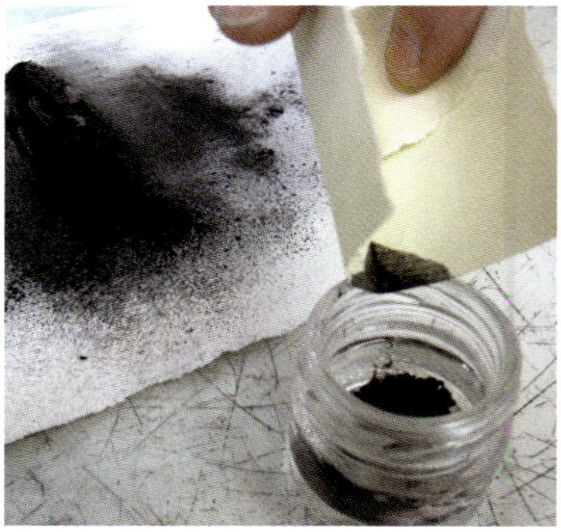

▲ **Mixing the toner and surgical spirit.**

▶ As a guide, white chalk can be used to map out a design on the plate. (As chalk is not greasy, it will not affect the plate.) The drawing is begun with a medium litho crayon by the artist Mary Dalton.

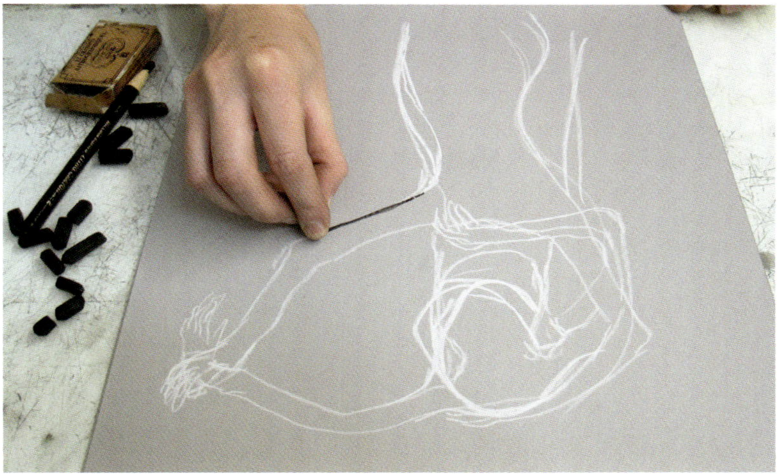

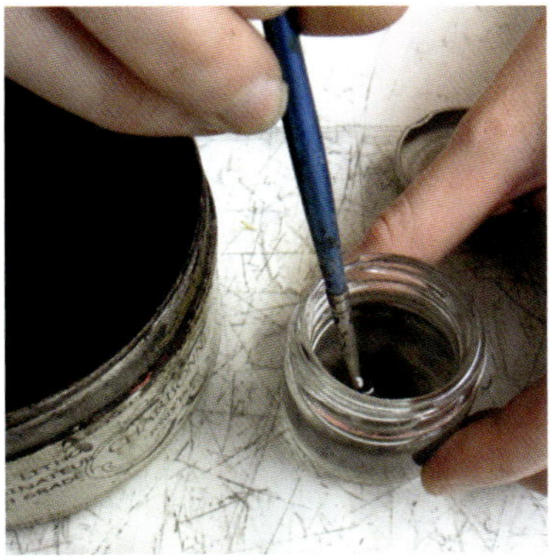

▲ Tusche is mixed with distilled water.

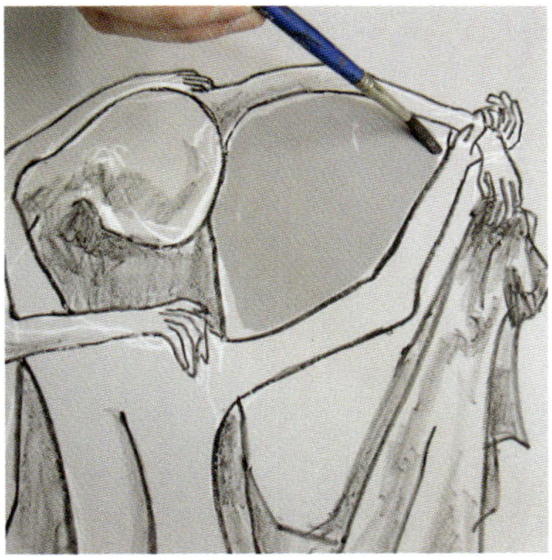

▲ Distilled water is brushed down.

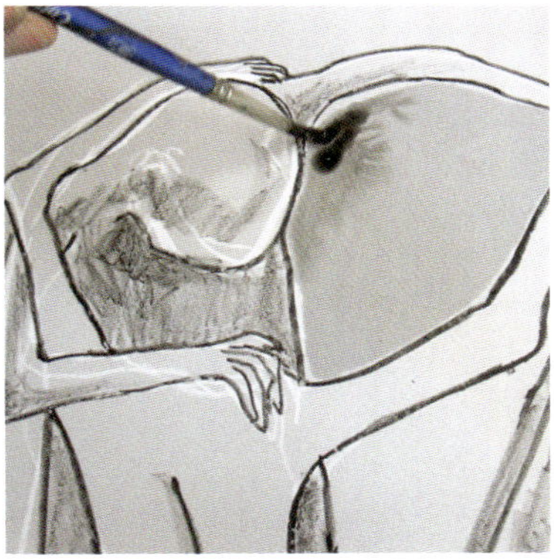

▲ The tusche mixture is pooled into the distilled water and allowed to disperse.

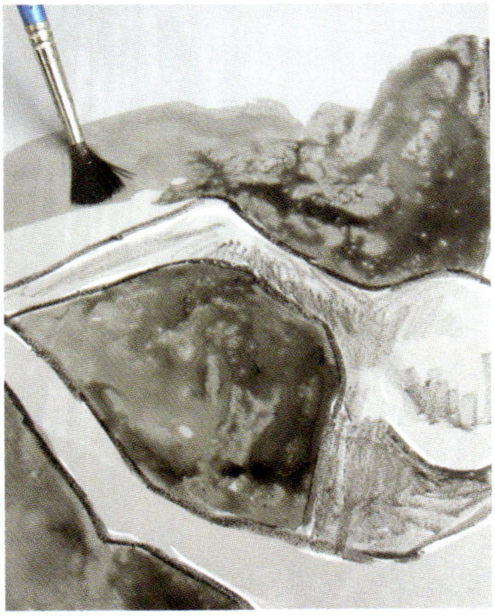

▲ Subtle washes are added using the toner/spirit mix.

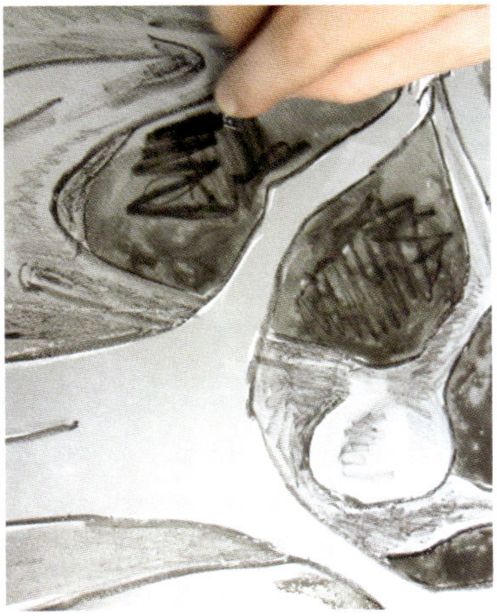

▲ Litho crayon is added over the washes.

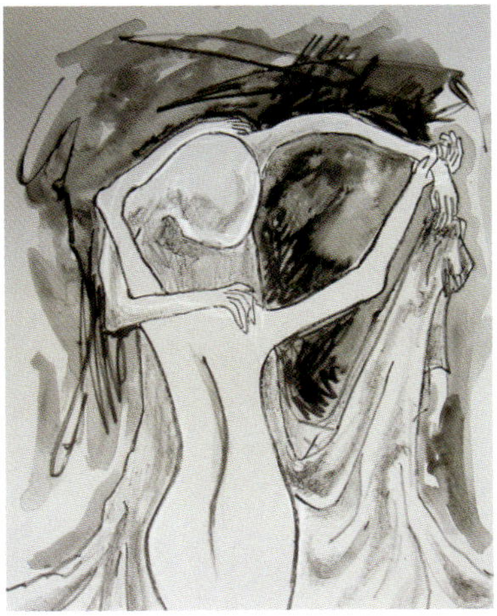

▲ The completed drawing ready for processing.

PROCESSING THE PLATE

As in all lithographic techniques, the main processing constituent applied to the plate is gum arabic. Gum arabic (gum is from the acacia tree and is used as a binder) creates a water-attracting, ink-repelling layer called the 'gum adsorb film' on the non-image area. The technical name for this process is 'etching the plate'. In the US, a gum etch has been specially formulated for plate etching called TAPEM (Tannic Acid Plate Etch Medium).

At the time of writing, TAPEM is not available in the UK but Paul Croft of the Aberystwyth University School of Art has developed an alternative recipe;

- 1920 ml gum arabic (ph4)
- 30 ml phosphoric acid (80% Ortho Phosphoric Syrupy Type)
  (This represents a ratio of 1:64.)

It is recommended that beginners use 50:50 TAPEM:gum arabic. For experienced lithographers, the American TAPEM gum etch or UK TAPEM mixture can be adjusted using gum arabic to suit different types of drawing on the plate. Strong, greasy, drawn areas will require full strength (pure TAPEM) and delicate washes will require a 50:50 mix of TAPEM and gum grabic diluted with more gum arabic to make a weaker etch.

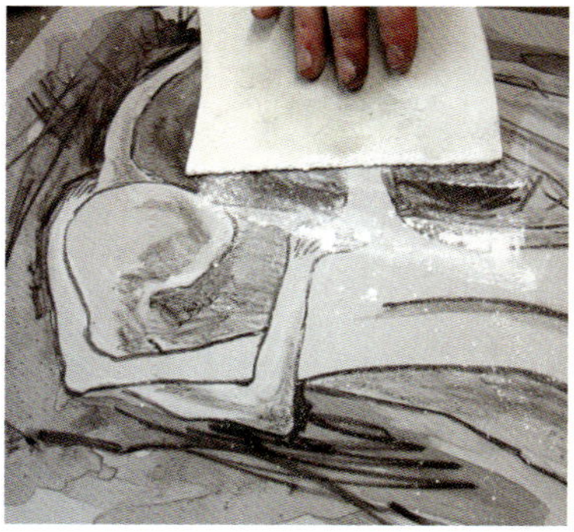

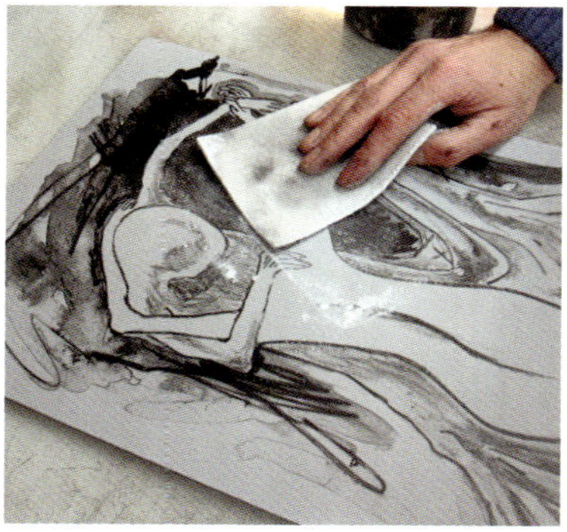

1 The finished drawing is dusted with French chalk.

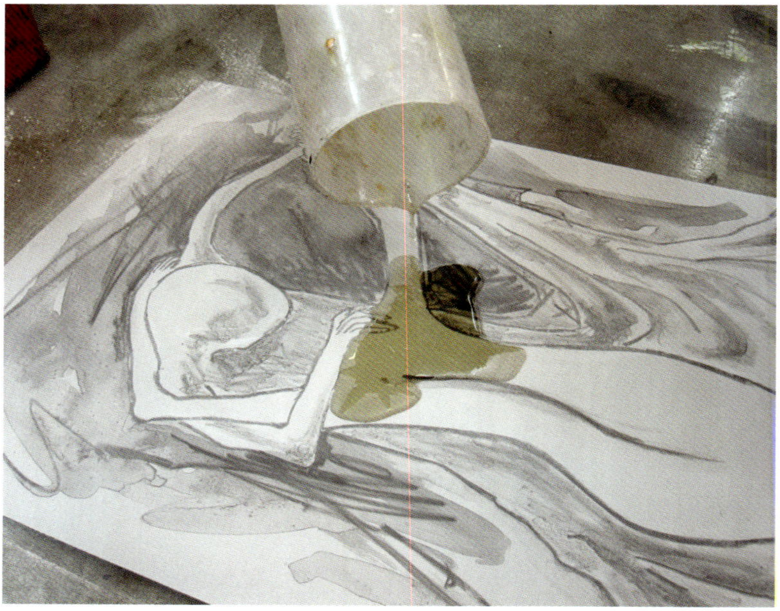

2 The whole plate is now covered in gum etch (TAPEM mixture). Use a clean, soft cloth to cover the entire surface and then buff the gum down to a thin layer. This is important as gum must not be lying over the drawn areas – these will need to be washed out through the gum. Imagine you are polishing furniture: buff the gum until it is almost dry! Allow the plate to sit for at least half an hour.

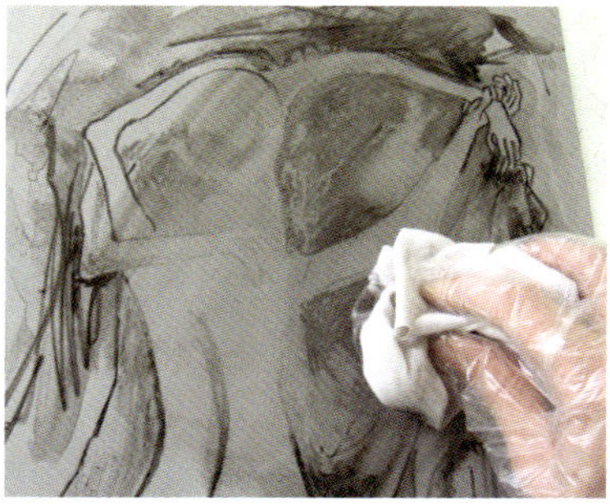

3 The drawing materials are now washed out with lithotine or white spirit. Finish off with acetone (a solvent used for cleaning and degreasing) to remove any traces of grease.

4 To reinforce the image, a base of shellac must be added. This permanent layer helps to stabilise the image during printing. In the US, a product such as Deep Etch Laquer V is formulated for this task. In the UK, use Button Polish or French Polish. Pour a little onto the plate and buff down to a thin layer. The shellac is then cured by heating the plate for approximately 10 minutes. Do this on a hotplate or in a preheated oven (120°C/250°F). Allow the plate to cool.

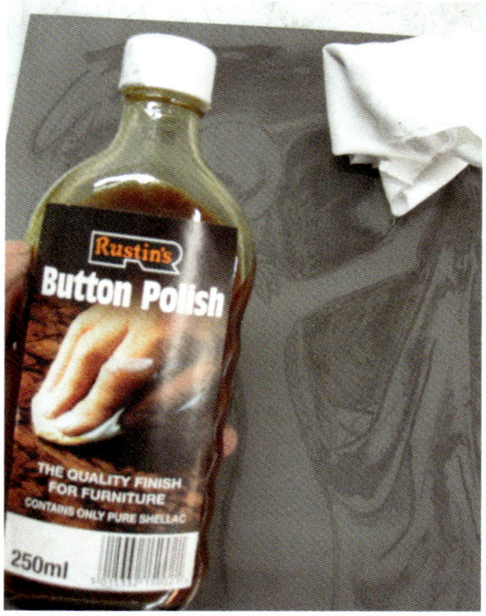

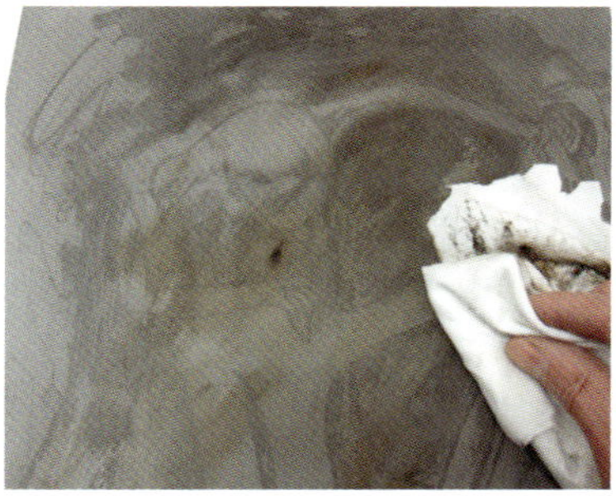

5 Rub a little asphaltum into the image. This will act as a greasy 'key' for the printing ink.

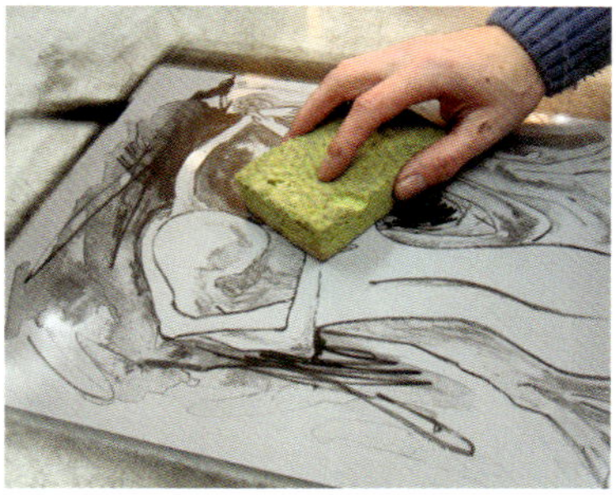

6 Using a clean sponge, buff the plate with gum arabic. Dry with a hair dryer. Using a clean sponge dampened with water remove the gum film.

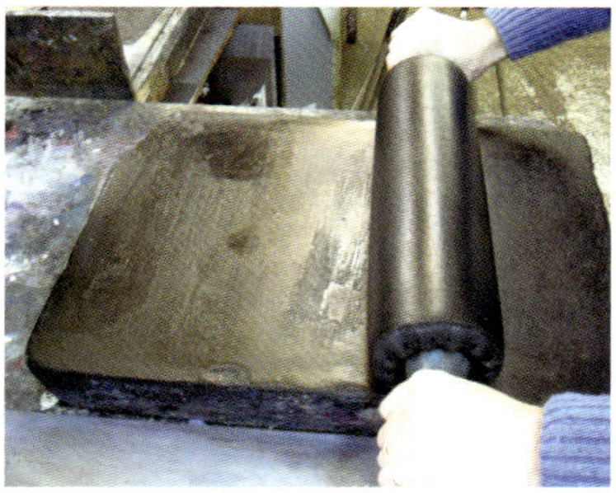

7 Keeping the plate evenly damp, roll the plate in non-drying proofing black. We recommend a mix of Senefelder's Crayon Black and Roll-up Black. Use a leather nap roller.

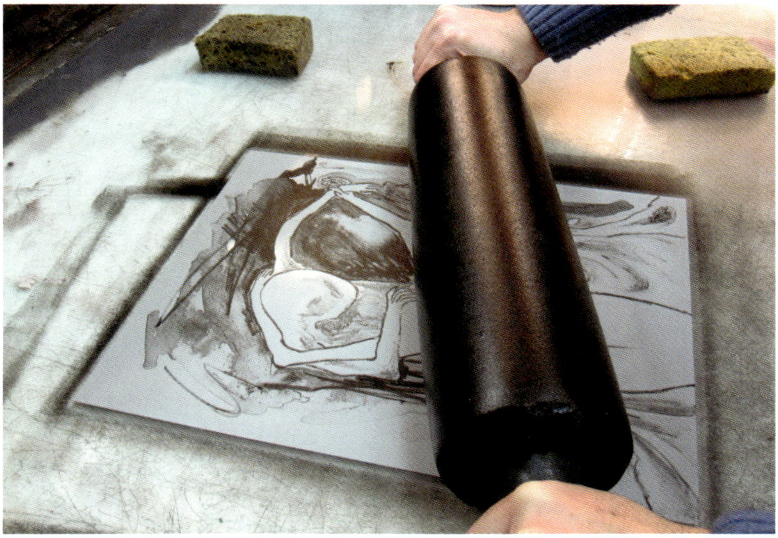

8 Ink the damp plate with a thin layer of proofing black, making several roller passes from different directions.

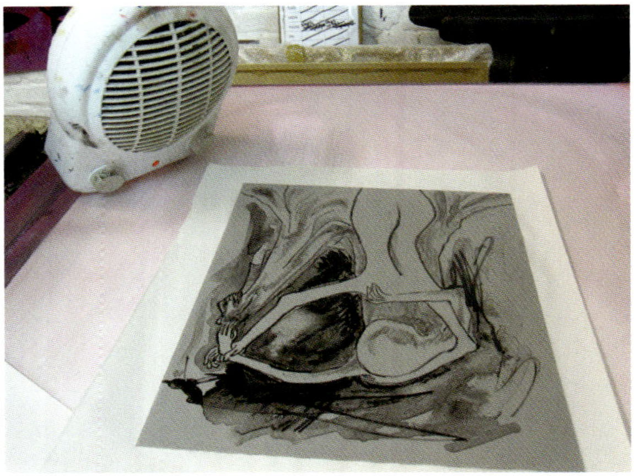

9 Dry the water layer with a fan or hairdryer.

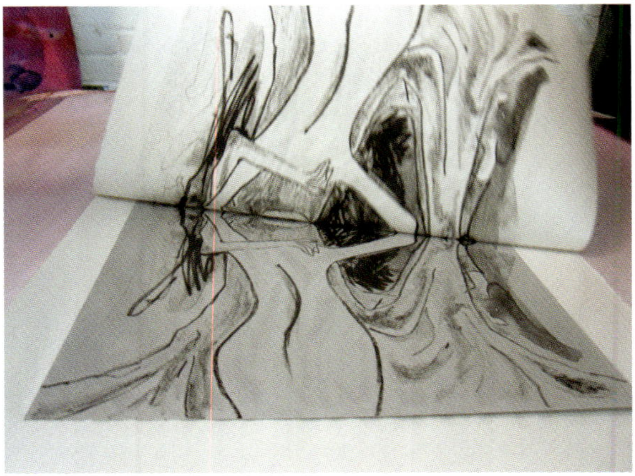

10 The image will need building up to a full-strength black by inking and printing several times onto newsprint.

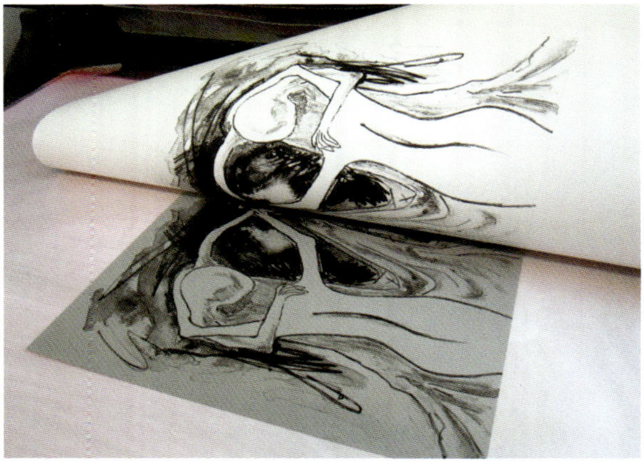

11 The plate is now ready for a second gum. The purpose of this is to stabilise the image for an edition of several prints. We recommend a gum etch of 50% gum arabic and 50% atzol. If an edition is not desired it is possible to run off a few prints onto good quality paper without doing a second etch.

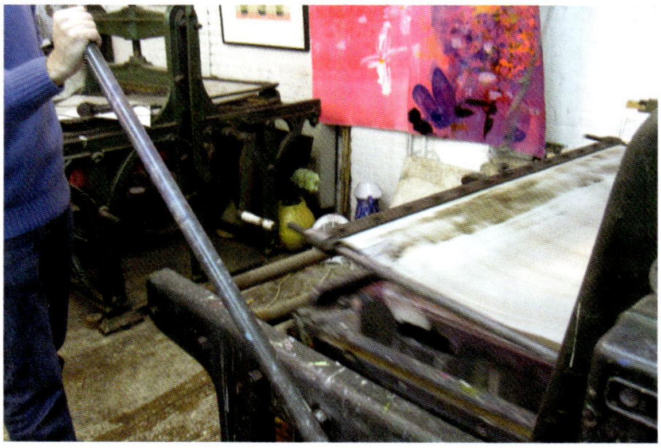

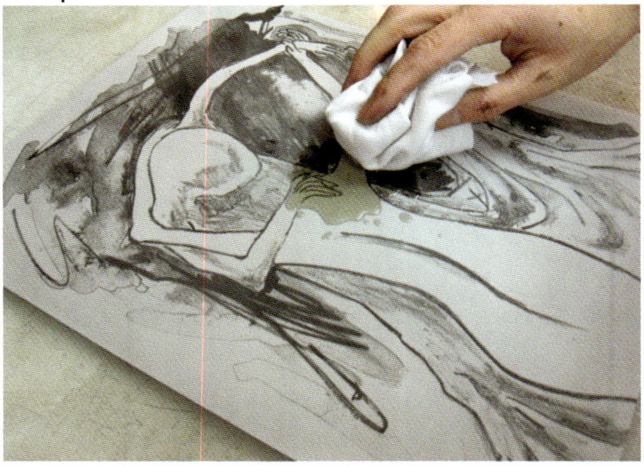

12 For the second etch dust the plate with French chalk and re-gum the plate with gum etch made from 50% gum arabic and 50% aztol. Dry the plate. Wash out the black proofing ink on the plate with white spirit or lithotine, rub in a little asphaltum and begin building up the image with black or colour lithographic relief ink. Print proofs onto newsprint. A Thomas Mann direct litho press (see picture left) was used to print the image in this sequence.

EDITIONING AND PRINTING IN COLOUR

If you want to print the image in colour, dust the image with French chalk and gum it. Dry. Then wash out the black ink with white spirit or lithotine and rub asphaltum onto the image. Remove the gum using a sponge dampened with water. Keep the plate damp and roll up the image in your chosen colour. This page shows the image being rolled up in red lithographic relief ink.

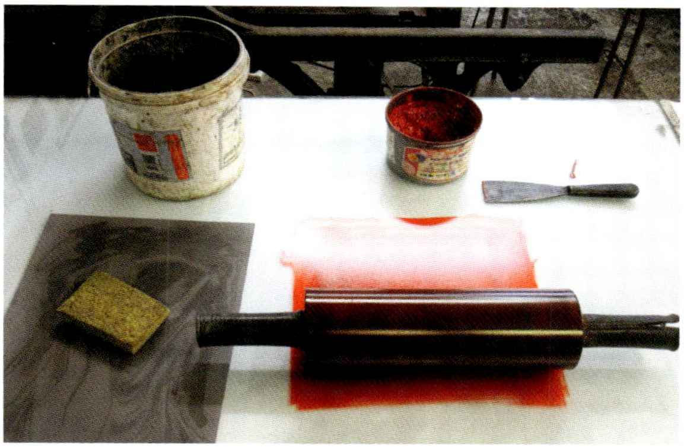

▲ The proofing black must now be washed out and replaced with a colour (or black, if required).

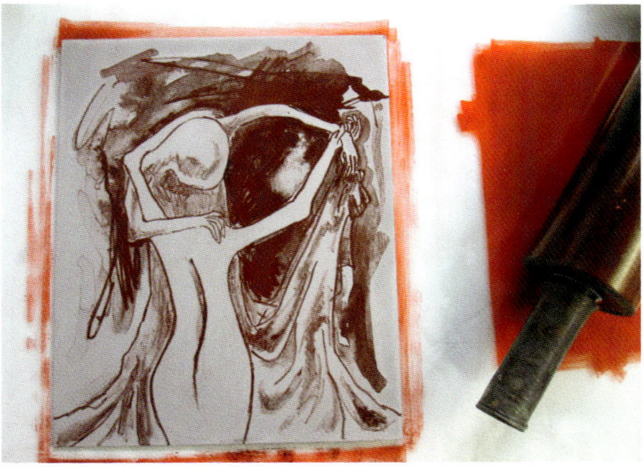

▲ The plate after inking in red.

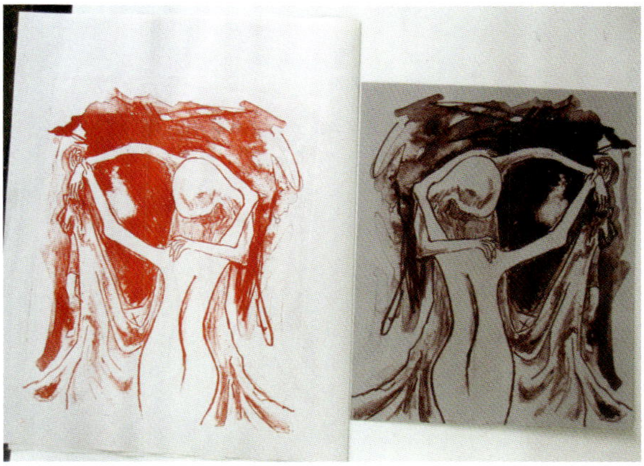

▲ Proof the plate onto newsprint until the image has reached full strength.

REGISTRATION

A backing sheet and the T-Bar method of registration ensure that images are printed squarely on the sheet and that colour layers line up accurately (see p.160). Each colour layer must be drawn on a separate plate of the same size. Chalk paper is used to transfer the key design onto another plate (see p.151).

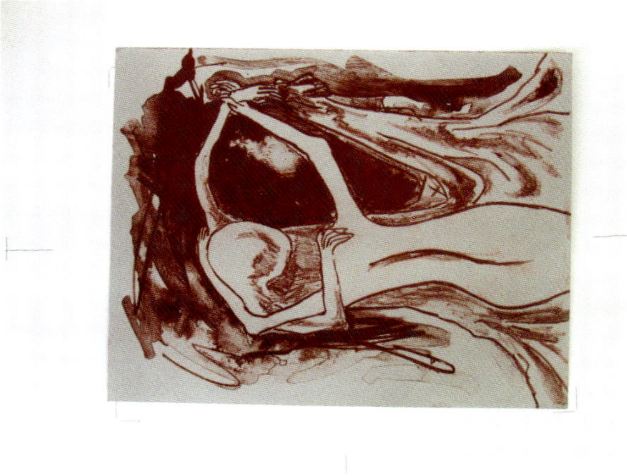

▶ Take a sheet of paper that is larger than the paper to be printed on. Place the printing plate in the centre and using a pencil, draw round the corners. At the top end of the backing sheet, draw a long 'T'. On the two other, sides draw a line. Image courtesy of artist Mary Dalton.

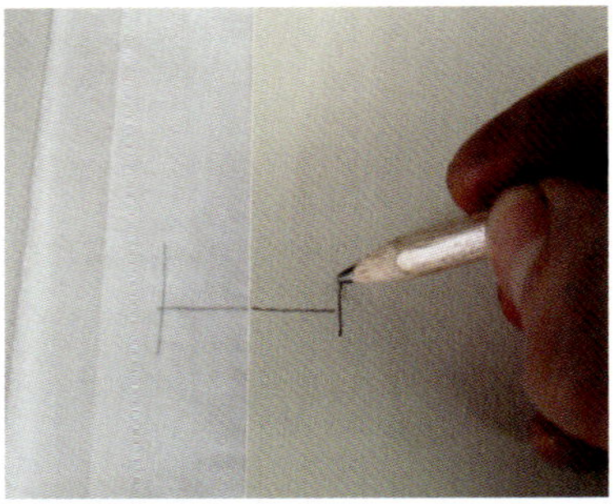

▲ As each printing sheet is laid down, transfer the 'T' and the two lines to the back of the sheet. Use the backing sheet throughout the whole edition: it has the plate position and the paper position marked on it.

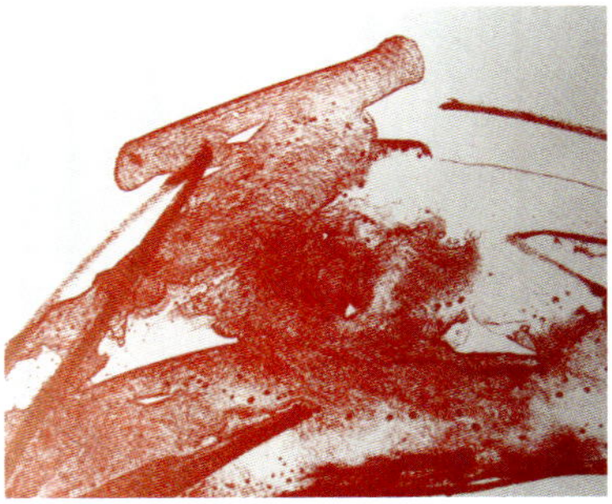

▲ Detail of tusche and toner washes printed in red.

MAKING CORRECTIONS TO AN ALUMINIUM PLATE

At the drawing stage, corrections may be made. Use acetone with a rag or cotton bud to remove all traces of grease from the plate surface.

Once there is ink on the plate, corrections must be made *after* the shellac layer. (See step 4 describing the application of the shellac layer on p.169).

If the shellac layer has been added to the plate, corrections are made using Positive Deletion Fluid. This is different to acetone as it is a commercial deletion fluid used for offset aluminium plates. It can, however, be used on hand-printed and processed aluminium grained plates. This is illustrated on p.180.

Counter-etching aluminium

If drawing is to be added, then the gum adsorb film must be removed so that the surface will be sensitive to grease once more. The plate must be inked in proofing black and dusted with French chalk before carrying out this procedure. To mix a counter-etch solution, take ¼ teaspoon of anhydrous citric acid and mix it with 300 ml of water. Heat the solution in a microwave until it is approximately 80°C. With the plate flat in the processing sink, pour half the solution over the plate. Use a soft brush to move the solution over the plate for two minutes. Rinse the plate with water and dry it quickly to prevent oxidisation. Repeat this process using the remainder of the counter-etch solution to ensure the plate is fully prepped for drawing. Once drawing is added, the plate can be etched and proofed as described on pp.169–71 beginning from step 5.

ZINC PLATE LITHOGRAPHY

The steps for making a lithograph on zinc are very similar to the steps used for aluminium plate lithography. Zinc plate lithography has its own chemicals and gum etch. Prepasol is used to counter-etch or prep a plate, it should be pre-mixed in two dilutions (20:1 and 7:1 respectively). Erasol is a caustic solution for making corrections and can be applied neat with a cotton bud or a stiff brush (but do wear eye and hand protection). Atzol is a gum etch (equivalent to TAPEM) and is usually mixed 50:50 with gum arabic. Victory Etch (this is acified gum) is a strong gum etch that is sometimes used to clean a plate when the plate is under proofing black, and it is also useful if a plate is scumming up during printing.

As mentioned above, zinc plates may be used three or four times for separate drawn colour layers. Once a drawing has been printed, the whole plate is treated with Erasol to destroy all grease content. The plate is then prepped again (with 7:1) and is ready to use like a new plate. A 'ghost' image of the previous drawing often remains and this is a useful guide for drawing the next colour layer.

PROCESSING

Prepping (also referred to as sensitising or counter-etching)

This process prepares the plate to accept grease.

1 Wet plate with water. Pour on the Prepasol solution 20:1 (20 parts water to 1 part prepasol) and rock the plate to rinse the entire surface of the plate with the solution. Dry plate.
2 Gum margins to make a one inch border around all the edges of the plate. Dry.
3 Draw. (Use chalk, red Conté® crayon or rouge/red oxide-dusted tracing paper to map out design.)
4 Dust image with resin and French chalk.

Note that resin (also called 'rosin') protects the drawing. The talc (French chalk) helps the gum applied to the plate draw in closer to the edges of the drawn image.

De-sensitising (1st etch)

This process separates greasy image areas from water-retaining non-image areas.

1 Gum the plate with gum arabic/gum etch. (This is a 50:50 mixture.)
2 Buff down to a thin, even layer and then leave the plate to dry for at least 30 mins (we recommend longer, if possible).

WASH OUT AND PROOFING

This process replaces the drawing material on the plate with ink.

1 Wash out the image with turpentine (if turpentine is not available, use white spirit or lithotine) and a rag.
2 Apply a thin layer of asphaltum or clear wash-out (turpentine, white spirit or lithotine) for light colours. This gives the ink a greasy surface to key onto.
3 Remove the gum layer with water and sponge.
4 Begin rolling up the plate with proofing black, keeping the plate damp at all times.
5 Proof onto newsprint: three to five printings will be needed before an image is strong. Examine proofs and decide whether to add drawing, erase or move onto edition paper.
6 Dust image with resin and French chalk. If the plate inked up cleanly, re-gum it, following the steps for the 1st etch (de-sensitising) on p.173. If scumming occurred during inking the plate you will need to make a solution of 50% Victory Etch and 50% water. Distribute this solution over the entire surface and leave for two minute. This will clean and stabilise the non-image areas where the scum is occurring.
7 Dry the plate and dust with French chalk, then gum it with a 50:50 solution of gum arabic and aztol. Dry the plate. The plate is now ready for printing in black or colour, or it can be stored until you are ready to print it.

PRINTING IN COLOUR

To print an image in colour, mix up your preferred shade, prepare the paper and then follow the wash-out sequence as in the steps above. As with proofing non-drying black ink, proofing colour strength needs to be built up over three to five pulls.

Erasing

Roll up the image in non-drying black and resin and chalk the image. To erase small areas, use a stick or rubber hone dipped into Erasol. You can then gum etch the whole plate.

To erase the *whole plate*, remove all ink and gum. In a sink, pour on Erasol and rub it into image with a rag. Pour on fresh Erasol and leave for a few minutes before scrubbing again. Rinse plate with water and prep with strong prep in a 7:1 solution (seven parts water and one part Prepasol).

Note that you must use goggles and heavy-duty rubber or nitrile gloves at all times when working with Erasol.

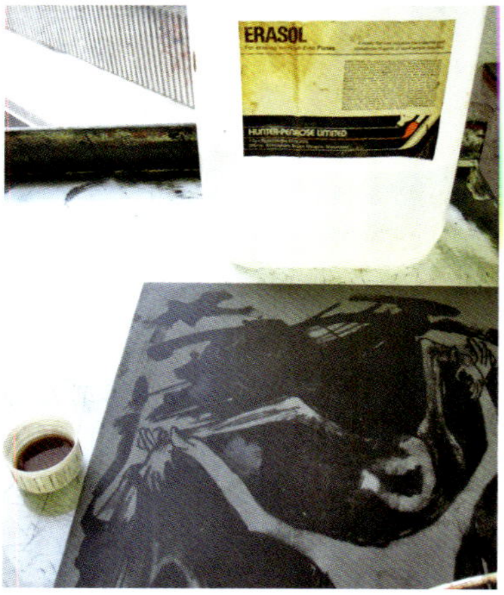

▲ Using Erasol to erase a small area on a zinc litho plate.

Adding drawing

Place the image under non-drying black, resin and French chalk. Next, prep the plate with a 7:1 Prepasol mixture (seven parts water and one part Prepasol). Dry the plate and redraw.

STORING PLATES

Always store plates under non-drying black ink. Chalk and buff with plain gum arabic.

At the end of a printing session, the plate must be stored in proofing black, French chalk and gum. To do this, strip the coloured ink from the plate by running it through the press onto newsprint several times (we have found there is no need to wash out the remaining colour). Next, ink the plate in non-drying black ink before applying the chalk and gum. Once the gum is dry, wrap in newsprint and store the plates horizontally in a drawer to prevent them from becoming dented or warped.

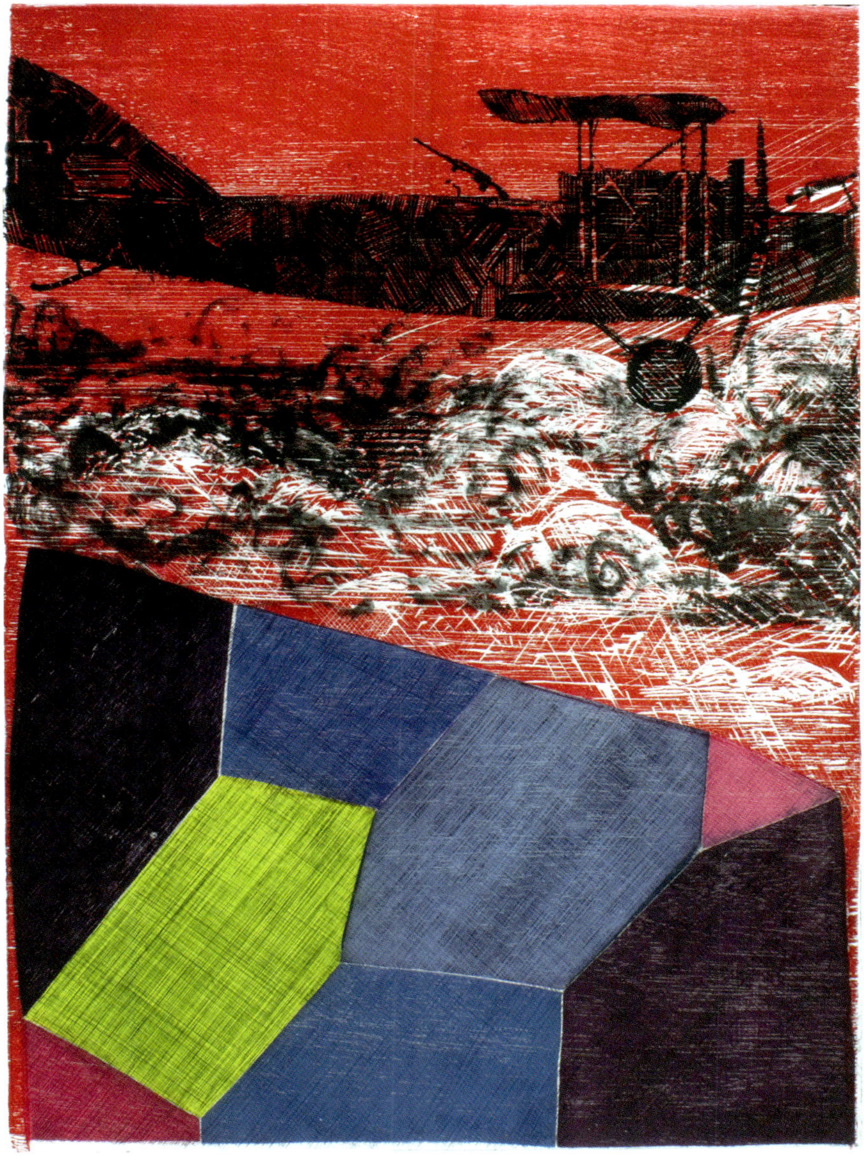

▶ **Colin Gale, *Sagittarius Rising*, 2010. Lithograph woodcut and etching, 76 x 112 cm (30 x 44 in.).**

▶ Rachel Gracey, *Wimbledon Common*, 2000. Lithograph from a zinc plate, 76 x 112 cm (30 x 40 in.).

◀ Petrina Wright, *Untitled*, 2011. Collage on paper (left) with lithograph (below) printed from a zinc plate, 76 x 56 cm (30 x 22 in.).

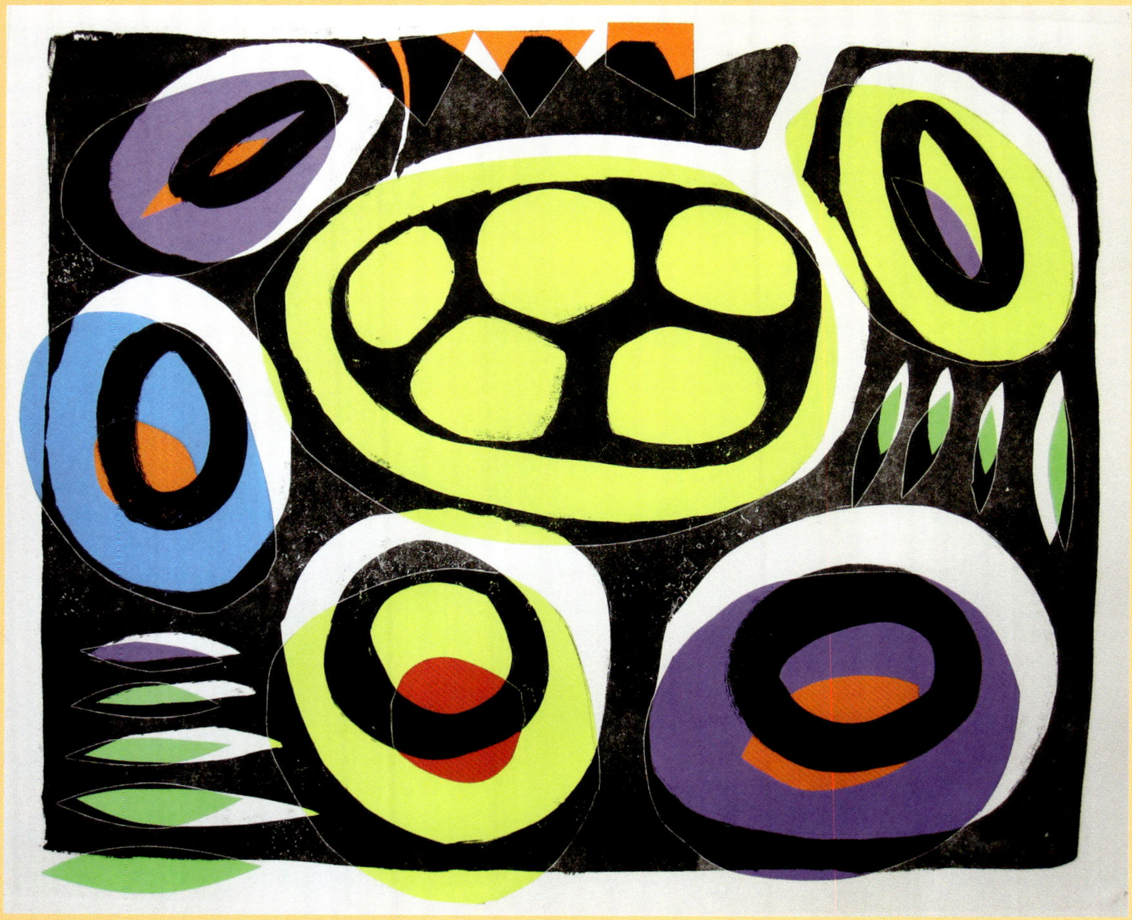

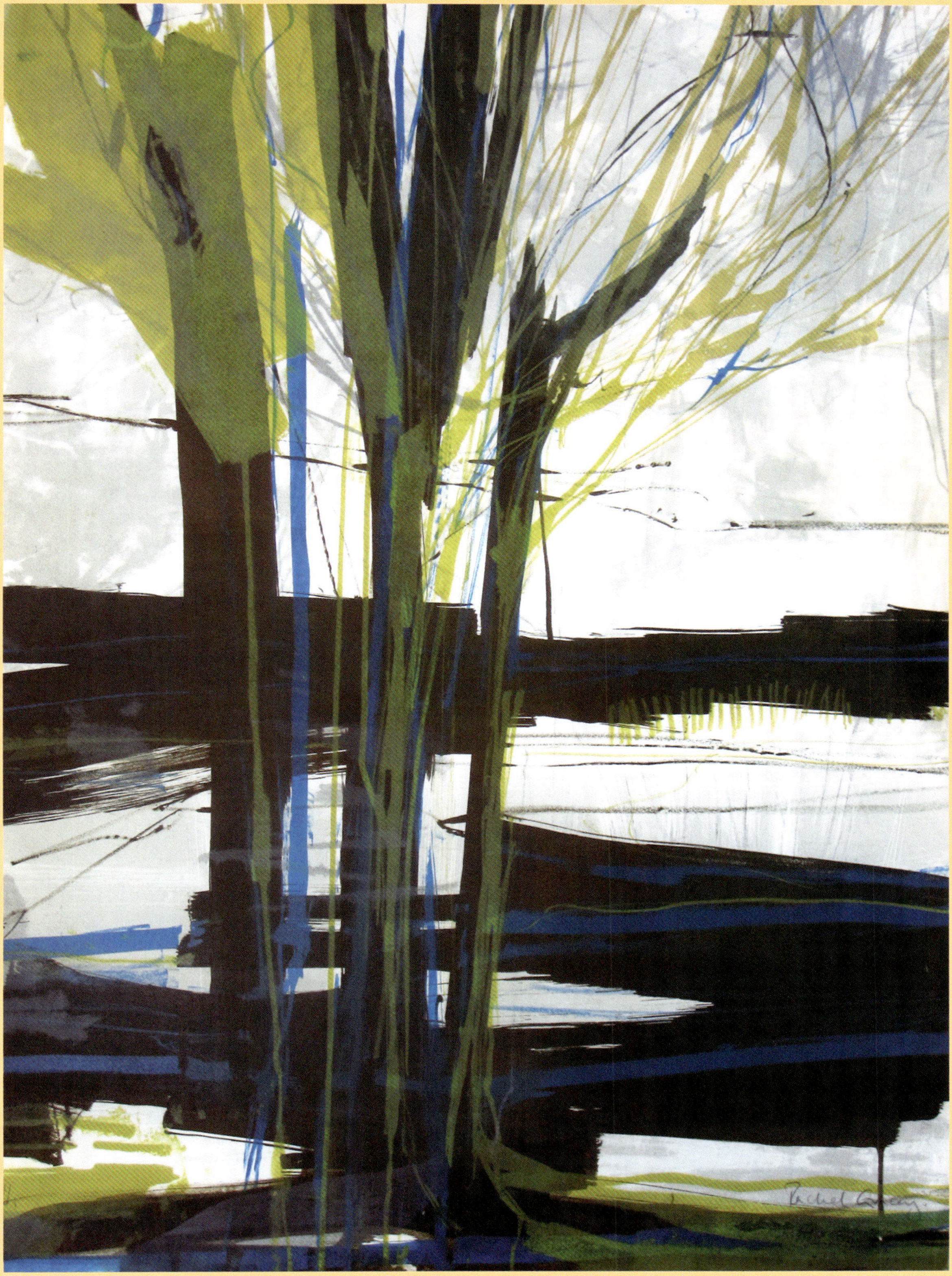

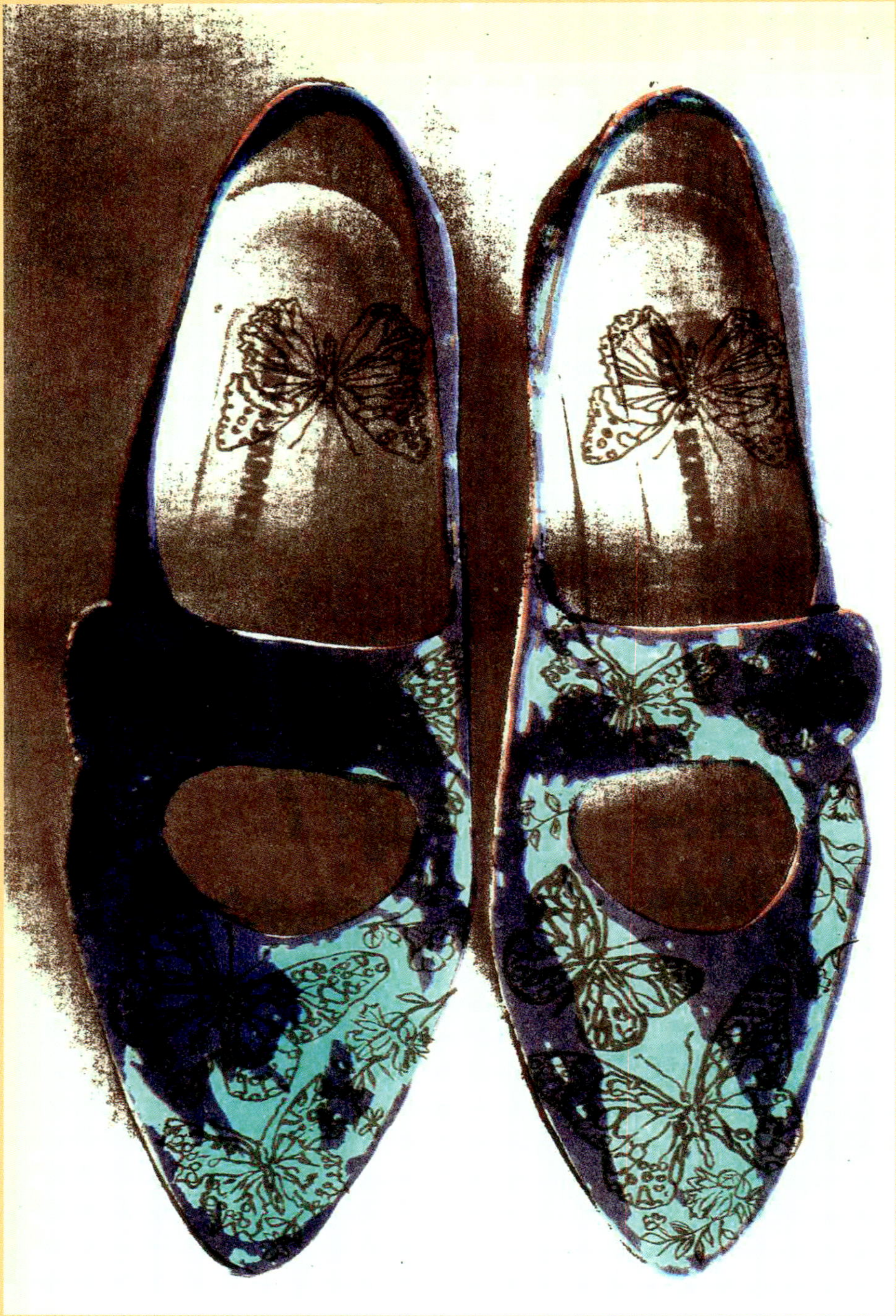

photolithography

PHOTO LITHO PLATES AND PRINTING ON AN OFFSET PRESS

Hand-operated offset presses were for many years used for proofing commercial litho plates. In today's commercial printing industry, this is no longer done. The offset process used by artists is similar technically, but a million miles away idealogically. Commercial lithography deals with reproduction and in great quantities. Artists draw or paint an image and then choose the printing press they want to use in order to offset that image from the plate to a specific paper. That the image is a photo-based one that is made and then printed from a photo litho plate is the artist's intention – it is an original print.

The offset machine has two beds, one for the plate and one for the paper. A cylinder roller that has a rubber blanket wrapped around it picks up the ink from the plate on the first bed (the image is now on the rubber blanket on the cylinder) and continues its roll to deposit or roll the image onto the printing paper on the second bed.

The main advantage for the artist printmaker is that the image is printed the way it appears on the plate and not in reverse, as occurs in the traditional 'direct' processes of stone and plate lithography. The offset press is used mainly with photo litho plates but can be used for ball-grained aluminium and zinc plates.

MAKING A PHOTO LITHO PLATE

Photo litho plates are made for the commercial offset industry. They can be purchased in quantities of 30 plates from commercial graphic ink and plate suppliers. Printmakers use positive working plates. These products are not expensive as they are made in such large numbers, but their supply may soon become more limited as companies are using CTP (computer to plate) systems, which means hand-processed plates are no longer needed. In fact, Kodak stopped making photo litho plates in 2010 but we are assured by our suppliers that plates will still be available in the future.

Photo litho plates can be printed on a direct litho plate, an offset press or an etching press.

◀ **Carole Hensher, *Shoes*, 2009. Lithograph printed from three photo litho plates on an offset press, 27 x 35 cm (10½ x 13¾ in.).**

PROCESSING A PHOTO LITHO PLATE

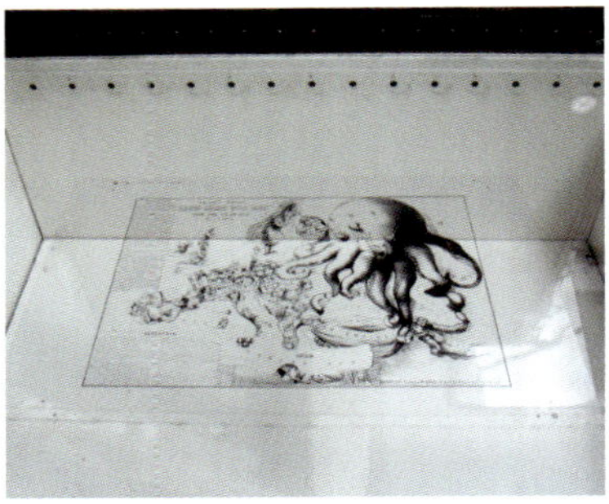

▲ A positive artwork is placed on the glass of the exposure unit. If the image is to be printed on a direct press, the positive is placed right-reading (as it should print finally). If the image is to be printed on an offset press, the positive must be placed down in reverse (so that it is right-reading on the plate). Artwork positives are discussed in on pp.130–2.

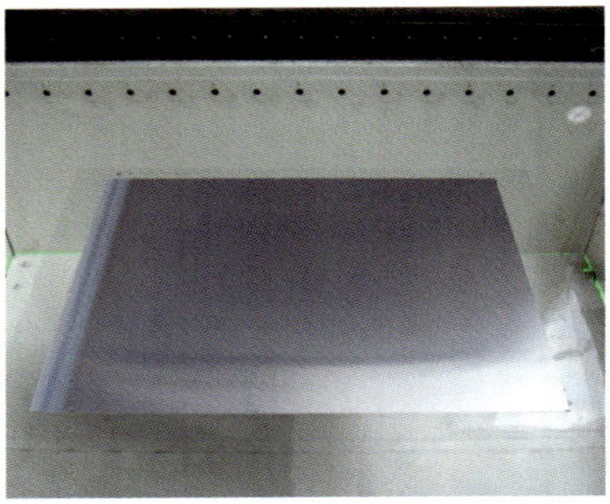

▲ The plate is placed face down on the positive art work and exposed. A test strip should be made to ascertain the correct exposure time.

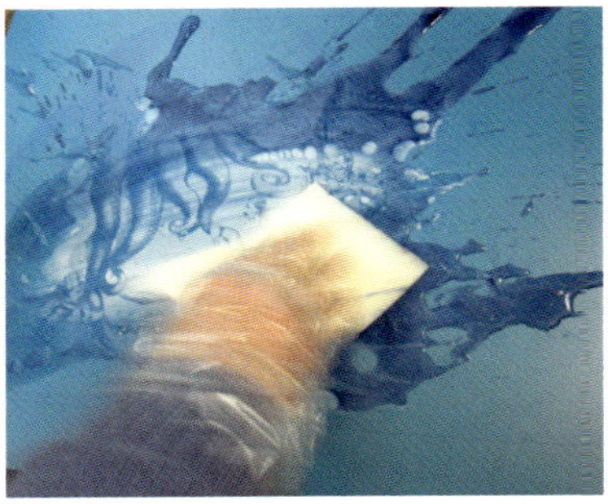

▲ The exposed plate is placed in the processing sink. Positive developer is poured onto the plate and distributed quickly using a soft cloth.

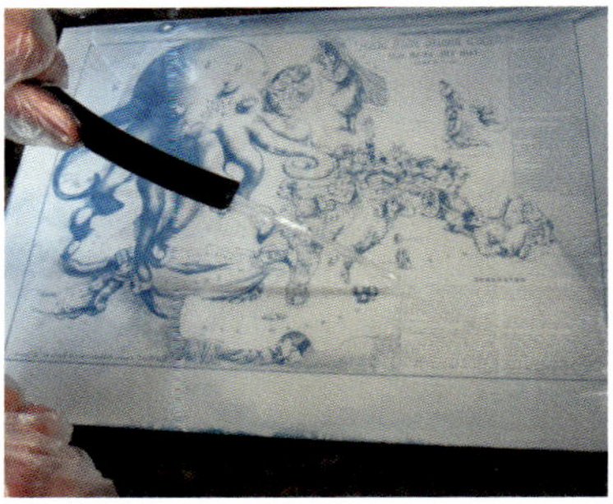

◀ Once the image is developed, the plate is rinsed with water and dried. Once dry, the plate is coated thinly with plain gum arabic. To print the plate, rub in a little liquid asphaltum over the image or use a little of the printing ink thinned with pure turpentine. (This will act as a key for the ink.) Remove the gum arabic and roll the plate up with printing ink. The image will need to be built up by printing onto newsprint in the standard way for lithography. It is not necessary to proof photo litho plates in non-drying black as the image is permanently fixed on the plate after developing.

CORRECTING MISTAKES ON ALUMINIUM PLATES

Positive Plate Deletion Fluid is also used on ball-grained aluminium plates that have been fully processed.

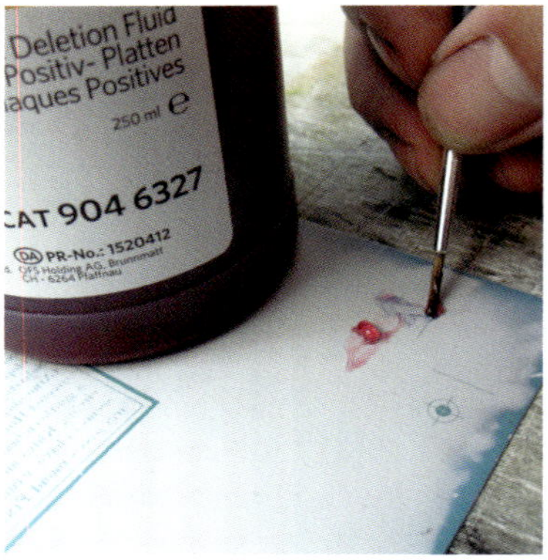

▶ Any blemishes, spots or image areas that you wish to remove can be taken away using Positive Plate Deletion Fluid. This is a ready-made product that looks like red jelly. It is painted directly on to the marks to be removed and sponged away with water. Wear eye protection when using this product.

PRINTING ON AN OFFSET PRESS

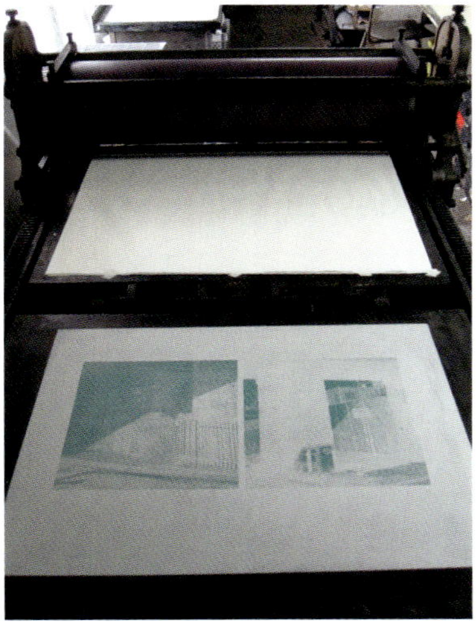

▲ A hand-operated offset press with plate and printing paper in place.

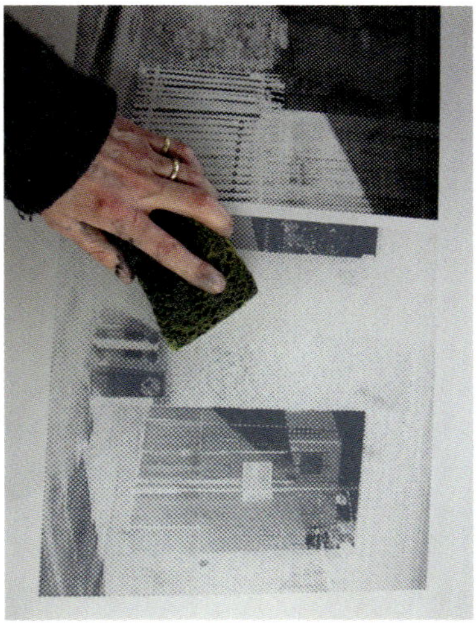

▲ The printing plate is damped with water, then rolled with ink.

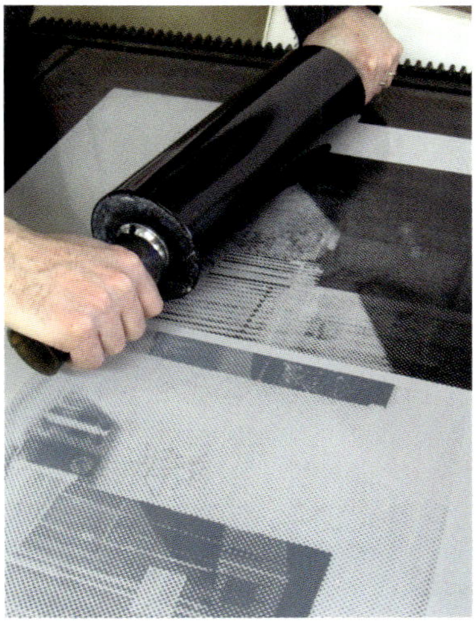

▲ This image – comprising two pixelated photographs – is inked half in black and half in dark grey.

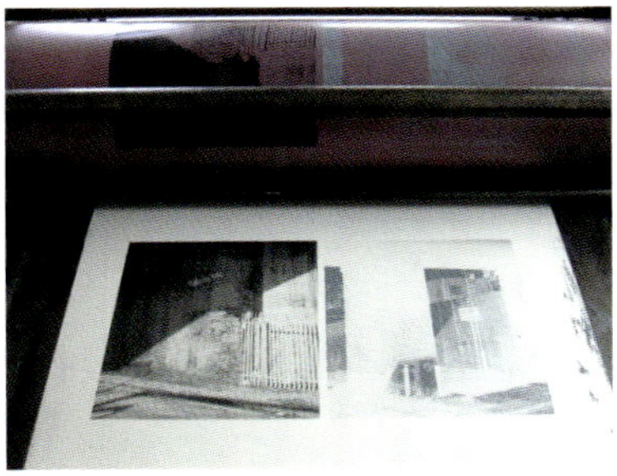

◀ The ink transferred onto the roller cylinder.

▼ Trevor Abbott, *Untitled*, 2010. Lithograph printed in two colours from one aluminium plate, paper size 76 x 56 cm (30 x 22 in.).

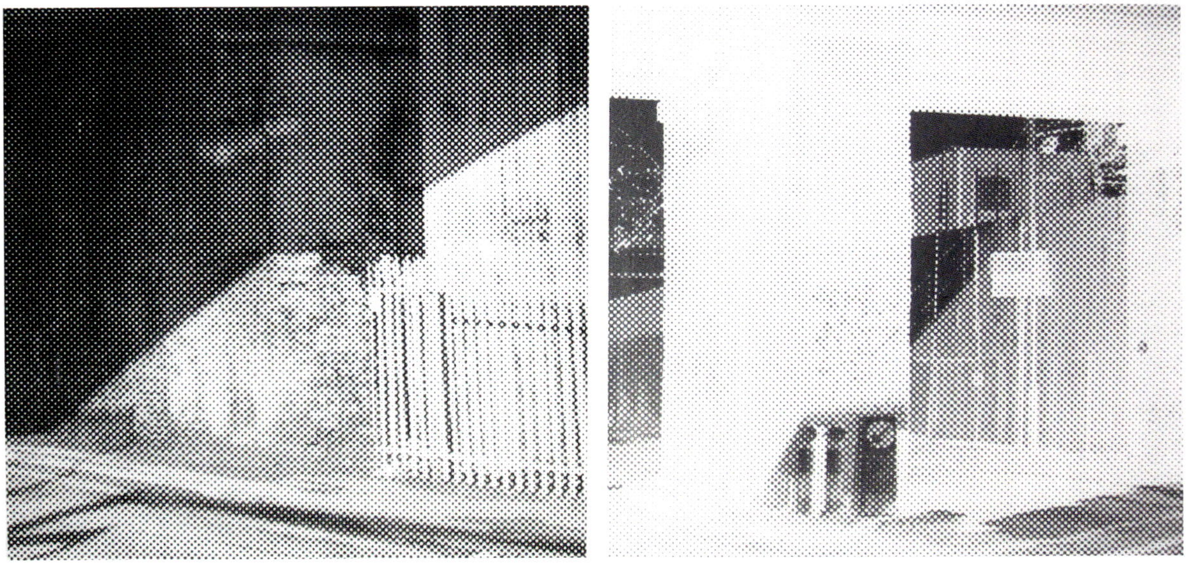

REGISTRATION ON AN OFFSET PRESS

Using an offset press has a number of benefits. Not only are images printed 'the right way round', but registration is much easier. The printing plate and printing paper are always in a fixed position on the two beds, meaning the image is always printed in the same place each time the roller passes over the plate and then onto the paper. This in itself makes printing considerably faster than it is on a direct press. Accurate registration is achieved by printing the image onto a sheet of clear acetate of substantial thickness which is taped to the bed on which the paper lies. It is now possible to place the printing paper in the correct position by sliding it under the acetate which has the image from the plate printed onto it. The acetate is then flipped back from the surface of the bed so that the corrected, registered paper can be printed onto. If the paper has cut edges, its position can be registered by sticking tabs of thin paper to the bed at the corner and one side. Each sheet is then laid down registered to these tabs.

Registering a proof of *Salman Rushdie as D.I.Y. Zola* by Tom Phillips

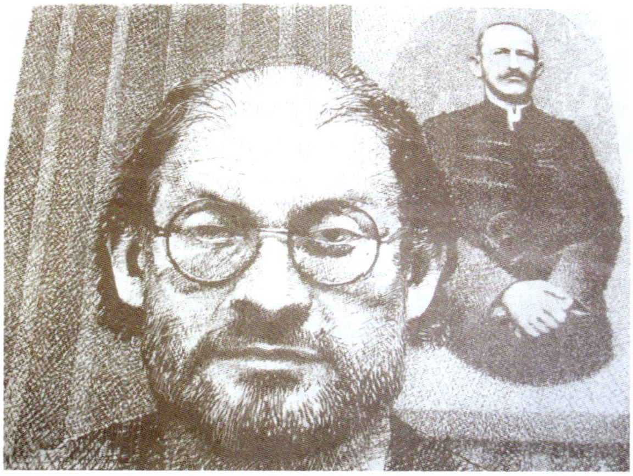

▲ The first brown layer.

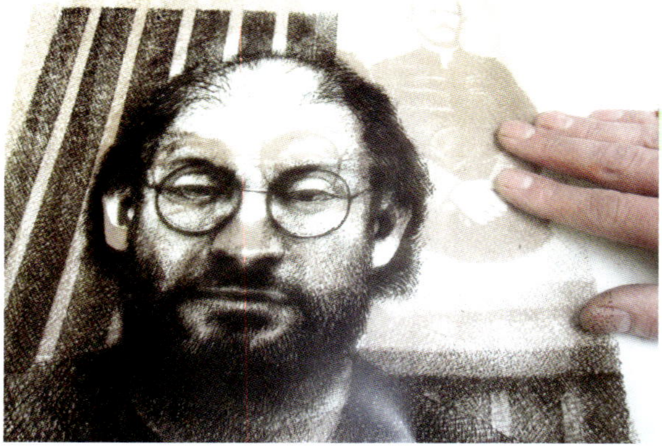

The black is printed onto the fixed acetate sheet. The sheet with the first colour layer is slid under the acetate and manoeuvred into position.

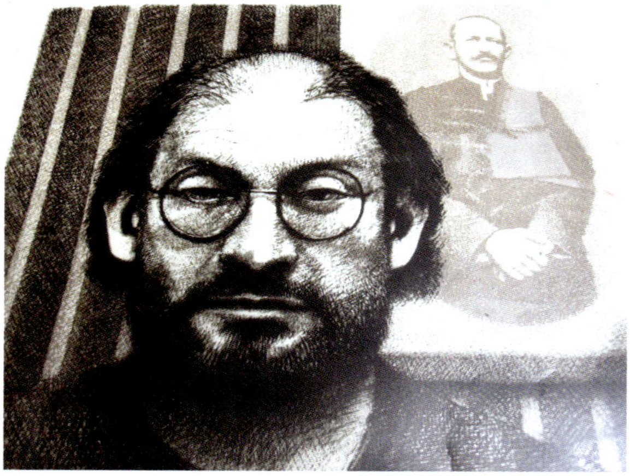

◀ The print is now in register. The acetate is flipped back and the press is run, dropping the black layer on top of the brown. As the paper used had deckled edges, each print was registered using the acetate. After proofing, it was decided to add a third colour of yellow ochre which was printed first, underneath the brown layer.

▶ Tom Phillips's *Portrait of Salman Rushdie as D.I.Y Zola* lithograph, 1994, 56 x 76 cm (22 x 30 in.), printed from three aluminium photo litho plates on a hand-operated offset press. The drawings were made on grained acetate using pen and ink and plumtree opaque liquid.

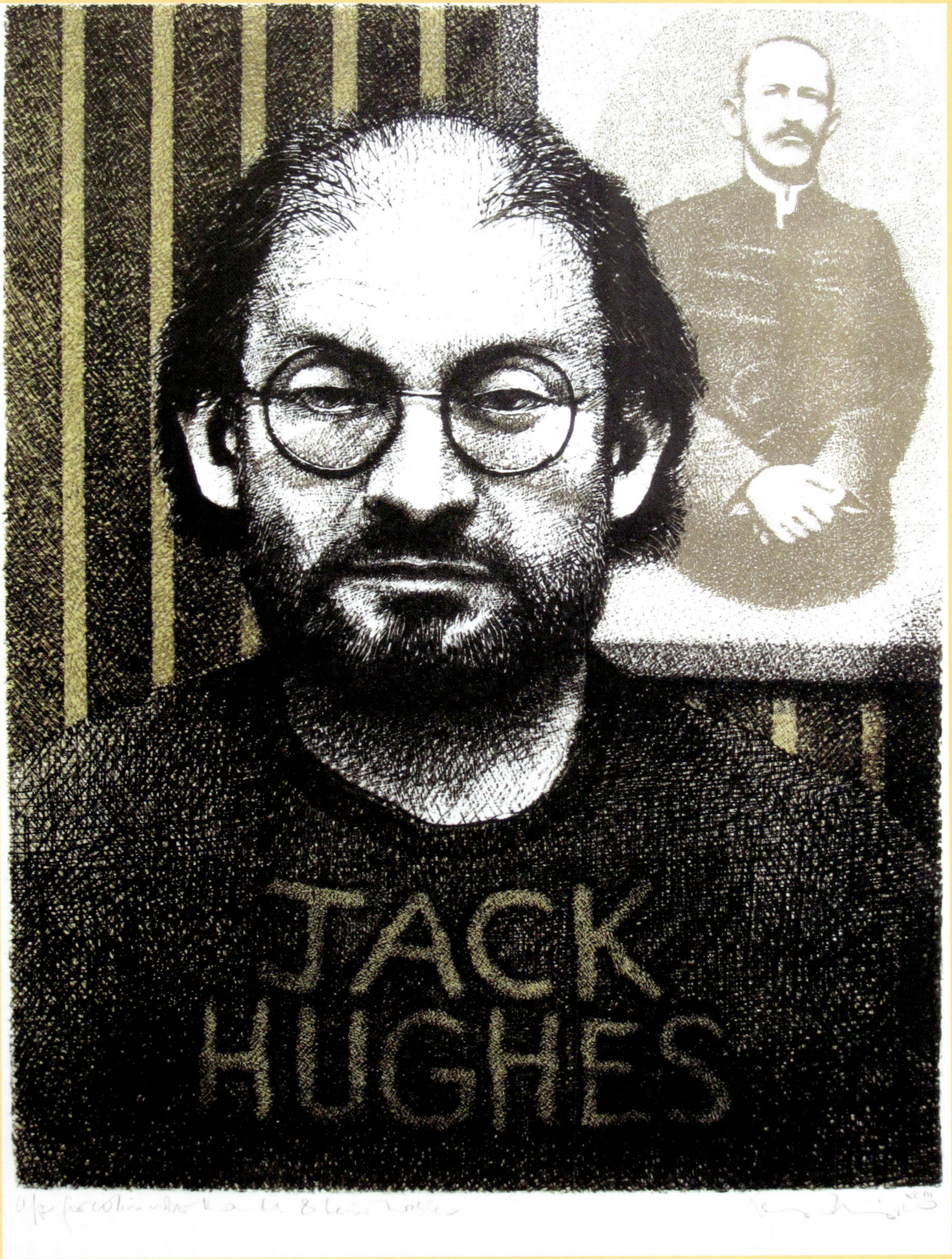
JACK
HUGHES

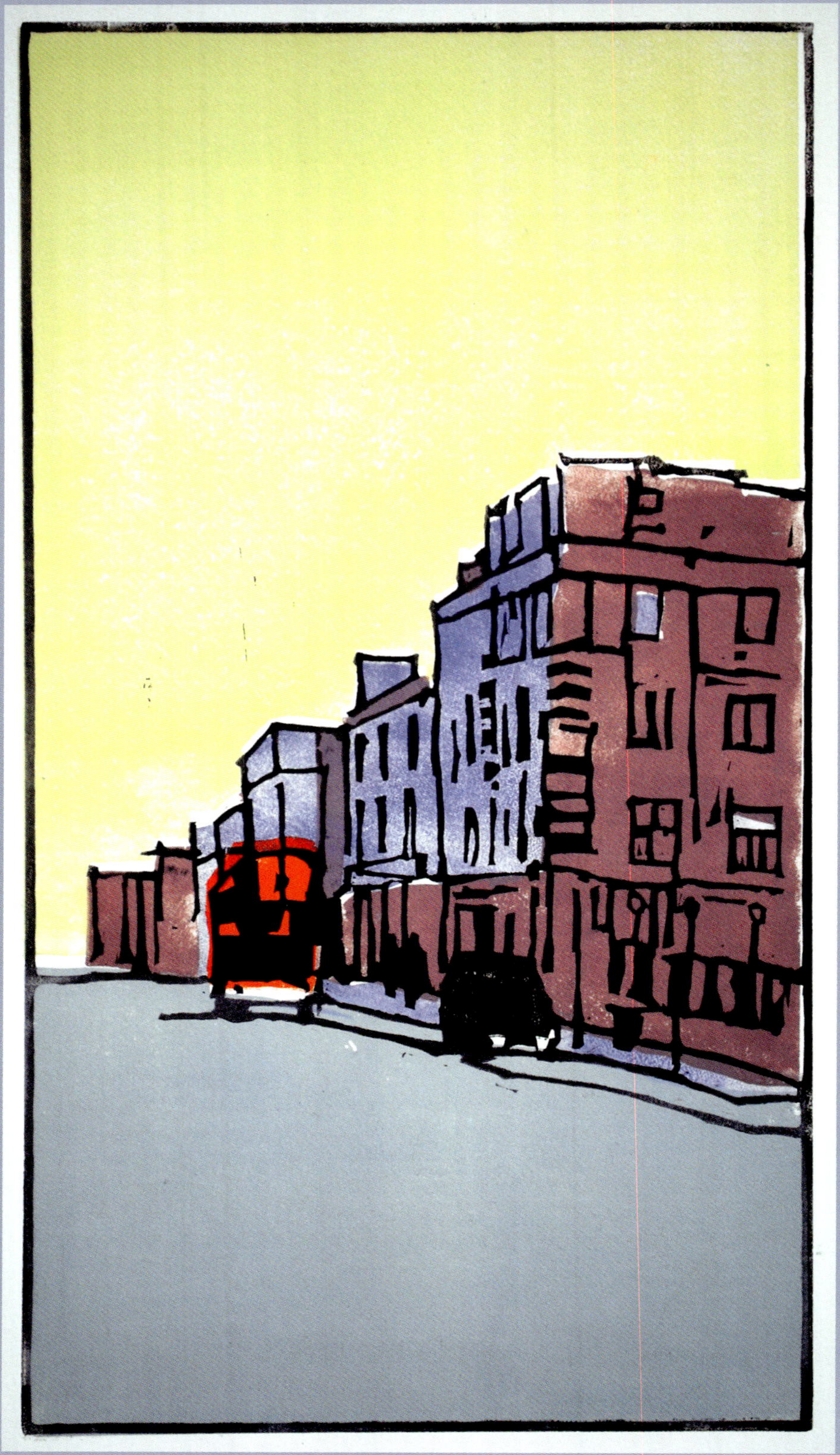

7

screen printing

Screen printing is a stencil process. Stencils have been used for centuries to duplicate patterns on walls, textiles and paper. Crude stencils were cut from thin metal and card, and colour was applied using a stiff brush. The problem of bridging 'floating' areas – the middle of the letter 'O', for example – always hampered the making of very fine imagery. The Japanese are credited as the first to use elaborate cut paper stencils that were held together by strands of human hair or silk. This approach led directly to meshes of silk (and later, of nylon) being held and stretched to a wooden frame.

◀ Natalia Avdeeva, *Bus*, 2011. Screen print using hand cut stencils, 22 x 32 cm (8¾ x 12½ in.).

Today, stencils are attached to nylon mesh and coloured ink is pushed through the open areas using a blade called a squeegee, onto the paper or material beneath.

Screen printing was always a commercial activity but over recent years it has been replaced by commercial lithography and inkjet technologies.

It was not until the 1960s, when the Pop Art movement began, that screen printing was seen as a legitimate means of artistic expression in its own right. Artists nowadays have a wealth of technical choices with the use of photographic emulsions applied to the mesh. Hand-drawn and painted stencils, as well as photographic and computer-generated imagery, can all be used as a base for creative work.

EQUIPMENT

Screen printing equipment generally falls into two categories. The first is a basic, low-tech mobile set-up, where screens are clamped onto home-made base boards. These can be used on a table top and removed and stored away vertically when not in use. This set-up is perfect for classrooms where multiple use is needed or for individuals printing in a home-based studio.

The second category of equipment is for professional use. If large print sizes and quantities are required, a dedicated screen vacuum table is used. This consists of a bed or table with a counterbalanced metal frame to which screens of different sizes can be clamped. The squeegee used for printing is also clamped to a mobile arm referred to as a 'one-arm squeegee', which holds the squeegee at the correct printing angle and facilitates smoother, even printing. The screen bed surface has hundreds of holes drilled through it, allowing air to be sucked through the holes when the vacuum pump is on. This suction holds the printing paper in place, ensuring accurate registration and also that the paper does not stick to the under-side of the screen when it is raised.

▼ There are various ways to clamp a screen to a base board. These include shop-bought clamps or improvised versions such as a hinge and rod.

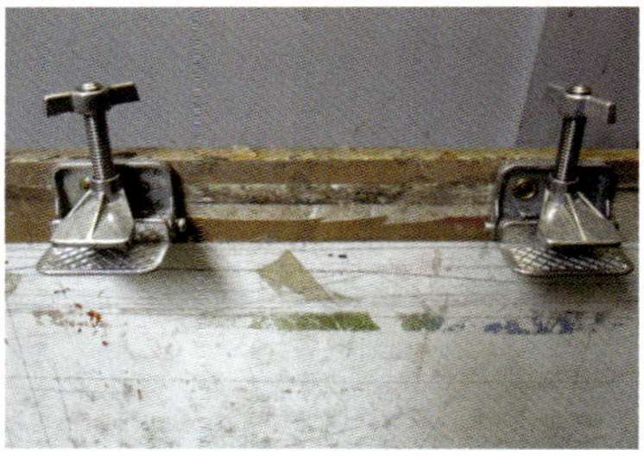

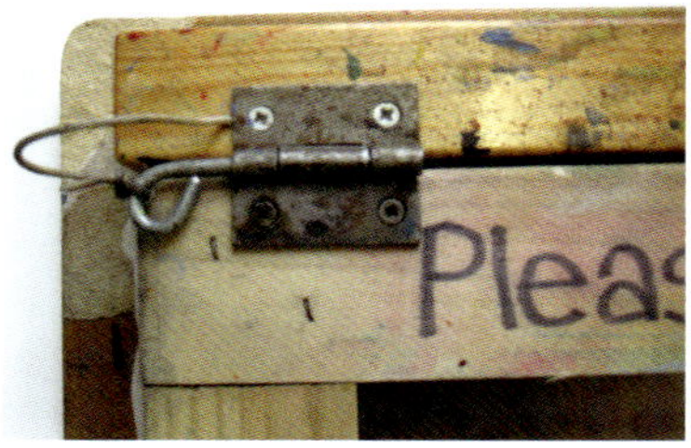

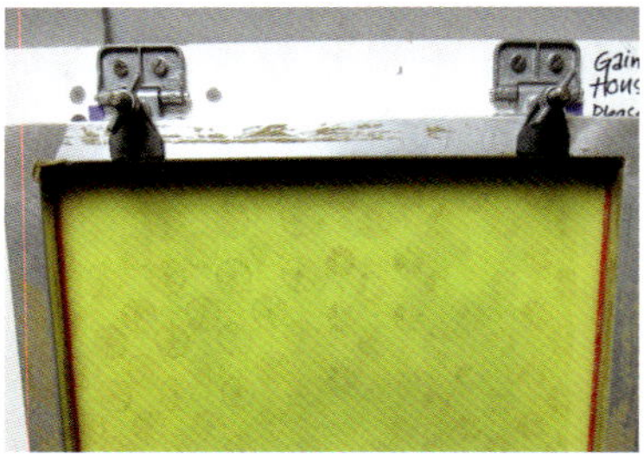

Screens and mesh

Screens frames are constructed of wood, steel or aluminium. Aluminium would be our preferred option: it is lightweight and does not rust or warp. Screens need to be stretched professionally to ensure correct and even tension.

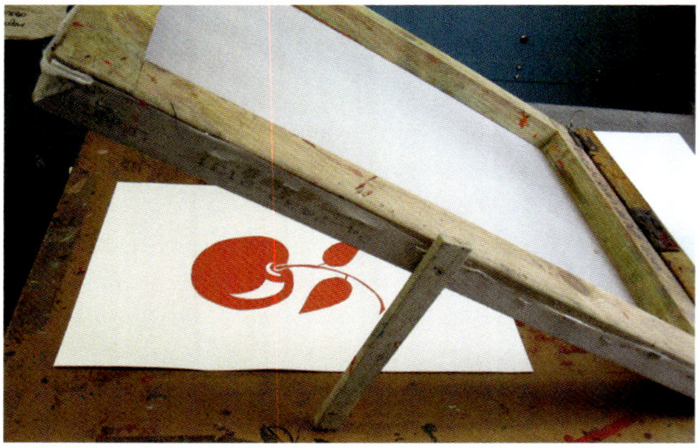

▶ Screen and base board. Note the wooden 'leg' that enables the screen to stand proud of the baseboard.

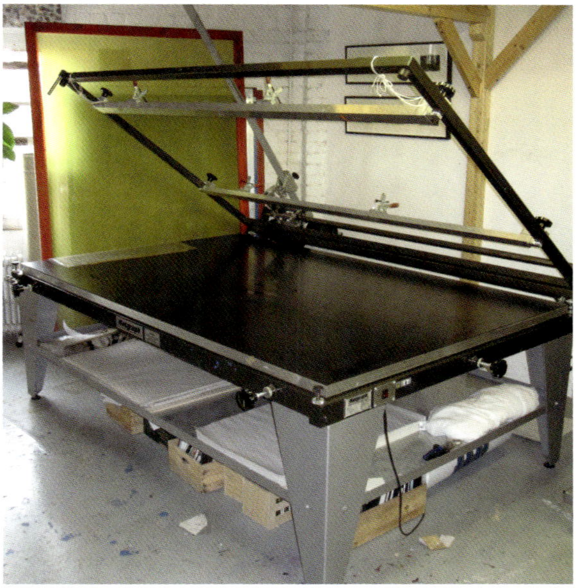

▲ A large screen bed by Natgraph.

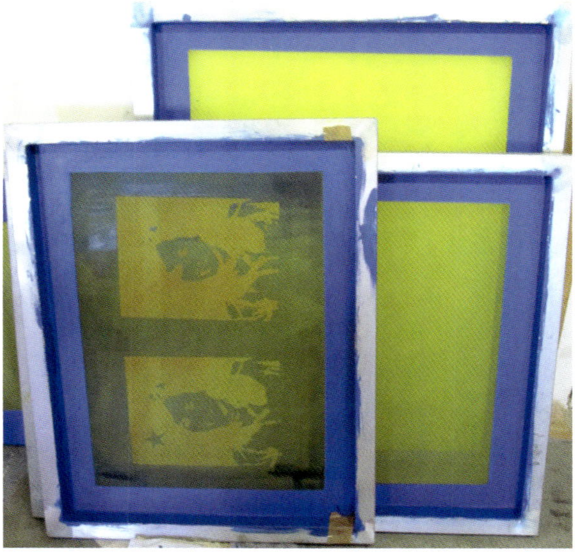

▲ Aluminium-framed screens.

The mesh is monofilament polyester. Mesh comes in different grades represented by a number and a letter. The number refers to threads per centimetre; the letter 't' refers to standard and 'hd' for heavy duty. For water-based screen printing, 120t mesh is standard for fine work. 90t is also commonly used and suits heavier colour work. It should be noted that the higher the mesh count, the more fragile the screen mesh is (the nylon fibres are finer) and the easier it is to damage.

Note that tensioned mesh is very fragile and sharp objects damage it easily. It is best to use only plastic implements when you are cleaning or placing ink on the screen. Store screens carefully in a vertical wooden rack when they are not in use.

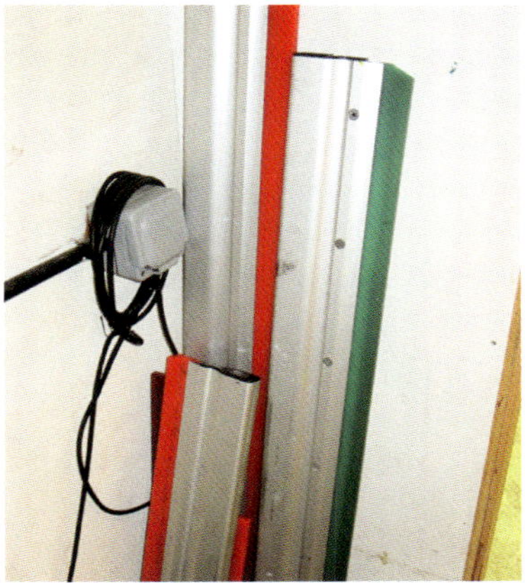

▲ A selection of aluminium squeegees. The green blades are medium grade; the red are a softer shore.

Squeegee

The squeegee pushes ink through the mesh and onto the paper. It is a simple piece of equipment consisting of a wooden or aluminium handle which holds a rectangular section of urethane blade (this comes in a variety of lengths). The blades come in various degrees of hardness, referred to as 'shore'. The most typical shore for an artist to use, and one good for general use on paper, is medium 70–75 and is coloured green. It is essential that the edge of the blade which presses down onto the screen mesh is sharp, true and has no nicks as this will directly affect the print quality of the image.

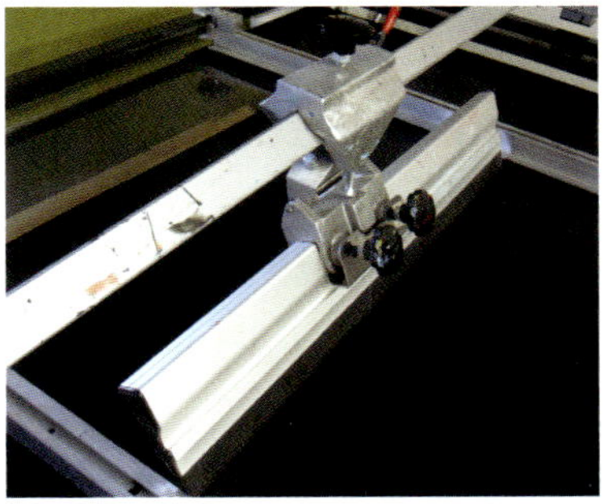

▶ A one-arm squeegee unit.

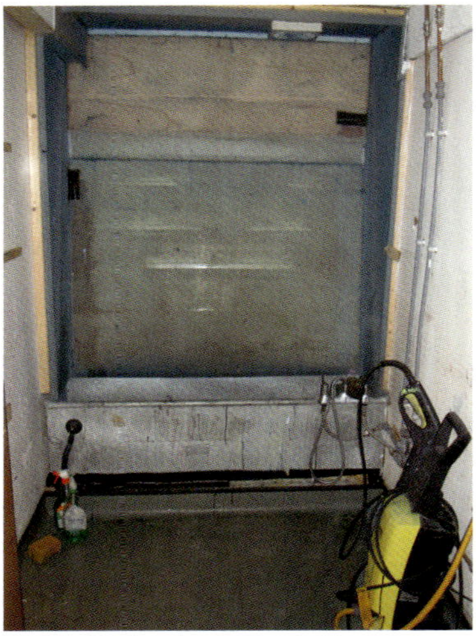

◀ A washout booth and high pressure washer.

▼ A floor-standing sprung drying rack.

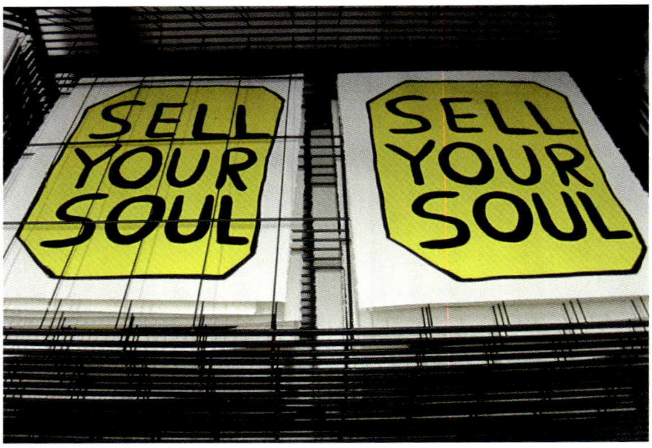

Pressure washer

Pressure washers are an essential piece of screen printing equipment. They are used to keep the screen meshes open and free of dried ink and old stencil material. Any blockages in the screen mesh will prevent ink passing through the intended areas of the mesh onto the paper. These items are now inexpensive to buy as they are sold in large numbers for car and patio cleaning. Select one that is at least 100 bar pressure. Over the years, a good washer will save a lot of money in cleaning products and chemicals.

Drying racks

Once printing commences, each paper sheet is printed quickly and in quantity so it is essential to have drying space closely accessible. There should be minimal delay in placing prints to dry before pulling the next print, or ink may dry on the screen, blocking the mesh and necessitating cleaning of the whole screen. The best drying system is the sprung, floor-standing drying rack. These are available in sizes from 46 x 61 cm (18 x 24 in.) to 132 x 203 cm (52 x 80 in.). Prints are placed horizontally on the wire racks which are spring-loaded, allowing each single rack to be lifted quickly when full so the next rack can be used. Prints dry safely without damage or sticking together.

INKS

In recent years, there has been a wholesale move towards water-based inks for screen printing due to health and safety concerns regarding oil-based screen inks. Oil-based screen inks dry as solvents evaporate into the local atmosphere. Together with the highly toxic chemicals needed for cleaning (screen wash), they create a hazard through inhalation and skin contact.

Although it is possible to protect against these hazards by good extraction systems and by following health and safety procedures, all education institutes and the vast majority of open access studios have now switched to water-based screen inks.

Health and safety

On the health and safety/toxicity issue, it should be noted that water-based inks also have an impact on our environment as do common household cleaning products.

In his book *Water-Based Screen Printing* (London: A&C Black, 2000), Steve Hoskins sums this up expertly:

> *'...solvent screen printing was unhealthy for the user. The solvents necessary were toxic and consequently carried many health warnings. Therefore, the substitution of solvents with water-based products is an extremely sensible move for the user. However, environmentally, there is probably little to choose between solvent and water-based inks. Both are petrochemical products, plus acrylic resins do not break down easily, to a certain extent, causing disposal problems. The acrylic residue can be filtered from the water system but still must be disposed of in other ways.'*

Some studios which edition, such as Advanced Graphics and Coriander in London, and individual artists still favour oil-based inks as they do provide some advantages over water-based inks. For example:

- The superior opacity of ink coverage.
- The fluidity and handling of the ink during printing.
- The ease of use with water-soluble screen fillers and the wider choice of papers (there is no problem with paper cockling i.e. where the water content in the ink permanently distorts the page sheet).
- The choices of substrates that oil-based ink readily adheres to.

It is, however, only a matter of time before the manufacture of oil-based inks for the paper and board market will cease completely. The enormous amount of digital equipment available and wide format printing will render screen printing products and equipment unviable commercially.

USING WATER-BASED INKS

Water-based inks consist of a base of acrylic polymer emulsified with water by a small amount of solvent (approximately 2% ethyl acetate as used in cosmetics) to which is added colour pigment.

The ink is supplied ready-mixed or as a clear base to which is added acrylic paint or liquid pigment. Water-based ink has been used for many years for textile screen printing, but the ink is not always suitable for working on paper as the water content is high and causes paper cockling. The colour used is actually a dye, not a pigment, which makes the colour 'fugitive' (not permanent).

There are three popular water-based ink systems currently in use and they are described below. The choice of system and brand vary from studio to studio. How do artists and students decide which to use? Personal preference gained by experience is a big factor but there is a large variation in costs too: if you are buying systems in from the US and Europe, there will be import costs to consider.

Acrylic paint and transparent base

This system uses a transparent base or acrylic medium, to which is added artists' acrylic paint, typically in a 50:50 ratio. A wide range of colours is available, all can be mixed together and they will be very familiar to handle to many artists who paint. To increase the opacity of ink, up to 75% acrylic paint to 25% base may be used. Conversely, for transparent colours, you will need to use a greater percentage of base to paint.

Acrylic paints are available in both student quality and professional quality and the purchase price reflects this. The difference between the two is the quantity and quality of the pigments used, which in turn reflect the strength/hue of colour in the final result. The transparent base is purchased from suppliers such as Daler-Rowney®, Golden and Lascaux®, in bottles or buckets in quantities ranging from 500 ml to 5 litres. It is more economical in the long run to purchase the base in the larger quantities if long-term storage is not an issue.

This system is the most economical to use by far and is easy to handle for the beginner or student. Experienced screen printers who have used oil-based methods may find the consistency of the ink frustrating as it does not have the fluidity they are used to. The acrylic paint system has a consistency similar to wallpaper paste, meaning that ink must be scraped from the screen's inside frame as prints are pulled. However, the ink is very slow drying on the screen which is actually a bonus: it is very forgiving to the inexperienced printer.

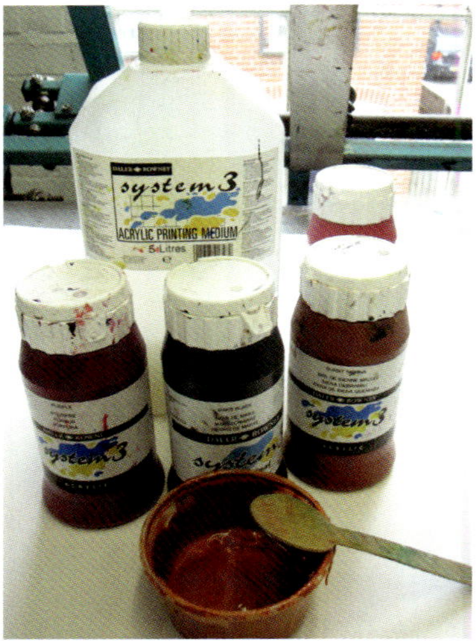

▲ **Daler-Rowney® System 3 Acrylic Printing Medium with acrylic paints and mixed ink in plastic container.**

Liquid pigment and transparent base

Brands such as TW Graphics WB1000 consist of water-based pigment concentrates, which are added to a transparent base. When mixing these inks, always begin with the clear base and then add the pigment. Good, strong colour intensity is achieved with approximately 20% of the pigment concentrate. Extra opaque colour intensity may be achieved by adding white concentrate to the printing base. Owing to the more liquid nature of this product, it will feel more familiar to those used to oil-based systems. The cost is higher than the acrylic paint system previously discussed. This system would be our choice as an ink for use in a professional studio: it scores highly in colour range, mixing quality and colour intensity.

Ready-mixed screen inks

Ready-mixed water-based inks are the most expensive option, but obviously have the convenience of being pre-prepared. They can be used straight, but many artists do combine them with a transparent base, which has the advantage of retarding the drying time as well as being cost-saving (the base is cheaper than the ink). Well used and well known brands include Hunt Speedball® and Sun Chemical®.

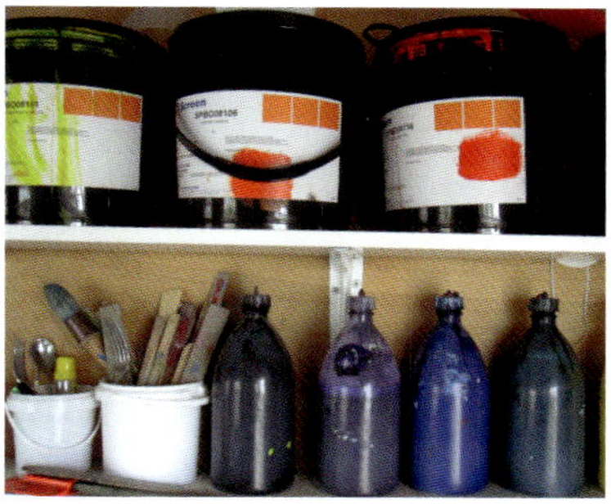

▲ Sun Chemical® is now the world's largest ink manufacturer.

Mixing inks

The ideal mixing container is a plastic container with a resealable lid. Utensils for mixing should also be plastic or wood – anything metallic will rust! The ideal mixing container is perhaps the yoghurt pot. These can be purchased in bulk online from catering suppliers. Buy small pots with snap on lids if you can: large pots lead to ink wastage as there is a tendency to mix too much ink for the job.

The majority of inks require no thinning. Do not be tempted to add water to an ink: it will curdle as the water will attract bacteria. Mixed inks have a good shelf life for many months if sealed from the air.

PAPER FOR SCREEN PRINTING

Owing to the water content in water-based inks, it is essential to choose a paper that has the ability to control the moisture that water-based inks contain without cockling. Generally, it is wise to select a mould-made paper of 250gsm or 300gsm. We have found that paper designed for watercolour painting performs extremely well. Two good examples include Arches® Aquarell and Fabriano® Artistico.

GETTING STARTED

Stencil making

Any stencil for screen printing consists of open areas which let ink pass through the mesh and onto the paper, and solid or blocked areas which stop ink passing through.

Stencil making comes in various forms: they can be cut, hand-drawn or even utilise digital imagery through photo-sensitive screen emulsions.

The simplest stencil is the paper stencil and it is the way most artists are introduced to this medium. Thin paper (such as newsprint), kitchen grease-proof paper or glassine (a glossy, semi-transparent paper) are all suitable.

To begin with, a paper sheet as large as the inside dimension of the chosen screen frame is needed. A design is cut using a sharp craft knife or scalpel. The cut-away areas are those that will print. This method offers a very inexpensive way of working and although it is relatively simple to execute, some surprisingly complicated and intricate images can be produced. This method is suitable for small editions of up to 20 only as the paper stencil may begin to deteriorate thereafter.

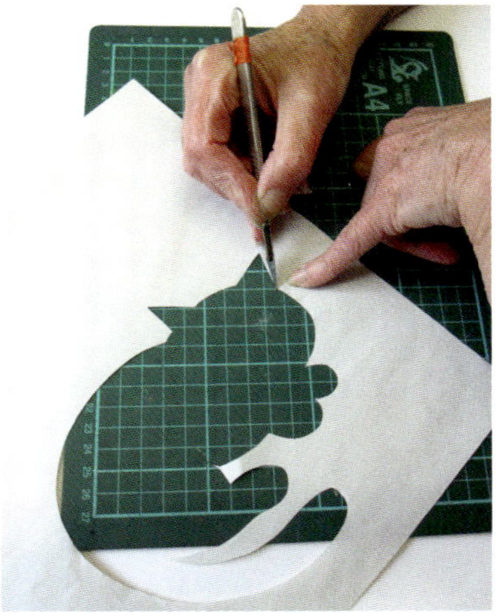

▲ A newsprint stencil being cut with a scalpel. Note the use of a cutting mat.

FILLER STENCIL

Filler stencils are painted directly onto the screen mesh. This is known as a negative working process, which means that the areas painted on the mesh will not print. A product such as Speedball® Screen Filler is painted on the screen mesh with a soft brush. (A guide may be drawn onto the mesh with a soft pencil.) Alternatively, a drawing may be positioned under the mesh to act as a guide. The screen must be elevated by a few millimetres from the drawing to ensure the filler does not stick to the drawing or design: a piece of mount card is thick enough to do this job effectively.

▼ **Sue Molineux painting on screen filler. Note the 'master' or key design. The key design was placed under the mesh and 2B pencil marks were drawn on the mesh as a guide for where to paint the filler.**

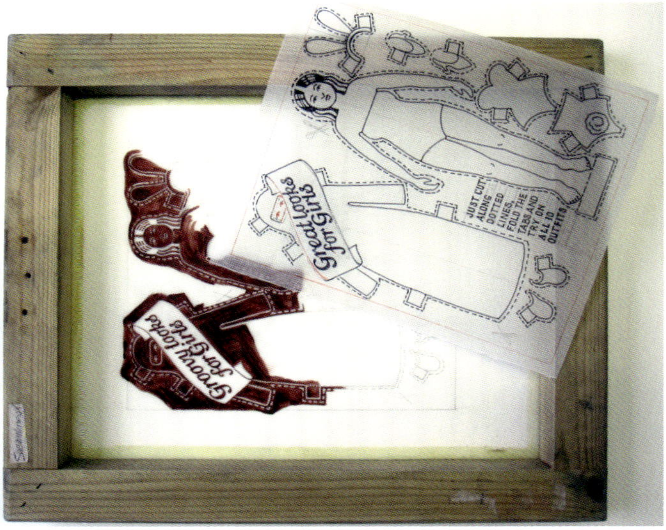

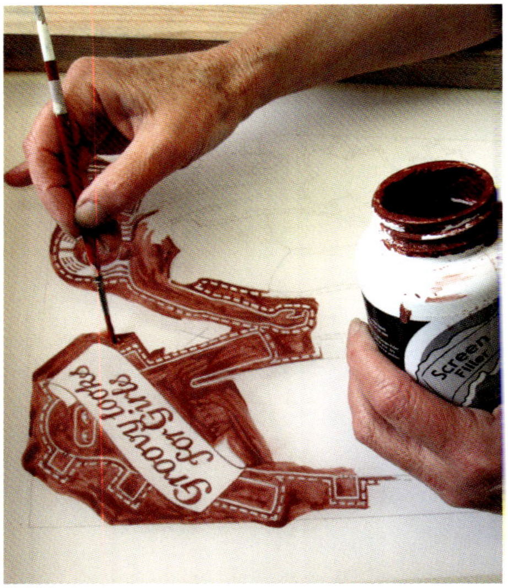

▼ **Sue Molineux, *Choices*, 2011. Screen filler and newsprint stencils, 22 x 30 cm (8¾ x 11¾ in.).**

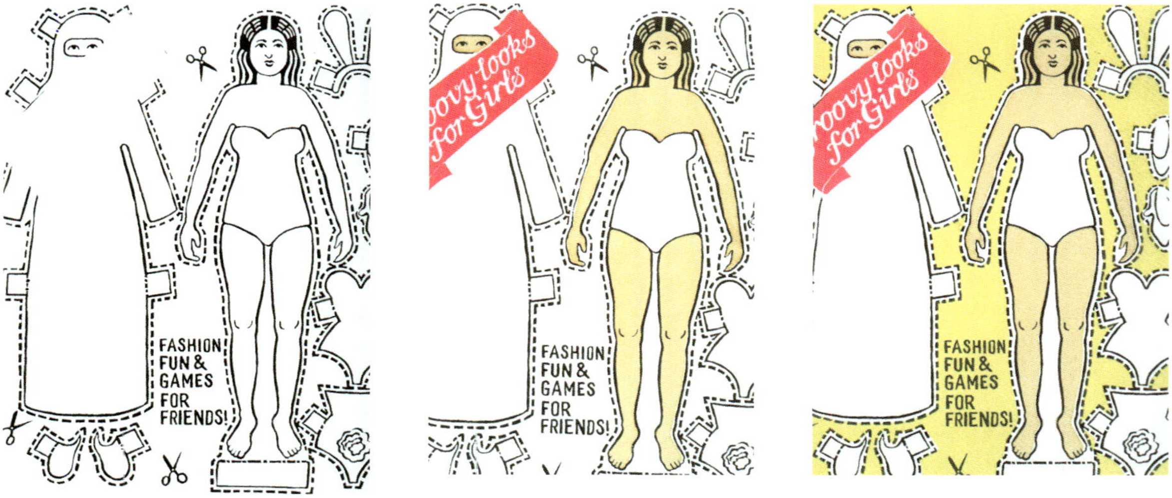

A screen print is built up in separate layers. Each colour layer is printed on paper sheets to the required edition size. In the case of paper stencils, these are thrown away after printing and the same screen is re-used for the subsequent colour layers.

Screen Drawing Fluid

Screen Drawing Fluid is used with screen filler. It is a positive working method, meaning that the marks painted are those that will print.

It is used as follows:

- The Screen Drawing Fluid is painted onto the screen mesh and allowed to dry.
- Screen filler is then applied on the same side of the screen using a piece of card or a small squeegee.
- A thin layer of filler is applied in one pass. (Multiple passes will prevent washout out of the drawing fluid.)
- After the screen filler is thoroughly dry, both sides of the screen are sprayed with cold water to remove the Screen Drawing Fluid.

PHOTO STENCILS

Direct photo stencils (or direct stencils) have a light-sensitive polymer emulsion coated onto the screen mesh.

The coated screen is then exposed to UV light in an exposure unit (see p.196) together with opaque art work in the form of a drawing or painting on grained Mylar® or a digitally-produced acetate or photocopy. The artwork is called the 'positive'.

The dark drawn or printed marks on the positive block the UV light and the emulsion here stays soft. The non-image areas that do receive UV light are hardened.

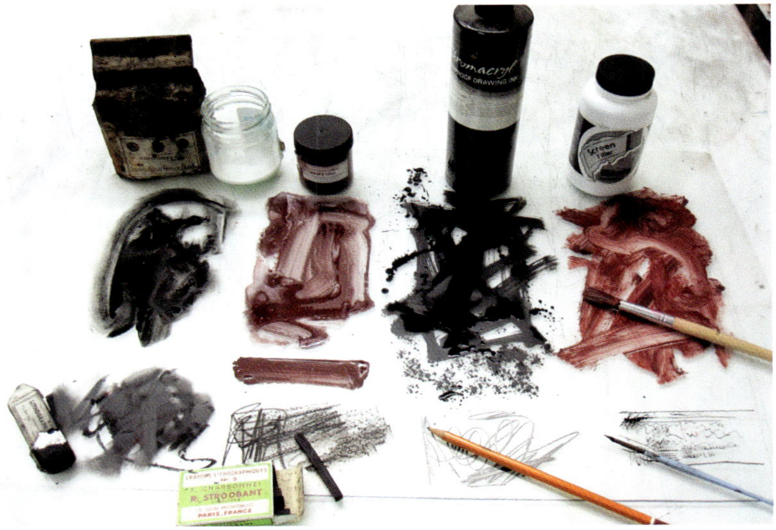

▶ **A hand-drawn positive.**
A True Grain (Mylar®) sheet with marks (top left to right): black pigment and PVA, glue, liquid photo opaque, black drawing ink, Speedball® Screen Filler.
Bottom left to right: lithographic rubbing crayon, lithographic crayon stick, pencil, dip pen using opaque black ink.

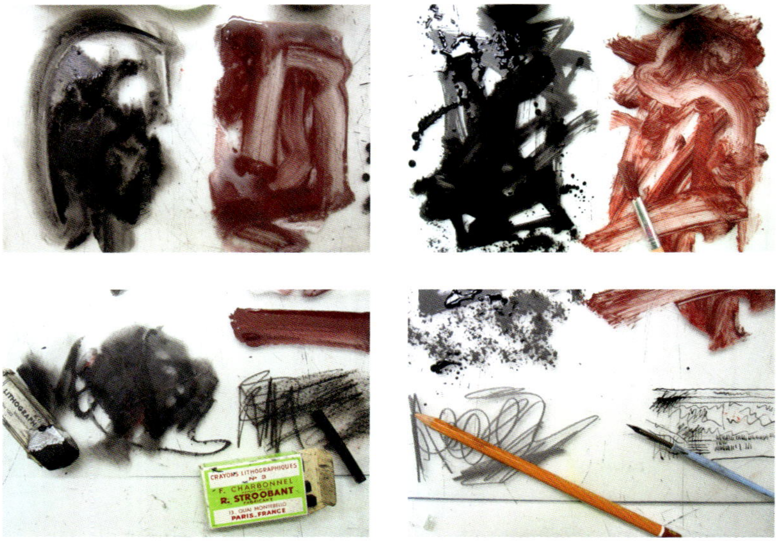

◀ Some of the varied marks possible when preparing a hand-drawn positive.

The exposed screen is washed with water and the soft, unexposed image areas wash away, creating open mesh areas. This is the image that will print.

The advantage with this method is the wide range of marks and imagery that can be printed – everything from the subtlest of halftones to calligraphic, painterly textures. This type of stencil is very stable on the screen, meaning large editions can be pulled.

Coating a screen

First, it is important to check that the screen is clean and free of any blockages in the mesh, such as dried ink or old stencil material. The best way to gauge this is to hold the screen up against a window and check that light can be seen through all mesh areas.

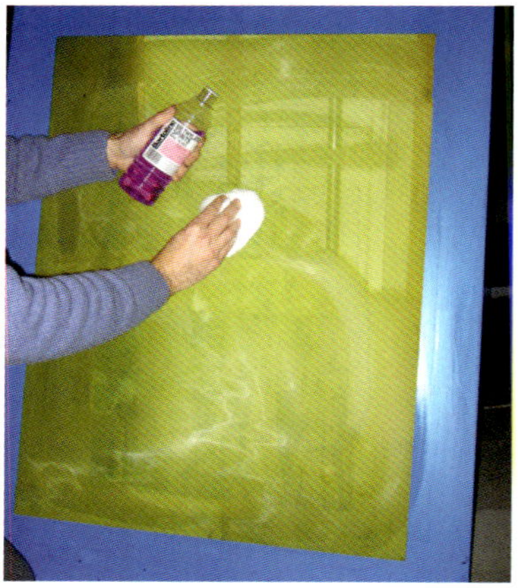

▲ Degrease the mesh using methylated spirit.

The screen mesh is now degreased using some cotton wool soaked in methylated spirit.

The light-sensitive emulsions most commonly used for general studio use are called Diazo-based. They come in two parts: the emulsion and a small bottle of sensitiser that is added to the emulsion to form the light-sensitive compound. They have a wide exposure latitude, meaning they are very forgiving of different types of art work positives.They are commonly supplied in 1 litre or 5 litre containers. Once mixed, the emulsion will last for three to four months if kept in a refrigerator.

The emulsion is applied to the screen using an aluminium coating trough. This is a U-shaped blade or scoop with detachable plastic ends.

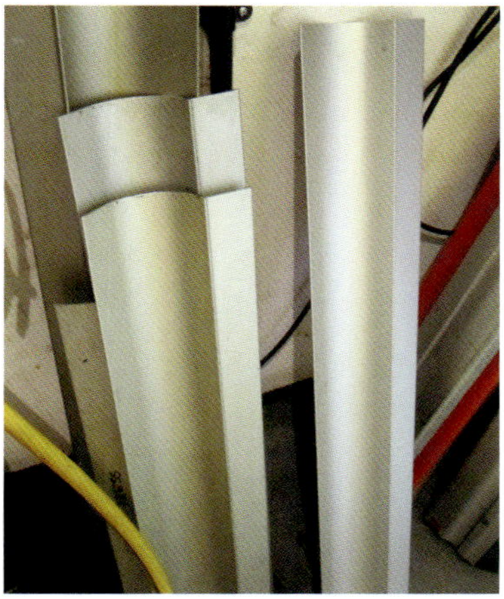

▲ Aluminium coating troughs of varying lengths to suit different screen sizes.

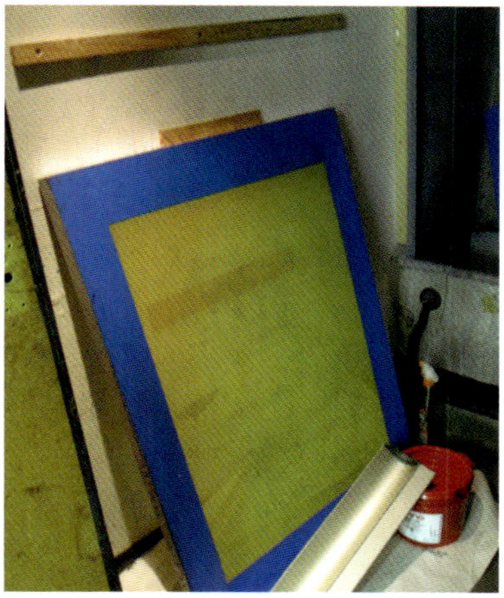

▲ Screen batons.

Tip

Fix strips of wood to the wall, so that screens can be wedged against them during coating. Have two or three batons of varying heights to accommodate different screen sizes. These are a great aid during coating, as the screen cannot move when the coating trough is pushed against it.

Next, the emulsion is poured into the trough and pressed against the back of the screen mesh (the back of the screen will be in contact with the paper during printing). Pulling up firmly from bottom to top creates a thin layer of emulsion which is deposited on the mesh. This procedure should be carried out in subdued lighting away from direct sunlight. One coat is sufficient, in our opinion, so ignore manufacturers' guidelines regarding multiple coatings: we feel they have no benefit and are a waste of the product.

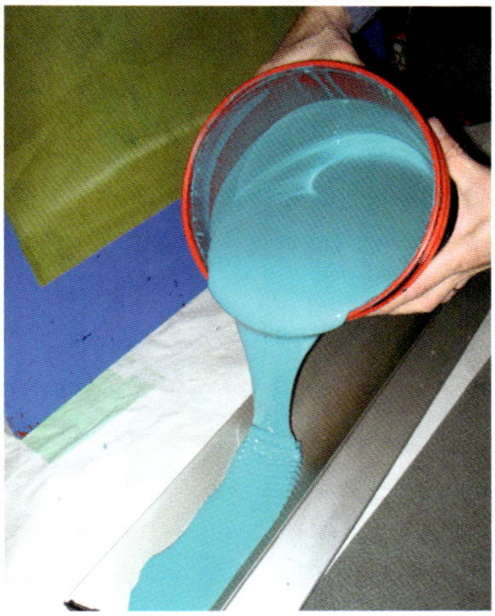

▶ Filling the coating trough with emulsion.

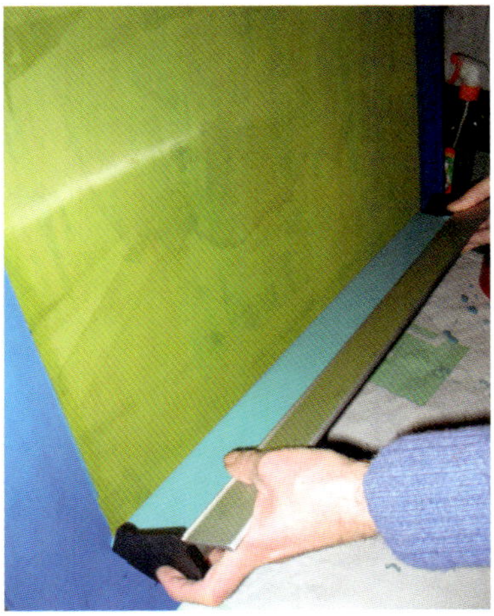

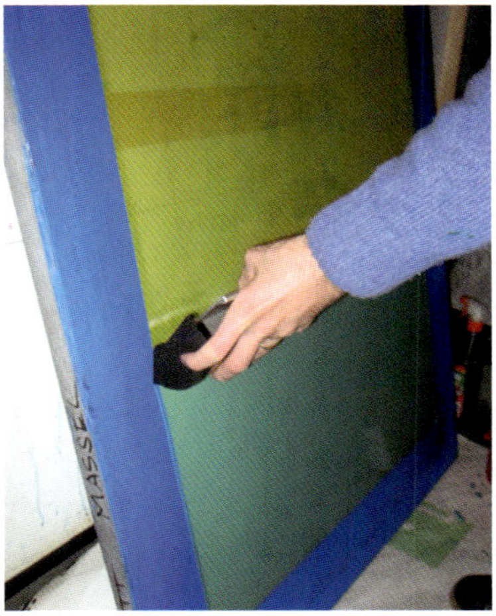

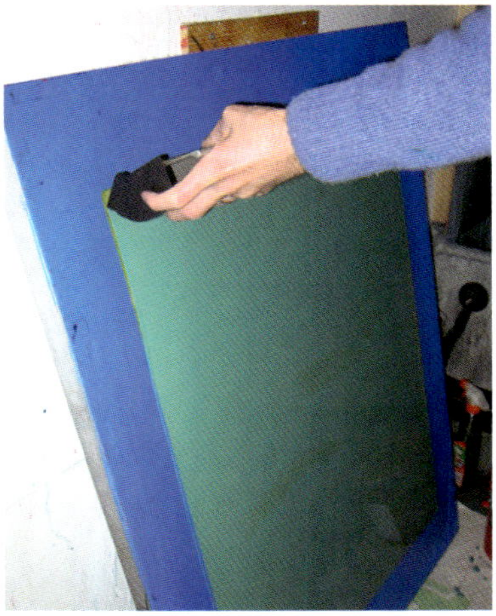

▲ LEFT TO RIGHT: Coating a screen with photo emulsion.

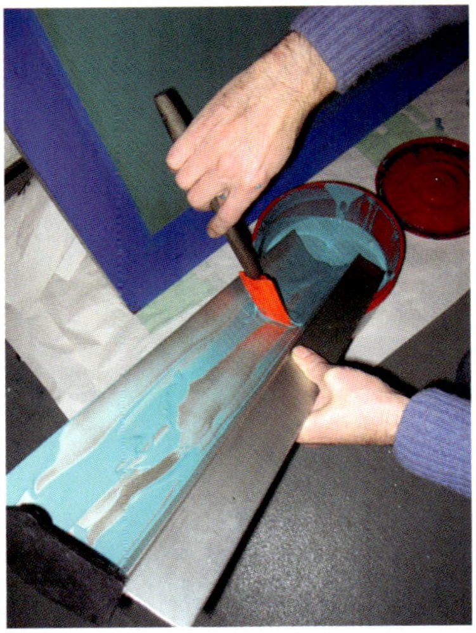

▲ The excess emulsion is returned to the pot.

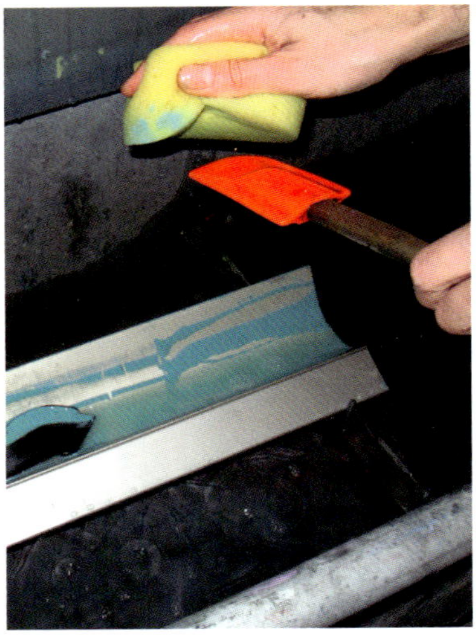

▲ It is important to wash the coating trough and spatula immediately.

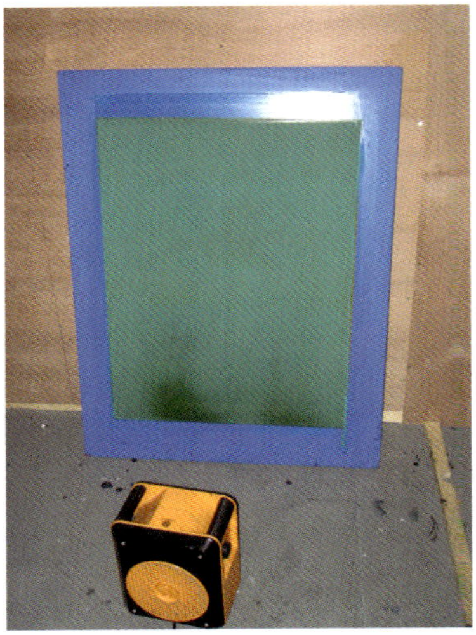

▲ The screen is dried with an electric fan.

Excess emulsion from the coating trough is immediately poured back into the container and the lid replaced. The coating trough should be cleaned with water before any emulsion dries. Ideally, the coated screen is dried horizontally in a heated drying cabinet but if space does not permit, a fan heater in a darkened room or cupboard will suffice. Remember contact with daylight will begin to expose the emulsion!

EXPOSING AND DEVELOPING THE SCREEN

When the screen emulsion has dried, it is exposed in a UV light box along with the artwork positive. A positive can be hand-drawn, painted or output digitally/painted or digitally outputted, ideally onto clear acetate or Mylar®. Computer print-outs on thin paper (80gsm) can be used if exposure time is increased slightly to compensate for the opacity of the paper. (The light source will read the paper as a grey tone, so more exposure light is needed to 'burn' through this.)

The positive is placed onto the glass of the exposure unit face-up, just as it is intended to print.

The screen is placed over the positive. The rule is always 'emulsion to emulsion', meaning that the emulsion on the screen mesh should be in contact with the emulsion (ink print-out or drawing) on the positive.

The vacuum in the exposure unit ensures a good contact between the mesh and the positive. The screen is exposed for a number of seconds and minutes in older units; in newer UV units, the exposure time is given in light units.

Light units are extremely accurate as they compensate for how cool or warm the UV bulbs are. Exposure times vary with different units so it is

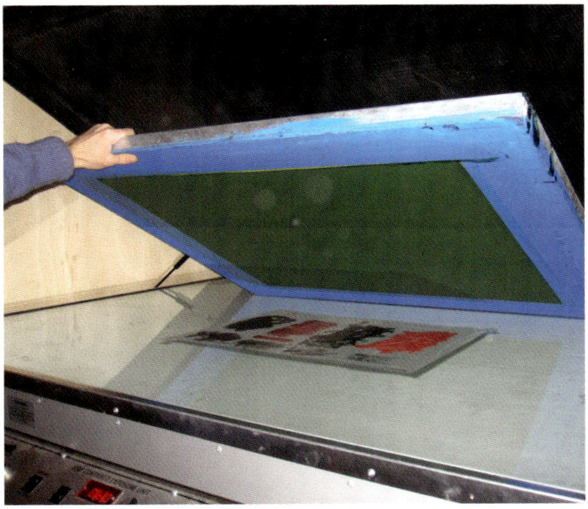

▲ The screen being placed over the positive in the exposure unit.

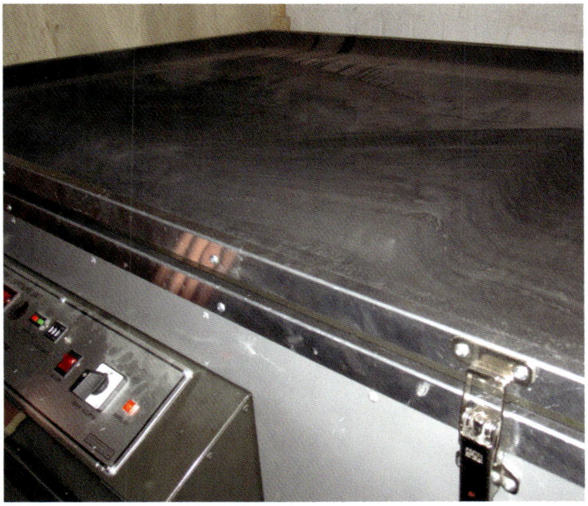

▲ The rubber cover is vacuum-formed over the screen.

impossible to give a guide here, but standard times will almost certainly have been recorded by other users or technicians. Light from the unit hardens the emulsion in the non-image areas. The actual image area (dark and tones) remains unexposed, so the emulsion stays soft and is washed out by the spray of water.

Exposure times

Exposure times can be confusing for the beginner. In a nutshell, there must be enough exposure time to harden the emulsion without losing image detail and resolution. Subtle marks, washes and weak positives must be given less exposure time, however, as they are not opaque enough. .

The examples below show the same positive exposed to 70 light units and 45 light units respectively. The shorter exposure gives more detail. In this case, 70 units represents an over-exposure.

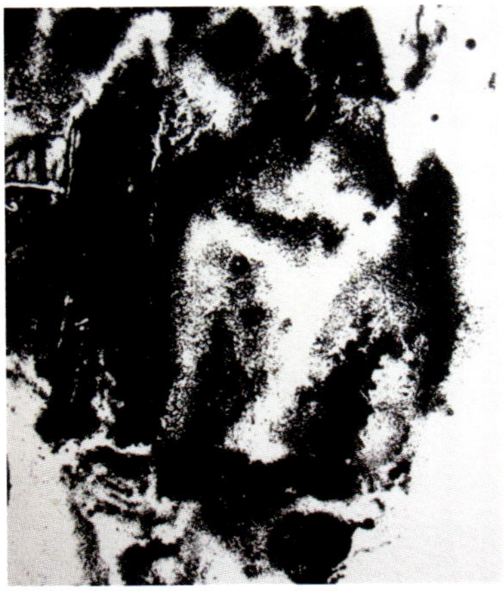

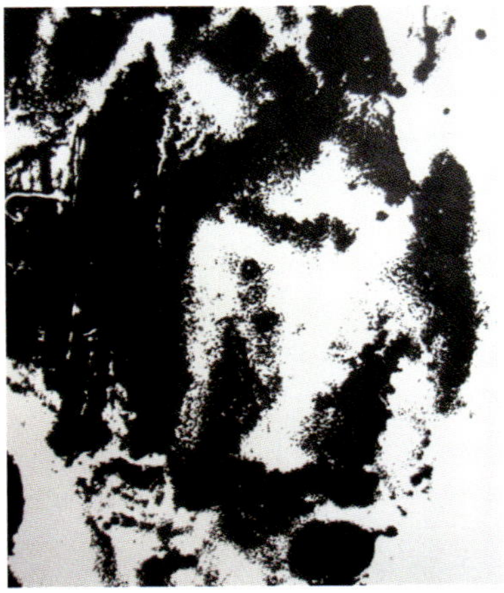

◀ LEFT: 40 units. A good resolution.

RIGHT: 70 units. The image is over-exposed.

Washing out the screen

Once the screen has been exposed, it is placed in the washout booth so that the image can be developed. Wet the screen on both sides with a waterhose. Under no circumstances use a pressure washer, as it will strip the emulsion. Wash out the screen from the back side (i.e., the side that was coated with the emulsion). Gently spray the screen with water and the soft, unexposed areas – those areas where the drawing was blocking the light – will wash away.

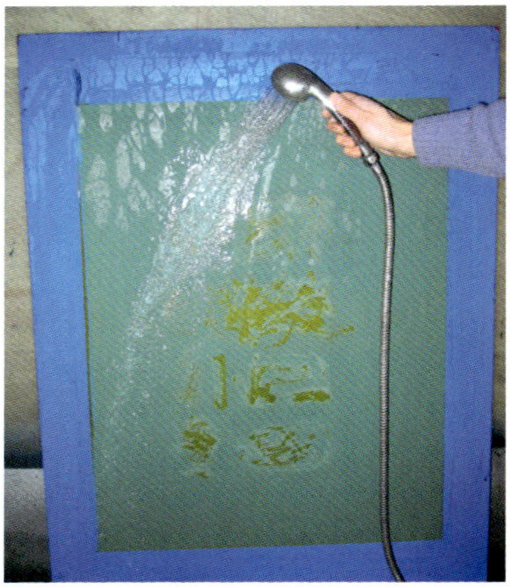

▲ Developing the exposed image using a shower-type water hose.

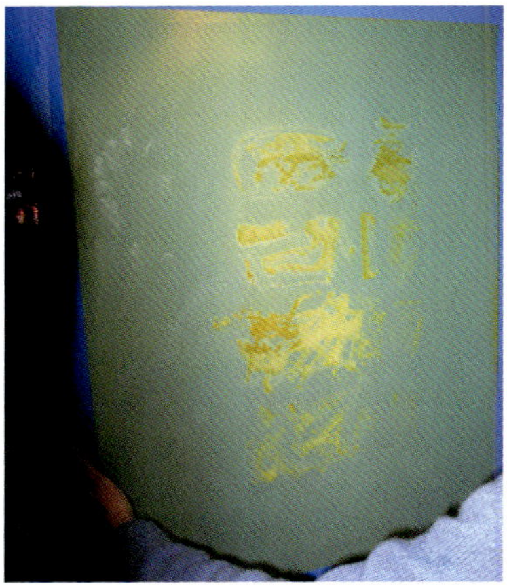

▲ Hold the screen up to a light source to check the progress of the washing out.

PRINTING

The golden rule before printing is to be prepared. Have everything ready: enough ink mixed, paper stacked close by and a bucket of water, sponge and cleaning fluid ready to clear any blockages during printing and also to clean the screen immediately after the final print is pulled Remember that the ink is acrylic-based and will be extremely difficult to remove from the mesh if allowed to dry for any significant length of time (five minutes or more).

Clamp the screen in place on the printing table. The printing table is adjusted so that the screen mesh is raised approximately 4 mm above the screen bed. This position is called 'snap'. It is important that the screen 'snaps' away from the paper as the squeegee passes: an even deposit of ink needs to be made, so that the paper does not stick to the mesh.

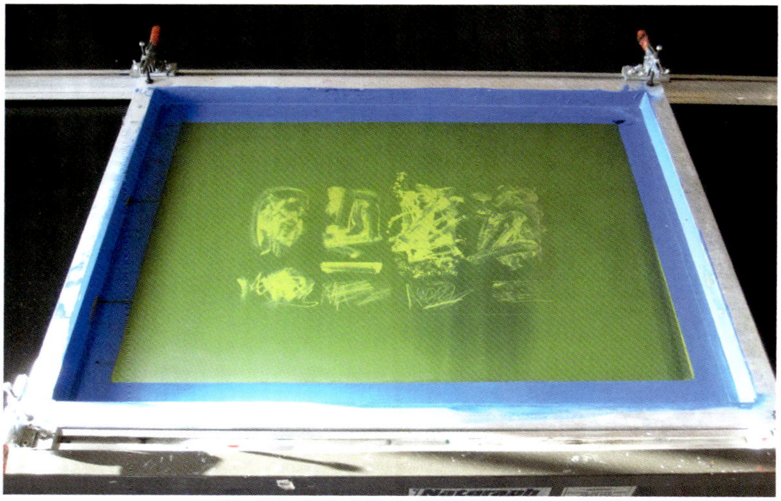

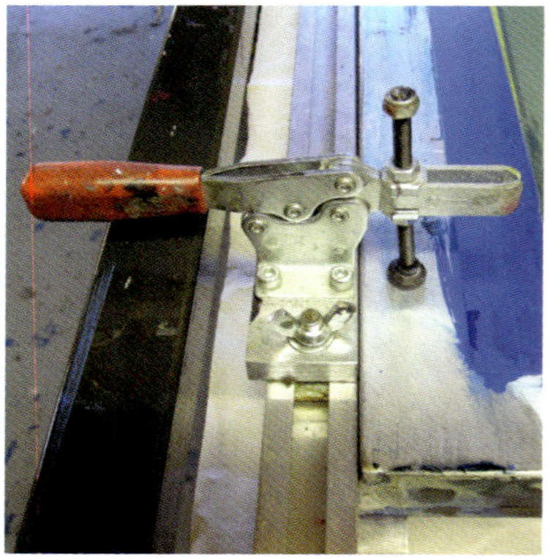

◀ The screen is held in place using the screen clamps. Detail above.

Use plastic packing tape to seal the edges where the screen mesh meets the frame and also where there are open areas of mesh which have not been coated with emulsion. The tape ensures that no ink can bleed through the screen onto the printing paper or screen bed.

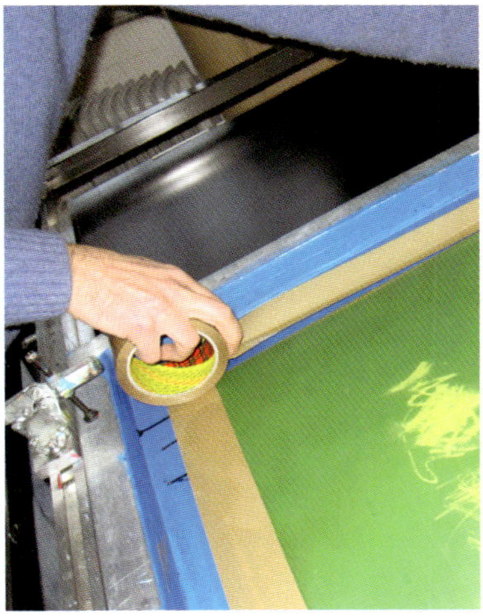

▶ Open areas of mesh are sealed with packing tape. Avoid the cheaper brands of tape: they are too sticky and can be difficult to remove.

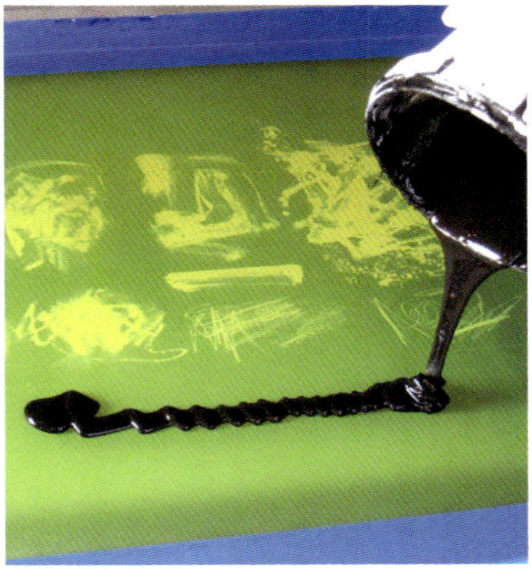

▲ The ink is poured onto the edge of the mesh.

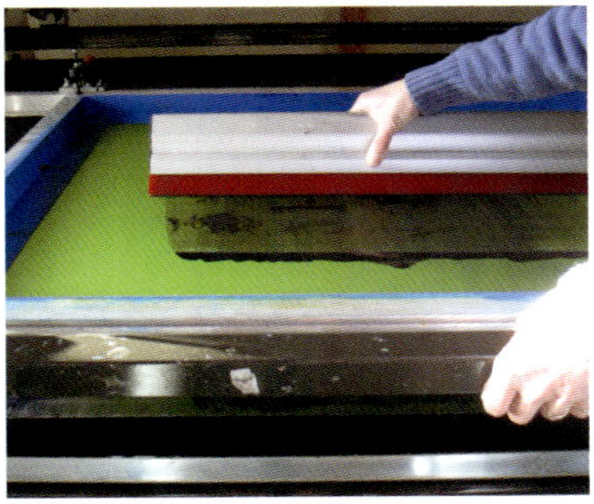

▲ With the screen raised slightly, the ink is flooded across the mesh.

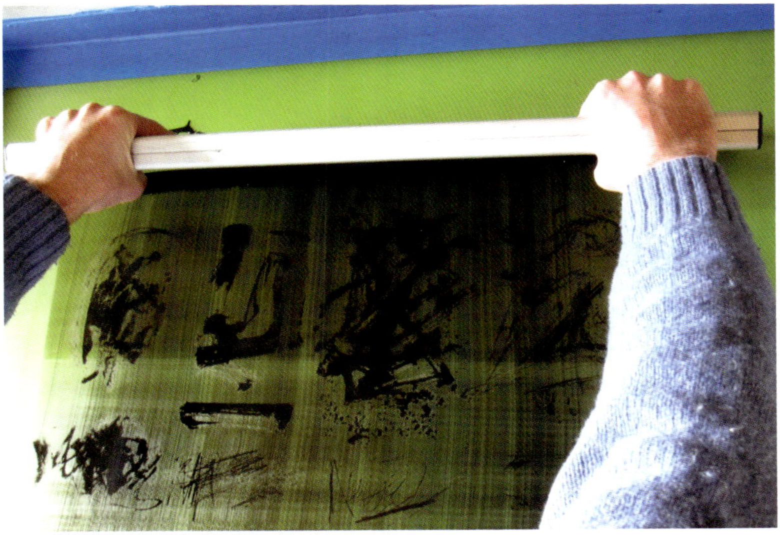

▶ With firm, even pressure the ink is pulled, which pushes it through the open areas of mesh.

REGISTRATION

Registration is used to ensure the image is printed squarely and correctly on the paper. The Mylar® is taped to the bed on one edge so that it can be flipped back before printing commences. The ink is poured onto the screen near the edge closest to your body. The frame is then raised from the bed with one hand and the ink is pushed across the screen using a squeegee (this is called 'flooding'). Lower the screen and pull the ink firmly towards the body with the squeegee, which should be at an angle of approximately 45 degrees. This action pushes the ink through the open areas of the mesh.

This first pull is made onto a transparent sheet of Mylar® with a printing sheet of paper underneath it. This creates the registration template or key. This is necessary for placing the image in the correct place on the printing paper and if more than one colour is used in the design of the image.

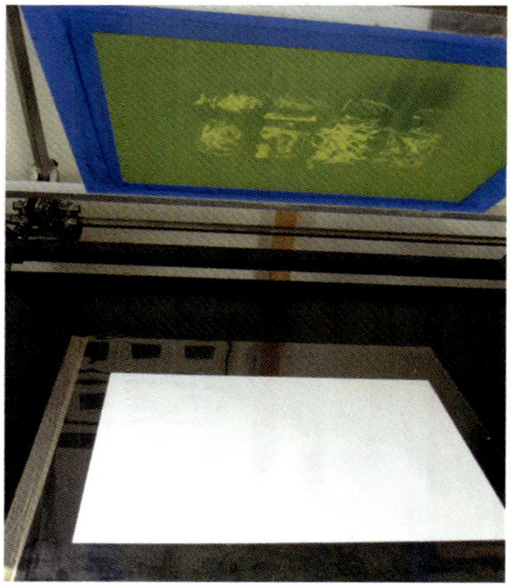

▲ A taped piece of Mylar® for registration, with printing paper underneath.

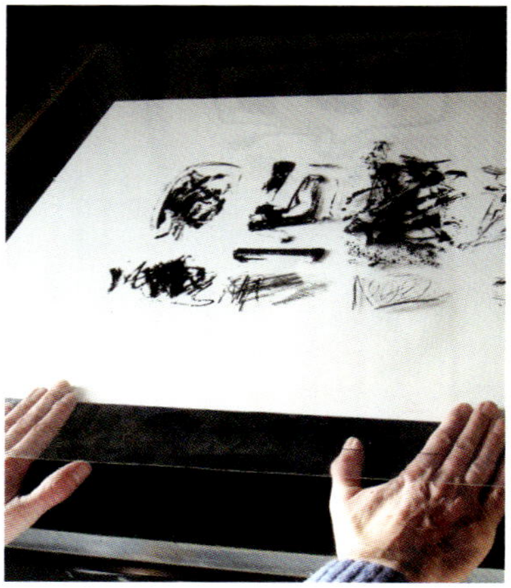

▲ The first pull is made onto the acetate and the printing paper is slid into position.

▲ Three card tabs are used to register the paper.

The image has been printed onto the registration Mylar® and the printing sheet can now be slid into position so that the image lies squarely on the sheet with equal margins.

The Mylar® is now flipped to the side and three registration tabs are butted up to the printing paper. Use slips of card that are backed with double-sided tape. Mark one corner with two tabs and place the third on the bottom leading edge. These tabs ensure that each sheet is placed in exactly the same place in relation to the fixed screen. The paper used should have cut edges to ensure accuracy in registration. Paper with deckled edges may be used, but a registration tolerance must be accepted as deckles are not uniform. Deckles may be trimmed, or a notch may be cut out to accommodate the registration tabs.

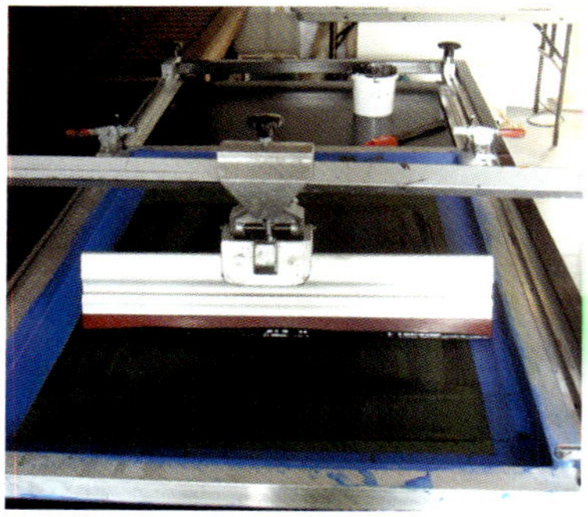

▲ A one-arm unit in printing action.

Once the registration is in place, printing should begin immediately. Each sheet is printed individually and then stacked in a drying rack. Fresh ink is added to the screen as needed.

If the screen bed is fitted with a one-arm unit, use it: it saves both energy and time compared to holding the squeegee by hand. The squeegee is held at the correct angle as it is swept horizontally across the screen.

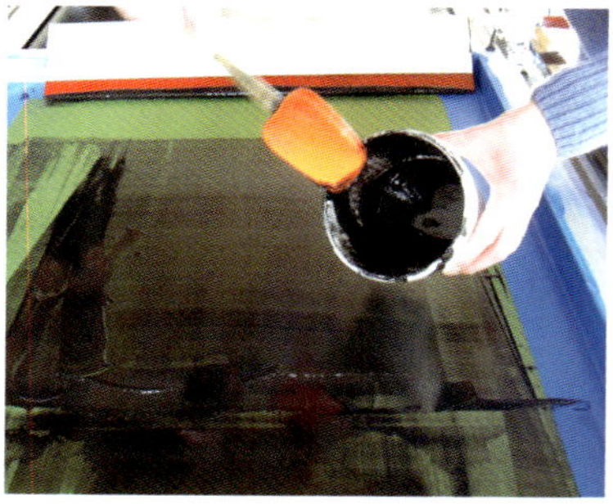

▲ Excess ink is returned to the pot for future use.

CLEANING UP

When printing has finished, begin cleaning up straight away to prevent ink drying on the screen and equipment. First, scoop up excess ink from the screen using a plastic palette knife and return it to the mixing pot. It will be fine for future use if sealed in an airtight container. Place newsprint under the screen and begin cleaning with sponge and water. Household domestic cleaner such as Mr Muscle® will aid the cleaning procedure and paper towels are absorbent and disposed of easily.

Reclaiming the screen

When a screen is finished with, it is cleaned by stripping the emulsion with a screen-stripping solution and blasting with a pressure washer. Place the screen in the washout booth with the back of the screen facing you. It is advisable to wear goggles and ear protection. Pour on the liquid screen photo emulsion remover and distribute it evenly with a sponge. Allow the screen to 'sit' for several minutes. Hose down the screen to remove the chemical stripper and begin systematically to wash away the stencil material with the pressure washer. Check the screen by holding it up to the light and examining the mesh for any remaining blockages.

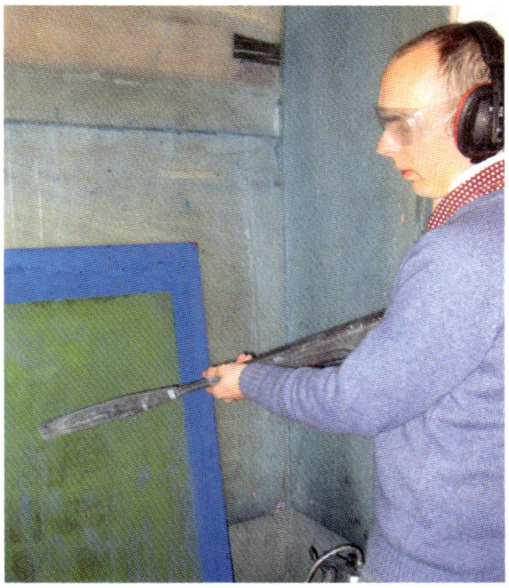

▲ Wear eye and ear protection when reclaiming a screen.

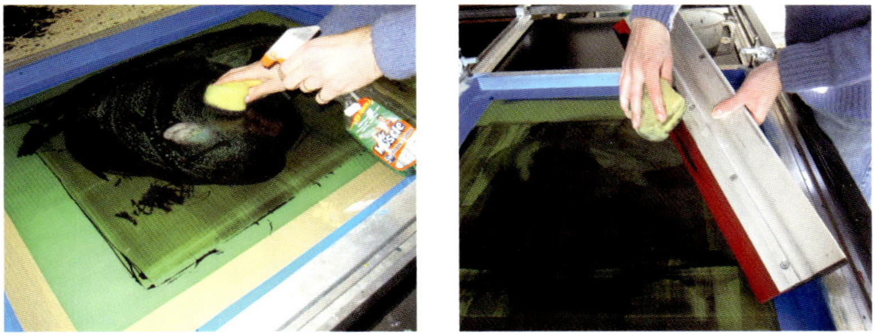

▲ Cleaning screen and squeegee.

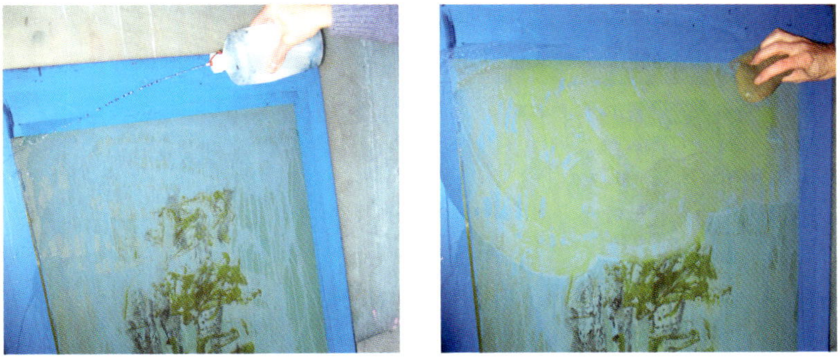

▲ Applying screen photo stencil remover.

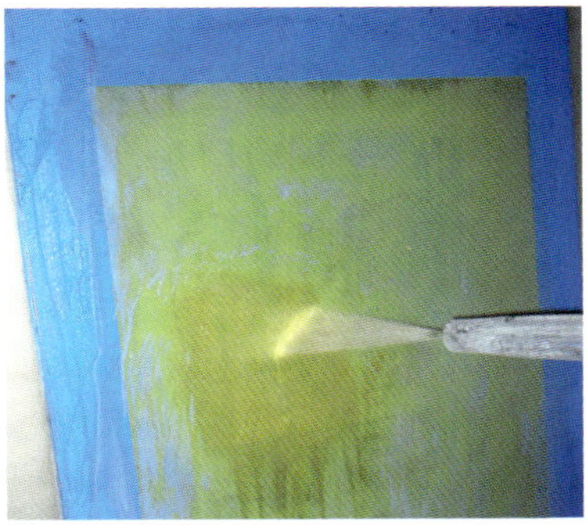

▲ Stripping the emulsion with a pressure washer.

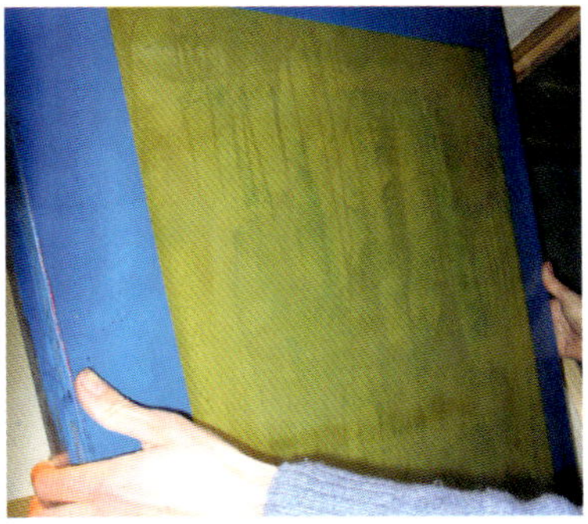

▲ The screen mesh should have no blockages when examined against a light.

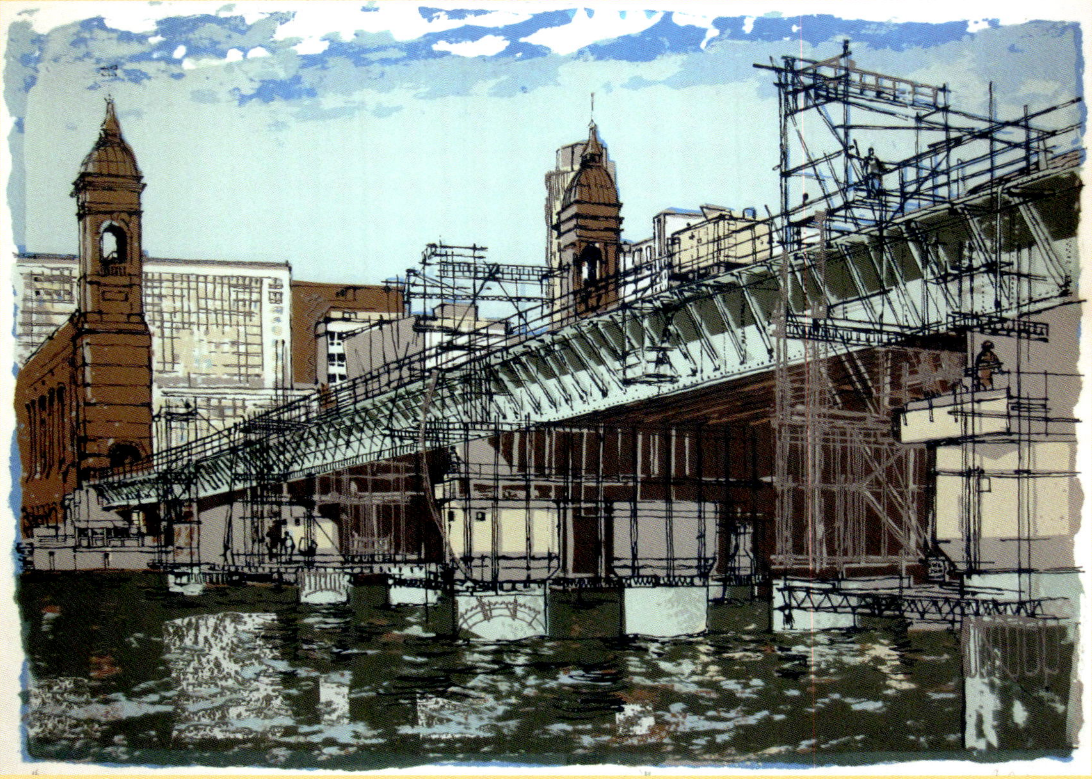

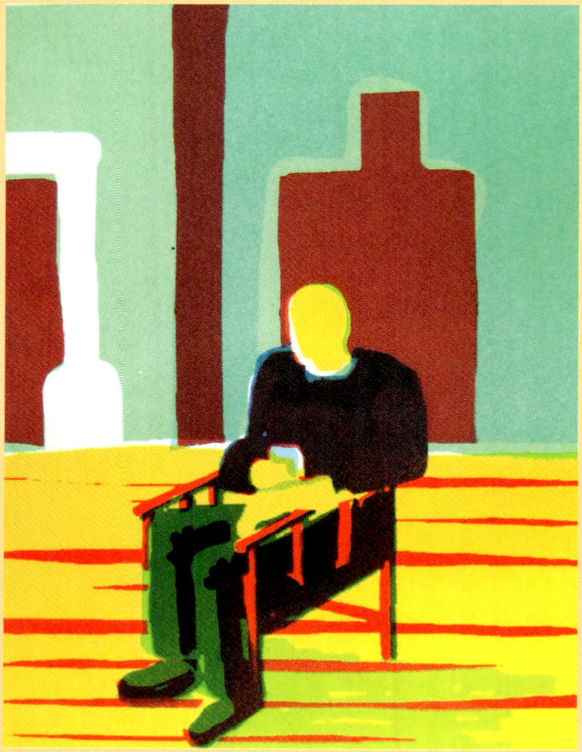

▲ Ray Gale, *Blackfriars*, 1985, Hand-cut stencils, 46 x 40 cm (18 x 15¾ in.). Eight hand-cut stencils using glassine with one photo-stencil for the final line work which was drawn with pen and ink onto matt drafting film.

◀ Scarlett Massell, *Untitled*, 2011. Water-based screen print using hand-cut paper stencils, 29 x 42 cm (11½ x 16½ in.).

▶ Sue Molineux, *Dad's Sardines* and *My Hero*, 2010. Water-based screen prints using hand-cut stencils and filler stencils, 30 x 22 cm (11¾ x 8¾ in.).

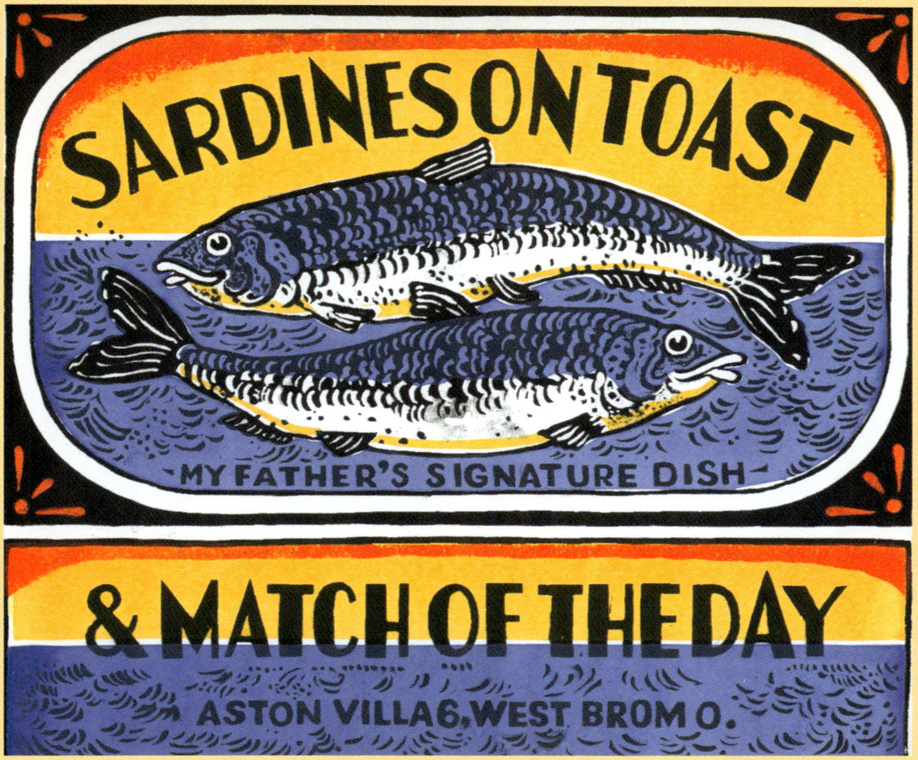
SARDINES ON TOAST
MY FATHER'S SIGNATURE DISH
& MATCH OF THE DAY
ASTON VILLA 6, WEST BROM 0.

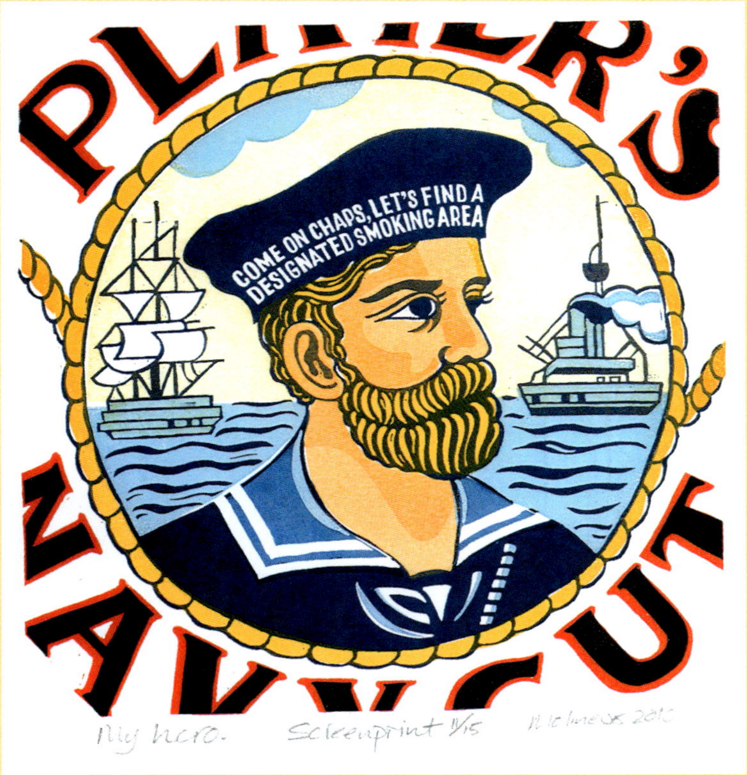
COME ON CHAPS, LET'S FIND A
DESIGNATED SMOKING AREA
NAVY CUT
My hero.
Screenprint 11/15

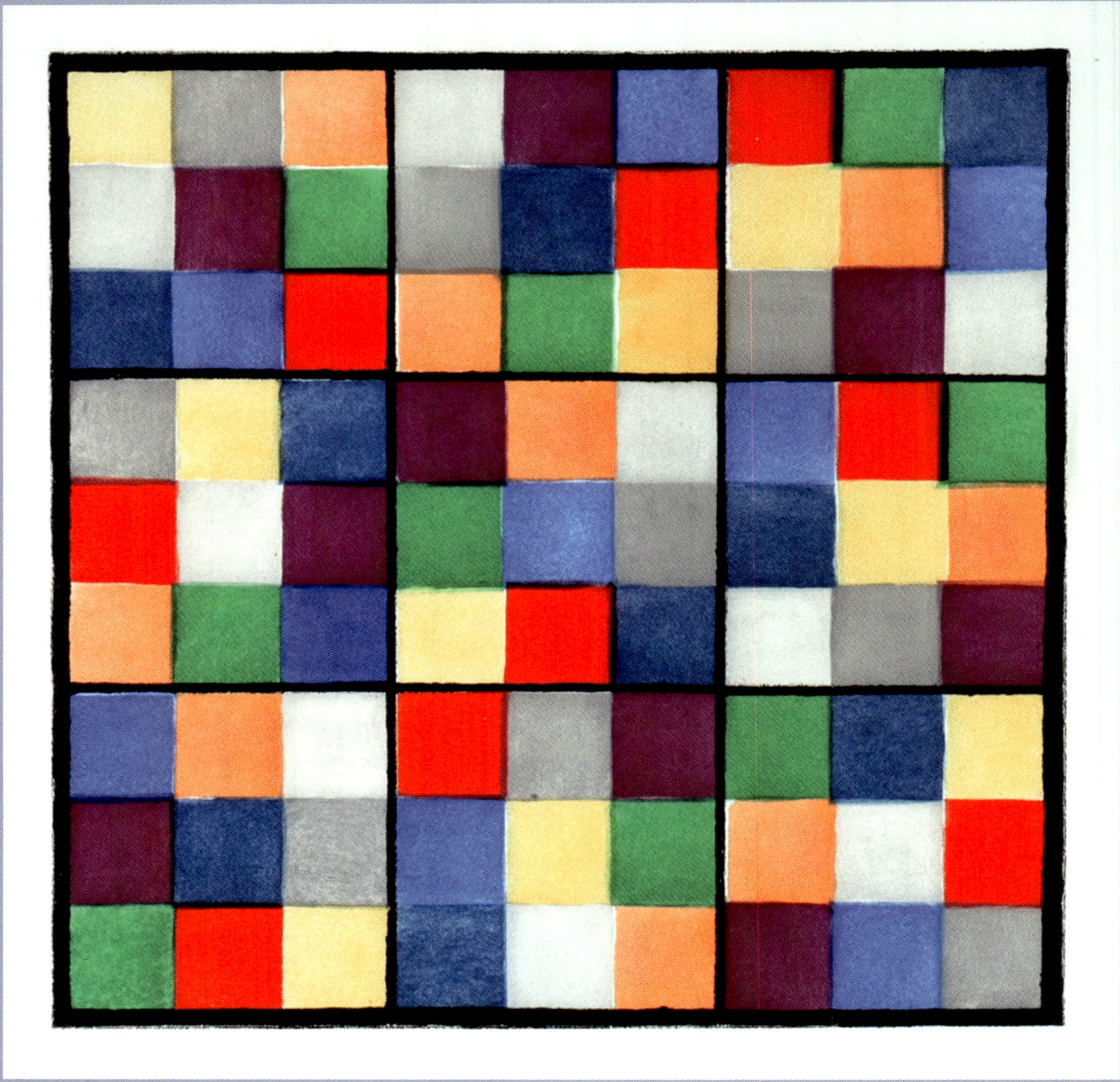

8

ink

Using ink is what makes printmaking special and what sets it apart from any other art practice.

Traditionally, ink is made from pigment and copperplate oil.

Today, many new water-washable inks are being created, such as Charbonnel® Aqua Wash. This is a traditional oil-based ink that has been altered so that it will emulsify (the ability of an immiscible substance to be dispersed in a miscible substance) – water and soap can be used to clean up these inks as a result. Water-washable inks are completely different to acrylic-based inks which can also be cleaned up with water but offer very little in environmental terms.

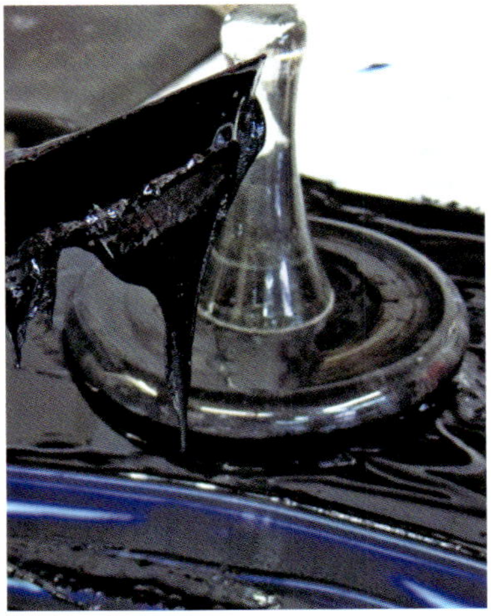

◀ Tom Phillips CBE, RA, *Suduko*, 2006. Etching, 27 x 27 cm (10½ x 10½ in.).
Colour plays a vital role in the printed image.

▶ Hand-mixed oil-based ink. The texture of this is quite grainy and its viscosity is quite short, judging from the way it is clinging to the palette knife.

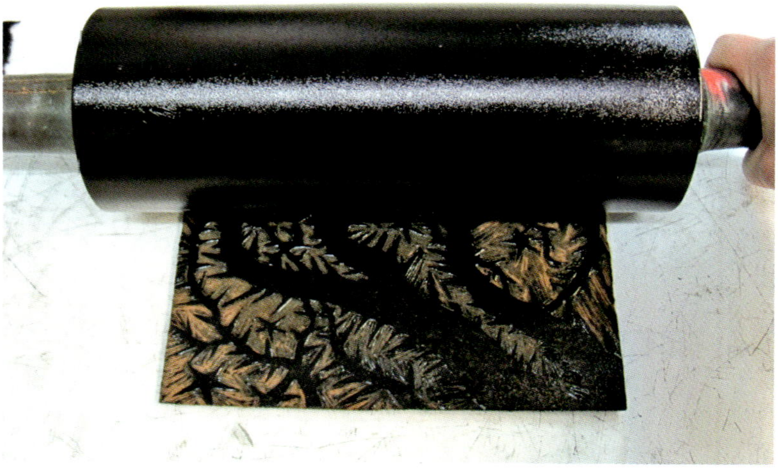

▲ Almost all inks are designed for a specific purpose. Lithographic relief ink is most often used for relief printing and lithography. It is also used for monoprinting.

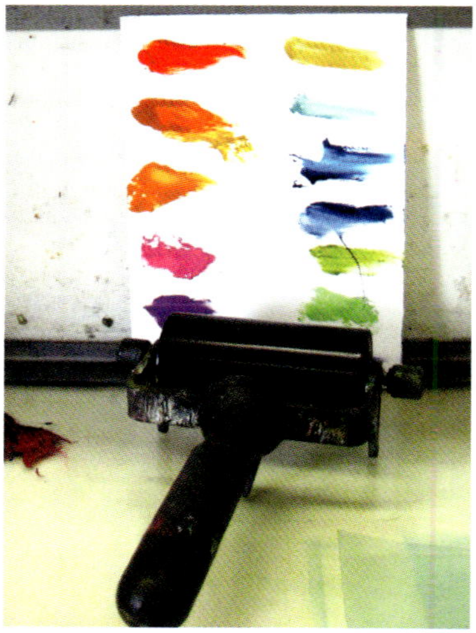

▲ All printmaking studios use a variety of printmaking inks and equipment and it is polite to respect each studio's ways of working. Always ask the workshop supervisor if you are unsure of something in the studio you are working in.

> *'Traditional oil-based ink, on the other hand, is biodegradable. Made from linseed oil, a natural sustainable product made from the flax plant, a simple ink will have possibly a small proportion of magnesium carbonate or talc and perhaps some wax, all readily occurring products that are chemically inert.'*
>
> Steve Hoskins, *Inks*, A&C Black, 2004

Copperplate oil is made from linseed oil. It is available in three strengths: thin (weak), medium and thick (heavy). Thick copperplate oil is the most viscous and thin copperplate is the least viscous.

Viscosity refers to the stickiness of the ink or how runny or how thick it is. Very dry ink is called 'short' ink. It has very little viscosity but adding copperplate oil to it will increase this. Very sticky ink is called 'long' ink. It has extreme viscosity.

Lithographic inks and relief links are 'long' inks. They need to be extremely sticky to cover surfaces very thinly. They have very high viscosity. Etching inks are mostly 'short' inks. They need to be easily wiped from a plate's surface. They have much less viscosity than long inks.

Thin copperplate oil is the best weight oil to add to ready-mixed inks. Medium and thick copperplate oil are most often used when you mix your own inks by hand from dry pigments.

Lithographic and relief inks are specifically designed to work for those processes and etching inks are specifically designed to work for intaglio processes.

What you actually choose to do with your inks is your personal choice: in the main, you can mix and match them as you see fit. In some cases,

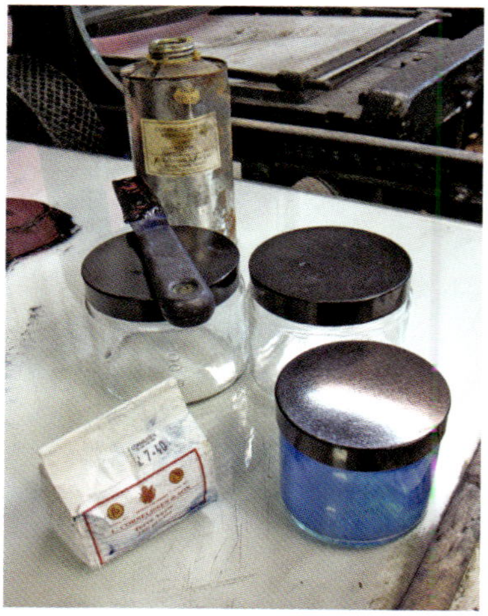

▲ Traditionally ink is made from copperplate oil and pigment.

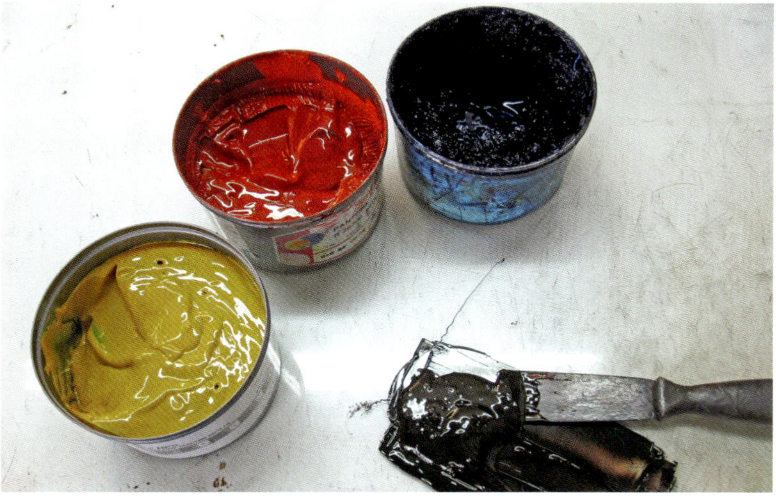

◀ Lithographic relief inks are 'long' inks. This means they have a high viscosity.

however, an ink is designed for a unique purpose, such as non-drying roll-up black for use in lithography. You would not use this ink to ink an etching plate with: it just would not be suitable.

There are many etching inks available from a wide range of different manufacturers. The same goes for lithographic relief inks. Commercial lithographic relief inks are often used for lithography, relief printing and monoprinting. (See Chapter 6.)

Good quality oil-based etching inks and lithographic relief inks should be of a dependable consistency. We are happy to recommend inks from Charbonnel®, who have much expertise in this area.

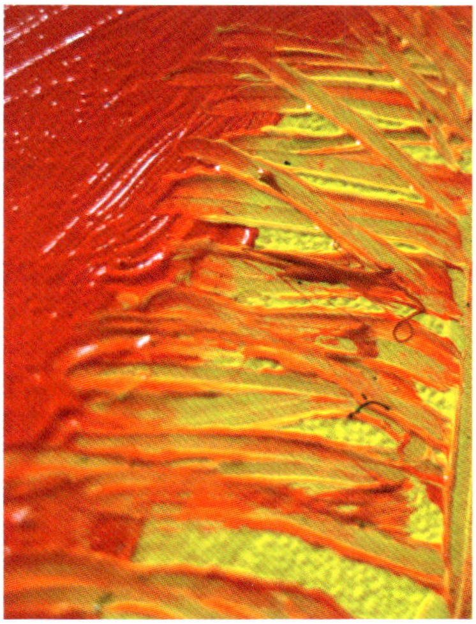

▲ Ink colour is beautiful.

Charbonnel® inks (in descending order of intensity):

- 55985 – Strong black well suited to drypoint, aquatint and mezzotint – difficult to wipe.
- 71303 – Warm black, with hints of red. It is not as difficult to wipe as 55985.
- Luxe C – Used as 55989 but easier to handle, black with hints of blue.
- F66 – Medium intensity black, no problem in handling all types of etching.
- RSR Concentrate – Compact black, useful for deeply engraved or bitten line.
- 55981 – (Carbon Black) Same intensity as RSR but less compact.
- Doux – Weakest black. Easiest to wipe.
- Noir vignette – a relief ink, a long ink suitable for surface rolling

Graphic Chemical inks:

- Intense black – Heavy, compact, strong black, difficult to wipe. Good handling all types of etching.
- Blue black – An easy to wipe, cold plate black with blue tint (of ultramarine).

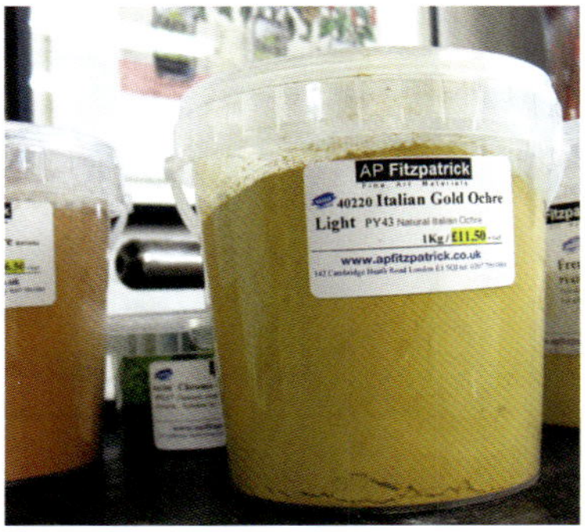

▲ Pure pigment (in dry powder form) is used for mixing ink by hand.

Intaglio Printmaker is an ink supplier based in the UK (they also ship abroad). They sell their own inks as well as other brands.

Other UK suppliers include:

- L. Cornelissen & Son
- T. N. Lawrence (suppliers of both etching and lithographic relief inks)
- Hawthorne Inks
- Gibbon Inks (who are now owned by Sun Chemical®. Sun have also taken over Marler, Coates Lorrilleux, Ault and Wiborg)

Some international suppliers include:

- Graphic Chemical Company
- Gutenberg®
- Charbonnel®
- Gamblin
- Speedball®
- Rembrandt
- Caligo Safe Wash
- Akua

Inks are available in tins, cartridges and as powder pigment (sold in plastic containers, paper bags and tins).

Etching inks are available in myriad colours. Colour charts are available from all manufacturers and can be a great aid in selecting a colour or colours. Experimenting with colours that appeal to you is the best way of learning about them and getting the best from them.

This is also true of selecting the best manufacturer's ink for you. All etching inks are different in small, individual ways specific to that manufacturer. It is only by trying out particular brand names that you will be able to decide what works best for your style of printing.

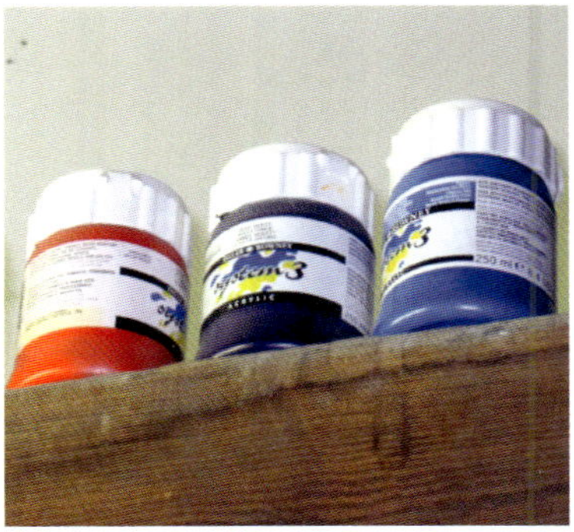

▲ System 3 inks are acrylic-printing ink made by Daler-Rowney®. They are used for screen printing.

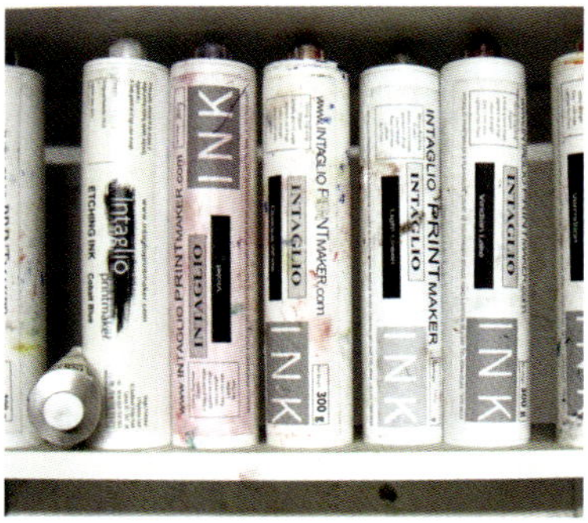

▲ Cartridges are a convenient way to store colours and keep them from drying out. A calking gun is used to dispense the ink.

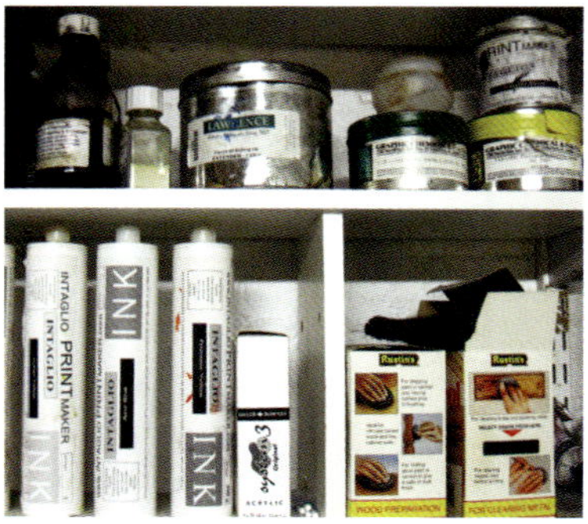

▲ Each manufacturer will package its ink in a different way. The container should be airtight and inks should be stored in a cool, dry place when not in use.

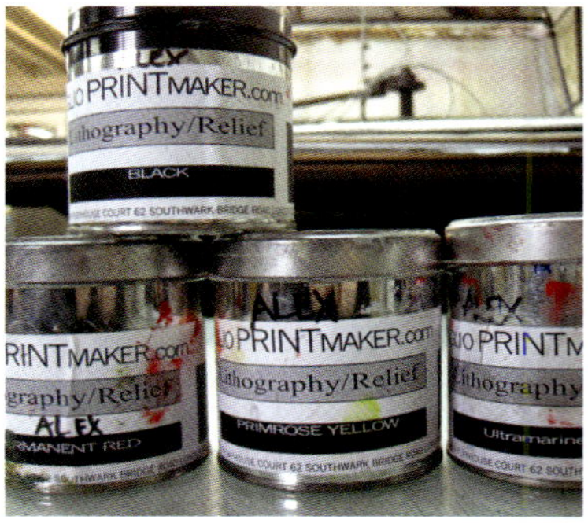

▲ Relief inks.

Working in a printmaking workshop means being able to tap into the knowledge and experience of others. Printers in professional studios make it part of their job to know what inks are suitable for specific types of work, so feel free to ask.

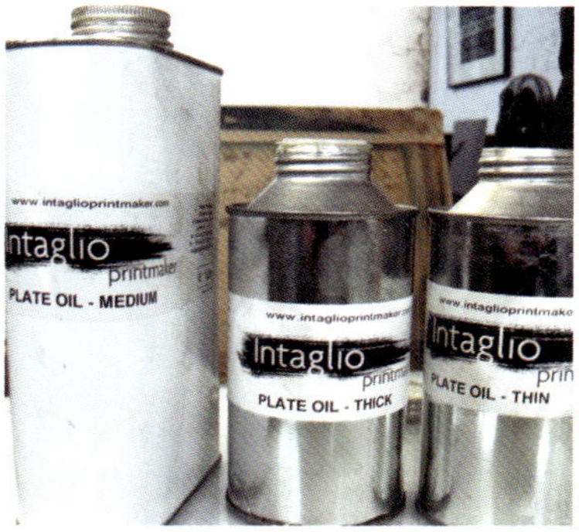

▲ A pigment's individual characteristics will determine how much copperplate oil to add to them and how long you will have to spend mixing or grinding them with a muller. (If the pigment is fine enough you may not have to use a muller.)

MAKING INK BY HAND

To make ink by hand, you will need dry pigment, copperplate oil, a muller (see pictures below), a large glass-topped surface, palette knives and empty storage containers (both metal tubes or glass jars are suitable). If a glass-topped surface is not available, very large lithographic stones can be used. (Ink was traditionally ground on lithographic stones in workshops and large stone slabs are kept in workshops specifically for this purpose. Non-drying roll-up black for lithography is stored this way – it is rolled out on the surface of a lithography stone and covered with greaseproof or acetate.)

Pigments look like dry powder and can be fine or coarse. Some pigments are greasier than others. All of these characteristics will determine how much copperplate oil you will need to add to them, which type of copperplate oil you should add to them, and how long you will have to spend mixing or grinding them with a muller. (If the pigment is fine enough, you may not have to use a muller at all.)

You will have to experiment with each individual pigment colour and copperplate oil to learn each pigment's viscosity (how long or short they are).

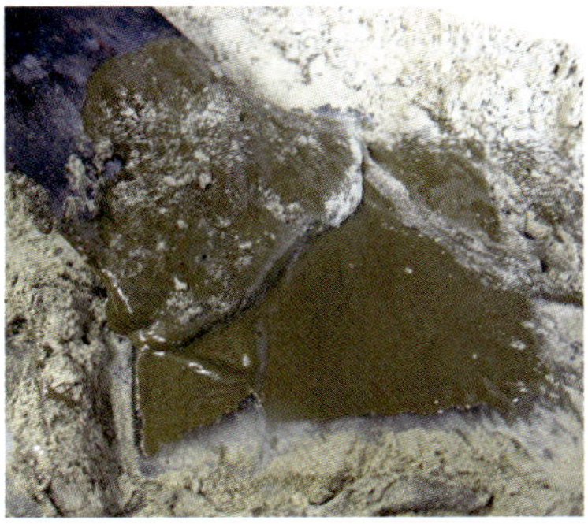

▲ Artists can mix their own ink by hand using pure pigment. You will also need copperplate oil (thin, medium and thick) palette knives and a glass muller. Place a small amount of pigment on the glass, coat the palette knife with oil, and mix the ink by pushing the palette knife into and across the dry pigment until all is blended.

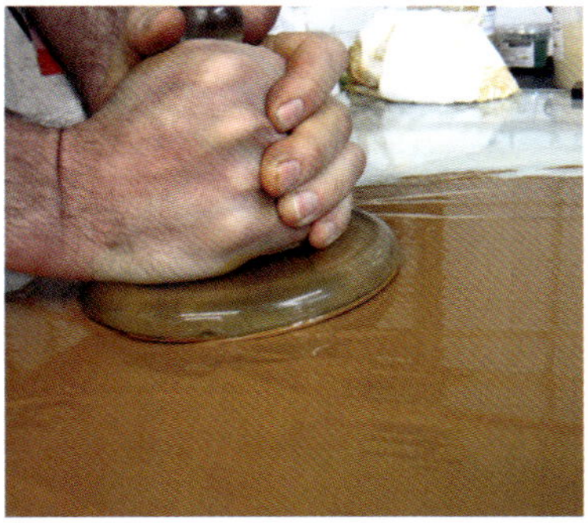

▲ Place the glass muller in the blended mixture and stroke back and forth across the mixture on the glass. This motion grinds the mixture to the desired texture. Continue to do this until the mixture is grit free and smooth.

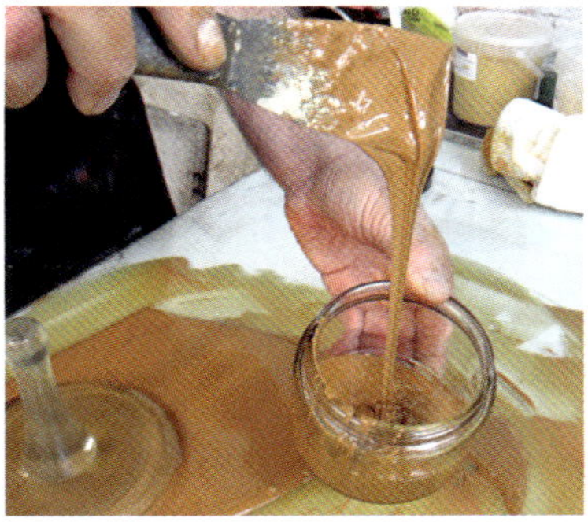

▲ When the pigment and copperplate oil is mixed to the desired consistency, it is lifted from the glass and stored in airtight containers. As coloured ink is so beautiful, glass jars are the perfect way to display it (you can also see the other colours easily when you need them).

COLOUR THEORY

Colour theory complements how inks are used.

The colours you use, and how you combine them, are both important elements in making your print look and 'feel' exactly how you want it to.

The very simple use of monochrome can be as exciting and dynamic as complicated colour schemes based on theory and the use of a colour wheel. Remember that there are three primary colours (red, yellow and blue) and all other colours (other than metallics and fluorescents) can be made from combining them in various ways.

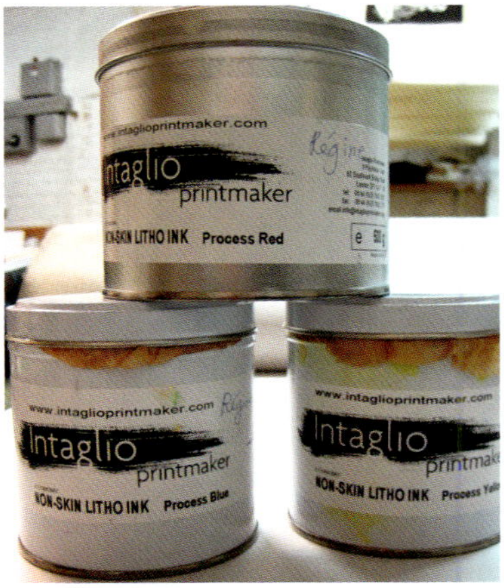

▲ Inks are made by a variety of manufacturers. Experiment with many brands until you find an ink range you enjoy using.

▶ Ink colour combinations are fun to create. This technique is known as a rainbow roll. More than one colour is rolled onto the roller at the same time.

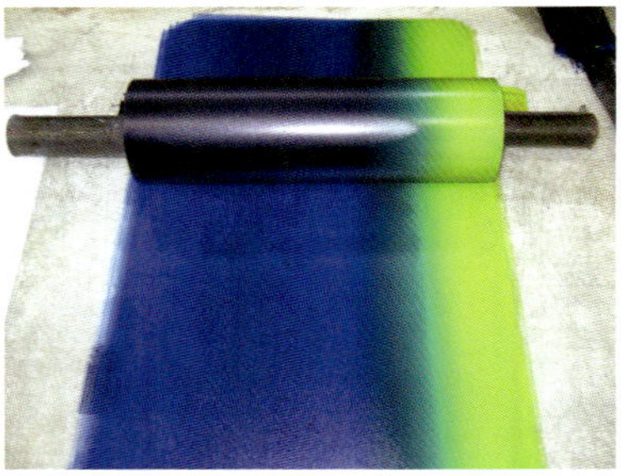

▼ The rainbow roll on a carborundum® plate.

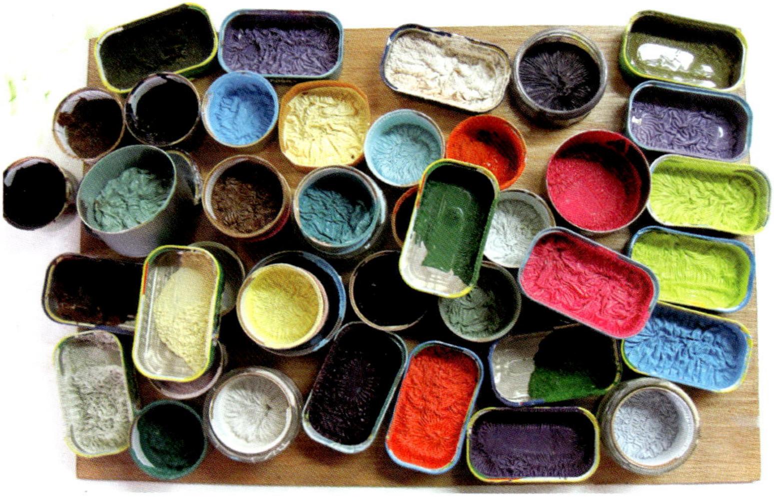

◀ Not all colours can be purchased ready mixed. The artist may have to make the colours needed. Storing colour swatches in tins and making notes how they are mixed is a great way to remember how to make a colour at a later date.

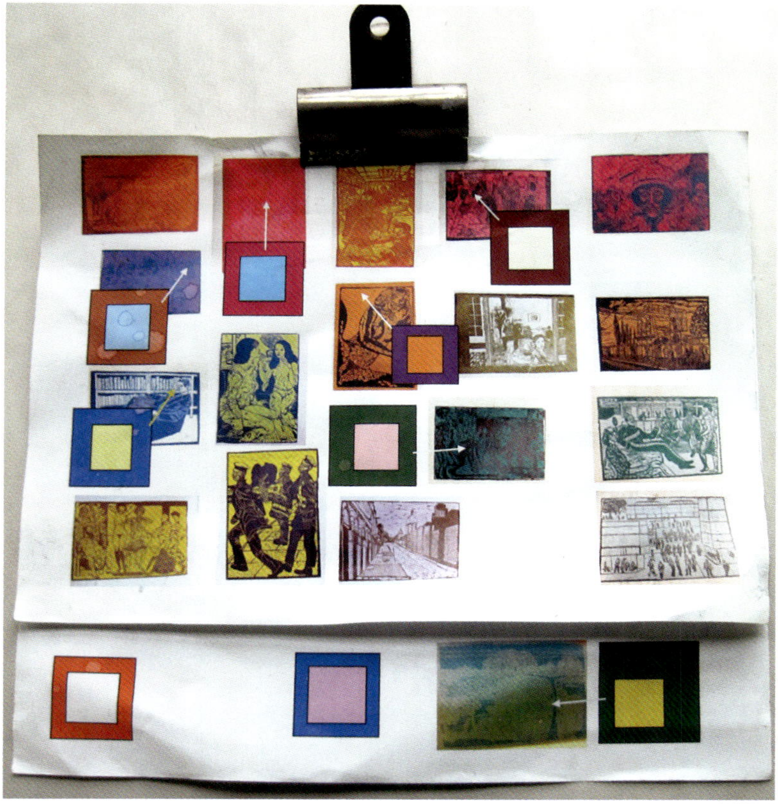

▶ This picture shows the artist Rahil Sheik's colour plan, which is used to work out how each colour will be used in his linocut images.

▼ Artist Helen Clark working on a monoprint at Artichoke Print Workshop.

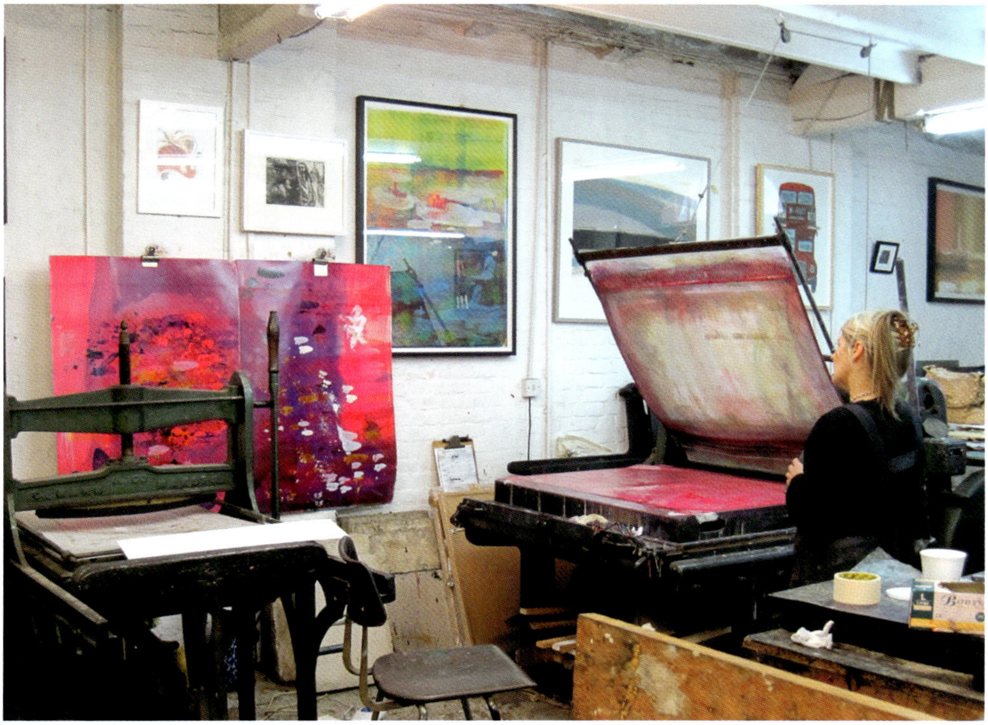

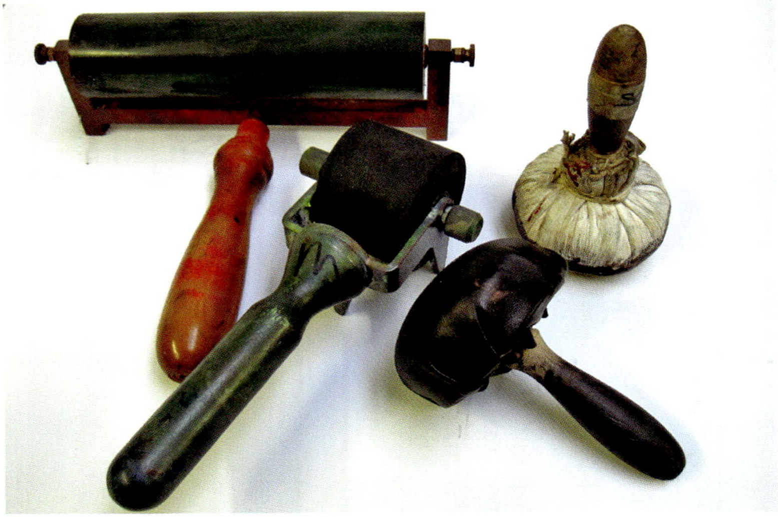

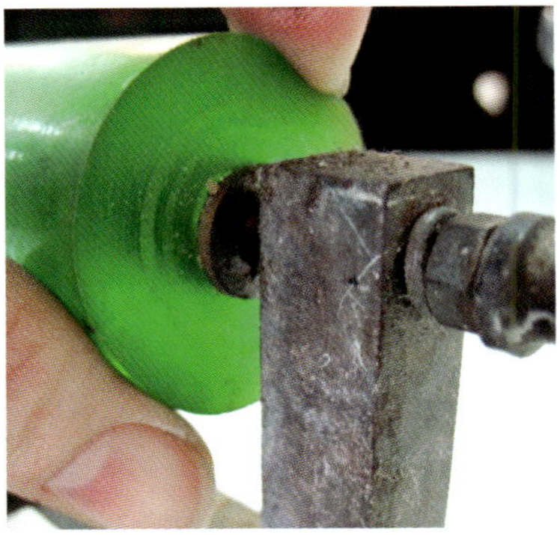

◀ Rollers (detail above) come in different sizes. Dabbers are rounded, mushroom-shaped tools with a handle and an end covered in soft leather.

HOW TO APPLY INKS

Leather dabbers, rubber squeegee, muslin, scrim (or tarlatan) and stiff card (mount board cut to a small convenient hand-held size) can all be used to ink a plate.

Nitrile PVC rollers are the most popular for this exercise, as they are hard-wearing. Most small rollers 5 to 25 cm (2 to 10 in.) are mounted into steel frames (brayers with locking screws and a handle). Larger rollers 30 to 36 cm (12 to 14 in.) and specialist rollers can be made to your specifications. The rubber varies in hardness and softness, and this is measured in a unit called shore.

25 shore = standard
30 shore = soft
40 shore = firm
70 shore = extra hard

INK ADDITIVES

Ink additives are substances added to inks in order to modify their texture, consistency and viscosity (hardness and softness). The most commonly used are cobalt driers, plate oil, magnesium carbonate, French chalk and manganese driers.

The composition of ink causes it to dry at different speeds depending on the amount of driers already present in it. Inks can be mixed by hand or by machine in larger, commercial quantities. Some inks, such as Senefelder's Crayon Black, purposely have no (or very few) driers. This is so that images can be kept on lithographic stones for long periods of time between uses. Drying times must always be taken into consideration when printing complicated images.

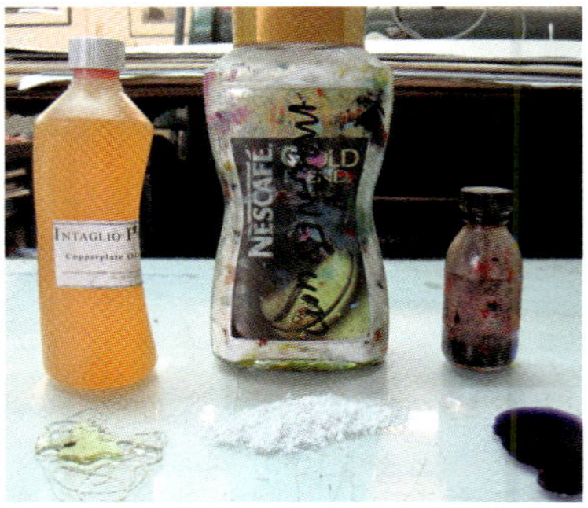

▲ From left to right: copperplate oil (thin), magnesium carbonate and cobalt driers.

INK TEST

One of the most common questions about ink is 'what can it be suitable for?'. We were asked to do a product test of Gamblin Ink. Here are the results from the questions/expectations we had of the product. The product test was published in the respected professional magazine *Printmaking Today* and is reproduced courtesy of the author, Megan Fishpool.

Gamblin Ink
Papers tested:
Japanese Block Printing Paper 90gsm, Somerset Satin 300gsm, Whatman 180gsm, Hannemuhle 280gsm, BFK Rives 180 gsm, Tissue, Newsprint

Presses used:
Nipping Press, Sprung-roller press, Hand-burnishing with wooden spoon and wooden barren

Substrates tested:
Wood Block, Wood Engraving, Perspex relief block, Linocut

Ink modifers used:
Lithographic relief extender (mixture ink 70%, extender 30%)

The quality of printing results on the blocks tested was very good. In particular, the ink on the surface of the perspex was excellent. The texture/consistency of the Gamblin ink is misleading – loose and runny. You do not need a thick layer – using too much will clog the cut lines on the block. The ink is easy to roll out. The pigmentation of the ink is intense. It stains your hands heavily like a dye but it cleans up very well. When mixed with lithographic extender (an oil-based transparent white), the consistency stayed stable and the ink rolled out evenly.
Two disadvantages were found (note: we write from the perspective of a professional printmaking editioning studio):

1) The printed surface marks VERY easily. Touching up blemishes is impossible as the ink does not allow you to blend a mark in. The blemish mark is still visible once the ink has dried. Which leads on to the second disadvantage.
2) Drying time. All of the test prints were still not dry after 10 days. This presents a problem for storing the prints and for letting a client take the prints away safely, especially if the prints are needed for a project deadline.

All in all, it is a good quality ink – easy and enjoyable to print with. It captured beautifully the details in the wood engraving and united superbly with the surface of the Perspex block. Given the available container size, using it for large scale woodcuts and linocuts would not be practical, but for small-scale work it is extremely suitable.

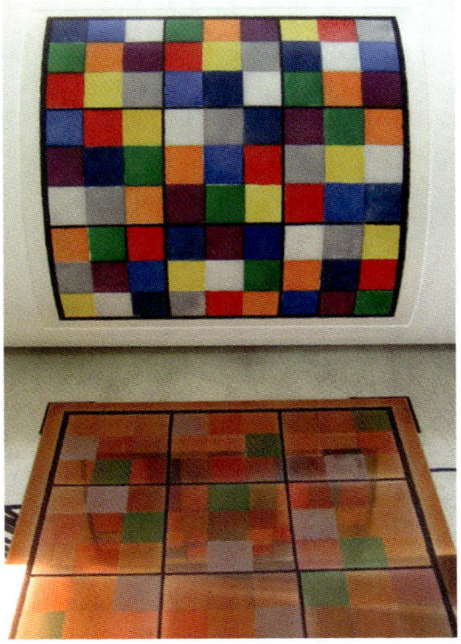

▲ **A complicated nine-colour aquatint image on five copper photo etching plates inked à la poupée, made for the artist Tom Phillips CBE, RA, and printed by Megan Fishpool and Colin Gale at Artichoke Print Workshop.**

Water-based inks have been available for many years. Inks which can be used with water can be known by a dizzying array of names, including water-based, water-soluble, water-mixable, water-washable and water-washable oil-based inks.

All of these inks are engineered to clean up with water (while the ink is still wet). They are similar to traditional oil-based inks but differ in the way they adhere to the plate surface and to how they react to water. Most are thinned with specially made mediums in order to achieve flow and gloss. Adding water to these inks tends to make them stiff and pasty. Most of these inks now being manufactured have greatly improved pigment vibrancy.

WATER-BASED AND WATER-SOLUBLE INKS

It is important that an ink that has an affinity with water (rather than solvents) is dependable, has a quality pigment content and works well for whichever process is required – whether this is intaglio, relief, lithography or screen printing. How an ink behaves with water is crucial to its successful use and to the ease and enjoyment of use for the artist.

All manufacturers present their products differently, whether they are water-affiliated or oil-based products. Inks that are used with water are used for several reasons, the most important being they smell nice and that you can use water to clean them up without solvents.

Water-affiliated products can be split into two categories. Water-soluble substances dissolve in water; water-based substances can be dispersed by water: two completely different characteristics. The make-up of an ink used with water is important – for example, many printmaking processes require the printing paper to be dampened so it is vital that the printing ink is not water-soluble. If it were, the ink would be dissolved by the dampness of the paper and the image would bleed and run into an indistinct mess. Water-based inks are made with a vegetable oil base. Vegetable oils are used because they add the necessary lubricity and emulsifying elements, and because of the oil content the inks actually repel water, and do not absorb it, let alone dissolve in it.

Like oil-based inks, water-based inks are not 100% biodegradable because they are mixed with pigment.

▼ Water-soluble inks will be labelled as such and with that description and are available in small, easy to handle tubes that can be transported without fuss. They are now used in the majority of schools. Open-access studios allow artists to bring their own printing inks, which means that both water-based inks and oil-based inks may be so used if the artist so desires.

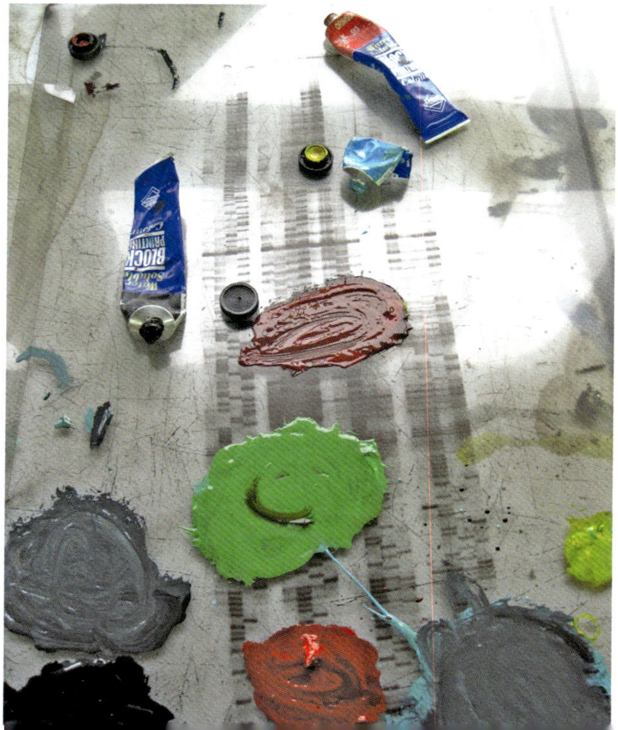

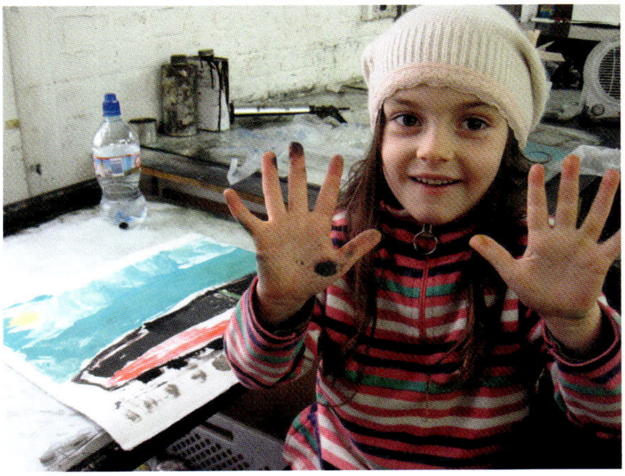

▲ Clarissa Newell-Nebbia shows that water-soluble inks are fun to use and easily cleaned up with water from working surfaces (and hands)!

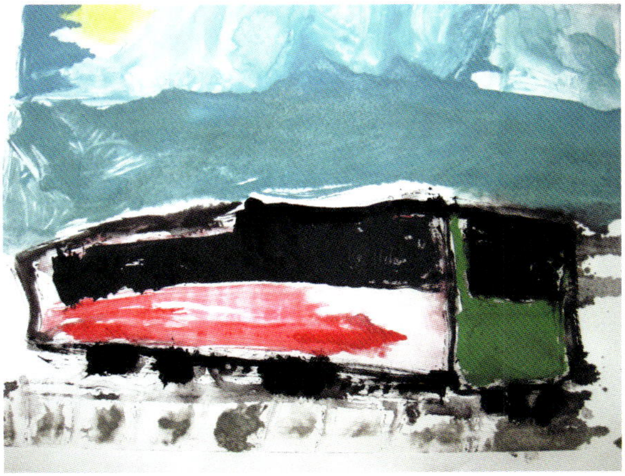

▲ Water-soluble inks need to be used with dampened paper. If the paper is too dry, the image will not offset onto it. If it is too wet, it will dissolve the image into a blur. This image was printed at Artichoke Print Workshop. You are never too young or too old to learn to print.

OIL-BASED INKS

Most oil-based printmaking inks are made with copperplate oil. Copperplate oil is made from linseed oil (flax seed), which is the most readily available, biodegradable pure plant oil, and is not hazardous.

Oil-based inks are usually cleaned from surfaces using solvents such as white spirit or lithotine. For those who prefer not to use solvents to clean oil-based inks, ordinary vegetable oil can be used to remove the ink. Place the vegetable oil directly on the plate surface (or glass top surface) and wipe with a clean cotton cloth until all ink is removed. Next, spray the surface with a solution of liquid soap diluted with water (50% Fairy Liquid® and 50% water is a good mixture). This removes the greasy vegetable oil residue.

Like water-based inks, oil-based inks can be easily cleaned away with water. A wet cotton cloth will remove oil-based ink very quickly from glass, metal or plastic surfaces. This is because of the emulsifying capability of all ink: it won't mix with water, so a wet cloth will displace it from the surface it is on. Linseed oil/vegetable oil can be used to remove ink from plates. Use diluted washing-up liquid soap to clean any remaining oily residue from the plate.

As a professional printmaking editioning studio, we are asked to print many projects. We have to decide on the best products and equipment for those projects. We still use traditional oil-based inks for the majority of our editioning projects and we do this with the artists' full agreement. We use the products and equipment that give the most consistent and trusted results when printing with them. Knowing how to achieve the results you want for any image you make in printmaking will at some point lead you to use ink! Understanding how and why an ink works is a very important part of printmaking.

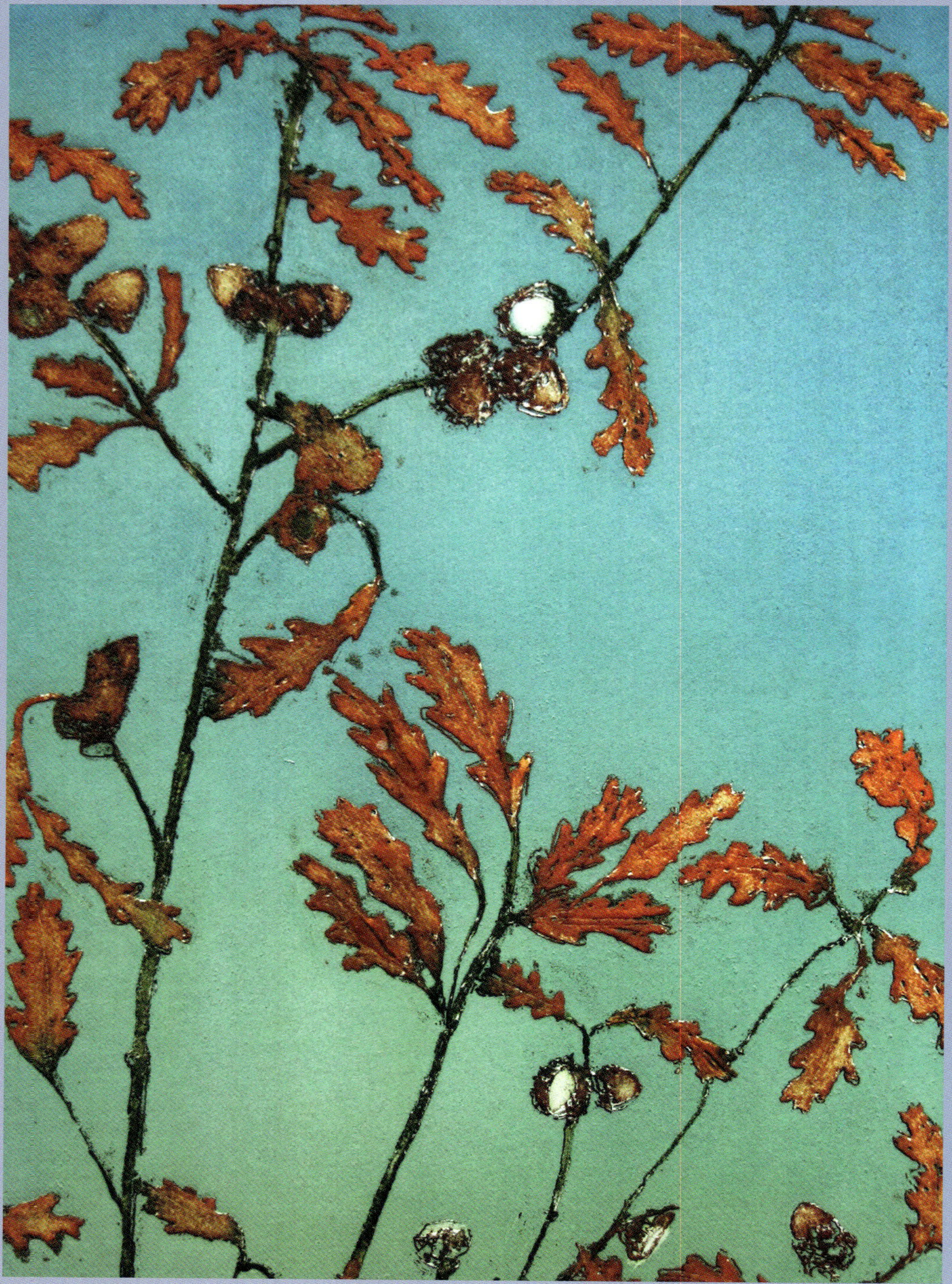

9

viscosity printing

Viscosity printing uses both relief and intaglio techniques on the same plate. The master printmaker Stanley William Hayter (1901–88) invented this technique in the 1960s.

◀ **Peter Wareham, *London Plane*, 2009. Open bite on steel, 36 x 28 cm (14 x 11 in.).**

In any printmaking technique, it is possible to print many colours to create a single image. Single colours can be applied on plates and printed in complicated plate registration sequences. Several colours can be applied to a single plate at once with a technique called à la poupée, and of course a printed image can be hand-coloured (or tinted).

In viscosity printing, all of the colour is applied to the plate prior to the printing of the plate. This is its only similarity to à la poupée printing. To make this process successful, the viscosity (runniness) of the ink and the hardness and softness of the rollers used are crucial.

Viscosity printing is a complex procedure. The ink mixtures and sequence in which they are printed is vital for a successful printed image.

There are three main points to remember about viscosity printing.

1 The plate has different levels of etched marks and tonal areas.
2 Different amounts of copperplate oil need to be added to the ink to create its viscosity.
3 The hardness and the softness of the rollers dictate how the ink interacts (or makes contact) with the surface of the plate.

There is a correct sequence to use when applying the different viscosity of inks to the plate.

1 Ink and wipe the plate so that the ink is pushed into the lines of the plate. Use the scrim (tarlatan) to do this.
2 A hard roller is used with the runniest ink.
3 A soft roller is used with the thicker ink.

We have always used oil-based etching inks for viscosity printing. Oil-based inks are designed to be able to be thinned with copperplate oil and/or linseed oil and their ability to stretch into a barely perceptible layer across a printing plate is one of their most remarkable characteristics.

Many workshops now use water-based inks, as the clean-up method for these inks is preferred. We have included the instruction for a variation on viscosity printing with Akua water-based inks.

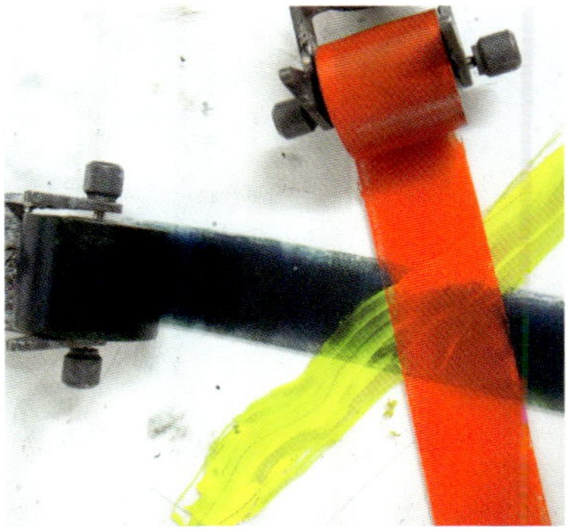

▲ The basic principle of viscosity printing is that each colour used represents a different ink viscosity. And each roller chosen to apply that colour of ink to the plate is selected specifically for its hardness or softness.

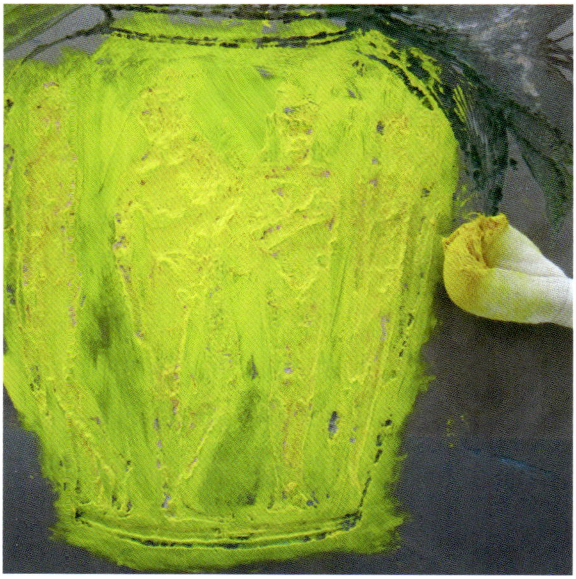

▲ First, the intaglio colour is applied to the plate. Ordinary etching ink is used. (For this picture sequence, Intaglio Primrose Yellow is shown.) A teaspoon of thin copperplate oil has been added to the ink to make it less sticky. A scrim dolly is used to work the colour into the extreme texture of the plate. This plate has also been wiped à la poupée: note the green and brown ink on the plate surface.

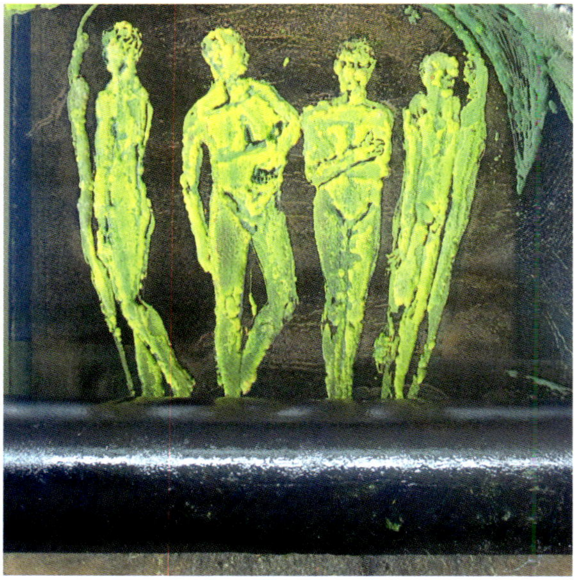

▲ The second (hard) roller has the runniest ink on it (blue). Thin copperplate oil is added to this second ink colour to create its viscosity. This roller passes over the surface of the plate with barely any pressure at all. You do not want the ink on the roller to be pushed into the textures on the plate: it needs only to coat the uppermost surface of the plate.

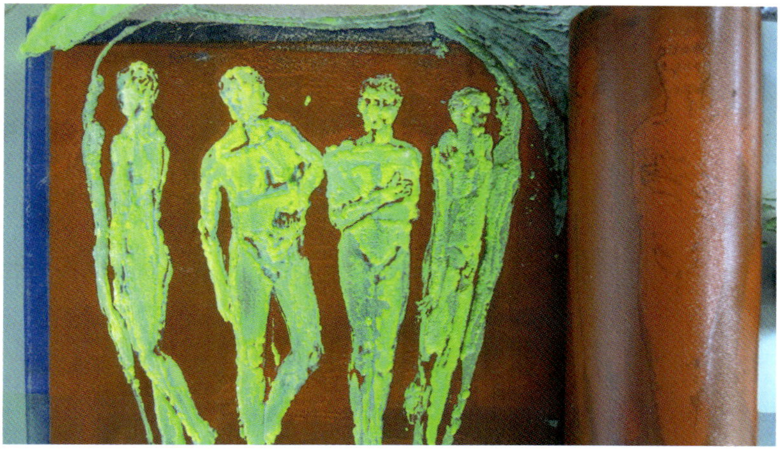

◀ The soft roller is rolled up with the third ink (red). Medium copperplate oil is added to this ink colour so that its viscosity is less runny than that of the second ink colour (blue). The soft roller is able to push the ink into the mid-level of textures on the plate. You will need to apply some downward pressure on the roller when rolling it across the plate's surface. The ink applied from this roller (red) will not mix with that of the ink applied with the hard roller (blue).

Try this simple sequence for viscosity printing using Akua-Kolor water-based inks.

Paint your design directly on the plate using Akua-Kolor straight from the bottle. Next, paint Akua Retarder straight from the bottle on areas of no colour. The Retarder is a medium that acts as a resist – it covers one substance and repels another substance. Spread a little Akua-2 water-based intaglio ink on an ink slab in a line about 2.5 cm (1 in.) thick and the length of your roller. Roll out the ink until the roller is evenly coated. Pass the inked roller lightly over the surface of the plate. The Akua-2 intaglio ink will not adhere to the first layer of Akua-Kolor or to the Akua Retarder.

You will need to experiment with all water-based printing inks to use for viscosity printing.

Manufacturers of water-based inks make many additives, such as converters, oil converters and blending mediums. It is best to purchase any (or all) of the additives manufacturers recommend for their products with the inks and have a go! The printing sequence order for viscosity printing remains the same. (See Chapter 8, p.208, for a list of manufacturers of water-based inks.)

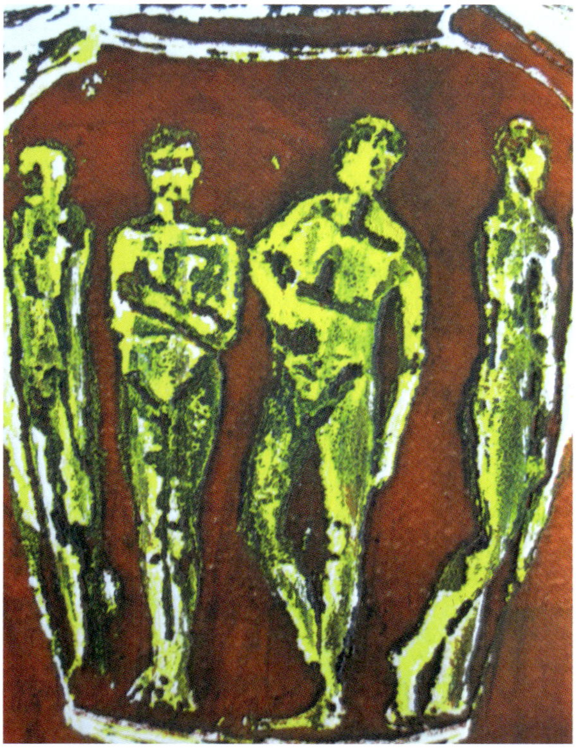

▶ The final three-colour viscosity image using oil-based inks, by artist Peter Wareham.

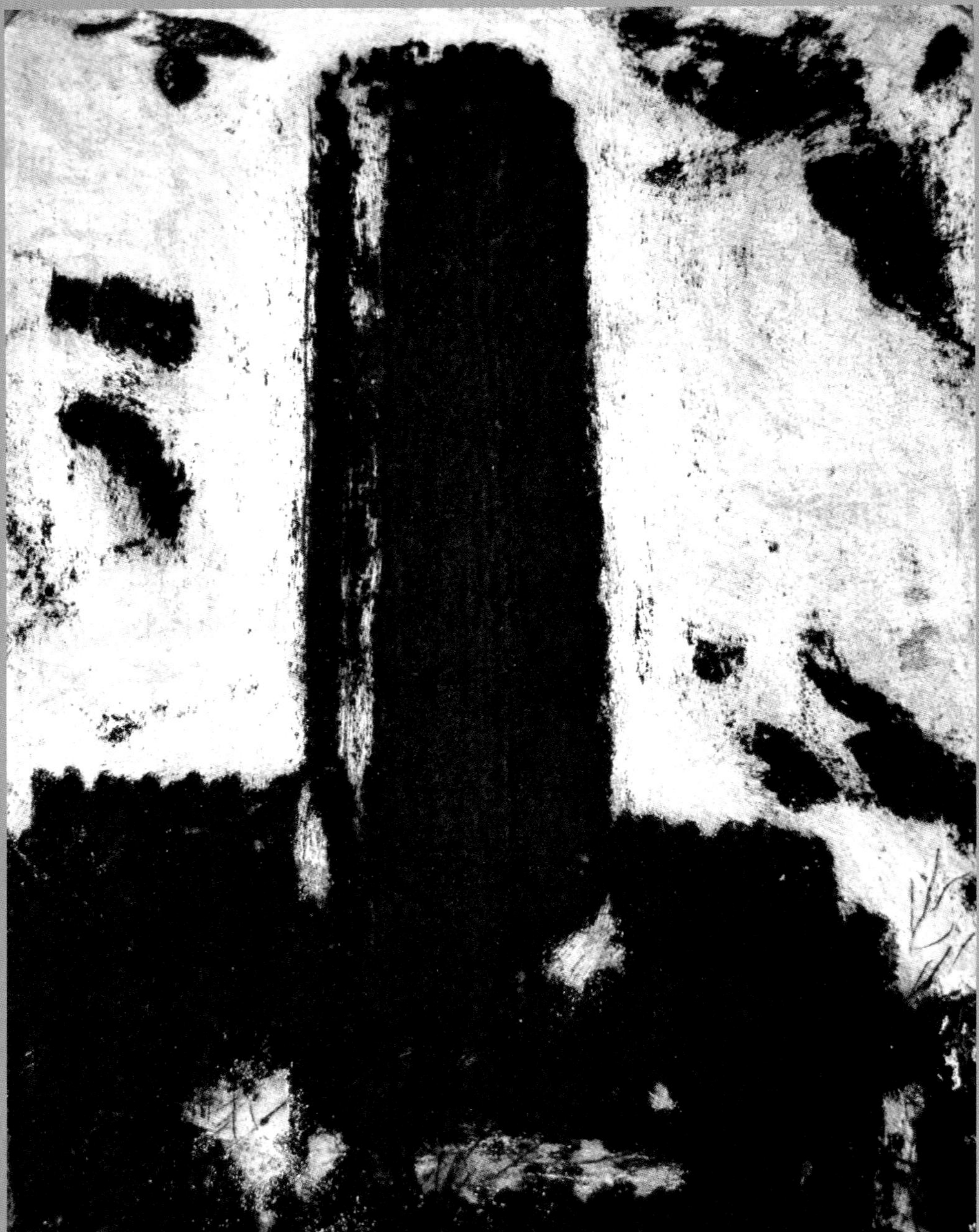

10 collagraph

The collagraph plate consists of both positive areas (raised areas on its surface) and negative areas (areas which have been cut into it or removed). This means that the plate can be treated as both a relief plate and an intaglio plate, which provides the artist with a variety of ways in which to apply ink to the surface.

◀ **Rachel Lindsey Clark, *Bankside*, 2005. Carborundum® and steel, 24.5 x 35 cm (9½ x 13¾ in.).**

The variety of surface textures sometimes makes it difficult to print a collagraph plate by hand. Most images taken from collagraph plates are done by using a printing press.

Extremely textured plates need to be printed with caution using a fixed-roller press, making sure that the pressure is appropriately adjusted. When using any press, take great care with the printing blankets: the most common collagraph disaster involves inappropriate collagraph textures damaging them.

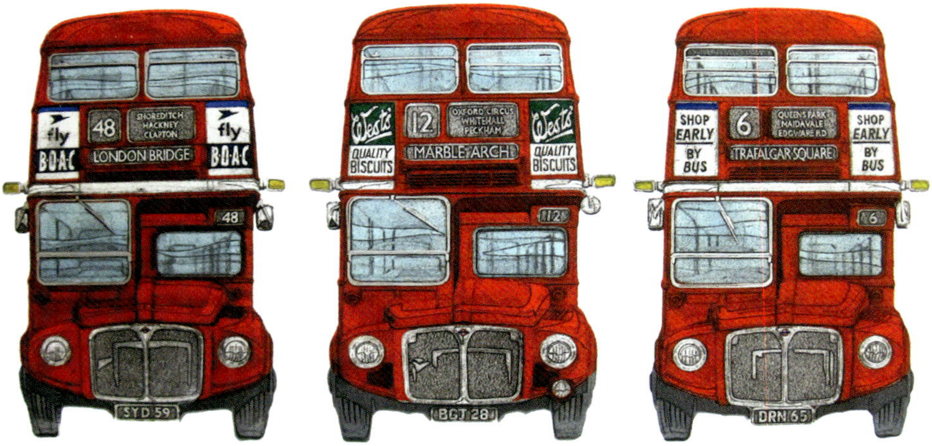

▲ **The collagraph technique enables intricate and graphic images to be created. Barry Goodman, *Three Routemasters*, 2010. Collagraph, 76 x 112 cm (30 x 44 in.).**

Making a collagraph plate is done by attaching different materials of various textures and shapes to the plate with adhesive.

'Collage' is from the French word *coller*, which means to glue. It is a process in art whereby the artist uses a variety of materials – such as pieces of fabric, distinctive papers, photographic imagery and so on – and arranges them compositionally. They are then stuck down onto the selected backing (this can be paper, canvas, wood, etc.). The act of making a collage is exactly what you need to keep in mind when you are making your collagraph plate.

Collagraphy is a printmaking process in which a collage of various materials are glued on to a printing plate and then coated with a protective layer of waterproof or solvent-resistant varnish. This protective coating enables inks (whether water-based or oil-based) to be applied to the surface of the plate and subsequently easily removed.

The word *collagraph* (*collograph* is also used) is derived from the Greek word *koll*, *kollo* or *kolla*, meaning to glue, and *graph* meaning the activity of drawing.

People often confuse the term collagraph with the term collotype, which is a type of photographic print. According to the Victoria and Albert museum website (www.vam.ac.uk, 2011) 'The collotype process was used between about 1870 and 1920. A glass plate was coated with sensitised gelatin and exposed under a negative. Light passed through the negative would harden the gelatin on the glass plate. The unexposed gelatin would absorb the water when washed and the exposed would repel it. The washed glass plate would be coated with ink, adhering to the exposed gelatin and printed onto fine paper.'

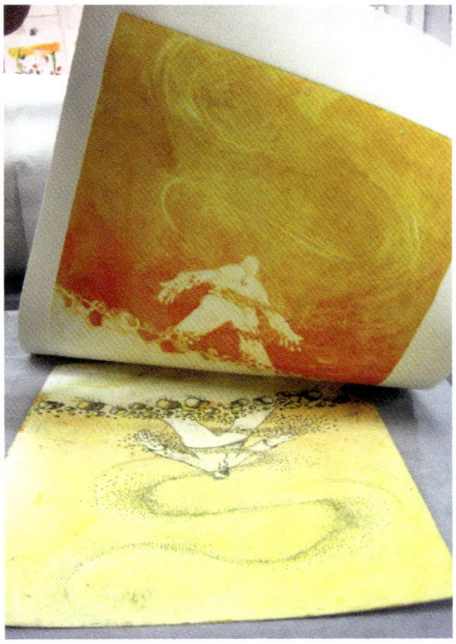

▲ Collagraph is a time-consuming but rewarding technique. The time taken to make an exceptional printing plate is well worth it! This image is made using two collagraph plates and one intaglio plate.

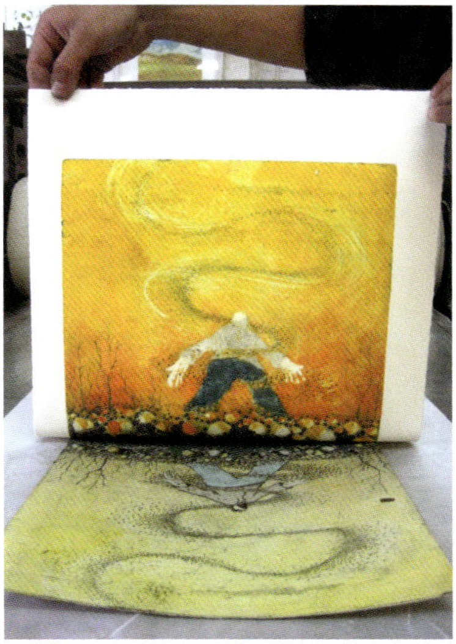

▲ The second collagraph plate is registered on top of the first collagraph plate printed.

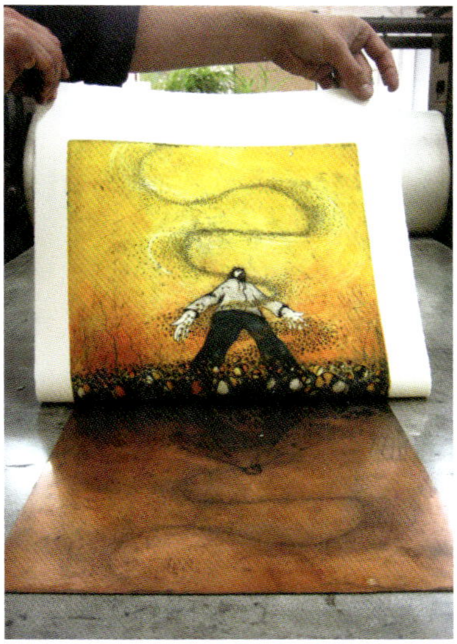

▲ The final plate is a copper intaglio plate. The etched line adds a deliberate network of information in this image by Staffan Gnosspelius.

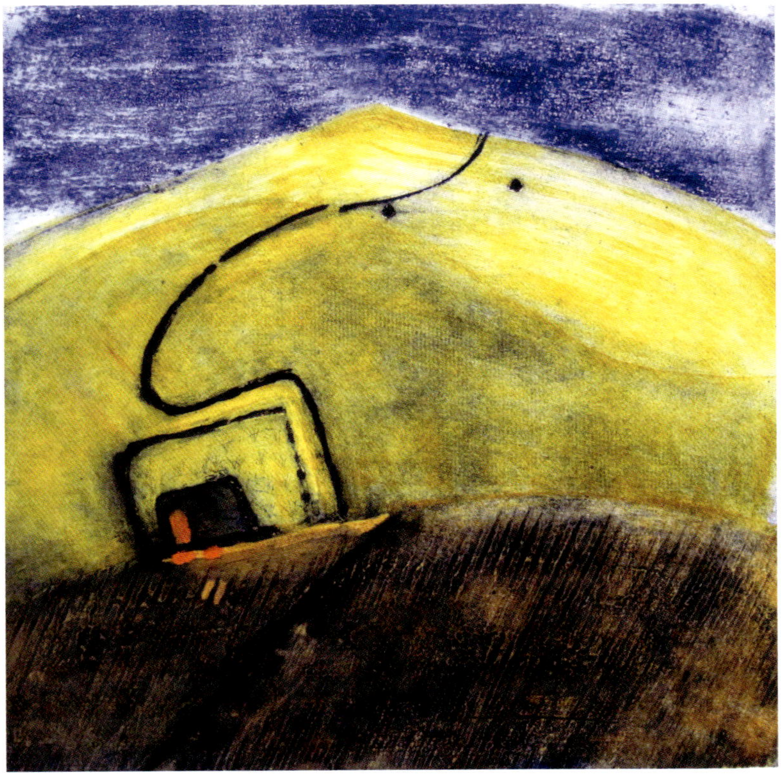

▲ Scrim adhered to a cardboard substrate. Note the artist has chosen to make it perfectly flat and even on the surface of the substrate.

◀ Margaret Auerback, *Landscape (blue)*, 2000. Collagraph, 40 x 39 cm (15¾ x 15¼ in.). Corrugated cardboard disappears into the foreground in this landscape collagraph.

The composition and the textures that you arrange on your collagraph plate will dictate how the final image will take its shape on the paper. The ink you use further enhances the textures.

Depending on how innovatively you use your chosen textures, corrugated cardboard can look like corrugated cardboard and scrim will look like scrim. It's how you incorporate those very distinctive textures into the plate's design that makes a collagraph image successful.

ADHESIVES

A range of adhesives are available and include those listed below.

PVA (polyvinyl acetate)

This bonds paper, card, textiles, leather, fabric and wood. It cleans up easily with water and is non-flammable. PVA is readily available in a variety of squeezy bottle or container sizes with nozzles making it easy to apply and control.

Rice starch glue (paste)/Pritt® Stick

Rice starch is made of wheat starch or rice starch. It is a highly purified adhesive and is used for adhering very fine papers, archival papers, museum mounting and bookbinding. It is water-based and should be applied as the thinnest coating as possible to the paper when using it for Chine-collé. Pritt® Stick is a solvent-free solid glue. It is perfect to use with paper and is often used for Chine-collé.

Contact adhesive

Fast acting and ideal for attaching non-porous materials to porous material or like-to-like materials, such as leather, plastics and carborundum® grits. Contact adhesives work on the basis that each surface is coated lightly with the adhesive and then each surface is let to semi-set for five to ten minutes before the surfaces are joined together. The join takes a few hours to dry and become permanent. EVO-STIK is an excellent contact adhesive which comes in large tins. It can tolerate heat if you need to warm a plate for the inking-up process.

Epoxy glues

The strongest adhesives known, epoxy glues are used to join together non-porous materials. Epoxy glues most often come in two parts: a resin and a hardener. Both must be mixed together before the adhesive can be used. Examples include Araldite Rapid®, Araldite®, J-B Weld® and EVO-STIK® Liquid Metal.

Note that Super Glue® (cyanoacrylate) is *not* recommended for use on collagraph plates. It is a glue specifically designed for plastics and we do not recommend the handling of it as a general purpose adhesive. Super Glue® is not used in schools.

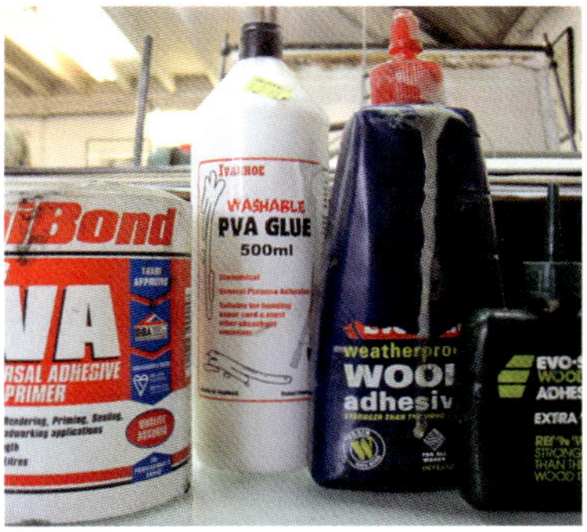

▲ EVO-STIK, PVA and wood glues. These are typical brands and readily available.

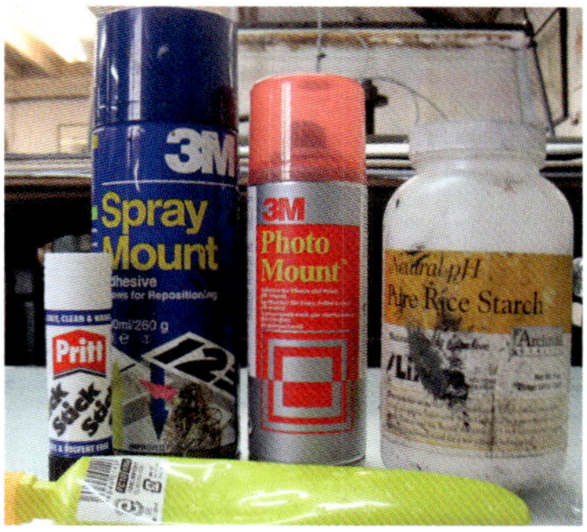

▲ Pure Rice Starch (available as dry powder) and as a ready-mix in tubes. Pritt® Stick and aerosol spray adhesives are also shown. All of these adhesives can be used for Chine-collé.

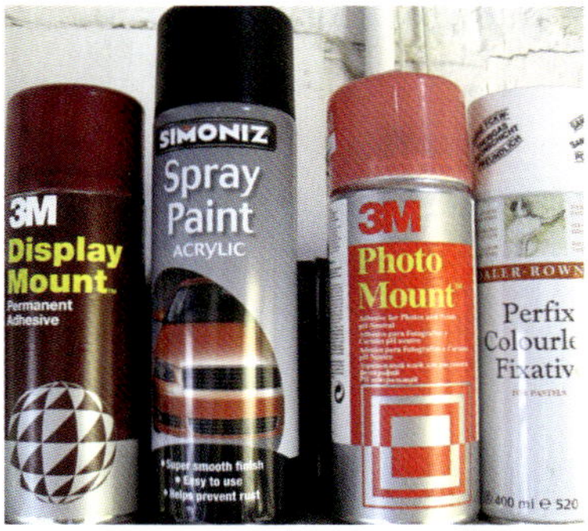

▲ Spray Mount, Photo Mount™, Display Mount™ and Fixative. They are favoured by many artists to use for Chine-collé because you do not have to hold the paper down as you have to when you apply a liquid or solid adhesive. These adhesives have a distinctive smell and should always be used with courtesy in a communal studio.

Spray glues

These are low-tack aerosol adhesives. They are designed to be able to move and reposition paper and photos before the adhesive dries. As a result, they are not particularly effective at attaching textures to the plate. Textures that have been applied using spray guns may pull away from the substrate surface and need repairing. Spray Mount® and Photo Mount® are examples of aerosol adhesives and are readily available from art stores.

These sprays are used because the adhesive does not cause buckling on photo paper or lightweight papers such as tissues. Do note, however, that they are extremely messy. The spraying causes the adhesive to drift onto all surrounding surfaces in the print studio.

Never apply spray mount at the bed of the printing press. The excess spray coats the bed of the press with a fine film which picks up blanket fluff and dust which then ruins the surface of clean printing paper being used by others. It can be cleaned away with white spirit.

Fixative

Fixatives are not suitable for collagraph as they have no adhesive qualities.

Adhesive tapes

These add texture and are useful for creating uneven layering. They can be cut and torn.

We do not recommend them to be used as the sole adhesive for securing textures to the collagraph plate, however. The use of cleaning agents or solvents on the collagraph plate can affect these materials and cause them to deteriorate as their adhesive backing is very low tack.

Sometimes even the application of the shellac or varnish that seals the surface of the card can damage or dissolve the adhesive on the tapes. The main reason for choosing to use adhesive tapes on a collagraph plate is for the variety of textures they provide.

Masking tape is textured, tears easily and will create soft tones. Packing tape and sellotape are smooth, shiny and wipe clean. Gum strip is semi-smooth, tears easily and creates light tone.

All of these tapes come in a variety of widths.

CREATING TEXTURES ON A COLLAGRAPH PLATE

To create texture on a collagraph, consider using some of the following tools and equipment. All can be found in DIY stores, hardware stores and printmaking studios:

- Wood filler
- Pre-mixed fillers, such as texture paste, and ready-mixed plaster
- Gesso
- Woodcut tools/drypoint needle
- Palette knives – these can be used to draw into gesso or pastes and shape them
- Dremel® drill – this has a variety of versatile attachments
- Hammer – use with punches, nuts bolts, bottle caps and hard shapes that can be embossed into the surface of the printing substrate with force to create dents, impressions and deep marks
- Scissors
- Cutting knives/scalpels
- Cork floor tiles
- Sandpapers – for cutting, tearing, layering
- Wood splinters, wood shavings
- Carborundum®
- General rubbish – sweep up the floor and have a look at the everyday rubbish that will have collected. All of the small gritty bits of the working day can be incorporated into the surface of the collagraph. It is easy to embed them into a plate coated with plaster, gesso, texture paste, wood filler and so on.

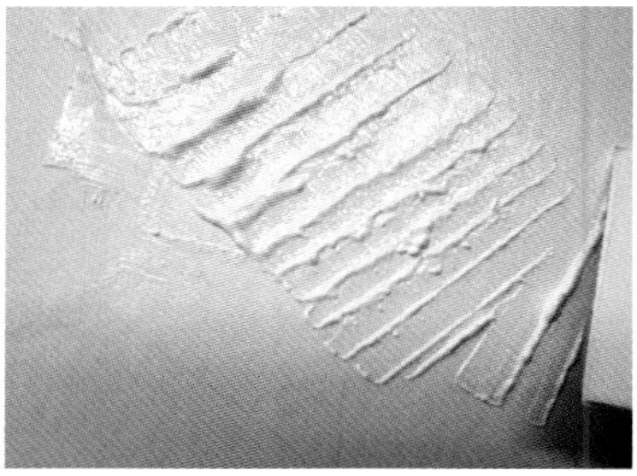

▲ Gesso can be used to create painterly marks on the collagraph plate.

SEALING THE COLLAGRAPH

Shellac and/or varnish is necessary to use to seal the surface of the collagraph plate.

You may also use gesso (Winsor & Newton® or Daler Rowney® are two excellent brands) or PVA glue applied as a very thin coating.

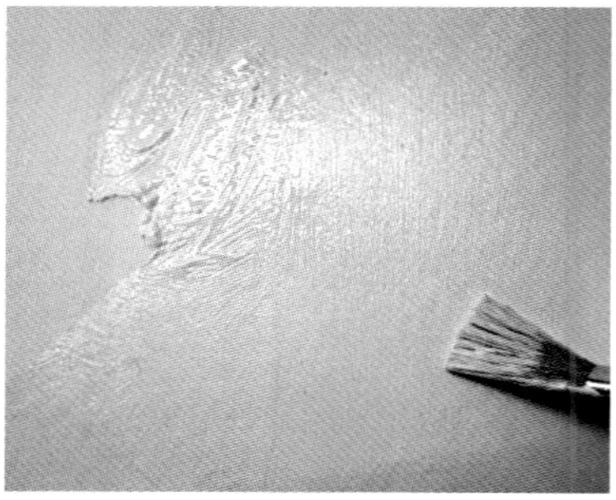

▲ Gesso is also used to seal the card surface. A gesso-sealed card surface provides plenty of plate tone.

Varnish

Varnishes are hard, tough, waterproof polyurethanes soluble in white spirit. Both matt and semi-gloss varieties are suitable. Ronseal® and Blackfriars make water-soluble, low-odour varnishes which dry quickly (30 minutes) and are easily cleaned away with water.

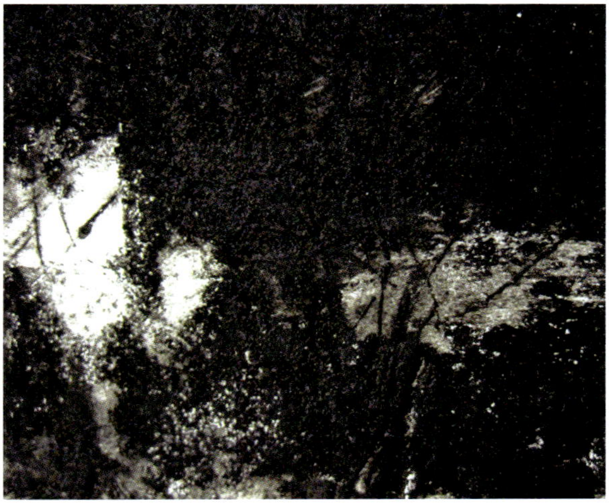

▲ Carborundum® grit texture.

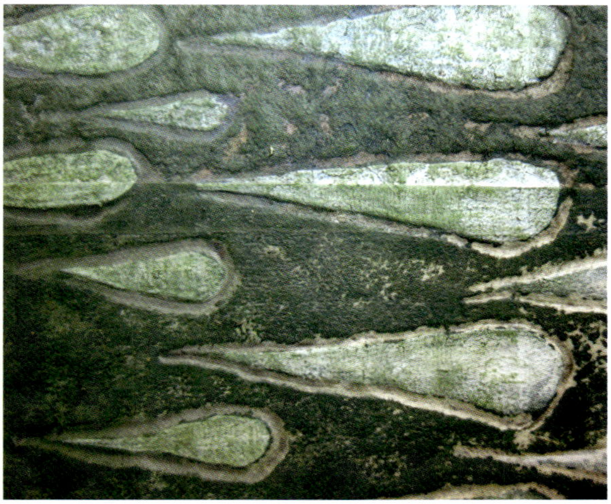

▲ Heavily embossed hand-painted shapes with PVA.

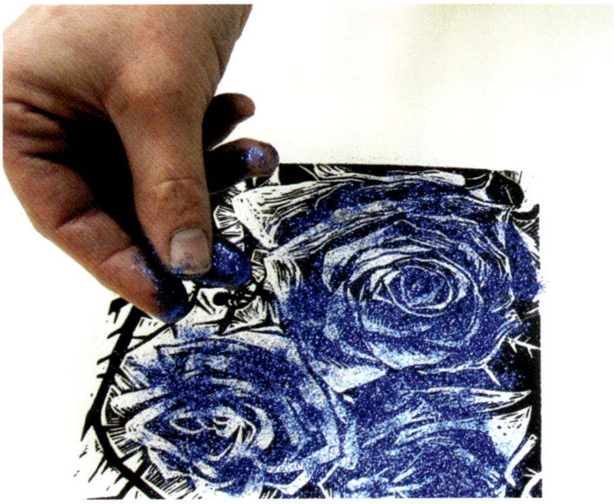

▲ Decorative glitter texture.

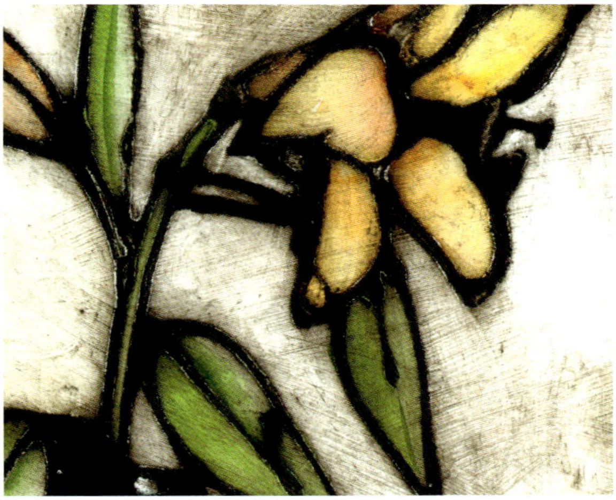

▲ Image outline is drawn with PVA.

Shellac
Shellac is a thin, single resin solvent-based varnish soluble in methylated spirit. Button Polish by Roberson's is excellent.

Gesso
You can make your own by combining whiting powder with PVA glue. It is also available ready-mixed in art stores.

PVA
PVA needs a *very* long time to dry – many days – before it can be inked and printed. If it is not completely dry, the damp paper will stick to the surface and the pressure of the printing press will laminate it permanently to the card. You only have to do it incorrectly once to remember not to do it again.

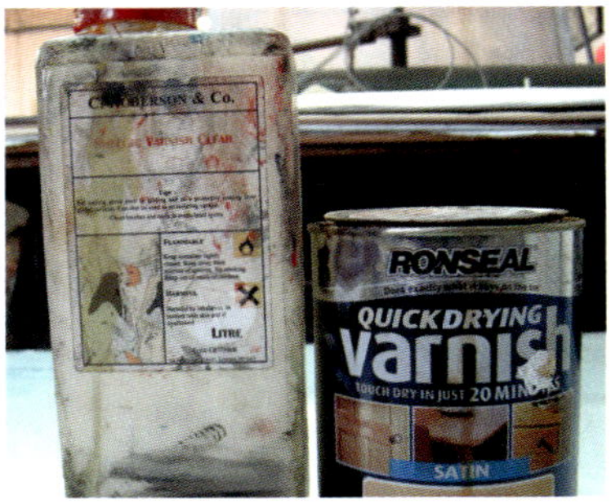

▲ **Shellac and varnish are the two most popular ways of sealing the surface of a collagraph.**

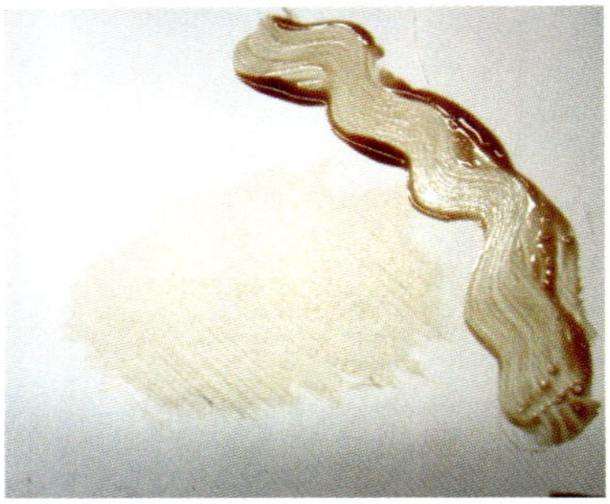

▲ **Varnish creates a smooth, glossy (optional) surface. It is available as a water-based product.**

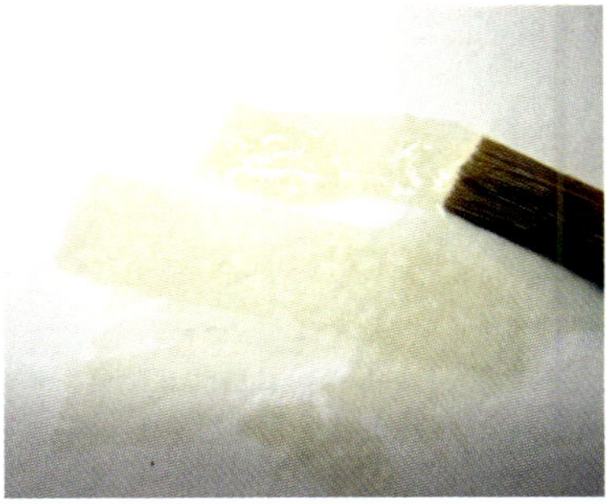

▲ **Shellac creates a matt surface. It is quickly absorbed into the substrate.**

The pictures above are of shellac and varnish applied to clean, bare card. Each coats the surface differently. Shellac is matt (non-shiny) and barely perceptible on the surface. The card absorbs it immediately, which is a bonus. It is impossible to create thick layers of shellac. Varnish is much thicker. Even matt varnish creates a sheen on the surface of the card. It is not completely absorbed into the card and takes much longer to dry the thicker it is applied to the card surface. Gesso creates a matt, textured layer. It is used if you want to have all-over tone in your final design with no highlight areas.

Gesso (made from plaster of Paris and glue) is used to coat the substrate and create base surface to apply ink to. It protects the textures on the plate and creates a tough, durable moisture-resistant surface on the substrate. This is vital as the printing inks applied to the surface – whether they are water-based, water-soluble or oil-based (or even water-washable oil-based, which is now available from Charbonnel®) – must have a surface on which they can be applied with ease and from which they can be easily removed.

Tip

After you have made the collagraph plate and it is completely dry, it is a very good idea to dust the entire surface of the plate with French chalk and run it through the printing press. Use an inexpensive but thick piece of paper. This ensures that all the adhesives and varnish or shellac on the plate really is dry. If it isn't, excess adhesive, varnish or shellac will ooze out from under textures and you will see it on the scrap paper you have just used. Collagraph plates take *many* hours to dry. This is because the various items used to create the plate have a range of drying times. Blind emboss printing the plate before you ink it for the first time also sets (crushes) the textures into the shapes they will actually print as.

It is important that the substrate is well sealed so that the various textures do not fill up with too much ink. This can be a disaster as the pressure exerted by the press can cause the excess ink hidden in the depths of the collagraph textures to ooze out and run where it is not wanted – across the image area. And even worse, if too much ink is present, it floods out from the printing paper onto the bed of the press and the blankets. Not good!

INKING THE COLLAGRAPH

You can ink a collagraph plate using scrim (tarlatan) or muslin. The cloth is often made into shaped bundles called 'dollies' (see picture on p.87).

Inking a collagraph plate can be quite a vigorous activity. A well-made collagraph plate will hold up well to any heavy-handedness needed to work the ink into the textures on the plate surface. The textures become set and defined the more frequently the plate is printed from. Collagraph plates are extremely durable substrates to print from, even though they seem fragile (they are most often made from lightweight card or mount board). Edition sizes are the choice of the artist. They can be as small as 10 and an edition of 30–40 can be taken happily. An edition of 75 is even possible.

Equipment used to ink a collagraph plate
Rollers
Cotton buds
Toothbrushes
Cut card shapes (mount board offcuts are best suited for this)
Rubber squeegee blade

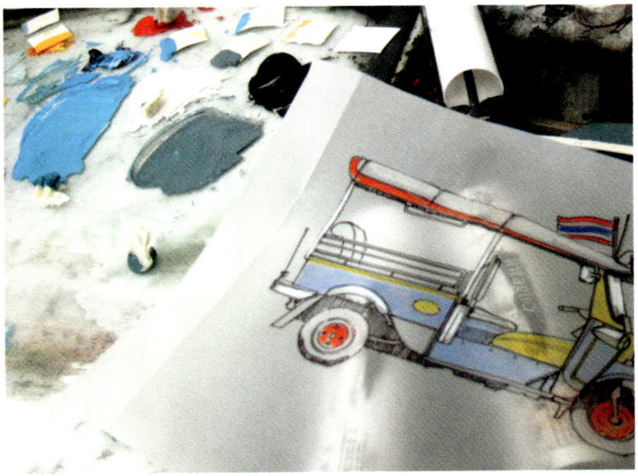

▲ Ink can be applied with scrim (tarlatan), muslin, cloths, cotton buds, mount card cut into easily handled small squares, or cut portions of squeegee rubber. Scrim dollies are a very efficient way to ink a collagraph.

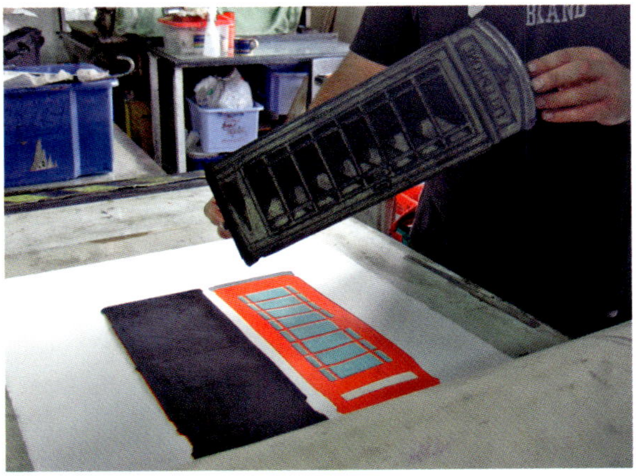

▲ The second collagraph plate with the main image details inked in black ink is printed on top of the assembled coloured sections of collagraph plates to create the final image. A larger ball of scrim that fits comfortably in the hand is used to do this.

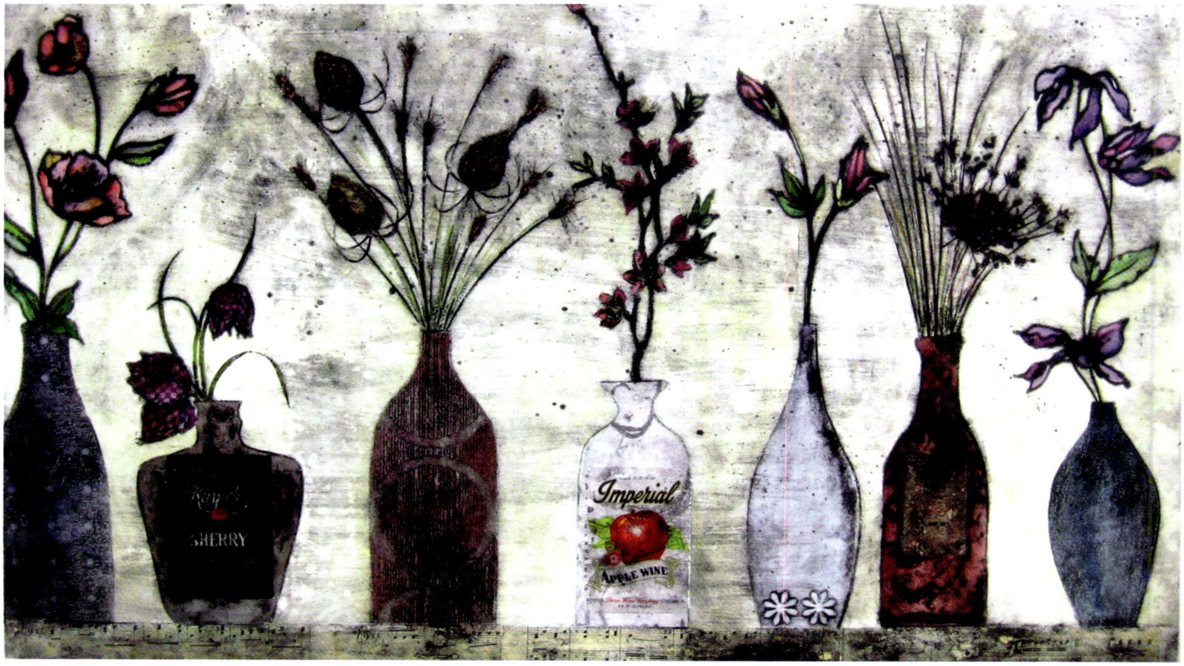

▲ Vicky Oldfield, *Flowers From the Hedgerow*, 2010. Collagraph, carborundum®, Chine-collé, 117 x 56 cm (46 x 22 in.).
It is possible to create loose lines and rough marks that resemble bold charcoal lines using the collagraph technique.

REPAIRING A COLLAGRAPH PLATE

Collagraph plates can become damaged. Textures can come unstuck from the surface. They are easily re-glued to the surface and the area recoated with the shellac or varnish used to seal the surface of the plate.

CARBORUNDUM®

Carborundum® (silicon carbide or aluminium oxide) is a synthetic abrasive. Different grades of carborundum® grit create very successful tonal areas and grainy areas on the collagraph plate.

Glue mixtures of carborundum® and PVA can be painted directly onto the collagraph plate. Or alternatively, the plate can be coated with PVA and the grit sprinkled directly on top and left to dry.

The carborundum® grit can be layered. After a first layer of glue and grit is applied and dried, a second layer can be applied. After that layer dries, a third layer can be applied and so on. This builds up soft layers of gritty shapes that punch a rich texture into the paper's surface when it is printed.

Carborundum® grit holds an enormous amount of ink, which means that as a texture, it provides handsome, dark tonal areas in an image's composition.

▼ Grit is a very useful collagraph texture. It combines with PVA to make excellent grit mixtures which can be painted quite freely on the plate or shaped into chunky, bold marks.

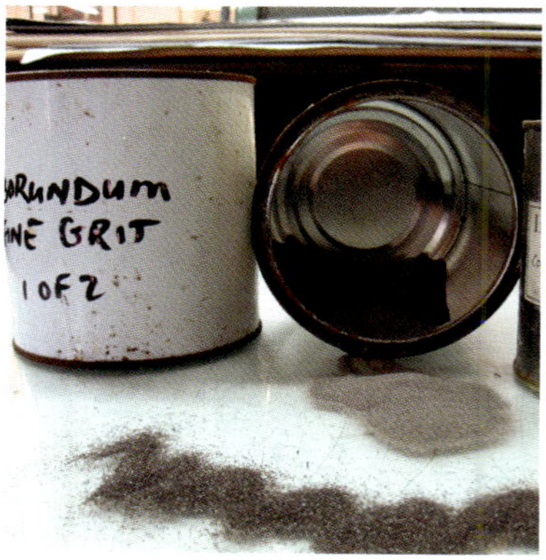

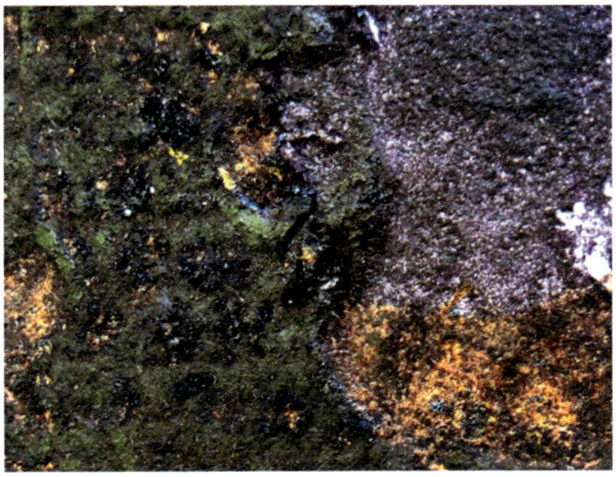

▲ This paper has been embedded with extremely coarse textures. Note the pocking and gritty, sand-like detail.

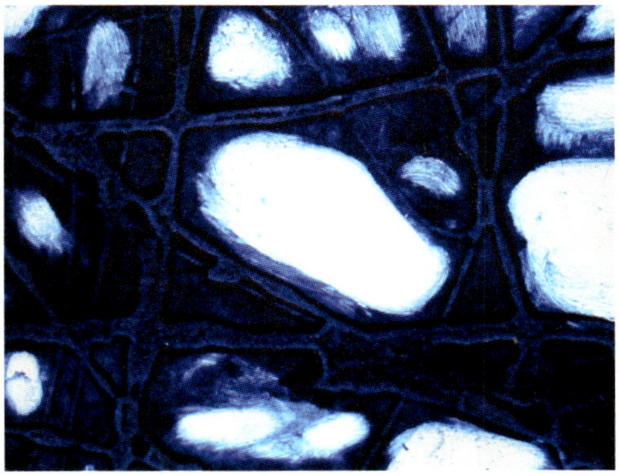

▲ The textures in this paper are very simple and repetitive. It is the loose way the blue ink has been scrimmed on the plate which creates the soft tones.

▼ Kate Boxer, *Backy*, 2009. Carborundum® and fluorescent marker pen, 70 x 63 cm (27½ x 24¾ in.).

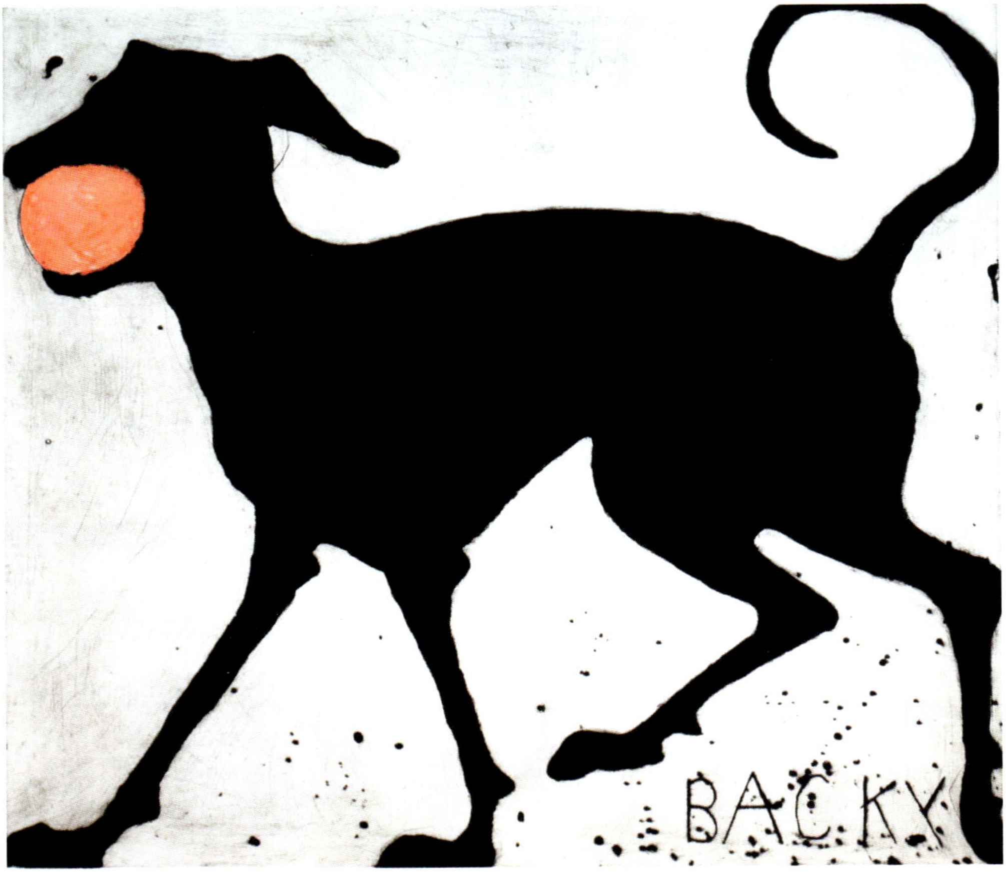

CHINE-COLLÉ – APPLIQUÉ TEXTURE IN AN IMAGE

Chine-collé is a wonderful way of adding textures and colours and of creating odd surface anomalies that cause a zingy dynamic with an unexpected use of material. Silver and gold leaf, textured handmade papers, Japanese tissues and fine fabrics can all be incorporated into a printed surface. They are placed on the inked plate before the dampened paper is overlaid and printed as normal.

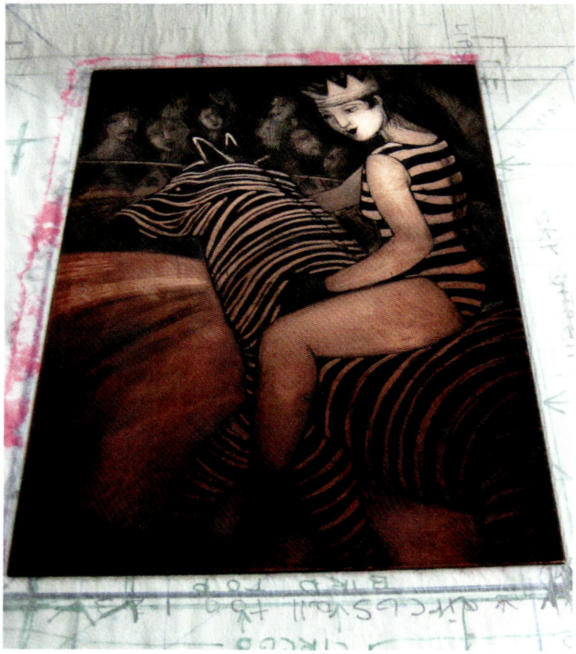

◀ In this picture the etching plate has been inked with black etching ink and wiped using soft scrim. The highlights on the plate are very visible. This way of wiping the plate was chosen by the artist, Sandra Millar, so the vibrant colour of the tissue would not be overwhelmed by excess plate tone.

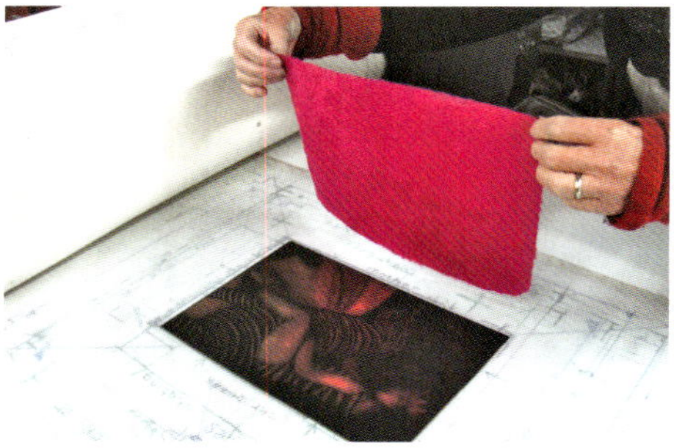

▲ The tissue paper, which has been lightly coated all over on one side with rice paper paste, is placed on top of the etching plate, glue side facing up.

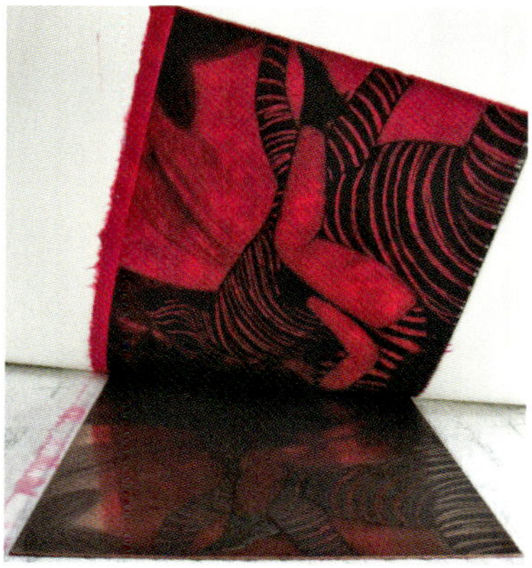

▲ The picture shows the striking colour that is now behind the image on the plate.

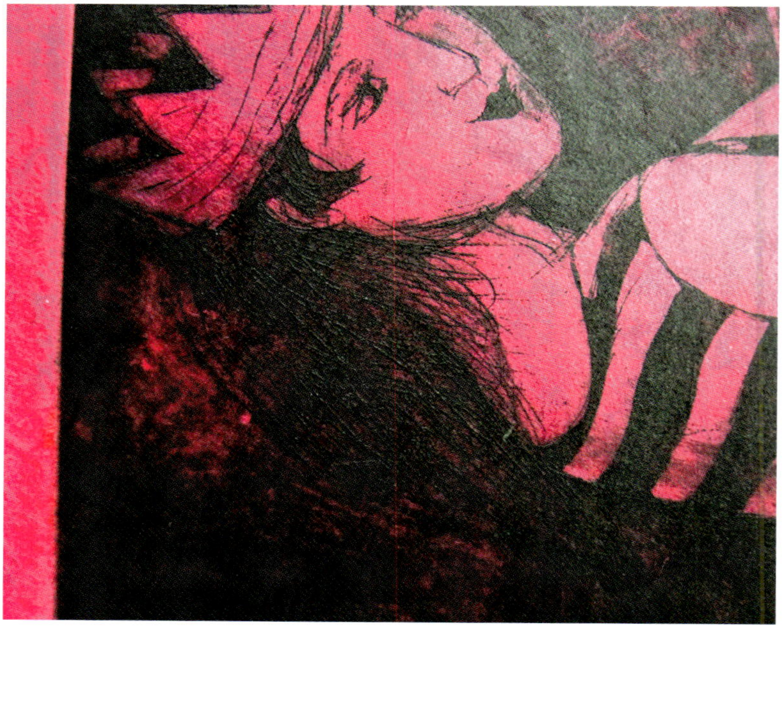

▶ A close-up of the inked lines that have been printed.

EMBOSSING

Embossing is a well-loved printmaking technique and many artists take advantage of its striking, subtle and clean look when using it to make prints. It is a very simple process.

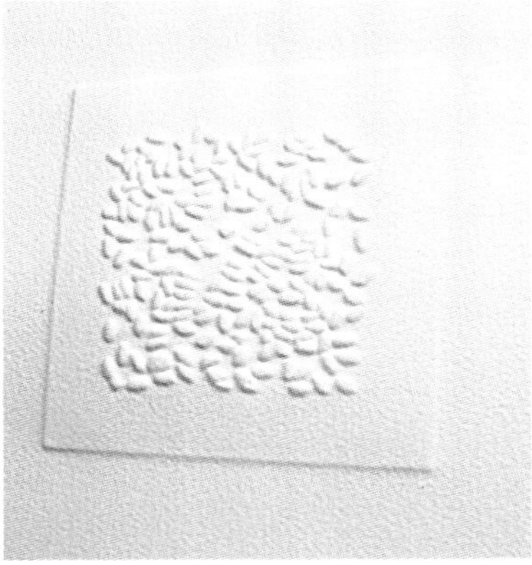

▲ **The deep impression of the plate's textures are seen here clearly.**

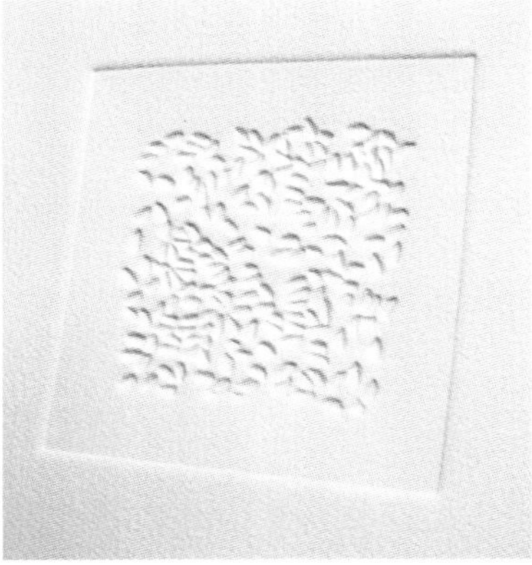

▲ **Each image shows that an embossed texture can look attractive when viewed from either side of the printing paper.**

You need to use good quality cotton paper. (It is best to dampen the paper with water.) Choose a paper that has some softness and has a fair amount of weight to it. 20–80gsm paper is incredibly lightweight and thin and may not hold the emboss that is pressed into it.

Paper choice is ultimately up to the artist and any paper should be experimented with, but there will be good reasons why some papers are more successful to use than others. For example, if the texture of the emboss material is too extreme or rough, it will tear or damage the paper when you try to remove it. (This is one reason why wood pulp paper is not a suitable choice. It is very difficult to place shapes into wood pulp paper successfully as it buckles, creases and tears as soon as it is placed in water for dampening.)

Using a printing press to emboss

Sprung-roller press

This press is ideal for embossing as it can be raised and lowered to fit a variety of block heights, plate thicknesses, found objects and random surfaces such as fabrics and textiles.

Fixed-roller press

This is suitable for embossing standard plates, woodcuts and collagraph plates. Even with the pressure taken off a fixed-roller press completely, the clearance between the bed of the press and the roller is not great. Plates that are too thick and objects that are too large cannot be put through them – there is too much risk of damaging the blankets and the roller.

Nipping press

Very suitable for embossing, although using it will require some physical exertion from the artist. Tightening the nipping press to exert pressure on the paper and the block being embossed from is hard work.

By hand

Again, hard work. Mostly unsuccessful, but hey, knock yourself out and have a go!

The collagraph is a rewarding medium. Sharp, detailed images can be obtained from it as can vibrant, eclectic, punchy, all-singing, all-dancing collagraphs.

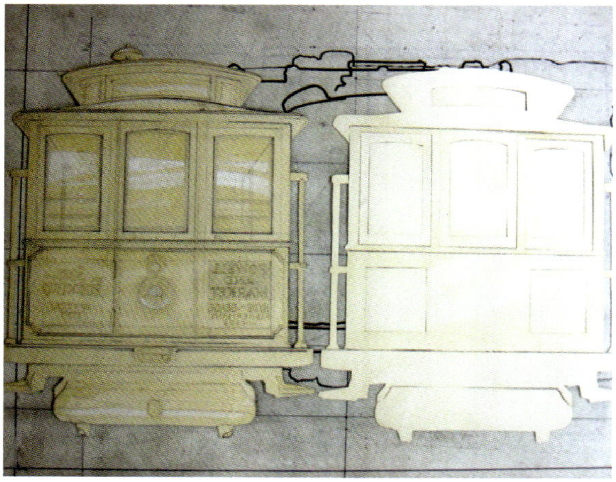

▲ This picture shows two collagraph plates made by the artist. The plate on the left is cut and layered with great attention to detail and lettering. The plate on the right is the image broken down into block shapes which represent each colour needed in the image.

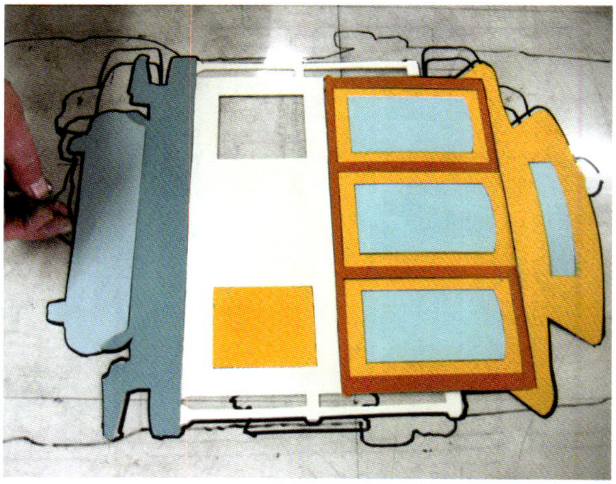

▲ The collagraph plate can be inked with several colours. The colours needed for this image have been cut into separate areas and inked individually with a specific colour. They are then correctly pieced together (like a jigsaw puzzle) and printed as a whole.

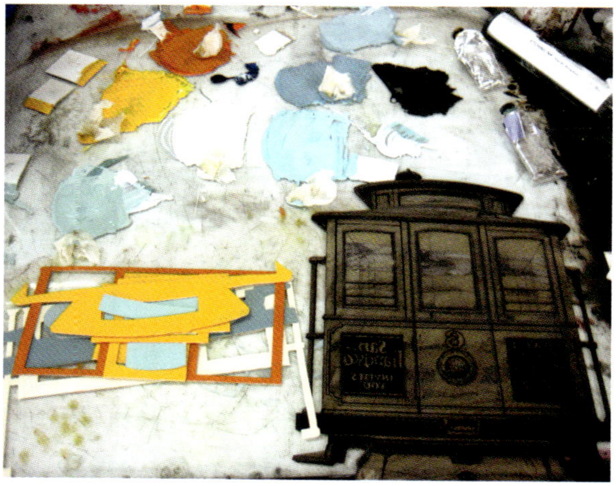

◀ This photo shows the plates with the colour inks and the black ink which has stained the card from the repetitive printings. Note that it is wise to leave a collagraph plate that is inked only in one colour to surface-dry as only the stripped-away colour remains on its surface. Cleaning the plate with a solvent is unnecessary. The texture of the collagraph is in no way diminished by doing this.

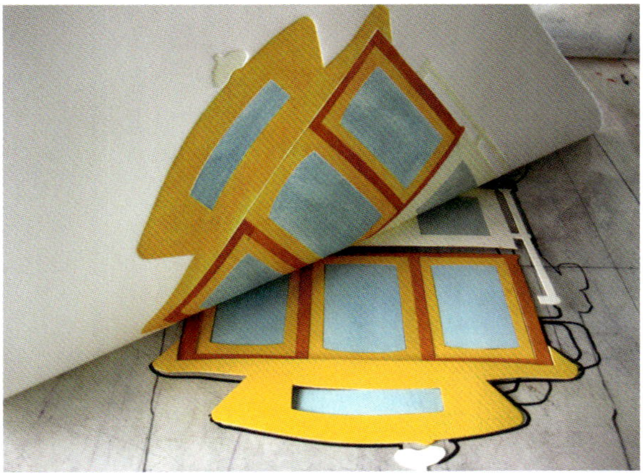

◀ This picture shows the jigsaw layout of the colour plates being printed. The lightweight card used by the artist Barry Goodman creates a pleasing emboss in the paper.

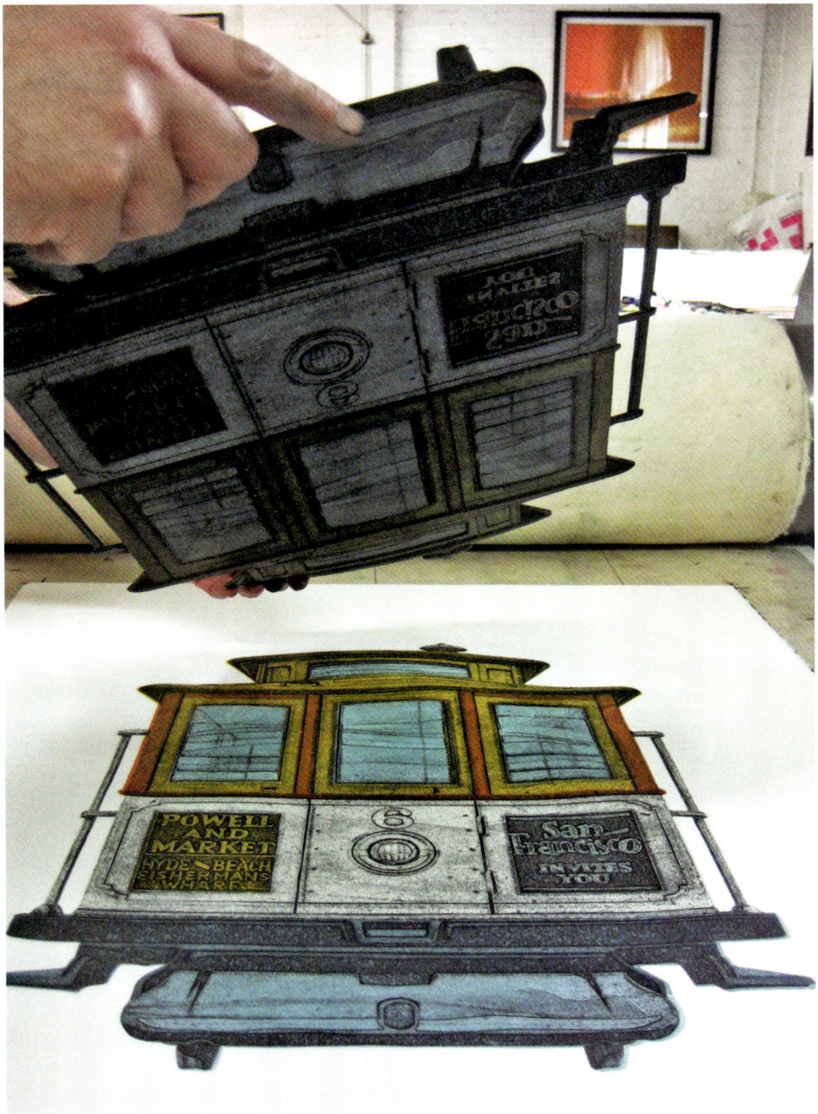

▶ The hotplate can be used to warm the ink on the collagraph plate. This ensures the ink is worked into all the textures areas on the plate. This is a black detail plate that has printed on top of the colour shapes printed in the previous picture.

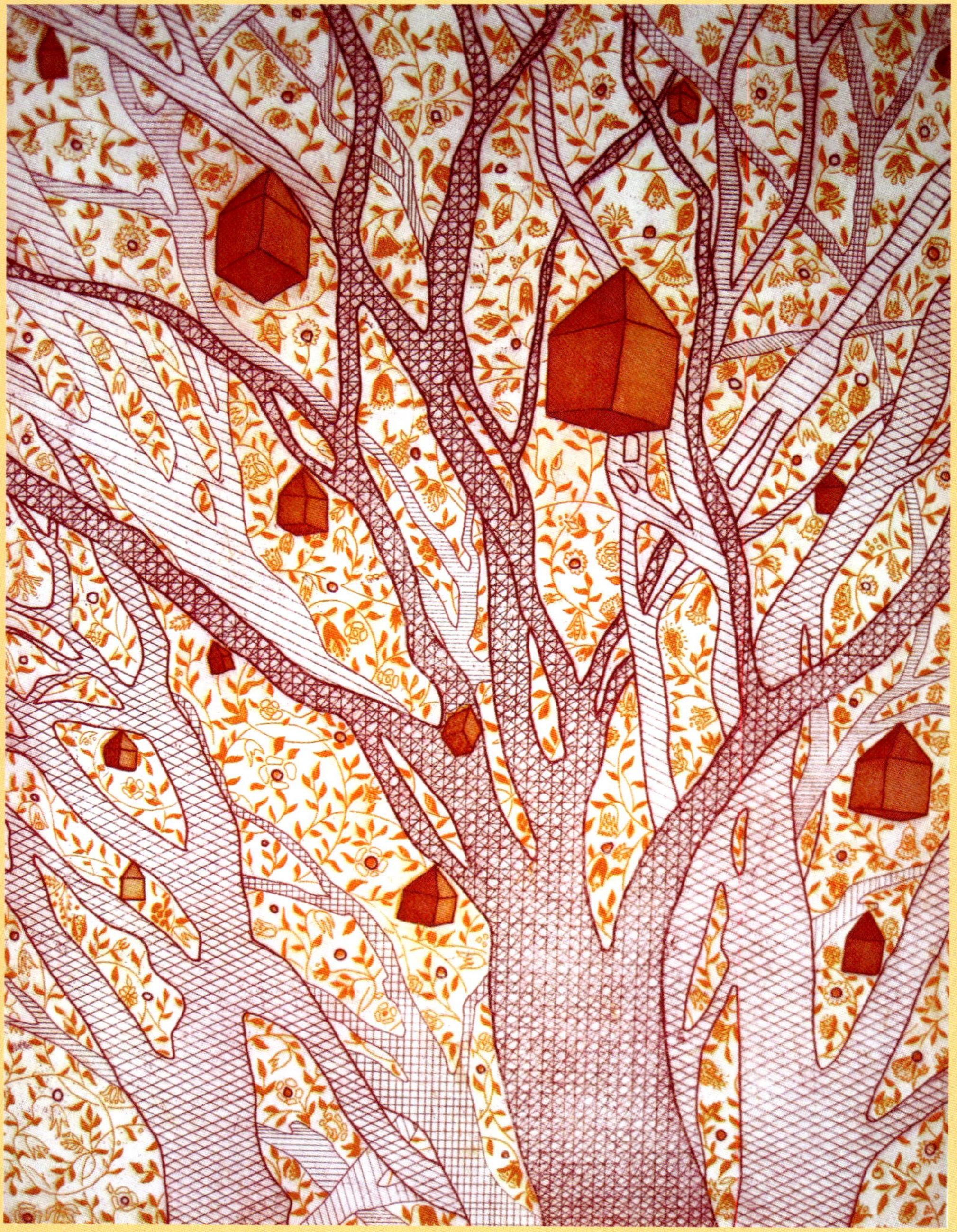

▲ Giulia Zaniol, *Candy Brothers*, 2010. Etching, Chine-collé, 36 x 49.5 cm (14¼ x 19½ in.).

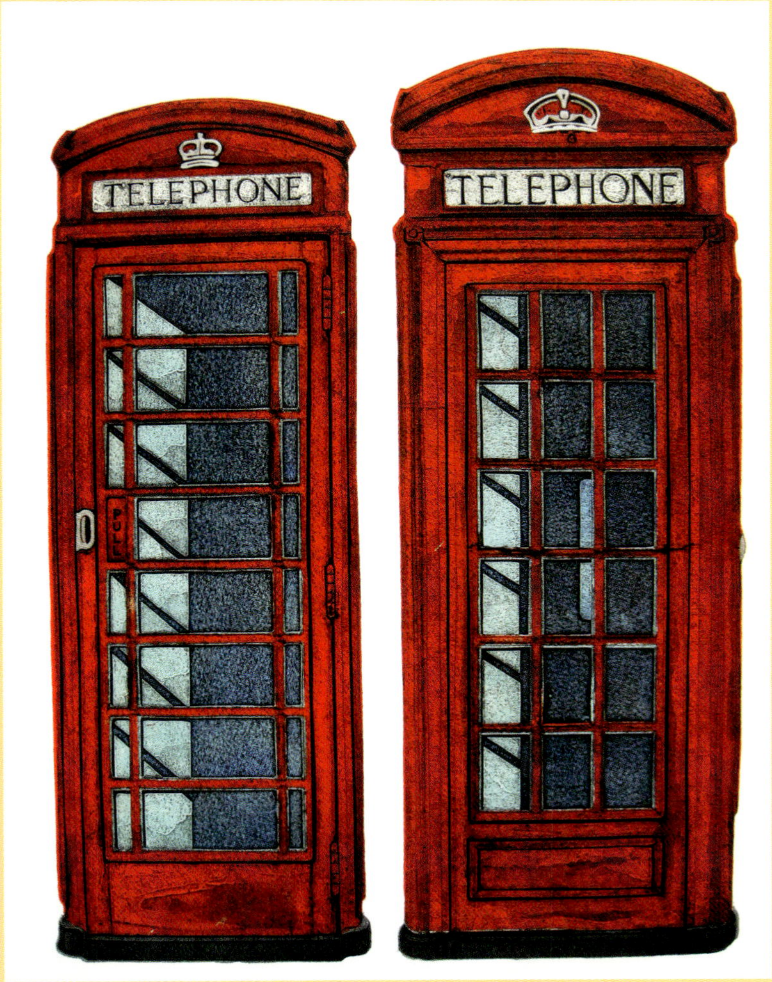

▲ Barry Goodman, *Callbox*, 2010. Collagraph, 55 x 47 cm (21½ x 18¼ in.).

▶ Barry Goodman, *VW*, 2010. Collagraph, 76 x 56 cm (30 x 22 in.).

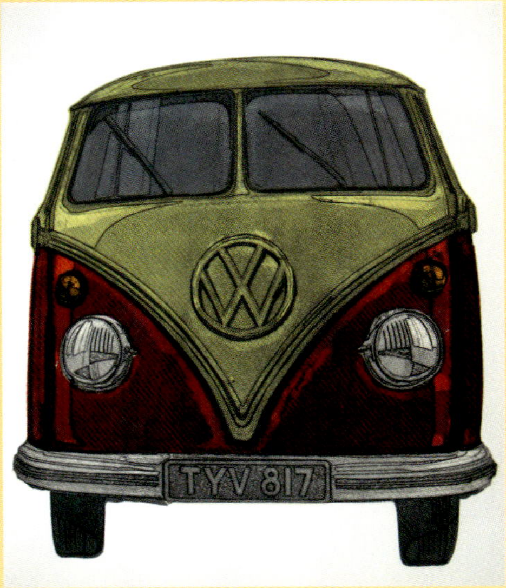

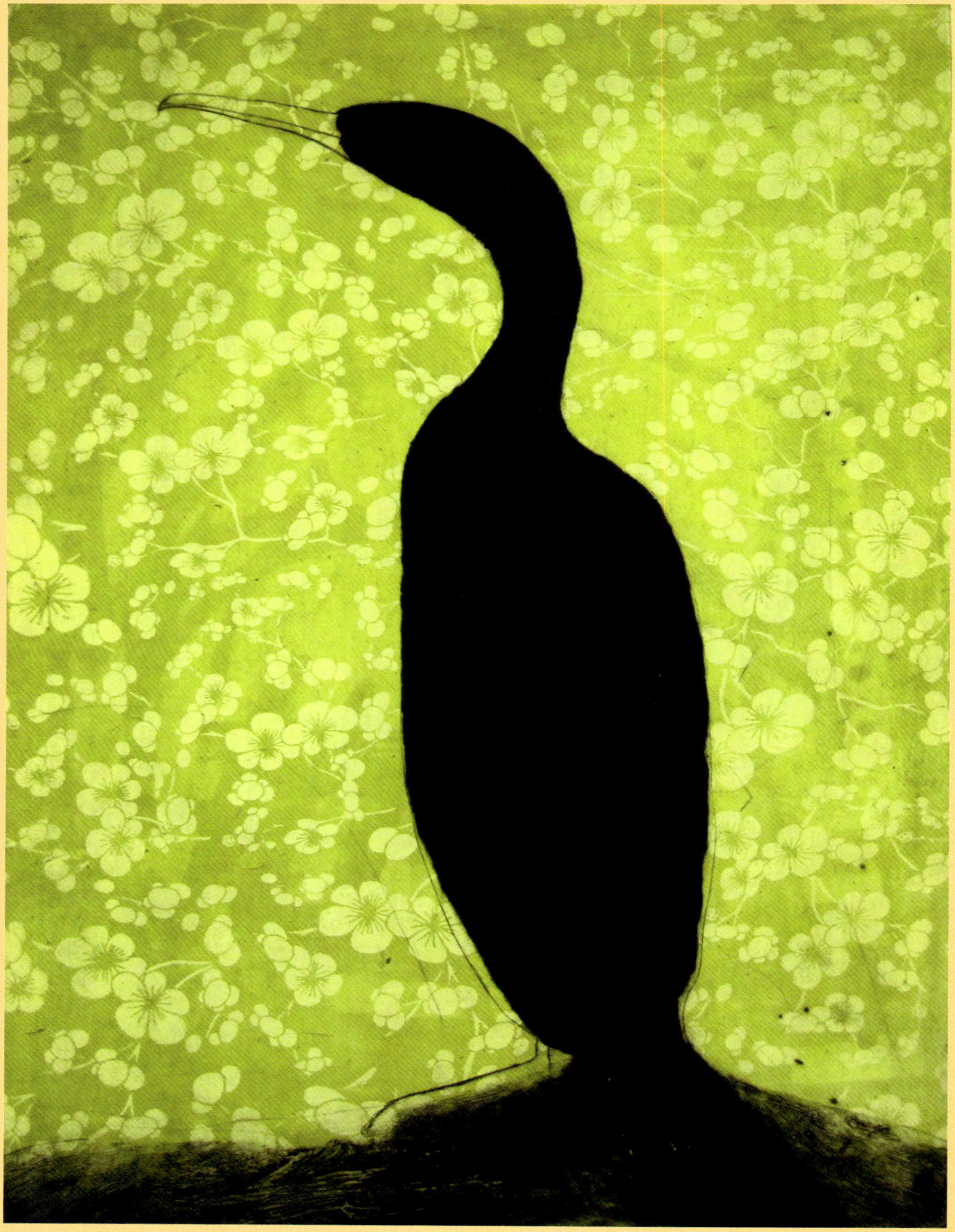

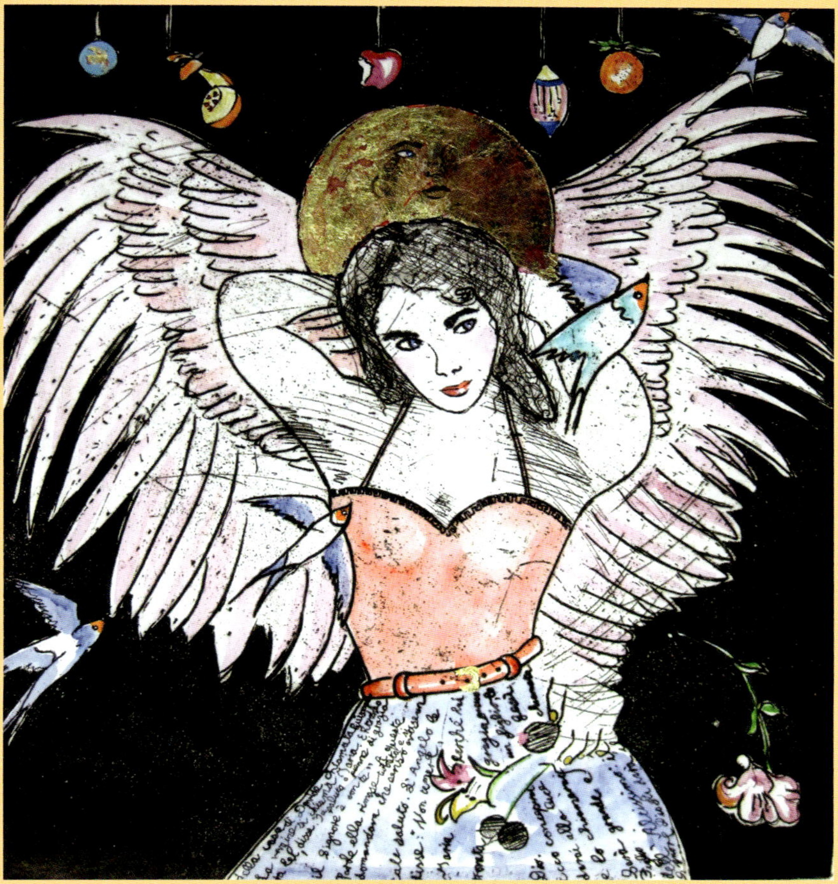

◀ Kate Boxer, *Cormorant*, 2009. Carborundum® and Chine-collé, 48 x 76 cm (19 x 30 in.).

▶ Linda Sutton, *Annunciation with Elizabeth Taylor*, 2011. Hand-coloured etching and Chine-collé, 44 x 49 cm (17¼ x 29¼ in.).

Detail below.

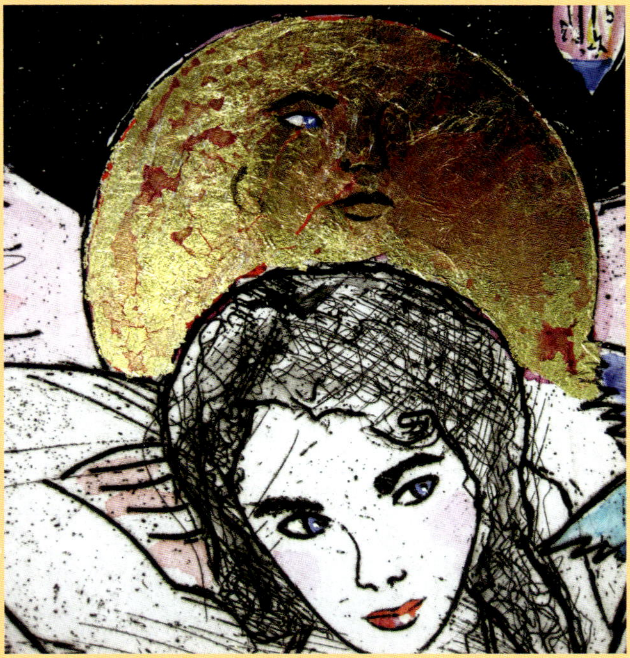

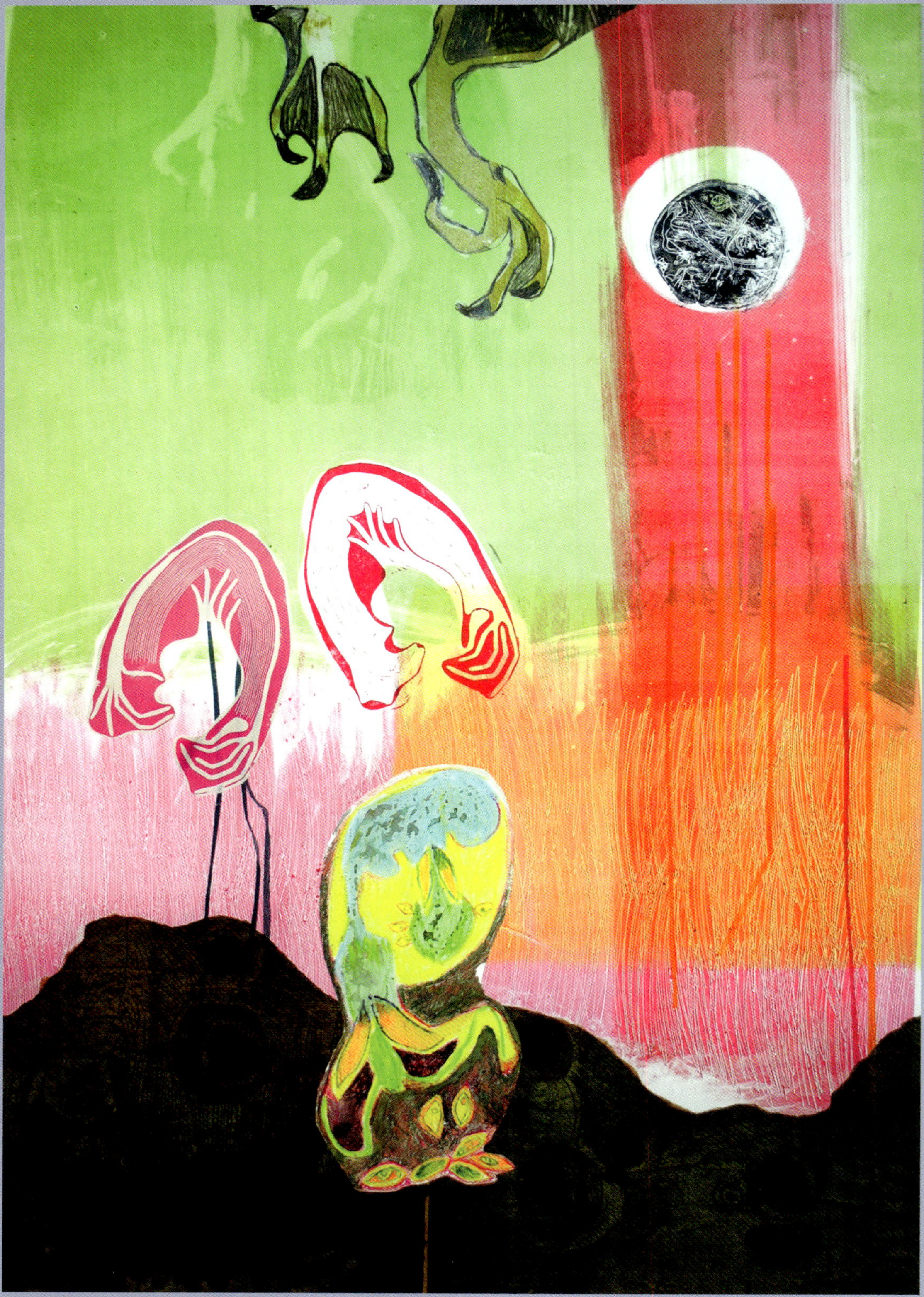

11

monoprinting

The monoprint is a versatile and enduring favourite with almost every printmaker. It is a spontaneous and immediate way to make an image in either colour or monochrome. The process is refreshingly simple: the printmaker freely paints, draws or wipes the inky design directly onto a substrate. As its name implies, the monoprint is a unique image. There is no other like it. It exists as a singular image that cannot be identically repeated.

◀ **Mary Dalton, *Untitled Pink and Green*, 2011. Monoprint, 76 x 114 cm (30 x 44¾ in.).**

Monotype and monoprint. Is there a difference? Historically, yes, but in today's usage of the two words, no. Both terms are used to describe the technique used in printmaking in which a single print is created by painting with inks onto any non-absorbent surface.

Monoprints offer a quick and immediate way for an artist to create an image, but it is also true that complicated monoprint images can take days to complete. It may take many hours or days to add all of the artist's desired colours and layers to the image.

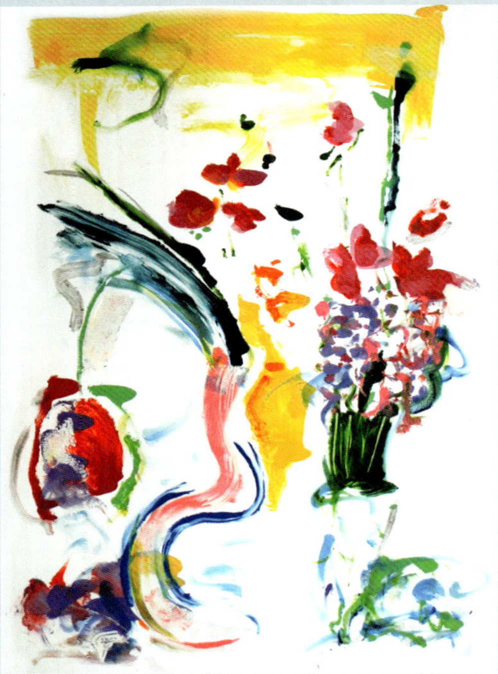

A monoprint is a singular image.

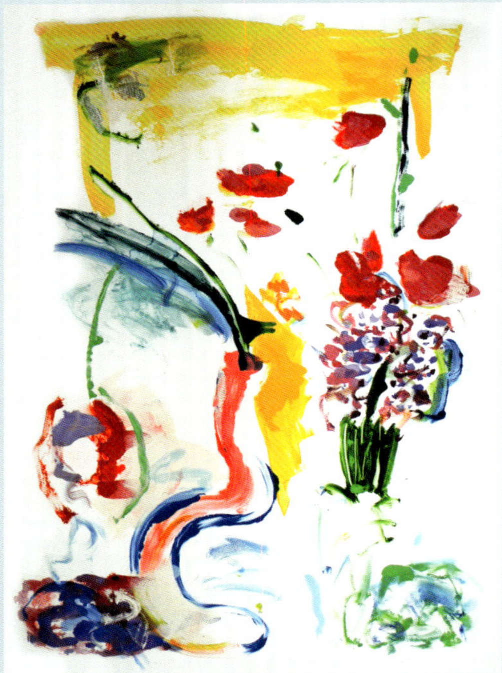

You may try as hard as you like but it is not possible to make a second identical image.

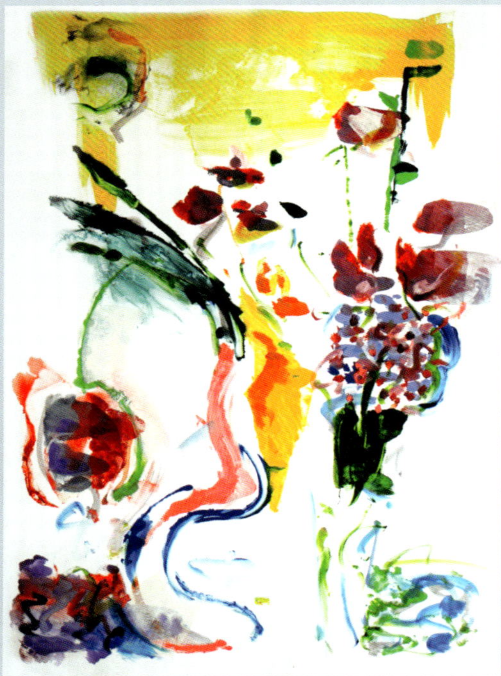

Or a third one....

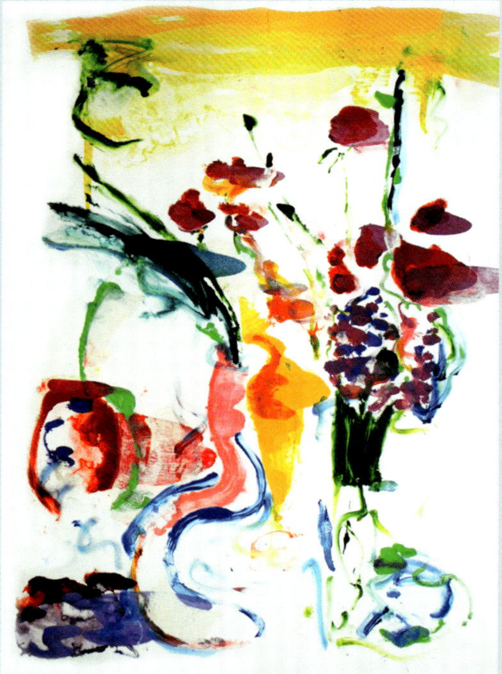

Or a fourth one... they will all be different! They may all seem to look the same but they are all unique hand-made images. Monoprint sequence courtesy of Helen Clark, 2010.

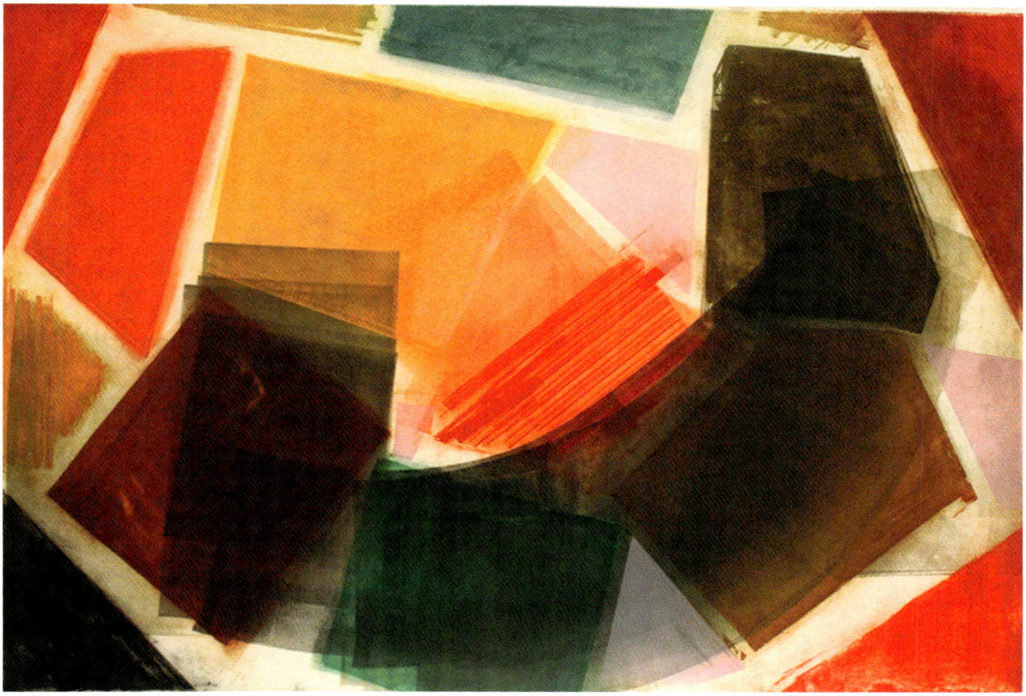

▲ Colin Gale, *Untitled Colours*, 2009. Monoprint, 117 x 76 cm (46 x 30 in.).

INK

Ink (and ingenuity) are the printmaker's most important tools when it comes to making a monoprint. How you place the ink on the surface on which you are making your monoprint is what gives the image its depth, texture and composition.

Ink is not at all like paint. Oil paint and acrylic paint are heavy and thick in comparison. Artists love to paint *impasto* (i.e., very thickly)! Piling paint on the canvas or board is fun and because of its heavy body weight and thick texture, it can be stacked on. Ink does not do *impasto*. No matter how thin and flat you think you are painting your oils or your acrylics onto the surface of a canvas, a layer of ink goes on even thinner than that. Why? Ink is designed to coat a surface that is then rolled under a roller of great weight on a printing press.

The ink palette

As ink is the medium most artists choose for making a monoprint, having a palette of colour to use is important. Ideally, you have the colours you want to use laid out and ready to go. Whether you use water-based ink, water-soluble ink or water-washable oil-based or oil-based inks – ink is your key tool. (See Chapter 8 for more information.)

Ready-mixed colours can be used, or you can choose to mix your own. Depending on the idea you have in mind, it can take as long to mix all of the colours you want to use as it does to make the monoprint!

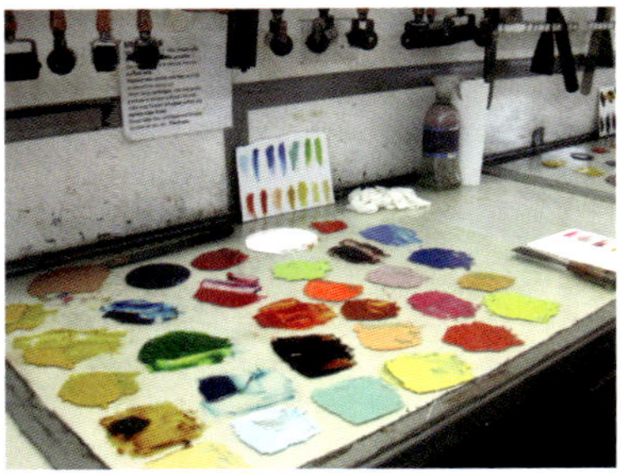

▲ Everyone's ink palette of colour will be different, whether you mix your own colours or use ready-mixed.

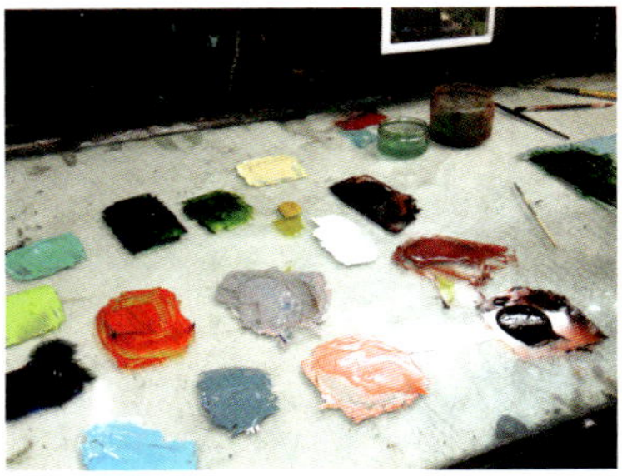

▲ New colours are constantly being made as they are blended and mixed on the plate all the time.

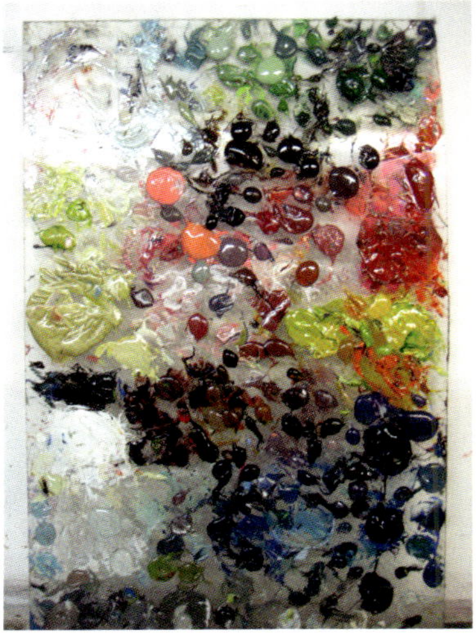

▲ Ink palettes are personal to each artist. This acrylic sheet makes an excellent support for these oil-based ink colours. The palette looks like a box of Smarties!

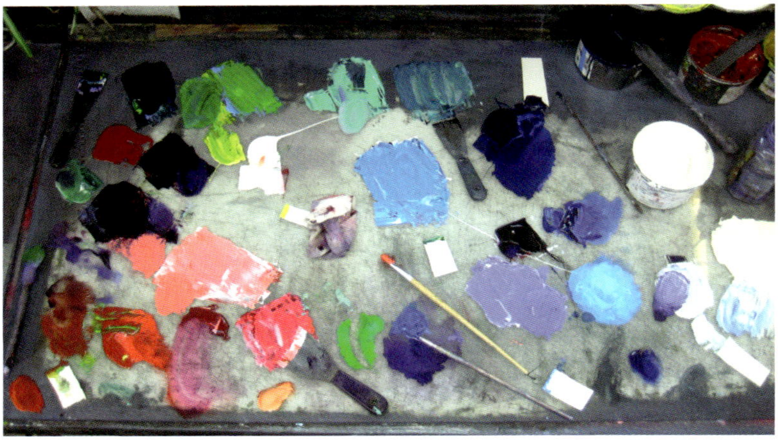

The monoprint must be printed *before* the ink dries. In the case of water-based ink, water-soluble ink or water-washable oil-based, this means very quickly. Oil-based inks allow the artist a much longer time to work with the image as their drying time is considerably slower.

Monoprint ink wash

Loose, painterly marks are often desired in monoprints. This is achieved by adding white spirit to oil-based inks and the appropriate manufacturer's mediums (e.g. Caligo/Akua) to water-based inks. The reticulated wash is one of the most popular wash looks amongst artists.

'Reticulated washes' is the collective name used to describe the application of any water-soluble solution to make a loose-textured mark in an image. A reticulated wash has a certain 'look' that is very attractive. The marks made have a fine, delicate net-like pattern, and they flow well because they are liquid.

You can use any of the following as wash materials for a reticulated wash: Indian ink, gouache, tempera paint (also known as egg tempera), powdered tempera paint, and poster paints. Lithographic tusche (a greasy liquid used to make ink) can also be used. You will need a 'carrier'

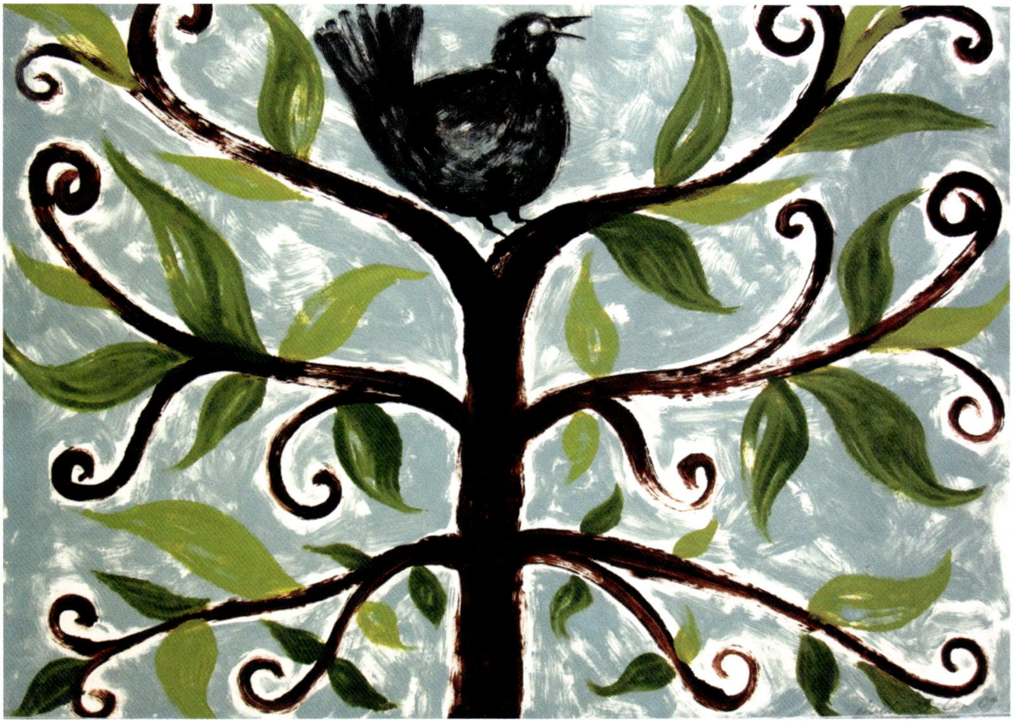

▲ Michaela Owen, *Blackbird*, 2009. Monoprint, 76 x 56 cm (30 x 22in.).

for your wash material. A carrier is a substance that the wash material will float in or semi-dissolve in.

Distilled water or de-ionised (DI) water (chemically pure water or nonionic surfactant) is an excellent carrier for your chosen wash materials. Available from DIY stores (it is used for car batteries), it can also be found in the laundry/detergent aisle at any supermarket. (It is used in irons to create the steam element.)

To make the wash material (e.g. Indian ink) bond better with the carrier (e.g. distilled water) you need to break the surface tension, which can be done by adding a very tiny drop of washing up liquid or glycerine (a sugar alcohol available in liquid form from any food store, usually in the baking section). Adding either one of these to the mixture will increase its ability to adhere to the printing surface. You need very little: one drop to 300 ml of tap water will be suitable.

Ink and solvents

Solvents such as white spirit, turpentine and (odourless) mineral spirits can be used to dilute oil-based inks to a thin loose consistency so it can be painted with quite freely. Note that a touch of pure linseed oil can be used to dilute oil-based inks. We have found it is a good alternative to using white spirit and is favoured by artists because it lessens the need to use other solvents which some people are reluctant to use.

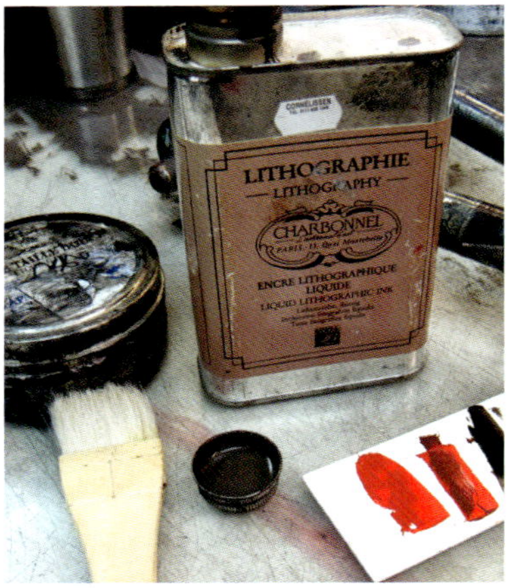

▲ Lithographic tusche is an effective mark-making liquid. It can be diluted with solvents and with distilled water to create reticulated washes.

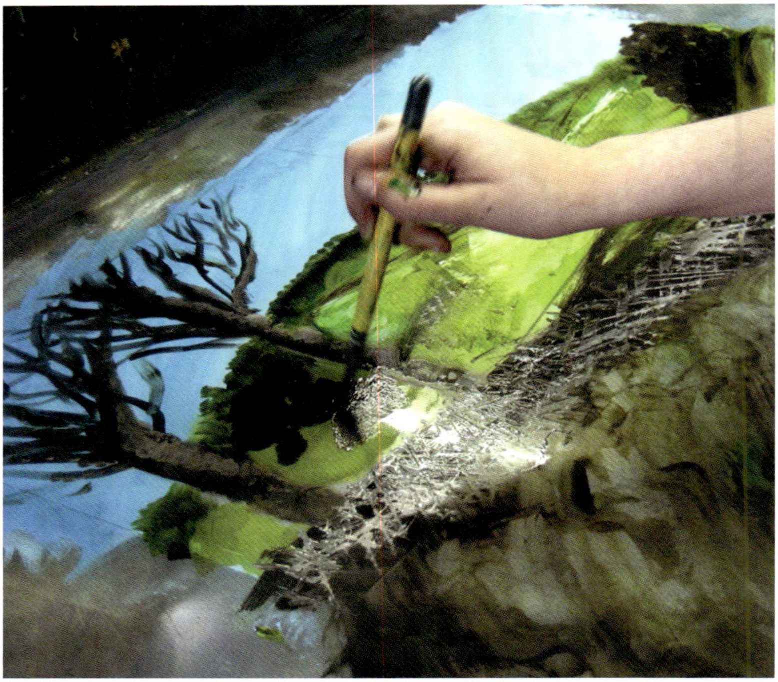

▲ The artist Sarah Redman is using an oil-based ink diluted with white spirit to make this monoprint. You need *very little* solvent to loosen the ink to a consistency suitable for painting.

BRUSHES, ROLLERS, DRAWING IMPLEMENTS AND PALETTE KNIVES

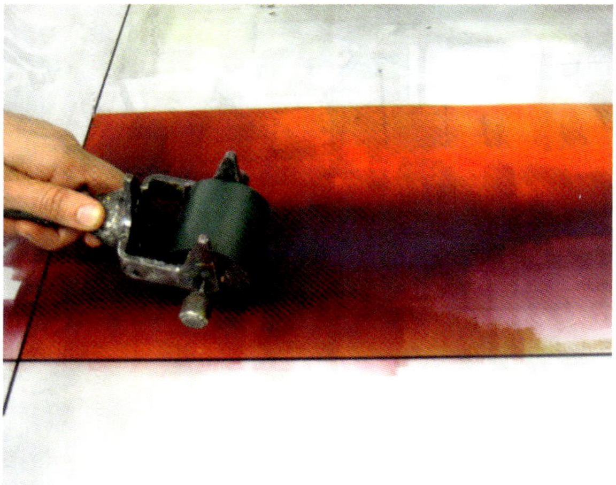

▲ Rollers are an essential tool for achieving flat areas of colour.

▶ Assortment of brushes, palette knives. Bristle and soft nylon, all sizes and shapes.

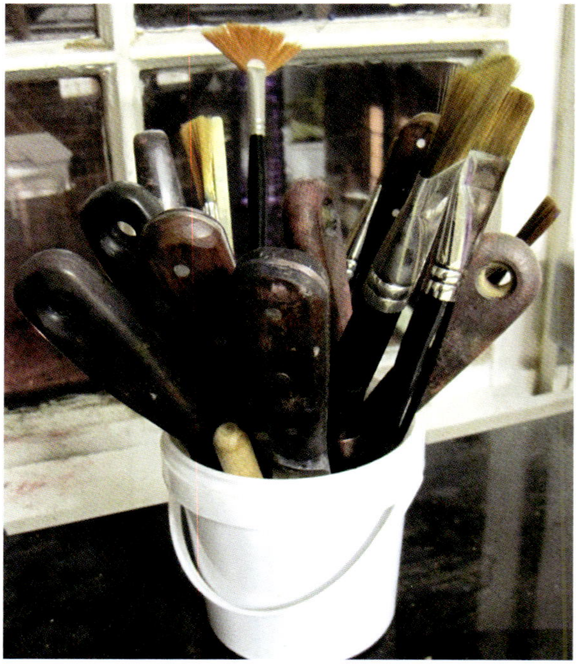

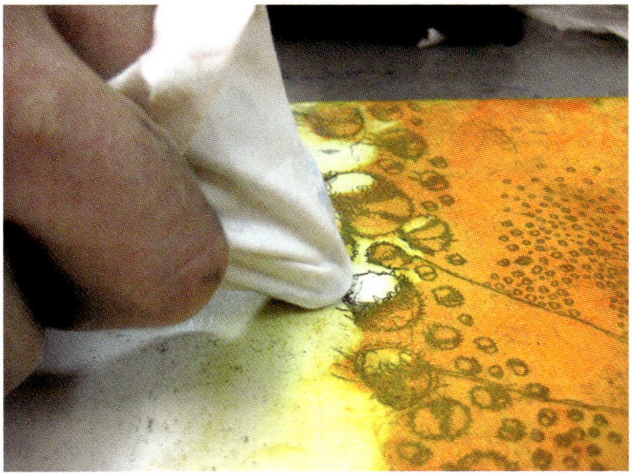

▲ Cotton rags/cloths and paper towels remove ink as well as add ink.

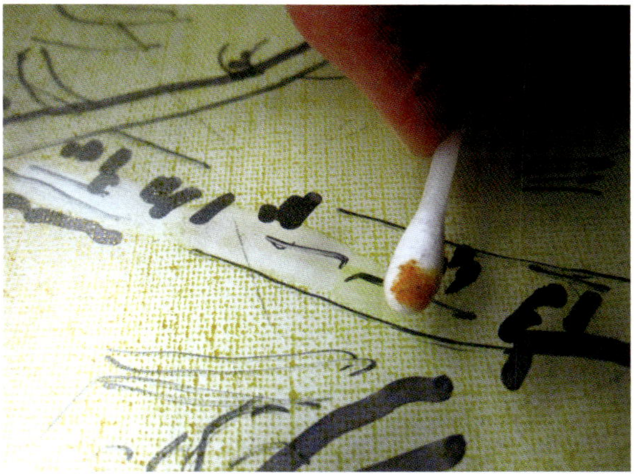

▲ The cotton bud is very effective in adding small ink marks or removing ink.

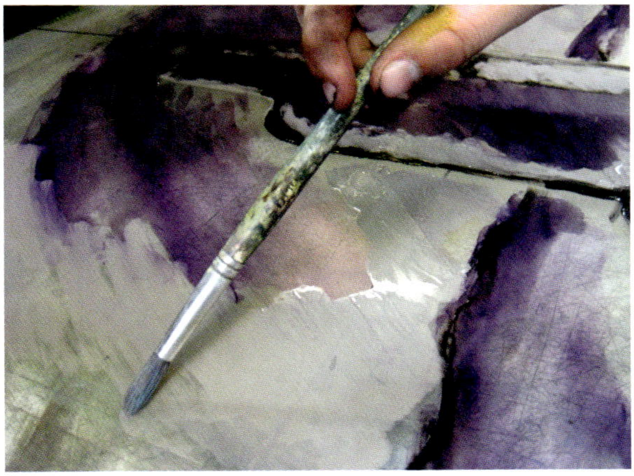

◀ Using a brush is a very direct and free way of working.

WATER-SOLUBLE CRAYONS/PENCILS

Water-soluble crayons and pencils used with damp printing paper create controlled and graphic-styled images. The dampness of the printing paper gives this particular way of making a monoprint a quality totally different from ordinary wax crayon marks on dry paper. Shading and blending, tonal marks, cross-hatching and line work are all softened by the effect the damp paper has on the pigment of the water-soluble crayons and gives images made this way a striking charcoal-like quality. If they are dissolved in water, they take on a 'watercolour' quality.

Always use a good quality water-soluble pencil or crayon. Quality is paramount to a successful image. Inexpensive crayons have a high wax content and low pigment content, which means they will print poorly: it is more difficult for the damp paper to work successfully with them and thus they will not always give a satisfactory colour-rich image.

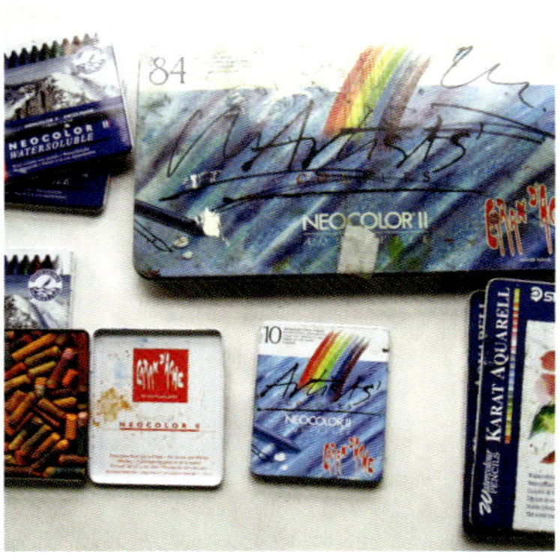

▲ An assortment of water-soluble tins. Caran d'Ache® and Stabilio® crayons are very good.

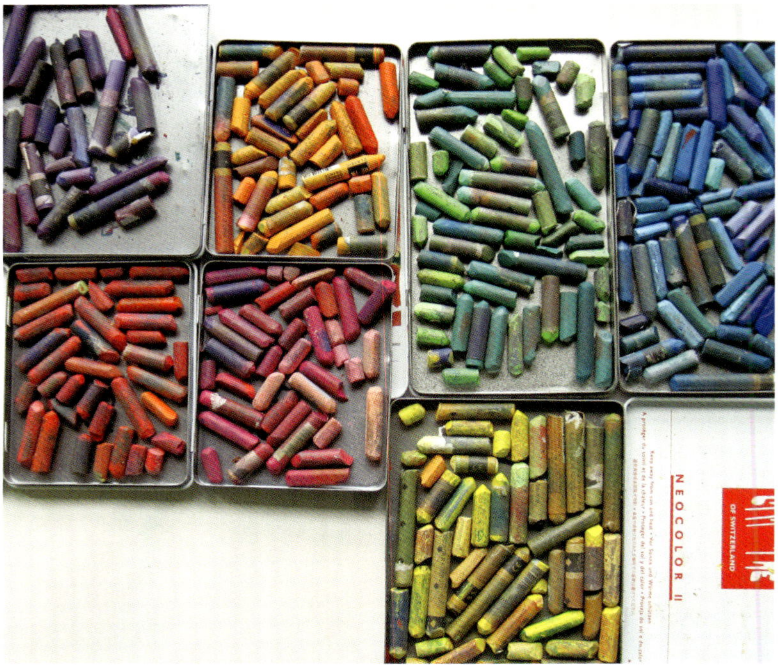

▶ Breaking the crayons into all sizes and shapes makes drawing with them easier. You are not restricted to drawing a singular line because the crayon has a point!

To create successful water-based images:

1 Avoid pressing down too heavily with the crayon when making the marks: if too thick a crayon mark is made, the dampness of the paper will not be sufficient to successfully moisten the crayon mark to allow it to be printed onto the paper.

2 The best paper to use is Whatman and BFK Rives. They have a soft smooth surface and excess water can easily be blotted away.

3 If burnishing a water-based image by hand, using a lighter weight paper (90–190gsm) will make the transfer of the image more successful.

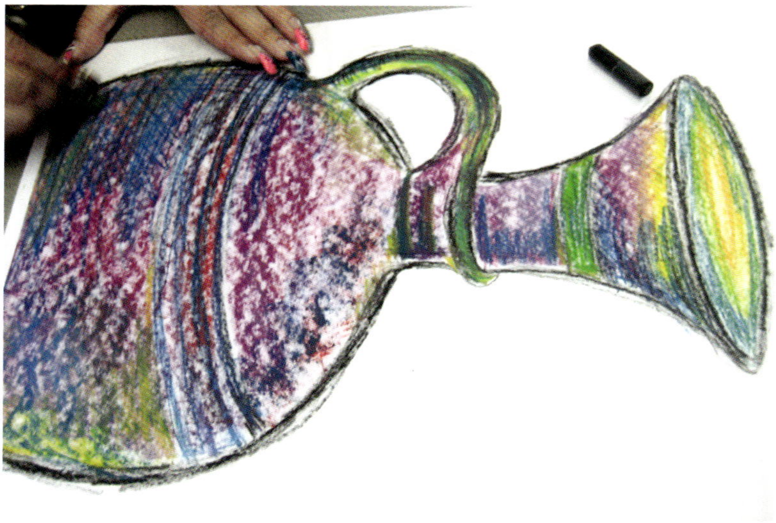

◀ Crayon marks are very distinctive. The dampness of the paper saturates the water-soluble marks on the printing substrate as it is run under the roller of the press. The pressure offsets the marks onto the printing paper. The dampness of the paper will be different every time, so the printed marks will be different each time you print a water-soluble drawing.

SUITABLE SURFACES FOR MONOPRINTING

In theory, a monoprint can be made on any unmarked substrate surface. Steel, copper, zinc, aluminium, any type of card or acetate (True Grain or Mylar®) should work, as would even another sheet of paper (printing an image from an already printed image is known as 'counter printing').

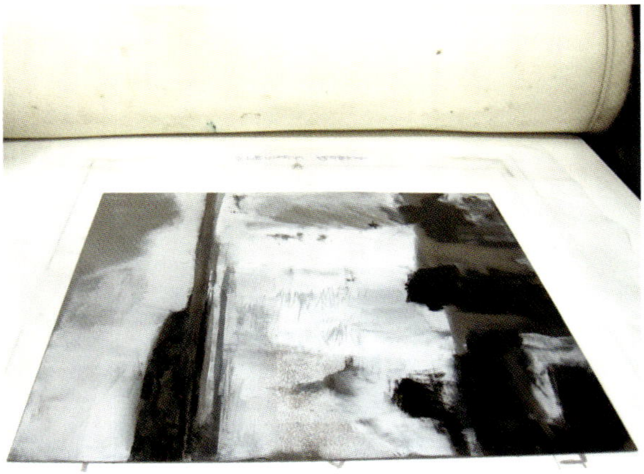

▲ Steel is an excellent substrate for use in monoprinting. It has a natural grain to its surface and so holds ink well. You can roll up the entire surface first and then work back into it with rags, brushes and more roller marks.

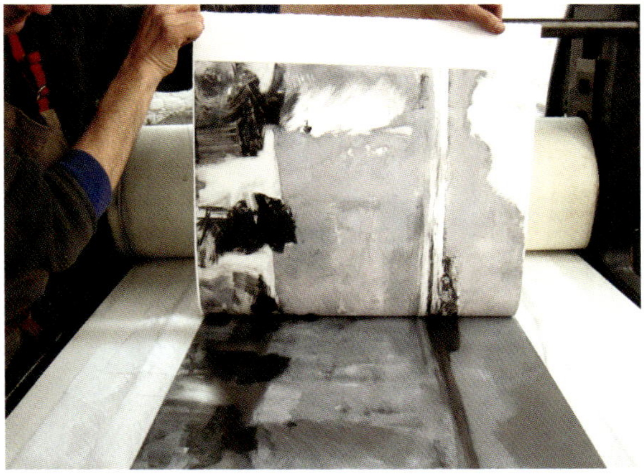

▲ An etching press is entirely suitable for monoprints. Depending on how much ink has been put on the substrate surface, the pressure of the press may have to be adjusted so that the image is not crushed (this would result in the ink being smeared across the plate in the direction of the press bed).

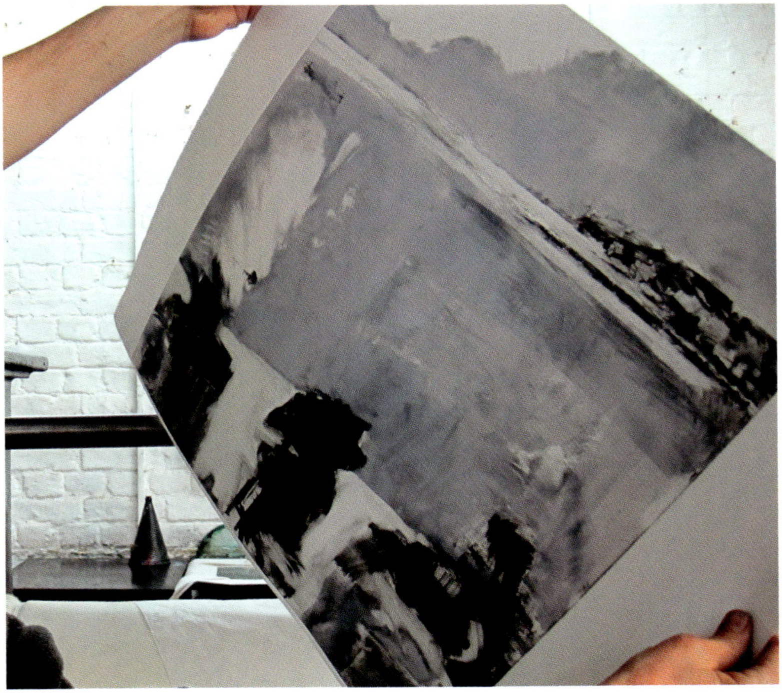

▶ A monochrome monoprint is very striking. Monochrome means to work in black and white and the tones the two create together. You can also use a monochromatic colour monoprint: this is an image that has been made using only one colour (such as blue) in addition to black and white.

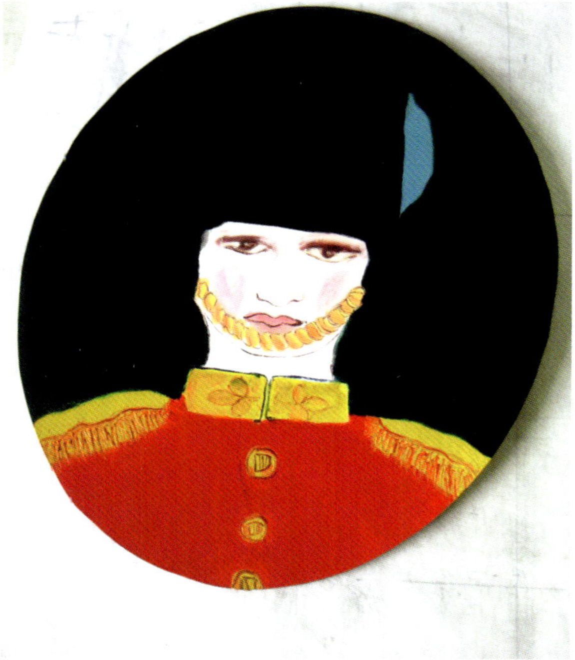

◀ Cardboard that has been sealed with gesso, shellac or varnish makes a very successful print base. Helpfully, it can be cut into irregular shapes. This plate is made by the artist Maria Carleton. It is inked with oil-based lithographic relief inks (the artist's choice).

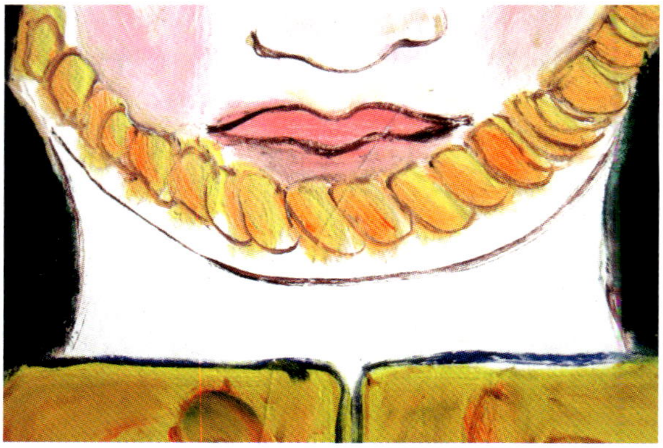

▲ A detail of the painterly marks. The gestural marks are the same as you would use when painting.

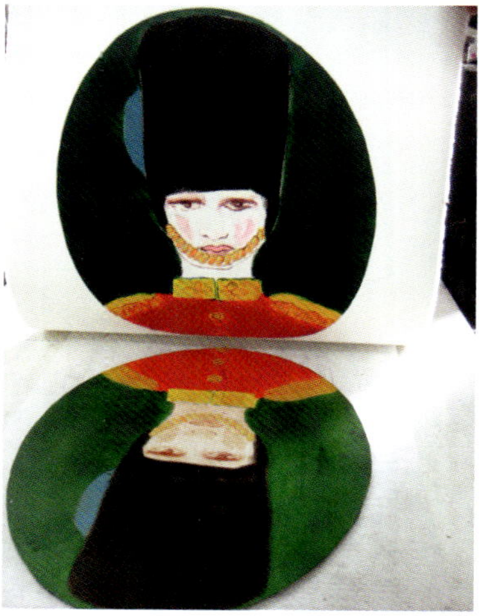

▲ The monoprint is being printed on a Rochat 81¼ x 137¼ cm (32 x 54 in.) etching press.

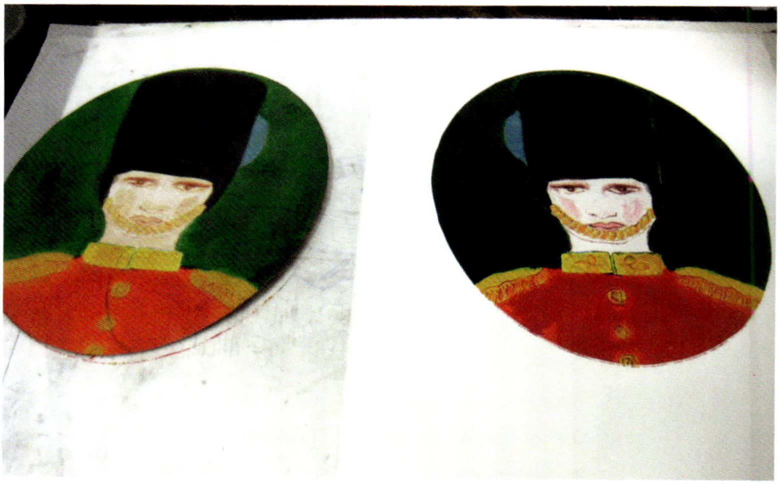

▲ The final monoprint and the image ghost on the cardboard base. It is a good picture in which to explain what a 'direct printing' is. The printed image is a mirror image of the painted image on the base.

MONOPRINTING WITH THE OFFSET PRESS

The advantage of using the offset press is that the artist can make the image without having to consider creating the image back to front (reversing it).

The offset press itself is designed to reverse the image for you.

MONOPRINTING WITH DIRECT LITHOGRAPHIC PRESS

Working on the direct lithographic press means the artist must work on the image in reverse, remembering that when it is printed onto the paper from the plate, it will be the correct way around.

It is often helpful for the artist to draw or sketch the image first as a guide. If the printing substrate is transparent, this is extremely helpful. Draw the image on the transparent acetate using a permanent marker. (The marker pen can be easily removed using methylated spirits or Mr Muscle®.) Remember to turn the acetate over before you begin working on it or otherwise you will not have actually reversed the image.

▶ LEFT TO RIGHT: The direct litho press is very easy to use and because of the size of the printing bed, offers the artist the advantage of scale: the Mann Direct we use at Artichoke is 114.3 x 91.5 cm (45 x 36 in.) and comfortably prints Double Imperial size paper (81.5 x 112.5 cm/32 x 44¼ in.). The loose black ink line is being made on a thin acrylic or plastic sheet. It is very shiny and smooth. (The back of True Grain can be used as only its front side has a textured grain.)

A monoprint in progress is placed on top of the painted marks on the acetate.

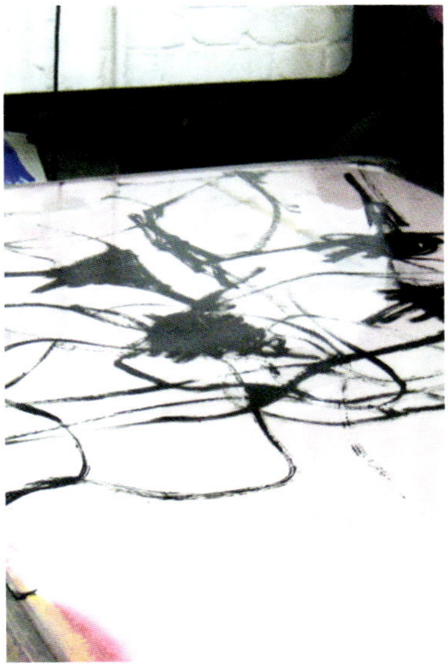

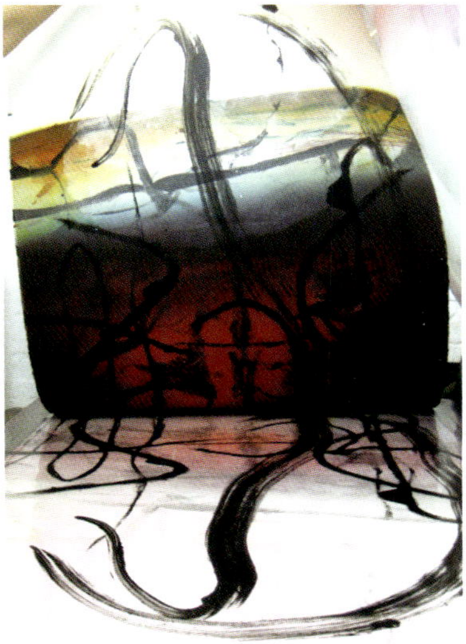

▶ LEFT TO RIGHT: The artist Sophie Layton is making a series of monoprints using the same colours and textures in each. A detail of texture has been used in the image. Note that it is not possible to put thick, textured objects through a direct litho press. It will damage the tympan and scraper bar, which are designed to print a thin, flat litho plate (litho plates and Mylar® have no pronounced edge) and the necessary sheets of printing paper and packing.

The artist continues with the monoprint series. A layer of inked colour made using a roller is printed onto the image.

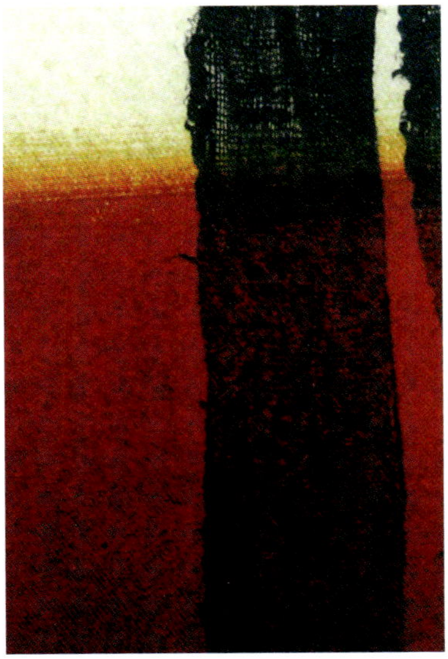

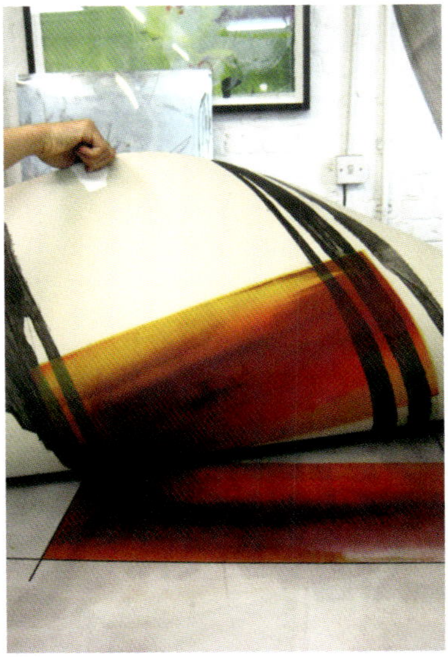

PRINTING MONOPRINTS WITH A NIPPING PRESS

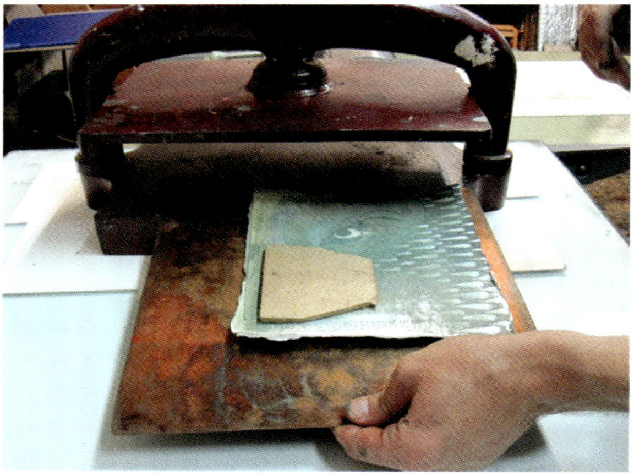

▲ A nipping press is suitable for small-scale work. The pressure is applied by screwing down the top plate to exert pressure on the paper on top of the printing base. In this picture, the artist is choosing to add colour to just a small area of the image.

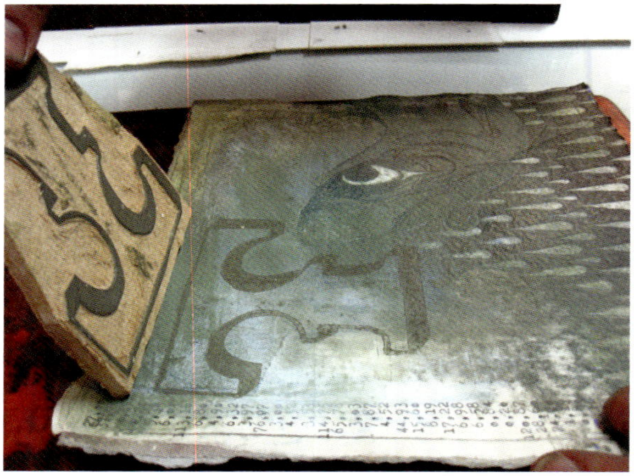

▲ The new shape is visible on the image's surface.

▼ The artist Staffan Gnosspelius has created a variety of individual images using monoprint layers of colour and texture from handmade blocks and True Grain templates.

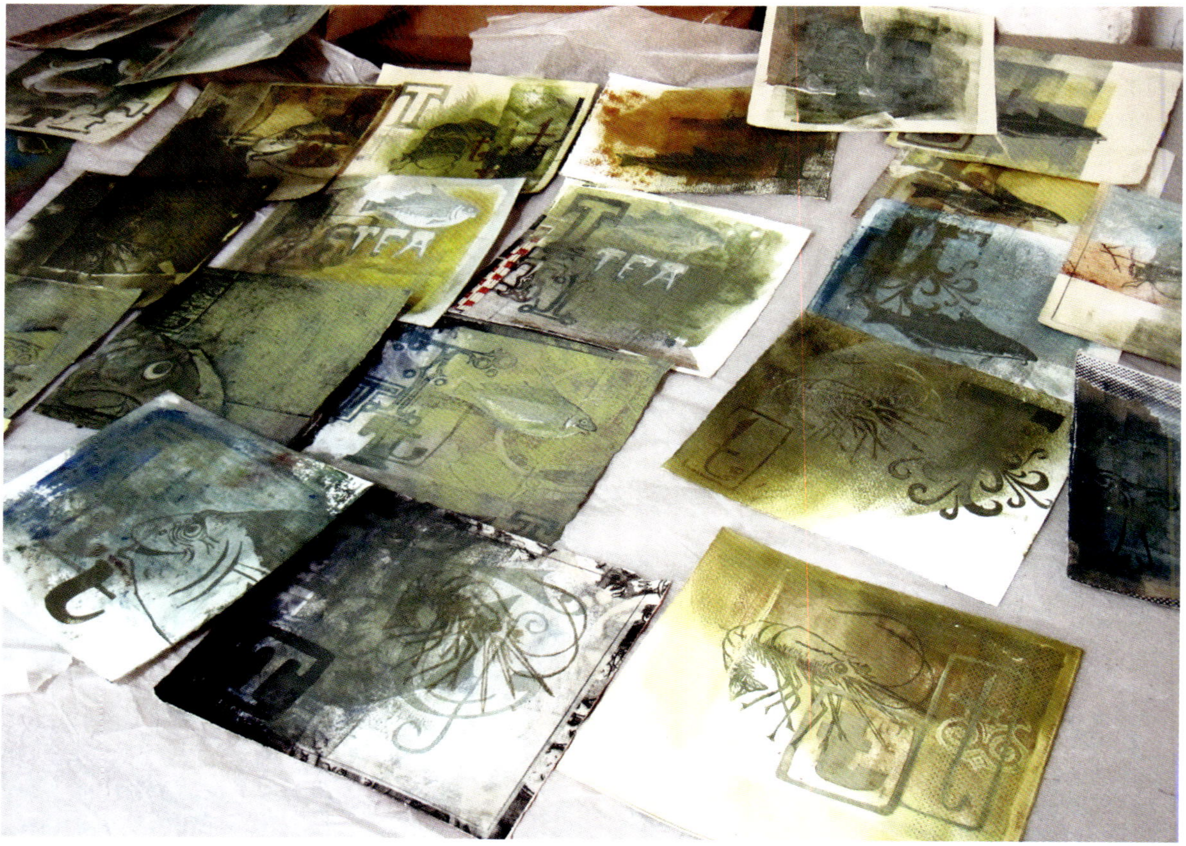

WORKING ON TRUE GRAIN

It is helpful to draw an image on clear Mylar® (True Grain) with a permanent marker pen. This enables you to follow a template for applying the colours to your design. True Grain is an acetate with grain on just one side, which holds the ink tightly to the surface of the acetate, enabling you to layer more colours before printing.

The grained texture on the true grain creates a 'key' for the ink to be securely held, similar to how the aquatint grain gives a key for ink to be held on the smooth, polished surfaces of copper and zinc plates.

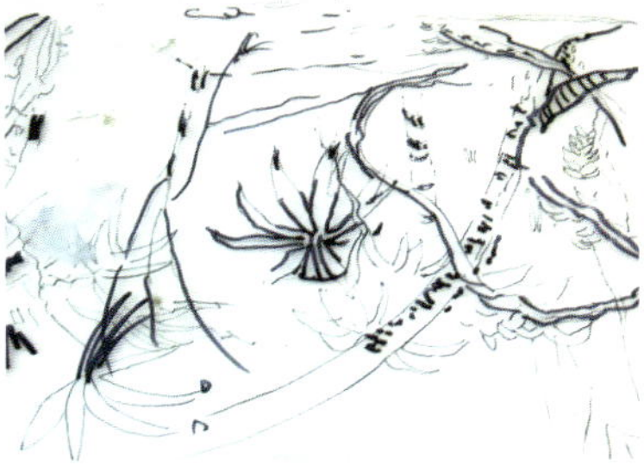

▲ The permanent marker pen drawing is seen clearly and creates a helpful template to guide the artist when applying ink.

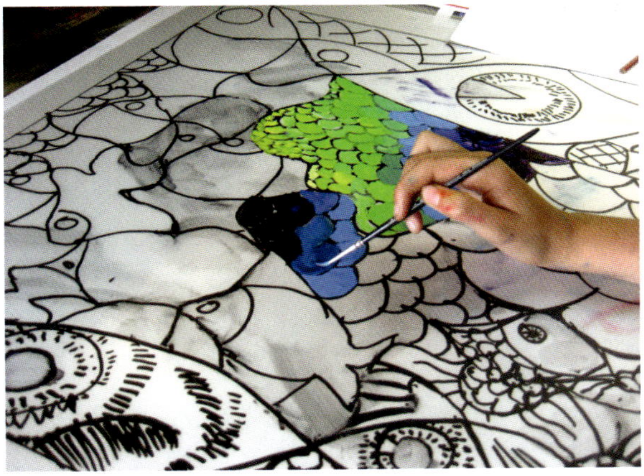

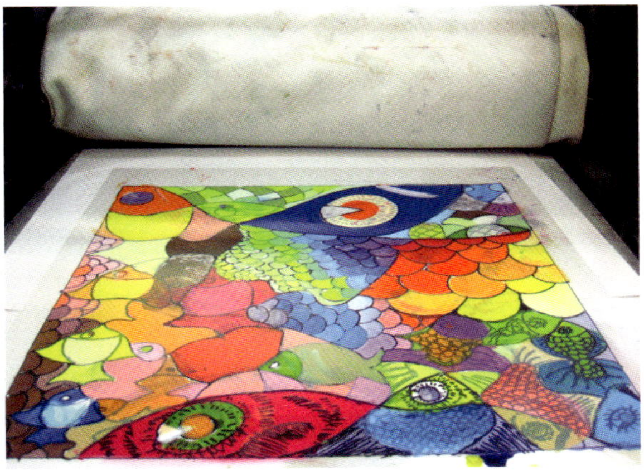

▲ LEFT TO RIGHT: The artist is creating a complicated colour design. The ink used is diluted with a very little solvent (white spirit). This loosens up the ink enough to make fluid, painterly marks.

Adding opaque white to colours reduces their transparency.

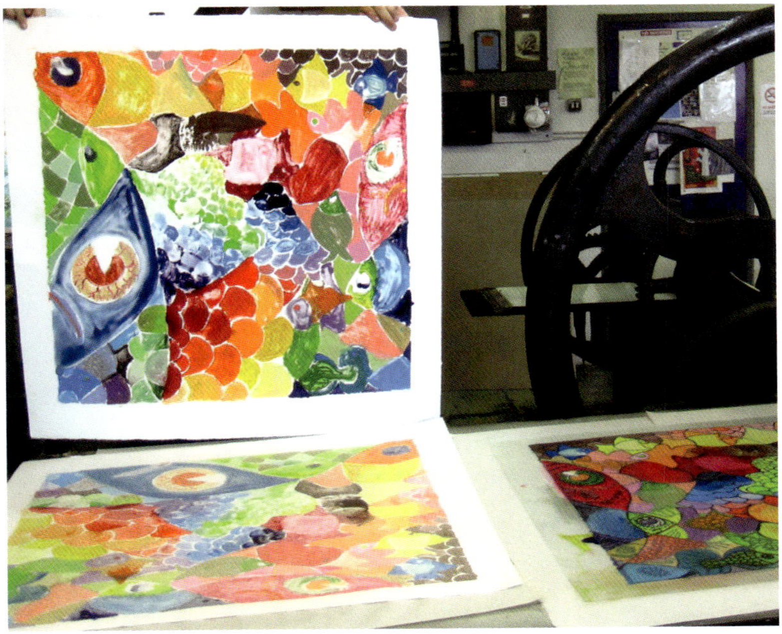

▶ The finished monoprint has been printed. It took the artist Sarah Redman several hours to mix all of the colours and paint the entire image. It is printed in one pull.

MONOPRINTING USING A LINO BLOCK

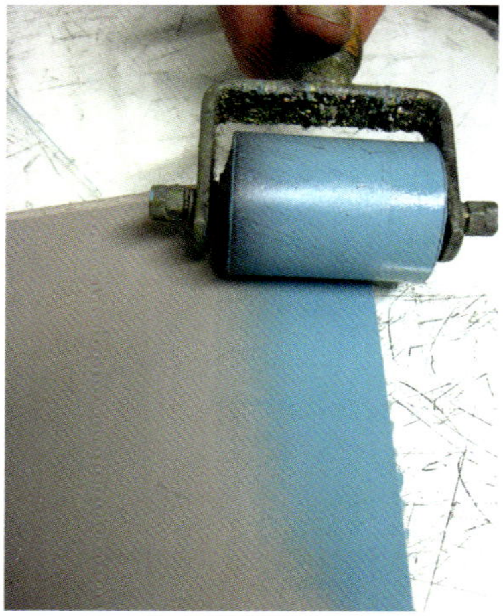

▲ Lino blocks can be used for monoprinting. They can be rolled up directly with different colours.

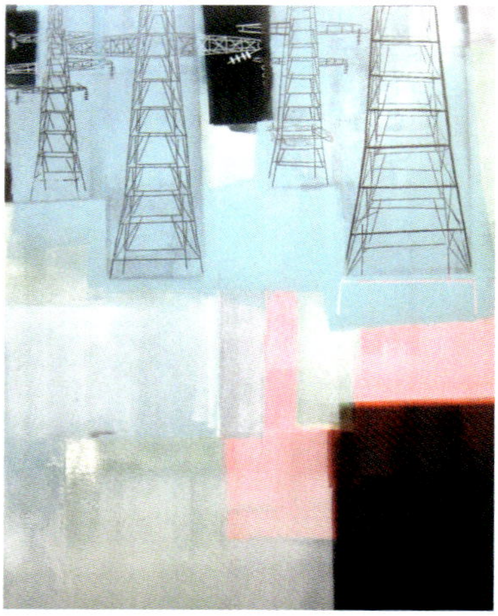

▲ The background in this image is taking shape. The lino block had been rolled with several colours. The image lines cut into the block are a strong feature.

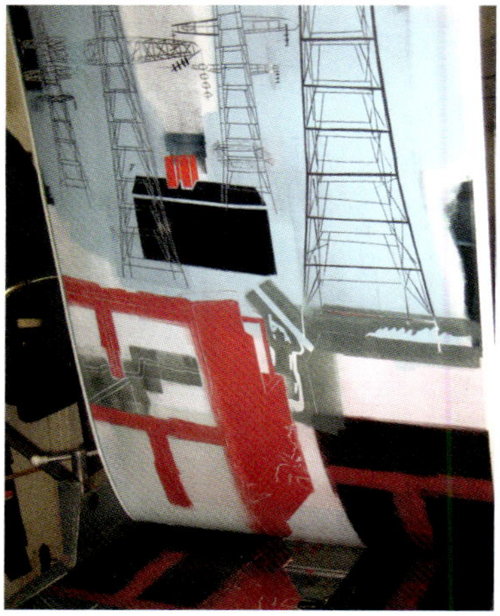

▲ The layer of new colour is printed into the progressing monoprint.

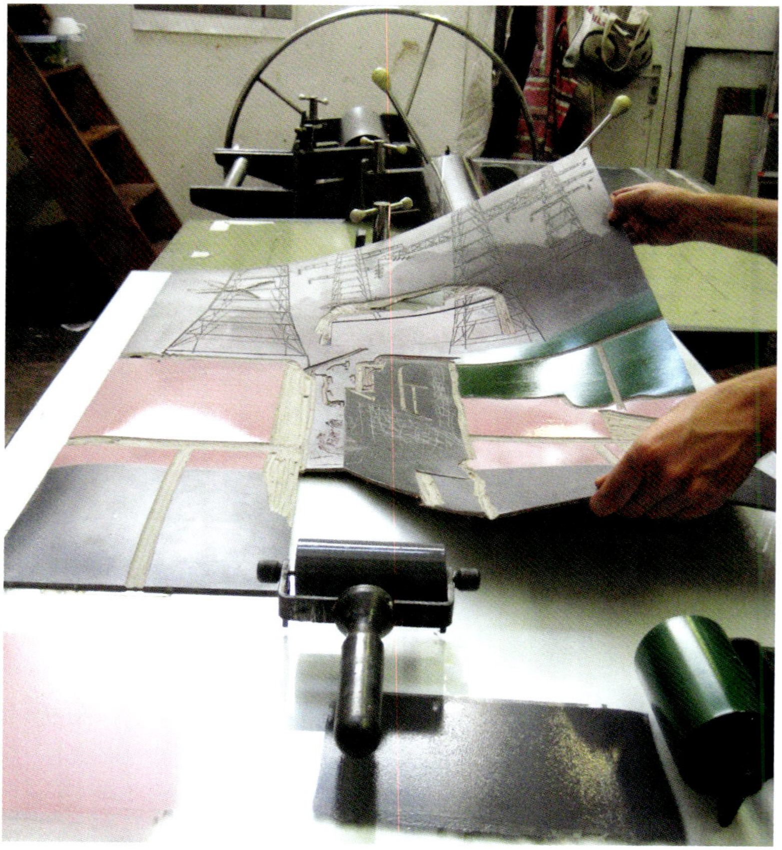

▶ The lino block can be cut and altered as needed to develop the image. Areas are obliterated by over printing. New shapes are added to the image to change existing ones.

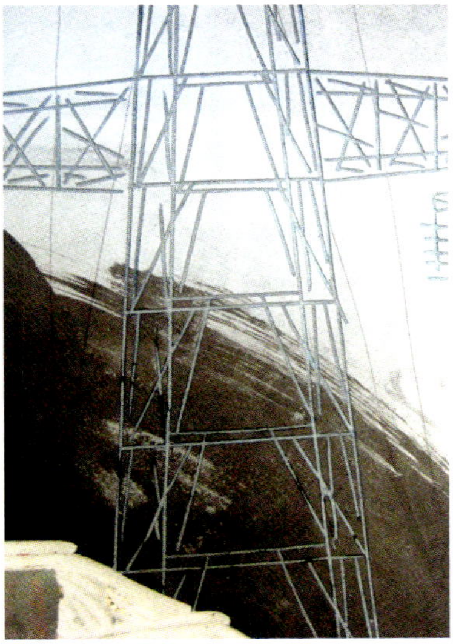

▲ The linocut block has new lines cut into the existing image to further alter the image.

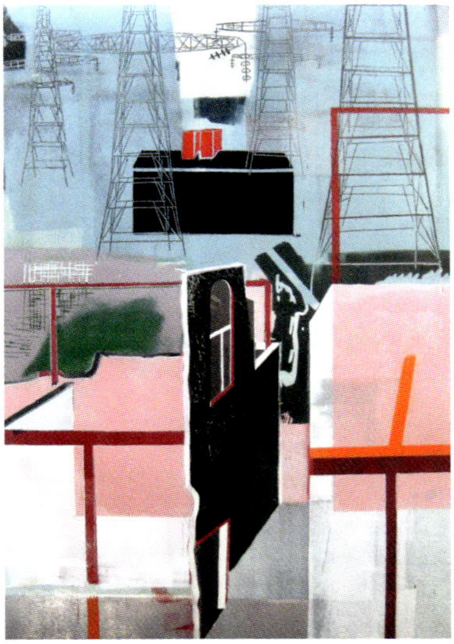

▲ The linocut monoprint has progressed. A complicated image is evolving.

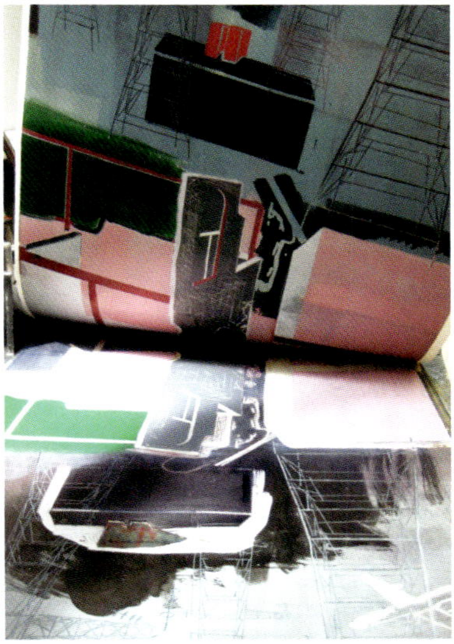

▲ A new layer of green ink has been added.

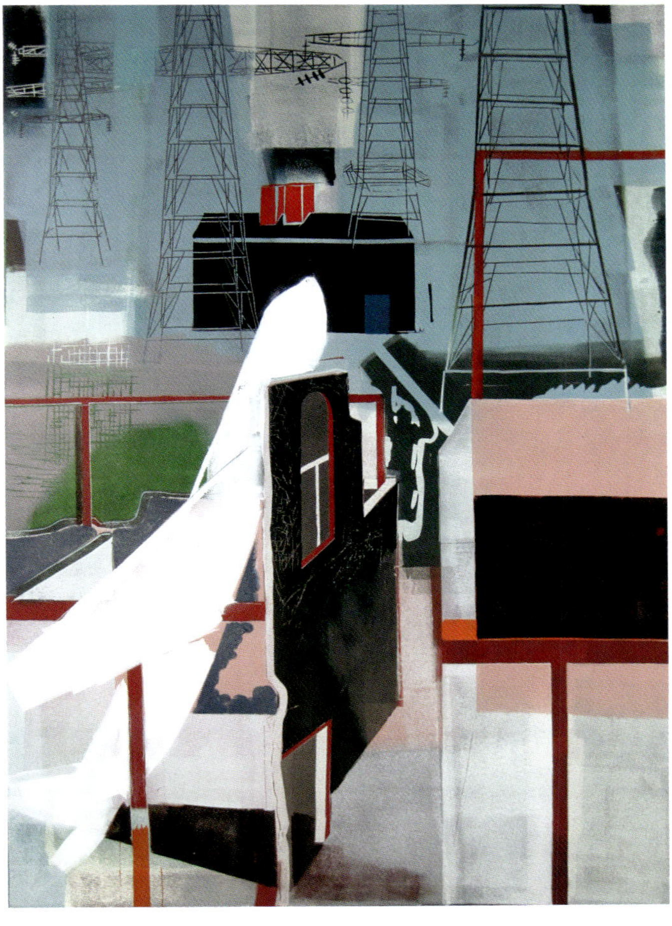

▶ The final print shows how far the image has metamorphasized! An airplane completes the artist's design.

Michael Kirkman, *Airplane*, 2011. Linocut monoprint, 112 x 76 cm (44 x 30 in.).

MONOPRINTING WITH A COMBINATION OF MEDIA

▶ The artist Mary Dalton is making the large-scale monoprint in this picture sequence. The image is 91.5 x 289.5 cm (36 x 114 in.). The image covers the entire paper surface all the way to its edges (a bled print). The print here is placed on the bed of the etching press ready to have another monoprint layer added to it. The paper is as wide as the press bed but considerably longer. This means it cannot be run all the way through the press and removed. The artist needs to plan the layer that will be printed into the image next, as the print will have to be rolled back through the press to remove it.

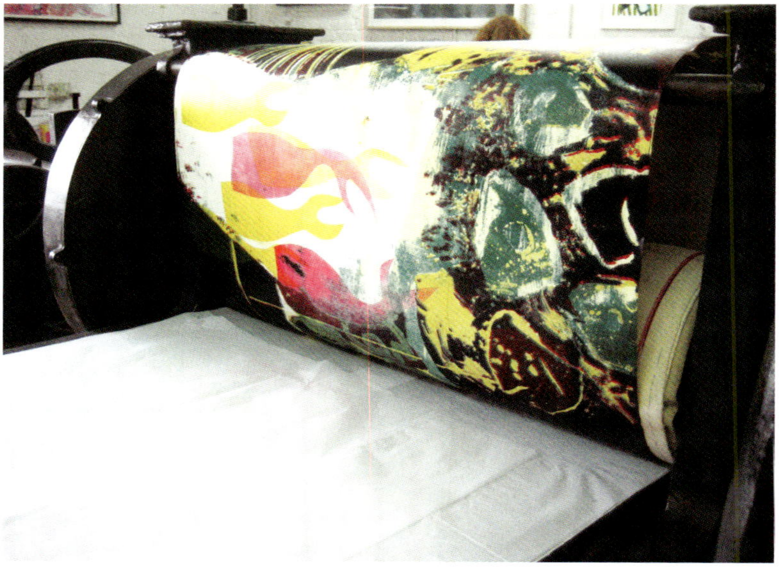

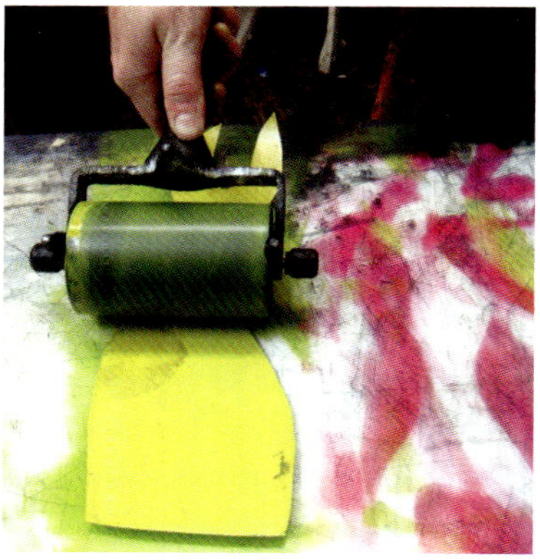

▲ Cut shapes of photo litho plate are inked with a roller.

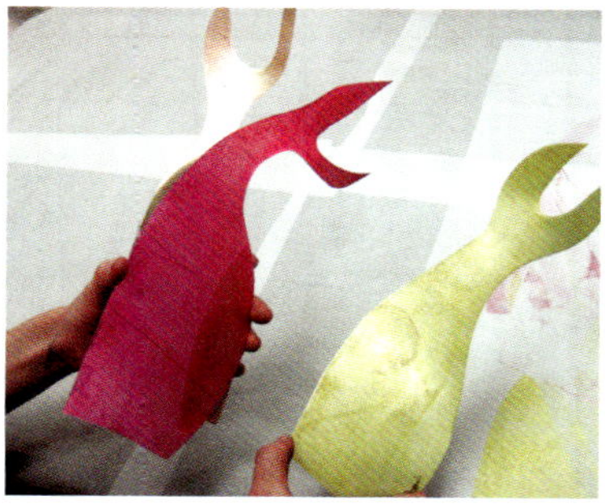

▲ Old photo litho plates make great bases to monoprint on. They are easily cut by hand with scissors.

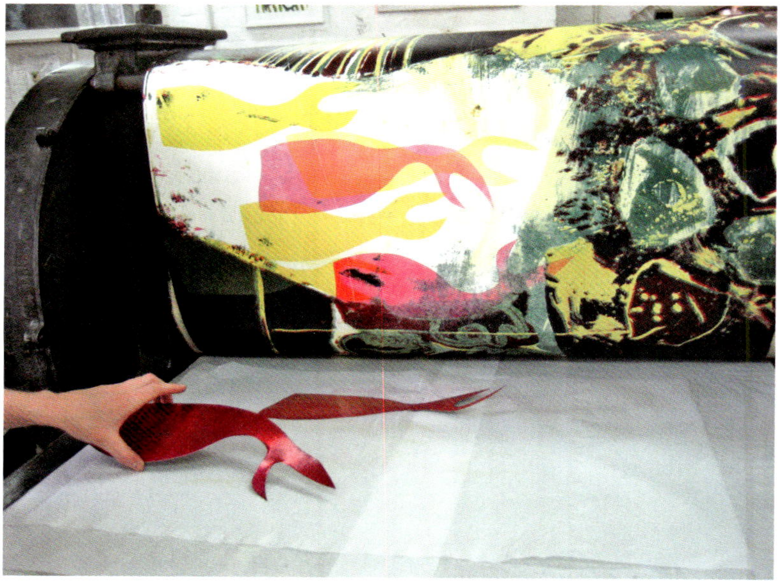

▲ The artist Mary Dalton places the inked shapes ink-side-up in position on the press bed.

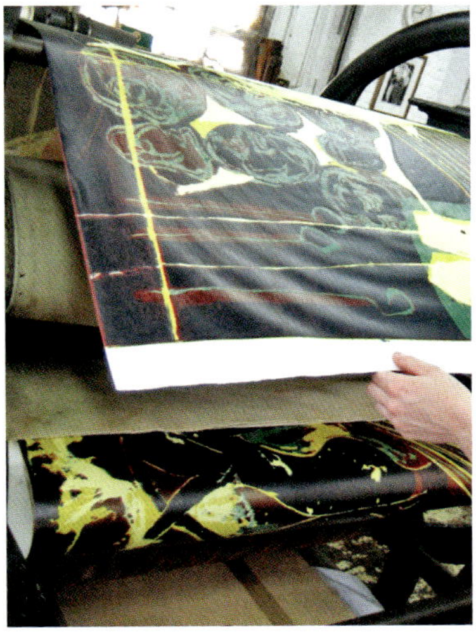

▲ The extremely long piece of paper can be seen draped over the press.

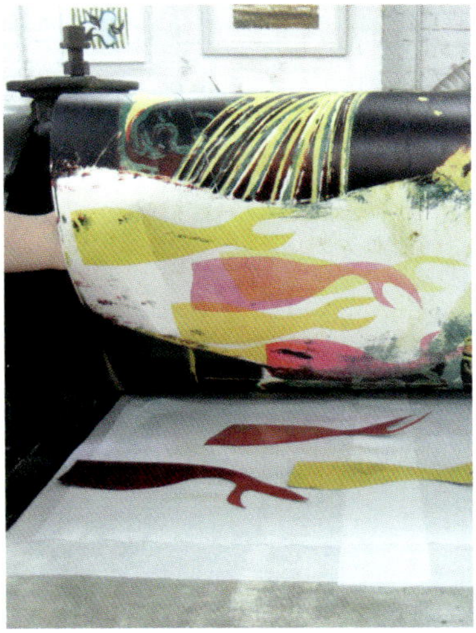

▲ The paper is gently pulled down onto the inked shapes. Great care is taken not to move them out of position as the paper drops down.

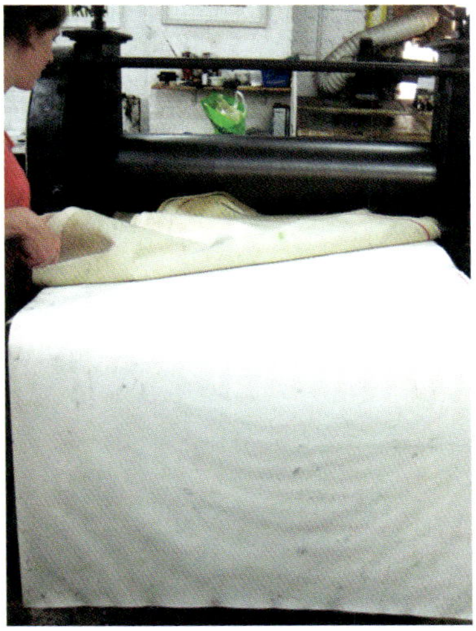

▲ The length of the paper is considerably longer than the length of the bed of the press and the printing blankets.

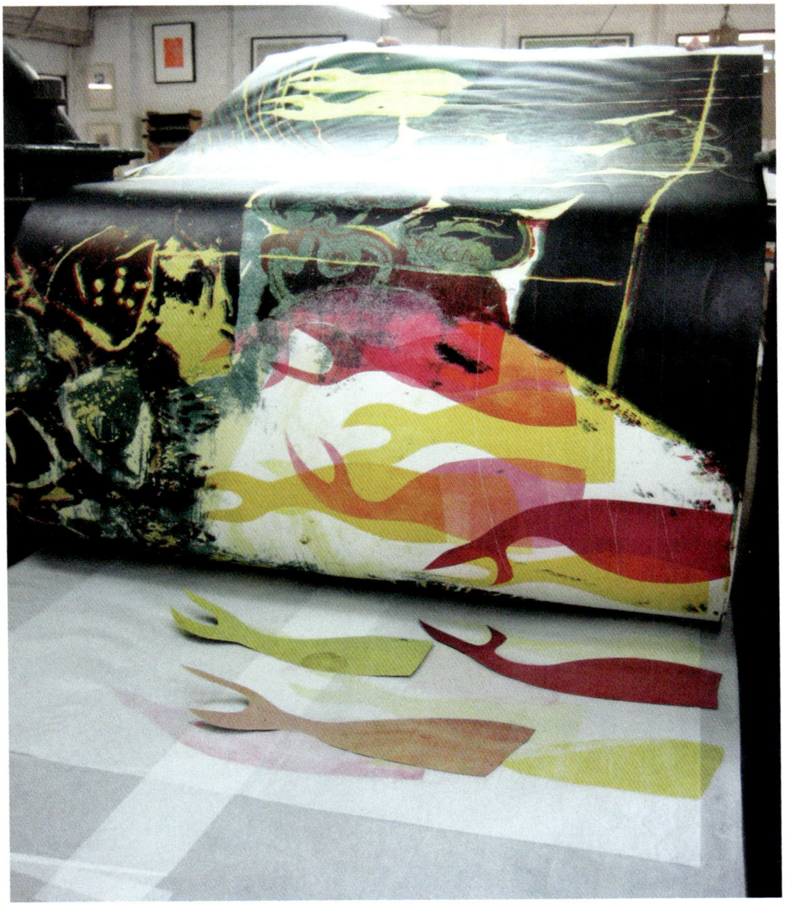

▶ The new layer of colour shapes is printed into the monoprint image. Remember, the paper will have to be rolled back through the press in the opposite direction to remove it. This print has monoprint layers made using wood blocks, acetate offsets, photo litho plate imagery and cut shaped blocks like the photo litho shapes in this sequence.

MONOPRINTING WITH LITHOGRAPHIC ROLL-UP BLACK

The roll-up black stone used in lithography offers a way of making a very simple monoprint. It has a very distinct texture and like the ink rolled on the glass top surface, will have textured tone as well as the strong drawn line of the image.

Lithographic ink on glass

A simple way of making a monoprint is to roll ink onto a glass surface. Lay a sheet of paper on top and draw on it as per the roll-up black technique. The advantage is you can roll any colour of ink you want onto the glass.

USING ALTERNATIVE MEDIA

It is always good to think outside the box. Alternative media can be used for monoprints.

Have a go at printing using food colouring, fabric dye and or live plant colour.

If you are working in an open access or shared studio, always ask the managers if it is possible to experiment. This is courtesy especially as printing blankets, blotters and so on are such expensive items to replace if they become damaged through staining or if the crushed result becomes embedded in their surfaces.

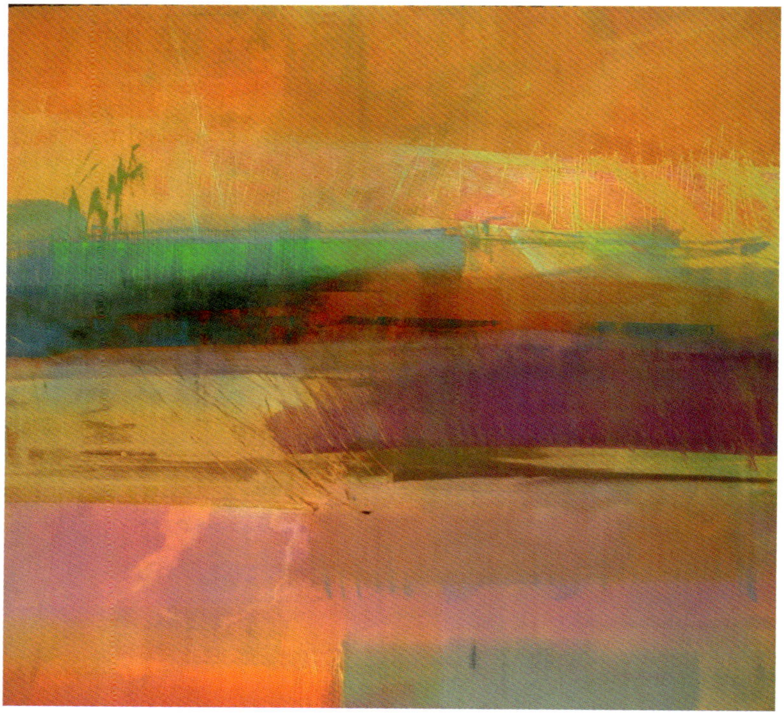

◀ **Megan Fishpool, *Stravinsky*, 2009. Monoprint, 60 x 60 cm (23½ x 23 in.).**

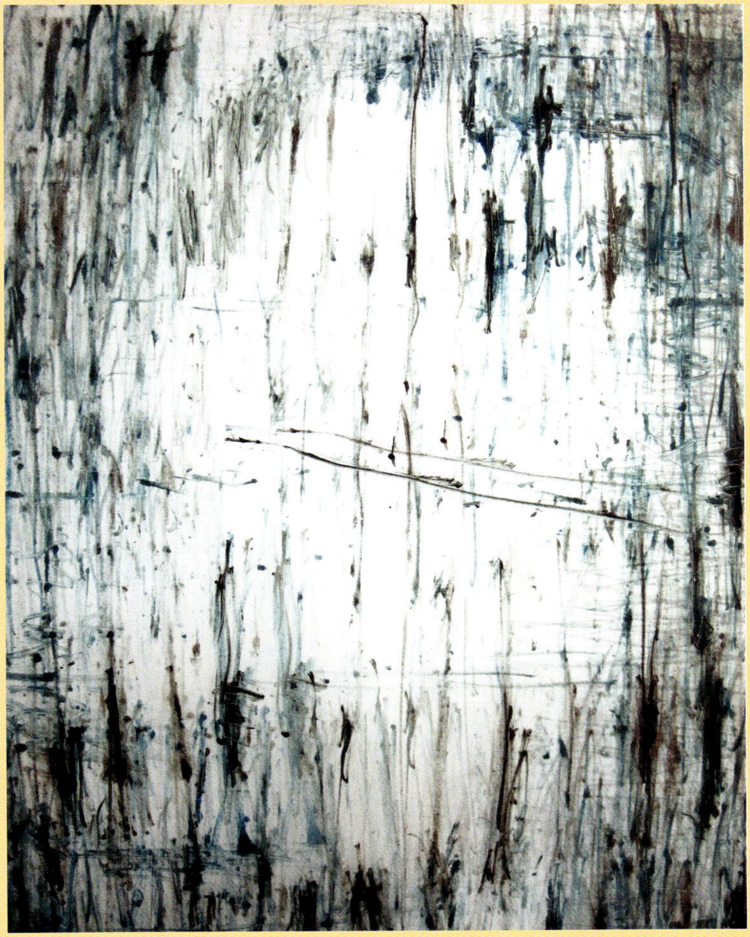

▶ Stephanie Newell-Nebbia, Untitled, 2011. Monoprint, 56 x 76 cm (22 x 30 in.).

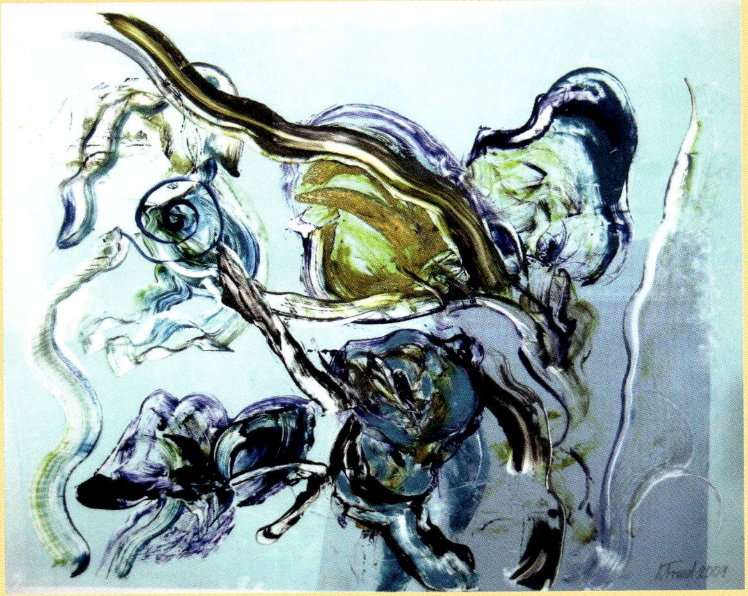

▶ Lucy Freud, *Cambodia*, 2009. Monoprint, 76 x 76 cm (30 x 30 in.).

MONOPRINT TEXTURES

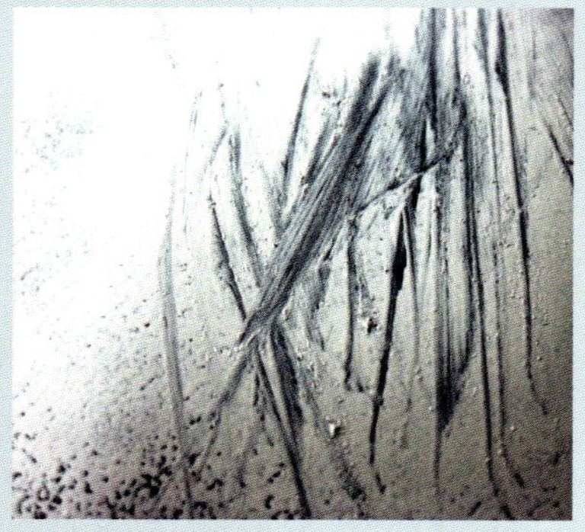

Bristle brush.

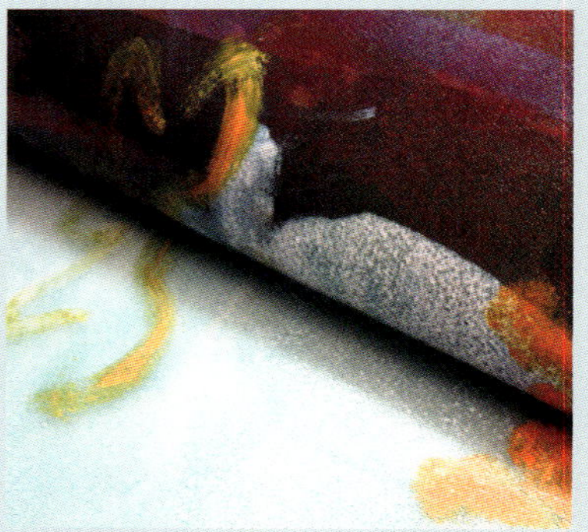

Lithographic relief ink.

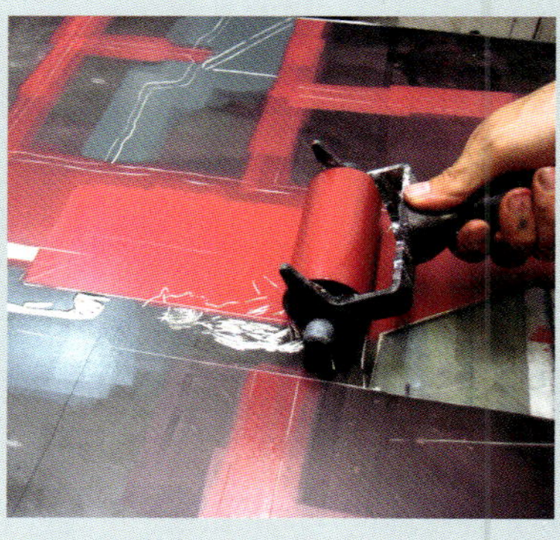

Lino block.

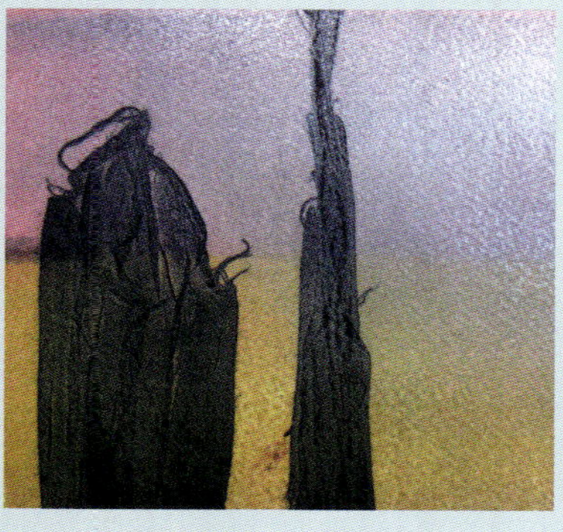

Tarlatan (scrim).

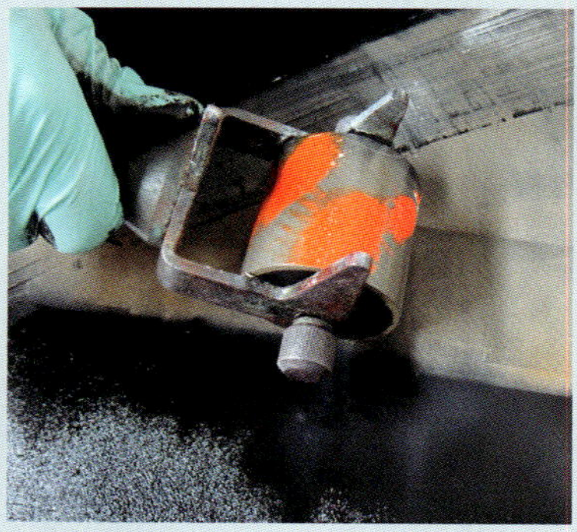

Small roller.

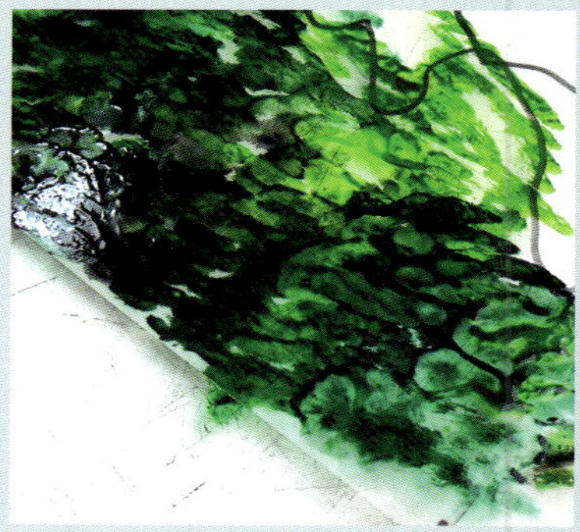

Solvent diluted oil-based ink.

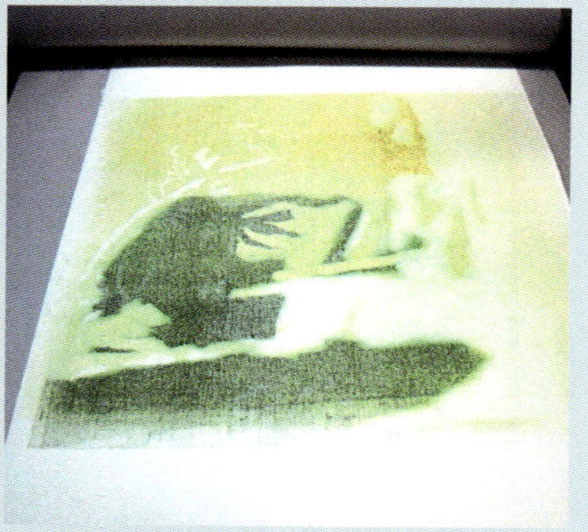

Fabric.

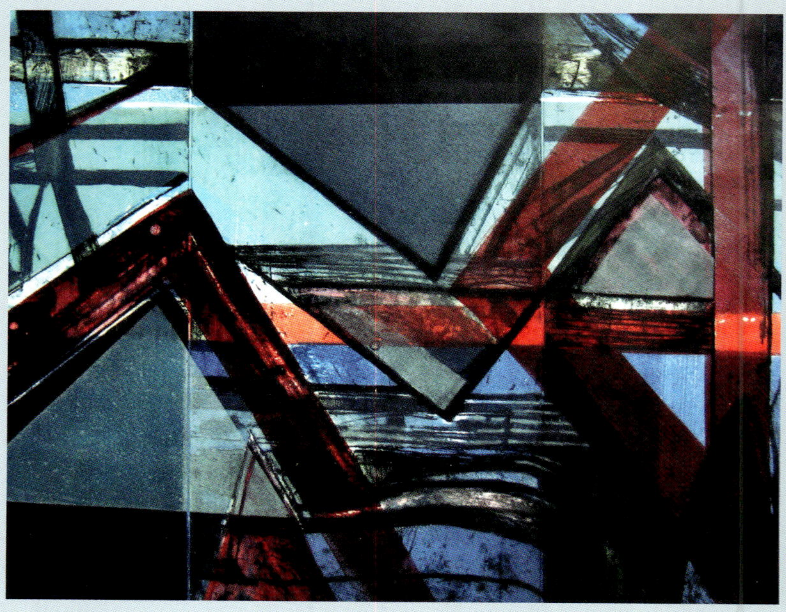

Etching ink.

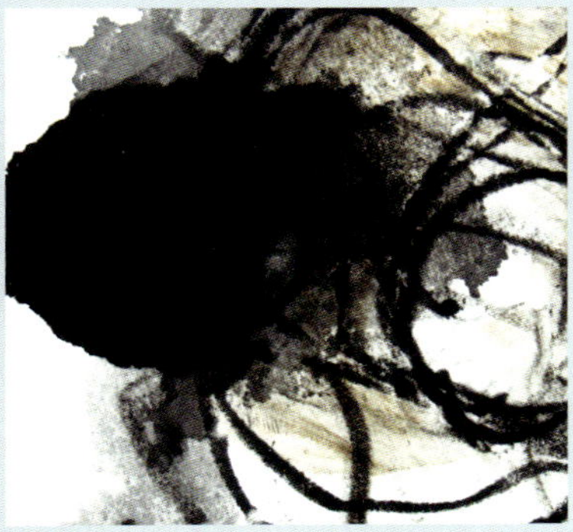

Lithographic tusche.

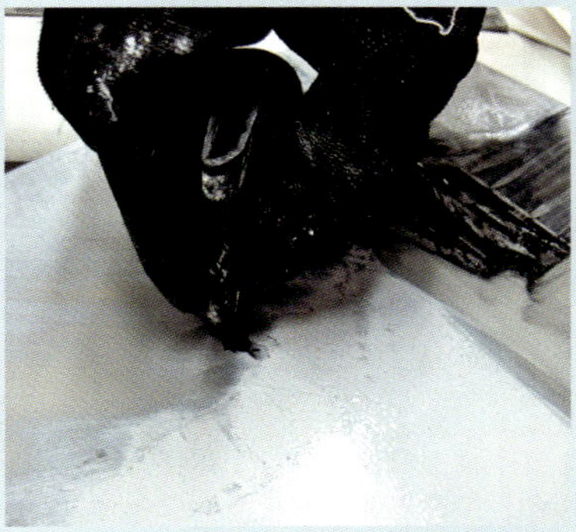

Mount board card.

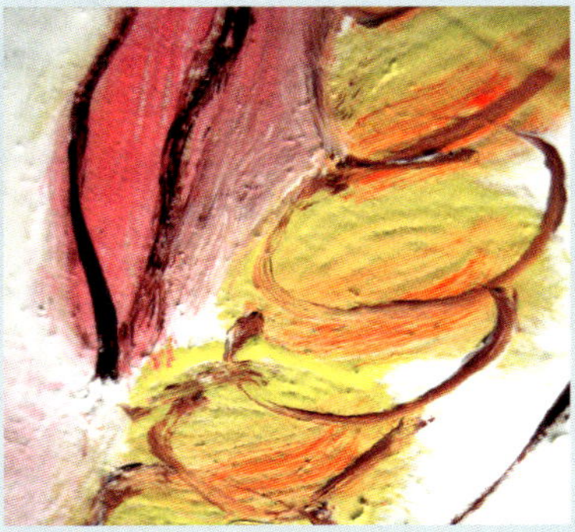

Daler-Rowney® nylon brushes.

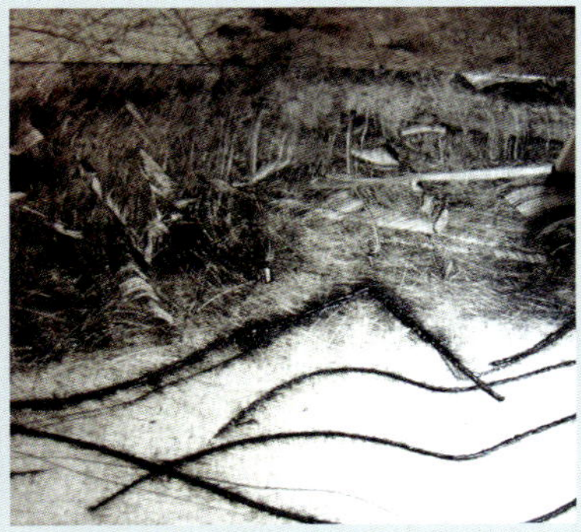

Plate tone and cut card.

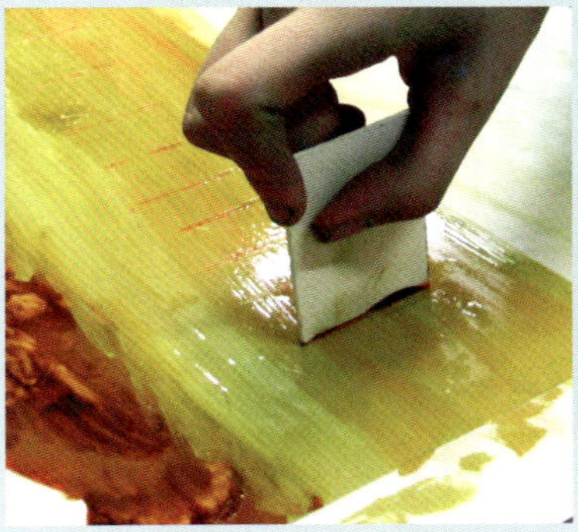

Cut card smearing ink.

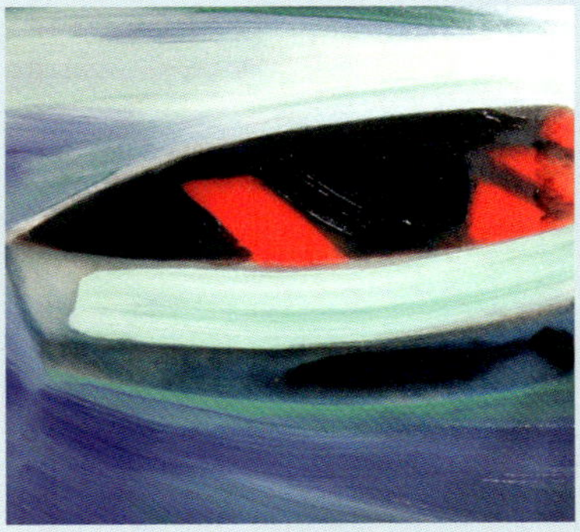

Dry brushing oil-based ink.

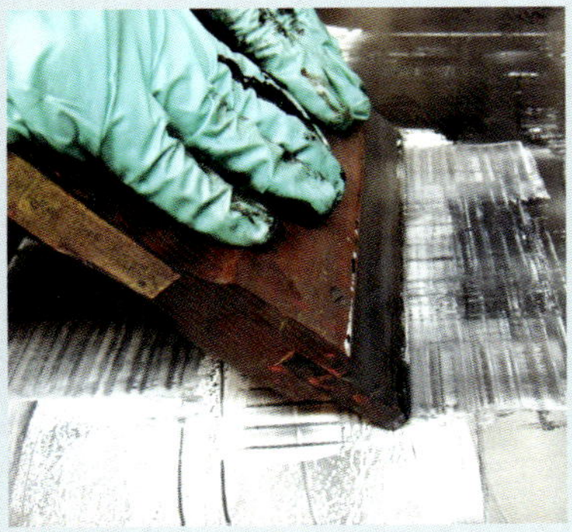

Squeegee.

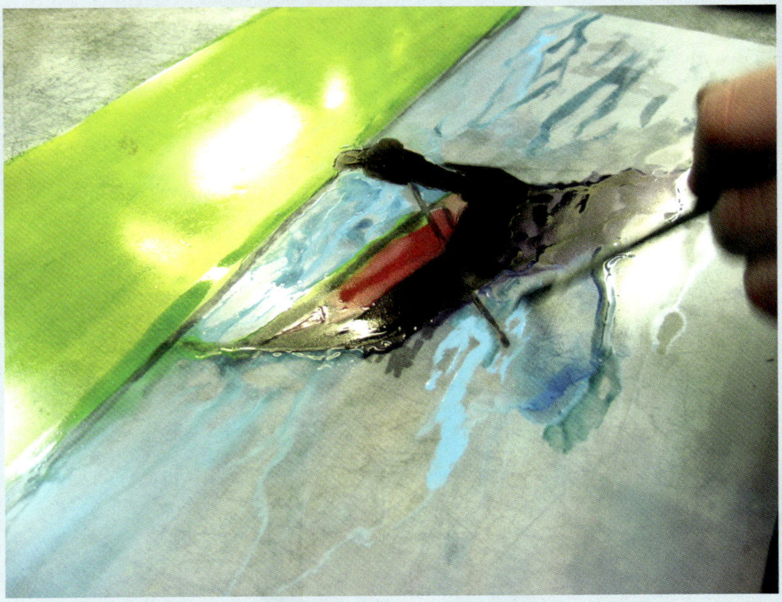

Extended ink and solvent.

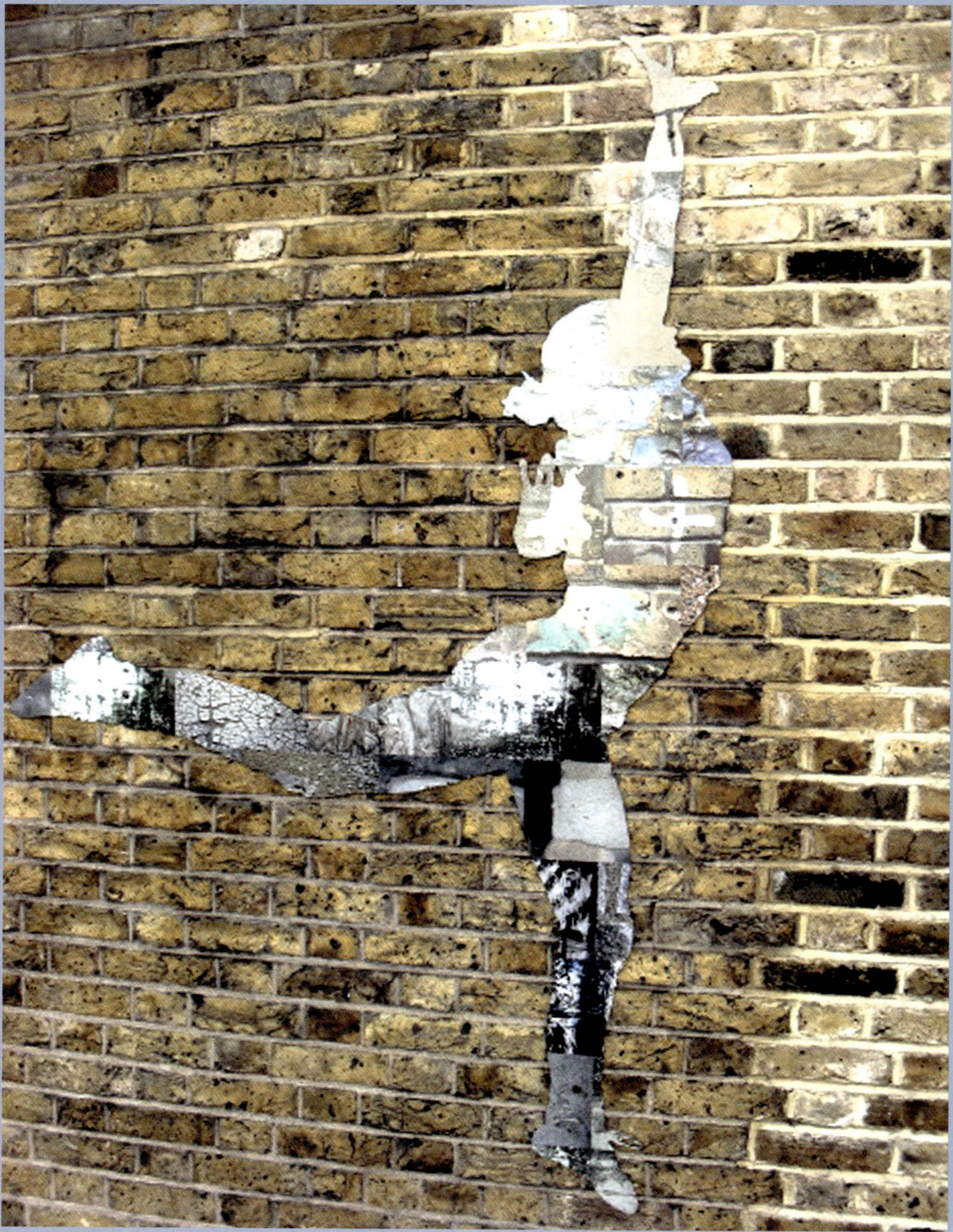

12

software

Technology is amazing. Graphic printing techniques have enabled pictures to be manipulated and presented anew in many digital forms. Electronic devices are constantly being upgraded and adapted to enable the 'output' of creative ideas that have been visualised with software (computer-controlled programs or applications).

◀ **Barton Hargreaves, *Untitled*, 2010. Digital archive print, 121 x 76 cm (47½ x 30 in.).**

Whether used by high-end graphics bureaux, digital ateliers, grand format printing studios or a home-based digital studio, software is the creative tool that imaging technologies rely on. Hardware is great but without software, the whole digital creation process stops. The only requirements for all digital printing are a scanner, a printer and a computer – and of course image processing applications (software).

So what does software do? Software is a collection of data that tells digital equipment – anything from computers and mobile phones to security and sat nav systems – what to do. That's simple enough. There are now thousands of computer software programs – software programs that draw, paint, mess things up, make things light and dark, make things large or small, edit, resize, take pictures of pictures you have already made, change the space/time continuum – you name it. (You would not be reading this book without the use of software.)

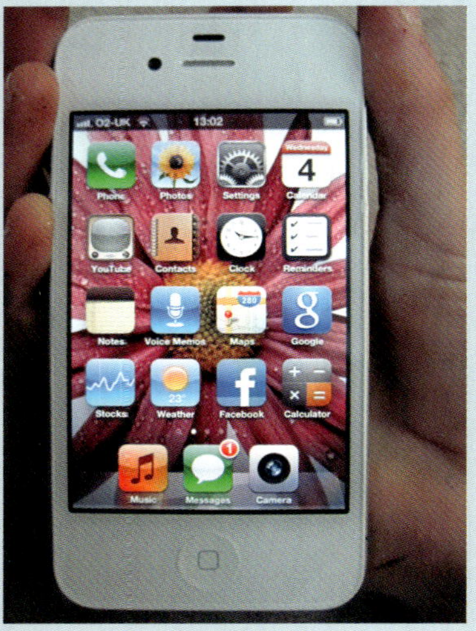

Portable technology.

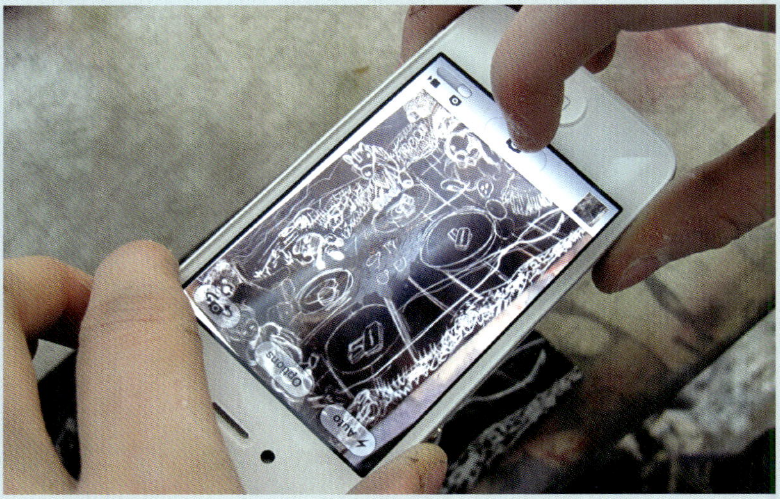

Taking a picture of the etching that has been made.

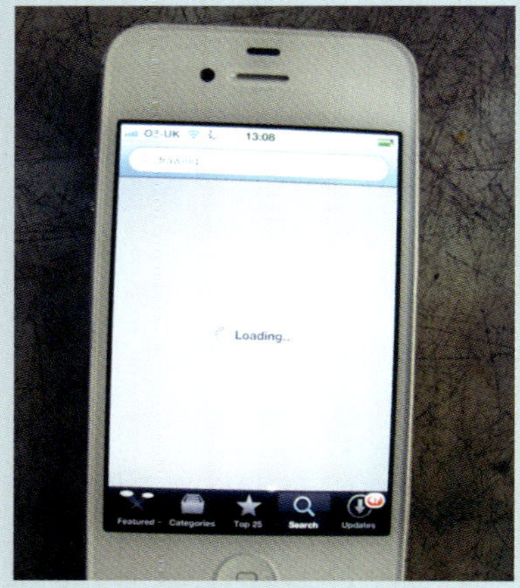

Drawing on it.

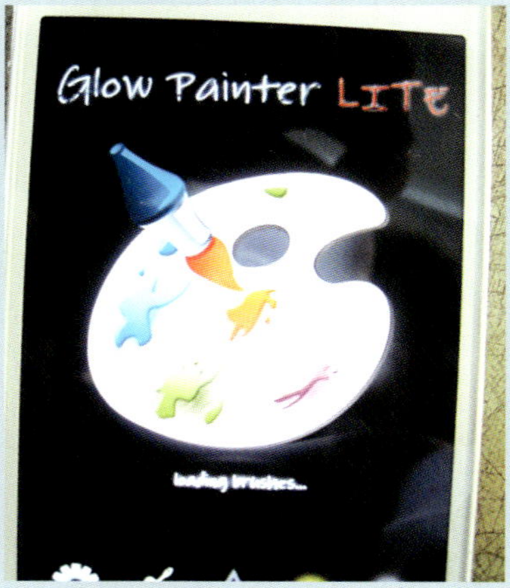

Painting on it.

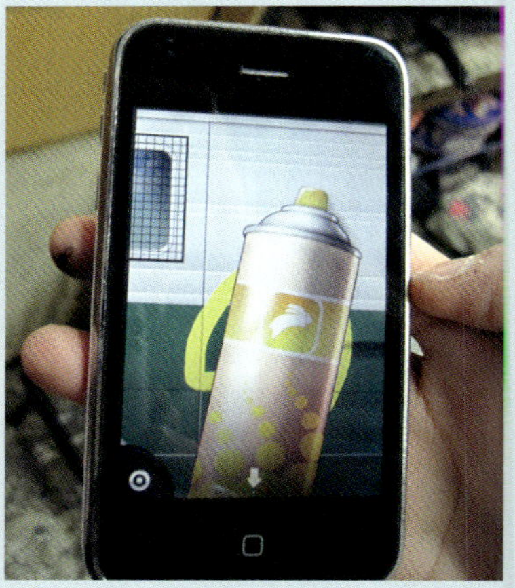

Choosing the yellow paint.

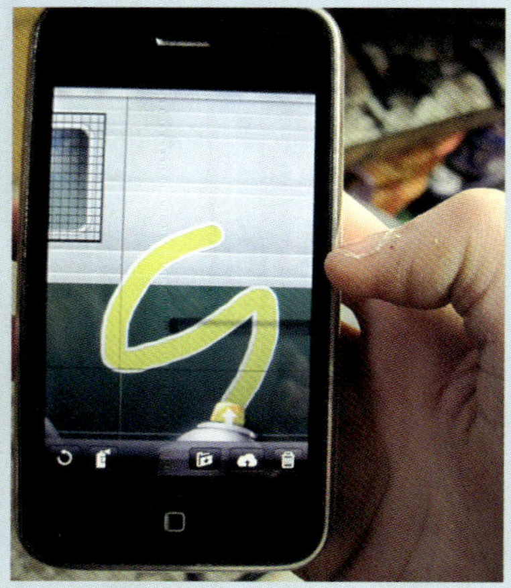

Using the yellow paint.

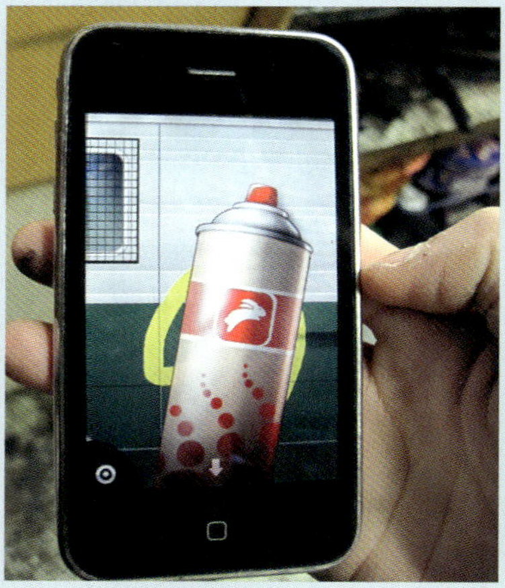

Choosing the red paint.

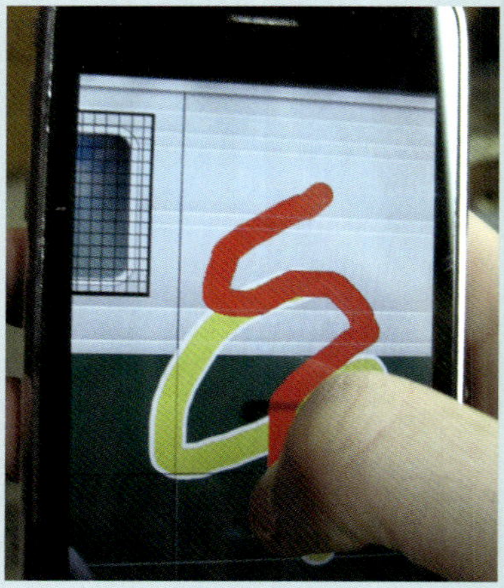

Using the red paint.

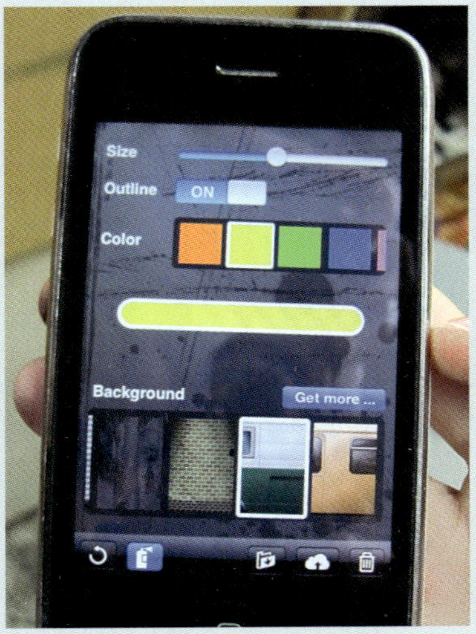

Drawing with light.

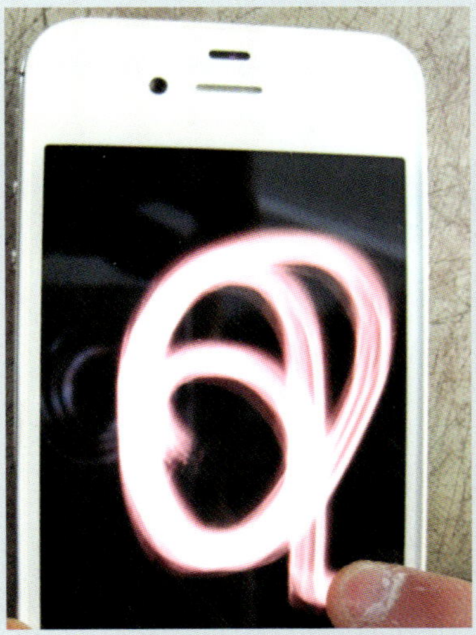

Moving light on the screen.

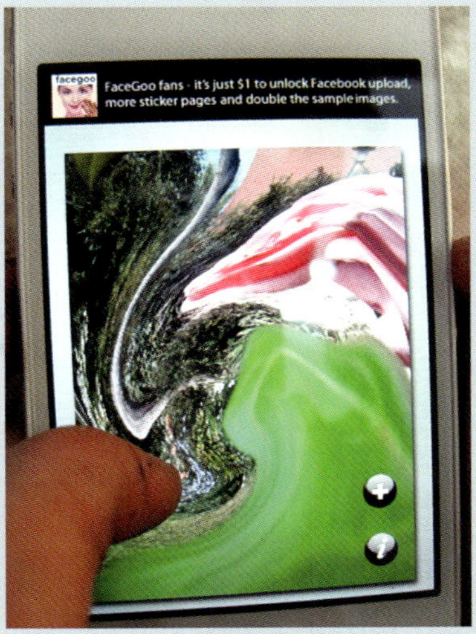

Smudging the picture like Francis Bacon.

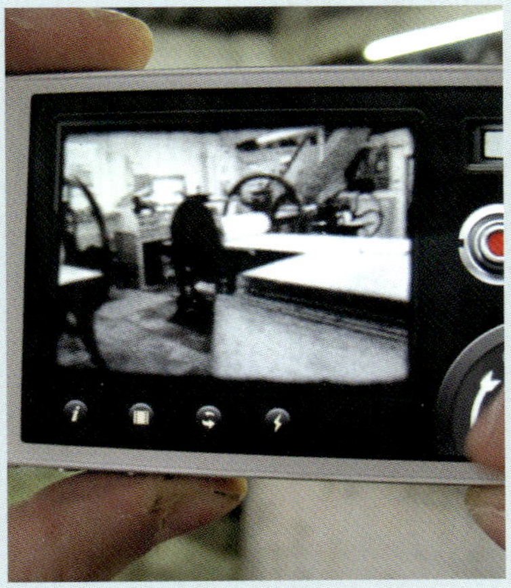

Turning the studio into a black and white image.

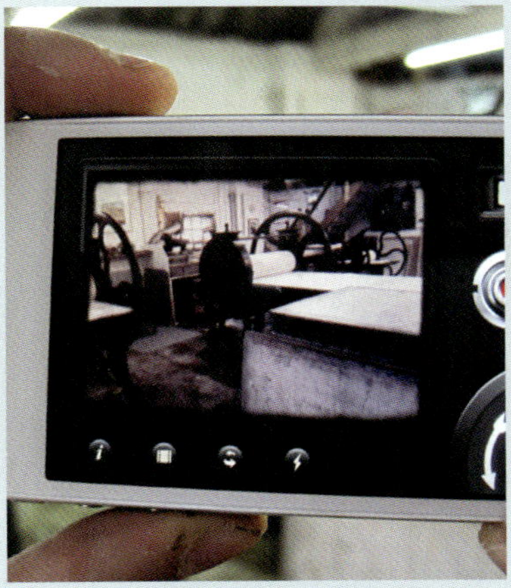

Turning the studio into an almost sepia image.

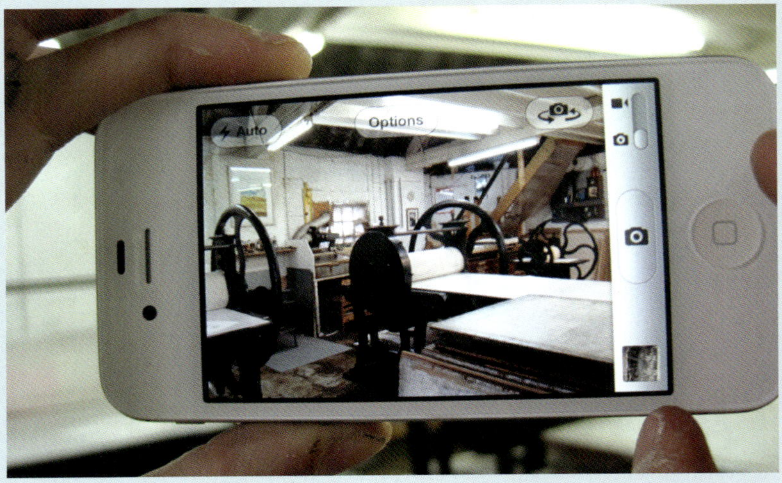

◀ Turning the studio into a colour image.

What is paramount in making any image is the influence and effect a stimulating idea has on the senses. That should never be sacrificed at the expense of technical interest.

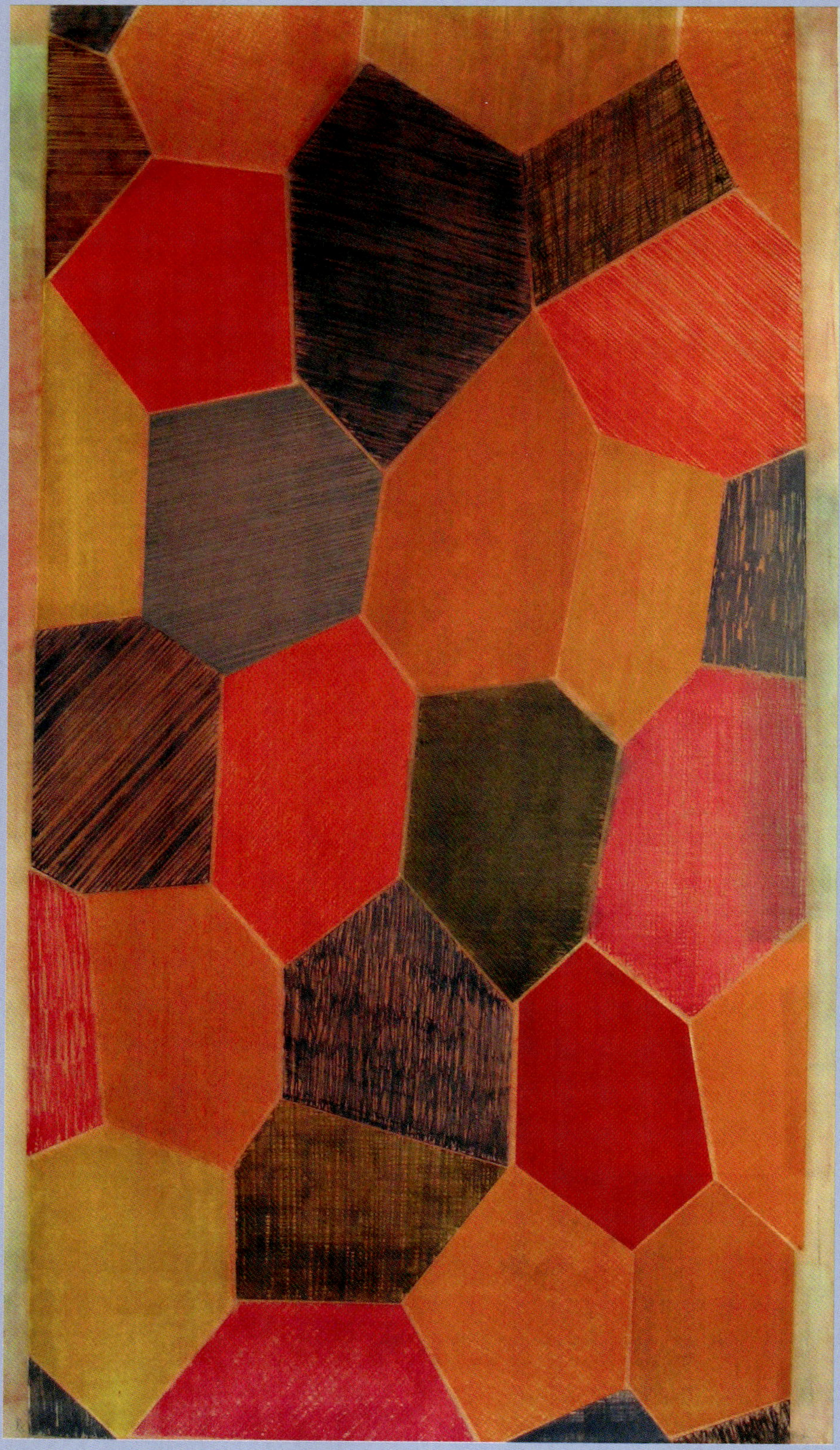

Colin Gale, *Lozenge*, 2008. Monoprint, 70 x 112 cm (28 x 44 in.).

glossary

acid a strong corrosive liquid used in the etching process. The two most common acids are nitric acid for biting zinc and steel plates and ferric chloride used for biting copper plates. It reacts with the surface of the metal and creates fumes, hence it must be used in a covered tank with an extractor fan. It is also used in stone lithography.

acetate clear thin Mylar® or plastic used for making stencils, or for registration, or as a surface for outputting inkjet images from a printer.

Akua Kolor modifers water-based products by Akua: blending medium thins Akua intaglio ink, retarder slows the drying rate of Akua inks, transparent base transforms Akua Kolor into a intaglio ink or relief ink, tack thickener adds tack and thickens Akua inks.

à la poupée method of inking a plate with more than one colour of ink. The colours are inked and scrimmed individually onto the plate one at a time. They can be deliberately blended to create mixed colour areas.

AP Artist's proof. 10% of the edition.

aquatint etching technique in which a resin dust is added to a plate by heating it onto the surface. The acid only bites the plate in the areas between the dust particles, thus creating a tonal value on the plate. The length of time the plate is left in the acid determines the depth/darkness of the tones.

Arkansas stone fine-grained whetstone used for grinding, sharpening and polishing.

asphaltum bitumen substance used to preserve plates from corrosion. It is often used as a ground (stop out varnish) and for coating the backs of intaglio plates. Liquid asphaltum is used in lithography – being buffed onto the surface before the image is rolled up in black ink. It is a base for the ink to adhere to.

bon à tirer (B.A.T.) translated literally as 'the good pull', this is the proof that the printmaker commits to and signs to confirm how the edition will look.

baren Japanese tool, usually large, circular or oval shaped and covered in bamboo, used for hand burnishing.

bevel the angle that is filed onto the edge of an intaglio plate before printing. The angle is usually 45 degrees. This ensures that the edges do not cut through the printing blankets on the bed of the press. It also allows the edges to be easily cleaned and wiped free of unnecessary ink that will dirty the printed emboss of the image.

bite/biting/bitten the 'action' of the acid on the surface of the metal plate when it is the mordant bath.

biting time length of time a plate is left in the mordant to be 'bitten'.

block printing surface referred to in relief print such as the lino block or wood block.

burin tool used for engraving.

burnisher smooth, curved tip tool used on metal plates to polish an area that has been removed by a scraper. A burnisher can be used to highlight an area within an area or to lighten and area that is too dark.

burr the wisps of metal that a drypoint needle pulls up when it is drawn through and into the surface of a metal plate. These edges of torn metal hold the etching ink and create a dramatic line. The burr is extremely delicate and wears away quite quickly, due to the pressure from inking and printing the plate. Drypoint editions are quite limited in number.

carborundum® grit used to regrain stones in stone lithography. Also used with an adhesive such as PVA, to create texture on collagraph plates. Carborundum® grit comes in different grades, usually: fine, medium and course and extra fine.

chine collé technique where additional paper of a different colour, texture or shape to the supporting paper is bonded to the surface of the supporting paper using a suitable adhesive. An inked plate is then printed onto these additional papers to complete the image.

chipboard See **MDF**.

Citra-solv® plant-derived degreaser containing D-Limonene (clear liquid from the peel of the orange). It can also successfully transfer toner from laser prints to substrates with the aid of a press.

collagraph (also collograh) print made from a block or matrix on which collaged materials with varying textures have been glued. The matrix is then sealed with shellac and dried before printing.

copper metal used for intaglio processes. It is available with a polished surface. It lends itself well to clean, even-width lines due to the way the ferric acid bites into the surface. Aquatint on copper is a joy! The biting times for copper, whether with lines or aquatint, are much longer than for zinc or steel.

counterprint offsetting the printed image onto another printing surface by placing that surface directly on top of the first printed surface.

dabber leather-covered cushion with a handle, used for inking.

deckle edge rough and feathery edge of a piece of paper made in a mould.

dolly tool that turns on a vertical handle, usually made of tarlatan, which is used for inking.

drypoint the technique where only a needle with a sharp tip or roulettes is used to make marks in the surface of a metal plate. No acids are used when making a drypoint.

drypoint needle metal tool with a sharp tip that is used to make marks in the surface of metal. The movement of the needle across the surface of the metal creates a mark which has a characteristic trait called a burr (see **burr**).

dpi (Dots per inch.) Measure of the density of a digial image, which determines its resolution. The resolution is crucial to the quality of the image when it is outputted.

driers additives such as magnesium powder or cobalt driers used to quicken the drying time of printing inks.

eps (Encapsulated post script.) A digital file format used to transfer graphic images within compatible applications.

emboss a raised design created by pressing damp paper onto the surface of a matrix and passing it through a printing press.

engrave an incised mark made with specific tools on a block of material such as copper fine grained wood. No acid is used.

etching intaglio process in which an image is created on a metal plate using acid. The plate is first covered with an acid-resistant ground or varnish. Lines or textures are then drawn into the ground, exposing the plate. The exposed metal from the drawn areas are what the acid 'bites' (see **bite**).

etching blankets felted and tightly woven wool cloth that is cut to size to fit the bed of a printing press. A standard set of printing blankets contains one swanskin (the thick, woolly top blanket) and two fleeces (thinner, more smooth-grained felts). They help to push the dampened printing paper into the grooves and lines of the etching plate.

extender a carrier for ink that is transparent and has no colour pigment. It creates a less intense version of the full strength ink colour. It does not change the density of the ink (i.e. it does not thin the ink. (See **thinner**). Also known as transparent white.

ferric chloride alkaline solution used for biting copper etching plates. It can also be used for zinc and aluminium if mixed to the correct ratio. It produces no fumes.

gesso a mix of plaster of Paris and glue used to create texture on a matrix.

Gamsol pure refined mineral spirit (OMS) that is odourless because the aromatic solvent has been removed. It is capable of totally evaporating.

gauge the thickness of metal or wood. Metal plate is best at 1.6 mm or 2mm thickness. Wood is best at 2mm thickness.

gouge tool with a v-shaped tip used for woodcut, linocut or engraving.

ground used to protect the surface of etching plates and to cover the surface of a plate so that an image can be drawn or impressed onto it. They are wax based or bitumen based and can be hard, soft or liquid.

gum arabic a natural material sourced from the acacia tree, used in lithography for processing the image on a plate or stone.

half tone screen (or half tone) simulates a continuous tone by breaking down and reproducing an image into dots of various sizes to represent detail and tone. The dots represent resolution. The quantity of dots is known as DPI (dots per inch) or LPI (lines per inch).

hand burnish printing without a press with a baren or wooden or metal spoon, using the pressure of your hand.

hotplate a metal surface with a heating element underneath used when appying a ground to the surface of the plate. The temperature of a hotplate can be adjusted to suit both hard and soft grounds. A soft ground requires a cooler temperature than a hard ground.

Imagon (Imagon HD) is a photopolymer film used for imaging purposes. Imagon films are developed using soda ash amd water. Imagon Ultra is also available which has a quicker exposure time.

intaglio a printing process that involves using metal, plastic or card plates; printing inks; cutting tools; grounds and varnishes; mordants; and a printing press. Cutting or etching lines and textures on the plate then pushing ink into the lines and textures on the plate with scrim and then wiping the plate to a desired inkiness makes the image. Damp paper is placed over the plate and it is rolled through a printing press with etching blankets.

jigsaw a power tool used for cutting metal plates into shapes, and also to cut wood.

letterpress a process of relief printing with metal or wooden type set into blocks of text.

lino/linocut a matrix on which the image made is cut into a linoleum tile block.

lithotine petroleum solvent that contains a small amount of pine oil. It is used in lithography for general clean-up and washing-out ink. It is usually used before applying asphaltum to the plate or stone. It can also be used as a second etch (see p.160) as it can penetrate gum arabic.

magnesium carbonate is usually in a powdered (ground) form and is used to stiffen ink.

matrix the substrate from which the printmaker makes the printing plate. Suitable materials to use include wood, Perspex, metal and card.

MDF (Medium density fibreboard.) A manufactured composite wood base. Similar to chipboard, except with a much finer, smoother grain. It is available in different thicknesses. (See **gauge**.)

monochrome a single colour used in a print design.

monotype a unique, one-off print made by printing on an unmarked surface of metal, acetate or thin Perspex.

monoprint commonly acknowledged to be a unique print taken from a printing matrix that has a marked surface that remains unchanged though each inking of the plate is done to deliberately to create a unique variant.

mordant also Dutch Mordant. (See **acid**.)

Mylar® see **acetate**.

muller tool made of stone or glass with a flat base used for grinding powder pigments on a smooth, flat slab usually made of stone or glass.

nap roller a leather roller used for roll-up black ink in lithography. Roll-up black ink is non-drying. Hence the nap (meaning the raised, hairy underside of the leather) roller is ideal, as the hairs of the nap roller are easy to revive in the rolling up process. See p.156.

newsprint an inexpensive wood pulp paper used in printmaking for proofing and blotting (also used for printing newspaper).

nitric acid (HNO_3) mordant used to etch copper, zinc and steel. Combined with water to create solutions of different strengths. It is also used in lithographic etches.

offset an image printed from a key plate then offset via a roller onto a second printing matrix. This makes it possible to print the drawn image the same way round as when it was drawn and not in reverse.

open bite a process in etching where a large area of the plate is left exposed to the mordant without aquatint or with disregard to the biting time. Unexpected shapes and patterns are created in these open areas.

PETG plate (Polyethylene Terepthalate Glycol.) Plastic printmaking plate used as an alternative to Polycarbonate plates. A PETG plate is softer than a Polycarbonate plate.

Perspex thick acrylic sheeting used for drypoint. It also makes an excellent cover for fume cupboards.

piezo a piezo inkjet head or nozzle differs from a traditional thermal inkjet nozzle in the way that it pulses to create the necessary pressure to produce the ink as a droplet. Piezo inkjets work on the principle that droplets of ink fluid are forced from the nozzle via an electric pulse rather than a heated element. This means you can have a greater variety of ink cartridges in the printer printing your image; six or eight colours at the same time instead of only four.

planography another name for lithography. Also photoplate lithography.

pixel the smallest actual element of an image made of light, as seen on a computer screen.

planography another name for lithography. Also photoplate lithography.

Plate general term for the matrix in a printmaking process. (See **matrix**.)

power tool electric tools such as the jigsaw, drill, soldering iron, or sander that can be used on a variety of matrixes to mark and shape them.

polymer plate a plate that has a light sensitive emulsion or light sensitive film coating on its surface that can be exposed to UV light or sunlight with artwork to transfer an image onto the plate.

Pritt stick® a water-based adhesive used for paper particularly chine collé.

proof the trial or working impressions taken in the process of making a plate.

PVA glue water-based glue; thinner than wood glue and thicker than Pritt® Stick.

registration the means by which the paper and printing block are accurately aligned for the precise fitting of all shapes and colours in the image.

relief print made by taking an impression from a matrix in which only the upper surface of the matrix has been inked.

rice paste water-based paste used for chine collé.

roulette a tool with a spinning wheel tip that is textured with fine lines or dots. This creates textured areas on a plate when it is rolled across the surface.

scrim See **tarlatan**.

shellac varnish used to seal the surfaces of card or wood. It is also used as a coating in lift gounds/sugarlifts and as a protective coating on metal plates in the etching process.

rice starch museum quality adhesive; neutral pH.

rosin (powdered) powder form of tree sap used in etching aquatint boxes to dust plates. Also used in plate/stone lithography in processng plates.

steel metal used for intaglio processes. It is a coarse metal and has a heavy surface tone that makes it ideal for colour etching. The biting times for steel are similar to zinc.

methylated spirits solvent used for aquatint resin removal. Also used to remove Button Polish, shellac, French Polish and permanent marker pen.

soldering iron tool in which the heated tip is hot enough to melt soft metal flex or burn wood to create alternative marks on a printing matrix.

stencil designs cut from paper, acetate or thin card and applied to a plate, block or screen. Ink is then applied through the open areas of the design. The uncut areas of the stencil act as a suitable barrier or mask.

tarlatan an open weave cotton fabric that is stiffened with starch (also called scrim) used for wiping intaglio plates.

thinner additive that thins or dilutes inks, such as water for water-based inks. Oil-based inks are thinned with copperplate oil (thin, medium or thick) linseed oil, turpentine or white spirit.

tusche ink supplied in stick form, as a paste, or ready-mixed for use in lithography.

wheat starch museum quality adhesive; neutral pH.

whiting chalk in powder form used to degrease intaglio plates. Usually used in combination with a dilute solution of ammonia to create an effective degreasing solution. Also, a coating for the hand during hand-wiping of a plate.

white spirit solvent used for cleaning ink from plates and removing grounds and stop out varnish.

woodcut print made from wood that has been cut as plank length, for example plywood or composite board, such as MDF, or hardboard. The surface is cut and it is commonly printed using the relief printing process.

wood engraving a print made from the end grain or cross grain of a hardwood such as apple or boxwood.

Z*Acryl a thinner version of Imagon photopolymer film that is processed in the same way. See **Imagon**.

Z*Acryl hardground emulsion water-soluble acrylic polymer used as an alternative to asphaltum-based grounds. It can be used in an airbrush to create aquatints as an alternative to powder rosin.

zinc metal used for intaglio processes. It is usually highly polished and is suitable for clean, sharp images. It is ideal for aquatint as the biting times for zinc are extremely short compared to copper.

index